FROM WAR TO WAR

FROM WAR

A STUDY OF THE CONFLICT
FROM THE PERSPECTIVE OF COERCION
IN THE CONTEXT OF INTER-ARAB
AND BIG POWER RELATIONS.

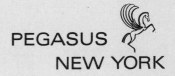

PEGASUS
NEW YORK

TO WAR

The Arab-Israeli Confrontation, 1948-1967

Nadav Safran

To "the tribe"

ACKNOWLEDGMENTS

I owe a very heavy debt of gratitude to my assistant, Jean Christian Lambelet. Throughout the years of struggling with this book, he has given me loyal and reliable help and has stoically endured my impositions on his own work and leisure time.

I am also grateful to my colleague, Richard W. Bulliet, my assistant, Shaul Bakhash, and my former student and present young friend, Theodore H. Moran for various kinds of help they have given me. Malcolm Peck has also assisted me in a previous incarnation of parts of this work.

The Ford International Studies Grant administered by Harvard provided me with the wherewithal to pay for some of the assistance I received, and the Center for Middle Eastern Studies of that same institution has contributed its bit.

Barbara Henson, Caroline Esfandiari, and Brenda Sens, "the girls" at the Center, have typed and retyped every draft of the manuscript. Despite their occasional attempts to improve on it, I am thankful to them.

My wife has been the unknown soldier of the long struggle that produced this book.

CONTENTS

Introduction / xv

I. The Evolution of the Arab-Israeli Conflict
Introduction / 21
The Origins of the Jewish-Arab Conflict to 1948 / 23
The War of 1948 and Its Immediate Results / 28
The Failure of the Postwar Peace Efforts / 36
The Festering of the Conflict / 42
The 1956 Explosion: Origins and Aftermath / 47

**II. The Pattern of Inter-Arab Relations
and the Arab-Israeli Conflict**
Introduction / 57
On the Origins of Pan-Arabism / 59
Pan-Arabism in World War I and After / 61
The Arab League: Its Origins and Politics / 63
Pan-Arab Appeals Over the Heads of Governments / 68
Pan-Arabism as Integral Unity / 70
Arab Unity as the Handmaiden of Social Revolution / 74
Nasserite Egypt and Arab Unity / 78
Inter-Arab Relations and the Arab-Israeli Conflict / 83

III. The Big Powers and the Middle East
Introduction / 89
Prelude to the Cold War in the Middle East:
    1945–1950 / 92
  General Features / 92
  Soviet Pressure and American Involvement in the
      Periphery / 94
  Britain's Abortive Effort to Organize the Heartland / 96
The Cold War in the Middle East: 1950–1958 / 100
  General Features / 100
  The Extension of the American Containment Policy to
     the Middle East / 101
  The Extension of the American New Look Policy to
     the Middle East / 103
  The Soviet Breakthrough in the Middle East / 106
  The Early Balance of Terror and the Climax of the
     Cold War in the Middle East / 111
The Powers and the Middle East in the Fading Cold
    War: 1960 and After / 119
  General Features / 119
  The Changing Big Power Interests and the Regional
     Conflicts / 123
  The Soviet Union / 123
  The United States / 131
  Third Powers / 137

IV. The Dynamics of Arms Buildup: Defense Expenditures
Introduction / 143
Egypt / 147
  Explanation of the Phases / 149
Israel / 156
  Explanation of the Phases / 161
Syria / 169
Iraq / 175
Jordan / 179
Lebanon / 182
Kuwait / 185
Saudi Arabia / 188
Summary and Conclusions / 190
  Dynamics of Arms Buildup / 191
  Strain of the Arms Buildup / 191
  Effects on Relation of Forces / 198

V. The Arms Buildup: Evolution of Armed Forces
Introduction / 205
Egypt / 206
Israel / 217
Syria / 227
Jordan / 232
Iraq / 235
Saudi Arabia / 239
Yemen / 242
Kuwait / 244
Lebanon / 245
Summary and Conclusions / 247
   Pattern of Arms Accumulation / 247
   Anticipated War and Likely Patterns / 249
   Balance of Forces / 253
Addendum on Population and Balance of Forces / 256

VI. To the Brink and Over: The May–June 1967 Crisis
Introduction / 266
The Chronological Skeleton of the Crisis / 268
The View from Cairo / 271
The View from Tel Aviv / 303

VII. The Six Day War (June 5–10, 1967)
Introduction / 317
The Armed Forces of the Opponents on the Eve of the
     War / 317
The Air War / 320
The Land War / 330
   The Egyptian Front / 332
   A Note on Naval Warfare / 353
   The Jordanian Front / 355
   The Syrian Front / 370

VIII. The War and the Future of the Arab-Israeli Conflict
Introduction / 383
The War, Pan-Arabism, and the Conflict / 385
The War and the Relative Position of the Belligerents / 390
   Syria / 391

Jordan / 392
Egypt / 395
Israel / 403
The War, the Superpowers, and the Conflict / 409
Conclusions: To War Again or to Peace at Last? / 417

Appendix A   Sources, Methods, and Comments / 421

Appendix B   The Armed Forces of Egypt, Syria, Jordan, and Israel on the Eve of the War / 435

Appendix C   The Opponents' Military Hardware / 445

Index / 453

TABLES

Table I: Egypt's Defense Expenditures, 1950–1965 / 148
Table II: Israel's Defense Outlays, 1950–1966 / 158
Table III: Syria's Defense Outlays, 1952–1965 / 170
Table IV: Iraq's Defense Outlays, 1952–1965 / 177
Table V: Jordan's Defense Outlays, 1953–1965 / 180
Table VI: Lebanon's Defense Outlays, 1953–1966 / 183
Table VII: Kuwait's Defense Outlays, 1957–1966 / 186
Table VIII: Kuwait: Foreign Assets and Reserves / 188
Table IX: Saudi Arabia's Defense Outlays, 1959–1967 / 189
Table X: Defense Outlays as a Burden on National
                Economies / 193
Table XI: Recent Outlays on Defense, Investment, and
                Education / 194
Table XII: Defense Expenditures as Percentages of
                Government Educational Outlays / 195
Table XIII: Defense Expenditures as Percentages of Gross
                Investment / 195
Table XIV: The Cost of the Arms Race Over and Above
                "Normal" Defense Spending / 197
Table XV: Index of Egypt's and Israel's "Real" Defense
                Outlays and Percentages of GNP Spent on
                Defense / 199
Table XVI: Egypt's "Real" GNP as Compared to Israel's / 201
Table XVII: Combined "Real" Defense Expenditures / 203
Table XVIII: Evolution of Egypt's Armed Forces / 217
Table XIX: Evolution of Israel's Armed Forces / 228
Table XX: Defense Expenditures and Real Armed
                Forces / 254

Appendix

Table A: Comparative; "Real" Defense Expenditures;
                Israel and Each Arab Country / 433
Table B: Total Defense Expenditures Over Various
                Periods / 434
Table C: Average Annual Growth Rate of GNP / 434

FIGURES

Fig. 1   Egypt's Defense Outlays as Percentages of GNP / 150

Fig. 2   Egypt: "The First Phase" / 151

Fig. 3   Egypt: "The Second Phase" / 151

Fig. 4   Egypt: "The Third Phase" / 153

Fig. 5   Egypt: "The Fourth Phase" / 155

Fig. 6   Israel: Defense Outlays as Percentages of GNP / 159

Fig. 7   Egypt compared with Israel: Defense Outlays as Percentages of GNP / 160

Fig. 8   Israel: "The First Phase" / 162

Fig. 9   Israel: "The Second Phase" / 163

Fig. 10   Israel: "The Third Phase" / 164

Fig. 11   Israel: "The Fourth Phase" / 166

Fig. 12   Syria: Defense Outlays as Percentages of GNP / 172

Fig. 13   Egypt, Syria, and Israel: Relative Defense Outlays as Percentages of GNP / 173

Fig. 14   Egypt, Syria, and Israel: Defense Outlays in 1962 U.S. dollars / 174

Fig. 15   Israel compared with Its Neighbors: Defense Outlays in 1962 U.S. dollars / 176

Fig. 16   Iraq compared with Israel and Egypt: Defense Outlays as Percentages of GNP / 178

Fig. 17   Jordan: Defense Outlays as Percentages of GNP / 181

Fig. 18   Lebanon: Defense Outlays as Percentages of GNP / 184

Fig. 19   Kuwait: Defense Outlays as Percentages of GNP / 187

Fig. 20   Saudi Arabia: Defense Outlays as Percentages of GNP / 190

Fig. 21   Arab States and Israel: Defense Outlays as Percentages of GNP / 192

Fig. 22   Egypt/Israel: Trends of Relative Exertion and Yield / 200

MAPS

Israel: Armistice lines, 1949
    —and Cease-fire lines, June 10, 1967 / 20

Egyptian Front: Physical map / 333

Egyptian Front: Initial Egyptian deployment / 335

Egyptian Front: Israeli offensive / 341

Jordanian Front: Physical map / 357

Jordanian Front: Initial Jordanian deployment / 359

Jordanian Front: Israeli offensive / 363

Jerusalem: Israeli offensive / 369

Syrian Front: Physical map / 371

Syrian Front: Initial Syrian deployment / 373

Syrian Front: Israeli offensive / 377

INTRODUCTION

Readers who are accustomed to skim over introductions should keep in mind one thing about this book: It is written from two different "historical" perspectives. The first five chapters were written over a period of two years before the June 1967 war, and have been left intact except for editorial changes and the addition of some footnotes. The last three chapters, dealing with the origins, course, and consequences of the war, were written during the year that followed it. This situation calls for a certain effort at adaptation on the part of the reader, but should not, hopefully, disrupt the logical continuity of the discourse.

The book was originally intended to be a study of the Arab-Israeli conflict as a confrontation; that is to say, as a struggle centering on the manipulation of various forms of coercion in the service of policy, and of policy in the service of enhancing the means of coercion. War, as the ultimate form of coercion, was therefore naturally a central focus of the study before the specific Six Day War broke out. Admittedly, the drift of the argument of the chapters completed before June 1967, although it allowed for accidental developments, ruled out the likelihood of a deliberate war for many years ahead; but the fact that such a war did take place, far from invalidating the previous argument, gives more point to the question why it nonetheless took place, especially in view of its outcome.

The choice of coercion as the focus for this undertaking was not due to any general conviction that force is the key determinant in the affairs of nations, but was rather the consequence of reflection on the facts of the dispute between Israel and its neighbors as it unfolded over the last two decades. War has been used as a continuation of policy in many international conflicts besides this one, but in few if any others has policy been used as a continuation of war, to the extent that it has in this case. Yet notwithstanding its obvious importance, no systematic study has been done of the dimension of force in that conflict in all the voluminous literature on the subject.

While focusing on the role of coercion, we have tried to take due account of the role of "emotion." All too often the latter has been used simplistically as the sole ground for explaining the behavior of Israelis and Arabs, particularly the latter; we want to avoid this shortcoming, and also the opposite extreme of thinking of our subjects as behaving exclusively in terms of a simple calculus of coercion. The general view taken in this study is that Israelis and Arabs, like all people, act on the basis of an interplay between emotional considerations and coercive pressures that is somewhat akin to the economic interplay of demand and supply. A given degree of emotional commitment sets a threshold that coercive pressure must reach in order to induce "rational," that is to say, calculated, behavior, and vice versa. In the Arab-Israeli conflict, the degree of emotional commitment has been high, indeed. But this has not meant that either side was emotionally "incapable" of yielding, but that efforts by one party to affect the behavior of the other necessitated the marshaling of vast means of pressure. Although individuals sometimes "crack up" or commit suicide rather than submit to the pressures of reality, in the case of nations, this has seldom if ever happened.

The unfolding of the Arab-Israeli confrontation over the last twenty years has been critically affected by two other constantly evolving conflicts: the rivalries and clashes among the Arab states, centering on the issue of the meaning and mode of realization of the pan-Arab ideal; and the conflict among the big powers, centering partly on local interests but consisting mainly of an extension of the Cold War to the Middle East. The elucidation of the evolution and dynamics of the Arab-Israeli confrontation, therefore, requires extensive attention to these other struggles, and this is done throughout the study.

The book is logically divided into four parts. The first, consisting of three chapters, analyzes the main lines of evolution of each of the three conflicts in terms of its proper environment while highlighting the effect of the other two on the Arab-Israeli conflict. For example, one of the central themes of the analysis is that a conjunction of circumstances in inter-Arab and big power relations produced in the mid-fifties a critical escalation of both the issue at stake in the Arab-Israeli confrontation and of the means with which the confrontation was henceforth carried out.

The second part, consisting of two chapters and an addendum, analyzes the Arab-Israeli confrontation as reflected in defense expenditures over a long period of time and as these in turn are expressed in grand strategies and real armed forces. The analysis seeks to discern the pattern of the competitive buildup of arms as related to the shifting perceived needs and objectives of each of the participants; to highlight the burden of the competition on the parties and their relative capacity to withstand it; to reflect on past shifts in the balance of forces and suggest some projections for the future; and to deduce from changes in the nature and level of armament and other factors the likely general pattern of war. The addendum discusses the question of population and its relation to the past and prospective balance of forces.

The third part consists of two chapters which deal with the origins of the May–June 1967 crisis and with the war that ensued. The discussion of the crisis, while relating its beginning and development to the analysis of the preceding two parts, does not pretend that the analysis had forecast it. The underlying theme of the discussion, on the contrary, is precisely the question why Nasser defied and challenged Israel when he did, when everything in the preceding analysis, including his own evaluations, suggested that he shouldn't have. The discussion of the war analyzes the size, deployment, maximal and minimal objectives, and the strategies of the belligerents, as well as the course of the fighting and its outcome. It implicitly highlights the dramatic expression in action of much that had been discussed earlier academically.

Finally, the last chapter examines the effect of the war on the main elements that have affected the Arab-Israeli confrontation in the past and reflects upon the implications of the change for the future of the Arab-Israeli conflict. The analysis shows that several of the elements have changed deeply in a direction that favors a final settlement; but it also points out that such a consummation is still contingent upon the form into which other elements, still fluid at present, will jell. Of these, the most crucial is the prospect of American-Soviet cooperation to help a settlement.

Cambridge, Massachusetts
August, 1968

FROM WAR TO WAR

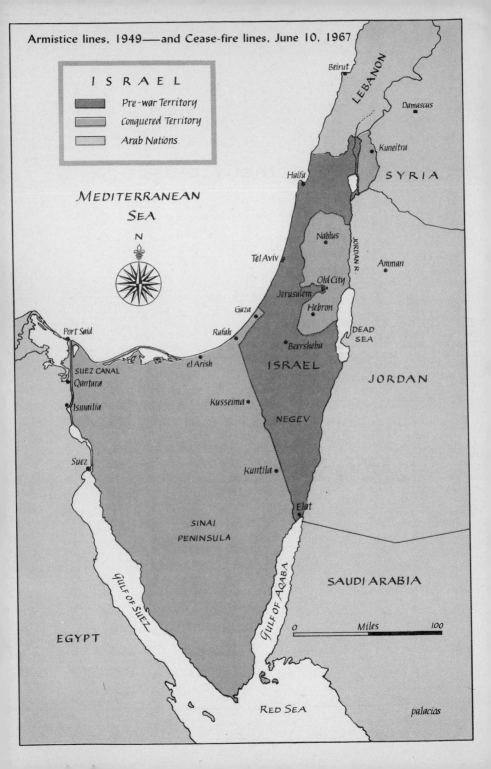

Armistice lines, 1949——and Cease-fire lines, June 10, 1967

ISRAEL
- Pre-war Territory
- Conquered Territory
- Arab Nations

MEDITERRANEAN SEA

N

LEBANON
Beirut
Damascus
Kuneitra
SYRIA
Haifa
Nablus
Tel Aviv
Old City
Jerusalem
Hebron
DEAD SEA
JORDAN R.
Amman
JORDAN
Guza
Rafah
el Arish
Beersheba
ISRAEL
Port Said
SUEZ CANAL
Qantara
Ismailia
Kusseima
NEGEV
Suez
Kuntila
Elat
SINAI PENINSULA
GULF OF SUEZ
GULF OF AQABA
SAUDI ARABIA
EGYPT

Miles
0   100

RED SEA

palacias

The Evolution of
the Arab-Israeli Conflict

Introduction

Discussions of the Arab-Israeli conflict are replete with interpretations
that attempt to explain it as a moral, psychological, legal, or political
"case" abstracted from history. According to these interpretations, the
conflict involves two sets of incompatible claims, attitudes, and points
of view. On the Arab side, there is the prescriptive right to a land inhabited for more than a thousand years, the right of self-determina-
tion, the shock to the dignity of a once great people seeking to make
its place in the modern world, the fear of Israeli expansionism, the
plight of one million refugees. On the Israeli side, there is the indissolu-
ble bond to the land that had been the cradle of the Jewish heritage,
the urge of Jews barred from the nations of Europe to reconstruct a
national life of their own in the land of their ancestors, their interna-
tionally recognized right to a share of Palestine, and their struggle for
survival as a political entity and a culture.

This abstract approach to the Arab-Israeli conflict may be of some
use in suggesting the reservoir of motives from which the parties draw.
It is of little use, however, and tends in fact to mislead, in any attempt
to understand the concrete unfolding of events and to formulate a policy relevant to the conflict. It fixes on feelings and emotions to the ne-
glect of changing realities and facts which interact with these and
greatly affect their practical implications. It assumes a single set of issues throughout the time in which the problem has existed when in

fact these have changed and the conflict has evolved through a number of critically different identifiable phases.

One major watershed in the nature of the conflict occurred in 1948, when the state of Israel was established, thus transforming what had up to then been a clash between the Arab and Jewish communities of Palestine into a contest between national states: Israel on the one side and the Arab countries on the other. Each of these major phases is further divisible into two distinct stages. In the first phase, there was a period up to about 1933 when Britain, as the mandatory power in Palestine and wielding great influence in the Arab world, had virtually full discretion to decide the Palestine issue on its own merits as it conceived them and in keeping with its broader national interests. The conflict entered a second stage a few years later when the growing strength of the Arab and Jewish parties imposed severe restrictions on Britain's discretionary power and turned what had been a problem of adjudication into a political issue of managing conflicting forces. The partition plan recommended by the Royal Commission in 1937, the persistent failure of Britain to coerce either the Arabs or the Jews to accede to "British" plans for a settlement of the conflict, and the partition resolution finally adopted by the United Nations in 1947 all reflect this phase of the conflict.

Once the state of Israel was established in 1948, the conflict entered a new phase and became a dispute between sovereign states. This at once had significant implications for the course of the conflict within the region and the manner in which it was viewed. The 1948 war ended in a defeat for the Arabs but not in formal peace. While the state of no-peace allowed the conflict to fester, the issues at stake between Israel and the Arab states were for some time mainly of a residual character and did not suggest war as an inescapable necessity. In the years 1956–1958 this situation changed drastically and the Arab-Israeli conflict entered a new stage.

When Nasser emerged as the most powerful leader in the Arab world and as he transformed Egypt's commitment to pan-Arabism from a loose form of cooperation with Arab states to a commitment to integral Arab union, the Egyptian-Israeli confrontation changed from a dispute over residual issues to a clash of destinies between the two countries. In this new stage, which has lasted to the present, the destruction of Israel became an imperative for the realization of Egypt's national-Arab destiny.

Viewed in this fashion, it is clear that the nature of the Arab-Israeli conflict was different in 1938 from what it had been when the Balfour Declaration was issued in 1917, different in 1948 from what it had been in 1937, and different again in 1958 from what it had been a decade earlier. Each transformation had, in turn, quite different possibilities and limitations and therefore very different diplomatic implications.

The Origins of the Jewish-Arab Conflict to 1948

The earliest organized claim of Jews to Palestine goes back to 1897. In that year, the first World Zionist Congress, assembled in Basel, Switzerland, at the initiative of Theodor Herzl, declared as its objective the establishment of a Jewish National Home in Palestine secured by public law, and set up an organization to pursue this objective systematically. At that time, Palestine was under the control of the Ottoman Turks and was inhabited by nearly half a million Arabs and some 50,000 Jews. No Arab voice was raised then to protest against the Zionist claim, and the Ottoman sultan, the sovereign master of Palestine, far from taking umbrage at it, received Theodor Herzl to discuss his organization's program before politely turning it down. All the efforts of Zionist diplomacy to get third parties to intercede with the Ottoman government to change its attitude proved of no avail until World War I broke out. In the meantime, several thousand Jews from eastern Europe had somehow made their way into Palestine and had begun practical nation-building work. In the absence of a political authorization, however, this work was bound to have little more than a symbolic significance.

World War I transformed the prospects for the Zionists. Once the Ottoman Empire joined Germany and Austria against Britain, France, and Russia, its defeat was expected to end its dominion in the entire Middle East, including Palestine. Before this actually came to pass, the Zionists went to work on the British, who bore the brunt of the fighting in the area and had shown some sympathy in the past for the idea of a Jewish homeland, in an effort to persuade them to sponsor the charter they needed to build their National Home in Palestine. Thanks to the exertions of Chaim Weizmann, the Zionists finally succeeded, and on November 2, 1917, the British government issued the Balfour Declaration, which said:

> His Majesty's Government view with favour the establishment in Palestine of a national home for the Jewish people, and will use their best endeavours to facilitate the achievement of this object, it being clearly understood that nothing shall be done which may prejudice the civil and religious rights of existing, non-Jewish communities in Palestine, or the rights and political status enjoyed by Jews in any other country.

The Declaration was eventually approved by Britain's allies and was incorporated in the terms of the Mandate over Palestine granted Britain by the League of Nations.

The Balfour Declaration is now viewed by Arab nationalists and by some historians as the root cause of the Arab-Israeli conflict. This is indeed true in that without it Zionist settlement of Palestine on a large scale would have been impossible; it is not, however, true insofar as it implies that the Balfour Declaration made the emergence of Israel inevitable. Between one event and the other there were many intervening causes that were by no means predetermined and that depended decisively on choices made and avoided by several participants, including the Arabs themselves. Consideration of these choices is very useful for an understanding of the Arab-Israeli conflict.

By the time the Balfour Declaration was issued, there was already an incipient Arab nationalist movement that hoped to inherit from the Ottomans control over the Arab-inhabited territories. Britain, through its High Commissioner in Egypt, Sir Henry McMahon, had already promised the authorized leaders of the movement, Sherif Hussein of Mecca and his son Faysal, that it would support Arab independence in most such territories in exchange for their launching a revolt against Ottoman authorities. Excluded from the promise was a vaguely defined Mediterranean coastal area to which the French allies of the British had laid claims. Advocates of the British, Jews, and Arabs have since debated *ad nauseam* the question whether Palestine was part of the territory excluded from the area of Arab independence; but no one until recently ever really questioned the underlying premise of Britain's discretion to promise or not to promise Palestine at all. Implicit in this omission is a recognition of the political reality that prevailed at the time, which was that the fledgling Arab nationalist movement was so weak and so dependent for the realization of its aspirations on the British as to leave the latter completely free to act, bound only by their own conscience and judgment. As it was, the British felt that, regardless of the McMahon promise, they could induce the Arab leaders to accept the Balfour Declaration with the properly reassuring interpretations in exchange for the vast benefits they were to get outside Palestine. When they actually elicited such approval from Emir Faysal (later King Faysal I of Iraq) on several occasions, they satisfied themselves as well as the Peace Conference that the experiment of the Jewish National Home was feasible and right.

The British retained a decisive measure of discretion over the fate of Palestine for some fifteen years after the approval of the Mandate by the League of Nations. Arab nationalism did little in that period that

was apt to persuade them to reverse their Jewish National Home policy altogether. To be sure, the movement had reversed Faysal's
guarded approvals of the Balfour Declaration shortly after they were
given and had explicitly reasserted on numerous occasions its claim
over Palestine. However, after 1920 it had broken up into weak segments as a result of the division of the Arab territories into several political entities under French and British control, and each segment
became absorbed in local struggles. The Palestinian part of the movement had hardly any strength. As the application of the Mandate proceeded, there were sporadic manifestations of violent resistance, as in
1920, 1921, and 1929; but these were always confined to particular
localities and focused on specific issues so that those who were so disposed could view them as specific incidents susceptible to specific reme-
dies rather than as indications of a gathering insuperable opposition
to the Mandate as such. It was not until 1937, when the Palestinian
Arabs finally rose up in arms over the entire country in an explicit revolt against British authority, that a Royal Commission of Inquiry
came to the realization that the Mandate was unworkable—that it
could not be applied without constant and massive use of force against
the Arabs. By then, however, the situation within Palestine had so
altered that the idea of the Jewish National Home could no longer
simply be abrogated. A point of no return had been reached.

When the British issued the Balfour Declaration, the Jewish population of Palestine numbered some 56,000 against an Arab population of
600,000. In the course of the next fifteen years, the Jews made important strides in organizing themselves for community self-government,
creating a labor movement, pioneering new forms of settlement, establishing a Hebrew educational system, creating a national press and so
on; but on the crucial issue of numbers, they had grown by only some
120,000 for a total of 175,000 by 1932 as against an Arab population
that had grown naturally to 800,000. Up to that point, the British
could have probably reversed themselves on the Jewish National Home
policy had they so chosen without undue concern about Jewish reaction. They did not choose to do so, not, as some contemporary Arab
spokesmen like to think, because of a sinister imperialist interest in
foisting a puppet Zionist state upon the Arabs, but because they saw
no reason to retract a moral-legal obligation they had assumed when
Arab resistance to it had seemed relatively inconsequential. Five years
later, the Arab revolt dissipated all illusions on that score; but by then
the British had lost most of their freedom to retreat because the capacity of the *Jews* to resist such a retreat had grown greatly in the meantime. Hitler's rise to power had induced a migration of German and

central European Jews to Palestine in hitherto unprecedented numbers, swelling the Jewish population in the country to 400,000 by 1937
and triggering an acceleration of development in all spheres of Jewish
national endeavor. A policy reversal then would have meant not only
reneging on a moral-legal obligation at a moment when the rationale
for it seemed greater than ever but would also have required no less
force to apply than was necessary to suppress the Arab revolt. In short,
from that moment on the Palestine problem ceased to be for the British primarily a matter of adjudication between rival moral-legal
claims and became instead a *political* issue, a question of the art of the
possible, in a situation in which two nationalist movements capable of
offering strong armed resistance were bent on pursuing conflicting objectives. This is why the Royal Commission, after reaching the conclusion that the Mandate was unworkable, did not simply go on to recommend its nullification but found it necessary to recommend the
partition of the country into an Arab state, a Jewish state, and a
British enclave.

The course recommended by the Royal Commission was to be recommended again ten years later by the United Nations Special Commission on Palestine—evidence that its logic had become inescapable.
In the meantime, however, and as if to test this logic by trying to escape it, the British government sought to pursue a different course.
The Zionist leadership, reluctantly acknowledging the strength of Arab
resistance to the Mandate, had accepted the partition proposal in principle and prepared to haggle over its application. The Arab leadership,
on the other hand, vehemently rejected it and insisted on the full recognition of the Arabs' right to the whole of Palestine. In the face of
this opposition the British government dropped the proposal and continued to search for alternative solutions. In February 1939 it assembled a conference in London, to which for the first time representatives of the then independent Arab states as well as the Palestinian
Arabs were invited, together with Palestinian Jews and representatives
of world Jewry, to discuss a settlement of the problem. The Arabs refused even to sit together with the Jews, and the conference got nowhere. By that time it had become apparent that Britain was going to
be involved in a world war, and some kind of decision on Palestine
had become imperative in view of the forthcoming contest. The British government, believing Arab good will to be essential for the war
effort and taking for granted Jewish opposition to Hitlerism, proclaimed
unilaterally a policy that practically reversed the Balfour Declaration.
The policy, which came to be known as the White Paper of May 1939,
did not go so far as to promise the liquidation of the Jewish establish-

ment in Palestine, as the Arab leadership had wished, but it froze its
size at its then existing level and envisaged the creation of an independent state of Palestine with an Arab majority after a ten year transition period, if a constitution were adopted that guaranteed the rights
of the Jewish minority. It was now the Jews' turn to pass to defiance
and resistance.

Jewish resistance to the White Paper policy was confined in the early years of World War II to evading and violating its provisions restricting land purchase and immigration. But as the war receded from
the Middle East, these efforts were supplemented by terrorist attacks
against British police and military personnel and installations. After
the war, as the British government continued to apply the White Paper policy while searching for possible alternatives, Jewish resistance
grew more intense. It combined with a universal wave of sympathy for
the Jews, roused by the spread of knowledge of the Nazi holocaust, to
exert an enormous pressure on the British authorities to permit massive immigration of survivors of concentration camps immediately. The
British tried to suppress the resistance and play for time in order to attempt a solution of the Palestine question in the context of a broader
settlement of their Middle Eastern problems. But after two years of
vain effort, they decided to turn over the whole Palestine question to
the United Nations.

The United Nations appointed a commission of eleven representatives of states with no interest in Palestine (Australia, Canada,
Czechoslovakia, Guatemala, India, Iran, the Netherlands, Peru, Swe-
den, Uruguay, and Yugoslavia) to inquire and make recommendations.
The majority of the commission recommended partition while the minority advocated a federal state with autonomous Arab and Jewish provinces. While the General Assembly debated these and other proposals, the representatives of the Arab countries and the Palestinian Arab
leadership refused both recommendations and insisted once again on
absolute Arab sovereignty over Palestine. This position left the delegations of most countries, unable to ignore the reality of the Jewish presence in Palestine, with no alternative but to opt for one of the two
proposals of the commission; and since partition depended much less
than federation on Arab cooperation, the statutory majority voted for
it on November 29, 1947. Literally at the last moment, Arab representatives sought to forestall what had become an obvious majority for
partition by coming out in support of the federal plan, but by then it
was too late. Had the Arabs adopted this tactic earlier, it is almost certain that neither plan would have mustered the required two-thirds
majority, and the whole matter would have been left open. That they

did not do this, and that they did not accept earlier British proposals of compromise, was undoubtedly due in part to their belief in the absolute rightness of their cause. But this rigid posture was also the result of weak political organization and rivalries among the leadership, which put a premium on intransigence and exposed the advocates of greater flexibility to political loss.

Their absolutist moral position having failed of recognition, the Palestinian Arabs now fell back on the only alternative such positions usually leave their adherents and, with the assistance of the neighboring Arab countries, resorted to arms to prevent partition. The fortunes of the ensuing civil war were initially favorable to the Palestinian Arabs to such an extent that the United States government became convinced by March 1948 that partition, for which it had voted and lobbied, was impracticable, and submitted to the General Assembly a proposal for a United Nations trusteeship over Palestine. However, while the United Nations became entangled in a discussion of trusteeship and how it could be enforced, the Jews of Palestine, having received a shipment of Russian arms and enjoying greater freedom of action as British withdrawal from the country continued, launched a series of offensives that reversed the tide of the war, decisively defeated the Palestinian Arabs, and brought most of the area allocated to them by the partition plan under their control. On May 15, 1948, they proclaimed the establishment of their state, Israel, which was immediately recognized by the United States, Soviet Russia, and other nations. The Jews barely had time to celebrate; for no sooner did they proclaim their state than armies of the neighboring Arab countries crossed the Palestine borders in another attempt to nullify the partition resolution by force. The Jewish-Arab conflict over Palestine thus became a war between the Arab states and Israel. The conflict entered a new phase.

The War of 1948 and Its Immediate Results

The War of 1948 constitutes an indispensable subject of study for anyone wishing to understand the intricacies of the Arab-Israeli conflict it inaugurated. We cannot, in the limited space we are able to devote to the subject, undertake the detailed analysis the war deserves. We will therefore have to content ourselves with a few comments and observations aimed at highlighting those aspects most pertinent to understanding its outcome as well as the subsequent attitudes of the participants regarding the problems it bequeathed.

The first observation is that, Transjordan aside, the leaders, soldiers, politicians, writers, journalists, not to speak of the common people of the Arab countries, had had no contact with the Jewish community in Palestine and therefore had but a faint idea of its composition, organization, achievements, guiding ideals, aspirations, and strength. The Arab governments had been drawn into the diplomatic arena of the Jewish-Arab conflict only a short time before and did not expect to become directly involved in it militarily. In any case they were so certain of their superior strength that they did not think it worthwhile to assemble more than perfunctory intelligence at the very last moment before the opening of hostilities. The Arabs' almost total lack of nonbelligerent contact with the enemy's people and country, and the Israelis' only slightly less sweeping lack of contact with the Arab states, was to continue after the war and to provide what is probably a unique example of nations at war that had never known one another in peaceful commerce. This mutual ignorance accounts for much of the extreme fluctuation in the sensitivities and mutual assessments of intentions that has been characteristic of the parties to the Arab-Israeli conflict.

The near-success of the Palestinian Arabs, despite their primitive equipment, training, and organization, in preventing the establishment of the Jewish state had convinced the Arab governments that a small regular force could succeed in destroying Israel. They therefore initially entrusted the task of military intervention to Transjordan's 6,000-strong Arab Legion alone. King Abdallah, who disposed of British advice and intelligence and whose British-officered Legion had served in routine duties under the Mandatory administration in Palestine, knew better than this. He therefore overtly accepted the mandate of his Arab League partners while he covertly maintained contact with the Jewish side with a view to arranging for the Arab Legion to take over only the parts of Palestine allocated to the Arabs by the partition plan. In the event, this modified partition scheme was nullified by the sudden decision of Egypt's King Faruq, against the advice of his government, to send his troops to Palestine, which in turn induced the other Arab governments to follow suit and led to the adoption of a common plan of action aimed at destroying Israel or constricting it to the narrowest confines. However, the Arab governments remained under the impression that the task could be accomplished with only a small proportion of the forces they intended to engage. Their decision to participate jointly in the action was more a function of their mutual suspicions—which in retrospect proved not to be misplaced—than of an estimate of military requirements.

The woeful underestimation of the Jewish forces was due to the Arabs' faulty, static conception of Israeli strength. Generalizing from their own condition, the Arab leaders thought of the Jewish forces *in being* at the time they decided to invade, in April 1948, as constituting the total forces they would have to confront. In fact, because of the extraordinary cohesion and spirit of the Jewish community of Palestine and the foresight of its leaders, who had accumulated vast stores of arms and equipment on ships in foreign ports ready to move as soon as British authority in Palestine ceased, these forces grew at a very rapid rate from one week to another. It is a rarely known fact that already by the beginning of the war, the Jews—numbering 700,000 in all—had far more men (and women) mobilized than the Arab countries, whose population was 40 times more numerous, and that they maintained and increased this numerical superiority in the course of hostilities. If the Arabs had a chance of winning the war, it was in the first few weeks, when the Israeli forces were not yet adequately organized and had not yet received and assimilated all the equipment they had accumulated. Once they missed this chance, they were condemned to worse and worse defeat the longer the fighting persisted.

The Palestine war was not, like "normal" wars, a free contest of force; it was repeatedly interrupted by truces and cease fires imposed from the outside. Officially, the war lasted about eight months, from the time of the invasion to the time Egypt sued for an armistice. Actual fighting, however, took place during only about one-fourth of that time, in four intervals spread over the entire period. The course of the war is best described by reference to each of these phases separately.

The first phase of fighting lasted four weeks and was the most critical of the entire war. Although the Israelis had more men and women in the field at the time, the Arab armies had an overwhelming superiority in firepower, were much better organized, equipped, and supplied, had the strategic initiative, and were able to occupy key undefended positions. The Israeli troops had had little experience in large-scale operations, were awed by guns, tanks, and planes against which they had not yet fought, and their best units were already exhausted by six months of fighting in the civil war against the Palestinian Arabs. Victory was within reach of the Arab armies had they coordinated their battle plans and pursued them with determination. As it was, however, their disunity enabled the Israelis to switch their forces from one front to another to deal with critical situations as they developed, while the timidity of the Arab commanders enabled the Israelis to stem dangerous possibilities with little more than dash and tactical initiative. By the time the Arab governments felt compelled to obey a United Nations injunction to keep a month-long truce, they had definitely failed to win. Their armies had occupied most of the portions of Palestine allocated to the Arabs plus some small Jewish portions, the Arab Legion had Jerusalem under siege, and the Egyptian army had cut off the Negev by several thin and long lines of positions; but they had failed to destroy the Jewish fighting strength and to develop a serious threat to the heartland of the Jewish state in the coastal plain, Jezreel, and the upper Jordan valley. In fact, they had succeeded in capturing only half a dozen Israeli villages.

Both sides used the month-long truce to rest, reorganize, and reinforce their troops, replenish their supplies, and improve their equipment in spite of a United Nations embargo and the presence of supervisors intended to prevent the parties from altering the size and equipment of their forces. The Israelis, however, took much greater advantage of the respite than the Arabs. For one thing, they were much more adept, from the White Paper days, at smuggling in men and equipment under the nose of supervisors than were the Arabs. For another thing, they already had equipment and men assembled in Europe on which to draw, whereas the Arabs could only improvise. Furthermore, they had considerable unutilized or underutilized reserves at home which they now mobilized and trained, whereas the Arab countries could only reshuffle their existing forces so as to allocate somewhat greater proportions of them for the forthcoming fighting—the bulk of the Arab forces during, before, and after the truce being tied to internal security tasks at home. Finally, the Israelis needed the time to organize their hastily established state and army and to rest their troops much more than the Arabs. The results showed themselves clearly when the fighting was resumed.

The second phase of fighting lasted for ten days. In the course of it, the Israelis were able to hold the Egyptians at bay in the south while they launched small attacks in the north and a major offensive in the center, against Transjordan's Legion. In the latter front, they made considerable territorial gains and opened the way to besieged Jerusalem; and though the Arab Legion eluded destruction, it was forced to pass to the defensive and fell under very heavy pressure from which it was saved only by a second cease-fire imposed by the United Nations. Henceforth, the Arab Legion and the Iraqi contingent that worked in close cooperation with it had their hands full consolidating their positions for defense and were incapable of initiating any large-scale offensive operations. The Syrians had already been contained in the previous stage in a small bridgehead in eastern Galilee, and the Lebanese and irregular Palestinian and volunteer forces held on passively to a sizeable rectangle in central Galilee. The Egyptians remained the most formidable force and still retained intact their lines that cut off the Negev.

The second cease-fire had no time limit. It was supposed to be final and to permit the settlement of the conflict by diplomatic means with the help of a specially appointed United Nations Mediator, Count Folke Bernadotte. However, in October 1948, fighting broke out for the third time, in this instance only between the Israelis and the Egyptians, except for some secondary Israeli action against the irregulars in central Galilee.

Hostilities began when the Egyptians responded to Israeli provocations that served to justify a major, carefully planned offensive designed to secure control of the Negev. The Israelis had been prompted to take this action by a proposal submitted by Bernadotte to modify the partition plan so as to give Israel all of Galilee (instead of Eastern Galilee only) and, in exchange, to give Jordan the Negev in addition to the Palestinian territory it already occupied. The Israelis believed that the Bernadotte plan rested on the military status quo between them and the Arabs, and they therefore set out to destroy it by altering the military situation. In a brief, energetic campaign in which they enjoyed the elements of surprise and initiative and were able to have at least tactical numerical superiority everywhere, the Israelis were able to shatter the Egyptian front, capture most of the Negev, trap the best third or fourth of the Egyptian forces into a pocket, and drive the rest of the Egyptian army back to an untenable arc stretching from Gaza to Asluj, some twenty miles south of Beersheba. In the north, the Israelis cleared all of central Galilee in a fifty-hour campaign and moved beyond the international borders of Palestine to occupy some Lebanese villages.

While the Egyptian army was being mauled by the Israelis, the other Arab armies stood perfectly still, thus marking the disintegration of the Arab coalition. The disintegration had already begun in the wake of the previous phase of fighting. Transjordan, which was the main beneficiary of the Bernadotte plan, had wanted to avoid that phase altogether by acquiescing to the prolongation of the first truce indefinitely; but the Egyptians, resentful of the proposal to give the Negev to Jordan, had forced their partners to resume the fighting on the grounds that the Arabs could still win. The actual fighting proved the Egyptians to be wrong, but it was Transjordan that paid for the mistake in significant territorial losses. Therefore, it decided to avoid further entanglement through the ill-considered actions of Egypt and, together with its Iraqi partners, remained passive while the Israelis acted against Egypt. As for the Syrians, they were in no position to do much anyway, while the Lebanese and the irregulars, as we have seen, were not even allowed to sit still and lost Galilee to the Israeli attack.

The last phase of the fighting occurred in December 1948 and the first days of the next year and lasted about two weeks. On November 16, 1948, the Security Council had ordered the parties to the conflict to conclude armistice agreements. When the Egyptians refused, the Israelis launched an offensive intended either to secure their acquiescence or to complete the destruction of their army in Palestine. As in the previous offensive, the Israelis prepared their attack by provoking the Egyptians, and the Egyptians obliged by responding and giving the Israelis the legal cover for breaking the truce. As in the previous phase, the other Arab armies sat still while the Israelis concentrated their by now superior forces against the Egyptian front. The Israelis easily broke up the Egyptian lines and drove into the territory of Egypt proper in a flanking movement aiming at el Arish. The entire Egyptian army in Palestine was thus reduced to one complete pocket left over from the previous phase and another almost complete pocket extending from Gaza to el Arish which the Israelis were pounding. With nowhere to retreat, the Egyptians did some of their best fighting in the entire war, but they were saved from a heroic doom only by their government's timely agreement to conclude an armistice to end the war. The fighting stopped on January 7, 1949, and by February 24, the Egyptians had separately signed an armistice agreement with Israel. Other Arab governments followed suit: the Lebanese in March 1949, the Jordanians in April, and the Syrians in July. The Iraqis simply withdrew from Palestine, transferring their positions to the Jordanians, without concluding an armistice with Israel.

The war had far-reaching consequences that have affected the long-run politics of the area in many crucial ways as we shall see throughout this study. At this point we need to note three basic and immediate results: the reallocation of territory, the reshuffling of population, and Arab disunity.

The war involved a far-reaching modification of the United Nations partition plan. The Arab state envisaged by that plan failed to emerge, and the territory allocated to it was divided by the armistice agreements between Israel, Jordan, and Egypt. Israel got the largest share, some 2,500 square miles, which it formally annexed to the 5,600 square miles allotted to it by the partition plan. Transjordan acquired 2,200 square miles, which it formally annexed before the conclusion of an armistice, transforming itself into the state of Jordan. Egypt retained control of the Gaza Strip, some 135 square miles, which it held in the status of Egyptian-controlled territory. As for Syria and Lebanon, the international frontiers of Palestine became the armistice lines between them and Israel. Jerusalem, intended by the partition plan to be under an international regime, was divided between Israel and Jordan. Several small demilitarized zones were created between Israel and Egypt, Jordan, and Syria.

The war also involved a major reshuffling of population. Over 700,000 Palestinian Arabs who had lived in the area that came under Israeli control were displaced in the course of the fighting both before and after May 15, 1948, and ended up as refugees in Jordan (about 60 percent), the Gaza Strip (20 percent), and Syria and Lebanon (20 percent). The armistice agreements, while acknowledging the territorial changes, said nothing about the refugees; but a United Nations resolution of December 11, 1948, before any armistice had been concluded, had ruled that those among them wishing to return and live at peace with their neighbors should be allowed to do so. A major controversy has since raged whether the refugees had left the territory under Jewish control of their own accord or had been compelled to leave by threat and force, the implication always being that the answer to this question is a key determinant to the solution of the problem. This implication is unwarranted as we shall argue further on; nevertheless, it may not be irrelevant to address ourselves briefly to the question anyway.

On the basis of first-hand observation it can be said that until about the end of May–early June 1948, the refugees from areas under Jewish control *left,* and left in the face of persistent Jewish efforts to persuade them to stay. From that time on, they were *expelled* from almost all new territories that came under Israeli control. The number of refugees involved in each phase was approximately equal. The reason for this apparently odd behavior of Israelis and Arabs is rather simple. Until about the end of May, the Jews were not sure that they would be able to make the partition resolution stick in the face of actual and anticipated armed Arab hostility. They consequently had an interest in the Arabs' remaining in the territories under their control since this would have meant a *de facto* acceptance of partition on their part and would have discouraged the Arab states from attacking or pursuing the war energetically by placing so many "hostages" in Israeli hands. For exactly obverse reasons the Arab leaders, confident at this stage in the victory of the regular Arab armies, were eager to have the Palestinian Arabs leave what they considered temporarily Jewish-occupied territories, and urged them to do so. By the time it became clear, with the cease fire of June 11, 1948, that the Jewish state had survived the war, the motivations were completely reversed. The Palestinian Arabs, unwilling to leave their homes and properties with no hope of return, now wanted to stay; while the Jews, having survived the attempt to destroy their state, thought it advantageous to have in it a homogeneous population and proceeded to push the Arabs out.

People with an incomplete knowledge of the facts have argued that even in the first stage the massacre perpetrated by the Irgun in Dir Yasin on April 9, 1948, had caused a stampede among the Palestinian Arabs, who did not differentiate between the dissident Irgun and the official Jewish Haganah, and that consequently it can be said that they fled under the threat of force, real or imagined, in both stages. But the fact is that much before Dir Yasin there were several *mutual* massacres—in the refineries and in Balad al-Shaykh notably—that were reported and exaggerated with relish in the press, and by the soldiery and population *of the side that committed them* without causing any stampede. Indeed, such are the instincts released by war that people on each side took "credit" loudly for massacres they never committed except in their imagination. Furthermore, after Dir Yasin and when the tide of the war had turned in favor of the Jews, the Arabs did not want to leave their homes in areas that fell to the Israeli forces notwithstanding the tales of real and alleged massacres, and had to be physically kicked out. The fear and terror argument, plausible as it sounds, and probably relevant in some individual instances, simply does not accord with the main facts.

A third and no less crucial result of the war was its crystallization of Arab disunity even in the face of a common enemy. The disunity was latent in the disparity of objectives sought by the various Arab countries. Transjordan, backed by Iraq, had wanted to intervene militarily in order to secure for itself the portions of Palestine allocated to the Arab state by the partition plan while Egypt, backed by Saudi Arabia, had sought to foil Transjordan's plan by nullifying partition altogether or securing as much territory as possible for a client Palestinian Arab state. These differences, temporarily papered over, began to manifest themselves as soon as the limits of the joint Arab military advance became apparent; then, Transjordan wanted to stop fighting and hold on to its gains while Egypt wanted to continue in the hope of achieving its objective. When the resumption of hostilities led to losses for Transjordan, it definitely decided to sit out the next round, leaving the Egyptian forces to be defeated and pushed out of the Negev. Finally, the quarrel broke into the open as Transjordan formally annexed the territory under its control while Egypt set up a Palestine Arab government in Gaza which laid claim to the entire country, and formally pulled out of the war by signing a *separate* armistice with Israel. This

last act left the other Arab countries generally, and Jordan particularly, to face the Israelis alone in working out armistice agreements under the implicit threat of resumption of a war they could only lose.

The Failure of the Postwar Peace Efforts

Even before any armistice agreements had been concluded, the United
Nations General Assembly had appointed a Conciliation Commission,
composed of representatives of the United States, France, and Turkey,
and had charged it with the task of assisting the parties concerned to
achieve a final settlement. The Commission went to work before the
last armistice agreement, between Israel and Syria, was signed and invited representatives of Israel and the four neighboring countries for
talks in Lausanne where it acted as a mediator to bring about a peace
agreement. After months of effort, the Commission succeeded on May
12, 1949, in getting the Arabs and the Israelis to agree on an agenda
and a basis for discussion, known since as the Lausanne Protocol. In
this, both sides agreed to accept the United Nations partition resolution as a basis for discussing the boundaries question, after Israel had
undertaken to take back 100,000 refugees as a good will gesture prior
to any negotiation of the whole refugee question. But this was the limit of the Commission's achievement; from that point on negotiations
bogged down beyond retrieval and the two sides tried thereafter to
qualify away even the limited degree of agreement that had been
reached.

Because the only open and formal peace attempt between Israel and
its neighbors failed on account of the refugees and boundaries questions, most people concerned with the Arab-Israeli conflict academically or diplomatically have come to view these two problems as the
real issue between the Arab states and Israel. Countless efforts have
been made by well meaning mediators, especially American, to resolve
the conflict between Arabs and Israelis on the basis of this premise;
and when all these efforts failed, the conclusion was drawn that the
problems were intractable rather than that the premise was wrong. A
more realistic analysis, however, would easily show that the conflict
has persisted not because of these problems, but because key Arab
countries had no desire for peace for reasons which have varied over
the years, and could not be compelled to make peace in view of peculiar circumstances. The problems of the refugees and the boundaries,
in other words, have been symptoms rather than causes of the persistence of the conflict.

That the issues in themselves are not intractable is evident not only from the obvious compromise forecast in the Lausanne Protocol but also from the more interesting attempt at peace between Israel and Jordan. As the Lausanne negotiations headed toward deadlock, Israeli representatives secretly met with King Abdallah of Jordan and his advisers over a period of several months in the winter of 1949 during which they thrashed out the terms of a peace treaty between the two countries including a settlement of these two issues. The agreement was particularly significant since the majority of the refugees were located in Jordan and since the thorniest boundaries problems existed between the two countries. Nevertheless, a mutually acceptable settlement was reached because both sides had important gains to expect from peace—Israel's being obvious, and Jordan's involving the consolidation of its territorial annexation, the injection into the economy of large amounts of refugee compensation money, and acquisition of an outlet to the Mediterranean through free port rights at Haifa. The treaty did not come to fruition because the opposition to peace at home and in other Arab countries deterred any Jordanian prime minister from putting his signature to the agreement and because King Abdallah was assassinated in July 1951 for pursuing the attempt. This turn of affairs says something about the attitudes of those involved toward peace and toward the Jordanian monarch, but it does not alter the conclusion that the refugees and the boundaries are not insuperable problems and are not the cause of the failure of a settlement to materialize.

As far as Arab governments other than Jordan's are concerned, the problems of the refugees and the boundaries may have been the real issues for perhaps a few months right after the termination of the war. They, as everyone else, assumed at that time that peace followed naturally upon armistice, and they wanted some concessions on these questions in order to preserve their self-respect and to justify themselves before home public opinion, from which they had endeavored to hide the magnitude of the disaster suffered. However, in the course of wrangling for these concessions through the United Nations intermediaries, they discovered a new truth which has guided their position ever since. They learned that if hitherto in history peace had followed upon armistice, it was because of the implicit sanction held by the party that had proved stronger in the war to resume it and thereby impose greater evil upon the weaker party. Since in this case the party that had proved stronger was hamstrung by the United Nations and other powers and unlikely to apply the usual sanction, there was no need to go on from armistice to peace unless there were specific gains to be had from it. And the Arab governments of the time saw little to gain and much to lose by making peace.

On the side of gains, there was the prospect of restoring land and rail communications between Egypt and the other Arab countries. But this benefit was of marginal importance since very little trade passed over these routes, which were used mainly by tourists, and tourist movement could be easily diverted to sea and air routes. Another potential gain was the resettlement of at least some refugees. But, again, the urgency of this problem became greatly reduced once international relief assumed the burden of supporting them, and the refugees did not much bother the "host governments" in other respects. Jordan was, in fact, glad to accept its refugees as additional subjects to its otherwise minuscule population along with the Palestinian territory it gained. Egypt segregated its refugees in the Gaza Strip across the Sinai Desert away from its own population centers. Syria had ample room for the 70,000 or so who fled to it. Lebanon was the only country to which the 80,000 refugees it received, who were mostly Moslem, presented a serious problem in that their absorption would disrupt the delicate balance between Christians and Moslems on which the country's political existence rested; but Lebanon had the least to say on the subject of peace, partly because of its size and partly because its half-Christian population made it suspect in the eyes of other Arab countries. As for territorial concessions that might be gained through peace, these appeared at the time to have little value to any country except perhaps Jordan, which was disposed to make peace on other grounds anyway. The one and only real incentive to make peace, that of avoiding the burden of mounting defense expenditure, did not appear at the time as a real issue for reasons to be explained later.

On the other hand, peace presented a number of material disadvantages from an Arab point of view. Lebanon would have had to share Beirut's transit trade with Haifa. Both Lebanon and Syria would have had to share with Israel, if not to lose altogether to it, the benefits derived from providing passage to oil pipelines and sites for refineries. Israel, with its more advanced economic and technological infrastructure, generally bid fair to serve as regional base and headquarters for international business in the area that would otherwise be forced to distribute itself in several Arab countries. Furthermore, an Israel at peace with its neighbors, using its nodal position as a means of bargaining for favored status for its trade, was apt to prove a strong competitor for area markets that a country like Egypt, seeking to industrialize, eyed for itself.

Far more important than these disadvantages, however, were the psychological, political, and security liabilities of peace. We have already referred to the fact that the Arab countries went to war so confident in their military superiority that they expected their armies to become involved more in police-type operations (this was how their representatives in the United Nations represented their intervention) than in serious warfare. The attitude of a country like Egypt was reflected in the very thin deployment of its troops from the Palestinian borders to Jerusalem along positions that were meant more to establish political claims than a real frontline. In these circumstances, defeat at the hands of the "Zionist gangs" was so humiliating that the Arabs found it very difficult to admit it. Though forced to sign armistice agreements that "objectively" consecrated their failure, Arab leaders developed the rationalization that as long as they did not sign peace treaties, the game was not over yet. As Azzam pasha, then Secretary General of the Arab League, put it in an interview with a journalist:

> We have a secret weapon which we can use better than guns and machine guns, and this is time. As long as we do not make peace with the Zionists, the war is not over; and as long as the war is not over there is neither victor nor vanquished. As soon as we recognize the existence of the state of Israel, we admit by this act that we are vanquished.[1]

This attitude of the Arab leaders was not only a device to protect their wounded dignity but was also a means of political and physical survival. Having aroused their peoples to a high pitch of enthusiasm for the cause of Palestine, fed them on anticipatory communiqués of victories, and hidden from them the deterioration of the military position as much as they could, they could not make peace without putting themselves in a critical position. For in the situation they had placed themselves, peace would have meant either a gratuitous concession of most of Palestine to the Jews after a war fought precisely to prevent that injustice, or it would have meant a definitive acknowledgment of defeat, which could only be attributed to the awful mismanagement of the war by the governments. The consequences for those responsible did not have to be guessed. Egyptian Prime Minister Nuqrashi pasha had been assassinated by a member of the fanatic Muslim Brethren organization for having accepted a mere cease-fire, before Egypt had signed the armistice agreement. The entire Syrian regime

---

[1] Wolfgang Bretholz, *Aufstand der Araber*, Munich, 1960, p. 215.

was overthrown by a military coup also before it had authorized any armistice. Prime Minister Riad al-Solh of Lebanon was assassinated for showing moderation even though Lebanon had played a minor role in the entire war. And King Abdallah of Jordan was assassinated on the suspicion that he wanted to make peace.

Reinforcing the internal pressures against peace were those deriving from the strange state of inter-Arab relations. These relations were ruled by the myth of Arab unity, which, while not strong enough to make possible positive common action, was sufficiently strong to justify the interference of the leaders of the various Arab countries in each other's affairs and the obstruction of each other's policies. Thus a government like Jordan's, which found it in its interest to conclude peace, and a government like Lebanon's, which might have reached the same conclusion, were put under pressure to desist by the governments of Egypt, Syria, and Saudi Arabia, whose countries were differently affected by the outcome of the war and faced different policy choices.

The totally unexpected defeat of the Arab states resulted not only in the loss of most of Palestine, but also produced a national security problem which appeared to some of them, at least, to be best met by abstaining from making peace. Given the ignorance of Israel among the Arab elites outside of Jordan, the shock of defeat at its hands when victory had been taken for granted tended to swing feelings to the opposite extreme and to give birth to exaggerated notions about the capacity of the Israelis, their cleverness, the international support they could command, the means they could muster, and the ambitions they entertained. Consequently, the Arab states, especially those immediately bordering on Israel, felt impelled to think of ways and means to protect themselves against possible future Israeli expansion. Jordan's monarch was inclined to protect his country by concluding peace with Israel and relying on his mutual defense treaty with Britain to deter the Jewish state from breaking it in the future. Lebanon too might have chosen the path of peace and reliance on formal or informal international guarantees. But Egypt and Syria mistrusted informal international guarantees as much as they mistrusted the worth of a peace treaty with Israel, and feared formal international guarantees even more than they feared Israel. They could therefore only fall back on collective Arab security arrangements, which had the merit of being better served by abstention from making peace, so problematic on other scores. For peace would legitimize Israel's entry into the Middle Eastern political arena and allow it to maneuver freely among the rival Arab states and with interested outside powers in order to promote its suspected expansionist designs; whereas by refusing to recognize it and by ostracizing it, Israel could be prevented from aligning itself with some Arab states against others and a measure of caution could be imposed on outside powers in their dealings with it. A condition for the successful application of this policy was, of course, that no Arab state should be allowed to make a separate peace with Israel.

The line favored by Egypt and Syria had the further appeal of leaving open for the Arab countries the possibility of future *offensive* operations. Given the apparent glaring disparity in gross size, numbers, and resources between Israel and the Arab states, or even between Israel and Egypt alone, it was impossible for the Arab elites and governments not to entertain the notion that, with better planning and preparation, it should be possible in the future to reverse the decision of arms of 1948 and take revenge, wash out the humiliation of defeat, and restore justice all at once. Such feelings were not necessarily incompatible with the sense of fear of Israel discussed before, since the one nourished itself on apparent future possibilities while the other fed on recent and present experience. Indeed, the same ambivalence, only with a confident arrogance feeding on the past and a deep anxiety nourishing on future possibilities, is to be found on the Israeli side. The refusal to make peace, though not necessarily guaranteeing freedom of militant action in the future, at least rendered it less difficult by keeping the "case" of the Arab-Israeli conflict open.[2]

These impediments to peace found a convenient cover of legitimacy in Israel's refusal to abide by the United Nations' resolution on the return of the refugees and, to a lesser extent, in its refusal to return to the partition boundaries. For Israel could not meet these resolutions integrally without jeopardizing its existence. Taking back the bulk of the refugees in addition to the Arabs already living in the country would have meant being faced with an enormous minority with irredentist aspirations, and none knew better than the Israelis what this could mean, since they themselves had been such a minority in Palestine.[3]

As for the partition boundaries, these were totally indefensible since they divided each of the two states envisaged by the resolution into three sections connected with each other by literally no more than points on the map. They had been adopted on the entirely unwarranted assumption that Arabs and Jews would acquiesce to them peacefully

[2] This paragraph may be taken as a summary of Nasser's position now, in the wake of the catastrophic defeat of June 1967. Who said history does not repeat itself?

[3] The temptation to annex territory may be obscuring this truth from many Israelis now.

and cooperate with each other. Therefore, the Arab states needed only to insist on absolute compliance with United Nations resolutions on the refugees and the boundaries in order to avoid a peace they did not want or could not conclude and at the same time shift much of the blame onto Israeli intransigence.

To summarize, then, the collective refusal of the Arab states to make peace after the armistice agreements was due to a complex set of reasons that could not themselves be articulated diplomatically but that could be served by an insistence on the integral application of United Nations decisions on the refugees and partition. These reasons included the unlikelihood of Israel's resort to force to compel the Arab states to come to terms, the paucity of material inducements for making peace and the counterbalancing of these by material disadvantages, the psychological reluctance to admit defeat, the fear of the leadership to confront an outraged public opinion that had been encouraged in its expectation of easy victory, the mutual deterrence of the Arab governments against making separate peace and defense arrangements, the apprehensions that peace would enhance the possibilities and therefore the dangers of Israeli expansionism coupled with the mistrust of external guarantees, and, finally, the seduction exercised on some governments by the seemingly superior potential of the Arabs leading them to wish to keep the issue open until 'such time as a shift in the balance of actual power would permit a radical reversal of the situation and the restoration of "justice." It is important to note that of all these reasons motivating the Arab governments collectively, only the last was of an offensive nature in that it involved not merely saying no to peace but looked forward to a time when the situation might be reversed. Even this, however, was *in the early postwar period* more of a vision for the future than a blueprint for action, since it entailed no sense of the desired contingencies and capacities and of ways and means to bring them about. Thus while the lack of formal peace left the conflict open, there was not, at this stage, an active Arab commitment to a resumption of hostilities or to the total destruction of Israel.

The Festering of the Conflict

We have just seen that the Arab governments justified their refusal to make peace to the world on one level and to themselves on another level. There was yet a third level on which they justified the perpetuation of the no-peace status, this one involving their relations toward their own people. On this level only the last among the reasons that had motivated the governments was stressed. Although the governments knew that the desire for revenge bore no concrete prospects of realization in any foreseeable future, they found it difficult to resist the temptation of courting favor among their people and scoring points against rivals by suggesting that it was an imminent plan on which they were actively engaged. Two consequences flowed from this: One was that the Arab governments were constantly impelled to give to their peoples and to each other earnests of their ultimate offensive intentions in the form of miscellaneous acts of harassment against Israel. The other was that Israel, acting on the principle of caution, took the Arab leaders at their word to their own peoples, viewed all real or feigned harassments as parts of a general scheme for its destruction, and responded to them accordingly when it could. The net result was a constant process of mutual irritation, which kept the conflict festering rather than allowing the healing hand of time to work, and gave rise to a number of secondary causes for potential unintended general eruptions.

The most comprehensive harassment measure was the Arab boycott of Israel. This was initially directed against Israeli trade with Arab countries but was gradually extended to embrace all Israeli activities and to cover all countries that could be reached. Thus non-Arab firms doing business with Israel were in principle and in varying degrees in practice barred from doing business in and with the Arab states. Ships and aircrafts calling on Israel were denied the use of Arab facilities. Travelers to Israel were subjected to more or less stringent restrictions if they wished to visit Arab countries. Pressure was put on many countries that had achieved sovereignty since 1948 not to recognize Israel or to refrain from having diplomatic or trade relations. All official or semi-official contact between Israelis and Arabs on third party soil was shunned, even in the sports arenas. The material damage inflicted on Israel by the boycott and the sacrifices supported by the Arabs because of it are not susceptible to accurate estimation except for the shutting off of the oil pipeline from Kirkuk, Iraq, to Haifa. But there is no doubt that the boycott had the effect of perpetuating the atmosphere of mutual ignorance, distance, and hostility.

A particularly grave extension of the boycott took the form of a partial blockade of Israel in the Suez Canal and the Gulf of Aqaba. Israeli ships, barred from the Suez Canal during the war, continued to be barred after the armistice on the grounds that Egypt remained formally at war with Israel. A 1951 ruling of the Security Council rejected the Egyptian argument and enjoined Egypt to desist, but instead of complying, Egypt went on in the years that followed to bar even goods to and from Israel carried on third-party ships. As for the Gulf of Aqaba, Egypt began in 1949 by placing coastal guns at the tip of the Sinai peninsula controlling the entrance to the strait, then moved on to interfere with traffic to and from the budding Israeli port of Elath, and ended up in the next few years by barring such traffic altogether. The combined effect of the Suez Canal and Aqaba blockade was to cut Israel off from convenient access to Asian and African markets and suppliers generally and Persian oil sources particularly, forcing it to buy the one to two million tons of oil it needed in remote and more expensive markets. Such was the gravity with which the Israeli government viewed the Aqaba blockade that in 1955 it decided in principle to go to war to remove it and left the execution to a convenient time, which came in October 1956.[4]

Since then, the Gulf has remained open, with United Nations troops posted in the Egyptian positions that formerly blocked it. Israeli trade through Elath has become of major significance, especially after the construction of an oil pipeline from Elath to Haifa that supplies Israel's requirements of Persian oil and provides an added outlet to international markets for it. A renewal of the Egyptian blockade is therefore virtually certain to be a *casus belli*, thus demonstrating clearly how a secondary harassment issue could become the cause of a general conflagration.[5]

Another issue that contributed to keeping the Arab-Israeli conflict festering, that was one of the reasons for Israel's going to war in 1956, and that is likely to be the cause of unintended war in the future, is the more or less continual flaring-up of Israel's borders with this or that Arab state. The problem has its roots in two causes. One stems from the demilitarized zones established by the armistice agreements between Israel and Egypt, Syria, and Jordan. Without going into the baffling details, the issue here is essentially that Israel views these zones as falling entirely under its sovereignty except for their demilitarized status, while the Arab countries concerned, especially Syria, deny the Israeli claim and dispute many of Israel's specific acts in those areas either on the basis of that denial or on the grounds that they alter the military situation. These disputes have often resulted in shooting and major skirmishes, which have in turn become the cause for retaliation and further violence.

The other cause of the problem stems from infiltration of Israel's borders by small groups of Arabs coming from Jordan, Syria, or the

[4] See Moshe Dayan, *Diary of the Sinai Campaign*, New York, 1965, pp. 12–13.
[5] This was written long before the crisis of May 22, 1967, and the war that followed it.

Gaza Strip. Initially, these groups consisted primarily of unorganized refugees sneaking across the wide-open border for stealing or smuggling purposes, occasionally killing a Jew on their way, though a few groups from the outset existed primarily to kill and destroy. The Arab authorities did not exert themselves overly to stop this traffic from their side and some may have even connived at various times and places to facilitate it. Eventually, after the number of Jews killed by infiltrators exceeded two score a year for a couple of years, the Israelis struck back in October 1953 in the first major retaliatory raid across the border by regular army units. Henceforth, border incidents resulting from infiltration fell into a pattern that has persisted to the present day. Random crossings for stealing and smuggling declined as a result of greater control on the Arab side and ceased to be a major problem. On the other hand, organized infiltration for espionage, sabotage, and killing assumed central importance and became a continuation of policy by other means, turned on and off in accordance with politico-military considerations and treated differently by different Arab countries.

The Jordanian government on the whole not only avoided sponsoring this type of infiltration itself but did all it could to prevent Palestinian refugees organized and armed by initiatives from outside Jordan from undertaking it. Not that the Jordanian government was less hostile to Israel than the others, but it rightly feared that such groups might turn against it as well as against the Israelis and realized that its long borders were particularly vulnerable to Israeli retaliatory attacks that could escalate into a large-scale war Jordan could only lose. Nevertheless, the government could not always seal the borders, especially when infiltrators were aided and abetted by Egypt or Syria through client Palestinian organizations, and for considerable intermittent periods, therefore, the Israeli-Jordanian border flared up with raids and counter-raids.

The Egyptian authorities tended at first merely to wink at infiltration undertaken for all sorts of purposes from the Gaza Strip under their control. But after a murderous Israeli retaliatory raid on Gaza in February 1955, the Egyptian government responded defiantly by launching a deliberate raiding campaign from Gaza and Jordan in which groups of two and three well-trained raiders (*fida'iyyun*) penetrated deep into Israeli territory to ambush lone military vehicles, mine roads, sabotage installations, and kill civilians. Israeli retaliatory attacks only increased the defiance of the Egyptian authorities and the murderousness of the raids, until finally Israel took advantage of a favorable conjuncture to launch an all-out invasion of Sinai and the Gaza

Strip in October 1956. The *fida'iyyun* raids were not the only reason prompting Israel to launch the Sinai campaign, but they were an important consideration since all other measures to deal with the terrorists had proved ineffective. Since then the Egyptian-Israeli border has been almost perfectly quiet under the supervision of the United Nations Emergency Force.

With Syria, border incidents have been numerous enough but until quite recently were not due to infiltration. The reason for this is that the demilitarized zone between the two countries offers Syria adequate opportunities for needling Israel when necessary without resorting to infiltration, especially since the Syrian forces sit on high ground and can hit Israeli targets without having to cross the border. Recently, however, the Syrian authorities seem to have decided on a campaign of infiltration through the Lebanese and Jordanian as well as the Syrian borders aimed at carrying a guerrilla war into Israel as a strategy for the final recovery of Palestine. The dangers of escalation into large-scale war are therefore particularly real in this sector.[6]

Lebanon has not only abstained from taking part in the border warfare but has taken measures to prevent infiltrators originating within its boundaries as well as elsewhere from crossing over into Israel. Consequently, with one or two minor exceptions the Lebanese-Israeli border has been quiet ever since the war of 1948.

Finally, one more issue which arose out of the persistence of the conflict and contributed in turn to exacerbating it is the dispute over the Jordan River waters. The sources of the river are found in Syria, Lebanon, and Israel, and a major tributary flows into it from Jordan. The river itself flows in Israel and Jordan and its waters are indispensable for these two countries. In order to avoid conflict over the sharing of waters and to promote cooperation by indirect means, the United States sponsored a plan for the integrated exploitation of the river for the benefit of all the riparian countries. After prolonged efforts from 1953 to 1955, Eric Johnston, the author of the plan and special representative of President Eisenhower, got the parties concerned to agree to it "on the technical level," including the allocation of percentages of available water. But the whole project eventually ran afoul of political objections on the part of Syria, which sought to prevent Israel from reaping the large benefits accruing to it from the plan even at the cost of the equally large benefits for Jordan and the much smaller ones for itself. In the event, Israel launched its own project for ex-

[6] This is exactly what came to pass in May–June 1967. The slide to that war, as may be seen in Chapter VI, began with Syrian-supported raids and Israeli threatened and actual retaliation.

ploiting its share of the river's waters through a large-scale diversion project. As the work reached the completion point in 1964–1965, Syria appealed to all the Arab governments to respond to what it perceived as an Israeli challenge. Egypt reacted by calling a "Summit Meeting" of all the Arab heads of state in Cairo in January 1964, which adopted a several-years-long program to divert the sources of the river while strengthening the Arab armed forces and creating a Unified Arab Command to meet the expected Israeli reaction. The summit project quickly got bogged down in inter-Arab disagreements; and when Syria attempted to start the work by itself, Israeli planes raided the site and destroyed the equipment used. The other Arab countries kept still and Syria stopped the work, but the potential for a future conflagration on this score remains open.[7]

The continuation of the Arab-Israeli conflict in the years ahead is certain to breed other secondary issues that may become themselves the causes for large scale armed encounters. One such issue may already be in the making in Israel's construction of a 24-megawatt nuclear reactor in Dimona, which is capable of producing enough fissionable material for making one or two nuclear bombs a year. Already the construction of the reactor has elicited solemn warnings from President Nasser of Egypt that if Israel should proceed with the manufacture of a bomb, the Arabs would launch a pre-emptive war.

The 1956 Explosion: Origins and Aftermath

We have already made several allusions to the Sinai-Suez War in the course of our previous analysis; but since this episode was a critical landmark in the Arab-Israeli conflict it might be worth our while to take a closer look at its causes, its course, and its consequences.

Successive Egyptian governments after the 1948 war, we have seen, had many reasons to avoid making peace with Israel, but, sporadic acts of hostility notwithstanding, they were under no strong compulsion to seek a resumption of the war or to plan for it. There was, to be sure, the psychological need to seek revenge and wipe out the humiliation of defeat, but several factors conspired to assuage this need and deny it the possibility of meaningful expression in terms of concrete planning for war.

In the first place, the need for revenge was itself mitigated by the fact that, as long as King Faruq reigned, the Egyptian governments

---

[7] In the June 1967 war, Israel made sure to capture the source of the river in Syria.

were under pressure to deny or minimize the fact of defeat for reasons we have already explained; and when a new regime came to power in 1952 with a vested interest in acknowledging and even exaggerating the defeat in order to damn its predecessors, it did not, by the same token, feel responsible for righting that defeat, at least in any immediate sense.

In the second place, Egyptian governments and the public became reabsorbed immediately after the 1948 war in the much more important and closer-to-home task of completing Egyptian independence by getting rid of the British base on the bank of the Suez Canal and settling the problem of Egypt's relations with the Sudan. Adding to this distraction were the internal upheavals that culminated in the revolution of 1952 as well as the preoccupation of the new regime in the two years that followed with the task of consolidating its position in the country and dealing with the power struggles within its own ranks.

Finally, the diplomatic and military conditions for a war policy appeared to be extremely unfavorable, especially after May, 1950. On that date, the United States, Britain and France jointly issued what came to be known as the Tripartite Declaration by which they pledged themselves to ration the supply of arms to the Arab countries and Israel so as to prevent the development of an arms race and the creation of an "imbalance" between the antagonists, and also made themselves the guarantors of the armistice borders against any attempt to alter them by force. Since the Middle Eastern countries had no significant military industries of their own, since the authors of the Declaration included the main traditional arms suppliers to the area, and since they had, in the presence of 80,000 British troops along the Suez Canal and otherwise, a visible and credible capacity to intervene forcefully in pursuance of the declared policy, the Tripartite Declaration appeared to rule out effectively any war alternative.

In the course of the years 1955–1956, two series of developments took place that seemed to remove or weaken all these limitations while providing the Egyptian leadership with reasons to contemplate a war-oriented policy. Already in the summer of 1954, the Egyptians had reached an agreement with the British on the evacuation of the Suez Canal base after an earlier agreement had disposed of the problem of the Sudan. By the fall of 1955, the British had completed their evacuation, thus removing the buffer of 80,000 troops that had stood between Egypt and Israel and freeing the Egyptian government to turn its attention to other arenas, including Israel.

A more important series of events began with the conclusion of an arms deal between Egypt and the Soviet Union, announced in September 1955. Having come to power through a military coup and lacking other support at the outset, the new regime in Egypt had made the strengthening of the armed forces one of its basic objectives. This objective, neglected for a while for lack of means and other preoccupations, was revived by a sudden flare-up of the Israeli border in the early months of 1955, which seems to have made Nasser and his colleagues particularly conscious of their military weakness. The Egyptian government pressed the United States for a prompt answer to a long standing request for arms but met with a response it considered unfavorable. Just then, an apparently unrelated development came to fruition that gave the Egyptians the chance to acquire all the arms they wanted from Soviet Russia.

That development had to do with an alliance project promoted by Britain and the United States, subsequently known as the Baghdad Pact, which aimed at joining the Arab countries with Turkey, Iran, Pakistan, and the two Western powers in a Middle East defense grouping. For reasons explained elsewhere in this study, the Egyptians began by suggesting an alternative plan based on a purely Arab grouping that would cooperate with the West, and ended up after their plan was spurned by launching an all-out diplomatic and propaganda attack against the government of Iraq, which adhered to it and sought to recruit other Arab countries. The Egyptian campaign succeeded in stalling the progress of the Pact after inflicting on Britain and Iraq severe diplomatic defeats in Syria and Jordan. But the most important result of the campaign was its effect on Soviet Russia. The Russians, who had their own reasons for vehemently opposing the Baghdad Pact, had previously viewed the military officers' regime in Egypt, which had started out with very friendly relations with the United States, as a mercenary, opportunistic government eager to sell its services to the imperialist powers but haggling only over the price. As the Egyptian campaign against the Baghdad Pact unfolded, the Soviet leaders began to revise their earlier assessment and to think of Egypt's rulers as possibly useful tacit allies in the endeavor to frustrate the Western plans and destroy the Western positions in the Middle East. Knowing the Egyptians' wish for arms, they agreed to provide them, and in quantities and on terms that were extremely alluring. The Egyptians hesitated for a while out of concern for their relations with the United States and fear of the Russian embrace, but then they took the plunge.

The conclusion of the deal was of momentous import to the entire politics of the Middle East. We shall have occasion later on to dwell on its significance for inter-Arab relations and for the big power rivalries in the area; here we shall concentrate on its consequences from the perspective of the Arab-Israeli conflict.

The deal, the execution of which had begun by the time it was announced, immediately shattered the limitation on the *level* of armament imposed by the Tripartite Declaration. Whether it was also to destroy the Declaration's *balance of power* principle and its *diplomatic security guarantee* depended on the signatory powers' willingness to provide Israel with weapons to counter the Egyptian acquisitions and their readiness to give a meaningful reaffirmation of the guarantee. Events showed that they were willing to do neither at a time when action might have stopped a conflict they did not want, and that they, after a fashion, then proceeded to do both when this was apt to make things worse. Not for the first nor for the last time in international affairs was the bad choice of the moment for hesitation and the moment for determination to lead to disaster.

As soon as the deal was announced, Israel asked the three Western powers, and Russia too for good measure, to be allowed to purchase modern equipment to counterbalance the new Egyptian weapons. The United States, to whom Britain and France looked for a lead, promised to give "sympathetic consideration" to an Israeli shopping list; but five months later the "consideration" was still continuing though the "sympathy" had apparently gone out of it. For at the end of February 1956, Secretary of State Dulles told the Senate Foreign Relations Committee that, "without prejudice" to Israel's arms request, he thought that it should rely for its safety not on arms (and implicitly not on any specific big power guarantee) but on the "collective security" of the United Nations.

The diplomatic reaction of the big powers was no less distressing to Israel. Prime Minister Eden did try at first to get the United States to "put teeth" (his own words) in the Tripartite Declaration and obtained in response the appointment of a dental committee (my own words); but as the committee got shoved by the Americans into oblivion, Eden turned round and urged the Israelis to make territorial and other concessions to the Arabs in order to avert war. The United States not only procrastinated on the arms request and implicitly diluted the purport of its diplomatic commitment by virtue of the Tripartite Declaration, but decided to redouble its effort to woo Nasser by offering to help him build the Aswan Dam. The French government kept its counsel, but its concern with the implications of the arms deal seemed to lie elsewhere, judging by the hurried trip Foreign Minister Pineau made to Cairo in an attempt to persuade Nasser not to dump his obsolete arms in Algeria. The conclusion drawn from all this, by Egyptians and Arabs as well as by Israelis, was that the diplomatic and the arms balance limitations on war of the Tripartite Declaration had gone by the board along with its limitation on the level of arms.

While this picture was gradually unfolding, the arms deal was having an electrifying effect in the area itself. Nasser, hitherto a rather obscure conspiratorial type disliked by those who knew him for his overthrow of the popular General Naguib and his ruthless suppression of the Muslim Brethren, turned into an all-Arab hero and a master of the Arab street, overnight. Whatever his own motives for the conclusion of the transaction, the Arab masses saw in it only the prospect for a successful showdown with Israel before too long. Nasser cashed in on his mastery of the streets in order to isolate Iraq and prevent the accession of Syria and Jordan to the Baghdad Pact; but he was also impelled to respond to expectations placed in him with regard to Israel by immediately adopting a tough line toward it. This took the form of extreme verbal attack, and of *fida'iyyun* missions for sabotage and murder deep inside Israel. As the Israelis responded with massive murderous raids, there developed a momentum for war that rolled on independently of the circumstances that had started it.

In the spring and summer of 1956, the diplomatic constellation that had left Israel isolated and anxious for six bleak months underwent a profound change in its favor though not because of Israel itself or for anything it did. The detailed reasons for the change need not concern us here except in the briefest outline: The French, having failed to make a bargain with Nasser on Algeria, began to sell arms to Israel in fairly large quantities on the theory that the enemy of an enemy is a friend. The United States, displeased with Nasser's continuing war on the Baghdad Pact and irked by his success in promoting an overturn of the government of Jordan in March 1956, openly associated itself with the French action. Nasser, hoping to discourage further change in America's position and seeking to ensure for himself an alternative source of arms, recognized Communist China. Secretary of State Dulles, irked by Nasser's boldness and pressed by Congress, emerged from a prolonged period of sullen reappraisal to cancel abruptly the United States' offer to help Egypt build the Aswan Dam. Nasser, anticipating such a step, as he later revealed, reacted swiftly by nationalizing the Suez Canal in July 1956. With this, the thrusts and counterthrusts reached the point of a showdown: Britain and France, the principal shareholders in the Suez Canal Company and the main users of the waterway, were determined to make Nasser "disgorge," while the United States backed its allies formally and sought worriedly to "defuse" the crisis.

We need not concern ourselves here with the three-month-long effort led by Dulles to settle the Canal crisis by diplomatic means except to point out that it resulted in alienating the British and French governments from the American and impelled them to decide to take military action on their own against Nasser. Before translating this decision into operative plans, the French explored on behalf of themselves and their British allies the possibility of Israeli participation in the envisaged action. Whether under different circumstances the Israelis might have held back is a question few, other than committed people, would venture to answer. It was certain, however, that under the *existing* circumstances the Israelis found the opportunity irresistible. First, the memory of their recent isolation at a moment of peril was still fresh in their mind, especially the effort of the three Western powers to wiggle out of the commitment to their security they had assumed in the Tripartite Declaration. Second, largely because of the feeble reaction of the Western powers to the arms deal, a war psychosis had gripped the area that expressed itself in furious incursions across the borders and in military-diplomatic preparations that brought the Syrian army under Egyptian command and were soon to do the same with Jordan's army. For Israel to hold back in these circumstances would have only given time to the Egyptians to assimilate more fully the vast amounts of weapons they had received and to avail themselves of the great strategic advantage to be derived from effective control of the forces in Syria and in the Jordanian bulge. Moreover, there were the *fida'iyyun* raids that could not be controlled by conventional limited action, and there was the old sore of the blockade of the Gulf of Aqaba and the closure of the Suez Canal. Finally, there was the hope that the newly opened French source of vitally needed arms might open wider through Israeli participation and the fear that it might close if Israel abstained. Under these circumstances, the surprising thing is not that Israel joined, but the tough bargaining with the French and the British that Ben Gurion engaged in before agreeing to participate.[8]

As is well known, the war began on October 29, 1956, with a drop of Israeli paratroopers near the Mitla Pass, some 30 miles east of the Suez Canal, which was followed by a dash by a mobile column across

---

[8] Ben Gurion insisted among other things on obtaining written evidence of the British and French collusion, arms from France, air cover for Israel.

southern Sinai to join with the paratroopers. This movement was designed, according to plans worked out in advance, to give an "excuse"
to the British and French to intervene in order to "protect" the Suez
Canal. The Israelis, whose recent experience had made them extremely
suspicious, made no significant further moves until their secret allies
actually delivered their incredible ultimatum on the next day, requiring them and the Egyptians to stay ten kilometers clear of the Canal on either side and announcing that Franco-British troops would be
landing anyway in order to secure uninterrupted navigation. Were the
British and the French to have second thoughts, the Israelis wanted to
be in a position to withdraw and claim that their action had been
merely a large-scale retaliatory raid. As things turned out, the ultimatum was given, the Israelis naturally accepted it since they lost
nothing by doing so, and the Egyptians rejected it since they lost nothing by doing so either. The Franco-British air forces then began
pounding Egyptian airfields, military concentrations, and lines of
communication prior to the landing of troops in Port Said three days
later, and the Israelis launched an all-out attack along their entire
front.

While this action was taking place, the diplomatic front came alive.
In the United Nations, the United States assumed a leading role in
marshaling opposition to the Franco-British-Israeli action that expressed itself in a series of quickly and overwhelmingly adopted resolutions calling for immediate cease-fire and withdrawal of foreign
forces from Egypt. The Soviet Union, while seconding the United
States' effort in the United Nations, sent a series of notes to the attacking powers culminating in one to Israel that questioned its future existence, and one each to France and Britain brandishing the implicit
threat of using rockets against them if they did not desist immediately
and withdraw their forces. By November 6, Britain and France agreed
to cease fire immediately and to withdraw as soon as a United Nations
Emergency Force, decided upon two days before, could take over their
positions. Israel had actually ceased fire earlier, and on November 8 it
agreed to withdraw from *most* of the territory it had occupied.

The general course of the fighting was quite different on the Franco-
British front along the Suez Canal and the Israeli front in Sinai. On
the former front, the allied command operated ponderously and cautiously as if time were not a factor at all. It spent three precious days
in preparatory air action and then proceeded to execute elaborate
landing and consolidation operations before finally breaking out of
Port Said southwards. It acted like a dentist anesthetizing his patient
completely and putting him through preparations for major surgery

before pulling out his tooth. By the time their governments could no longer resist issuing a cease-fire order on November 6, the Franco-British forces were less than one-third of the way down the 100-mile long Canal. The Israelis, on the other hand, once they ascertained that the British and the French were indeed intervening, thrust themselves upon the Egyptian front, made a number of breakthroughs, and pushed on relentlessly without much concern for by-passed positions until they reached the vicinity of the Canal in the west and Sharm el Sheikh in the south within less than one hundred hours. The speed of their movement converted an intended Egyptian strategic retreat into a rout.

The merit of the Israeli performance in Sinai from a purely military point of view has been wildly overvalued or grossly underestimated by outside observers. However, this is not of so much interest to us as the conclusions drawn by the parties to the conflict themselves; and here, surprisingly, the views of *responsible* Israelis and Egyptians have not been very far apart. Notwithstanding different interpretations of detail, both sides essentially recognized that Franco-British intervention neutralized the Egyptian air force, tied one hand of the Egyptian command, led it to issue a retreat order to large units that had not been overrun, and had a generally demoralizing effect on the troops. Nevertheless, both sides also agreed, the Israelis made the most of the situation through the application of great skill and drive, but for which they might not have achieved their objectives *in the time allotted them* by circumstances, and this might have made a considerable difference materially, morally, and politically. This agreement was sustained by the contrast both sides made with the Franco-British action, where the high command failed to avail itself of its at least equally favorable odds over the Egyptians to achieve fast enough the objective it had set for itself.

An interesting aspect of the conflict was the inaction of other Arab countries. Iraq's passivity was not surprising since it was at that time at odds with Egypt and allied to Britain. With regard to Jordan and Syria, which had at least nominally put their troops under Egyptian command, the inaction was less understandable. Shortly after the war, Nasser claimed that the Syrians had wanted to intervene but that he had dissuaded them on the grounds that since his troops were about to retreat from Sinai, he did not wish to leave them exposed to the Israelis by themselves. A similar explanation for Jordan's nonintervention was given by Muhammad Hassanein Haykal, Nasser's confidant and editor of *al Ahram,* but only ten years later.

Whether these explanations were true or not, the Israelis and the world at large doubted them, and the Egyptians subsequently acted as if they did not believe them themselves, as we shall have occasion to see.

Of the many momentous consequences of the war, we need to concern ourselves at this point only with a few that seem essential for understanding the subsequent course of the Arab-Israeli conflict. The war relieved Israel of what might have been an immediate grave threat but did nothing to further a solution of the conflict; on the contrary, the defeat inflicted by the Israelis upon the Egyptian army deepened the Arab desire for revenge, and their collusion with Britain and France gave substance to the Arab conviction that Israel was a tool of imperialism. It temporarily upset the military balance in the area by destroying much Egyptian equipment and putting out of action several Egyptian divisions; but the Russians immediately began to make up for the lost equipment and the rebuilding of the army was quickly resumed. The war did not alter the territorial situation either, since Israel was forced to cede back all the terrain it had captured. Israel did achieve free passage through the Gulf of Aqaba, but even this was more a factual gain than a juridically sanctioned accomplishment. Supporting it was the presence of United Nations troops at Sharm el Sheikh, at the entrance of the Gulf, and an assurance on the part of the United States that it would uphold the exercise of the right of innocent passage by Israel and other nations in what it considered to be international waters. But, on the other hand, the Egyptians did not formally acknowledge Israel's right, and they could, at their discretion, dismiss the United Nations troops. So far they have not done this because they have not felt themselves prepared to confront an almost certain showdown with Israel, and possibly the United States; but the moment they feel ready for a showdown with the one and doubtful about the intervention of the other, they would not need to look far for a provocation to start a war.[9]

The Egyptians' forbearance of United Nations troops at the tip of the Gulf of Aqaba and along their border with Israel bespeaks what is perhaps the most important consequence of the Sinai War for the Arab-Israeli conflict. It reflects a determination on the part of Nasser not to allow himself again to become compromised by current incidents, secondary issues, and the clamor of Arab opinion into a war with Israel, as he had in the course of 1956. To this decision he has so far stuck with remarkable firmness in the face of repeated taunts by his Arab enemies, the manifest impatience of his Arab fans, and the

[9] Written in the summer of 1966.

frequent eruptions of border warfare between Israel and Syria and Jordan. This does not mean that Nasser has avoided unwitting war in order to tread unwittingly on the road to peace with Israel. On the contrary, Egypt's commitment to the goal of integral Arab unity, which took place shortly after the Sinai War, engaged it more than ever before to the ultimate destruction or dismemberment of Israel.

The Pattern of Inter-Arab Relations and the Arab-Israeli Conflict

Introduction

Although the Arab-Israeli conflict has been a crucial factor behind the process of arms buildup in the Middle East with its concomitant pattern of politics revolving on threat and deterrence, it has not by any means been the only one. Two other factors have decisively contributed to the process both independently and through their added effect on the Arab-Israeli conflict itself. One of these, to be discussed in this chapter, is the complex course of inter-Arab relations in the years since World War II. The other, to be discussed in the next chapter, is the course of the big power rivalry in the Middle East during the same period.

Unless a completely deterministic view of history is taken, it is easy to imagine a process of competitive arms buildup and its concomitant style of politics taking place in the Middle East in the absence of the Israeli factor and solely as a result of relations among the Arab countries in interplay with big power politics. Perhaps the western Arab world, with which we are not concerned in this study, provides a good illustration of this proposition. Morocco, Algeria, and Tunisia have been only marginally concerned with the Israeli problem; yet, despite the multitude of ties that bind them and despite an impressive record of assistance on the part of Tunisia and Morocco to Algeria during its struggle for independence, Algeria's regime and its political orientation have led its neighbors to eye with suspicion the growth of its armed power and to seek to counter its buildup. Already one short but sharp, large-scale armed encounter has taken place between Morocco and Algeria (in 1963) to give substance to the mutual fear and suspicion.

Another way of confirming our proposition may be to look in a summary fashion at the last decade's record of the use of armed forces and violence among the Arab countries with which we are directly concerned. Without any connection to the Arab-Israeli conflict, the following took place:

1. Egypt at one time or another sent troops into Syria, Iraq, Kuwait, the Sudan, Algeria. Its armed forces have been engaged in hostilities in Yemen since 1962. Its air force has raided Saudi Arabian territory several times. It has attempted to instigate or support revolution in Syria, Lebanon, Iraq, Jordan, Saudi Arabia, and Yemen, not to speak of the western Arab world.

2. Syria has sent troops into Iraq and Jordan on some occasions and has attempted to instigate rebellion in both of them on other occasions.

3. Iraq has sent troops into Jordan, has massed troops to threaten Syria, and has attempted to instigate coups and rebellions there on more than one occasion.

4. Saudi Arabia has sent troops into Jordan a number of times, into Kuwait once, has supported with money and arms the royalists in Yemen against the Egyptians and the republicans since 1962, and has attempted to instigate rebellion and political assassination at one time or another in Syria, Jordan, and Egypt.

5. Jordan has sent troops into Kuwait, massed troops against Syria, and supported the Yemeni royalists at different times.

Almost all the troop movements across international boundaries mentioned above took place at the invitation of the government of the country into which they marched. However, they were nearly all intended to bolster one Arab state against another Arab state or one Arab government against segments of its own population supported by other Arab governments. The threats, air attacks, and instigations to rebellion were of course of a different category, being unsolicited by the governments on the receiving end. But action in both categories obviously expressed politics of threat and deterrence and called for the building of military capabilities on a competitive basis. That such buildup could reach impressive magnitudes is indicated by the fact that at one point Egypt had up to 70,000 troops in Yemen and that at one moment in 1966 Saudi Arabia ordered $400 million worth of military equipment to meet a perceived threat from Egypt.

Conflicts and clashes among the Arab countries have been in some instances of the kind that underlies disputes between any neighboring countries. The great majority of them, however, have had their roots in the very "Arabness" they all profess to share. The great irony of the Arab peoples has indeed been that their sense of Arab community has developed sufficiently over the years to make some of their governments, states, and political groupings feel entitled to meddle in the affairs of others in its name, thus heightening tension, friction, and conflict among all, but that this sense has not developed enough to impel all governments, states, and political groupings to renounce or modify their particularistic interests, views, and orientations for the sake of achieving real unity. The principles of sovereignty and territorial integrity of states have thus been subverted in the name of the higher principle of a single Arab political community before that principle had acquired a generally acknowledged standing and meaning. This state of suspension might have been terminated if one country, grouping, or leader had developed the required strength to override particularistic resistances and impose unity. However, the one likely candidate for such a role, Nasser of Egypt, has himself been caught in an intermediate position: While he felt too strong to compose his differences with others, he has proved too weak to impose his conception on them.

We cannot in this work do full justice to the fascinating and intricate history of inter-Arab relations. However, since we need to achieve some understanding in depth of these relations in terms of their connection with the arms buildup and the Arab-Israeli conflict, we have decided to follow here the same "topical approach" we have used in our discussion of the Arab-Israeli conflict. To elucidate the paradox of heightened inter-Arab conflicts *because* of inter-Arab affinity, we shall focus our attention in the selection of topics and in their treatment on the evolution of the idea of pan-Arabism and will follow this with an attempt to relate our discussion to the Arab-Israeli conflict and the arms buildup.

On the Origins of Pan-Arabism

Pan-Arabism is a term that does not have an exact equivalent in Arabic and does not have a precise meaning in English.[1] When we speak

[1] Arabic writers from the beginning of this century have translated pan-Arabism as "Arab league"—*jami'ah 'arabiyyah*—on the analogy of pan-Islamism, a European term which preceded it—*jami'ah islamiyyah*. But a contemporary Arab

here of pan-Arabism, we take it in its broadest historical sense and mean by it an idea and a movement that recognize a close affinity among Arab peoples (not well-defined) and seek to give that affinity some meaningful political expression. The nature of that expression may range all the way from limited cooperation among some Arab entities to the constitution of a single nation embracing all the Arabic speaking peoples.

As is the case with any idea susceptible of many meanings, the idea of pan-Arabism has been traced back by scholars to several different sources. Some have seen its beginnings in the thoughts, dreams, and policies entertained by Ibrahim pasha, son of Muhammad Ali of Egypt, during the period he governed Syria on behalf of his father in the 1830's. Others have traced it back to Syrian Christian Arab writers of the last quarter of the nineteenth century who are credited as the intellectual progenitors of Arab nationalism. Still others find its origins in some mysterious English conspirator who insinuated to Khedive Abbas II of Egypt (1892–1914) the idea of establishing and heading an Arab caliphate. Whatever the historians may believe about paternity and birthdate, the important point from our perspective is that all the versions at least implicitly consider the origin of the idea of pan-Arabism to be causally linked to the process of disintegration of the Ottoman empire. Concepts of solidarity are often best understood by reference to the concepts *against* which they are asserted; in this case, pan-Arabism defined a solidarity principle that was in opposition to the broader principle of Ottomanism, itself resting largely on the idea of Muslim solidarity.

On the origins of pan-Arabism as a political movement rather than as an idea historians are more in agreement. They see its first manifestations in the demands made by Arab notables and members of the Ottoman Representative Assembly established after the Young Turk Revolution of 1908 for equal Arab representation, decentralization of government, and autonomy of the Arab regions. The notion of Arab regions did not include Egypt, which already enjoyed an autonomous status within the Ottoman empire and was under British occupation.

The rebuff of the Arab notables by the Young Turk leaders created

---

would understand by *jami'ah 'arabiyyah* the organization called the Arab League rather than the concept of pan-Arabism. For that concept he would probably use some term that translates as "Arab unity," which he would also use for the very specific idea of integral political merger! All this sounds, and is, very confusing; this is why we should stick to what *we* mean by pan-Arabism and remember that a contemporary Arab may have some difficulty in rendering that meaning back into his own language.

an estrangement between the two groups that favored the formation of some small secret societies that sought complete Arab independence. Neither the group seeking decentralization nor those seeking independence had gotten very far by the time World War I broke out. For they were essentially composed of partly westernized officials and notables or army officers without considerable power or backing. The great bulk of the Arab population and most of its leaders considered themselves loyal subjects of the Ottoman sultan-caliph and acted accordingly in the trying years of the war.

Pan-Arabism in World War I and After

The war brought new forces into play that gave the idea of pan-Arabism a fresh chance even as they transformed its content.

Britain, which had been committed through most of the nineteenth century to a policy of preserving the integrity of the Ottoman empire for reasons of national interest, now found itself at war with its protégé. As part of its effort against its new enemy, Britain sought to detach from the Ottoman empire its Arab portions by the time-tested method that had already reduced the empire to a shadow of its former self: playing on the ambitions and fears of local rulers and encouraging nationalist groups in order to bring about secession and revolt. British agents made contacts with all sorts of Arab groups but in the end settled upon Sherif[2] Hussein, the guardian of the holy cities of Mecca and Medina. Hussein, who suspected the Ottoman government of plotting his dismissal, was eager to cooperate and had the advantage, from the British point of view, of being of exalted religious descent and holding a position of great religious dignity. He could therefore be used to deflate the call to Holy War issued by the Ottoman chiefs, which the British greatly feared because of its possible impact on the Muslim subjects of their empire, especially in India. That Hussein was a traditional man out of touch with the younger Arab generations and with the nationalist spirit was one of his disadvantages; but the British attempted to remedy this by pushing forward his son, Faysal, and encouraging the latter to establish contact with the secret Arab nationalist societies and to adopt their nationalist phraseology.

The deal which the British worked out with Hussein required him to proclaim a revolt against the Ottoman empire and rally Arab forces to fight it (which he did in June 1916) in exchange for their promise "to support Arab independence" in the Arab-inhabited territories of

[2] Sherif is the title of a descendant of the prophet Muhammad.

the empire except for the not wholly Arab area "west of the districts of Damascus, Homs, Hama, and Aleppo," on which the French had claims acknowledged by the British. The agreement did not, as is often mistakenly suggested, envisage a single Arab state to be set up in the area of Arab independence. Indeed, it spoke explicitly of Arab governments in the plural, and subsequently the Arab nationalists themselves proclaimed two states in addition to the Kingdom of Hidjaz. Nor was independence conceived as precluding "advice and assistance" on the part of outside powers. It was understood, however, without its being written down, that the several Arab states would all be united by a dynastic link through Hussein's house.

The incredibly complex story of the fate these promises met in the postwar years as they became entangled with other British commitments and interests has been told many times and need not be repeated here. For the purpose of outlining the evolution of pan-Arabism and the pattern of inter-Arab relations, it will suffice to make the following brief observations:

1. The idea of a number of dynastically linked Arab states covering the Arab-inhabited territories of the Ottoman empire never achieved more than an ephemeral nominal existence. Hussein proclaimed himself king of the Hidjaz with the agreement and support of the British. An Arab nationalist congress in Damascus proclaimed his son, Faysal, king of Syria, including Palestine, and another son, Abdallah, king of Iraq, in the teeth of British cautioning advice. However, Abdallah never set foot in Iraq, and Faysal's reign in Damascus was brought to a brusque end by French troops who marched from the coast and established French rule throughout Syria, exclusive of Palestine. The latter country became a British mandate and Britain was enjoined to fulfill the terms of the Balfour Declaration. As for Hussein himself, he became alienated from the British, proclaimed himself caliph of the Arabs, became involved in a war with Emir Ibn Saud of the neighboring principality of Najd, lost his kingdom to him, and went into exile.

2. The Hashimite (Hussein's) family and the aspirations it espoused were, however, saved from complete bankruptcy by the British. They arranged to make Faysal king of the new state of Iraq, which they had established under their mandatory control, and they made his brother Abdallah emir of the hastily constituted principality of Transjordan, also under their mandate.

3. The new Hashimite rulers were grateful to the British for restoring their fortunes after complete disaster, but they and their descendants never ceased to look upon the domains once promised by

the British to Hussein as their unredeemed patrimony. With respect to
the Hidjaz, this attitude nurtured a deep hostility between the House
of Hashim and the House of Saud, which has been a central motif of
Arab politics until recent years. With respect to Syria and Palestine,
the situation was different. In both of these countries many influential
families retained a sense of loyalty to the Hashimites and saw them as
the bearers of the idea of Arab unity and its proper focus; but the consummation of the Hashimite aspirations was obstructed by the presence of the French in one case and the British commitment to the
Zionists in the other. When these obstacles began to be removed in
the crucible of World War II and its aftermath, the Hashimite rulers
rushed back with schemes for uniting Syria and Palestine under their
aegis; but by then new forces had emerged, mostly from within the
Arab camp itself, to oppose them.

4. Throughout the period discussed so far, Egypt had very little association with the pan-Arab idea. Whatever thoughts Ibrahim pasha
may have entertained with regard to the Arab world during his brief
tenure as governor of Syria in the 1830's, these came to an end after
his forces were compelled to withdraw from there in 1840. All the intellectual and political development of Egypt for the next hundred
years centered either upon Egypt itself or upon Islam as the essential
foci of identity. The few instances of pan-Arab interest, mostly ema-
nating from ambitious monarchs, were the exceptions that proved the
rule. Thus the secret interest of Abbas II in an Arab caliphate was denounced by Muhammad Farid, leader of the Egyptian Nationalist Party.
Similar expressions of interest by King Fuad in the early 1920's were
opposed by all Egyptian political parties of the time and evoked a remark by Sa'd Zaghlul, leader of the massive Wafd party, that is still
remembered in Egypt today: Asked why he did not support a union
of the Arab countries, he answered because zero plus zero equals zero.
Finally, when King Faruq played with the same idea in the 1930's and
1940's, the Wafd attempted to undercut his efforts by supporting the
much wider project of the Arab League that explicitly preserved the
sovereignty of the member states.

The Arab League: Its Origins and Politics

The formation of the Arab League in 1945 constitutes an important
landmark in any survey of pan-Arabism and inter-Arab relations. This
institution, maligned by its own members even more than by outsiders,
gave the pan-Arab idea its first formally organized expression. It affili-
ated at the outset all seven Arab countries that were formally indepen-

dent at the time and has since been joined by each of the six Arab countries that gained independence afterwards. It has endured to the present, surviving momentous upheavals and political change in all the Arab countries and becoming nearly the oldest existing political institution in the Arab world. Out of the Arab League much more powerful streams of pan-Arabism have branched; but the League has remained the only expression of pan-Arabism that is universally shared by all Arab countries.

Of course, this record of longevity and comprehensiveness has been attained at the cost of catering to the lowest common denominator. In the political sphere, even with regard to those issues that were generally recognized as properly its own, the League has been paralyzed or condemned to failure from the outset by the existence of rival blocs and conflicting purposes. Indeed, its very creation may be said to have been a "plot" by some Arab countries to frustrate the realization by the Hashimites of a meaningful but restricted Arab unity by thrusting in its place a broader but greatly diluted pan-Arab ideal.

The two decades since the crystallization of the post-World War I settlement had witnessed very little change in the pan-Arab idea and in inter-Arab relations. Events such as the bombardment of Damascus by the French in 1925 or the revolt of the Palestine Arabs in the late thirties evoked echoes of sympathy and inspired flurries of support on the part of some governments and private groups; but no important development on the level of thought or action could take place as long as the Arab countries were under different regimes of political dependence under British and French political control. The main political energies of the Arab peoples and leaders were absorbed in local political struggles and in efforts to wrest a greater degree of independence from the occupying powers.

World War II caused a crucial change in this situation. It removed the French from the Levant and the Italians from Libya, leaving Britain for the first time the sole big power in the Middle East. At the same time, the exhausting burden the war had imposed on Britain, on the one hand, and the renewed and intensified nationalist pressures it had stirred, on the other hand, made a revision of the entire political status of the area inescapable. As soon as this became apparent, after the declaration of the independence of Syria and Lebanon, even before the end of the war, the Hashimite governments rushed in with pan-Arab schemes that intended to pick up the thread where it had been left at the end of World War I. Nuri al Said, Iraq's perennial prime minister, produced a plan for a union of the Fertile Crescent comprising Iraq, Syria, Lebanon, Transjordan, and Palestine; while Emir Abdallah produced his Greater Syria plan, designed to unite Syria, Lebanon, and Palestine to his Transjordan.

The Hashimite projects stirred opposition in various quarters. Opinion in Syria was generally favorable to the idea of Arab unity, but the hundred families that inherited power from the French were reluctant to surrender it so soon to the Hashimites and their courtiers. The Christians of Lebanon, who constituted half the population, were not too eager to be reduced to a tiny minority in a large Muslim state. King Ibn Saud saw a threat to his dynasty and realm in an enlarged and strengthened Hashimite state. King Faruq of Egypt considered that if there were to be any grouping of Arab states he was more entitled to head it than the Hashimites. All these apprehensions eventually yielded suggestions of forming an all-embracing but more loosely bound Arab grouping that would take the wind out of the Hashimite plans.

The British, whose dominant position in the area gave them many critical levers with which to affect its politics, were actively interested in the idea of some kind of Arab grouping as a base on which to reorganize their position in the area. They too were inclined to pick up the thread where they had left it some quarter of a century before. At first they looked with favor upon the schemes of their trusted Hashimite friends as a means for securing their own position and extending it to the Levant, newly rid of the French. However, in the face of the opposition from Arab countries and quarters where they had additional interests to protect and promote, the British decided to throw their weight behind the idea of a broader and looser scheme in the hope of securing through it their interests in the whole Middle East. This stand and the active mediation efforts of able British agents proved decisive. In 1944 two conferences, attended by representatives of Egypt, Saudi Arabia, Yemen, Transjordan, Syria, Lebanon, and Iraq, were successively held in Alexandria and Cairo and produced the organization that came to be known as the Arab League.

The charter of the Arab League was designed more to put obstacles in the way of the Hashimite dreams than to provide means of inter-Arab association. It explicitly stressed the principle of the full sovereignty of all members and established the rule that decisions taken by the organization were binding only upon those members who accepted them. It did not rule out tighter unity arrangements among some of its members by mutual consent, but it indirectly made the likelihood of such arrangements more difficult in at least two ways. In the first place it weakened the pressure for unity that the Hashimites might be able to exert on such states as Lebanon and Syria by providing in effect a collective guarantee of the sovereignty of each state. In the second place, on the excuse that all members ought to be given the chance to join any more advanced unity arrangement, it forced the Hashimites into the position of having either to put their projects on the agenda where they could be discussed to death, or to by-pass the League and open themselves to the charge of working conspiratorially.

The Arab League was officially established as an instrument for inter-Arab cooperation that might gradually lead to greater and greater degrees of Arab association. But even in the sphere of cooperation the League was beset from the beginning by the internal antagonisms and contradictions that marked its birth. Nowhere was this demonstrated more dramatically and with more disastrous results than in the League's armed intervention in Palestine. In the civil war that broke out after the passage of the 1947 partition resolution, the Arab League decided to support the Palestinian Arabs with money, arms, and volunteers. However, each of the Arab countries that responded to the decision sought to dispense its assistance primarily to rival client groups in order to promote through them its influence and ambitions in Palestine. When, partly due to the resulting uncoordination of effort, the Palestinians went down to defeat, the Arab League decided to authorize King Abdallah of Transjordan to send in his Arab Legion to fight the Zionists upon the termination of the British Mandate. As we have already indicated, Abdallah intended to use his army in order to secure for himself the part of Palestine allocated to the Arabs by the partition plan and whatever additional territory he could capture; but the suspicion that such was his motive led King Faruq to press his government to commit Egypt's armed forces to the war, as much to frustrate Abdallah's plans as to fight the Zionists. This move, in turn, induced the governments of Syria, Lebanon, and Iraq too to send their troops to what promised to be a parade to Tel Aviv. The results of this improvised, uncoordinated effort guided by contradictory political objectives have already been discussed: military defeat, loss of Arab territory to Israel, hundreds of thousands of refugees, Egypt left to fight repeated Israeli offensives alone, annexation of the remainder of the Palestinian Arab territory by Transjordan, bitter feuds and mutual recriminations among the Arab governments, a wave of political assassinations, immediate collapse of the Syrian regime and, four years later, of Faruq's regime.

The Palestine fiasco destroyed any vestige of British influence on the League and came very close to destroying the organization itself. The League was saved only by the revival of the Hashimite schemes of political union with Syria as a result of the sensed need among leaders of that country to seek in union the means of protection and revenge against Israel. To prevent the Hashimites from capitalizing on Syria's needs, their opponents came forward with a project for a collective security pact among all League members, which was eventually concluded and marked the resuscitation of the organization. Thus, ironically, the very rivalries that had brought the League to the verge of destruction turned out to be the reason for its salvation. This desire of all to be included lest some should go off on their own was also to be the ground for the League's enduring.

Neither the Mutual Security Pact nor any of the numerous other collective political, economic, and military initiatives undertaken by the Arab League throughout its existence have been of any practical consequence in themselves. Except for the general boycott of Israel and for a modicum of cooperation in the United Nations, the Arab League has been rent by disagreements even over important international issues, where cooperation was recognized as one of its proper central functions. Yet, the record of the League's failures as an active political organization should not obscure its very important passive achievements in this very sphere or its success on other levels.

The Arab League scored two fundamental achievements: It gave the idea of pan-Arabism an institutionalized expression that made it part of Arab daily life, and it broadened the purview of the concept "Arab" to embrace Egypt and other countries that had not previously identified themselves as Arab and were not so considered by others. Regardless of divergent interests and positions, the Arab League provided a forum before which all Arab governments had at least to justify their policies from an all-Arab point of view. The importance of this fact in implanting and reinforcing a consciousness of general pan-Arab standards is all too often obscured from the sight of those, including the Arabs themselves, who dwell exclusively on the departures from these standards and their violation in practice. Equally underestimated has been the contribution to the development of this consciousness made by the League's very extensive activities in the social and cultural spheres.

Besides these achievements, which might be called strategic from a pan-Arab point of view, the League's contribution on what might be called the "tactical" levels of inter-Arab relations has not been altogether negligible or negative. It has played the role of a miniature United Nations, giving the parties to a dispute at least an additional instrumentality for diplomatic action, allowing for mediation where positions were not too far apart, making possible face-saving solutions when other means had led to a stalemate, providing convenient auspices for "summit meetings," mounting peacekeeping operations through Arab League "presence," as in the conflict between Iraq and Kuwait, and so on. These accomplishments of the League had much to do with the fact that no country or group of countries would take the responsibility for killing the organization though some of them could have done so, and that no country or group of countries withdrew from it except to come back to it later.

Pan-Arab Appeals Over the Heads of Governments

The Arab League had been conceived as an organization for pan-Arab cooperation among sovereign states rather than as a popular movement, as its full name in Arabic carefully specified (*Jami'at al Duwal al 'Arabiyyah*, literally, The League of the Arab *States*). It was meant to transact business of common Arab interest on a government-to-government basis and did so for the first eight or nine years of its existence. This understanding did not preclude some governments from working secretly on pan-Arab projects on a bilateral basis, nor did it preclude some governments from working secretly with the opposition behind the back of some other government, as the Iraqis repeatedly attempted to do in Syria. What mattered, however, from the point of view of the evolution of pan-Arabism, was that the Arab publics or peoples were overtly engaged only through their governments.

It was therefore a new and very consequential development when governments involved in disputes over issues alleged to be of common Arab concern began to go openly and systematically over each other's heads and to present their case directly to the people of the opponent. This development, as well as others we shall presently consider, did not cancel the framework within which the League was supposed to operate, but simply bifurcated from it and unfolded side by side with it. It added a new dimension to inter-Arab relations, which entailed at least implicitly the assumption that the Arab peoples formed one single constituency and the Arab countries one common homeland. This represented an advance over the pan-Arab idea embodied in the League; but it also meant that disputes between governments became more profound and antagonisms more bitter since it put the existence of governments at stake.

This development took place in 1954–1955, and the responsibility for it lay with Nasser's government. The issue over which it first occurred was the dispute between Nasser's Egypt and Nuri al Said's Iraq over the latter's intention to join what came to be known as the Baghdad Pact and to draw other Arab countries into it. The two sides felt their vital interests were involved and compromise proved impossible to achieve. The Saudis, ever fearful of the Hashimites, sided with Egypt as did Yemen. Lebanon took a traditional neutral position, while Syria and Jordan, still undecided, were courted and pressured by the two parties.

Nasser, having recently come to power through a coup d'état, felt no legitimist scruples about appealing to the Iraqis, Syrians, and Jordanians over the heads of their governments. The appeal took the form of a massive propaganda campaign, using newly established powerful broadcasting facilities, in which the Iraqi leaders were depicted as tools of imperialism and defectors from the Arab cause. The Saudis backed Egyptian propaganda with liberal distribution of bribe money in Syria and Jordan. The combined Egyptian-Saudi pressure succeeded fairly easily in Syria, where a government favorably inclined toward the Pact gave way peacefully to one that aligned itself with Egypt. In Hashimite Jordan, however, the campaign was harder and lasted longer, and it was not until mob violence had erupted and two Jordanian governments had fallen within a week that the king took a stand against the Pact and veered in the direction of Egypt.

The success of the Egyptians in isolating the Iraqis was facilitated by two events that lent special weight to Nasser's appeal to the Arab peoples over the heads of their governments. The first was the announcement in September 1955 of the arms agreement between Egypt and Czechoslovakia (actually Russia), concluded by Nasser to counter the military advantages Iraq was expected to gain from its membership in the Pact and to grapple with the deteriorating situation on the border with Israel. As previously indicated, the Arab masses saw the acquisition of the weapons and the implicit promise of Soviet political support that went with it as offering the prospect of a triumphant confrontation with Israel; and Nasser, as the architect of the move, was thrust into the position of all-Arab hero. The second event was the announcement by the United States in December of the same year of its willingness to support the construction of the mammoth Aswan Dam, the master project of Egypt's regime. This move was viewed in the Arab world as crucial not only because of the intrinsic importance of the Dam but also because of its political implications. After having just defied the West with his arms deal, Nasser was able to obtain from the United States massive economic support instead of hostility. With such a man, it appeared, nothing was impossible. The test of Nasser's sudden enormous popularity was demonstrated in Jordan, with the devastating effect already described.

Once Nasser was thrust into the limelight of the Arab world, he no longer needed to make any special effort to direct the Arab masses away from their governments; they responded to his moves almost spontaneously. By the same token, he was no longer as free to determine his own actions as before but had to act the role in which the Arab imagination had cast him. He had to act boldly and win or to make believe he did; and he had to assume responsibilities that he had not anticipated.

The need to act boldly and win was clearly dramatized in the Suez episode. Having been rebuffed by the United States' withdrawal of the offer to help build the Aswan Dam, Nasser responded with the sensational move of nationalizing the Suez Canal. The Arab masses did not wait for their governments to give them a cue as to how to react; they cheered Nasser's move and forced even the most reluctant of their governments to give public support to his decision.[3] The same pattern was repeated when the French and the British in collusion with Israel invaded Egypt to regain control of the Canal; the mobs sacked French and British institutions before their governments decided to break off diplomatic relations or adopt other measures indicating displeasure. As for the defeat of the Egyptian forces at the hands of the Israelis, this was easily explained away to a public eager to believe, especially since in the final account Nasser ended up in possession of the Canal and with the invading forces out of Egyptian territory.

Pan-Arabism as Integral Unity

The enormous appeal of Nasser to the Arab publics across political frontiers and over the heads of hostile governments had in fact burst the boundaries of the conception of pan-Arabism as cooperation among sovereign states. The question after Suez was whether these shattered boundaries were to be restored to the *status quo ante* or whether the notion of pan-Arabism was to be given new and all-encompassing lines of demarcation. The answer to this question emerged in the course of the year or so following the liquidation of the Suez war and was, unequivocally, that pan-Arabism was now to signify the ideal of integral unity of the Arab countries.

The merger of Egypt and Syria in the United Arab Republic in Feb-

---

[3] Anthony Eden, Britain's Prime Minister at the time, told in his memoirs how the news of Nasser's nationalization of the Canal reached him at a moment he was with Nuri al-Said. The Iraqi premier, upon being told the news, urged Eden to strike at Nasser, and strike hard. Yet officially and publicly, Nuri found it necessary to proclaim Iraq's support for Nasser's move. (See Lord Avon, *Full Circle*, Boston, 1960, p. 18.)

ruary 1958 and the federation of Iraq and Jordan in the Arab Union shortly thereafter were convincing expressions of the new resolution and the political pressures it engendered; yet no Arab country, with the possible exception of Syria, had deliberately sought this particular answer at that time. It came about as the unanticipated result of a struggle, involving the United States and the Soviet Union as well as the Arab countries, in which the issue was not Arab unity but rather the containment and defeat of the unwritten alliance between Nasser and the Soviet Union.

The politics of the big powers in the Middle East will be discussed in the next chapter, but for the sake of our present analysis we must refer to certain aspects briefly here: As the French and the British were pulling out of the Suez Canal zone in failure, the United States government woke up in alarm to the realization that there was little left to resist the extension of Nasser's political hegemony over the entire Middle East. The other Arab governments were intimidated by Nasser's popularity and divided among themselves, and the British and French were no longer in a position to shore them up after the collapse of their Suez venture. Given Nasser's dependence on the Soviet Union for political and material support, his success in dominating the area was seen in the United States at that time as tantamount to Soviet control of it.

To ward off the threat, the United States in January 1957 improvised the so-called Eisenhower Doctrine, by which, in the guise of resisting communism, it sought to rally and stiffen the timid Arab governments and to roll back Nasser's influence where it was already established. The policy seemed to work well for a while: It encouraged the Saudi government, which had hitherto been allied to Nasser because of its hostility to the Hashimites, to detach itself from him; it caused the Lebanese government, hitherto fearfully neutral, to align itself with the Doctrine and hence against Nasser; it even succeeded in April 1957 in helping King Hussein of Jordan get rid of his pro-Nasser government and reorient his country in a pro-Western direction. From then on, however, the policy hit only snags and failures that more than outweighed the accomplished gains.

Encouraged by the success in Jordan, the United States had sought, in the summer of 1957, to promote the overturn of the Syrian government, which had solidly aligned itself with Nasser and had cooperated closely with Russia on its own. The plot misfired, and the United States, badly compromised, sought to salvage the situation by putting pressure on Syria through Sixth Fleet maneuvers and movement of Turkish, Iraqi, and Jordanian troops on Syria's borders. As the Soviets made threatening noises, and the Egyptians jumped into the fray by sending troops into Syria at a cautiously chosen moment, a big war scare developed. Eventually, the crisis, which had been sadly lacking in plausible justification, was defused by the Arab countries themselves in October 1957 in the context of a United Nations meeting. However, it marked the failure of the American-led effort to roll back Nasser's influence, which was then left free to reassert itself more strongly than ever before. The first consequence was Syria's complete merger with Egypt.

Syria's bid to merge with Egypt had not been solely the result of the 1957 diplomatic crisis. At the bottom of it was an intricate tangle of internal politics involving the Communists, the Ba'th party, various army groups, and powerful political personalities, in which a coalition of forces led by the Ba'th sought in union with Egypt an escape from being out-maneuvered by its rivals. However, the crisis provided the climate for consummating the Ba'thist design. By scaring the Syrians, it made them generally feel an urgent need for strength in union, while its outcome made Nasser appear stronger than ever and therefore a natural refuge. Nasser himself had not, up to that point, sought integral unity with any Arab country (except the Sudan, but that was long ago and had no connection with pan-Arabism), and when confronted with the Syrian bid, he hesitated before accepting. It apparently took him some time to recognize the extent to which his previous tactics and his success in appealing to the Arab publics across legal boundaries had narrowed his choices. His eventual acceptance of the Syrian bid, logical as it was, nevertheless marked a crucial turning point in Arab affairs. It formally established integral unity as the goal of pan-Arabism and concomitantly escalated inter-Arab relations to a new level of tension by exerting heavy pressure on the independent Arab governments to comply with the new objective or risk condemnation and hostility as enemies of the supreme Arab aspiration.

The resultant shift in the state of inter-Arab relations was immediately reflected in a succession of moves and events that followed upon the formation of the United Arab Republic: The Hashimite governments of Iraq and Jordan, seeking to comply with the objective of Arab unity while creating for it a new pole of attraction, federated themselves in a new entity called the Arab Union; Yemen joined with the United Arab Republic in a loose confederation; in Saudi Arabia, the ruling establishment fell into confusion and emerged from it by transferring effective power from King Saud, who had become too closely identified with an anti-Nasserist policy, to his brother, Faysal. However, the pressures generated by the new situation were best seen in the events that transpired in Lebanon, immediately after the formation of the United Arab Republic, and in Iraq, after the overthrow of the Hashimite dynasty four months later.

Lebanon's politics from the time it achieved its independence in 1945 had rested on a delicate balance between the Muslim and Christian halves of its population. In foreign affairs, this balance reflected itself in a policy of solidarity with the Arab countries matched by close ties to the Western world. As long as solidarity with the Arab neighbors meant cooperation on issues of common interest within the frame of the Arab League, this policy worked well. However, the emergence of Nasser as an all-Arab figure put this approach under heavy stress by attracting the Muslims toward greater identification with his policies and driving the Christians to seek protection from his excessive influence through closer ties with the West. The formation of the union between Egypt and neighboring Syria brought this pressure to the breaking point by escalating the issue in the minds of the contenders from a matter of policy orientation to a question of the very existence of Lebanon as a sovereign entity. The result, working itself through a maze of strictly local and personality quarrels, was civil war. For several months Lebanon teetered on the verge of dissolution, until the outbreak of revolution in Iraq in July 1958 brought the United States Marines hurrying into the country in response to an outstanding invitation by its Christian president. American troops stayed in the country long enough for Lebanese good sense and genius for compromise to reassert themselves several months later and to restore Lebanon's traditional neutrality.

The Iraqi revolution destroyed the Hashimite dynasty and replaced it with a military regime headed by General Kassem. Kassem repudiated the Baghdad Pact, reoriented Iraq's foreign policy toward Russia, abolished the union with Jordan, reversed the budding cooperation with Saudi Arabia, and proclaimed his solidarity with Nasser's United Arab Republic. Yet it is indicative of the heightened level of pan-Arab expectations that this reorientation, which would have been considered a brilliant victory for pan-Arabism months before, was no longer considered sufficient by Nasser and much of Arab opinion because it stopped short of integral unity with the United Arab Republic. It was not that Kassem disassociated himself from the objective of integral Arab unity; he merely sought time to consolidate his position in Iraq and bargain for a more significant role in Arab affairs than he thought was assigned to him by Nasser. In any case, the difference between the two kindred regimes of Iraq and Egypt became the cause for a renewal of the feud between the two countries on a level of intensity far exceeding that which had characterized the fight between Nuri al-Said and Nasser. Where these two had fought primarily a battle of diplomacy and propaganda, Nasser and Kassem fought a merciless war of active mutual subversion, instigation of revolt in each other's domains, and threats of military intervention. Nuri al-Said's "crime" was that he had veered away from Arab solidarity by joining the Baghdad Pact; Kassem's "crime" was that after correcting Nuri's deviation he stayed put and by doing so became the *kassem* (divider) of the Arabs.

Arab Unity as the Handmaiden of Social Revolution

The adoption of the goal of integral Arab unity converted the idea of pan-Arabism into the idea of Arab nationalism. Like other nationalisms, Arab nationalism either assumed that an Arab nation existed objectively and sought to assert itself, or else at least took it for granted that the potential constituents of such a nation aspired to form one. This premise confronts all nationalist movements with the need to answer the question why, if the nation exists objectively or is desired by all, it does not *actually* assert itself; and this question, in turn, impels proponents of the nationalist idea to define the obstacles and enemies. Because the definition of the obstacles and enemies suggests the strategy to be pursued, and because the strategy determines the character of the movement, the answer to the question becomes central to a full understanding of the movement under consideration.

As integral Arab unity became the operative objective to which nearly all Arabs paid at least lip service, Nasser and his followers had to confront these questions. Immediately after the formation of the United Arab Republic, it was quite easy for them to identify the enemy that obstructed the achievement of the goal as hostile foreign powers and local rulers who were their hirelings. When, in the wake of the Iraqi revolution (thought at first to have been the work of Nasser's partisans) Arab nationalism seemed about to sweep all the Arab countries, did not the American Marines land in Lebanon and British paratroopers descend on Jordan at the request of their rulers to prevent such an outcome? However, subsequent events showed this explanation to be at least incomplete and raised questions requiring a redefinition of enemies, obstacles, and strategy. In the first place there was the case of Kassem's Iraq, as oriented toward Russia as Egypt and therefore presumably equally "free" of foreign control, yet opposed to union under Nasser. Then there was the shattering case of Syria's secession in 1961 from the union that already existed and was controlled by Egypt itself.

The answer devised to explain these events, particularly the latter, marked another turning point in the evolution of the idea of Arab nationalism and inter-Arab relations: It was that the capitalists in alliance with feudalists and colonialism were the true obstacle to unity because they were bound by the very nature of their interests to oppose it. It followed that the achievement of the supreme goal of Arab nationalism required the launching of a "class struggle" and internal revolution to eliminate the obstructionists. Thus the promotion of revolution became the prerequisite for Arab unity, and the Arab world was divided into two mutually hostile camps—states ruled by revolutionaries, ostensibly prepared for union, and states ruled by conservatives who had to be overthrown before union could have a chance.

The process by which this development took place is as interesting and as significant as the development itself. It involved a series of steps connected with policy decisions made by Nasser. Since Kassem's Russian orientation made him immune to the charge of being a lackey of imperialism, and as he survived a succession of plots and attempted uprisings, Nasser began to explain his opponent's resistance to Arab unity by claiming he was the captive of the Communists of Iraq, whose interests were best served by Arab disunity. Attacking Kassem on this score, however, eventually angered the Russians and led Premier Khrushchev to make a severe and rather humiliating public reprimand of Nasser in the early spring of 1959. Nasser courageously responded with a verbal counterattack citing Russian interference in internal Arab affairs; however, in view of his dependence on Russia for arms and Russia's commitment, only a few months before, to help in the financing and construction of the Aswan Dam, Nasser had little choice but to change course and confine his fight against Kassem to verbal sniping operations. At the same time, he sought to mend his fences with the United States for added insurance.

With the drive for Arab unity checked in Jordan and Lebanon with the help of the West, and in Iraq with the help of the East, Nasser turned his attention inward to the task of consolidating "the base" of Arab nationalism in Egypt and Syria. (This switch is reminiscent of Stalin's decision to consolidate socialism in one country after the world socialist revolution had been checked.) In Egypt, his action was straightforward and drastic. Starting from the accidental fact that many of the most important enterprises in Egypt had been taken over by the government from their previous British, French, and Jewish owners in the course of the 1956 war, Nasser decided to consecrate the predominance of the public sector and officially to adopt socialism and the principle of planned economy. Once this was proclaimed, the requisites of planning, the need to mobilize capital resources for development, the logic of events, bureaucratic empire building, and the feared or actual opposition of the Egyptian capitalists combined to lead the government further into taking a succession of ever more drastic measures of nationalization, socialization, and confiscatory taxation that culminated in the draconian decrees of July 1961. The task of political consolidation was served by the same measures when it did not actually inspire them, insofar as these measures deprived potential opponents of the regime among the well-to-do classes of the economic means of threatening it, and provided the government with the wherewithal to bestow benefits and patronage upon the less privileged classes and thus gain their support.

In Syria, the path of consolidation was much more tortuous and ultimately led to disaster. Whereas in Egypt political and economic consolidation went hand in hand, in Syria they contradicted each other, at least immediately and in Nasser's mind. To establish his control in Syria firmly, Nasser thought it necessary to eliminate the socialist Ba'th party, which had been the chief promoter of the union and expected to build its political fortunes in Syria and the rest of the Arab world upon it. Nasser, therefore, insisted on the dissolution of all political parties and the creation of a single political organization—the National Union—which he packed with anti-Ba'thists and bourgeois elements. He also maneuvered the Ba'thists out of influential positions in the administration and the army and replaced them with men beholden to him. Eventually he drove his erstwhile partners to resign from the government and withdraw into impotent sulking. Other important groups and individuals in the army and outside it were neutralized by similar tactics and by posting people in honorific jobs away from their power base. When he thought he had a clear field, he issued the drastic socialist July decrees, which he sought to apply to Syria as well as Egypt. But with the Ba'thists and other influential leaders who might have supported such measures eliminated, Nasser had only the broken reed of the Syrian bureaucracy to rely upon for their application in the face of the resentment and opposition of a much more vigorous and well-entrenched bourgeoisie than the one he had known in Egypt. The result was that members of that class, in alliance with dissatisfied and ambitious army officers and in tacit connivance with the alienated Ba'thists and others, engineered a military coup d'état which terminated the Egyptian-Syrian union. A hastily planned effort to restore the union by military force collapsed in the face of the general indifference of the Syrian public.

It was in a post-mortem speech about the Syrian secession that Nasser enunciated the theme that Arab nationalism could achieve its goal only through the triumph of the alliance of the toiling classes, the soldiers, the intellectuals, and the "patriotic capitalists" against the alliance of "exploitative capitalists," feudalists, and colonialists, which he held to be responsible for the secession. Whatever the analytical value of Nasser's diagnosis of the Syrian fiasco, his prognosis marked the injection of yet another dosage of tension and turmoil in inter-Arab relations. For it proclaimed that henceforth the realization of the pan-Arab ideal called not only for the overthrow of reticent governments and the elimination of independent states, but also the abolition of types of regimes and the transfer of power from class to class.

The first practical application of the new doctrine occurred in Yemen, where in September 1962 a group of military officers overthrew the Imam-king and called for Egyptian support. Nasser, true to his recently proclaimed doctrine of unity through social revolution, responded immediately by sending in a small number of Egyptian troops to help the revolutionary regime and restore the drive for Arab unity, stalled since the Syrian secession. In retrospect it appears that Nasser could have hardly chosen a worse place to test his doctrine. For the "toiling people" of Yemen, who were supposed to be yearning for unity, actually threw their support in bulk behind the deposed Imam, while the revolutionaries, who were supposed to lead the people toward the fulfillment of their aspiration, gained only limited and precarious backing. In the face of the resistance of the Imam's rag-tag forces, financed and armed by the Saudi government, Nasser found himself forced to escalate the Egyptian commitment to a point where it reached an estimated 70,000 troops armed with the best modern equipment. Yet all this effort proved of no avail and the Egyptian forces, greatly reduced from their maximal strength, are still battling in Yemen after having been forced to go on the defensive and confine themselves to a relatively small enclave.[4]

If Yemen demonstrated the excessive simpleness of the proposition that it was the feudalists who obstructed the otherwise universal popular yearning for unity, two Ba'thist "revolutions" that took place in Iraq and Syria in February and March of 1963 demonstrated the even greater simpleness of the notion that the advent of revolutionary socialists to power would lead to the realization of unity. To be sure, the newly installed revolutionaries immediately sent delegations to Cairo to explore the possibility of a tripartite union and, after prolonged and

[4] The Arab-Israeli war of 1967, which took place after this chapter was written, has since forced Nasser to withdraw his troops altogether, leaving the Yemeni republicans to fend for themselves as best as they could.

agitated discussion, an agreement was actually concluded providing for a tight federation of the three countries. But the projected union never got off the ground and within months gave way to a cold war between the Ba'th and Nasser. The Ba'thists, remembering their experience with Nasser in the United Arab Republic, had wanted to consolidate their position in Syria and Iraq and effectively unite the two countries before translating their agreement with Egypt into practice. They had in fact hoped to use the very agreement with Nasser as a means to neutralize his sympathizers in the two countries and thus facilitate their own entrenchment. However, Nasser had suspected and feared this from the very outset, and as soon as he thought his suspicions confirmed, demurred publicly and then repudiated the agreement while putting the blame on the Ba'th.

The Ba'thists continued for a while with their efforts to unite Syria and Iraq, but a split within the Iraqi Ba'th gave the opportunity to President Abdel Salam Aref to pull a coup d'état that got rid of all Ba'thist factions. In Syria too the Ba'th split more than once, but various factions have continued to succeed one another through military coups to the present. Iraq under Aref signed another unity agreement with Egypt but little came of it in practice. Nor did periodic talk in Syria about a rapprochement with Egypt lead to more than the restoration of diplomatic relations, which had remained severed since the break-up of the United Arab Republic, and the signing of a mutual defense treaty in November 1966.

Nasserite Egypt and Arab Unity

Our survey of the development of inter-Arab affinity and conflicts has shown that it was the emergence of Nasser as the dominant figure in Arab politics that had provided the main impetus to the evolution of pan-Arabism from the concept of limited cooperation enshrined in the Arab League to the concept of integral unity that received partial embodiment in the formation of the United Arab Republic. Our survey has also implicitly brought out the key paradoxical point that as long as Nasser did not seek integral Arab unity as such, that objective seemed to be forcing itself upon him; but that the moment he formally committed himself to it after the formation of the United Arab Republic, its full realization seemed constantly to elude his grasp. Because of Nasser's central role in the processes we have broached, it behooves us to conclude our analysis with a recapitulation of the considerations that have ruled Nasserite Egypt's commitment to Arab unity. The recapitulation should also prepare the ground for the discussion of the connection between inter-Arab relations and the Arab-Israeli conflict, since Egypt played a key role in both.

The key feature of Egypt's commitment to the cause of integral Arab unity is that this commitment was not the result of a previously planned action or even premeditated intention. It was rather the accidental by-product of Nasser's successful tactics in appealing for the support of the broad Arab publics for moves and policies he had undertaken pragmatically on behalf of Egypt's national interest as he perceived it. It was only after he accepted the Syrian bid to unite that he began to think of union itself as a strategic objective, to which he wedded Egypt's entire future economic and social, as well as political, development. This change of strategic objective necessitated far-reaching changes in tactics; but Nasser was never able fully to effect them, largely because he was too addicted to the tactics and mental dispositions that had served him so well up to the point of the formation of the United Arab Republic. This explains why the initial move toward integral Arab union has proved so far to be also its last manifestation.

Looking back some years after Egypt's commitment to integral unity, many writers thought they found it all anticipated in Nasser's 1955 meditations called *The Philosophy of the Revolution*, where he speaks of destiny beckoning to Egypt to fill a vacant role in the three overlapping circles of the Arab world, the Muslim world, and the African continent. However, the briefest reflection on this much-cited and little-understood passage should reveal that Nasser did not think of Egypt's role in the Arab circle in terms of integral unification with other Arab countries any more than he thought of its role in the other circles in terms of an impossible integral unification with the Muslim and the African countries. What Nasser clearly had in mind was a role of diplomatic leadership that would rebound with benefits upon its performer, and this he tried to achieve, perhaps with greater zeal and success in the Arab circle than elsewhere, until the Syrians forced him to make a fateful decision by offering to merge their country with him.

We have already discussed the events that thrust Nasser into a position of political pre-eminence in the Arab world and made the Egyptian-Syrian union a logical step: His successful fight against the Baghdad Pact, the arms deal and tacit political alliance with Russia, the nationalization of the Suez Canal, his survival of the tripartite invasion of 1956, and his success in escaping the isolation that the Eisenhower Doctrine sought to impose on him. Nasser's moves and actions in all these instances were undertaken with a view to Egypt's national interest as perceived by him, though he managed to mobilize behind them general Arab support and reap from them credit as an Arab leader. His war on the Baghdad Pact provides a good illustration of the point since this was the base from which he rose, the bridge to the arms deal and alliance with Russia, and much else.

The issue of the Baghdad Pact stemmed from the urgent interest shown by the West, led by the United States, in organizing a Middle Eastern alliance as part of the global strategy against Soviet Russia and international Communism. Nasser's initial opposition to the project of the pact was due not to any hostility to the West or friendship to Russia but to the fact that this particular project competed with an alternative plan of his own, which envisaged an exclusively Arab alliance that would, however, maintain close political, economic, and military links with the West. Such an alliance, sponsored and naturally headed by Egypt, would put Egypt in a position to receive large-scale economic and military assistance and bestow upon it and its leader great prestige.

Nasser's proposal was in effect very much akin to the original *British* conception of the Arab League, and he was therefore confident that the West would buy the plan if it lacked a better alternative. His ire against Nuri al-Said was aroused precisely because the latter spoiled his game by giving the West the alternative it preferred, thus allowing it to by-pass and ignore Egypt. In seeking to foil Nuri's effort, it was natural for Nasser to attack his opponent for breaking up Arab solidarity, as envisaged in the Arab League Pact, for conceding to the West positions it did not need to have, for exaggerating the Soviet and Communist danger in order to justify his misdeed, for pretending falsely that his move would help the Palestine cause, and for acting against the true wishes and interests of his own people and the Arabs generally. All these themes were logical weapons for Nasser to employ in fighting for *Egypt's* interest; but they all happened also to be themes that appealed greatly to the Arabs and the Russians, and they gained for him political credit with the former and military, economic, and political assistance from the latter. The same kind of considerations could be shown to have been operative in each move and situation up to the merger between Syria and Egypt.

The formation of the United Arab Republic did not immediately lead to any profound alteration of Nasser's basic mode of thinking. It did of course immediately commit Egypt to the cause of integral Arab unity and did impel him to try to capitalize on the momentum generated by the union with Syria in order to extend its scope to other Arab countries, particularly to Kassem's Iraq. However, all the evidence indicates that at this stage he still thought of union as merely another, albeit more important, tactical move that could enhance Egypt's and his own political standing in the world and in turn yield large returns in prestige and economic assistance. It was only after his drive to extend the union got stalled in Iraq and brought him into conflict with Russia that he had the chance to reevaluate his thinking about the significance for Egypt of integral Arab union.

The checks he encountered in Iraq led Nasser to turn his main attention to an effort to consolidate the union and reorganize and develop the resources of the United Arab Republic. This effort, we have seen, led to the adoption of socialism and a planned economy, which in turn induced Nasser and the men of his regime for the first time to think seriously and concretely of Egypt's future development in terms of the resources made available directly by Arab unity itself. Neither he nor his helpers ceased to think of union as a means of courting economic and military assistance from the big powers; but this usefulness of union came to be viewed as secondary, especially as the friction with Russia over Iraq suggested that outside assistance might be too precarious a base on which to plan economic development. The foundation of Egypt's development was to rest on Arab unity directly.

We have already seen that, ironically, the measures that were meant to facilitate the development of the joint resources of the two "provinces" of the United Arab Republic proved to be the final blow that led to the Syrian secession. This disaster did not, however, alter the conception already established, which linked Egypt's future to the resources to be made available by union. On the contrary, with the Egyptian economic experience in subsequent years, this conception changed from convenience to necessity and from a disposition of thought to an imperative. As the execution of the first five-year plan fell considerably short of the objectives, as improved demographic figures showed an acceleration in the rate of growth of the population, which was already close to 3 percent, as the prospects of capital imports for the second five-year plan fluctuated drastically with the ebb and flow of current international politics, the conviction grew that the future livelihood of Egypt, not to say its progress, depended inextricably on access to the land and capital resources of sister Arab countries.

Although the merger with Syria signified the crucial step of Egypt's commitment to the cause of integral Arab union and although it subsequently led to the change we have described in the conception of the significance of Arab union for Egypt, it did not produce appropriate changes in Nasser's thought and tactics to suit the new circumstances. Though reputed to be a pragmatist and a brilliant tactician, he was in fact unable to adjust and adapt the dispositions that had brought him success up to the moment the United Arab Republic was formed to the situations he faced after the union. For example, he had risen to pre-eminence in the Arab world up to the point of union by associating his opponents with the hated foreign domination and attacking both. When the Iraqi revolution clearly removed Western influence from that country without throwing Kassem into his arms, he could only fall back on this same tactic and accuse Kassem of being the tool of the Iraqi Communists. And when the Russians rebuked him for trying to press Iraq into union by such methods, he essentially gave up. He did the same thing after the breakup of the United Arab Republic when he diagnosed the reason for the secession as the alleged community of interest between the capitalist-feudalist secessionists and imperialism and proclaimed thenceforth a "new" kind of struggle.

In the years before 1958, Nasser's approach was to clothe his pursuit of Egypt's national interest in pan-Arab justifications. The immense success he reaped from this tactic disposed him to assume that what was good for Egypt was *ipso facto* good for the Arabs. This disposition led him to pursue in Syria *Gleichschaltung* policies that sought to impose on that quite different country the same type of political system, the same economic-social policies, and the same methods of administration that he had applied in Egypt. When disaster ensued, Nasser did not blame the medicine but the patient, and instead of deciding in future instances to change the former he resolved that the patient must be changed. This inability to penetrate his own premises and revise his assumptions led Nasser to the forced conclusion of "class struggle," which landed him into the Yemen impasse one year after the secession.

Finally, Nasser had attained impressive accomplishments through boldness and willingness to take risks, which presupposed his dominance and freedom to maneuver as single leader. Confidence in his own charismatic power and capacity for political manipulation led him to brook no partner or rival in Syria, to attempt to destroy the very forces that had brought the country into his arms, and to replace them with more amenable clients. Nineteen months after the Syrian secession, the will to exclusive dominance dissipated the next great opportunity to take a decisive step toward Arab unity presented by the Ba'thist revolutions in Iraq and Syria in February and March 1963, respectively. No one who has read the nearly one-million-word record of the "unity talks" between Nasser and two dozen representatives of "revolutionary" Syria and Iraq could fail to be struck by Nasser's relentless effort to dominate the entire proceedings. With his very first sentences he turned what was meant to be half-negotiating conference and half-constitutional convention of the representatives of three states into something more akin to seminar sessions, of which he was the stern and rather pedantic leader and which were relieved from time to time by moments of fraternization when he acted like big brother. His interlocutors included some of the very Ba'thist leaders he had eased out of power after they had brought Syria into the union with Egypt. They remembered then that they had forgotten what a union with Nasser would mean and repented their coming to Cairo.

The minutes of the "unity talks" were published by Cairo after the collapse of the projected union in order to show, among other things, how towering was Nasser's stature by comparison with his interlocutors. True: Nasser was too strong to compose his differences with other Arab leaders seeking unity, but he was also too weak to impose unity on his own terms. This summarizes the status of Arab nationalism in recent years.

Inter-Arab Relations and the Arab-Israeli Conflict

Our analysis of inter-Arab relations, which has centered on the evolution of pan-Arabism, has focused primarily on the impetus given to that movement by Arab participants. These participants were, of course, often prompted by developments outside the sphere of pan-Arabism, but we have taken these developments more or less as given and have not dwelt much on them in order to stick closely to the pan-Arab perspective. As we reach the concluding point of this chapter, it behooves us to turn our attention for a moment to a brief specific summary of the interaction between the pattern of pan-Arabism, which we have just considered, and the dominant features of the Arab-Israeli conflict, discussed in the previous chapter.

The evolution of pan-Arabism as we have depicted it has had a critical impact on the nature of the Arab conflict with Israel, while that conflict has in turn had a very important effect on the fate of pan-Arabism and the course of inter-Arab relations.

The commitment of Egypt to the cause of integral unity, which transformed pan-Arabism into Arab nationalism, had the coincidental effect of "escalating" the Arab conflict with Israel from a clash over residual issues left over from the 1948 war to a clash of destinies. At the stage when pan-Arabism meant inter-Arab solidarity, the existence of Israel was essentially a humiliating reminder of the failure of the Arab states to protect the rights of the Palestinian Arabs. But at the stage when pan-Arabism came to mean a striving led by Egypt for integral unity, the existence of Israel became additionally a physical barrier frustrating the realization of that unity. The very presence of

Israel and the fulfillment of Egyptian-led unity thus became mutually exclusive, in practice if not in theory.[5]

Prior to this development toward integral unity, the Arab-Israeli conflict could, in principle, persist indefinitely in the stalemate state of neither war nor peace. After it, the conflict had to be ultimately resolved on the basis of one of two alternatives: either, on the one hand, by the disappearance of Israel as a political entity or by the transformation of its identity as a Jewish state; or, on the other hand, by a drastic mutation of Arab nationalism that would either leave Egypt out of any united entities east of Suez or water the concept of Arab nationalism down to some much looser notion.

A look at the surface course of events involving Egypt and Israel in the period spanning the two stages of pan-Arabism under discussion would seem to suggest an opposite interpretation of the evolution of the Arab-Israeli conflict. It would show that incidents of hostile initiatives between the two countries were most numerous before the moment of "escalation." The closing of the Suez Canal, the blocking of the Gulf of Aqaba, the boycott, the *fida'iyyun* action and the Israeli raids, and finally the all-out war of 1956—all took place before Egypt's commitment to integral unity. On the other hand, the period since then has been marked by a perfectly quiet border between the two countries and no new hostile initiative except the project to counterdivert the Jordan's waters, which was pushed through by Syria against Egyptian reticence and came to naught anyway. Many who base their views on the record of such events have reached the conclusion that the conflict between Egypt and Israel had so simmered down as to permit the hope that it might cool off entirely in the not too distant future. Quite a few diplomats of interested countries were among these.

Actually, the undeniable drop in the temperature of the conflict was precisely the consequence of its deterioration. For as long as Egypt's dispute with Israel was fundamentally emotional, it could find satisfaction in actions that had spite as their only purpose; once the dispute came to assume a fateful strategic significance, however, more purposeful action was called for, and acts that merely gave vent to hostile feeling had to be subordinated to long-term strategy and, if necessary, suppressed for its sake. This view of the situation would suggest that

[5] In principle, the existence of Israel need not conflict with Arab unity. There is nothing to prevent Syria, Jordan, Iraq, and Egypt, for example, from proclaiming their unity. In practice, however, unity is most unlikely to come about in this manner. It is likely to require maneuvers and movements of men and goods that are severely hampered by Israel's presence.

the Egyptian self-restraint would probably continue as long as the deliberate strategy for a confrontation held the promise of success; but the moment that strategy would appear hopeless, the acts of spite would most likely be resumed with redoubled vigor because of redoubled frustration.

The true signs of the evolution of the Egyptian-Israeli conflict from a clash over residual issues to a clash of destinies may be seen in the arms buildup amply documented in this study. They may also be seen in the formal position of Egypt with regard to the Palestine problem: Prior to the union with Syria, Egypt, along with the rest of the Arab League, stood for the application of the United Nations resolutions on partition and the return of the refugees, which admitted the right of Israel to exist; after the union, this line was abandoned for one that clearly intimated the liquidation of Israel under a variety of formulae, such as "the restoration of the Arab rights in Palestine" or the "liquidation of the Zionist aggression in Palestine." The signs may be seen most clearly, however, in the multitude of pronouncements defining the Arab objectives made by Nasser to his own people, in Arab councils, and in discourses with foreign individuals in official and unofficial positions.[6]

[6] For example, on November 25, 1965, Nasser explained in a speech to his people that:

> Among the reasons [of the imperialists] for perpetuating this plot [Israel] was their desire to isolate Egypt behind the insulator of the Sinai Desert from the rest of the Arab world . . . so that it should be easy for Israel to confront torn and separate Arab fronts and so that it should be easy for them, in turn, to deal with an Arab world split in the middle. But the assertion of Egypt's Arab identity [what we called Egypt's commitment to Arab unity] dealt a severe blow to the imperialist plan. . . . The hope for the complete liquidation of this imperialist plot and for eradicating its evil roots from Arab soil now rests on the prospects of the Arab revolution. *(al Ahram,* November 26, 1965.)

A short while later, Muhammad Hassanein Haykal sounded this theme again in a column in which he tried to justify the heavy burden of defense expenditure assumed by Egypt. After referring to the danger confronting Egypt from imperialist powers and from Israeli expansionist ambitions, he went on to say:

> In addition to Israel's expansionist danger, that country blocks the gate between the Arab east and the Arab west which begins with Egypt. This is a situation which cannot possibly be accepted in the long run no matter what the perils. . . . The results of the 1948 war were sad enough . . . but a greater cause for grief was what happened in 1949, after the armistice, when the Israeli forces advanced to Aqaba and established themselves on this gulf on the Red Sea. This Israeli step, which took place without sufficient Arab awareness and without effec-

The increased emphasis on the necessity to liquidate Israel reflected an increased consciousness of the gravity of the obstacle in the path of Arab unity that that country represented. In the period of rapid political movement that followed the formation of the United Arab Republic and reached its climax in the Iraqi revolution of July 1958, it was easy not only for Nasser but even for unsympathetic outsiders to believe that Arab nationalism was irresistible and that Arab unity was inexorably on its way to prompt achievement.[7] The problem of Israel could be ignored then by Egypt because it was thought that Arab unity would take care of it one way or another. However, as the euphoria subsided, and the dream of rapid unity gave way to the expectation of a prolonged and difficult struggle for its realization, Israel's existence as a wedge separating Egypt from the eastern Arab countries began to have telling effects. Israel, for example, stood in the way of any massive movement of people and goods between the Egyptian and the Syrian "regions" of the United Arab Republic, which might have permitted the consolidation of the union. Also, its presence unwittingly encouraged the secessionists in Syria to launch their coup d'état by shielding them against any massive Egyptian military action to restore unity. The abortive Egyptian attempt to save the union, initiated with the drop of a company of Egyptian paratroopers in Latakia and the preparation of a naval expedition, only drove deeper home the impossibility of circumventing the Israeli roadblock.

Israel hampered the prospects of Arab unity in even more telling and humiliating ways. At many points during and after the union with Syria, it was in Egypt's power to bring about a revolution in Jordan and a union with that country; but the realization that Israel, for what it considered to be vital security reasons of its own, was bound to intervene militarily to prevent the occupation of the West Bank by an Arab power other than Jordan deterred Egypt from availing itself of the opportunities. The great moment of hope for Arab unity in the spring of 1963, following the Ba'thist coups in Iraq and Syria, was also forfeited because Egypt, isolated from the Fertile Crescent by Israel, could not count on any direct communications to allow it to regain later what it might concede at first in the way of political autonomy for

tive Arab response, shut the gate tight and completely between the Arab east and the Arab west. . . . The duties of the Egyptian defensive capacity are . . . to deter any Israeli expansionist effort, then to open the connecting gate, then to move on to the real and legitimate liquidation operation of the aggression which is constituted by the fact which exists now in occupied Palestine. (al Ahram, January 7, 1966.)

[7] See, for example, the editorial in *The New York Times*, July 15, 1958.

the two Ba'th groups. Still later, a unity agreement with the Iraq of Abdel Salam Aref remained a scrap of paper because Israel's presence divided the partners. It was a realization of this state of affairs on Nasser's part that had led him to see in the initially fortuitous intervention in Yemen the possibility of a wide flanking movement that might achieve Arab unity by advancing from a base in Yemen, through Arabia, Iraq, and Syria before confronting Israel. It is not clear, in view of the nature of Yemen's terrain and in the light of the resistance offered by the Yemeni tribesmen, whether Egypt might have won that war if it had thrown into it more than the 70,000 troops it had there at one point; but Israel's tying down of most of Egypt's troops prevented it from doing so. In any case, the morass of the Yemen war must have driven home to Nasser more painfully than anything else the frustrating impact of Israel on all his efforts to achieve Arab unity.

The relationship between Israel and pan-Arabism had another and obverse effect. If Israel's existence has so far constituted a stumbling bloc in the way of Arab unity under Egyptian leadership, it has on the other hand decisively contributed to preventing the complete death of pan-Arabism under the impact of inter-Arab conflicts. Whenever inter-Arab relations reached a point of crisis, the common hostility to Israel and the need to deal collectively with some features of that hostility either came to the rescue or were deliberately used to prevent the crisis from definitively disrupting the pan-Arab cause. After the debacle of 1948, for example, Syria's felt need to provide for its defense against Israel led to the conclusion of the Arab League Mutual Security Pact, which saved the Arab League from total destruction and gave a new lease on life to that organization. Throughout the years since 1948, the boycott of Israel and other expressions of hostility were the only constant common Arab activities. The break between Iraq and Egypt over the issue of the Baghdad Pact failed to attain the dimensions of a breach reaching deeper down in society largely because "society" in all the Arab countries was aroused by the prospects of an encounter with Israel seemingly opened up by the Soviet-Egyptian arms deal. Most tellingly perhaps, in 1964–1965, when inter-Arab relations had been at their nadir after the enunciation of the doctrine of inevitable struggle between the "revolutionary" and the "reactionary" regimes and classes, when Saudi Arabia had been fighting by proxy with Egypt for over two years, and when virtually each of the eastern Arab governments was at odds with most others and calling for their overthrow, the completion by Israel of its Jordan River diversion project provided the excuse for a series of Arab "summit" meetings that temporarily restored a sense of Arab solidarity. In short, the existence of

Israel provided a net that saved pan-Arabism from getting smashed to the ground each time the attempt to rise high above it toward integral unity brought inter-Arab relations tumbling down.

Israel's unsought role of keeping pan-Arabism alive yet preventing it from achieving fulfillment in integral unity has had the strongest impact on Egypt specifically since Egypt has been the center that has held together the Arab front against Israel and since its present government has taken the lead in striving to achieve integral unity. Egypt has been unable to realize Arab unity largely because of Israel's existence; yet without Arab unity, Egypt by itself has so far been in no position to contemplate practically the destruction of Israel. Egypt's attempt to go around Israel and achieve unity by way of the Yemen detour shows all signs of having hit a dead end. Whether it can, through greater exertions, place itself in a better position in the future to face Israel alone constitutes one of the questions the next chapters should answer.

The Big Powers and the Middle East

Introduction

In discussing the Arab-Israeli and the inter-Arab conflicts in the previous two chapters, we noted that either one of these two conflicts could, independently, have generated a competitive arms buildup in the Middle East. We also made the point that the meshing of these conflicts in actual practice intensified and escalated the arms race. However, none of the parties involved in either conflict could have pursued a policy of threat and deterrence and expanded its military stockpiles without the intervention of outside powers. None of them possessed an armaments industry equal to such a task; all of them have had to rely on outside suppliers. Even the limited arms industry developed in recent years by Egypt and Israel was made possible only by technological assistance and expertise from outside the Middle East.

The contribution of outside powers to the arms buildup took several forms. In Turkey and Iran, which lie on the periphery of our study, outright arms grants were a very important factor. In the case of the Arab states and Israel, this form of assistance was much less important as it was limited to a few countries for emergency situations or short periods of time and involved relatively small quantities.[1] Examples of this form of arms provision would include shipments made by the United

---

[1] These observations were written before the Six Day War. Since then, the Soviet Union has made massive shipments of arms to Egypt and Syria, which may be wholly or partly free of charge. If that should prove to be the case, it would constitute a crucial new departure with far-reaching implications.

States to Iraq under the Baghdad Pact, to Jordan and Lebanon during the crisis period of the Eisenhower Doctrine, and the secret shipments from Germany to Israel in 1958–1963.

The principal form of arms provision to the Arab states and Israel has been sale, in which political and economic considerations were mixed in varying doses at different times. Generally speaking, economic considerations have always taken second place, although in recent years the defense establishments of the Western powers have actively promoted arms exports as a means of supporting domestic military industries and of correcting the balance of payments. In all cases, however, the selling powers have considerably facilitated the purchases by budget subsidies, as in the case of American and British contributions to Jordan; reduced prices and easy credit terms, as in the case of Soviet deals with Egypt, Syria, and Iraq; or government loan-guarantees to the arms industries concerned and similar devices, as in the case of most British, American, and French sales.[2]

But the contribution of the outside powers to the process of arms buildup in the Middle East has not been confined to providing the weapons and the financial assistance to facilitate buying them. Economic assistance of a purely developmental nature has been a relevant factor as well; for insofar as such assistance has permitted the states of the area to divert to the purchase of arms resources that would otherwise have been used for development, it has also been a contribution to arms escalation.

Furthermore, the outside powers have stimulated the desire and need for arms. In pursuing their political objectives, the big powers have become involved in the area's disputes and conflicts, supporting the Arabs or the Israelis, backing one Arab faction against another or one regime against its rivals, and even taking sides in the internal power struggles of individual countries. This type of activity, by intensifying the Arab-Israeli and inter-Arab disputes and converting them to a certain degree into extensions of the great power struggles being waged on a global scale, has increased the instability and tension of the area and accelerated the scramble for arms.

Naturally, this great power role in the arms buildup and in the politics of threat and deterrence in the area was itself the product of their own interests in the Middle East, conceived here in its broadest sense

[2] For an example of the activities of the U.S. Defense Department in promoting arms sales in recent years, and the reasons for them and circumstances under which they were carried out, see the series of reports in the *New York Times*, October 26, 1967, and following issues.

to include both the peripheral countries bordering on Russia (Iran and Turkey) and those of the "heartland" (Iraq, Egypt, Syria, Lebanon, Jordan, Israel, and the Arabian Peninsula). These interests were complex and variable. Their evolution was related to developments in weapons technology and communications, concomitant strategic concepts, the constellation of great power alignments, and, of course, the changing situation in the area itself.

Once again, we shall account for the role of the great powers in the Middle East through a topical approach rather than a continuous historical narrative. The selection of topics will be designed to throw into relief the changing objectives of the great powers, the policies they pursued to attain them, the entanglement of these policies in the politics of the area, and the manner in which this entanglement stimulated the politics of force and the accumulation of arms among the Middle East states. More specifically, we shall divide our analysis into three broad phases, as follows: (1) A period of flux following World War II and continuing until roughly 1950; (2) a period during which the Cold War was extended to the Middle East and reached its highest intensity —from 1950 to 1958; (3) a period from 1959 to the present in which the Cold War began to wane in the Middle East and the world at large. Each of these three periods will be subdivided into key topics and episodes.

The reader will notice that our discussion will focus heavily on developments in weapons technology and strategic thinking among the big powers and the impact of these on their Middle East policies. This particular perspective has never before been applied systematically, even though all writers on the Middle East have unfailingly spoken of the strategic importance of the area. The reason for this is probably that the influence of changing strategic concepts on the policies of the powers has been an implicit rather than an explicit one. It cannot necessarily be demonstrated that after each significant breakthrough in weaponry or new stage in strategic thinking, policy makers sat down and translated the new strategic concepts into diplomatic aims and policies in the Middle East. However, as we shall presently demonstrate, recurrent crises continually forced policy makers to distinguish between aims that remained vital and those that had become obsolete, and this ensured a constant and semiconscious process of policy adaptation to new strategic and political realities.

Prelude to the Cold War in the Middle East: 1945-1950

GENERAL FEATURES

It had become apparent, even before the end of World War II, that the old international political order in the Middle East was finished and that in its place had developed a new, fluid situation. The hallmarks of this new situation were two: a transformation of the relative positions in the area of the great powers and a powerful nationalist upsurge that swept most of the Middle Eastern countries. These two developments revised the limits and possibilities of the great powers' policies in the area.

The transformation of the relative positions of the powers had two critical facets. First, in the territories of the northern periphery of the Middle East—Greece, Turkey, and Iran—the crucial development was the adoption by the Soviet Union of a revisionist policy involving the exertion of pressure on its Iranian and Turkish neighbors and supporting the Communist-instigated civil war in Greece. This policy, in turn, brought forth a second critical development: decisive United States intervention, which made the United States for the first time a Middle Eastern power. Second, in the heartland—including the Arab states and what was to become Israel—Britain's emergence as the sole great power, after the expulsion during the war of the Italians from Libya and the French from the Levant, was the most crucial change. This change inspired the British government to attempt, singlehandedly, the reorganization of the entire region on the basis of cooperation between Britain and a united Arab world, an ideal that had been frustrated at the end of World War I by contradictory commitments to the Zionists and the French.

In the early postwar years events in the periphery and the heartland seemed to the powers concerned to have only a limited and tenuous connection; but subsequently the powers were repeatedly to attempt to affect their position in one region by moves in the other. This growing interconnection was to become a key to their Middle East policies as a whole.

With regard to the nationalist upsurge, each of the three great powers involved was affected differently by it in the early years. Nationalists everywhere viewed the United States positively, largely because at that point it had no obvious imperialist tradition and no national interests or commitments in the area. In later years, the United States was forced to make choices and assume commitments that embroiled it in regional rivalries and internal disputes, but until that time, everyone in the Middle East wished the United States to take an interest in their country in hopes of gaining its support against other big powers. Thus Turkey and Iran welcomed American intervention as a counterweight to Russian pressure. In Palestine, the Zionists yearned for United States involvement to counter British policy. Elsewhere in the heartland, though American support of the Zionists was resented, this did not keep nationalists and governments from seeking United States support against Britain.

Russia, as already suggested, was feared and resented by the Turks and the Iranians. Its position in the heartland, although ambiguous, was on balance suspect as well. On the one hand, Russia's clean slate in the region preserved it from the kind of active resentment directed at Britain and France. Moreover, the wartime alliance had prompted the allied propaganda machinery to create a favorable image of Russia. During the war, for the first time, diplomatic relations were established between Russia and the Arab countries. But on the other hand, fear of Bolshevism as a social system and of Communist atheism, combined with an awareness of Russia's pressures on its neighbors, more than countered these factors.

It was Britain, traditionally the dominant and since the war the predominant power in the area, which received the full brunt of nationalist wrath. But the situation was not a simple one. For one thing, due to its position and influence, Britain never lacked friends, genuine and otherwise, among the ruling classes in the various Middle Eastern countries. These were known in the jargon of the time as "moderate nationalists" and were willing to cooperate with the British on whatever terms seemed optimal under the circumstances. Under the circumstances prevailing at war's end, they and the British agreed that far-reaching concessions to nationalist feelings were called for.

For another thing, Britain held important bargaining cards that were considered valuable even in the eyes of militant nationalists. In the heartland, there was the British position in Palestine, which could be used to gain Arab good will; in the periphery, more particularly in Iran, there was the still considerable British capacity to help resist Russian pressure. Thus, the British government could hope that despite rising nationalist pressures, the Middle East could still be reorganized on solid and enduring foundations. Events were to show what an ill-founded hope that was.

SOVIET PRESSURE AND AMERICAN
INVOLVEMENT IN THE PERIPHERY

The Soviet Union's adoption of a more aggressive policy toward Iran, Turkey, and Greece in the immediate post-war years stemmed from strategic interests and a policy pattern that went back to Czarist times. In Russian eyes, these countries controlled the most convenient approaches to the Russian heartland and offered the only all season outlets for Russian shipping. Three times in its modern history—in 1712, 1812, and 1941–1945—Russia foiled would-be conquerors from the west by strategic retreats across the steppe; whereas the naval invasion of the Crimea in 1853–1856 had led to defeat, and Anglo-American reinforcements via the Persian Gulf and the Iranian plateau had tipped the balance in favor of victory in World War II. Consequently, Russia had historically followed a consistent policy toward Turkey and Iran: When it felt itself strong, it attempted to deny these countries to potentially hostile powers by seeking to gain direct control over them and reach for their sea outlets; when it felt itself weak, it sought to deny them to other big powers by trying to make them into neutral buffers. Soviet policy in this regard differed from Czarist primarily by the addition of an ideological justification: to promote the world Communist revolution and to protect the Communist center against capitalist encirclement and counterrevolution.

In the years of civil war and instability immediately after the Bolshevik revolution, the Soviet leaders endeavored to secure Russia's southern approaches by cultivating the good will of its neighbors and seeking to neutralize them. They helped Ataturk in Turkey eject the Allied Powers, defy the British, and defeat the Greeks; and they likewise helped the Persians combat British influence while renouncing by the treaty of 1921 almost all the concessions gained by Czarist Russia. In the same treaty, however, appeared an indicative clause permitting Russian intervention in the event of the occupation of part of Iran by foreign troops hostile to the Soviet Union.

Later, in connection with the Ribbentrop-Molotov Pact of 1939, Russia tried with little success to gain a free hand in this area. Then, when the tables were turned in the course of the war, they tried bargaining with the Allies for support on the Turkish Straits question and succeeded in extracting general promises of assistance in revising the Straits regime. When the war ended, the Russians felt relatively powerful and acted accordingly. In Iran, the presence of Soviet troops was used as a lever in an attempt first to build a pro-Soviet political movement and subsequently to support a secessionist puppet regime in Azarbaijan, the key northern Iranian province controlling access to the Caucasus. In Turkey, they worked for revision of the Straits regime and the "recovery" of the eastern Anatolian area of Kars and Ardahan, which they had conceded in the twenties. Besides their strength, the Russians banked on Allied wartime promises and the isolation and unpopularity of Turkey stemming from its "pro-German neutrality" early in the war.

This aggressive revisionist policy proved to be a blunder, for it provoked an American reaction in support of Iran and Turkey which made the United States for the first time in history a power in the region. First, the United States threw its diplomatic support behind Iran on the question of Russian troop withdrawal, agreed upon at the wartime Teheran Conference, and then on the Azarbaijan question when these issues came up before the United Nations. This brought the two great powers into the arena for the first time as rivals rather than as allies. In the event, the Russians thought it better to retreat, thus allowing the Persian army to snuff out the secessionist regime in Azarbaijan. At least implicitly, the United States was now involved as a guarantor of Iranian sovereignty against the Soviet Union, a position that was to be formalized in subsequent years by a variety of multilateral and bilateral agreements. Regarding Turkey, the United States first joined with the British, recently allied with Turkey, in bolstering Turkish resistance to Soviet demands, and then in the spring of 1947 formally extended American protection through the Truman Doctrine to Turkey and also Greece, then suffering a Communist-supported civil war. The net result was that the Soviets, by inducing the most powerful naval power in history to extend its influence into the area, jeopardized their defensive interests while intending to promote their offensive interests.

A consequence of this boomerang effect was that in ensuing years the Soviets endeavored to minimize the damage done and obviate further American involvement by adopting a moderate, rather passive policy toward the Middle East. Their policy regarding the creation of Israel was an exception to this rule, made possible only by the identity of their position with that of the United States.

Though content to leave the Middle East heartland in the care of the British, the United States had occasionally supported the specific interests of American groups there. One was the interest of American oil companies in securing what they considered a fair share of Middle East oil concessions; another was the interest of American Jews in repealing British rules restricting Jewish immigration to Palestine in order to allow survivors of the Nazi massacres to go there. Immediately

after the war President Truman had pleaded with the British government for the immediate admission to Palestine of 100,000 Jewish war
survivors, a move that commanded general support in the United
States. For reasons soon to be discussed, the British first procrastinated
and then sought to evade the request. Finally, when American pressure continued to mount, some unfortunate remarks by British Foreign Secretary Bevin converted the issue into an open clash between
the American and British governments over Palestine policy.

This clash and Jewish defiance and terror forced the British to place
the whole Palestine issue before the United Nations where the United
States vigorously supported the termination of the British mandate
and the partition of the country into an Arab and a Jewish state. The
Soviet Union backed the proposal as well, as a means of expelling the
British from Palestine immediately and as the only plan likely to command the required majority. In the face of armed Arab opposition to
the partition resolution and systematic British obstruction, the Soviet
Union added to its determined diplomatic support of the Jews arms
and facilities that contributed decisively to their final victory.

The result of this active Russian intervention, predicated upon the
improbability of any American counteraction, seemed much like that
produced by their pressure on Turkey and Iran. Once the Jews established their state, they turned, for a number of reasons, not the least of
which was their ties to American Jewry, to the United States for economic and other kinds of support. Since the Soviet Union subscribed
then to the Zhdanov Doctrine according to which everyone not exclusively pro-Soviet was *ipso facto* hostile, it saw this as joining the enemy camp. Russian indignation at this betrayal, manifested in verbal
attacks followed by a full-fledged anti-Semitic and anti-Zionist campaign, did eventually bring about a real Israeli effort to join the American camp for protection, thus making the Russian suspicions self-ful-
filling. This new boomerang in Soviet Middle East policy confirmed
the advisability of a cautious approach toward the area. This was
reflected in Russian passivity during the succession of Middle East
crises from the end of the Palestine war to the middle of 1955, including the Iranian oil nationalization crisis that wracked that country
between 1951 and 1953.

BRITAIN'S ABORTIVE EFFORT
TO ORGANIZE THE HEARTLAND

From the vantage point of the late fifties and the sixties, Soviet support of nascent Israel in 1947–1948 appears strange indeed. Even given

the desire to see the British evicted from Palestine, the risk of antagonizing the Arabs still makes this policy seem incomprehensible. But one must keep in mind how Russian and non-Russian eyes then viewed the heartland, for that vision was completely dominated by the British presence and by apparent British success in organizing the entire Middle East, with Arab cooperation, firmly and durably under British hegemony.

Britain emerged from the war as the sole power in the Middle East. Italy, a presence in the area only since its consolidation of Libya after World War I, had been defeated and dispossessed. France, Britain's main Middle Eastern rival, since World War I in the guise of an ally, had been bluntly ejected from Syria and Lebanon in 1945 when the British ordered De Gaulle's government to stop suppressing nationalist risings, thus forcing it to concede independence and evacuate the two countries. Later, in the early days of the North Atlantic Treaty Organization, the United States and Britain were to invite French participation in major policy moves in the Middle East; but this invitation was more from courtesy than from any sense that France was still a Middle Eastern power. By 1953–1954 all pretense was dropped, and France was excluded from plans for a northern tier pact. Looking back from the late fifties and early sixties, with France in a strong position in Israel, and even more from more recent years, with De Gaulle apparently thriving on American and British difficulties in the area, the "Anglo-Saxons" may appear to have been premature in writing France out of the Middle East. Nevertheless, there is no doubt that in the decade after the war France was not an important factor in the area. Britain was indeed alone, buoyed up by the prestige of victory and armed with treaties of alliance with Egypt, Iraq, and Transjordan, a mandate over Palestine, and a network of military bases everywhere. Moreover, it had friends, was credited with liberating Syria and Lebanon, and was godfather of the Arab League, which it viewed as a promising policy instrument.

In view of all this, the Russians, probably generalizing from their own comparable position in eastern Europe, considered Britain's position in the Middle East heartland unassailable, except in or through Palestine, where presumably the latent conflicts between the imperialist-capitalist powers had come to a head.

In reality, the surface appearance of the British position was deceptive. Generally speaking, Britain was exhausted financially and psychologically and was thus under immense pressure to trim the costs and commitments of empire just when nationalist demands everywhere were making an increase necessary. As a consequence, in less than two years, Britain abandoned the defense of Greece and Turkey and conceded independence to India, Pakistan, Burma, and Ceylon. In the Middle East heartland specifically, Egyptian and Iraqi nationalists violently contested Britain's treaty rights; and in Palestine Jewish defiance and terrorism proved beyond the capacity of 100,000 British troops to suppress. The British government, under the aegis of Foreign Secretary Bevin, was not blind to these difficulties, although it was confident that it had the means to reconcile British interests and nationalist demands in a sound and lasting new order in the area.

Oil, communications, and imperial defense were the main British interests in the area after the war. The oil concessions helped Britain's foreign exchange balance as well as supplying revenue and vital oil. Furthermore, the Middle East was a necessary link with commitments and crucial trading partners east of Suez, and any dream of an empire revitalized in the new Commonwealth hinged on secure transit through the Middle East. Foreign Secretary Bevin believed that all these interests could be adequately safeguarded if three conditions were met: (1) if rival powers were kept out of the area; (2) if independence demands were essentially met; and (3) if Britain could obtain by consent of Middle East governments a centrally located military base. The first and second conditions were complementary and seemed to present no problems. The third ran somewhat counter to the second but appeared attainable in exchange for the benefits of the first two. Palestine was a potentially disrupting special problem; but if handled correctly, which Secretary Bevin was certain he could do, it also offered potential leverage for attaining the three conditions.

In pursuit of his objectives, Bevin entered into negotiations for treaty revisions with Egypt, where he sought to gradually liquidate the Suez Canal base in exchange for a free hand in the Sudan; with Iraq, where he sought to confirm the presence of British air bases in return for dropping all other limitations on Iraqi sovereignty; and with Transjordan, where he sought to turn a mandatory relationship into one of alliance. Simultaneously, he attempted to ward off the return of rival powers to the heartland by fostering the Arab League; and he explored the possibilities of a collective treaty with it that would be more palatable to the nationalists than individual treaties. Meanwhile, he put off his party's pre-election promise to repeal the White Paper policy on Palestine, thus holding out to the Arabs, at least implicitly, the promise of a favorable British stand in return for their cooperation.

Except for a successful redefinition of relations with Transjordan, Bevin's vision of a new order failed to materialize. Painfully negotiated treaties with Egypt and Iraq were torn up by street mobs and opposition groups for falling short of absolute nationalist demands. The idea of a collective treaty ran afoul of inter-Arab problems and proved no more attractive to Arab leaders than bilateral treaties. In Palestine, Bevin had attempted to gain time and ease up American pressure by setting up a joint American-British commission of inquiry, but when the commission unanimously favored the admission of 100,000 Jewish immigrants and the removal of other White Paper restrictions, his effort backfired. Jewish terrorism and American pressure intensified and drove Bevin to make intemperate remarks about American motives and Jewish character that soured Anglo-American relations and caused him political trouble at home. Compounding the difficulties was the fact that the various British offices concerned with Palestine—the Foreign Office (Bevin's), the Colonial Office, the War Office, and the British authorities in Jerusalem—pursued different and conflicting approaches and objectives. Finally, in despair, the British government turned the entire problem over to the United Nations in hopes of obtaining either a new, clearer mandate or a way out that would not jeopardize its relations with the Arab countries.

With the United Nations partition resolution imminent, the British set dates for terminating the mandate and evacuating the country. The resolution was finally adopted on November 29, 1947. During the remaining six months or so of British control in Palestine, Bevin acted to gain Arab good will and salvage his Middle East policy. He refused to cooperate with the United Nations. In the civil war that broke out between Jews and Arabs, he sought to use the British military presence in favor of the Arabs. The resulting chaos almost killed the partition plan by convincing the United States that it was impracticable, but the rapid loss of control by London over British officials on the spot and the eagerness of the British military to disengage, with the concomitant military success of the Jews, reversed the trend. The Jews brought most of the area allotted them under control and on May 15, 1948, proclaimed their state.

Before this had come to pass, however, Bevin had encouraged King Abdallah of Transjordan to send his British-officered Arab Legion into Palestine on the heels of the mandate to secure for himself at least the allotted Arab area. This, Bevin hoped, would give Transjordan access to the Mediterranean and make it a suitable site for a British base. The entry of other Arab countries, with contradictory objectives, into the war threatened this "reasonable" way for Bevin to obtain his base. On the other hand, it gave him an opportunity to put all the Arab countries in his debt by extending to them British support at this crucial moment, and thus to improve the odds for successful treaty revisions. Accordingly, he helped the Arab states with arms, diplomacy, and delaying tactics at the United Nations for as long as possible. But the Arab military effort faltered, and Britain realized that every day's fighting imperiled their position and the chances of Transjordan keeping what was already won. Thus, finally, it fell in with the United Nations arms embargo and cease-fire resolutions.

Britain's change of policy, though helpful in intent, was interpreted by the Arabs, except for King Abdallah, as a betrayal and a new example of British perfidy. Bevin's last effort, the invocation of the 1936 Anglo-Egyptian treaty against the Israelis when their assault on remaining Egyptian positions carried them into Sinai, was repudiated by the Egyptian government, which preferred armistice negotiations to an admission that the treaty with Britain was alive or useful. Henceforth, Britain was saddled by the Arabs with the blame for their defeat; and the Palestine issue, through which Bevin had sought to gain Arab good will, became instead another major Arab grievance against Britain.

Immediately after the war, Arab attention shifted back to the British. In Egypt, the British garrison of 80,000 in the Suez Canal base was deprived of supplies and subjected to guerilla attacks before a new Egyptian government unilaterally terminated the 1936 treaty. In Iraq, the pro-British government could maintain itself against attempted coups only by emergency measures. British credit with the Syrians for helping them to independence was dissipated. King Abdallah of Jordan was assassinated by a Palestinian for seeking peace with Israel.

On top of all this and quite independently of the Palestine problem, Iran erupted early in 1951 with anti-British feelings, focused on Britain's control of Iranian oil. Prime Minister Razmara was assassinated and the oil industry nationalized. Thus, within five or six years of the end of World War II, Britain's effort to organize the Middle East had failed completely. What appeared to be incontestable hegemony had fallen like a house of cards.

The Cold War in the Middle East: 1950-1958

GENERAL FEATURES

The collapse of Britain's Middle East policy impelled the United States, by then fully engaged in a global struggle with Russia, to extend its involvement in the area from the periphery to the heartland in an effort to stem the instability and tension in that region and to organize it as part of the emerging Western bloc. American global strategy, and consequently Soviet global strategy, was thus extended to the entire Middle East. In short, the Middle East was brought fully into the nexus of the Cold War.

Basically, this meant that the conflicts of the area became intertwined with the East-West struggle. At first, this amounted to little, due to Russia's inability to respond effectively to the extension of American involvement; but with the Soviet penetration of the heartland in 1955 through the Egyptian arms deal, the implications of this intertwining acquired momentous significance. Immediately, the Arab-Israeli conflict was exacerbated and after a year of tension exploded into war in 1956. An arms race was begun between Israel and Egypt that continues to the present day. At the same time, inter-Arab relations became increasingly polarized along East-West lines, except for moments of apparent anti-Israeli solidarity. Indirectly, this confluence of East-West, Arab-Israeli, and inter-Arab conflicts contributed to the emergence of Nasser as an all-Arab hero and to Egypt's commitment to the cause of integral Arab unity. This, in turn, converted the conflict between Egypt and Israel into a clash of destinies and greatly intensified inter-Arab struggles. Needless to say, all this had a feedback effect on the over-all relations between the superpowers themselves, but this does not concern us here.

Because the most crucial feature of the period under discussion was the drawing of the Middle East into the global East-West struggle, the following observations will center on the main strategic-diplomatic phases of that struggle and the manner in which they meshed with the area's problems.

THE EXTENSION OF THE AMERICAN
CONTAINMENT POLICY TO THE MIDDLE EAST

During the years of Britain's failing effort to organize the Middle East, tension between the United States and the Soviet Union had developed into a Cold War. What with the Berlin blockade, the communist coup in Czechoslovakia, the tension over Tito's defection from the Communist camp, and the final triumph of the Communists in China, the United States had become convinced of Soviet aggressive, expansive ambitions and had developed what came to be known as the "Containment Policy." In the words of the architect of that policy, it consisted of "the adroit and vigilant application of counterforce at a series of constantly shifting geographical points corresponding to the shifts and maneuvers of Soviet policy."

The weapons of Soviet foreign policy being visualized as subversion, coup d'état, and incitement to Communist insurrection, the Containment Policy was defensively armed with economic recovery and development programs designed to reinforce the fabric of threatened societies, military programs to boost the capacity of their governments to suppress disorder, and American-backed alliances pooling the resources of several countries to provide mutual insurance and to stiffen the will to resist. In Europe, this policy found expression in the Marshall Plan and the North Atlantic Treaty Organization.

The Middle East was viewed as an area vulnerable to Communist influence and vital to the recovery of Europe. Most European oil came from the Middle East, and a great deal of European trade passed through it. The possibility of disruption here thus constituted a serious enough menace even without the added military consideration of the area's position on NATO's flank. Since the British proved unable to secure the area, the United States found it necessary to try to extend the containment belt through it.

Since the Arab-Israeli conflict had contributed greatly to the failure of Britain's stabilization effort in the area, it appeared necessary as a first step to bring that conflict under control. Moreover, a pooling of Arab and Israeli resources seemed to fit well with future defense plans. Thus, in May 1950, with efforts at peace between Israel and the Arabs at a standstill, the United States, with Britain and France, issued the Tripartite Declaration, in which the three powers undertook to oppose any attempt to revise existing armistice lines by force and to ration arms shipments to the area. Indicative of the character of the Declaration as a preliminary step to further plans was the clause in it that defined the criteria to be followed by the powers in providing arms. These included the legitimate self-defense needs of the countries of the area and arms needed "to permit them to play their part in the defense of the area as a whole."

The defense arrangements foreshadowed in the Declaration were delayed by the outbreak of the Korean War a few weeks later. But the willingness of the Communists to use force in Korea gave the United States and its allies added impetus to return to the project once the fighting died down there. Moreover, Middle Eastern tensions were once again high. Iran had nationalized the British-owned oil industry and ushered in an era of political turmoil and near chaos. In Egypt, the government was preparing to abrogate unilaterally the 1936 treaty. On October 13, 1951, the United States, Britain, France, and Turkey formally proposed to Egypt the formation of a Middle East Defense Organization (MEDO).

The proposal was intended to provide for the needs of containment in the Middle East while ending the hated British occupation. The Anglo-Egyptian treaty of 1936 was to be terminated, and the British Suez Canal base "internationalized" by being transferred to the alliance, consisting of the initiating powers, the Arab states, and certain British Commonwealth members. The Egyptian government promptly turned down the proposal, arguing that termination of British occupation under such conditions would amount to a substitution of multiple for single occupation. Instead it proclaimed the unilateral abrogation of the treaty.

Egypt's rejection of MEDO killed it even though the possibility of an alliance without Egypt was talked about for a little while. The United States and its allies were stymied, but an unexpected chain of events in Egypt gave them a breathing spell. The 1936 treaty being defunct, guerilla action against British troops in the Canal zone intensified, and tension in the entire country mounted to hysteria. In a skirmish in the zone British troops killed some forty Egyptian policemen, whereupon the mobs in Cairo vented their fury by burning and looting scores of foreign establishments in the city on January 26, 1952. King Faruq used this "burning of Cairo" as an excuse to dismiss the Wafd party government with which he had a continuing feud. For six months thereafter the "national struggle" was suspended as one government followed another. Finally, on July 23, 1952, a group of army officers overthrew the entire regime. After a period of consolidation, negotiations with the British were resumed, but with the new government daring neither to accept terms that would impugn its patriotism nor to risk fresh agitation and guerilla action, the negotiations dragged on, and the status quo persisted.

THE EXTENSION OF THE AMERICAN
NEW LOOK POLICY TO THE MIDDLE EAST

Korea was the most dramatic application of the Containment Policy. Yet the experience of that war led ultimately to a drastic revision of that policy and to the development of a new, quite different approach.

The war seemingly demonstrated the validity of the assumption of Communist expansionism that underlay the Containment Policy; but it also underscored two severe limitations of that policy: that it left to the enemy the freedom to choose the time, place, and conditions of any confrontation; and that it involved the possibility of engaging America's conventional resources so heavily in one place as to make it impossible to face a threat in another unless a very large and costly military establishment were kept in permanent readiness.

Besides doubts about the wisdom of the Containment Policy, the war also raised the specter of a total conflagration. This induced Congress to loosen the purse strings and thus permit the launching of a vast nuclear and thermonuclear armament program. By 1953 this program gave the United States a distinct superiority over the Soviet Union. Although the Soviet Union had by then nuclear bombs and a delivery system, a pre-emptive strike by the United States could have knocked out this capacity. The United States, on the other hand, had developed the capacity to absorb a Russian first strike and still inflict unacceptable damage on the Soviet Union in a second strike.

The return of the Republicans to power after twenty years of Democratic rule helped to bring into sharper focus the doubts about Containment and the new options opened up by America's nuclear superiority. The Eisenhower administration had no vested interest, intellectual or psychological, in previous conceptions and was, indeed, eager to develop its own distinctive policy. Defense policy was subjected to a broad review that yielded an alternative approach dubbed the New Look. Strategically, the key feature of the New Look was that it no longer bound the United States to meet Communist aggression at the point of its occurrence or to use only conventional weapons. Instead, it declared that the United States would meet such aggression with massive retaliation by means and at places of its own choosing.

The New Look had important implications for American objectives and policies in the Middle East. The core of the policy, the credibility of American second-strike capacity, depended on ringing the Soviet Union with air bases from which American bombers could attack all Soviet bases. This accentuated the need for obtaining through alliances suitable bases in the Middle East among other places. As these were to be air bases, however, rather than complete military complexes as called for by Containment thinking, greater flexibility was possible in choosing allies. Thus, when Secretary of State Dulles found Egypt still cool to the idea of a Western alliance during a Middle East tour in the spring of 1953, he was not unduly disturbed; for on the same trip he got sympathetic responses from the "northern tier" countries—Turkey, Iran, Iraq, and Pakistan—which were anyway better located from the point of view of air strategy. Accordingly, he decided to work for a new Middle Eastern alliance based on these countries, and two years later the Baghdad Pact was born.

Although Secretary of State Dulles invented the "northern tier" alliance, the United States never signed the Pact but let Britain play the leadership role in it. The reasons for this abstention are not very clear to the present day. They seem to have been part of an overly subtle attempt on Dulles' part to gain the benefits of the alliance while avoiding its liabilities. In the event, the fact that the United States was behind it but not in it was to make the alliance more vulnerable to attack than it might have been, and to expose American policy to a confusion of purpose.

The proposal of a pact including Iraq had run into both the Arab-Israeli and the inter-Arab conflicts. The Israelis feared that Iraq's adherence would mean greater British and American military assistance to that country, which would make it a more dangerous enemy. They also knew that the alliance aimed at drawing other Arab countries and feared not only the further strengthening of their enemies but also the cooling of Western attitudes toward Israel for the sake of attracting Arab membership. The American and British reassurances that the Arab states were less dangerous to Israel within a Western alliance than outside it did not convince the Israelis, who could cite the arguments of Iraqi leaders, justifying their adherence to the Pact to their fellow-Arabs on the grounds that the Pact would strengthen the Arab position vis-à-vis Israel. Therefore, while the Pact was still pending, the Israelis tried to get their friends in the United States to oppose it; and when Iraq finally joined it early in 1955, they first tried to join NATO and, failing that, formally urged the United States to conclude with them a bilateral mutual defense treaty. American reluctance to enter such an alliance, which would jeopardize relations with the Arabs, confirmed the Israelis' sense of insecurity and strengthened their disposition to take reckless action to correct the situation.

This Israeli agitation and the realization that an alliance connecting the United States with Iraq would increase the pressure to do something for Israel played a part in Secretary Dulles' decision not to sign the Pact for the time being. Probably a more important part was played, however, by Egypt's refusal to join the Pact and its opposition to Iraq's adherence to it on grounds of Arab solidarity. This should have come as no surprise since the Secretary of State had in the first place conceived the "northern tier" idea in consideration of the obvious reluctance of the countries of the heartland to align themselves formally with the West. Nevertheless, once the idea began to be fulfilled, Dulles thought he could afford a temporary abstention with a view to mollifying Egypt and perhaps even inducing it to join, since the desired advantages and facilities of the Pact were available to the United States in any case.

Dulles' confidence in his capacity to handle Egypt and his ambition to achieve more than the goal he had set for himself by gaining Egyptian (and other Arab) adherence to the alliance were sustained by the good position that the United States enjoyed in that country at that time. On the first day of the coup d'état in 1952, the new rulers had successfully sought American intercession with the British to prevent any effort to restore the old regime by the intervention of their troops in Suez. Subsequently, the new government had endeavored in every way to cultivate American friendship and win American support for its position in the negotiations with the British for the evacuation of the Suez Canal base. The United States had responded favorably and had pressured its ally to accede to one Egyptian proposition after another until an agreement satisfactory to Egypt was finally concluded in the summer of 1954. Immediately afterwards, the Egyptians revived requests for American economic and military assistance they had made earlier, to which the United States had promised to give sympathetic consideration once the problem with Britain was settled. This close relationship between the new regime and the United States seemed to Secretary Dulles to be full of promise provided he did not precipitate things by immediately joining the Baghdad Pact. After all, had not the emergent leader of the new regime, Colonel Nasser, explicitly said more than once before that Egypt's place was naturally in the Western camp and that it only needed a little spell of full independence before committing itself? And was he not proposing, just then, before the conclusion of the Baghdad Pact, that the Arab countries constitute an all-Arab alliance linked to the West?

This reasoning might have proved sound, and Egypt might have been lured into some form of Western defense system, if the United States had not merely abstained from joining the Pact but had altogether held it in abeyance. Britain, however, needed the Pact urgently to replace its expiring bilateral treaty with Iraq. Furthermore, it was thought that its conclusion would help pressure Egypt to commit itself. As it was, the signing of the treaty, as we have observed in another context, dashed Egypt's hopes of itself leading an all-Arab alliance and promoted Iraq as the West's Arab intermediary, thus inspiring fierce opposition in Egypt, first on specifically Arab and then on general nonalignment grounds. The abstention of the United States, instead of pacifying Egypt, encouraged it to attack the Pact with much less inhibition than it would have ventured at this stage; and the vehemence of the attacks brought Egypt to Russia's attention.

THE SOVIET BREAKTHROUGH IN THE MIDDLE EAST

In the eyes of the Soviet Union, the American Containment Policy was but a euphemism for the old, aggression-bound, "capitalist encirclement," and the extension of the containment belt into the Middle East threatened to establish American power on the approaches to Russia's heartland. Yet, despite seething nationalist agitation and general turmoil following the Arab-Israeli war, the Soviet government of the time felt that it had little if any leverage in the area that could be used for countering American efforts. Threats and warnings against joining a Western alliance or incitement of local Communist parties, insignificant anyway except in Iran, were more likely to precipitate than to prevent the results Russia feared. Therefore, with one exception that in a sense proved their apprehensions, the Russians contented themselves in the Middle East with a passive policy of mild protestation and with the hope that the United States would become embroiled with the nationalists. Conceivably, the Korean conflict was ignited with the intent of diverting American attention to what was, in Russian eyes, a much less sensitive area.

The exception to the mild Russian response was their attitude toward Israel. Persuading itself that the Tel Aviv government was courting American favor and seeking to advance its interests through the Western regional defense projects envisaged for the Middle East, the Soviet government launched virulent attacks against Zionism and Israel, which quickly assumed the character of a vast anti-Jewish campaign. Jewish cultural institutions in the Soviet Union were suppressed and Jewish writers were banished or simply vanished; it was the time of the notorious Slansky trial in Czechoslovakia and of the Doctors' plot in Moscow. When some outraged individuals bombed the Russian embassy in Tel Aviv, the Soviet government promptly broke off diplomatic relations with Israel. Why Israel received this kind of treatment is partly due to the indignation of Stalin's government at what it thought to be ingratitude after all the help it had extended to the Jewish state in its birth struggle. There is no doubt, however, that this more or less understandable feeling triggered an explosion of latent anti-Semitism in parts of the Soviet establishment and served to focus the paranoiac fits that had become frequent with Stalin in his last years against the Jews in the domains under his control, whom he suspected of putting loyalty to Israel above loyalty to the Soviet Union and Communism. In any case, this violent reaction only resulted in prompting the Israeli government desperately to seek protection in the Western camp and in alienating or rendering ineffective the very strong organized sympathy for the Soviet Union that existed in Israel even among non-Communist leftist parties.

As we have seen, it was Egyptian nationalist opposition and not some Russian action that scuttled the American effort to organize the Middle East within the frame of the Containment Policy. In trying once again to organize the area in terms of the New Look Policy and strategy, the United States presented the Russians with a new and infinitely more dangerous challenge. Whereas in the previous phase the object of the policy was, at least ostensibly, to protect the area against the eventuality of Communist aggression, the New Look Policy openly avowed that the area might be used as a base for retaliation for something the Soviet Union might do elsewhere. Under the Containment Policy, the Middle East was to take care of itself and add little to America's over-all strategic capability; now it was to be organized with a view to playing a crucial role in America's over-all capacity to strike at Russia and to restrict the effectiveness of a Russian strike. Finally, whereas the MEDO proposal was stillborn because of Egyptian opposition, the peripheral countries most relevant to Russia's strategic posture seemed willing in advance to commit themselves to a "northern tier" alliance.

Nevertheless, despite the threatening nature of the projected new alliance, the Soviet government felt itself in no position to do much about it in the Middle East itself in the course of the two years that elapsed between its conception and its consummation in the Baghdad Pact. The death of Stalin in March 1953 did give his successors the chance to terminate the anti-Jewish, anti-Zionist campaign, restore diplomatic relations with Israel, and thus open up the possibility of enlisting on the Soviet side the very strong Israeli opposition to the projected pact. However, the Soviet Union was too compromised by recent actions to attract Israeli cooperation. Israel merely assured the Soviet government that it would not join any aggressive pact against Russia and then proceeded to oppose the Baghdad Pact on its own and in a way that violated, in Soviet eyes, the spirit of the assurance just given. As mentioned earlier, Israel's government attempted to protect itself against the effects of the pact by seeking admission to NATO and then by seeking a bilateral mutual defense treaty with the United States, both parties being in the Soviet book aggressive by definition. It is intriguing, though of course idle, to speculate about what course events might have taken in the area if the community of interest of the Soviet Union and Israel in opposing the Pact had actually served as a basis for a true rapprochement between the two countries.

Elsewhere in the Middle East, the deeply rooted suspicion of the Soviet Union on the part of Turkey and Iran inhibited Soviet action by making it liable to backfire. But an infinitely greater inhibition was the reality of American nuclear superiority and the belligerent disposition of circles in and close to the Republican Administration, who had spoken earlier for instance, of rolling back the Iron Curtain. Therefore, the tactic adopted by Stalin's successors was to generate in the world at large a climate of détente designed at once to minimize the chances of war under the condition of American nuclear superiority and to weaken the justification for any new alliances, in the Middle East or anywhere else. This tactic found expression in, among other things, the trips of Bulganin and Khrushchev to such focal countries as Britain, where they reassured the government about its interests in the Middle East and tried to persuade it that a new alliance was unnecessary; Yugoslavia, where they mended Soviet relations with Tito and eliminated a great source of tension; and India, where they promised assistance and encouraged Nehru to lead a nonalignment campaign among African and Asian countries, which culminated in the Bandung Conference of April 1955. At that conference, China's Chou En-Lai played a key role in promoting the adoption of the so-called Bandung Principles, which became the charter for nonalignment as a doctrine. The Russian détente campaign climaxed in the convening of the Geneva Summit meeting in July 1955.

In the meantime, the Soviet scientific-industrial-military establishment had been working full steam to close the power gap with the United States. By the time the Geneva Summit convened, the Soviet Union was near enough this objective for the deliberations at the conference to be strongly tinged with the notion that total war had become suicidal for both superpowers. By that time, too, the Soviet Union had already taken advantage of the greater freedom of maneuvering its new power position gave it to make its first effective countermove in the Middle East in the form of the arms deal with Egypt.[3]

We have already discussed in other contexts the immediate effects of the arms deal on the Arab-Israeli conflict and on inter-Arab relations. We have seen how it exacerbated Arab-Israeli tensions to the point of war and how it thrust Nasser into the role of Arab hero, which in turn led to Egyptian commitment to the goal of integral Arab unity and to intensified inter-Arab strife. In addition to these effects, the deal introduced Russia as a power in the Middle East heartland, a position it has retained and developed ever since.

Initially, the Soviet Union wanted no more than to encourage Egypt to stay out of the Baghdad Pact by furnishing the arms that the Arab advocates of the Pact argued were the principal advantage to be had from it. Thanks to Nasser's daring and American fumbling, however,

[3] News of the deal was released to the world in September 1955 but it has since become clear that it was actually concluded the previous May. This fact as well as other pertinent information concerning the whole episode was revealed by Muhammad Hassanein Haykal in *al Ahram*, April 14, 1967.

the Soviet Union was able to capitalize on the events put in train by the deal to achieve much more than it had hoped for.

The United States' view of the arms deal was also limited at first, although in a different way. It resented the fact that the deal had killed all hope of luring Egypt into the Western alliance and was irked by its disruptive effect on the Arab-Israeli conflict, which had been precariously stabilized by the Tripartite Declaration. But its chief concern was the fear that the deal might lead to Soviet-Communist control or takeover of Egypt. Accustomed to thinking of the Russians as masters of subversion and of leaders of young countries as inexperienced dupes, American policy makers addressed themselves mainly to the issue of saving Nasser from the consequences of his actions. Little did they imagine that, rather than becoming a Russian puppet, Nasser might actually use the Russians to his own ends and that those ends could be more devastating to Western interests than anything the Russians themselves could do.

The United States' effort to save Nasser and Egypt from Communist control was not even consistent. It alternated between threats and blandishments and secured only the worse effects of both. As soon as reports of the deal were confirmed, a special emissary was rushed to Nasser to warn him and press him to undo it. As Nasser took a defiant stance, the United States responded, not with retaliatory measures, but with an offer of support for the construction of the Aswan Dam in order to counterbalance Soviet presence. While the offer was being studied, Secretary Dulles became irritated by Nasser's continued attacks on the Baghdad Pact, his mounting intransigence toward Israel, and his recognition of Communist China and decided to withdraw the aid offer in a manner intended to insult and deflate Nasser. Nasser retaliated by nationalizing the Suez Canal Company, in which Britain and France had the main interest. For a while, the American Secretary of State went along with Franco-British threats of forceful action; but later he reversed himself and tried to defuse their resolve to use force. Finally, when Britain and France sought to by-pass American dilatory tactics by going to war in collusion with Israel, the United States took the lead in marshaling world pressure against them, thus compelling them to withdraw and leaving Nasser in undisputed control of the Canal.

The equivocal attitude of the United States not only emboldened Nasser and confused its allies and friends, but it also allowed the Soviet Union to convert its initial penetration of the area into a breakthrough with minimum risk to itself. In September 1955, the Soviet Union had proceeded so cautiously that the arms deal had been announced as an agreement between Egypt and Czechoslovakia instead of Russia. Presumably, this was to allow for a retreat without loss of face in the event of a drastic American reaction. The American response of competing for Egyptian favor through the Aswan Dam offer relieved Russian anxiety and encouraged them to support Nasser's attacks on the Baghdad Pact and to back his design to nationalize the Suez Canal Company. Again, during the crisis that followed nationalization, the Russians, while giving Egypt full diplomatic backing, were cautious not to commit themselves to any military assistance in the face of Anglo-French threats for fear that the United States might ultimately join its allies in military action. But when it became evident that, rather than supporting its allies, the United States was actively and energetically opposing their resort to force, the Russians came forward with barely veiled threats of nuclear reprisals and of sending volunteers to fight on Egypt's side. Thus did the deal concluded secretly in May and cautiously announced to the world in September 1955 become converted within a year and a half into a broad tacit alliance between Egypt and the Soviet Union, with the Soviet Union playing the role of patron of the country that was spearheading the struggle of the Arab nationalists against the West, its Arab stooges, and its Israeli lackey. In contrast with Russia's record of forceful support, the credit gained by the United States for opposing its allies in the Suez war appeared slight and was dissipated by the next swing of American policy toward Nasser.

THE EARLY BALANCE OF TERROR
AND THE CLIMAX OF THE COLD WAR
IN THE MIDDLE EAST

Already before the Suez-Sinai War, the acquisition of second strike capacity by the Soviet Union had rendered the short-lived New Look Policy and strategy obsolete. As long as the United States could absorb a Soviet first strike and still respond with a knock-out blow, it could effectively threaten nuclear retaliation for *any* Soviet encroachment. But as the Soviet Union became capable of absorbing an American first blow and still respond with a devastating strike, the American threat became unbelievable and ineffective, except as a retaliation against encroachment on vital positions.

This new relation of forces entailed a new complex set of strategic and tactical considerations. Since both superpowers were capable of inflicting unacceptable damage on each other in an all-out war, it became their supreme interest to avoid such war by avoiding any irreversible challenge to each other's vital-interest areas. However, abiding by this imperative was difficult in practice because, while some "vital-interest areas" of each were readily identifiable as such by the other, others, being in large measure a consequence of subjective determinations, could not be assessed with any degree of certainty. The difficulty was compounded by the realization on the part of each that the other was apt to *pretend* that some interests were vital when it actually did not consider them to be so in order to deter the opponent from challenging them. Considering the terrible consequences of miscalculation, the new situation might have led the superpowers to a gradual toning down of the conflicts between them and to a détente based on coexistence. However, while the desirability of such a consummation began to be discussed in earnest, the lingering hope on the part of now one side, now the other, that it might achieve a technological or diplomatic breakthrough that would fundamentally alter the situation in its favor stood in the way of fully realizing that possibility. In the meantime, while the conflict persisted, the new situation actually contributed to the exacerbation of tension rather than its reduction. For it encouraged each side to conduct probes in what it thought were "gray"—that is, doubtful—interest areas of the other and to respond to the probes of the other for as long as possible *as if* it considered the threatened interests vital in order to compel it to retreat. In other words, the new situation put a premium on a policy of brinkmanship for both sides.

The Middle East periphery—Turkey and Iran—having been directly or indirectly integrated in the American global defense network since 1946–1947, appeared to the Russians to be too important to the United States for them to risk direct probes against it. The Middle East heartland, however, where the Western hold was precarious, appeared to offer more promising grounds for probes which, if successful, could be traded for more favorable arrangements in the periphery. As the Soviet Union proceeded to test this idea and the United States reacted, the Middle East was plunged into the tensest period of its postwar history, and its own conflicts were raised to their highest intensity.

The first Russian probe after acquiring second-strike capacity was the arms deal with Egypt. In this instance, however, the inconspicuous use by the Russians of their new power position (recall the precaution of using Czechoslovakia as a front), unfamiliarity with the tactics suggested by the new power relations, and a misguided view of the real implications of the deal combined to misdirect the American response and prevent the development of a Soviet-American confrontation. However, after the United States had had an opportunity to rethink its global position in light of the new balance of power and had seen the outcome of the arms deal, it began to see things quite differently: The Soviet Union, it now became apparent, had not bothered with subverting and communizing Egypt but had instead used every opportunity to support Egypt's assault on the Western positions in the Middle East by extending over it, at least seemingly, the protective umbrella of its power. This was seen as probing by proxy to extend the initial successful Soviet penetration. At the same time, the erosion of British and French influence and the mushrooming of Nasser's popularity following the collapse of the Suez invasion made the United States aware that a proxy protected by Russia could constitute a formidable challenge to American and Western interests. Thus, to check Soviet-Egyptian probes and perhaps recover some of the lost ground, the United States adopted the tactics suggested by the new power balance and devised the Eisenhower Doctrine.

The idea of the Doctrine was to rally as many Middle Eastern countries as possible to the Western camp on the basis of minimum overt identification on their part and then to impress on the Soviet Union that these countries fell in the American vital-interest area and were therefore taboo to Soviet probes, direct or by proxy. However, the Administration's decision to dramatize its declaration of intent by seeking advance Congressional approval to use the armed forces of the United States to support it, as well as the necessity to manage the sensibilities of Middle Eastern governments who shied from an open breach with Egypt, forced the formulation of the Doctrine in terms that betrayed the fact that the United States was much less unequivocal about opposing "aggression by proxy" than aggression by the Soviet Union itself. The Doctrine spoke of using the armed forces of the United States to defend any country concerned that was threatened with aggression by a country under international Communist control. Although these terms made it unmistakably clear that open aggression by Russia would be resisted, they equivocated about what constituted a "threat" and what was comprised in the notion of "a country under the control of international Communism." This equivocation made for flexibility of interpretation, permitting the United States to counterprobe when possible or hold the line and retreat when necessary; but that flexibility also weakened the deterrent effect of the message as far as probes by Egypt were concerned and thus left the whole issue open to actual trials of strength and nerve.

We have already discussed the succession of crises that followed the application of the Eisenhower Doctrine from the perspective of inter-Arab relations, and we can therefore be brief in our treatment of these crises and their outcome from the standpoint of the big powers. At the beginning, the United States met with moderate success. All of the Arab countries surrounding Egypt adhered to the Doctrine, except for Jordan, whose king had become ever more a prisoner of a pro-Egyptian government since March 1956, and Syria, which had sided with Egypt at about the same time and had then concluded an arms agreement with Russia. The adherence of Saudi Arabia and Lebanon were particularly important since up until that point the former had sided with Egypt against the Baghdad Pact and the latter had been neutral in inter-Arab affairs. On the other hand, most of the adhering governments, Saudi Arabia in particular, sought to ward off any untoward events by stressing opposition to open Communist threat and underplaying any identification of Egypt with the Communist camp.

Next, to further isolate Egypt, the United States helped King Hussein of Jordan engineer a coup d'état against his own government in April 1957, probably through discrete assistance in planning and execution. While matters were still undecided, the Sixth Fleet maneuvered in the eastern Mediterranean as a warning to Egypt, Syria, and Russia to keep hands off. Thus, without undue difficulty Jordan was brought back into the Western fold, and thenceforward the United States assumed the burden of providing Jordan with an annual subsidy for military and budgetary support and became the guarantor of Hussein's regime.

Finally, to complete the isolation of Egypt, the United States, in cooperation with the Iraqis, attempted in the following summer to work the overthrow of the Syrian government by pro-Western elements. When the plot was uncovered, as we mentioned before, the United States invoked the Eisenhower Doctrine, suggesting that Syria was under Communist control and presented a threat to its neighbors, entitling them to call for armed American assistance. Once again the Sixth Fleet maneuvered in the eastern Mediterranean, while Turkish troops deployed on Syria's northern border and Iraqi troops prepared to advance to the Syrian frontier. This time the Soviet Union reacted with warnings that it would not tolerate aggression against Syria on the part of its neighbors. Egypt offered military assistance to its threatened ally and launched a massive propaganda barrage designed to rouse the Arab populations against the governments adhering to the Eisenhower Doctrine, which it portrayed as an instrument of imperialism. A typical confrontation thus developed that threatened to plunge the area and the big powers into war.

The crisis was defused when, from fear of war and public opinion, the Arab governments adhering to the Doctrine lost their nerve and denied that they viewed Syria as a threat and generally declared their opposition to any interference in another country's affairs. The anti-interference declaration, when subscribed to by Syria and Egypt as well as the other Arab countries, allowed the United States to pull out without loss of face. But the fact was that the Eisenhower Doctrine had crumbled at its first serious test as a means of checking Soviet gains by proxy. Those countries whom the Doctrine was intended to protect against presumably Communist-controlled Egypt and Syria had denied their need for such protection. Henceforth, American opposition to Egypt, if called for, had to be pursued directly and openly, exposing both the United States and its "accomplices" to the charge and the consequences of opposing the dominant current of Arab nationalism and its hero.

It was for this reason that the United States held back when, in the spring of 1958, the crisis of the Lebanese civil war broke out. As we indicated previously, the war was partly the result of Lebanese personality politics, but the identification of Lebanese Muslims with Nasser and the newly formed Syrian-Egyptian union played a major part in it. Nevertheless, despite the fact that Syria was supporting the Muslims and that the Christian president of the country was prepared to call for American help, the United States, chastened by the recent Syrian experience, chose to watch the situation closely rather than intervene during several months while the conflict simmered.

This posture was almost completely reversed after the outbreak of what was thought to be a Nasserist revolution in Iraq on July 14, 1958. The very next day, after eliciting an invitation from the Lebanese president, American Marine units landed in that country. Simultaneously, a Marine combat team from Okinawa was ordered into the Persian Gulf; a Composite Air Strike Group from western Europe was rushed to Adana, Turkey; air force tankers were deployed in forward positions; and the Strategic Air Command was put on increased alert level. In conjunction with these moves, British paratroopers landed in Jordan at the invitation of its king, and Turkish troops began to concentrate on Iraq's borders.

The nature, scope and timing of these moves, along with Iraq's crucial importance because of its oil, its strategic position in relation to Russia, and its being the bulwark of Western influence in the Arab Middle East, clearly suggested that even though the United States spoke only of its mission in Lebanon, it actually was seeking to place itself and its allies in a position from which they could intervene in Iraq if the opportunity arose. The evidence of men who participated in making or executing the decisions indicates clearly that the United States and its allies hoped for an invitation to act against the revolution from surviving men of authority in the old regime or from loyalist army units.

The reaction of Nasser and the Russians was directed particularly at the danger of Western intervention in Iraq. When news came of the revolution and the American moves, Nasser was aboard ship returning from a visit to Tito. Immediately, he returned to Yugoslavia, whence he flew to Moscow to consult the Russians and seek their support. From dawn to midnight he deliberated with Khrushchev and his staff; then he flew to Damascus, the second capital of the United Arab Republic, where he made public an order for general mobilization and proclaimed his determination to support the Iraqi revolution without reservation and with all the means at his disposal. Simultaneously, the Russians announced maneuvers on their southern borders and began to mass troops and equipment in the Caucasus, while their diplomatic and propaganda apparatus set to work to mobilize world opinion against what they termed "American aggression against the Arab world." Thus arose the second confrontation in ten months, this one of much greater seriousness because much greater interests were at stake and because all the parties involved had moved troops to the fringes of Iraq.

The crisis passed its peak when it became apparent that there was no loyalist force left in Iraq to call for help and that the United States would not use King Hussein's claim to be the constitutional chief of the Arab Union of Iraq and Jordan as an excuse to intervene. Since the United States had formally justified its actions by the Lebanese situation alone, it had no difficulty backing out without losing face. And after their "victory" in Iraq, Nasser and the Russians were quite content to leave Lebanon alone. American mediators required only bazaar-diplomacy to patch up the Lebanese crisis and send the troops home. The British had an even easier time leaving Jordan since by the time the option of intervention in Iraq had been foreclosed, their job of seeing King Hussein through the dangerous period of potential revolution was done.

Some six and a half years later, Muhammad Hassanein Haykal revealed in one of his Friday columns something of what went on between Nasser and Khrushchev during their long deliberations on July 16, 1958.[4] Since this information is not only specifically pertinent to the crisis itself but also sheds considerable light on the nature of Soviet-

[4] *al Ahram*, January 22, 1965.

Egyptian relations and on Soviet thinking on the Middle East, it is worthwhile to digress for a moment and dwell on it in some detail.

We should perhaps begin by mentioning that the revelations have a ring of authenticity, especially since they were not made for their own sake or in connection with a discussion of the Iraqi crisis as such, but were used as illustrative material in the context of a hero-worshipping column entitled "The Loneliness at the Summit . . . and its Tortures." Haykal, who was with Nasser on the ship taking him home from Yugoslavia and went with him to Moscow, gets to the main part of his story by way of some interesting details, such as the fear of Tito and the Russians for Nasser's personal safety from American naval movements and their urging him to return to Brioni and go home by some other way; and the indication that the initiative to go to Moscow was taken by Nasser after very careful deliberation.

The main part of the story consists of a concise summary of the discussion between Khrushchev and Nasser, such as might have been written down at the time by one of Nasser's aides for the record. Khrushchev told Nasser that the situation was critical. The West seems to have lost its nerve. It sees an imminent danger in the success of the Arab national movement. The collapse of the Baghdad Pact is a grave blow to its interests and influence; and the suddenness of the blow has caused it to lose all reason. Therefore, anything can happen. Frankly, Khrushchev concluded, the Soviet Union was not prepared for a clash with the West the consequences of which were unforeseeable.

Nasser responded that he was not asking Khrushchev to enter into armed conflict with the West, nor did he want or seek such a clash. What he wanted to know was how far the Soviet Union would back him up. To this Khrushchev replied that the Soviet Union would provide maximum political support, that it could muster tremendous international pressure against the possibility of a clash with Nasser, and that he believed the clash could be averted.

Nasser agreed that the clash could be averted but pointed out that the situation was so tense that a small mistake could make it uncontrollable. He promised that, for his part, he would try his best to keep things under control; but he pointed out that the side confronting him had lost its nerve. If the clash he was trying to avoid did come, the United Arab Republic could not shake off its responsibilities. Then, he reminded Khrushchev that if the West liquidated the Iraqi revolution, it was bound to turn next to liquidating the United Arab Republic. It would not stop halfway; it knew that the Arab revolution was all one impulse and one movement. He concluded by saying that he was not asking for what the Soviet Union could not give but wanted to know exactly what the position of the Soviet Union was going to be in view of this prospect.

Khrushchev then suggested an idea: He would declare that the Soviet army was going to hold large-scale military maneuvers on the frontiers of Turkey and Iran. Such a declaration would make the West take into consideration the possibility of Russian intervention. This would be useful. He asked Nasser what he thought of this, and Nasser replied, laughingly, that if it should not prove useful, it would not be harmful anyway. Then Khrushchev added, also laughingly, that he was not concerned about the West's thinking that the Russians were preparing for more than maneuvers; but that it was important that Nasser should not imagine something other than the truth.

It is clear from this scenario that the Soviet Union was consciously bluffing during the Iraqi crisis. It was almost convinced by the troop movements of the United States and its allies that the United States considered Iraq's membership in the Baghdad Pact a vital-interest area calling for hands off. The Soviet troop movement in the Caucasus was the last step the Russians were prepared to take. They also suspected that their Egyptian protégé might "deliberately misunderstand" this and warned him against it.

In addition, the scenario suggests that contrary to the assumption guiding American policy toward Egypt ever since the arms deal and reflected in the phraseology of the Eisenhower Doctrine ("a country under international Communist control"), Egypt was far from being an inert tool in Russian hands. Actually, it was the more daring of the partners, pressing forward its more reticent and cautious associate. Only after Nasser had raised the specter of the West sweeping away the Iraqi revolution, the United Arab Republic, and concomitantly the entire painfully acquired Soviet position in the heartland, did Khrushchev think of trying the military maneuver bluff.

Lastly, the scenario prompts a still more important reflection on the Soviets' conception of their interest in the Middle East. Although the interlocutors agreed that the stakes involved in the crisis were nothing less than the entire Soviet or Western position in the heartland, Khrushchev nevertheless made up his mind clearly and firmly that these stakes did not warrant carrying the confrontation beyond the point of bluffing with military maneuvers; and he warned Nasser that he would not be dragged into a clash by degrees.

Without a call for help from some Iraqi authority, would the United States have acted differently if it had known for certain that the Russians were merely bluffing and were determined to avoid a clash with the West? The question cannot be answered with certainty on the basis of the available evidence. On the one hand, it might be argued that the Eisenhower Administration would have been inhibited anyway by its own legalistic bent, its own opposition to its allies' invasion of Egypt less than two years earlier, and the fear of repercussions in Arab countries still under friendly regimes. On the other hand, without the added fear of a clash with Russia, the importance of the interests at stake, the risks already run in fighting Nasser, the possibility of dealing him a critical blow and of rolling back Soviet influence, and the ease with which the appearance of legitimacy could have been concocted might have led to forceful American intervention. Be that as it may, the fact that the United States wrote off Iraq and did not intervene marked the final failure in the succession of unsuccessful British, British-American, and American attempts since the end of World War II to organize the Middle East heartland in the frame of the Western alliance system.

The Powers and the Middle East in the Fading Cold War: 1960 and After

GENERAL FEATURES

The Iraqi crisis was the last major confrontation between the United States and the Soviet Union in the Middle East to the present time and thus marks a turning point in the superpowers' contest in that part of the world. This change was not due to any abatement in the frequency of regional crises. In the years since mid-1958 there has been the protracted struggle between Kassem and Nasser, the Iraqi threat to Kuwait, the Syrian secession from the United Arab Republic, the Kurdish war, the Yemen war, half a dozen coups d'état in Iraq and Syria, the Jordan waters dispute, and so forth. Neither was the turning point due to the withdrawal of one or both of the superpowers from the area. On the contrary, both took an interest in all the conflicts mentioned above; both committed even more military and economic assistance to countries in the area after 1958 than before; and each extended its involvement to countries or activities it had not previously been engaged in. The main reasons for the change were the renunciation by the United States of its effort to form a Western coalition in the heartland and, consequently, the loosening, not to say undoing, of the previous polarization that had pitted the Soviet Union and its protégés against the United States and its protégés, related to which was a loosening of the link between the Middle East heartland and its periphery. All three developments resulted from political-tactical considerations thrown up by the Iraqi revolution and its aftermath; but they were upheld and given a more basic rationale by diplomatic-strategic developments on the global level.

What we called the "early balance of terror phase" had seen the Soviet deterrent, especially after the launching of the Sputniks, rely increasingly on long-range missiles while the United States' deterrent had continued to rest primarily on long-range bombers. This situation had given the Soviet Union at least a theoretical advantage, for its missiles were sited either in its home territory or in contiguous countries under its firm control, whereas the American bombers and short-range missiles depended for optimal effectiveness on far-flung bases, some of them in countries that were vulnerable to internal upheavals and Soviet diplomatic pressure. In 1960, the United States essentially freed itself from this disadvantage by introducing into operational use its first batch of intercontinental missiles and commissioning the first two of a whole fleet of Polaris submarines. Thus, both superpowers came to have deterrents that were truly independent and virtually invulnerable.

Potentially, this change entailed two momentous effects for the pattern of international politics. First and more obvious, it bore the seeds of the disintegration of the alliance and alignment system of the Cold War. The superpowers no longer needed extensive alliance systems to maintain their basic deterrent posture, and the allies of both sides were apt to suspect that the superpowers would no longer be willing to risk a confrontation in order to protect vital allied interests. At the least, the allies were likely to feel that the weakening of mutuality of interest at the strategic level was bound to diminish drastically their influence with the relevant superpower. This, in turn, was apt to impel them to try to improve their bargaining power by forming subcoalitions within the alliance and adopting autonomous courses.

The second effect, in many ways related to the first, was the alteration of the pattern of competition between the superpowers. Both countries had independent and invulnerable deterrents based on a very high level of technology. By virtually foreclosing the possibility of a decisive alteration of the balance between them by a diplomatic or technological breakthrough, this situation was likely to scale down the intensity of their contest and to open up possibilities of agreement on diplomatic and military issues that had previously abetted the competition. At the same time, however, the reduction in the ultimate relevance of the contest, by lessening the fear of any particular encounter escalating into a full-fledged confrontation, was apt to create vast new areas and issues for competition, albeit of a modified character. Such competition was bound, for instance, to be selective and much more conscious of the concrete costs and returns of specific cases than in the past. Furthermore, it was certain to be keyed lower since the superpowers could be expected not to allow it to escalate.

These *logical* implications of the new situation did not become fully apparent in actual practice until after the Cuban missile crisis of 1962. There were some manifestations of these implications even before that: the restlessness of France, the Chinese-Soviet ideological dispute, and Khrushchev's enunciation of the doctrine that war between the capitalist and Communist camps was no longer inevitable and that violent revolutions were not indispensable to Communist takeovers. Three factors, however, had combined to suppress their full realization before 1962. First, there was the pressure exerted by the Chinese on behalf of revolutionary militancy that genuinely convinced some Russian leaders and forced the rest to compromise in order to avoid a complete breach. Then, there was the impact of the massive decolonization movement that brought into existence dozens of new countries, most of them favorably inclined toward the Soviet camp out of resentment for their former Western masters. This tended to impart buoyancy to Russia's view of the future and lend credence to the Chinese claim that a decisive Communist victory was possible. The final and probably most important factor was that of inertia. Established institutions and patterns of thinking and behavior tend to persist for some time after the premises underlying them have changed; in this case, where the balance of terror had existed previously and only the means of delivering weapons had changed, the change was less perceptible and inertia more applicable.

The Cuban crisis jolted all concerned out of their inertia and accelerated the process of adaptation to the new situation. In the East, the result was the consummation of the breach between China and Russia. China denounced Soviet betrayal of the revolutionary cause and claimed for itself the role of militant leadership. Russia denounced adventurism, deposed Khrushchev for his Cuban policy among other things, and talked less and less about even peaceful competition and more and more about the inevitability of cooperation. In the West, France under De Gaulle strove energetically and with some success to create a West European coalition as a balance between the superpowers and took more dramatic steps to loosen its ties with the United States and build new ones with the Soviet Union. Both the Chinese and the French proceeded to develop nuclear forces to bolster the independent roles they aspired to play in world affairs. The superpowers themselves, starting with the nuclear test ban treaty, worked ever more cooperatively to check the consequences of their arms race and contain dangerous conflicts until their momentum was checked by the Vietnam War. As an effort to persuade the Chinese of the futility of fomenting revolutions, the massive intervention of the United States in Vietnam may indicate the dilemma the superpowers will have to face next; either to cooperate in containing and taming China or to allow China's militancy to reverse the détente process and increase the chances of a frightful showdown.

The unfolding of the implications of the new strategic posture of the superpowers could not fail to affect the Middle East too. As control of parts of the area ceased to be a crucial feature of American strategy, denial of such control ceased to be a crucial objective of the Soviet Union. Consequently, the easing of the contest between the superpowers that had begun before the Iraqi revolution for contingent regional reasons continued and was reinforced by strategic considerations. But even though major confrontations between the superpowers were thus made much less likely, their rivalry did not stop. Indeed, the Middle East turned out to be one part of the world where reduced fear of confrontation encouraged more extensive competition motivated by secondary strategic and other considerations. This situation gradually shaped a new pattern of big power—Middle East relations.

A wide variety of considerations stimulated the continuation and extension of competition, all of which may be grouped under four headings: (1) inertia, established commitments, or the pressure to "protect" previous investments of effort with new investments; (2) real or imagined specific advantages, either material, such as oil; diplomatic, such as the support and friendship of countries of the area; or psychological, such as prestige; (3) vestigial ideological reasons, survivals of Cold War habits; (4) competition itself, or the reluctance to abandon acquired positions to the other side or to a third party, such as China or France. The means of competition remained essentially the same as before but were used more extensively: economic assistance, diplomatic backing in disputes involving countries of the area, and, most important for this study, the supply of arms.

The consequences of this competition for the Arab-Israeli conflict and for inter-Arab rivalries have been more detrimental than in the previous period precisely because the superpowers have had less at stake. The decreased likelihood of a local crisis escalating into a confrontation has made the superpowers more willing to risk involvement in such crises. At the same time, the sense that the superpowers may ultimately hold back to avoid a mutual confrontation has led the countries of the area to expect both more freedom of action and a greater exposure to danger in pursuing their interests, and therefore to wish to expand their own means of compulsion and defense. On occasion, the superpowers have hesitated and pondered over the mounting cost of their competition in the area and over its real value. So far, however, they have found it easier to continue their costly and unsettling rivalry than to check it by agreement.

THE CHANGING BIG POWER INTERESTS AND THE REGIONAL CONFLICTS

Between mid-1958 and the present a series of redefinitions of the positions of the superpowers in the Middle East took place, which, though gradual and undramatic from the perspective of the superpowers themselves, had very important consequences for the countries of the area. The first redefinitions were triggered by the local political changes wrought by the Iraqi revolution. Policies changed visibly although the basic interests of the superpowers did not. Subsequent redefinitions were affected by the evolving global situation as well as changing local configurations. These resulted not only in visible changes of policies but also in changes in basic interests, though the latter were sometimes almost imperceptible. In the remainder of this chapter, we shall outline these redefinitions and their impact on the Arab-Israeli conflict and inter-Arab relations. For the sake of clarity, we shall treat the superpowers separately.

THE SOVIET UNION

The first reaction of the Soviets to the Iraqi revolution was to attempt to advance the strategic objective they had been working for ever since their first penetration of the heartland in 1955: to neutralize the northern tier, or at least to deny the United States the use of bases in those countries. In the past, each real or pretended Soviet success in supporting their Arab protégés against the West had been followed by a Soviet proposal for some kind of big power agreement through which they sought to trade the successes for American concessions in the northern tier. In February 1957, for example, after the Suez-Sinai war, Foreign Minister Shepilov proposed a six-point plan calling, among other things, for an undertaking by the big powers to refrain from shipping arms to the Middle East and for the abolition of all existing military bases in the area. In January 1958, after the Syrian Crisis, the Russians proposed a summit conference on the Middle East and followed up with an appeal to keep the area free of nuclear weapons and missile bases. Feeling they had more to lose than the Russians, the United States and its allies had turned a deaf ear to these proposals. Now, in July 1958, after the Iraqi revolution, Khrushchev renewed the call for a big power meeting, thinking that perhaps the West was now convinced that he had enough assets to make a bargain worth while.

Khrushchev was correct up to a point. The United States did not dismiss his proposal out of hand as it had the previous ones. It still refused to have a summit conference in order not to alarm its Turkish and Iranian friends, but it expressed its willingness to discuss the Middle East at the highest levels within the frame of the regular United Nations General Assembly in the fall. The Soviets agreed and, in anticipation of the bargaining, proceeded to firm up their position by signing an agreement to help Egypt financially and technically in the construction of the first phase of the Aswan Dam and by providing Iraq with massive quantities of weapons and economic assistance. This action was in addition to an earlier arms agreement with Syria and to the acceleration of arms shipments to Egypt to make up its losses in the Suez-Sinai war.

The projected discussions never took place because in the meantime the Soviets adopted a major revision of their Middle East views. The previous objective of eliminating or restricting the American presence in the periphery remained, but the heartland was elevated to an area of intrinsic interest, not to be traded for concessions in the northern tier. The Soviet position thus became symmetrical with the United States' position at the time, which was to restrict Soviet penetration in the heartland without giving up its interests in the periphery. For the first time since the initial penetration in 1955, the Soviet interest in the heartland was defined as promoting Communism as well as fighting imperialism. Even after pursuit of this twin objective proved futile, the Soviet Union persisted in viewing its position in the region as an end in itself rather than as a means of achieving its objective in Turkey and Iran and strove to find new rationalizations for it. This view explains why the Russians not only backed out of the projected New York meeting but never renewed the call for a big power agreement on the Middle East; indeed, it explains why they turned a deaf ear to Western suggestions to the same effect in subsequent years.

The new Soviet approach to the heartland was triggered by Chinese criticism, but it was grounded in the circumstances of the region after the Iraqi revolution. We know that Khrushchev canceled his New York trip after a hurried, unscheduled visit to Peking and, in retrospect, that the Soviet-Chinese dispute over global strategy was already

sharp at that time. We also know that the Chinese particularly accused the Soviet Union of trying to reach an accommodation with imperialism and of lavishing aid on bourgeois regimes that suppressed
local Communists and even fought them beyond their boundaries. The
Chinese criticism fell on fertile ground not simply because the Russians wanted to avoid a breach but also because the situation in the area
lent credence to it. Reneging on the New York meeting, for example,
appeared justified by the addition of Iraq to Egypt and Syria in the Soviet sphere of influence, thus making that sphere worth preserving in
itself. Moreover, it was felt that with the collapse of the Baghdad Pact,
Iran would be more amenable to conciliation out of mistrust of the value of American support. As for the criticism of showing too little concern for Communists and Communism in countries receiving aid, the
point seemed well taken since the course of Iraqi revolutionary politics
was giving the Communists, for the first time in the history of the Arab
countries, a chance to play an overt important role. And since the narrow strip of Iranian and Turkish territory separating Iraq from the Soviet Union was largely inhabited by restless, pro-Soviet Kurdish tribes,
the potentialities of the situation seemed particularly hopeful. Finally,
supporting the Iraqi Communists and the regime that allowed them to
function appeared tactically advisable since the United States' renunciation of any effort to organize a pro-Western coalition in the
heartland made it less essential for the Soviet Union to suppress its
ideological interest for the sake of marshaling an anti-imperialist front.

The actual course of events proved to be anything but favorable to
the new Soviet approach. Far from making Iran easier to pry loose
from the West, the collapse of the Baghdad Pact alarmed its ruler
about encroaching Communist influence and the possibility of a Communist-inspired Kurdish uprising and drove him still closer to the
United States. Feeling that a refurbished northern tier pact without
Iraq, the Central Treaty Organization (CENTO), was not enough, he
sought greater insurance in a bilateral treaty with the United States.
The Soviet effort to forestall such a treaty or to obtain a pledge that
foreign missile bases would not be allowed on Iranian soil by offering
a nonaggression pact was rebuffed by the Shah early in 1959.

By that time, too, it had become quite apparent that the pro-Soviet
Arab camp was anything but united. Differing views regarding Arab
unity had developed into a deadly tooth-and-nail fight between Kassem and Nasser. The Russians, necessarily, took the side of Kassem and
the Iraqi Communists, which brought them into open conflict with
Nasser for the first time since they began to cooperate in 1955. With
the leverage of their economic and military aid, they were able to

force Nasser to relax his attacks on Kassem, but the encounter made Nasser aware of his vulnerability to Soviet pressure and of the long-run conflict between Communist interests and his own. This state of affairs induced him to look westward for a counterweight. The United States, for its part, which had been searching for ways to counter Soviet and Communist influence since the collapse of the Eisenhower Doctrine policy, saw in Nasser's need the opportunity it was looking for and went more than halfway to meet him. The resulting rapprochement broke the polarization that had underlain confrontations in the area since the beginning of 1957 and that had served Soviet interests so well.

The final disappointment of Russian expectations occurred when the Iraqi Communists, for whose sake they had risked so much, were toppled by Kassem himself. Early in 1960, in the process of reorganizing Iraqi political life and licensing parties, Kassem refused legal recognition to the regular Communist party and recognized only a small, dissident nationalist Communist group. This action was followed by official harassment, divisionary tactics, and subtle incitements that accomplished the disorganization of the party and hampered its ability to reconstitute itself effectively underground or behind nonpolitical fronts. Thus the new interest of actively promoting Communism not only gravely damaged the old interest of pushing the West out of the area but ended up itself in abject failure.

As the promising cause of Communism in Iraq turned into a costly disappointment, the Soviet Union entered the most frustrating phase of its relations with the Middle East heartland. Abandoning the field to the United States after all the pains taken to establish a position seemed out of the question. There was nothing to do but hold on and wait for better days. This approach, however, besides being difficult to justify to Chinese critics and like-minded members of the Soviet hierarchy, involved increasing costs and painful complications in the region itself. In other words, continuous embarrassments and mounting costs were required simply to try to stay in the same place.

To maintain their association with Kassem's regime, the Soviets were first compelled to acquiesce in its suppression of the Iraqi Communists, gaining the latter's resentment, and then to support Kassem's claim to Kuwait, thus incurring the displeasure of all the Arab countries. The same consideration was an important factor in their recognition of the secessionist regime in Syria and their continuation of aid to that country. This move yet further antagonized Nasser. When Kassem launched a murderous war against the Kurds, traditionally Soviet protégés, using Russian weapons and aid, the Soviet Union had to content itself with mild protests. This stance obviously alienated the Kurds. Ironically, all these difficulties endured for Kassem's sake proved to be futile: In February, 1963, a military coup led by Ba'thists overthrew and killed Kassem and followed up with a systematic slaughter of all known Communists of any stripe. The Soviets were left with no choice but to terminate their aid and presence in the country.

A less dramatic but perhaps more profound example of the tribulations of the Soviets during this period was their position on Arab unity. After siding with Kassem against Nasser, they felt compelled to justify their position by taking a stand on the question of Arab unity generally. They declared their support for Arab unity but excluded that kind of unity that refused to take into account the variety of conditions in the Arab countries and sought to impose itself by force and subversion —in other words, the type of unity pursued by Nasser. This position was made to appear quite hollow, however, by the contradictory stands the Soviets took subsequently on concrete issues: In the summer of 1961 they supported Kassem's effort to "unite" Kuwait by annexing it, belying their regard for diversity and free determination, and later in the year they recognized the secessionist regime in Syria, belying their solicitude for Arab unity. Then, a year later, they supported Nasser's armed intervention in Yemen in the name of Arab unity, and still another year later they found themselves at odds with the Ba'thists in Iraq and Syria, who were active advocates of the kind of unity the Soviets presumably supported. In every case, the position adopted was determined by opportunistic adaptation to current events. With the constant turbulence of Arab politics of the time, however, every concrete position taken seemed to contradict previous positions or to be swept away by sudden turns of events, making Soviet policy as a whole appear to be working against itself.

While their policy was thus at loose ends, the Soviets had to pay an ever higher price to achieve the negative objective of not being driven out of the area altogether. The higher price was due, in the first place, to the fact that, with footholds to protect in Yemen and Iraq as well as Egypt and Syria, they had more commitments to meet. In the second place, it was due to the fact that in each of these countries, actual or potential American competition and a conscious exploitation of that competition by the governments concerned constantly raised the ante needed to stay in the game. For example, America's commitment of $150 million a year to Egypt in wheat surpluses exerted heavy pressure on the Soviet Union to come through with support for the construction of the second phase of the Aswan Dam and with vast additional amounts for industrialization projects. And this support was on top of pressures to provide great quantities of military equipment on easy and risky terms, pressures that the Soviet Union could not resist, partly because of the danger of appearing to trifle with a matter that the customer countries considered vital and partly because arms supply was the one area in which it had an advantage over the United States. For while the United States was restricted by its commitments to Israel, Jordan, Saudi Arabia, and Libya from freely supplying arms to their potential enemies—Egypt, Syria, and Iraq—the Soviet Union had no such inhibitions. On the contrary, providing arms to the enemies of friends of the United States on an increasing scale offered precisely the best chance of embroiling those countries with the United States and undoing the rapprochement that had begun to take place between them.

Eventually even the Soviet policy makers, or at least some of them, were struck by the expense and apparent aimlessness of their Middle East policy, and this realization initiated a new phase in Soviet-Middle East relations. It seems that one of the charges made against Khrushchev at the time of his ouster in 1964 was that he had unduly committed his country to another large dose of aid to Egypt during his visit there earlier that year. In any case, it is certain that Middle East policy came under critical review at the time of his deposition. Clear evidence of this is that the new ruling group dispatched Shelepin, one of its leading members, on a fact-finding mission to Cairo. Further evidence is reflected in Egyptian concern about future Soviet aid as expressed in Nasser's speeches, in press articles, and in the hurried mission of Marshal Amer to Moscow to seek clarifications and reassurances. The Soviet policy review produced no apparent immediate change in practice, but it did result in a redefinition of Russian interest in the area that bore the potential of significant practical consequences in the long run.

Policy in the periphery was left unchanged, for it appeared to be developing satisfactorily. Iran, which in 1959 had refused to restrict its association with the United States, committed itself in September 1962 not to allow foreign missile bases in its territory and went on from there to explore with the Soviet Union ways and means of economic cooperation. In Turkey, the United States itself had taken the initiative, after the Cuban crisis, in dismantling missile bases, apparently reciprocating for the withdrawal of Soviet missiles from Cuba. This action prompted the Turks to adopt a more flexible attitude toward the Soviet Union and to discuss possibilities of economic cooperation. Strategically, of course, Turkey and Iran had become far less important than they had been a few years earlier, and the United States still remained in a predominant position; but nevertheless, this thaw represented a considerable improvement in Soviet relations with these countries and gave promise of further advances toward counterbalancing American influence in the future.

With regard to the heartland, the review redefined the Soviet interest in a manner that gave a new justification to Soviet investments and political efforts there. The change had already been broached implicitly by Khrushchev himself, but the new leadership converted what seemed to have been a typical Khrushchevian impulsive assertion into a deliberately adopted doctrine.[5] Observing the increasing radicalization of the regimes in Egypt, Syria, and Iraq, and with the Cuban example possibly in their mind, the Soviet leaders conceived that "progressive" nationalist regimes might, by a combination of internal necessity and conflict with neocolonialist and imperialist powers, evolve toward an acceptable type of Socialism. Thus, by assisting these countries economically and diplomatically, the Soviet Union could both deny any reassertion of American influence in them and acquire levers that could be used to stimulate or accelerate their evolution in the desired direction.

The specific results of the new approach are hard to assess. Some developments that took place in the region after its adoption seem to be definitely connected with it; others may or may not be. One of the latter was the rapid deterioration of Egyptian-American relations over a variety of issues, leading to a withering away of United States economic aid and to an increasingly open and emphatic identification of the United States as Egypt's sworn enemy. Another was the evident acceleration of "radicalization" in Egypt, on the verbal-ideological level if not so much on the policy-action level. Whether these developments would have taken place anyway or whether direct or indirect Soviet pressure was partially or wholly responsible for them is impossible to tell. Nor is it known whether the Soviet Union had anything to do with the coup d'état of February 1966 in Syria that brought to power an extreme left wing faction of the Ba'th. On the other hand, it seems clear that Soviet relations were an important factor in Nasser's decision to release the Egyptian Communists from jail and permit them to participate in politics as individuals, in the Ba'thist regime's allotment of one or two ministerial posts to avowed Communists, and in the for-

[5] In the course of his official visit to Egypt in 1964, for example, Khrushchev introduced a jarring note into the festive atmosphere by lecturing his hosts that there was no such thing as Arab Socialism and by expressing the hope that they would come around to dropping their nationalist inhibitions and joining the international family of Socialist countries.

mal adoption at a Ba'th party convention of Marxism as one of the sources of Arab Socialism.

The new approach also led unquestionably to greater Soviet involvement in inter-Arab affairs and in the Arab-Israeli conflict. There is some evidence, for example, that the Soviet Union took a greater interest in Egypt's war in Yemen after 1964.[6] Furthermore, during a visit to Egypt in May 1966, Prime Minister Kosygin himself mediated a reconciliation between Egypt and Syria, at odds since the 1961 secession, in order to enhance the position of the left Ba'thist regime. This was also intended to strengthen the Syrian position vis-à-vis Israel. The Ba'thist government had loudly proclaimed upon its accession the beginning of a guerilla war against Israel and had been supporting saboteurs and raiders inside Israeli territory in an effort to improve its position at home. The Russians had at first advised the Israelis to be patient and promised to restrain their Syrian friends, but as their promise bore no fruit and as Israel responded with retaliatory action, the Russians simply lined themselves up with the Syrians and condemned Israeli actions. The Russian-promoted reconciliation between Egypt and Syria issued shortly in a defense agreement between the two countries that served to strengthen the Syrian regime.

Whatever the specific results of the latest Soviet approach, there is no doubt that it generally contributed to the stabilization and improvement of Russia's position. According to the new formula, competition with the United States and promotion of Socialism could be complementary objectives instead of conflicting ones, as they had been in 1959 and afterward when the promotion of Socialism was considered dependent on the growth of Communist parties. In principle, encouraging and subtly pressing for the radicalization of regimes increased the likelihood of their becoming alienated from the United States, while encouraging clashes between them and the United States over issues on which the United States was committed, such as Israel's security and that of the regimes in Jordan and Saudi Arabia, improved the prospects of further radicalization. But the new approach had its disadvantages, too. The Soviet Union's much more intimate commitment to the general welfare of the specific regimes it assisted and its much more specific concern with their internal politics and economic and social policies implicated it more than ever before in the vagaries of inter-Arab politics and in the multitude of issues arising from the

[6] In September 1965, following a visit to Moscow, Nasser reported to the National Assembly that his trip resulted in a saving for Egypt of £.E. 200 million (about $460 million). This sum probably represents a retroactive Soviet contribution to the costs of the Yemen war.

Arab-Israeli conflict. Moreover, the closer the identification, the greater the risk that the Soviet position would not survive the overthrow of the protected regimes from within. And in the cultural context of the area, the greater the progress toward Soviet-approved Socialism, the more exposed the regimes themselves were apt to become. The danger was particularly grave in coup-prone Syria and Iraq, but even in Egypt the regime itself felt, and actually was, vulnerable to a religiously inspired revulsion against too close an ideological identification with Soviet-type Socialism.

THE UNITED STATES

The United States redefined its policies and interests after the Iraqi revolution in stages that corresponded to those of Soviet policy, but the substance of the redefinitions was not always the counterpart of the Soviet changes because the United States had particular commitments and interests of its own in the area.

After the Iraqi revolution, the idea of linking the periphery and the heartland in a single alliance was given up, and different objectives were developed for each region. The immediate objective in the northern tier was to check the damage caused by Iraq's withdrawal from the Baghdad Pact and to insure continued access to actual or potential bases in the region, which were then still necessary for maintaining the American deterrent. This aim was easily accomplished by the creation of the Central Treaty Organization (CENTO) and by the conclusion of a bilateral defense treaty with Iran, the one CENTO member not linked to the United States through an additional collective alliance.[7] These arrangements have formally persisted to the present, but their significance has been greatly eroded by the consequences of the new balance of terror. From being vital to maintaining the American deterrent, the United States' "presence" in Turkey and Iran became, from the American point of view, essentially an end in itself, a part of the global American sphere of influence. It committed the United States to resist any blatant, high-handed Soviet encroachment, but it left the Soviet Union free to woo the Turks and Iranians with economic assistance and diplomatic sweet talk.

In the heartland, the brief period of great Soviet expectations immediately following the Iraqi revolution corresponded with a period of American dejection and drastic retrenchment. After nearly a decade of

[7] Britain and Turkey were linked to the United States through NATO and Pakistan through SEATO in addition to CENTO.

vain effort, the United States finally gave up all thought of organizing a Western coalition in the region and fell back on the purely defensive aim of protecting its remaining positions in Saudi Arabia, Jordan, Libya, and Israel against what seemed to be an almost irresistible tide of Arab nationalist–Soviet pressure. As for the growth of native Communism, which the Soviet Union was then trying to promote, the United States could think of nothing to do but sit back and hope the Iraqi Communists would overplay their hand.

The opportunity for the United States to revise its aims and policies in a more positive direction came about mainly as a result of the complications in which the Russians became entangled by trying to push out the West and promote local Communism at the same time. The ground for the shift was prepared when the Eisenhower Administration, in its last year in office, reversed its hostile attitude toward Egypt and proffered it a limited amount of economic assistance. With the advent of the Kennedy Administration, this initial rapprochement, essentially an act of appeasement toward Egypt and a reflex reaction to its mild quarrel with the Soviet Union, became a focal point for a new approach to the region, quickly dubbed "preventive diplomacy" by State Department hands.

According to this new approach, Nasser was to be given massive economic assistance to help him make Arab Socialism a success. Such a success would not only undercut the appeal of Communism in the Arab countries by offering an alternative way of meeting those countries' economic and social aspirations, but would have the added advantage of identifying the United States with a supposedly indigenous Arab national ideology as opposed to the alien Communist ideology the Soviets were trying to thrust upon the Arabs. Nasser, in return, was expected to abstain from putting pressure on American positions in the region. In short, the United States would use a newly discovered community of interest with Arab Socialism to check the Russians, fight native Communism, and better protect its own positions all at once.

The new approach did not produce anything like the results expected of it. It did, however, in the few years it lasted, put the United States in the comfortable position of reaping benefits from the embarrassments that Soviet policy was then continually confronting. The United States, for example, could oppose Kassem's claim to Kuwait and find itself on the side of all the Arab governments against the Soviet Union; it could recognize the secessionist regime in Syria without being accused of hostility to Arab unity merely by waiting for the Soviet Union to recognize it first; and at no effort or expense to itself it could watch Soviet aims in Iraq being dashed by the overthrow of Kassem and subsequent Ba'thist opposition to the Soviet Union and the local Communists. Furthermore, the new approach gained the United States some latitude in its dealings with Egypt. It could, for example, take new initiatives favorable to Israel or defend the interest of Saudi Arabia without precipitating any immediate crisis. However, the accumulation of problems and disappointments gradually undermined the vision of the new approach and supplanted it with conceptions and policies of a quite different inspiration.

The key to the withering away of the new approach was perhaps the Egyptian military intervention in support of the Yemeni "revolution." Initially, the United States tried not to rock its relations with Egypt over the issue. It allowed itself to be convinced by its ambassador in Cairo, who symbolized the American-Egyptian rapprochement, that the new republican regime in Yemen was an established fact and that it deserved recognition since it stood for the kind of progress the Administration said it favored. In fact, however, the Imam of Yemen had survived the coup and, with the help of Saudi Arabia, proved able to mount very effective resistance against the republicans and the Egyptian forces supporting them. As the fighting dragged on and the Egyptians poured in more and more troops without being able to gain a decision, they naturally sought to get at Saudi Arabia itself through subversion and air attacks on alleged royalist bases in its territory. Since the Saudi rulers were traditionally friendly to the United States and since American oil companies had an enormous stake in Arabia's vast oil reserves, the United States was compelled to come to that country's aid. It warned the Egyptians to desist and deployed American air power to enhance the warning. Then it negotiated an agreement with Egypt calling for simultaneous Egyptian withdrawal and cessation of Saudi aid to the royalists. The accord, however, collapsed amid mutual accusations of bad faith. At this point, the United States appeared to Nasser to be denying him victory in the war by protecting the royalists' Saudi sanctuary, while Nasser appeared to the United States to be indirectly using American aid to fight a futile and ever more costly war that threatened its Saudi friend. Neither side was eager to let this lead to a crisis in their mutual relations, but the rapid deterioration of these was inevitable.

The Yemeni conflict also contributed indirectly to damaging American-Egyptian relations through its effect on the Israeli question. As the pace of their rapprochement increased after the advent of the Kennedy Administration, both countries had entertained hopes of altering the other's position on Israel. Then, as these hopes proved illusory, both countries tacitly agreed to put the issue on ice and not allow it to interfere with their developing relations. The Yemen war made this tacit agreement unworkable.

Even prior to that war, Egypt had launched a five-year program to double the size of its armed forces and had inaugurated it by concluding a new arms deal with the Soviet Union in 1961–1962. In view of the war demands, the Egyptians accelerated the program, and by the end of 1963 they had formed at least two new divisions. The Israeli reaction was to turn to the United States with requests for arms and diplomatic support. Although the United States had never before provided Israel with substantial quantities of weapons directly, it agreed on this occasion to supply it with Hawk ground-to-air missiles and reaffirmed its commitment to support the integrity and independence of Israel and the other Middle East countries. The Egyptians dared not react for fear of jeopardizing the continued flow of American aid, but their resentment of the United States deepened, and the link between the two countries became strained, the more so as it became clear that the Hawk transaction presaged further transactions by which the United States agreed to supply Israel with offensive weapons, such as tanks and bombers.

This departure from established policy regarding arms for Israel and the pressure applied to Egypt concerning the Yemen war were largely made necessary by the fact that the United States provided Egypt with $150 million a year in surplus food. Congressional criticism to the effect that the United States was helping a less than friendly country against its own friends, not to mention the widespread belief on Capitol Hill that granting aid entitled the United States to cooperation on the part of the recipient country, exerted constant pressure on the Administration to balance its help to Egypt by responding to Israeli requests for arms and political support, and to demonstrate displeasure whenever Egypt's position in world affairs ran counter to the American position. These occasions were rather numerous, for Egypt considered itself a leader of the neutralist bloc, identified with the colonized and former colonial countries, and needed now and then to please the Soviet Union in order to justify the aid it was receiving from that quarter. It was in connection with expressed American displeasure with Egypt's position on the Congo, for example, that Nasser publicly told the United States at the end of 1964 to take its aid and go jump in the lake.

The vision that underlay the American-Egyptian rapprochement in the early days of the Kennedy Administration fell victim to all these developments. The limits of America's identification with Arab Socialism and Arab unity became clear in the Yemen war. The accelerated arms buildup belied the notion that the Israeli problem could be put on ice. What with the Yemen war, increased arms expenditures, and faulty economic planning and execution, the Egyptian economy became ever more deeply mired in troubles, making a sham of the hope that it would become a model to be emulated in preference to the Communist or any other pattern. Finally, the friction between the United States and Egypt over these and other issues eliminated the possibility that Egypt could be won from the Soviet embrace. A few years after it began, all that was left of the rapprochement was economic assistance that had to be justified in terms of immediate cost and return. This did not prove to be an enduring bond.

The termination of American aid to Egypt in 1965 may be seen as marking the latest phase of American policy toward the Middle East heartland. It is significant for understanding that phase that this step could be viewed as a landmark only in retrospect. The United States did not cut off its assistance in a dramatic manner, as Dulles had cut off the Aswan Dam offer in 1956, but simply allowed the Egyptian request for aid renewal to get lost in a maze of formalities without ever saying no to it. There were no fact-finding missions by high officials, after the pattern of the Shelepin mission to Cairo in 1964 or the Dulles Middle East tour in 1953; no great debates, such as characterized Soviet global policy shifts and the early New Frontier days; and no new doctrines, like those associated with the names of Khrushchev and Eisenhower. The latest phase of American policy simply emerged out of a gradual and not altogether certain change in the perception of the Middle East situation under the impact of regional events and global trends, and out of a gradual extension and modification of the kinds of action taken earlier.

From the vantage point of the end of 1966, the dominant characteristic of the American approach appeared as a confident and pragmatic conservatism. The United States neither sought to alter systematically the existing situation in the area nor did it fear any sweeping hostile trend that might call for some elaborate "preventive diplomacy." Several developments underlay this mood: The general détente in relations with the Soviet Union in the wake of the Cuban crisis; the decline in the relevance of alliances and alignments to the basic positions of the superpowers and the consequent dwindling of the significance of rapprochements and alienations in themselves; the growing vested interest of the Soviet Union in world order to undercut the Chinese challenge and maintain the détente with the United States that permitted lower defense expenditures and speedier domestic development; and the relaxation of the anti-Western mood in the third world

countries following the virtual conclusion of the decolonization movement, the end of Soviet incitement, and the collapse of such flam-
boyant and adventurous leaders as Sukarno, Nkrumah, and Ben Bellah.
In the Middle East in particular, the American mood was sustained by
the fact that the combination of Nasser's Arab nationalist drive and
Soviet backing, which before had so effectively cramped the Western
position, had weakened greatly. In the first place, the two had learned
to suspect one another. Second, the Soviet interest in marginal gains in
the heartland became much smaller and had to be weighed against the
possibility of an American response causing incommensurate marginal
losses in the periphery. Third, the fire of Arab nationalism had been
greatly dampened by its accumulated failures. And finally, Nasser's capacity to create pressure on any issue except Israel had suffered drastically from the endless Yemen war and from growing economic difficulties at home.

The one major potential danger to the United States' position
seemed to be an explosion of the Arab-Israeli conflict into a general
war. Such an explosion could set the entire Middle East cauldron
boiling and endanger the oil interests, the friendly Arab regimes, and
Israel. Moreover, by gravely exposing the entire Russian position in the
region, it could lead to a confrontation between the superpowers.
However, even though there was no lack of causes for an Arab-Israeli
war, as we have seen in Chapter I, the balance of forces between
Egypt and Israel, Egypt's preoccupation with Yemen, and the cautious
approach toward Israel displayed by Nasser since 1956 militated
against his starting one, and unless he did, a general conflagration was
very unlikely.[8] In any case, to guard against this danger the United
States explored discretely with the Soviet Union and Egypt the possibility of stopping the arms race and consolidating the *status quo;* when
that effort failed, it strove more openly and consciously than ever before to insure Israel's having sufficient military strength and diplomatic
backing to deter war.

The United States also provided Jordan and Saudi Arabia with massive quantities of arms. This was in part a demonstration of even-hand-
edness between Israelis and Arabs, but the main reasons were specifically pragmatic: to reinforce the regimes of King Hussein, whose fall
might unwittingly set off an Arab-Israeli war, and of Saudi King Faisal,
who was faced with an Egyptian threat from Yemen and a developing
three-cornered struggle over the South Arabian Federation between
the British-backed conservative government, a Nasser-supported radical

[8] See Chapter VI for an analysis of the reasons why this prediction proved wrong.

nationalist group, and an autonomous radical nationalist front. Other United States interests in the region, such as Libya and Lebanon, could be protected by the Sixth Fleet or, in the case of Kuwait, by the British base in Bahrein.

To summarize, as the Cold War gradually faded, the United States came to conceive of its basic objective in the Middle East as keeping the peace in the area. This objective seemed best fitted to maintaining American presence, protecting specific interests in various countries, and meeting the long-standing commitment to the security of Israel. To this end, the United States kept alive its determination to support the independence and integrity of all Middle East countries; but it also relied increasingly on local balances to do the job. It thus sought to avoid an Arab-Israeli explosion by helping to maintain a certain balance of military power between the main opponents, and it attempted to check other sources of trouble by buttressing friendly Arab regimes militarily.

THIRD POWERS

Before closing this overlong chapter, we must say a few words about the interests and roles of other relevant powers in the Middle East, notably Britain, France, and China.

Britain's interest and role in the area up until the Suez war has been followed in some detail. We have seen Britain attempt to organize the heartland under its sole hegemony and fail; we have seen it working as an equal partner with the United States in the creation of the Baghdad Pact and in the attempt to recruit additional Arab members; and we have seen it diverge from the United States and cooperate with France in an effort to reestablish its position in the region by force after Nasser's seizure of the Suez Canal. After the disaster of this last venture, Britain was forced to sit back and let the United States alone make the next attempt to organize a Western coalition in the area in the guise of the Eisenhower Doctrine, about which it was not even consulted. When this attempt met its severest test in the form of the Iraqi revolution, the British eagerly responded to the American invitation to cooperate militarily in Jordan in hopes that the joint intervention would lead to the restoration of Iraq to the Western fold and to the collapse of the Soviet-supported Nasserite drive. When the United States disappointed these hopes, they finally gave up thinking in terms of policies and moves to shape the destiny of the entire region and sought, rather, to safeguard their minimal, specific remaining interests.

By that time, these interests consisted of two things: British oil holdings in the Persian Gulf basin, especially in Kuwait, and unhampered passage through the Suez Canal, which was the main route for Persian Gulf oil moving westward and for commercial and military traffic between Britain and east Asia. As the British saw things, their oil interests were potentially threatened by two forces: covetous neighbors, including Iraq, Saudi Arabia, and Iran, and the general Arab nationalist anti-imperialist movement stimulated and led by Cairo. Against the former threat, the British counted on a string of bases and client sheikhdoms along the southern and eastern coast of the Arabian peninsula and on a mutual standoff between the rivals. Egypt remained a threat, however, because it could, in principle, strike at the other British interest as well—movement through the Suez Canal. To guard against that threat, Britain discretely encouraged the formation of counterforces capable of preventing the establishment of Egyptian hegemony in the region while at the same time trying not to antagonize Egypt.

On the whole, the British have been quite successful in pursuing these more limited policies. They defended Kuwait against Kassem's threat and then passed the responsibility on to Saudi, Jordanian, and Egyptian troops commissioned by the Arab League itself. They successfully capitalized on Saudi fears of the Egyptian menace issuing from Yemen and South Arabia to convert a relationship of hostility due to a dispute over the Buraimi oasis into one of tacit alliance and cooperation. They supplied weapons to Jordan, Saudi Arabia, and Israel—including all the latter's major naval equipment—to help counterbalance Nasser's power. These actions did antagonize Egypt; the two countries have fought each other by proxy in Aden and South Arabia, and diplomatic relations have been severed. So far, however, the Egyptians have not dared to interfere with British traffic through the Suez Canal for fear of American as well as British reaction.

As we have seen, France's position in the Middle East was at its lowest ebb at the end of World War II as a result of its expulsion from Syria and Lebanon. But the French nevertheless continued to think they had interests that called upon them to play an active role in the area. These interests consisted of a very extensive cultural presence that fed French prestige, a limited share in the area's oil through a 23.75 percent slice of the Iraq Petroleum Company's operations, and, above all, a concern about the possible repercussions of the situation in the Middle East heartland on its position in North Africa. Partly because they acknowledged these interests and partly because of their alliance with France in NATO, the United States and Britain took France as an associate in their early efforts to deal with the Arab-

Israeli conflict through the Tripartite Declaration of 1950 and in their attempt to set up a Middle East Defense Organization. But the limits of "Anglo-Saxon" willingness to suffer French partnership were revealed in the next attempt to organize a Western coalition in the area. Because the French were by then involved in troubles in North Africa, the British and the Americans thought it "impolitic" to associate them with the projected alliance that eventually became the Baghdad Pact. The connection between the Arab heartland and North Africa, which was one of the principal reasons for French interest in the former region, was thus precisely the excuse used by the "Anglo-Saxons" to exclude France from it.

The Suez crisis and Dulles' handling of it gave the French a chance to break the Anglo-American front that had excluded them from the area and to reassert themselves by joining the British in military action. They also stood to improve their position in the Algerian struggle by hitting at Egypt, one of the most important sources of support for the rebels. As is known, however, the Suez war did not fulfill their expectations: Instead of reasserting French military and political presence, the war brought about a wholesale liquidation of French cultural institutions in Egypt and Syria; and instead of improving their position in Algeria, the Suez fiasco made it worse. As for the alignment with Britain and the dissolution of the Anglo-American front, that did not long survive the liquidation of the crisis.

The fact that France by then had very little to lose in the Middle East made possible a bold new policy to restore its presence in the area. Already before the Suez war, France had begun supplying Israel with considerable quantities of weapons, first to pressure Nasser to stop helping the Algerian rebels and then to build up Israel's military might for an eventual joint war against Egypt. When the war came and went without producing the desired results, these *ad hoc* measures designed to meet specific objectives were converted into a tacit broadranging alliance with Israel designed to secure a French say in Middle Eastern affairs and to build an enduring counterweight that would check Nasser's excessive interference in North Africa. As part of that alliance, France supplied Israel with massive quantities of modern weapons on a regular basis, joined the Israelis in cultural, scientific, and technological endeavors, including the building of a nuclear reactor at Dimona, and gave Israel political support in world councils. This policy was pursued for nearly a decade before showing signs of waning, as a result partly of its very success and partly of changes in the international political environment.

The French position in Israel meant that any potential big power scheme for settling Middle East problems had to have French support or risk being made unworkable. Such schemes, as we know, were never attempted in fact, but they were always being urged from many quarters and seemed the logical thing to do. But more important than the comfort of knowing they would have to be consulted by the big powers was the forcing of France on the attention of the Arab countries as a power to be reckoned with. While the Algerian war persisted, the reckoning the French wished the Arabs to make was the probability of suffering damage at their hands, through Israel, in retaliation for giving aid to Algeria. After the settlement of the Algerian conflict, the desired reckoning was that the Arabs should seek to appease a power that could do them harm from an invulnerable position. This the Arab states eventually began to do.

The Algerian war came to an end in the same year that the Cuban missile crisis occurred, and both developments affected the Arab disposition to appease and please the French. Arab states in both the Soviet and American camps feared that the détente between the superpowers in the wake of the Cuban crisis would lead to a decline in their bargaining position with their respective patrons. To compensate for this, they began to explore new sources of diplomatic maneuverability. France under de Gaulle, with its position in the budding European Community, its independent nuclear capability, and its intention of playing a global role independent of the superpowers, appeared as just that kind of source. By responding to the French desire to play a broad role in the Middle East, the Arab countries hoped to weaken France's commitment to Israel as well as to stimulate the kind of big power competition from which they expected to gain. From the French point of view, a strong position in the Arab Middle East combined with their influential position in North Africa seemed, with some imagination, to hold out the prospect of a standing in the entire Arabic speaking world worthy of French grandeur, and one to be appreciated all the more for its contrast with the waning Anglo-Saxon influence in the region.

So far, the rapprochement between France and the Arab countries of the Middle East has manifested itself primarily in visits to Paris by such Arab dignitaries as President Helou of Lebanon, King Hussein of Jordan, and Marshal Amer of Egypt, visits usually terminated with agreements to reinforce cultural and economic ties and expressions of mutual good will. The flow of French arms to Israel has not ceased, nor has there been any radical shift in French political support for Israel. There are numerous indications, however, that the French government is striving to take some distance from Israel in order to encourage this budding rapprochement. Whether this process would lead eventually to a diplomatic reversal or whether it would itself be stifled could not be foreseen at the time of writing.

China's interest in the Middle East dates only from the success of the Communists in that country and has been entirely a function of its ideological commitment and its implications. Until it became a member of a revolutionary Communist bloc engaged in global struggle with the Western "capitalist" bloc, China was isolated from the area by both history and geography. Prior to the ideological quarrel with the Soviet Union, Chinese influence was mainly indirect through its being a senior member of the Communist bloc. Since then, however, the Chinese have tried to construct for themselves an independent position in competition with the Soviet Union and, to a degree difficult to estimate, have had some influence on Soviet Middle East policies by means of their criticism and the weight they have within the Communist world.

Between the Communist takeover in China and Stalin's death, Soviet policy in the Middle East, as we have seen, was stymied by previous rebuffs and by a rigid conception of objectives and prospects in the area. This and the preoccupation with the Korean War deprived the Chinese of any role in Middle East affairs. But after Stalin's death, as Russia sought to mobilize neutralist feeling in the world to prevent being surrounded by American alliances and bases, the Chinese very usefully stimulated the convening of the Bandung Conference, in which several Arab states took part, and promoted its adoption of the principles of nonalignment.

Preliminary to the Conference, Chou En-Lai met Nasser in Rangoon and agreed to transmit to the Soviets his interest in acquiring Russian arms. This project materialized a few months later and proved to be a turning point in the history of the Middle East. Throughout the Suez crisis, the Chinese seconded the Soviet position, and during the 1956 war they spoke loudly of sending volunteers to help throw the invaders out of Egypt. Then, when the United States attempted to contain and push back Egyptian-Soviet influence in the heartland, China once again seconded the Soviet Union and provided Egypt with a modest grant to help it withstand American economic pressure. Not long thereafter, however, Chinese and Soviet views began to diverge, and China started to criticize the very policies it had hitherto supported.

We have already mentioned the circumstances that led the Soviets, after the Iraqi revolution, to renounce their recurrent efforts to reach an understanding with the West on the Middle East and, instead, to begin promoting the fortunes of Communist parties in Arab countries. As we pointed out, although the Russians had their own reasons to reconsider and revise their objectives and policies, it was Chinese pressure and criticism that triggered the revision. At the time, the condemnation of any effort to de-escalate the struggle with imperialism or to sacrifice revolutionary incitement to the expediency of cooperation with bourgeois nationalist regimes seemed to be motivated by rigorous adherence to Communist doctrine. In retrospect, these ideological invocations appear to have been useful sticks to beat the Russians with rather than indicators of what policies China might follow in the third world. For as the rift with Russia widened into a breach and the Chinese began to establish their own position in the area, they proved no more scrupulous than the Russians in cooperating with regimes that suppressed Communism. Indeed, they even supported the Ba'thist government that overthrew Kassem in 1963 when its brutal suppression of Iraqi Communists sickened the Soviet Union and forced it to cut its losses and pull out of Iraq.

In the sixties, the Chinese have tried without much success to win control of Communist parties in the Middle East, such as they are, and to outbid the Russians for the favors of established bourgeois nationalist governments. They have adopted the most extreme Arab position regarding Israel's existence and taken the Arab side on every specific issue or incident between the Arab states and Israel. They have given unequivocal political support and some material backing to the Palestine Liberation Organization—China, in fact, is the only non-Arab country to have accorded the organization semidiplomatic status. They have tried their utmost to play on the fears of Arab countries within the Soviet sphere of influence that the Soviet Union might trade their interests for an understanding with the United States. But so far, these efforts have availed the Chinese very little. Geography and economics have been against them. The temptation some Arab countries might have had to flirt with the Chinese in order to elicit more benefits from the Russians has run up against the fact that China does not now have the wherewithal in economic and military aid to make such a game plausible. That this situation might change in the not too distant future is the main reason we have bothered to discuss China's role in the area. A second reason is that, however fumbling China's efforts, they have to a considerable extent kept the Soviet Union on its toes and forced it to pretend that it is concerned with promoting Communism and to strive constantly to prove its loyalty to its friends in the area.

IV The Dynamics of Arms Buildup: Defense Expenditures

Introduction

In the preceding part of this book we have tried to analyze in historical perspective the evolution of the Arab-Israeli conflict and the main factors that meshed with it to produce a pattern of politics in which force, threat, and deterrence are the dominant features. In this chapter and the next, we shall endeavor to analyze, also in historical perspective, the thought and action of the Arab states and Israel in the military sphere, in an effort to see force, threat, and deterrence concretely at work in the area where they manifest themselves best. If we visualize the first part of this study as dealing with the anatomy of the politics of threat and deterrence in the Middle East, we might visualize the part we are about to begin as dealing with the physiology of these politics. And just as physiology must refer to anatomy in pursuing its analysis of the organism in action, so we shall have to refer to the material we have already analyzed in one form in examining the politics of force in action in the military sphere.

The first chapter in this new discussion will deal with the military effort of the Arab countries and Israel as reflected in their defense expenditures over a long period of time.[1] We shall pursue our analysis with three objectives in mind: (1) to demonstrate and explain the dynamics of the process of arms buildup in the area; (2) to highlight the

[1] Throughout this chapter and the next the terms "defense" and "military" when used as qualifiers have an identical meaning.

strain that this process has imposed on the countries involved; and (3) to try to gain an insight into the trend of the relation of forces among the antagonists, especially the Arab states and Israel. Although the orientation of this entire study is explicative rather than prescriptive, an understanding of these three questions should be particularly important for policy makers in all the countries concerned, particularly those who would strive to terminate or mitigate the necessarily dangerous pattern of politics of force in the Middle East.

The task we have set for ourselves in this chapter requires that we should look into the defense expenditures of the Arab states and Israel comparatively, both in terms of absolute amounts allocated for the purpose and in terms of the percentages of Gross National Product (GNP) that these amounts represented. Were we concerned merely with a *description* of the strains of the military effort on these countries we might have contented ourselves with data showing the proportions of GNP they spent over the years. Were we concerned only with a description of the changes in the balance of forces as reflected in relative defense spending, we might have used only data about comparative absolute defense expenditures. Our interest in analysis rather than just description and in both aspects of the problem and their interplay impels us to work with both kinds of data simultaneously. We must in this case visualize the governments concerned as acting under the impulse of two simultaneous considerations: The pressure for arms buildup they exert on each other, which is ultimately a function of the absolute amounts they spend by comparison with one another; and the constraints on the amounts they can spend, which are ultimately imposed by the size and growth of their GNP in comparison with one another. These abstract considerations will become hopefully clearer as we proceed with our concrete analysis.

Observers of the Middle East scene speak frequently of the accumulation of arms by countries of the area as an arms race. If the term arms race has any precise meaning—and it should have one—then its application to the area as a whole is misleading.[2] There is indeed an arms race that has been going on for over a decade between *some* countries, but the pattern of arms accumulation in the area as a whole is much more complex than a race. This writer lacks the imagination to suggest an appropriate alternative metaphor, but what has been

[2] Such a definition of an arms race should contain the following elements: a conflict between two parties believed susceptible of resolution by force; a perceived capacity of each of the parties to attain a certain relation of forces considered satisfactory in connection with its objectives; action by each without sufficient or proper estimate of the reaction of the other; freedom to act.

going on has been essentially a primary contest between Egypt and Israel that has tended to spill over on the Egyptian side and induce higher levels of armament among other Arab countries; this in turn has tended to induce Israel to try for an extra margin of safety in its competition with Egypt, which in turn has driven Egypt to raise its own level again, and so on. To complicate matters further, internal reasons apart from both the Egyptian-Israeli context and the Egyptian confrontations with other Arab countries have contributed to the felt need of these countries for more armed force and have thus swelled the secondary stream that has fed into Israel's motivations and calculations.

Two simple facts have underlain this odd situation. One has been the asymmetry between Israeli and Arab motives for the acquisition of arms. Israel has been prompted to accumulate arms by the sole motive of resisting Arab hostility, whereas the Arab countries have had a variety of other motives in addition to their hostility to Israel. An Arab country, for example, might have tried to develop its armed power primarily for internal or inter-Arab reasons that have had little to do with Israel—and we shall see that this has indeed been the case with some though they have tried to cover their motives with anti-Israeli rhetoric.[3] From Israel's point of view, however, the accretion constituted a potential danger against which it had to provide an appropriate margin of strength. The other fact underlying the situation has been that, while Israel has tended to add the forces of other Arab countries to Egypt's in its reckoning, Egypt has considered that it could not count much if at all on the accretion of power to other Arab countries in connection with its contest with Israel and has therefore sought to achieve a favorable balance with Israel all by itself.[4] This, for Egypt, has been a lesson of the bitter experience of having been let down by other Arab countries before; it has been a matter of pride and of claim to leadership; and it has been a function of the friction

[3] In a speech made on June 15, 1966, in Damanhur, Egypt, President Nasser, for example, after indicating his opposition to another Arab summit conference scheduled to be held in Algiers the following September, had this to say: "Arab reactionary elements cannot march with progressive forces even if the road leads to the liberation of Palestine, because reaction sees in these progressive forces a greater danger to it than Israel itself." (*New York Times,* June 16, 1966.) This statement is important as a public acknowledgment by the Egyptian leader of the point we are making here about the reasons for which some Arab countries may wish to acquire arms; but the point itself rests on more solid evidence than the testimony of a party to a quarrel, as will be seen below.

[4] See, for example, Haykal in *al Ahram,* September 25, 1964, where he not only indicates this to be Egypt's objective, but suggests that Egypt has actually attained it.

resulting from the pursuit of that very leadership claim. The result has been that disagreement has prevailed even with regard to the elements that ought to enter into the reckoning of the relation of forces between Egypt and Israel, which has put a built-in accelerator in the Egyptian-Israeli race.

These observations should help us to broach an answer in these introductory remarks to two questions that may be worth considering if only because propagandists of one party or the other have raised them: (1) Who has been "responsible" for initiating the race between Egypt and Israel, which has remained at the center of the accumulation of arms in the area?; and (2) who has been "responsible" for escalating it at various points? The answer to the second question should be quite easy in the light of our previous observations: Neither Israel nor Egypt has been responsible, but the different perspectives from which they were bound to view things. The one could not afford to discount much the strength of other Arab countries; the other could not count much on them.[5] As to the first question, there is no doubt that President Nasser's deal with the Soviets in 1955, which destroyed the limitations of the Tripartite Declaration, burst the dam and let the flood sweep in. But it should be said in fairness that in the restricted competition that went on between 1950 and 1955, the rationing powers had tended to adopt the Israeli perspective of balancing all the Arab states as potentially one force against it, which from the Egyptian perspective was not only humiliating but perilous. The irony was that the powers could not from *their* perspective have adopted the opposite course without creating the makings of an armed conflict they were intent on avoiding. For as they saw the situation, Israel was the *status quo* country and the Arab states were the ones bent on revision, and it therefore seemed wiser to err on its side than on that of the latter. As the Egyptians viewed things, however, Israel was not so certainly content with the *status quo*, or at least could not be relied upon to remain content with it in the longer run, even if it had been possible for Egypt to put up with being cut off by Israel from the other Arab countries.

We shall make one more procedural remark before going on to examine concretely the process of arms buildup as reflected in defense expenditures. The analysis of the previous chapters, especially of interArab relations, as well as the preceding remarks should make it clear that the concept of external defense cannot be separated from internal security as far as the Arab countries are concerned. The distinction be-

[5] The events of June 1967 justified both!

tween police and armed forces is largely a formal one since armies are heavily used openly or secretly for purposes of maintaining internal order on a regular as well as emergency basis. Armies not only engage in the suppression of riots and rebellions, but military intelligence sections have often had full charge of secret political police functions. There have been cases, for example, of transfers back and forth in the budgetary allocations for police and armed forces even before the idea of the inseparability of the two was given some official recognition in the Egyptian budgets, which since 1962 have lumped together "defense, security, and justice" under one heading.[6] We shall not go so far as to include justice administration into our calculations of defense expenditure, but we shall include police and gendarmerie; and since we must do that for the Arab countries, we shall also do it for Israel in order not to distort the comparisons, though in Israel police and defense are actually distinct and separate functions.

This judgment is only one instance among scores of more or less important decisions that we have had to make in the process of compiling the data to be presented below. Were we to present the rationale for each decision at each step as we went along, we would risk losing sight of the more important trends we seek to illuminate. Consequently, we have decided to present in the following pages only summary results of the data and to leave the discussion of the documentation and procedures used to arrive at them to an appendix.[7]

Egypt

A useful indicator of Egypt's military effort over the past 15 years or so is the size of its past defense expenditures. As is shown in Table I, column 2, defense expenditures have increased almost sevenfold in the course of the 15 years, 1950-1951 through 1964-1965. When allowance is made for the changing value of the Egyptian pound over that period by converting the defense expenditure into the appropriate dollar rates (column 3) we still get more than a fivefold increase. Both columns bring out the point that while the first two-thirds of this period, up to 1959-1960, were characterized by more or less drastic fluctuations up and down, the last third of it is characterized by more or less sustained large annual increases; in each of the three years from 1961-1962 to

[6] For example, in the Egyptian budget for the fiscal year 1951-1952, police allocations were reduced from £E 8.2 million to 2.7 million at the same time that armed force allocations were increased by 50 percent. A year later, the allocation to police was restored to its previous level.

[7] See Appendix A.

TABLE I: Egypt's Defense Expenditures, 1950-1965

1 Year	2 Defense Outlays (millions £E.)	3 Defense Outlays (millions U.S. $)[1]		4 GNP[2] (millions £E.)	5 Defense Outlays as percentage of GNP
1950/1	37.9	108.9		966	3.9%
1951/2	46.0	132.1	PHASE	973	4.7%
1952/3	44.1	126.6	I	905	4.9%
1953/4	44.2	126.9		963	4.6%
1954/5	57.9	166.3	PHASE	1,014	5.7%
1955/6	89.9	258.2	II	1,073	8.4%
1956/7	89.7	257.6		1,125	8.0%
1957/8	66.1	189.8	PHASE	1,195	5.5%
1958/9	76.8	220.5	III	1,256	6.1%
1959/0	82.2	236.0		1.372	6.0%
1960/1	102.5	294.3		1,467	7.0%
1961/2	109.8	315.3	PHASE	1,550	7.1%
1962/3	141.9	324.4	IV	1,679	8.5%
1963/4	208.0	475.5		1,894	11.0%
1964/5	251.6[3]	575.2[3]		2,058	12.2%
1965/6	(191.6)[4]	(438.0)[4]		...	...

[1] Conversion into U.S. dollars done by means of the official exchange rate (up to 1961-1962: 1.00 £E. = $2.8716; thereafter: 1.00 £E. = $2.286.) Due to the constant erosion of the Egyptian pound, this series tends to overestimate defense outlays in the one or two years before 1961-1962 as well as in recent years.

[2] GNP at current market prices.

[3] Provisional figure.

[4] Budget appropriation. Especially in later years, budget appropriations tend to seriously underestimate actual amounts spent, as can be seen from the following figures, which refer only to "Ministry of War/Armed Forces":

	Budget Appropriations	Actual Amounts Spent
1962/3	103.0	115.0
1963/4	116.3	176.8
1964/5	133.4	213.5

Hence the figure of 191.6 for 1965-1966 is probably much too small.

Sources, method, and comment: See Appendix A.

1964-1965, the annual increase was especially impressive, oscillating between £E. 30 and 60 million.

A more useful indicator of Egypt's military effort than these absolute figures in themselves is their relation to Gross National Product. This relationship gives us a measurable picture over time of the strain on the country's resources involved in the military effort as well as useful inklings about future possibilities and limitations. Looking at Table I, column 5, and casting regular glances at columns 4 and 2, we can distinguish clearly four phases: (1) a relatively low starting point in 1950-1951 rising and then falling mildly over the next three years; (2) a large spurt in 1954-1955 followed by an even larger one the next year, which is maintained for another year; (3) a great drop in 1957-1958, which is maintained with relatively minor fluctuations for two more years; (4) a significant spurt initiating a new regular trend upward. This picture is clearly illustrated in Figure 1. An important point to keep in mind is that, with the single exception of the year 1952-1953, a proportional rise in defense expenditure involves an accentuated growth in the absolute amounts spent on defense due to the simultaneous growth of GNP. The same reason cushions the fall in absolute amounts spent when proportional expenditure declines; it may even cause the former to rise while the latter declines, as happened between 1958-1959 and 1959-1960 for instance.

EXPLANATION OF THE PHASES

Analyzing the four phases brings out concretely the main factors that have had an important bearing on Egypt's buildup of its military power, previously dealt with abstractly and in different contexts.

The first phase points out above everything else the effectiveness of the Tripartite Declaration in limiting the possibilities of defense expenditure by imposing a rationing of arms supplies (see Figure 2). That it was this rather than the will of the Egyptian government that kept defense expenditure relatively low is indicated by the enormous spurt that took place when the Soviet Union broke the Tripartite rationing system. It is also indicated by the substantial increases at the beginning of this first phase and at the beginning of the next (that is, before the Soviet-Egyptian deal), pointing up the restlessness of the Egyptians under the limitations of the Declaration and their partially successful effort to break them. This means that the Tripartite policy still left room for maneuver and competition; nevertheless, for as long as it lasted, it managed to keep Egypt as well as other countries of the area within the limits of the defense spending of all but a few major world

powers, a situation that was to change drastically in the following
years.[8]

A point worth mentioning, though it is not included in the data of
Table I, is that the defense outlay for the fiscal year 1950-1951 repre-
sents a considerable reduction over the previous year both absolutely and in relation to GNP due to the elimination of half of a sum of
£E. 13.6 million allocated in 1949–1950 to the defense forces "in view

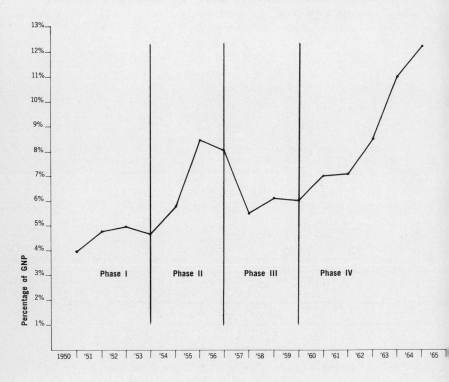

Fig. 1   Egypt's Defense Outlays as Percentages of GNP

[8] See Table X.

of the situation prevailing in Palestine." [9] This reduction reflects a fact worth recording for the historian but generally forgotten by hindsight commentators: that the Egyptians did for a short while after the conclusion of the 1949 armistice agreement with Israel tend to accept the results of the war as final. That moment did not last. In the next year, most of the remainder of the emergency allocation was permanently absorbed in the defense budget, to which some further additions were made as our data indicate.

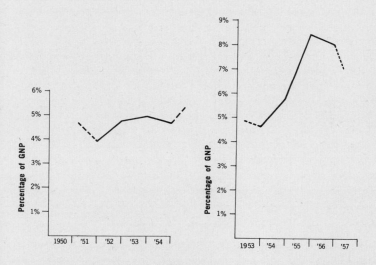

Fig. 2   Egypt: "The First Phase"   Fig. 3   Egypt: "The Second Phase"

The figures for the first period reflect in an interesting way the consequences of the military coup of July 1952. During the first two years, a combination of the power struggles within the ruling military junta, the purgings of unreliable elements in the army, the preoccupation of the new leaders with the effort to consolidate their hold on the country and to settle the problem of the British evacuation, and a serious economic setback produced a decline in the amounts spent on defense by the new military regime. In the first year (1952-1953) the expenditure on the armed forces specifically declined by a full 20 percent over the previous year, that is, the year just prior to the coup, but the drop

[9] Budget of the Egyptian State, 1954-1955 (Egyptian fiscal years begin at midyear).

was compensated by a more than threefold increase in police expenditure. Total defense expenditure in absolute amounts was still slightly lower than the previous year, though the decline of GNP caused it to be higher proportionately. In the second year the line was held in terms of absolute amounts spent, but the recuperation of GNP caused defense expenditure to decline considerably in proportional terms.

The second phase reflects very clearly first the accumulation of inducements to develop the armed forces and then the bursting of the external limitations on the realization of such intents with the conclusion of the Soviet-Egyptian arms deal (see Figure 3). The sharp increase in defense expenditure in 1954-1955, both in absolute and proportional terms, was the consequence of developments in the internal, regional, and international scenes that took place that year: the emergence of Colonel Abdel Nasser as supreme leader after defeating General Naguib, thereby ending the freeze on the level of armed forces imposed by mutual suspicions among members of the junta in the previous phase; the greater freedom to acquire equipment gained after agreement with the British on evacuation of the Suez Canal base and the status of the Sudan had been reached; and the increase in the felt need for a stronger defense establishment as a result of the suppression of the Muslim Brethren as well as all other political groupings at home, the occurrence of severe border clashes with Israel in which the Egyptian forces were worsted, and the desire to enhance Egypt's position in its effort to foil Iraq's attempt to attract other Arab countries into the Baghdad Pact. This complex of varied factors, which was henceforth to become typical of Egypt's moves, underlies the drastic increase in defense expenditures in absolute and relative terms the following year (1955-1956), as the Soviet-Egyptian deal opened up undreamt of opportunities for the acquisition of arms and escalated the competition for them in the area to new heights. The new level of expenditure was maintained at the same height for one more year in absolute amounts though the rise in GNP caused a slight proportional decline. This most probably reflects the spreading of the 1955 transaction of nearly half a billion dollars over a number of budgetary years corresponding more or less with rates of delivery, which were exceptionally high during the first two years.[10]

[10] This does not mean that actual payment was made over the same period of the spread of the deliveries. There is some evidence, indeed, that while deliveries under the first transaction were spread over a period of about five years, actual payments for it were to be made in installments over a 20-year period. In an article in *al Ahram* of December 21, 1965, Haykal argued that installments on the arms deal amounted to about £E 12 million (about $34 million) per annum,

The sharp drop in defense expenditure in relation to GNP that characterized the first year of the third phase (1957-1958) and the relatively low level of the next two years were to some extent merely the consequence of excessively high delivery rates in the previous two years
(see Figure 4). It seems that when the opportunity for acquiring mod-

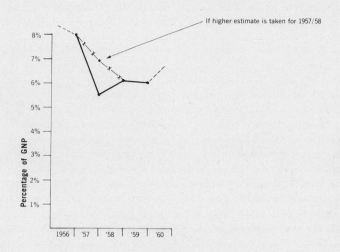

Fig. 4   Egypt: "The Third Phase"

ern weapons in large quantities arose, the Egyptian authorities were
fearful that it might not last and therefore sought to have as much of
the transaction delivered while the going was good. This, of course,
inflated the defense budget for the first two years in relation to the following. But the low rate of 1957-1958 is probably also the result of the
Egyptians' need for time to assimilate the massive quantities of new

comprising £E 8 million for one transaction and the rest for the other. There is
evidence from other sources that the first transaction amounted to somewhat
over $450 million, which, when divided over 20 years, yields just about £E 8
million ($23 million). As to how the second transaction, the value of which is at
least as high as the first, could be paid for in annual installments of £E 4 million remains mysterious. Either Haykal, quite understandably, is not telling the
whole story, or else the explanation is to be found in the cryptic remark made
by Nasser after returning from a trip to Moscow the previous September to
the effect that his trip saved the Egyptian people 200 million pounds ($450
million).

weapons already delivered, with which their forces, hitherto accustomed to British arms, were totally unfamiliar.[11]

The continuation of relatively low rates for the next two years probably reflected two factors: The formation of the U.A.R., which brought Syria's military resources under Egyptian control, thus mitigating Egypt's sense of urgent need for more force of its own, and the quarrel with the Soviet Union over policies toward Kassem's Iraq, which apparently limited the possibilities of getting equipment because of a Soviet go-slow policy toward Egyptian requests for arms and parts.

The fourth and last phase was characterized by a steady rapid growth of defense expenditure both in absolute and proportional terms over a period of five years, which seemed to signify the institutionalization of the arms escalation (see Figure 5). In absolute terms defense expenditure more than doubled during that period in current value and rose by 95 percent in dollar terms. Proportionately, the increase was by a very impressive 5.2 percentage points of GNP.

Underlying this rise was a whole series of factors, which may be summed up under the headings of more intensively felt needs and enhanced possibilities of meeting them. Under the latter heading comes, first, the restoration of harmonious relations with the Soviet Union, which reflected itself in the conclusion of several economic and technical aid agreements in the civilian sector as well of a new arms deal of comparable value to the first one in the military sector. At the same time that the new deal made weapons and credits available, a sharp increase in United States economic assistance under Public Law 480 probably enhanced Egypt's capacity to assume new armament burdens. A third factor under the same heading was the "socialization" of the Egyptian economy undertaken in 1961 and 1962, which gave the government direct access to most of the revenue-producing resources of the country.[12]

---

[11] It should be noted that the figure for 1957-1958 may be on the low side. Due to the complete change in Egypt's budgetary methods that took place in 1960-1961, no final figure was ever published for that year. The amount shown is said to be "approximate," that is, it is a provisional estimate of the amount actually spent; in previous years, "approximate" figures were regularly lower than final figures, in general by about £E 10 million. So if we assume that the margin of underestimation did not change in 1957-1958, we would come up with total defense outlays of £E 86.8 million instead of 76.8. Relative to GNP, these expenditures would then represent 6.9 percent instead of 6.1 percent. However, since absolute defense expenditures were then clearly in a phase of moderate increase or even slight decline, it is quite plausible that the margin of underestimation was less in 1957-1958 than in previous years.

[12] The effect of this move was partly practical, in that the government could

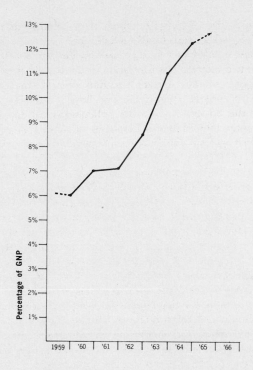

Fig. 5   Egypt: "The Fourth Phase"

Under the heading of more intensively felt need there was the urge to countermatch some of the superior equipment that Israel had acquired since 1956 in its effort to match earlier or contemporaneous Egyptian and other Arab acquisitions—in other words, the escalation of

help itself to the revenue of economic enterprises without having to worry about discontent due to increased taxation. But it probably was mainly psychological in that it made defense expenditure appear as a relatively small proportion of a total state budget now enormously, albeit artifically, inflated by the inclusion of the revenues and uses of economic enterprises. This self-deception is evident in several speeches of President Nasser in which he was wont to make comparisons of defense expenditures with other countries that had more conventional type budgets in terms of percentage of defense to total budget. For example, in a speech printed in *al Ahram*, November 13, 1964, he said that Egypt was spending 12 percent of its £E 1 billion budget on armed forces, or one-seventh on defense, while the United States was spending 50 percent and Israel 28 percent of their respective budgets.

the arms race. A particularly expensive item in this connection was the launching of a crash program to develop Egyptian surface-to-surface missiles after Israel had fired an experimental rocket into the atmosphere in the summer of 1961. Within three to four years the Egyptians, with the help of foreign technicians, had designed and produced at great cost two, and later three, V-2 type liquid-fueled missiles of apparently dubious military value. At least so far, the missiles have lacked adequate guidance systems to make them usable for selective bombing, and anything better than conventional explosives to make them economically usable for saturation bombing.[13]

In addition to the competition with Israel, developments in the Arab arena contributed greatly to the felt need for more armed power. The union with Syria had permitted Egypt to share with that country some of the defense burden, but the secession of Syria threw Egypt back upon its own resources since its leaders could not, least of all at that time, rely on the Syrians in a confrontation with Israel. But the most important intra-Arab factor was the involvement of Egypt in the Yemen war on the side of the republican regime in opposition to the royalists, who were supported by Saudi Arabia. We have been unable to find reliable estimates of the burden that this war added to Egypt's defense expenditures, but an idea may be had from the fact that Egypt had to create two entirely new divisions because of it, in addition to mobilizing some 20,000 reservists and maintaining and supplying for close to four years at the time of writing (summer of 1966) an army whose strength varied from 20,000 to 70,000 troops.

Writing in *al Ahram* on December 21, 1965, Haykal argued in justifying to his fellow Egyptians these defense expenditures, that Egypt was anyway bound to expand its military forces by 1965 in order to meet developments on the Israeli front, and that the Yemen war had mainly cost Egypt the price of creating two divisions three years ahead of time. This argument is interesting for its omissions and its context. But it is even more noteworthy for its failure to imagine that the creation of two additional divisions around 1962 might have had something to do with bringing about the situation on the Israeli front three years later that allegedly justified the new divisions retrospectively. This is precisely the type of thinking on which arms races flourish.

Israel

Israel's 1950–1966 defense effort cannot be assessed at all in terms of

[13] None was fired during the June 1967 war.

absolute value in Israeli currency since this has undergone a sharp process of erosion over the years that has brought its official dollar value in 1962 down to one-eighth of what it was 12 years before. A much better idea of that effort can be had if we convert Israeli values into dollars at the different rates of exchange that have prevailed over that period. This would show Israel's defense expenditures to have increased about fivefold between 1950 and 1966. But while this procedure is reasonable for pointing out broad trends, it is less than adequate for illuminating fluctuations within the trends since each of the five different rates of exchange that have prevailed during that period has provided only an uncertain resting point that was swept away before long. This leaves defense expenditure in relation to GNP as the most important indicator, with absolute amounts in dollars serving as useful support.

Israel's military effort over the recorded 16 years has gone through four distinct phases that correspond closely with the four phases observed in the case of Egypt. As can be seen in Table II, column 5, from 1950 through 1955 there was a period in which defense expenditure was high by international standards but low by comparison with subsequent periods and involving a few comparatively moderate fluctuations.[14] This was followed by a two-stage drastic spurt over the next two years that more than doubled the percentage number of the end of the previous period. Over the next four to five years there was a virtual plateau whose lowest point was still considerably higher than the highest point before the spurt. However, if one allows for the arms received free from West Germany (of which more in a moment), this third period was characterized by an initial mild fall followed by a climb to a plateau. Finally, from 1962 on there is a steady and fairly rapid trend upward. All this is clearly illustrated in Figure 6.

The correspondence in phases between Egypt and Israel reflects the decisive degree to which the military effort of the one has determined that of the other—in other words, the arms race between the two countries. Figure 7 illustrates this clearly. The figure seems to point out that from 1955 on Egypt was the one that set the pace while Israel has followed after some delay. One can understand this in light of the fact that Israel has been the power interested in the political *status quo* in Palestine and in the area at large while Egypt has been the power interested in changing that *status quo* in its favor. However, as we have previously warned, this point should not be pushed too far. For one thing, Israel, for whatever reasons, seems

[14] See Table X.

TABLE II: Israel's Defense Outlays, 1950-1966

1 Year	2 Defense Outlays (millions I.£)	3 Defense Outlays[1] (millions U.S. $)	Phase	4 GNP[2] (million I.£)	5 Defense Outlays as percentage of GNP
1950	31.3	87.6		458	6.8%
1951	54.1	151.5		698	7.8%
1952	75.5	75.5	PHASE	1,062	7.1%
1953	82.0	63.8	I	1,334	6.1%
1954	117.6	65.3		1,762	6.7%
1955	139.0	77.2		2,124	6.5%
1956	340.0	188.9	PHASE	2,534	13.4%
1957	255.0	141.7	II	2,943	8.7%
1958	279.2	155.1		3,373	8.3%
1959	341.9 (+27)[3]	189.9 (+15)[3]	PHASE	3,861	8.9% (9.6)
1960	375.5 (+36)	208.6 (+20)	III	4,346	8.6% (9.5)
1961	429.6 (+54)	238.7 (+30)		5,208	8.2% (9.3)
1962	549.2 (+105)	183.1 (+35)		6,243	8.8% (10.5)
1963	711.5 (+105)	237.1 (+35)	PHASE	7,528	9.5% (10.8)
1964	931.1 (+75)	310.4 (+25)	IV	8,692	10.7% (11.6)
1965	1,170.8[4]	390.3[4]		10,202	11.5%
1966	1,375.6[5]	458.5[5]		11,106[6]	12.4%

[1] Conversion at current official rate of exchange.

[2] GNP at current market prices.

[3] Figures between parentheses stand for amounts imputed for arms received free from West Germany.

[4] Partly a budget appropriation.

[5] Budget appropriation (if past experience is any guide, budget appropriations tend to exceed amounts actually spent).

[6] Our estimate (see Appendix A).

Sources, method, and comments: See Appendix A.

by the same token to have been the pace setter before 1955. For another thing, a response on the part of Israel to an Egyptian challenge could be so successful as to constitute a challenge in itself. This is the tragic element of any arms race: It bears within itself the dynamism for its own perpetuation.

In discussing Egypt we made the point that a proportional rise in defense expenditure is accelerated in absolute amounts and a proportional decline is cushioned by rising GNP. This is even more true of Israel because in its case GNP at constant prices has grown throughout the entire period under study at an annual rate of better than 10 percent on the average; GNP at current prices has grown even faster because of chronic inflation. This can be seen by looking at the middle

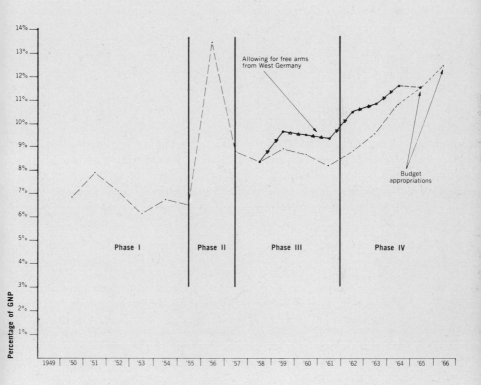

Fig. 6   Israel: Defense Outlays as Percentages of GNP

years between 1950 and 1965, for example: Whereas a 0.6 percent increase of relative defense expenditures in 1959 over 1958 yielded over $30 million in absolute amounts, the much larger percentage decrease in 1957 from 1956 (4.7 percent) yielded a decrease of only about $47 million in absolute amounts. The difference in the rates of economic growth between Israel and Egypt has other crucial implications that will be explored later on. Here we should mention this phenomenon

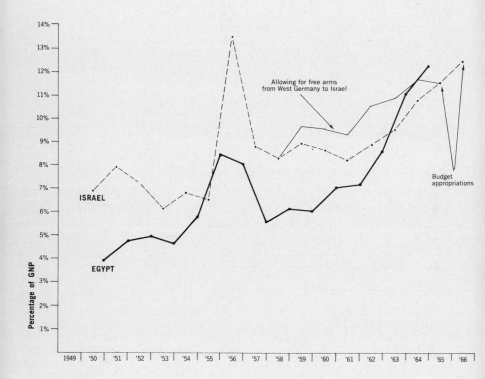

Fig. 7   Egypt compared with Israel: Defense Outlays as Percentages of GNP

only as another reason for caution in interpreting some diagrams so as to allocate ultimate "responsibility" for the arms race to one party or the other.

EXPLANATION OF THE PHASES

Up to 1963-1964, the percentages of GNP that Israel spent on defense have been higher than those of Egypt; but the difference has been greater in the earlier phases than in the last. This, of course, is due to the fact that Israel started its career with a much smaller GNP than Egypt's and sought to draw from it absolute amounts for defense that were competitive with those of Egypt as well as with those of other Arab countries; but as its economy grew very fast, it was able to draw the mounting absolute amounts it thought necessary without increasing the percentage of GNP devoted to defense as rapidly as Egypt.

The first and lowest phase of Israel's defense expenditure, in addition to being proportionally much higher than Egypt's, is divided into two subphases of three years each, in the first of which the rate of expenditure averaged 7.2 percent of GNP as against 6.5 percent average for the second, a not inconsiderable difference (see Figure 8). The first and higher subphase reflects the basic reorganization of Israel's defense forces that was taking place in these years. The Israeli army that had won the war of 1948-1949 had been an improvised force consisting of a combination of various nuclei of secret armed groups and a *levée en masse* more or less haphazardly equipped and organized in the midst of the fighting. It did not have the elaborate infrastructure of barracks, colleges, workshops, and the countless other items that go to make a normal military establishment; it did not have standardized equipment and did not even have proper uniforms. The partial realization of these tasks in the first three years made possible the reduction of the burden in the next.

For the first phase as a whole Israel spent on the average about $87 million a year as compared with an average of $132 million a year for Egypt in *its* first phase. For an Israeli population that averaged less than a million at the time, the period can hardly be looked upon as one of routine military activity under the shadow of the Tripartite Declaration. The expenditure of $152 million in the one year of 1951 in particular, even when allowance is made for the fact that the rate of exchange was sufficiently unrealistic to be devalued the following year, betrays the looseness of the rationing under the Declaration or the degree to which it could be circumvented. Nevertheless, it is very probable that but for the Declaration the expenditures would have been more; it is almost certain, for example, that Israel would have acquired large amounts of equipment to anticipate the exaggerated strength that was expected to accrue to Iraq from its membership in the Baghdad Pact.

The second phase with its drastic upward spurt essentially reflects

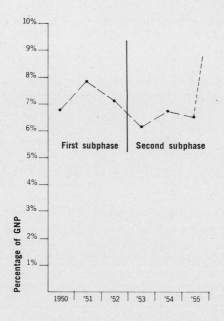

Fig. 8   Israel: "The First Phase"

Israel's response to the Soviet-Egyptian arms deal (see Figure 9). But its extraordinary magnitude is also the result of the expenditures involved in the Sinai campaign, and even more of the eagerness of the Israeli authorities to capitalize on the opportunity opened up by Israel's collaboration with France in that war in order to acquire all the modern equipment they could afford to buy while France was willing to sell. Israel's leaders were still obsessed with the painful memory of the five or six months after the Soviet-Egyptian arms deal when no government was willing to sell them the arms they felt they desperately needed. Here too the result was a hoarding of weapons that were

to become obsolescent, albeit to a lesser extent than in the case of
Egypt if only because the Israelis had the chance to select some of
their weapons with reference to what the Egyptians had already acquired and were stuck with.

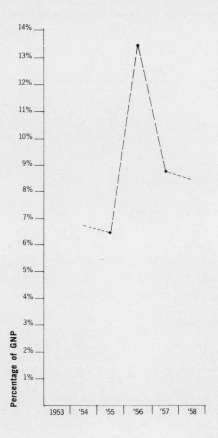

Fig. 9   Israel: "The Second Phase"

The third phase, with defense outlays oscillating between 8 and 9
percent for five years (between 8 and 9.6 percent if one allows for the
free arms from West Germany), is rather complex (see Figure 10). The
fact of the decline from the level of phase II reflected a series of factors working in one direction, while the high level of even the lowest

point reflected factors working in an opposite direction. The situation is further complicated by the fact that during most of this and the next phase Israel received a considerable amount of military equipment free from West Germany. What quantities and values were involved? Assuming we could estimate these correctly, how should they be

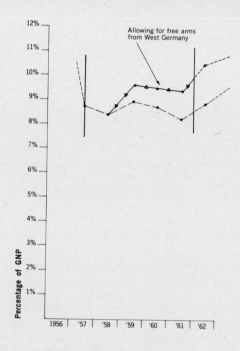

Fig. 10   Israel: "The Third Phase"

treated? Clearly the equipment should be taken into account when we consider the effect of the added military strength it provided Israel on the actions of Egypt and other Arab countries; but how should it be treated when we try to assess defense effort in terms of the economic-financial strain a country is willing to bear in order to meet it? Would Israel have bought any of the equipment if it had not received it free? How much?

We are not in a position to answer some of these questions at all and can only provide very tentative answers to others. In any case, since the German-Israeli deal straddled the phase we are now discussing as well as the next, we shall postpone considering it momentarily and concentrate now on the characteristics of the third phase that were not basically altered by the deal.

The fact of the decline in Israel's proportional defense expenditure from the peak of 1956 reflected the corresponding decline in Egypt's effort, the greater sense of security and confidence Israel gained from its military success in the Sinai campaign, the termination of the border warfare with Egypt, and Egypt's tacit earnest of its desire for calm given in its agreement to the stationing of United Nations troops on its side of the frontiers even though Israel had refused to allow them on its side. These considerations were reinforced by favorable political developments including Israel's tacit alliance with France, the renewal of the United States' moral commitment to the defense and integrity of Israel, the United States' effort, under the Eisenhower Doctrine, to isolate Nasser and contain his drive for Arab unity, and finally, after the Iraqi revolution of 1958, the renunciation by the United States of previous efforts to promote or support a Western-Arab alliance, which the Israelis had always viewed as detrimental to themselves, and the subsequent thawing of the Cold War in the Middle East.

That the decline in defense expenditure was not greater than it was considering all these favorable factors reflected Israel's concern over some countervailing tendencies. First there was the fact that Syria began to receive large shipments of Soviet weapons after concluding a deal of its own; as we shall see presently, there was an enormous spurt in the defense outlays of Syria in 1958, at a time Egypt was in its third, "low" phase. Then there was the fear of a collapse of Jordan that could trigger a general war in the area. Third, there was the formation of the U.A.R. by the union of Egypt and Syria that altered the strategic conditions by putting the two armies under a single effective command. Fourth, there was the formation of the Jordanian-Iraqi union that involved the potential danger of bringing Iraqi troops into the strategic West Bank of Jordan. Fifth, there came the turn of Iraq to acquire vast amounts of equipment from the Soviet Union after the overthrow of the monarchy and the termination of the Baghdad Pact. Although the rivalries and conflicts among the Arab countries and the tensions within them reduced the possibility of their ganging up on Israel, they did not, in Israeli thinking, preclude it altogether. A collapse of the regime in Jordan or a number of other contingencies could still bring all the Arabs together in a war against it.

Moving on to the fourth and last phase (see Figure 11), the proportional and absolute rise since 1961-1962 represented in part a response to the following factors: the new Egyptian-Soviet arms agreement, the rapid expansion of the Egyptian army in connection with the Yemen war and the spillover effect this had in Arabia, the tension over the diversion of the Jordan's waters, the creation of a United Arab Command and the formation of the Palestine Liberation Army, and the

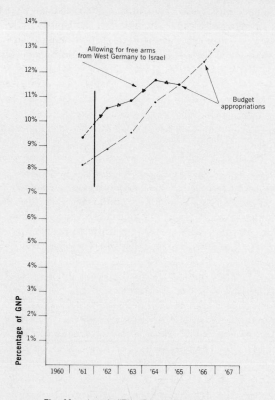

Fig. 11   Israel: "The Fourth Phase"

concerted effort of the Arab summit conferences to subsidize an accelerated expansion of the armed forces of Syria and Jordan. In part too it reflected the maturation of Israeli initiatives such as the nuclear reactor of Dimona, whose construction had begun in the previous phase.

Matching these motives and making their realization possible was the virtual disappearance of all limitations on the sources of weapons that had previously inhibited Israel to greater or lesser extents. Sometime in the late fifties and early sixties the market for modern weapons

outside the Soviet bloc became a buyers' market with potential suppliers competing for the gold of potential buyers. The reasons for this
are most probably connected with the desire of the great powers to
keep a modicum of production and development of conventional weapons going after their own demand for them had slackened due to
their switching to missiles as the mainstay of their strategic plans. This
as much as anything else probably underlies the United States' becoming in fact a major supplier of arms to the Middle East even while protesting its theoretical intention to avoid this role.[15] In any case, it is
clear that while in early 1956 it was necessary for France at least to
pretend that the United States had to relinquish its priority over
France's production before it could divert to Israel 24 Mystères, a few
years later Israel could buy as much as it could afford of the latest
equipment in France or elsewhere without any fuss. The opening up of
the market has worked too for those Arab countries that have not relied on the Soviet Union for their arms supplies, as is evident from the
recent *competition* between the United States and Britain to meet a
Saudi Arabian shopping list worth $400 million—a competition eventu-
ally resolved amicably by splitting the order fifty-fifty. This new situation has permitted Israel to go about strengthening its armed forces in
a more systematic way in accordance with preconceived plans instead
of acquiring more or less haphazardly whatever was available on the
market.

And now to the question of the free German arms and its
implications: Knowledge that Germany had been giving arms to Israel
leaked out early in 1965 and led immediately to a chain of crises between Germany and the Arab states, among the Arab states, and between Germany and Israel. Little is known about the details of the
German-Israeli deal, but a few pieces of evidence permit us to construct the main elements of it that are of interest to us.

In two articles by Haykal in *al Ahram* (February 5 and 12, 1965),
reflecting apparently the belief of the Egyptian government, the author asserted that there were two deals, the first originating in the Ben
Gurion-Adenauer meeting in New York in March 1960, and the second in 1964. The first was completed and the second was interrupted
when news of it leaked out. About the first deal, Haykal had no details. But about the second he said that its official value was $80 mil-
lion but its actual value much more. In evidence he produced a list of
items allegedly comprised in the deal, which included: 200 Patton

---

[15] See, for example, *The New York Times* of October 26, 1967. American arms
sales to the Middle East and South Asia burgeoned from $7.7 million in fiscal
year 1962 to $333 million in fiscal year 1967.

tanks, 200 armored carriers Hotchkiss, 30 carriers H.S., an unspecified number of Leopard tanks, 200 40-mm radar-guided AA guns, 72 105-mm "mobile" (self-propelled?) guns, 60 20-mm "mobile" guns M42, 36 105-mm Howitzers, 48 American F84 bombers, 27 observation planes, 15 helicopters S58, 24 Noratlas transport planes, six Jaguar torpedo boats, two 300-ton (sic) submarines, "and many other things as yet unknown."

On the other side of the frontline, an article in the Tel Aviv daily *Haaretz,* presumably passed by the military censorship, suggested that there was only one deal, which went back to 1958 (rather than 1960), was confirmed in the Ben Gurion-Adenauer meeting in 1960, and was "transformed" in 1964 before being interrupted at the end of that year.[16] According to the story, the deal was concluded in 1958 between Shimon Peres, then Deputy Defense Minister of Israel, and Franz Joseph Strauss, then German Defense Minister, during the latter's visit to Israel. Deliveries began that same year. The deal did not refer to any specific amount of money but comprised global quantities of equipment. Each year, Shimon Peres personally submitted to the German Minister of Defense a specific shopping list of Israel's needs and the German authorities met them almost fully. During the Ben Gurion-Adenauer meeting, the Israeli Prime Minister sought, and received, from the German Chancellor assurances that he knew about the deal and approved its continuation. Four years later, in the course of a visit to Tel Aviv of Dr. Biernbach, the still undelivered part of the global list was given a monetary value, apparently in connection with a German effort to normalize what had hitherto been a very special kind of operation. We should mention that the article was written at the height of the controversy between Israel and Germany about the interruption of the transaction and the German offer to give Israel monetary compensation for the undelivered equipment. One of the points the author sought to suggest was that the monetary value assigned to the remainder of the transaction in 1964 did not at all reflect its real value.

The main contours of the affair seem thus to emerge clearly from a combination of the two stories. There was one deal, going back earlier than the Egyptians knew, with a "transformation" in 1964 that the Egyptians have called a second deal. There is agreement between the Egyptian and the Israeli stories that the real value of the unfulfilled part was much higher than the $80 million nominal value assigned to it. In view of this agreement, the list provided by Haykal does

---

[16] *Haaretz,* March 18, 1966: "What Did Adenauer Actually Promise to Ben Gurion?" by Amos Ben Vered.

not seem improbable, especially since Israel has gone on after reaching a settlement with Germany to acquire many of the very items mentioned in it or similar ones, including 200 Patton tanks and 48 Skyhawk bombers, from the United States. As for the value of the equipment already delivered in the six years before the interruption, this can only be guessed at from the magnitude of the mostly undelivered part. An average of $25 to $30 million a year in real value would probably be erring on the underestimation side.

The addition of the freely received equipment to the Israeli arsenal could not but have affected, at least in part, the Egyptian efforts to strengthen and expand their armed forces after 1961. True, the value of this equipment was not reflected in the Israeli budget in an identifiable way, but the Egyptians must have observed concrete forces and equipment in being even more than budgets, and the real increase due to the German equipment could not have escaped them altogether.

As far as the pattern of Israel's defense expenditure, the addition of the value of the German equipment to the years 1959 through 1964 makes for a rise in the middle of the third phase and mitigates the sharpness of the rise in the fourth (see Table II and Figure 6 above). The new curve gives us a more accurate measure than the other of the strength the Israelis thought desirable to maintain and build in those years. It is not, however, a more accurate measure of the sacrifices the Israelis were willing to make in order to attain that strength level, since we have no way of knowing if they would have bought some or all of the arms they received free. Nor, for that reason, can we take the new curve along with other data as a measure of Israel's proven past capacity to spend on defense insofar as this is relevant for future forecasts.

Syria

The data on Syria's defense expenditure are somewhat more complicated than those of Egypt and Israel in view of the very heavy fluctuations of its GNP. This is because Syrian agriculture, the main source of its income, is heavily dependent on climatic conditions, unlike Egypt's, which can count on the steady irrigation made possible by the husbanded Nile. Israel, though subject to the same climatic conditions, is not so subject to the same consequences because agriculture does not constitute so large a part of its income and since much of it is based on an elaborate system of artificial irrigation. With Syria, therefore, we must pay particularly close attention to absolute in addition to proportional expenditures. Unfortunately, however, we have no reliable con-

TABLE III: Syria's Defense Outlays, 1952-1965

1 Year	2 Defense Outlays (millions £S.)	3 Defense[1] Outlays (millions U.S. $)	4 Defense[2] Outlays (millions U.S. $)		5 GNP[3] (millions £S.)	6 Defense Outlays as percentage of GNP
1952	86.2	23.0	39.3		...	...
1953	93.3	25.7	42.6	PHASE	2,141	4.4%
1954	89.9	25.1	41.0	I	2,188	4.1%
1955	104.8	29.3	47.8		2,017	5.2%
1956	166.3	46.7	75.9	PHASE	2,757	6.0%
1957	166.0	46.4	46.4	II	2,884	5.8%
1958	276.8[4]	77.4	77.4	PHASE	2,273 (2,704)[5]	12.2% (10.2%)
1959	271.3[4]	75.9	75.9	III A	2,195 (2,640)[5]	12.3% (10.3%)
1960	285.1[4]	79.7	79.7	PHASE	2,913 (3,601)[5]	9.8 % (7.9%)
1961	299.9[4]	83.9	83.9	III B	3,425 (4,083)[5]	8.8% (7.3%)
1962	339.7[4]	91.6	91.8		3,990	8.5%
1963	374.7[4]	98.1	98.1	PHASE	3,906	9.6%[6]
1964	405.8[4]	100.0	106.2	IV	4,999	8.1%[7] (10.4%)
1965	434.8[4]	107.6	113.8		5,268	8.3%[7] (10.2%)

[1] Conversion into $ at "free" exchange rate used for exports.

[2] Conversion into $ at official "controlled" exchange rate used for imports.

[3] Estimated GNP at current market prices (see Appendix A).

[4] Up to 1958, figures are closed accounts (that is, amounts actually spent). Starting in 1958, figures are said to be "estimates."

[5] GNP figures adjusted so as to eliminate the effects of the 1958–1961 slump due partly to adverse climatic conditions, but mostly to the union with Egypt.

[6] Percentage increase due mainly to slight fall in GNP.

[7] These percentage figures seem small and are probably underestimated. The source of the underestimation might be (1) the fact that defense outlays are here defense appropriations and not final closed-account figures, and/or (2) overestimation of Syrian GNP (see Appendix A.) The U.S. Department of State estimated that the share of defense in Syrian GNP was 10.4% in 1964 and 10.2% in 1965, the figures we give in parentheses.

Sources, method, and comments: See Appendix A.

version rate for Syrian currency prior to 1957 and after 1963, and we must resort simultaneously to two exchange rates, one used for exports, which is equivalent to a free exchange rate of the Syrian pound, and one used for imports, which is actually the government controlled exchange rate. Table III provides a summary of all the relevant data.

Despite these complications, the pattern of Syria's defense expenditure is easy to discern because it fits into the pattern of the Egyptian and Israeli efforts we have discussed at length. That is to say, it fits into it in the sense that it is made intelligible by resort to the same four phases we have used in the case of Egypt and Israel, not necessarily in the sense that the direction taken by Syria's defense expenditure in each phase was identical. Indeed, the most singular feature of Syria's pattern is that instead of taking a turn downward after the initial leap from the first phase, Syria's defense expenditures took still another immense leap and stayed very high before declining slowly and finally rising again mildly. This second leap was, as we have pointed out in our discussion of Israel, one of the principal reasons why the decline in Israel's proportional expenditures after the peak of 1956 was much less than that of Egypt after *its* peak.

Figure 12 illustrates the outlines of the Syrian pattern with a suggestion of only one correction of the distortions introduced by the fluctuations of GNP. If we go back to Table III and examine it in conjunction with the figure, we could easily see that the upward turn of the curve in 1955 was exaggerated by the *fall* of GNP while that in 1956 is very greatly understated by an extraordinary rise in GNP exceeding 30 percent over the previous year. By any calculation, the absolute rise in defense expenditure in 1955 was less than 20 percent over the previous year, whereas in 1956 it was more than 50 percent over 1955. Thus, Figure 12 understates the 1956-1957 increase in Syrian defense outlays. Indeed, 1956 and 1957 were the years when Syria made the equivalent of the major leap we have observed in the case of Egypt in 1954-1955 and 1955-1956 and Israel in 1956, largely in consequence of moves made by these countries (see Figure 13). On the one hand, the conclusion of the Soviet-Egyptian deal opened the door for the conclusion of a Soviet-Syrian deal (said to amount to $110 million). On the other hand, a combination of mounting tension in the area, Israel's acquisition of arms in response to Egypt's move, the Sinai-Suez war, and an intensification of internal and foreign intrigues in Syria itself enhanced the sense of felt need for more arms.

Why Syria went on after this spurt to make another enormous spurt (Phase IIIA) is a matter for wonder and speculation. Before indulging in either, we should remind the reader that the years in question, 1958 and 1959, were the first two years of the union with Egypt. We should also point out that in those years GNP took a very severe drop as a result of adverse climatic conditions and flight of capital and other influences connected with the union. For the purpose of gauging the strain imposed on the economy by heavy defense expenditure, the spurious drop in GNP is, of course, irrelevant; but even if we discount it, as we should for purposes of arms competition, we still come out with an absolute increase of 60 percent and a proportional increase of 44 percent in 1958 over 1957, the level being maintained with negligible change in 1959.

One speculation is that the enormous increase was due in part to the Egyptian-led effort to reorganize the Syrian defense establishment both for political reasons and in order to bring it in line with the Egyptian establishment, standardize its equipment, and so on.

Another is that the increase was partly due to Syria's bearing the

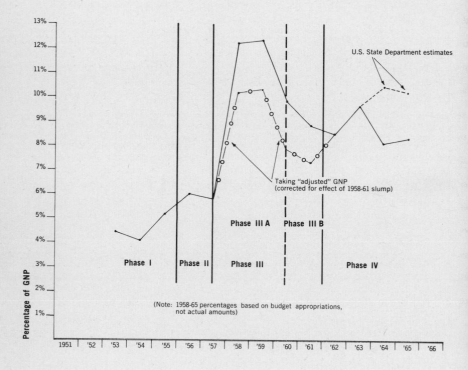

Fig. 12   Syria: Defense Outlays as Percentages of GNP

brunt of the intervention in the Lebanese civil war in the first half of 1958 and of the open confrontation with Kassem's Iraq after the latter part of that year. A third speculation, which actually is only a more general statement of the second and the first, is that the Syrians were made to carry a disproportionate share of the combined defense budget of the United Arab Republic.

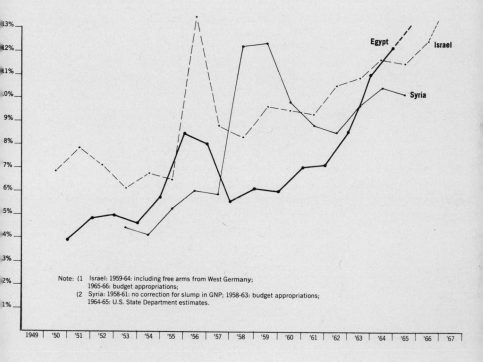

Note: (1 Israel: 1959-64: including free arms from West Germany;
         1965-66: budget appropriations;
      (2 Syria: 1958-61: no correction for slump in GNP; 1958-63: budget appropriations;
         1964-65: U.S. State Department estimates.

Fig. 13   Egypt, Syria, and Israel:
          Relative Defense Outlays as Percentages of GNP

Whatever the reasons for the second Syrian spurt, the fact itself could not fail to have its effect on Israel's action. We have already suggested that the difference in the pace of the movement of Egyptian and Israeli defense expenditure after 1957 was partly due to the Syrian

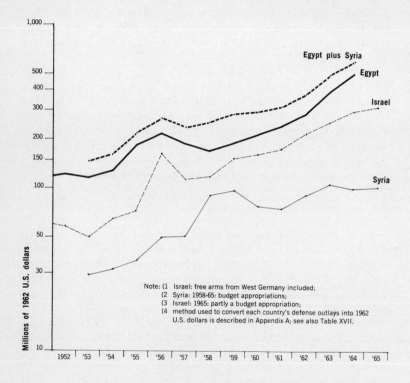

Fig. 14   Egypt, Syria, and Israel: Defense Outlays in 1962 U.S. dollars

spurt. That Syria was in those years integrally united with Egypt only enhanced the Israeli point of view that counted at least some of the forces of the smaller Arab countries as additions to the strength of the main Egyptian opponent. A concrete illustration of this is provided by Figure 14, which shows that when Egyptian and Syrian absolute defense expenditures (in 1962 dollars) are joined and their fluctuations are compared with those of Israel, the parallelism is striking, at least up to 1962. The same conclusion also obtains when Israel's defense outlays are compared to the combined expenditures of its neighbors, Egypt, Syria, and Jordan (see Figure 15).[17]

As is clear from Figure 12, the fall in Syria's proportional defense expenditures in 1960 and 1961 (Phase IIIB) is exaggerated by the erratic behavior of Syrian GNP during the 1958–1961 slump. Actually, as Table III shows, Syria's absolute defense outlays stayed at about the same level in all these years. Consequently, the years 1958–1961 really make up but one phase despite the fact that Figure 12 suggests two subphases.

The fourth and latest phase of Syria's defense expenditure, from 1962 on, probably involved a slow resumption of the upward process. At least, this would be the case if the estimates of the U.S. State Department are a better reflection of actual expenditures than our estimates, which are based on budget appropriations. This resumption of the upward movement was obviously related to the secession from the U.A.R. and the escalation in Syria's defense expenditures brought about by the competition between Egypt and Israel.

Iraq

Iraq's pattern of defense expenditure has been quite different from anything we have examined so far. Starting from a relatively high level in relation to GNP in 1952, it has gone on through 1962 accelerating absolutely at a measured pace and has tended to move upward proportionally without major jumps up or down—with two exceptions: one comparatively mild spurt upward in 1956, and a somewhat sharper one in 1959. These, however, were nothing like the big leaps and dives that characterized the patterns of Egypt, Israel, and Syria. Since 1963 a major spurt seems to be developing even if we make allowance for the fact that in that year the proportional rise was exaggerated by the fall in GNP and even if we take into account the fact that the figures for the subsequent years are somewhat inflated budget figures. Table IV below reflects these points clearly.

The most crucial point suggested by this pattern is that Iraq,

[17] In the later years, it would seem that Israel was being outpaced by the Egyptian-Syrian military effort, but this apparent gap probably reflects Egypt's intervention in Yemen. Part of the Egyptian expenditures incurred in connection with this intervention did enhance Egypt's potential capability against Israel (for example, the creation of two new divisions), but another part of these expenditures—the cost of supplying an expeditionary corps at the other end of the Red Sea, for example—surely did not add anything to Egypt's military potential. Hence, the Israelis could afford to discount the latter part of Egypt's military outlays.

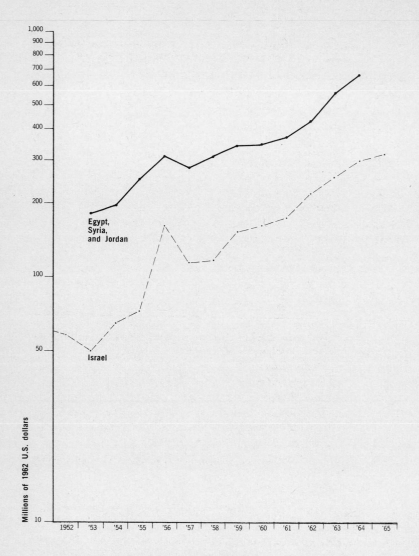

Fig. 15   Israel compared with Its Neighbors:
Defense Outlays in 1962 U.S. dollars (Note: See notes to Figure 14)

TABLE IV: *Iraq's Defense Outlays, 1952-1965*

1 Year	2 Defense Outlays (millions I.D.)	3 Defense Outlays[1] (millions U.S. $)	4 GNP[2] (millions I.D.)	5 Defense Outlays as percentage of GNP
1952	15.6	43.7	...	...
1953	19.0	53.2	286.9	6.6%
1954	20.0	56.0	331.7	6.0%
1955	21.8	61.0	341.7	6.4%
1956	27.1	75.9	389.4	7.0%
1957	29.7	83.2	413.1	7.2%
1958	31.0	86.8	436.2	7.1%
1959	35.8	100.2	452.6	7.9%
1960	42.4	118.7	502.8	8.4%
1961	44.9	125.7	557.3	8.1%
1962	48.3	135.2	600.8	8.0%
1963	58.2	163.0	587.6	9.9%[3]
1964	68.4[4]	191.5[4]	625.3	10.9%
1965	81.4[5]	227.9[5]	667.8[6]	12.2%

[1] Conversion at current exchange rate (1.00 I.D. = $2.80 for entire period, Iraq being in the sterling area).

[2] GNP at current market prices.

[3] Percentage increase partly due to fall in GNP.

[4] Partly a budget appropriation.

[5] Budget appropriation (judging by past experience, appropriations might well be higher than amounts actually spent).

[6] Our estimate.

Sources, method, and comments: See Appendix A.

notwithstanding the rhetoric of its leaders and its participation in the Arab League and summit meetings, has not been deeply involved in the Arab-Israeli conflict. Certainly that conflict has had something to do more or less indirectly with the upward trend of Iraq's defense expenditure; but it does not seem to have *specifically* guided Iraqi action. A look at the Iraqi pattern in juxtaposition with that of Israel and of Egypt as shown in Figure 16 immediately brings out the lack of any

178   THE DYNAMICS OF ARMS BUILDUP: DEFENSE EXPENDITURES

but minor or accidental relationships between the courses taken by
these two countries and that of Iraq.

The general lack of specific year-to-year correlation between Iraq's
moves and those of the other countries is partly explainable by geography, by the sheer physical distance from the arena of conflict. Iraq is
not contiguous to Israel and therefore neither fears Israeli aggression
nor is in a position to deploy its troops rapidly against Israel. This does

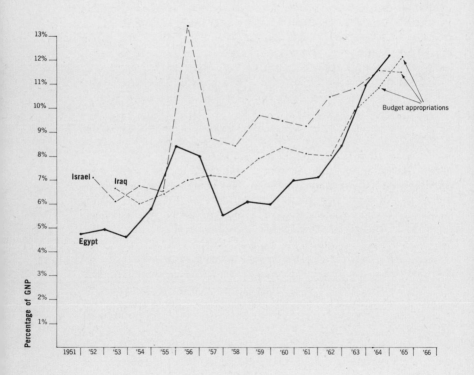

Fig. 16   Iraq compared with Israel and Egypt:
Defense Outlays as Percentages of GNP (Note: Israel's outlays include free arms from West Germany)

not mean that the Israelis, for their part, have seen things in this light and have not been concerned with Iraq's steadily growing armament.

The relative regularity of Iraq's defense expenditure reflects that country's independent course in another way. As a founding partner of the Baghdad Pact and its only Arab member, Iraq had had access through the middle of 1958 to a steady source of armament in Great Britain that obviated the need for any big spurts in defense expenditure. There was no need for Iraq to take advantage of newly opened up sources of arms by hoarding as much as possible as was the case with Egypt and Israel in 1955–1957. After Iraq pulled out of the Baghdad Pact and the new revolutionary government began to acquire arms from the Soviet Union in 1958-1959, it looked for a moment as though the Egyptian or Syrian pattern might be repeated. But as it turned out, the opening up of the Soviet source only pressed Britain to keep its channels open, with the result that there was no need to re-equip at once all the Iraqi army with Soviet weapons, and the spurt that occurred at that time remained relatively mild.

The initially high and steadily rising level of defense expenditure reflects at once Iraq's strong internal needs and its aspiration to play a leading role among the Arab countries. Strong disintegrative forces, such as the Shi'i-Sunni division and discontented Kurds who have repeatedly defied the central government, have necessitated an unusually high degree of reliance on military force to keep the country together. It is impossible to determine just what proportion of the defense expenditure was due to internal needs, but the fact that three of the five divisions that constituted the Iraqi army plus much of its air force had been engaged for over five years until 1966 in a futile effort to put down the latest Kurdish uprising suggests that most of it was. Also significant is the fact that one of the mild spurts in defense spending took place after the revolution of 1958, when the disruption of the previous order gave freer scope to the disintegrative forces in the country. As for Iraq's ambitions—and fears—in the Arab world, we have referred to them in the analysis of pan-Arabism and inter-Arab relations and need only recall them here: the Hashimites' aspiration to annex Syria, their old feud with the house of Saud, the rivalry with Egypt, the interventions in Jordan in support of the fellow-Hashimite monarch, the Nasser-Kassem quarrel, and Iraq's designs on Kuwait.

Jordan

Jordan's pattern of defense expenditure has been similar to that of Iraq in that it reveals no apparent connection to the Egyptian, Israeli, and

TABLE V: Jordan's Defense Outlays, 1953-1965

1 Year	2 Defense Outlays (millions J.D.)	3 Defense Outlays [1] (millions U.S. $)	4 GNP [2] (millions J.D.)	5 Defense Outlays as percentage of GNP
1953	9.3	26.0	39.9	23.3%
1954	10.2	28.6	53.6	19.0%
1955	10.5	29.5	57.4	18.4%
1956	12.8	35.9	75.9	16.9%
1957	13.5	37.7	76.3	17.6%
1958	15.9	44.6	88.9	17.9%
1959	20.1	56.4	99.1	20.3%
1960	19.1	53.6	105.7	18.1%
1961	18.6	52.2	127.1	14.7%
1962	19.0	53.3	130.8	14.6%
1963	20.6	57.5	137.6	14.9%
1964	21.0	58.9	160.6	13.1%
1965	21.1 [3]	59.1 [3]	180.5	11.7%

[1] Conversion at current exchange rate (J.D. 1.00 = $2.80 for entire period, Jordan being in the sterling area).

[2] GNP at current market prices.

[3] Partly a budget appropriation.

Sources, method, and comments: See Appendix A.

Syrian patterns. But this has been so for entirely different reasons. Geography, for example, which places Iraq at a safe distance from the Palestine conflict, puts Jordan in an exposed position at its very heart. If Jordan has not been involved in the leaps and dives of Egypt, Israel, and Syria, this has not been because of insensitivity to what these countries did, but because of lack of capacity to compete with them on a year by year basis due to two facts: (1) the country's poverty—Jordan's entire GNP has been less than Egypt's defense expenditure through most all of the last 15 years; and (2) its dependence on British and American subsidies for its entire defense effort.

Table V gives the figures for Jordan's defense expenditures in absolute amounts and as percentages of GNP. In absolute amounts the

figures are comparatively modest. They have risen quite slowly over
the years, except for the years 1957 through 1960, to reach somewhat
more than double the initial size in the course of 14 years. Proportionally, they have been extremely high—probably the highest in the

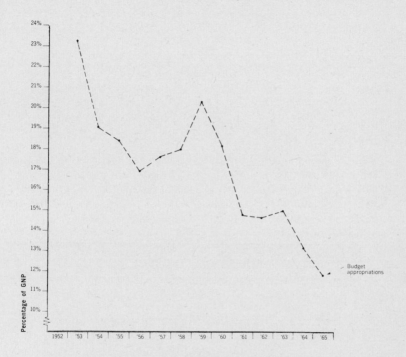

Fig. 17   Jordan: Defense Outlays as Percentages of GNP

world, averaging 19 percent through 1960 and about 14 percent in the
recorded years since.

The movement of the proportional expenditure is illustrated in
Figure 17. As may be seen even without juxtaposing the patterns of
other countries on it, it has been quite different. Its determining factor
has been the result of the interplay between the foreign subsidy and
changing GNP more than of any other influences. In the period
through 1956, the British provided a subsidy that increased less rapidly
than GNP year after year, thus resulting in a generally slight, propor-

tional downward trend. Then, after a confused brief interim in which Egypt, Saudi Arabia, and Syria failed to deliver fully on their promise to replace the British subsidy, the United States took over and contributed amounts that rose faster than GNP until 1960-1961, when the latter decisively outstripped the pace of growth of the subsidy. The increase in the American subsidy reflected the agitated years of Jordan's internal existence and relations with other Arab countries that reached their peak after the overthrow of the related Hashimite dynasty in Iraq in 1958 and the enormous pressures this put on Jordan.

The fact that Jordan's armed establishment has depended almost entirely on British and American subsidies of relatively modest magnitudes and that a good part of this establishment is tied down to internal security duties might have been thought to be sufficient reason for Israel not to reckon Jordan for much in its defense considerations. But two factors have prevented the Israelis from taking this view: One was Jordan's control of the strategically vital West Bank of the Jordan River, which compensated for the dearth of other military assets in the opportunities it offered, and the other was the possibility of an overthrow of the present regime and its replacement by another, which would both release Jordan's forces from dependence on America and throw them on the scales with those of Egypt and other countries.

Lebanon

Lebanon's past pattern of defense expenditure demonstrates clearly its deliberate decision to stay out of the area's game of power politics. With a GNP recently more than twice that of Jordan and larger in earlier years, Lebanon has lately spent half as much as Jordan on defense and less than that before. Being a small country with a fragile political system resting on a precarious balance between the Muslim and Christian halves of its population, Lebanon drew the wise conclusion to rely for its external security on diplomacy and collective security. This has permitted it until very recently to keep its defense expenditure at a low absolute and proportional level, just enough for the needs of internal security and order.

Such, however, has been the climate created in the area around Lebanon by the massive accumulation of arms that in spite of its military isolationism it has not altogether escaped rising military expenditure not only absolutely, which would have been understandable, but also proportionally. As Table VI shows, military outlays have increased about fivefold in absolute terms between 1953 and 1966 and have more than doubled in proportional terms during the same period. It is

TABLE VI: *Lebanon's Defense Outlays, 1953–1966*

1 Year	2 Defense Outlays (millions L.£)	3 Defense Outlays[1] (millions U.S. $)	4 GNP[2] (millions L.£)	5 Defense Outlays as percentage of GNP
1953	30.9	9.1	1,343	2.3%
1954	31.7	9.9	1,445	2.2%
1955	37.5	11.6	1,580	2.4%
1956	50.5	15.7	1,630	3.1%
1957	52.9	16.6	1,693	3.1%
1958	57.5	18.1	1,524	3.8%[3]
1959	58.3	18.5	1,880	3.1%
1960	62.8	19.8	1,961	3.2%
1961	74.1	24.1	2,057	3.6%
1962	85.7	28.5	2,135	4.0%
1963	95.1	31.6	2,265	4.2%
1964	106.5	34.6	2,366	4.5%
1965	118.9[4]	38.7[4]	2,477[5]	4.8%
1966	145.3[4]	45.8[4]	2,594[5]	5.6%

[1] Conversion at current exchange rate on free market.
[2] GNP at current market prices.
[3] Percentage increase largely due to fall in the GNP.
[4] Budget appropriations.
[5] Our estimate.

Sources, method, and comments: See Appendix A.

significant in this respect that one of the two minor spurts in the otherwise creeping increase occurred in 1956, following the escalation of arms levels in the area brought by the Soviet-Egyptian deal—the other being related to the civil war of 1958 both directly and through the decline in GNP it occasioned (see Figure 18).

Obviously Lebanon's pattern has been like nothing we have seen so far, though in the years since 1963 it has been under pressure from other Arab countries, working through the summit meetings, to increase its defense effort with unwelcome assistance from them. The data for recent years suggest that the pressure has succeeded to some extent, although the figures for 1965 and 1966 are based on budget appropriations, the amounts actually spent remaining unpublished as of the time of writing (summer of 1966). Another straw in the wind is Lebanon's announced intention to buy some 12 Mirage-III supersonic fighters from France, thus considerably upgrading an air force that had been all but negligible (see the following chapter). But as of the time

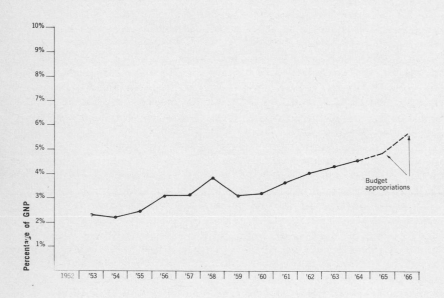

Fig. 18   Lebanon: Defense Outlays as Percentages of GNP

of writing no Mirage-III had been actually delivered. And it would not be out of character if in fact Lebanon's actual defense expenditures turned out to be less than had been appropriated in the recent budgets and if no Mirages were ever received. Should that be the case, Lebanon would remain, luckily for itself, of only hypothetical importance to the area's calculus of force.

Kuwait

Like Iraq, Jordan, and Lebanon, Kuwait has followed a pattern of defense expenditure that has had only a vague relation to the Egyptian-Israeli pattern. The limitations that have prevented Kuwait from conforming to the Egyptian-Israeli pattern are obvious: Kuwait's geography and the miniscule size of its population that rule out any significant offensive or defensive military capacity. Yet, because of its fabulous oil-derived wealth, Kuwait has not been permitted, since it attained its independence in 1961, to abstract itself from the currents and cross-currents of conflict in the area. The result has been a two-way pattern of interaction: In one direction, the conflicts have forced Kuwait into the general tide of high and mounting defense expenditures, and in another direction, Kuwait's surplus wealth has become a factor of actual and potential importance in the process of arms accumulation throughout the area. The latter movement is of far greater significance, especially for the future.

The absolute and proportional defense expenditures of Kuwait since before its independence are given in Table VII below.

The large magnitudes of the absolute defense expenditures for a city-state of about 500,000 people are unmistakable. Over the recorded period, Kuwait has spent on the average each year as much as Jordan, which has almost five times its population and is in a very exposed position. On a per capita basis, Kuwait spent in recent years about 15 times more than Egypt, a much higher proportion than the difference in per capita income between the two countries. Where and how these amounts are spent is a bit of a puzzle since Kuwait's tiny army could hardly absorb them. There is some evidence that the Kuwaitis stockpile arms for use by friendly interventionist forces in case of need, as is suggested in the British defense papers that fell into Arab hands and were published by Haykal in *al Ahram*, June 11, 1965, under the title, "British Staff Plans for Intervention in Kuwait." The same source also hints that large amounts must be spent on intelligence against the danger of internal subversion and external sudden attack, especially from Iraq's side. The danger of internal subversion may

TABLE VII: Kuwait's Defense Outlays, 1957-1966

1 Year	2 Defense Outlays (millions K.D.)	3 Defense Outlays [1] (millions U.S. $)	4 GNP [2] (millions K.D.)	5 Defense Outlays as percentage of GNP
1957/8	9.2	25.7	269	3.4%
1958/9	12.0	33.7	311	3.9%
1959/0	14.0	39.3	367	3.8%
1960/1	16.2	45.2	387	4.2%
1961/2	15.4	43.1	407	3.8%
1962/3	22.0	61.6	460	4.8%
1963/4	21.6[3]	60.5[3]	500	4.3%
1964/5	22.3[3]	62.4[3]	542	4.1%
1965/6	24.2[3]	67.7[3]	565	4.3%
1966/7	28.2[3]	79.0[3]	607	4.7%

[1] Conversion at current official exchange rate (K.D. 1.00 = $2.80 for entire period, Kuwait being in the sterling area).

[2] GNP at current market prices (see Appendix A).

[3] Budget appropriations.

Sources, method, and comments: See Appendix A.

well loom very large and make for considerable expenditures on internal security, since foreign workers from other Arab countries represent a large and growing fraction of Kuwait's resident population.

The movement of Kuwait's proportional defense expenditure is illustrated in Figure 19. The single moderate spurt in the trend upward reflects the confrontation with Iraq immediately after the proclamation of Kuwait's independence. Kassem then laid claim to Kuwait as part of Iraq's territory, which prompted the intervention of British forces, later relieved by Arab League troops.

As we have already suggested, the real importance of Kuwait does not lie, however, in its own defense effort in the sense discussed so far but in its diplomatic extension in the form of direct or indirect financial support for the defense effort of other Arab countries. The confrontation with Iraq, for example, was eventually terminated in 1963 when the Ba'th government that overthrew Kassem recognized Kuwait's independence and was simultaneously given an interest-free loan of $84 million. In somewhat less obvious ways Kuwait has bought the good will of other Arab countries by extending to them loans through the Kuwait Fund for Arab Economic Development. More directly related to defense matters, Kuwait has been one of the main sources for financing the plans of successive Arab summit meetings to divert the sources of the Jordan River, create the Palestine Liberation Army, and strengthen the armed forces of Jordan, Syria, and Lebanon. The magnitude of contributions such as these in the future will depend on political conjunctures, including the viability of Kuwaiti sovereignty, and thus cannot be known.[18] But in view of the vast resources

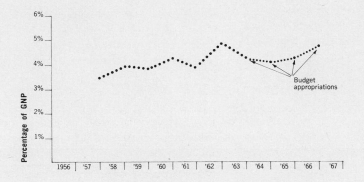

Fig. 19   Kuwait: Defense Outlays as Percentages of GNP

available to Kuwait, there is no doubt that they could be very significant. Not only have Kuwait's oil revenues been large and rising (more than half a billion dollars in 1964), but it has also been keeping vast and increasing amounts of assets and reserves abroad, as Table VIII indicates, much of which can be called in on short notice.

To put the magnitude of Kuwait's foreign assets and reserves into proper perspective, the 1963 grand total for the tiny city-state (1.577 billion dollars) was almost exactly equal to the *combined* total foreign assets and reserves of Saudi Arabia, Iraq, Egypt, Lebanon, Jordan, and Syria in the same year.

[18] Since the Six Day War, Kuwait, together with Saudi Arabia and Libya, has literally saved Egypt from economic-financial catastrophe through a massive subsidy.

TABLE VIII: Kuwait: Foreign Assets and Reserves (millions U.S. $)

Date	Revenue-Yielding Investments	Currency Board Reserves	KF-AED[1]	International Organization	Interest-Free Loans[2]	Sub-Total	Commercial Banks	Grand Total
3/31/61	637	–	–	–	–	637	305	942
3/31/62	952	90	–	–	–	1,042	392	1,434
3/31/63	988	98	42	14	–	1,142	389	1,531
11/30/63[3]	896	90	76	14	109	1,185	392	1,577

[1] Kuwait Fund for Arab Economic Development.

[2] Loans to Algeria ($16.8 million), Iraq ($84 million) and Egypt ($8.4 million).

[3] Rough estimate.

Sources, method, and comment: See Appendix A.

Saudi Arabia

Analysis of Saudi Arabia's defense effort is particularly fraught with difficulties and risks of major errors. Estimates of GNP are especially rough. Defense expenditure is dispersed in the budgets under no less than 11 separate items that suddenly appear, disappear, and reappear with disconcerting caprice. We could discover no information prior to 1958 or 1959; we can't even tell exactly which year it was since the budgets follow the Muslim lunar Hejira year. Nevertheless, after a laborious scrutinization and manipulation of the data, there did emerge, much to our surprise, a pattern that makes sense. It is summarized in Table IX below.

The very high level of defense expenditure in absolute and proportional amounts even at the lowest points reflects partly the basic problem of the Saudi political system, which embraces immense, loosely bound territories and several confederations of powerful, mostly nomadic tribes that comprise the vast majority of the population. It also reflects the rather primitive administrative state of the defense establishment, which includes a Military Division of the Presidency of the Council of Ministers, a National Guard, a Royal Body Guard, a Ministry of Defense, a Ministry of the Interior, a Department of Intelligence, a Mujahideen (Holy Warriors) Department, Frontier Forces, as well as other shifting administrative units.

The movement of the defense effort is illustrated in Figure 20. The high point from which our data start in 1958-1959 reflects the agita-

TABLE IX: *Saudi Arabia's Defense Outlays 1959-1967*

1 Year[1]	2 Defense Outlays[2] (millions S.R.)	3 Defense Outlays[3] (millions U.S. $)	4 GNP[4] (millions S.R.)	5 Defense Outlays as percentage of GNP
1959	412.2	109.9	3,360	12.3%
1960	338.1	82.7	3,568	9.5%
1961	329.0	73.1	4,220	7.8%
1962	361.4	80.3	4,623	7.8%
1963	477.1	106.0	5,140	9.3%
1964	636.1	141.3	5,817	10.9%
1965	748.4	166.3	6,457[5]	11.6%
1966	921.2	204.7	7,167[5]	12.9%
1967	1,371.8	304.8	7,884[5]	17.4%

[1] Both GNP and defense figures were given for Hegira years; these have been related to the Gregorian years.

[2] There is no indication in the sources consulted (see Appendix A) as to whether any of these figures are budget appropriations or amounts actually spent; however, the figures for the later years are surely budget appropriations (for 1967 it could not be otherwise).

[3] Conversion at current official exchange rate.

[4] GNP at current market prices (see Appendix A).

[5] Our estimate.

Sources, method, and comments: See Appendix A.

tion of the Saudi rulers after the collapse of the monarchical regime in Baghdad under what appeared at the time to be an irresistible populistic-military wave, which came after the no less disconcerting extension of Egyptian hegemony in Syria and the subversion of Lebanon. The subsequent decline reflects the gradual détente that came over the area in the next few years just as the sharp subsequent spurt upwards clearly marks the Saudi response to the Egyptian military intervention in Yemen.

The Saudi military effort, as far as the data we have shows, seems thus to be essentially determined by internal necessities and inter-Arab struggles. Nevertheless, such are the magnitudes of the effort that it could not remain without considerable effect on the Arab-Israeli confrontation. We have already seen that the resistance of the Yemeni royalists, which would have been impossible without Saudi support, has involved Egypt in the creation of two additional divisions, at least prematurely, and that this has had its effect on Israel. In a more direct way, the vast Saudi armament program launched in 1965-1966 with an

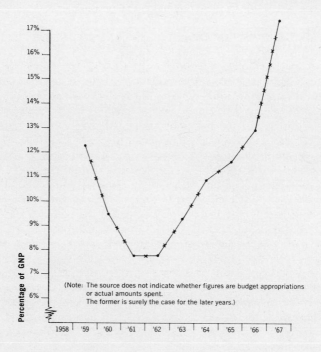

(Note: The source does not indicate whether figures are budget appropriations or actual amounts spent. The former is surely the case for the later years.)

Fig. 20   Saudi Arabia: Defense Outlays as Percentages of GNP

initial budget of $400 million could not be ignored by Israel. One day, the Israelis must think, the Yemen war will be over, but the Egyptian divisions and the modernized Saudi forces will stay; and against this day they had to provide.

Summary and Conclusions

The data we have just examined are pregnant with suggestions about many aspects of the politics of the Middle East and their future prospects. At the present stage of our analysis, however, we shall confine ourselves to making some summary observations and conclusions about the three objectives that have guided our investigation in this chapter: (1) the dynamics of the process of arms buildup in the area; (2) the strain that this process has imposed on the countries involved; and (3) the relative improvement or deterioration of the position of the main contestants as a result of their prolonged competition.

DYNAMICS OF ARMS BUILDUP

(a) The pattern of military buildup in the Middle East, as reflected in defense expenditure, has been the result of an unusual combination of factors at the center of which has been a primary race between Egypt and Israel, in which Egypt endeavored to attain by itself a position of military superiority over Israel, while Israel strove to provide against the military effort of Egypt *plus* any number of other Arab countries likely to join it in a hostile coalition. A dramatic illustration of this point was seen in Figures 14 and 15, which showed an uncanny constant relationship between the expenditures of Israel and a combination of its neighbors. The certainty that the decision-makers concerned did not deliberately plan things this way makes the outcome all the more remarkable.

(b) The pattern of defense exertion of all Middle Eastern countries together is given in Figure 21. The diagram brings out clearly that while specific correlations appear only between the Egyptian and Israeli curves, all the curves show an upward trend in 1955-1956, or shortly thereafter, and in the years after 1961-1962. This clearly reflects the spill-over effect of the Egyptian-Israeli race into the area as a whole, and the feedback effect on that race of arms buildup due to inter-Arab and internal tensions.

STRAIN OF THE ARMS BUILDUP

(a) On the basis of the data examined, which probably have missed some hidden defense expenditures, it appears that six out of the eight countries considered—Egypt, Israel, Jordan, Iraq, Saudi Arabia, and almost certainly Syria—have reached a point where they spent in 1964 higher percentages of their GNP on defense than any other countries in the world except the Soviet Union, including powers with global responsibilities and foreign policies such as the United States, Britain, and France. This fact is brought out by Table X. These six countries spent more than twice the percentage of countries like India and Indonesia, which have also been involved in grave international conflicts involving threat and deterrence. Even Lebanon's and Kuwait's defense expenditures in that year were comparatively high: Of the 35 other countries listed, no fewer than 24 spent a lower percentage of their GNP on defense than these two.

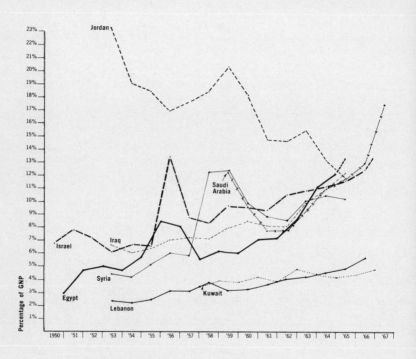

Fig. 21   Arab States and Israel:
Defense Outlays as Percentages of GNP
Note: (1   Israel: including free arms from West Germany;
(2   For all countries, data for later years represent budget appropriations
(see each country's table and diagram).

(b) These extraordinarily high percentages of GNP spent on defense would constitute a tragic drain of resources even for rich countries. For most Middle Eastern countries, with their miserable standards of living and their crying need for development resources, they are nothing short of catastrophic. Consider the pattern of outlays on defense, capital formation, and education of some of these countries in recent years as shown by Table XI.

TABLE X: *Defense Outlays as a Burden on National Economies*

Country		Defense Outlays (millions U.S. $)	As percentage of GNP
Middle East: Our Estimates for 1964			
	Jordan	59	13.1%
	Egypt (1963/4)	476	11.0%
	Iraq	192	10.9%
	Saudi Arabia	141	10.9%
	Israel	310	10.7%
	Syria	106	8.1% (10.4%)
	Lebanon	35	4.5%
	Kuwait	61	4.3%
Other Nations: Estimates of the Institute for Strategic Studies, London, for 1963–1964[1]			
	United States	52,400	8.9%
	United Kingdom	5,140	6.7%
	Portugal	176	6.2%
	France	4,062	5.1%
	Germany	4,607	5.0%
	Netherlands	618	4.4%
NATO	Greece	167	3.9%
	Canada	1,480	3.7%
	Norway	197	3.6%
	Turkey	235	3.5%
	Italy	1,510	3.3%
	Belgium	444	3.2%
	Denmark	225	2.9%
	Luxemburg	7	1.3%
	U.S.S.R.	40,000	14.8%
	Czechoslovakia	789	3.9%
WARSAW	Hungary	277	2.8%
PACT	Rumania	342	2.7%
	Poland	911	2.5%
	East Germany	650	2.5%
	Bulgaria	128	2.4%
	Australia	669	3.4%
	Pakistan	255	3.2%
SEATO	Thailand	75	2.5%
	New Zealand	86	2.0%
	Philippines	79	1.8%
	Yugoslavia	380	6.0%
	South Korea	165	5.8%
	Sweden	787	5.2%
	India	1,858	4.7%
OTHERS	Iran	197	4.1%
	Indonesia	980	3.9%
	Spain	473	3.3%
	Switzerland	292	2.5%
	Japan	669	1.1%

[1] Due to different definitions, the I.S.S. estimates may not be strictly comparable with ours.

TABLE XI: Recent Outlays on Defense, Investment, and Education

Country	1962	1963	1964
ISRAEL (million I.£)			
Defense expenditures	549	711	931
Gross investment [1]	1,985	2,210	2,691
Governmental outlays on education	284	425	495
EGYPT [2] (million £E.)			
Defense expenditures	142	208	252
Gross investment	300	372	...
Governmental outlays on education and health [3]	89	103	116
IRAQ (million I.D.)			
Defense expenditures	48	58	68
Gross investment	85	75	90
Governmental outlays on education	29	32	33
SYRIA (million £S.)			
Defense expenditures [4]	340	375	406
Gross investment	693	639	637
Governmental outlays on education [4]	84	92	113
JORDAN (million J.D.)			
Defense expenditures	19	21	21
Gross investment	22	20	19
Governmental outlays on education	3	3	4

[1] Gross domestic capital formation, without investment in inventories.

[2] 1962-1963; 1963-1964; 1964-1965

[3] No data could be found on actual expenditures on education only. Budget appropriations for education are as follows: 1962-1963: 60; 1963-1964: 61; 1964-1965: 86.

[4] Budget appropriations.

Sources and comments: See Appendix A.

(c) In proportional terms, the defense expenditures of these countries compared as follows with their outlays on education and investment:

TABLE XII:
Defense Expenditure as Percentage
of Government Educational Outlays [1]

Country	1963	1964
Israel	168%	188%
Egypt (as percentage of education *and* health outlays)	200%	219%
Iraq	181%	206%
Syria	407%	359%
Jordan	700%	525%

[1] Source: Table XI.

TABLE XIII:
Defense Expenditures as Percentage
of Gross Investment [1]

Country	1962	1963
Israel	28%	32%
Egypt	47%	55%
Iraq	50%	77%
Syria	49%	59%
Jordan	86%	105%

[1] Source: Table XI.

The figures speak for themselves, and we need only point out that the fantastic social and economic cost of the arms buildup incurred by Israel and the Arab countries—and by the latter, interestingly, much more than the former—is not even significantly mitigated by such secondary gains as the creation of investment and employment opportunities and the training of a labor force in sophisticated technology, which are often cited as by-products of high defense expenditure in advanced countries.[19] For one thing, the Keynesian argument of stimulating effective demand is inapplicable to poor economies such as those of the Middle East.[20] For another thing, most, if not all, the expensive military hardware of the countries under study has been imported rather than locally manufactured.

(d) We have already observed that the early sixties witnessed an escalation to a particularly high level of defense expenditure, but we have also noticed that the pattern of unusually high military outlays had already been set by 1955. This means that the sacrifices incurred by countries of the area have been accumulating year after year for that long. For nations like Egypt and Israel, the amounts involved have been staggering: Between 1955 and 1966 Egypt spent over 3.5 billion constant-value dollars while Israel spent nearly 2.5 billion.[21]

(e) Another, and perhaps fairer, way of computing the cost of the competitive arms buildup is to calculate that portion of defense expenditure which is over and above the amounts each country would have "normally" spent on its military establishment. Looking back at Table X, it would seem that 4 percent of GNP would be a generous "nor-

[19] Throughout our entire discussion of the cost of the arms race, the reader should keep in mind that credit arrangements and easy payment terms may delay the moment that cost has to be borne. But if credits may *delay* the economic impact of the arms race, they do *not suppress* that cost, which is simply shifted to the future and increased by the interests due. Furthermore, depending on the duration of the credits, actual payments may come close to new commitments after some years. In the months prior to the June 1967 war, when Egypt had all but completely exhausted its once substantial foreign exchange reserves and had to go begging for a small loan from the IMF/IBRD, it seemed that the moment of economic reckoning was fast approaching. The recent (June 1967) war may have created a new situation in that the Soviet Union may have agreed to write off old Egyptian debts. If this should be confirmed, it will surely make the Russians, who are more economy-minded than is often assumed, more careful in the future, for they should now realize that by selling large quantities of modern arms to Egypt on credit they may never "get their money back."

[20] Very few underdeveloped countries—and surely none of the Arab countries examined—have ever had or have now a problem of insufficient domestic aggregate demand; quite generally, the problem has rather been one of inadequate aggregate supply. Consequently, the Keynesian argument that increased public expenditures are needed to stimulate aggregate demand in times of recession does not apply to underdeveloped countries. In these countries, public expenditures increasing at too fast a rate can only generate inflationary pressures, which often must then be counteracted by direct controls. The case of Egypt's economy in recent years illustrates this very clearly.

[21] The complete data are presented in Table A and Table B in Appendix A. The utter and ultimate folly of it all was revealed in the Six Day War, when by Nasser's own admission 80 percent of Egypt's painfully accumulated equipment went up in smoke or was captured in the course of four days!

**TABLE XIV: The Cost of the Arms Race
Over and Above "Normal" Defense Spending** [1]

Year	Israel	Egypt [2]	Syria	Iraq	Jordan	Saudi Arabia
	Million constant-value dollars[3]					
1955	27.6	80.1	9.4	24.6	23.2	...
1956	113.4	111.8	15.8	34.4	28.9	...
1957	61.6	74.7	15.1	40.9	31.3	...
1958	60.7	52.8	59.5	38.9	34.6	...
1959	77.9	65.3	62.5	49.6	43.5	59.6
1960	78.3	82.4	44.4	63.3	39.2	45.3
1961	78.5	102.8	39.8	65.2	36.1	35.1
1962	99.9	138.9	46.8	67.2	37.9	39.0
1963	127.7	232.2	60.2	99.7	40.2	59.0
1964	171.0	325.6	75.8	125.4	38.5	81.7
1965	204.9	...	73.8	158.2	35.2	99.0
Total 1955–1964	896.6	1,266.6	429.3	609.2	353.4	...
(Index: Israel = 100)	(100)	(141)	(48)	(68)	(39)	
Total 1959–1964	633.3	947.2	329.5	470.4	235.4	319.7
(Index: Israel = 100)	(100)	(150)	(52)	(74)	(37)	(51)

[1] No cost was computed in the case of Lebanon and Kuwait, these two countries having spent less or only slightly more than 4 percent of their GNP on defense.

[2] For purpose of comparability, data for Egypt were converted to a calendar-year basis.

[3] Million constant-value dollars = million 1962 dollars

Sources and comments: See Appendix A.

mal" rate of defense spending for countries not involved in galloping arms races. Calculating the difference, making the necessary adjustments to allow for inflation, and converting the various currencies into constant 1962 dollars, we arrive at the figures of Table XIV. The vast amounts of "superfluous" expenditures involved speak for themselves.

(f) The most interesting and ultimately the most revealing question one could ask about the economic cost of the arms race is: What would have been the rate of growth of each country's economy if the *extra* amounts spent on defense because of the arms race had instead been integrally put into investment? What, in other words, is the *maximum* foregone growth? An adequate answer to this question could be attempted only by an elaborate econometric model for each country's economy—an undertaking well beyond the scope of this book. However, some rough calculations (described in Appendix A) suggest that the arms race caused the average 1955–1965 *per capita* growth rate of GNP to be cut by no less than 30 percent in the case of Egypt and by some 16 percent in the case of Israel (3.6 percent instead of 4.67 percent for Egypt and 6.1 percent instead of 7 percent for Israel). These, it must be kept in mind, are compound rates, so that a 30 percent or even 16 percent difference in average *per capita* growth rate makes for a great difference in the long run. We should, incidentally, note that here too the cost of the arms race in terms of foregone growth has been considerably higher for Egypt than for Israel.

EFFECTS ON RELATION OF FORCES

Turning now to the question of the change in the relation of forces between the Arab states and Israel as a result of the arms buildup, the data on defense expenditure suggest to us some very valuable insights. To be sure, the relative amounts of defense spending are only one variable in the equation of relative military power, which comprises among other things respective objectives, geostrategic features, strategic doctrines, a host of political, social, moral and technological factors, and even such issues as the respective costs of hardware, personnel, and overhead. Nevertheless, changes in relative amounts of defense spending constitute one important index of change in relations of forces even when the other pertinent factors too are changing; and when, as in the case at hand, most other factors have remained constant most of the time, the change in relative defense spending can be a critical index.

We shall come back to the other factors in any case, but for the moment let us just assume that they have remained equal, and that therefore relative military capacity is reflected in relative defense spending. This, of course, takes for granted the point that is clearly brought out in all our data since the 1955 arms deal that the countries involved in the arms buildup, especially Egypt and Israel, have actually allocated for defense all they actually thought they needed and could afford.

(a) With these provisions in mind, it seems clear from our data that insofar as Egypt's objective of matching or surpassing Israel all by itself implied improving or at least maintaining its competitive position vis-à-vis Israel in the realm of defense spending, then Egypt has deci-

TABLE XV: *Index of Egypt's and Israel's "Real" Defense Outlays and Percentage of GNP Spent on Defense*

Year	ISRAEL		EGYPT [2]	
	"Real" Defense Outlays [1] (million 1962 $)	Defense Outlays as percentage of GNP	"Real" Defense Outlays [1] (million) 1962 $)	Defense Outlays as percentage of GNP
1951	60.3 (100) [3]	7.8% (100) [3]	114.2 (189) [3]	4.3% (55) [3]
1952	58.6 (100)	7.1% (100)	121.8 (208)	4.8% (68)
1953	49.8 (100)	6.1% (100)	116.8 (235)	4.7% (77)
1954	64.8 (100)	6.7% (100)	129.0 (199)	5.2% (78)
1955	72.3 (100)	6.5% (100)	182.8 (253)	7.1% (109)
1956	161.9 (100)	13.4% (100)	217.6 (134)	8.2% (61)
1957	113.6 (100)	8.7% (100)	185.9 (164)	6.7% (77)
1958	116.8 (100)	8.3% (100)	170.9 (146)	5.8% (70)
1959	151.8 (100)	8.9% (100)	188.2 (124)	6.1% (69)
1960	161.1 (100)	8.6% (100)	214.3 (133)	6.5% (76)
1961	173.7 (100)	8.2% (100)	241.1 (139)	7.0% (85)
1962	218.1 (100)	8.8% (100)	285.1 (131)	7.8% (89)
1963	251.8 (100)	9.5% (100)	392.8 (160)	9.8% (103)
1964	295.4 (100)	10.7% (100)	501.4 (170)	11.6% (108)

[1] "Real" defense expenditures are the sum of all resources going to defense after price variations have been eliminated.

[2] For purpose of comparability, all figures for Egypt have been converted to a calendar-year basis.

[3] Figures in parenthesis are indices (base: Israel = 100 in each respective year).

Sources, method, and comments: See Appendix A.

sively failed. This fact is clearly brought out in Table XV, which gives
the relative real defense outlays of the two countries over a period of
14 years in both absolute amounts and percentages of GNP. The
table shows, for example, that although in 1951 Egypt was able to
spend 89 percent more on defense by exerting itself only slightly over

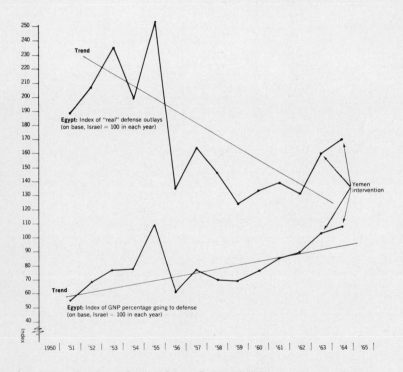

Fig. 22   Egypt/Israel: Trends of Relative Exertion and Yield (Note: Trend lines were fitted by hand.)

half as much as Israel, in 1964 it was able to spend only 70 percent
more by exerting itself 8 percent *more* than Israel, or nearly twice as
much as it did in 1951.

(b) A better way of seeing this is perhaps through a diagramatic picture of *trends* that cut across the rather large year to year variations.

Figure 22 brings out clearly in its bottom part the mounting exertions
of Egypt, understood as higher and higher percentages of GNP being
allotted to defense by comparison with Israel, while in its upper part

TABLE XVI: *Egypt's "Real" GNP as Compared to Israel's*

Year	Israel	Egypt
1950	100	449
1951	100	343
1952	100	305
1953	100	305
1954	100	257
1955	100	234
1956	100	221
1957	100	211
1958	100	208
1959	100	196
1960	100	194
1961	100	183
1962	100	176
1963	100	173
1964	100	168
1965	100	166

Note: "Real" Gross National Product (GNP) is the sum of all goods and services produced in an economy after spurious variations due to price changes have been eliminated. Consequently, real GNP can be thought of as the total resources in an economy.

Sources and method used: See Appendix A.

it points out no less clearly the smaller and smaller absolute amounts yielded by the increasing exertions in comparison with Israel. The conclusion is inescapable that insofar as military power is a function of defense expenditure, Egypt has been losing the arms race with Israel, and at a rapid rate. We have seen forecasts of this conclusion in our discussion of the comparative sacrifices imposed by the arms race.[22]

(c) The "secret" of the change in the relative power positions of Is-

[22] See Tables XII and XIII and point (f) above.

rael and Egypt as expressed in comparative defense spending is simply that Israel's economy has grown much faster than Egypt's over the last 15 years. Indeed, with an average rate of growth of better than 11 percent between 1953 and 1963, the Israeli economy experienced the fastest sustained rate of growth in the world.[23] The changing relationship of Egyptian and Israeli GNP's over the years is given in Table XVI. Again, the figures speak dramatically for themselves, and we need only add the obvious reminder that the fact that the *per capita* GNP of Israel has been from six to eight or nine times larger than Egypt's over the years has meant that identical percentages of GNP extracted for defense purposes mean much less strain for Israel than for Egypt.

(d) Because of the unique rate and duration of growth of its economy, Israel has also been able to sustain a favorable trend in the relation of forces between itself and any combination of Arab countries as measured in terms of defense spending. This improvement is clearly brought out in Table XVII, which gives indexed and absolute defense expenditures in 1962 dollars for Israel and selected combinations of Arab countries for a period of 12 years, except the combination of all the Arab countries for which we have data for only six years.

It can be seen that Israel's position in relation to any combination has improved more or less considerably over time. Columns 3 through 6, comprising the most likely or least unlikely combinations with Egypt, show a common pattern through the variation of data under them. All of them show a decline in the index relation to Israel from the high point of 1953, followed by a spurt in 1955 that falls short of the 1953 high point, then a period of nonuniform fluctuation ending uniformly in a spurt in 1963-1964 that, again, falls short of the previous spurt of 1955.

(e) With regard to future balance of forces, it is really best not to attempt any projections much as one may be tempted to do so. The number of imponderables is just too great. Let us content ourselves with pointing out that if past trends continue into the future for as little as five or ten years, their consequences would be momentous. They would signify, for example, that for Egypt to attain again the relation of forces (as expressed in defense spending) it had with Israel in 1963, it would need to unite with oil-rich Iraq by 1970. By 1975, it would take a union with Iraq and Syria to reattain the relation of forces of 1963, which Egypt considered then to be entirely out of line with its objective toward Israel.[24]

[23] See Table C in Appendix A.

[24] This assertion is based on some extensive projections that involved forecasting each country's GNP on the basis of various assumptions about future growth

TABLE XVII: Combined "Real" Defense Expenditures

Year	(1)	(2)	(3)	(4)	(5)	(6)	(7)	(8)	(9)
				Million constant-value $					
1953	49.8 (100)[1]	116.8 (235)[1]	145.9 (293)[1]	176.4 (354)[1]	208.6 (419)[1]	242.8 (488)[1]	126.0 (253)[1]	...	...
1954	64.8 (100)	129.0 (199)	160.5 (248)	194.8 (301)	226.3 (349)	260.5 (402)	131.5 (203)	...	...
1955	72.3 (100)	182.8 (253)	218.7 (302)	248.3 (343)	284.2 (393)	314.4 (435)	131.6 (182)	...	...
1956	161.9 (100)	217.6 (134)	267.0 (165)	297.7 (184)	347.1 (214)	385.7 (238)	168.1 (104)	...	...
1957	113.6 (100)	185.9 (164)	235.9 (208)	272.1 (240)	322.1 (284)	363.8 (320)	177.9 (157)	...	...
1958	116.8 (100)	170.9 (146)	262.2 (224)	259.0 (222)	351.2 (301)	396.8 (340)	225.9 (193)	...	...
1959	151.8 (100)	188.2 (124)	284.3 (187)	288.4 (190)	384.5 (253)	439.9 (290)	251.7 (166)	582.6 (384)	734.4
1960	161.1 (100)	214.3 (133)	291.7 (181)	335.3 (208)	412.7 (256)	464.2 (288)	249.9 (155)	606.1 (376)	767.2
1961	173.7 (100)	241.1 (139)	316.2 (182)	369.3 (213)	444.4 (256)	496.5 (286)	255.4 (147)	636.0 (366)	809.7
1962	218.1 (100)	285.1 (131)	376.6 (173)	420.3 (193)	511.8 (235)	565.0 (259)	279.9 (128)	725.7 (333)	943.8
1963	251.8 (100)	392.8 (160)	499.3 (198)	560.2 (222)	666.7 (265)	723.3 (287)	330.5 (131)	915.5 (366)	1,167.3
1964	295.4 (100)	501.4 (170)	600.8 (203)	700.5 (237)	799.9 (271)	856.5 (290)	364.1 (123)	1,079.4 (365)	1,374.8
1965	313.6 (100)	...	...	...	...	...	391.0 (125)	...	...

[1] Figures in parentheses are indices (Israel = 100 in each year)
(1) = Israel
(2) = Egypt
(3) = Egypt + Syria
(4) = Egypt + Iraq
(5) = Egypt + Iraq + Syria
(6) = Egypt + Iraq + Syria + Jordan
(7) = Iraq + Syria + Jordan
(8) = All Arab Countries (Egypt + Iraq + Syria + Jordan + Saudi Arabia + Kuwait + Lebanon)
(9) = Middle East (Arab Countries + Israel)

Source, method, and comment: See Appendix A.

rates and then estimating future defense expenditures by taking several "representative" percentages observed in the period 1950-1966. Under most combinations of assumptions (for example, average GNP growth rate and highest defense outlays/GNP ratio observed in the past), the results summarized in the text were shown to obtain in the fairly near future.

(f) Whether or not past trends continue into the future, our analysis in this chapter should at least have reconfirmed the point we made in previous chapters that beneath the surface "sameness" of the Arab-Israeli conflict there have been critical changes in some of its most important elements and components. Our analysis should also draw the attention of students and diplomats concerned with the future of the Arab-Israeli conflict to such factors as we have discussed here. These have been neglected all too often though they provide critical leverages for understanding and handling the problem.

(g) One final point about the implications for Egypt of the drastic deterioration of its power position (as reflected in defense spending) vis-à-vis Israel. Possibly, Egypt may reach the conclusion that the arms race has been costly and futile and be prepared to accept some scheme of arms control, especially if this should appear to be imposed by the big powers. More likely, given the nature of the regime and the fateful stakes its leadership has placed on the Palestine question, it will redouble its efforts to acquire the means to stay in the race another round and another, in the hope that an extraordinary temporary conjuncture of events may yet allow it to win its ultimate objective. We have recently witnessed Egyptian efforts through summit meetings to get the oil rich Arab countries to support the military effort of the poorer ones, near to Israel. Though this effort may be called a failure by now, others of a different variety can probably be safely predicted to follow.

The Arms Buildup:
Evolution of Armed Forces

Introduction

In the previous chapter we have tried to discern the politics of threat and deterrence as manifested in the military expenditures of the Arab countries and Israel. In the present chapter we shall attempt an analysis of the same issue as manifested in the evolution of the armed forces of these countries.

The object of this second analysis is threefold. First, it is intended to convey a more concrete picture of the pattern and dynamics of the arms buildup than is provided by the study of military expenditures alone. It will dwell on the evolution of the actual instruments of threat and deterrence and the general strategic considerations that have guided that evolution in the case of each country. For, although the actions and reactions of the governments concerned are *reflected* in the patterns of military expenditure, as our analysis in the previous chapter has tried to show, the actual motivation of these governments was affected by the development of the real armed forces of the countries they considered relevant rather than by their budgetary allocations and expenditures for defense. Second, by examining the kind of force being built up, we want to acquire some notion about the kinds of armed conflict being envisaged by the parties and, perhaps too, some indications about the likely patterns of future development of their armed forces. Finally, the analysis in this chapter is designed to check the conclusions of the previous chapter with regard to the balance of forces between the main antagonists in the Arab-Israeli conflict by juxtaposing financial-economic data with information about real military inventory. To the extent that significant correlations may be discovered between the two we will not only have confirmed our analysis with regard to past trends and present situation, but we will have provided a very useful means of attempting projections for the future. For, while it is impossible to make projections of military force from present real data except for the manpower component, it is possible, though admittedly difficult, to project economic-financial data for, say, a decade or so and thus get at real military force indirectly.

Ideally, our analysis of real armed forces should refer to their development year by year and phase by phase along lines parallel to our analysis of the economic financial data. This, however, is practically impossible not only because of the lack of information about real military establishments year after year but also because the financial and real aspects are not perfectly synchronized in real life anyway. Instead, we shall proceed by examining the evolution of real armed forces in terms of some specified periods that served as landmarks in their development. Since our analysis in the previous chapter has brought out that amidst the country by country variations there have been two major general spurts in defense spending since 1950—one in 1955–1957, and the other after 1962—we shall take these dates or approximate ones as our landmarks.

Before proceeding with our analysis we should caution the reader that in speaking of real military establishments we will be dealing with material that all countries in the world seek to keep secret and are under no compulsion to reveal regularly even to the extent that they are impelled to reveal the budgetary side of them. Consequently, in looking at the data we have gathered, allowance should be made for a certain margin of error. On the other hand, one should not underestimate the degree of accuracy that can be achieved in these matters despite the efforts of each state to keep its military affairs secret. A systematic screening and collation of exclusively open material and analysis of it with close attention to its context can still yield a picture that, whatever its operational value for general staffs, can be quite adequate for the purposes of our study.

Egypt

The general strategy that has guided the development of the Egyptian armed forces in the last ten years or so came about largely as a result of the fumblings and gropings of the Egyptian governments in the preceding seven or eight years. From the time of its creation by the

British occupation authorities in the 1880's until after World War II, the modern Egyptian army had been almost exclusively intended to serve internal security purposes. Egypt's external defense was the exclusive concern of Britain in theory and practice until 1936. By virtue of the Anglo-Egyptian treaty signed that year, British and Egyptian forces were in theory to share in Egypt's external defense but in practice Britain continued subsequently to assume sole responsibility. Thus, when German-Italian troops invaded Egypt in the course of World War II, the Egyptian armed forces took no part in the fighting except for manning anti-aircraft batteries against Axis planes raiding towns and installations behind the front line.

The first external assignment of the Egyptian armed forces came in 1948, when King Faruq and his government decided lightheadedly, without adequate preparation, and at the last moment, to intervene militarily in Palestine. The humiliating defeat of the Egyptian forces at the hand of the "Zionist gangs" and the failure of a peace settlement to follow the armistice agreement that terminated the fighting introduced the objective of confronting Israel as a second task for the Egyptian armed forces in addition to the task of internal security. External defense not related to Israel remained in practice in the hands of the British, though the Egyptians assailed Britain's position in Egypt altogether.

The Revolution of 1952 did not at first basically alter this situation. But its different handling of Egyptian policy suddenly resulted in 1955 in a situation in which Egypt confronted *de facto* entirely new defense contingencies. In that year, British troops finally evacuated Egypt after 72 years of occupation, leaving its government free to make meaningful foreign policy choices that could not but have strategic implications. The Egyptian government availed itself of this freedom within that year to commit itself to "positive neutrality" in the global struggle, which translated itself regionally into active opposition to the participation of any Arab country in the Western sponsored Baghdad Pact in the name of Arab solidarity, and in the conclusion of the 1955 arms agreement with the Soviet Union. These policies opened two new "fronts" for the Egyptian armed forces, making them an important factor in the intensified inter-Arab struggles as well as confronting them with the possibility of clashes with Western powers detrimentally affected by Egypt's opposition to the Baghdad Pact and by its military cooperation with Russia. In addition, the already existing Palestine and internal "fronts" became more critical, the former as a result of the removal of the buffer of British troops in the Suez Canal base and the acquisition by Egypt of vast amounts of modern weapons from Russia,

the latter by the probably justified fears on the part of the regime of
efforts by its aroused enemies in the Arab world and the West to subvert it from within.

The transformation in the tasks that needed to be met by Egypt's
armed forces implicit in the country's new diplomatic posture was
only vaguely sensed by the Egyptian leadership in 1955-1956. It took
the Suez-Sinai War, when all four fronts—the internal, the Israeli, the
inter-Arab, and the anti-Western—were activated, to make the leadership seize clearly the over-all general strategic picture and the inter-
connections between its elements. The ultimate politico-strategic
victory of Egypt in that war, notwithstanding whatever tactical defeats it suffered in it, encouraged the Egyptian government to accept
the challenge of having to operate on four interrelated fronts in the
future and to formulate its general defense strategy accordingly.

This summary of the evolution of Egyptian defense conceptions is
reflected in the following analysis of the development of Egypt's
armed forces since the Palestine War. At about the end of that war,
the Egyptian armed forces totaled some 55,000 men, more than 90
percent of whom were accounted for by the army and the rest by the
air force and navy. This, however, was only paper strength. In fact, after straining themselves, the Egyptian authorities at the time had been
able to field in the last stages of the Palestine war not more than
18,000 men, and half of these consisted of relatively second rate reserve
and garrison battalions plus 14 companies of Saudi, Sudanese, and
other volunteers. The rest of the army was occupied in (and only fit
for) maintaining internal security and servicing the units in Palestine.
The equipment was almost entirely British, mostly of pre-World War
II vintage, with some more modern additions, British and miscellaneous. An armored unit existed, equipped with a few score, mostly light
tanks in addition to bren-carriers and armored cars.

The operational air force at the end of the Palestine War consisted
of two squadrons of Spitfires—some 30 aircraft—and one squadron of
transport and bombers. The navy was negligible.

In the next five or six years, a more or less constant effort was made
to expand, re-equip, and strengthen the armed forces. Conscription
was applied more seriously, especially after the 1952 Revolution; the
old pasha-type officers were purged and were replaced by younger
ones with more recent military education; service was made more attractive by improvement of conditions and more rapid promotions.
About 80 former Wehrmacht officers were hired to retrain and reorganize the armed forces, and considerable quantities of new modern
equipment were acquired despite the limitations of the Tripartite

Declaration, bringing the armor stock of the army to 200 tanks, mainly Sherman Mark 3's, and replenishing the air force with 80 Meteor and Vampire jet warplanes.

The most decisive step forward, however, came with the arms deal of 1955. Information about the matériel involved varies wildly, and even authors who should know most are inconsistent themselves.[1] The confusion arises in part from the fact that informants do not distinguish clearly between various deals, between equipment ordered and equipment delivered, and available and operational weapons. A careful scrutiny of the sources suggests that by October 1956, the time of the Suez War, the following equipment had been *delivered:* 530 armored vehicles, including 230 tanks, mostly T-34's, 200 armored troop carriers, 100 SU-100 self-propelled guns; 500 artillery pieces; 200 jet planes, including about 120 MIG-15 fighters, 50 IL-28 medium bombers, and 20 IL-14 transport planes; a number of naval units, including two "Skoryi" type destroyers, some 12 motor torpedo boats, probably four minesweepers. The deal included a number of submarines, too, but none had been delivered as yet by October 1956.[2]

Not all this equipment was operational by the time of the Suez-Sinai War, and much of it was lost in the course of it. Nevertheless, for the purpose of describing the process of accumulation of military capacity in real terms, it is useful to include it all in the picture of the Egyptian military establishment on the eve of Suez. This picture was then:

(1) Total mobilized strength: 100,000
(2) National Guard: 100,000[3]
(3) Army: About 88,000, organized into five divisions (1st, 2nd, 3rd, 4th, and 8th) not all complete, or 18 brigades of which ten were infantry, three armored (one of which was a training cadre), three were

[1] For example, General Dayan, in his *Sinai Diary*, p. 4, indicates that Egypt received 200 fighters, bombers, and transport planes in that deal. Further below on the same page, he indicates indirectly that it received a total of 120 fighters and bombers. On p. 80, he says that Egypt received 200 MIG-15 fighters plus 50 IL-28 bombers.

[2] Dayan, *op.cit.,* pp. 4–5; A. J. Barker, *Suez: The Seven Day War,* (London, 1964) p. 59; Jane's *All the World's Fighting Planes, 1965–66,* pp. 71–73; E. O'Ballance, *The Sinai Campaign, 1956* (London, 1959) pp. 47–48.

[3] The National Guard was a largely improvised organization composed of volunteers on a part-time basis. Its training was sketchy, on a platoon and section basis. It had very little heavy equipment and not enough small weapons for all its members. It was mobilized after July 1956, and some units were sent to Sinai for experience and training in larger formation.

anti-aircraft, one was coastal defense, and one was medium machine gun.[4] In addition, there were three frontier guard battalions of some 3,000 men.

The equipment of the army included some 430 tanks, about half of them Soviet T-34 and JS-3 models and the remainder mostly Sherman Mark 3's with some British Centurions and French AMX's. Other armored matériel comprised 100 Soviet SU-100 self-propelled guns, some 200 Archers (17-pounder guns mounted on Valentine chassis and used primarily for anti-tank defense), 200 Soviet six-wheeled armored personnel carriers, plus several hundred British bren-carriers.

The air force comprised some 6,000 to 8,000 men and about 400 planes. The planes included the following: 120 MIG-15 fighters; about 85 earlier types of jets—Furies, Vampires, and Meteors; 50 IL-28 medium bombers; some 20 Halifax and Lancaster piston-engined heavy bombers; 20 IL-14 jet transports; about 40 Dakota and Commando piston-engined transport planes; and over 65 miscellaneous piston-engined trainers and retired planes.

The navy had begun to gather strength. It included some 3,000 to 4,000 men and the following warships: four destroyers, two ex-Soviet "Skoryi" type and two ex-British "Z" class; five ex-British frigates; two ex-British corvettes; four ex-Soviet minesweepers; and 30 motor torpedo boats (12 from Italy and Britain and the rest from Russia and Yugoslavia).

A comparison between the sets of facts and figures given shows that the Egyptian armed forces had certainly come a long way in the relatively brief period between 1949-1950 and 1955-1956, and that they had particularly achieved a breakthrough in terms of quantity and quality of equipment as a result of the 1955 deal with Soviet Russia. Nevertheless, it was not these years but the following ones that were the real formative period of the Egyptian armed forces. For one thing, much of the equipment acquired in 1955-1956, including most of the fighter planes, was lost in the Suez-Sinai War. For another thing, as we have already indicated before, the development of the armed forces

[4] The basic organization of a brigade in the Egyptian army followed at that time the British pattern. An infantry brigade comprised three battalions of four rifle companies each and an HQ and support company with machine guns, heavy mortars, and carrier platoons with a flame thrower section. Training battalions were alloted to most of the infantry brigades. Each infantry brigade had a battery of field artillery and an anti-tank gun company or a squadron of mobile anti-tank guns. An established infantry division comprised three infantry brigades plus command and support units.

could not follow a systematic rational plan while the Tripartite Declaration was effective because of the restrictions on the supply of arms,
and when the opportunity of the Soviet deal came the Egyptians
rushed to take advantage of it without much regard to their capacity
to absorb all the equipment they ordered. Thus it was that more than
a year after the massive deliveries of Soviet equipment had begun the
Egyptian forces had not yet assimilated very large parts of it: Of the
120 MIG-15's in their possession, for example, only 30 were operational by the time of the Suez-Sinai War and even this much was
achieved, it seems, only by switching crews of earlier jets, so that of
the 78 Vampires and Meteors held only 27 were operational.[5] In the
meantime, the mere reception of large quantities of equipment had
alarmed Israel and led it to acquire some equipment which, though
less plentiful, confused the Egyptian calculations even more because
some of it was of superior quality and all of it could be assimilated at a
much faster rate.[6]

More important than either of these considerations, however, was
the fact that the Egyptian leadership had had prior to the 1956 war
only a rudimentary conception of the general strategy that ought to
guide the development of the armed forces aside from the general notion of buttressing the internal order and confronting Israel. A full
conception emerged only after the British evacuation, the arms deal,
the Suez War, and subsequent events connected with them.[7] This conception envisaged clearly a threefold task for the Egyptian armed
forces apart from internal security, along with some more precise notions about the war strategies they necessitated. The tasks were now
seen as: (1) confronting Israel; (2) confronting potential Western aggressors; and (3) conducting operations connected with Egypt's pan-
Arab drive.

(1) The Suez-Sinai War demonstrated to the Egyptians how their

---

[5] The estimate of 30 operational MIG's is given in Dayan's *Sinai Diary*, p. 218.
A. J. Barker, who had access to British military sources, says that more than half
of the 270 Soviet planes received were operational by October 1956 (*Suez: The
Seven Days War*, p. 60.) Ten years later, in a speech commemorating the nationalization of the Suez Canal, Nasser confirmed that at the time of the Suez War
Egypt had only 30 fliers for the Soviet planes (see *al Ahram*, July 27, 1966). This
confirms the generally held view of the high quality of Israeli intelligence.

[6] In the course of the six months preceding the Suez War, Israel received some
60 Mystères from France. Of these it was able to put 16 in the air during the
war. Contrast this with the Egyptian performance reported above.

[7] In a speech made ten years later, Nasser confirmed the notion that a strategic
"plan" crystallized only after 1956. He, too, attributed great importance to this
fact for the development of Egypt's forces (see *al Ahram*, July 27, 1966).

conflict with Israel might be linked with conflicts they might have with powers from outside the Middle East. Hitherto they had realized that an armed clash with Israel was likely to bring international intervention; now they learned as a matter of fact and not as a point of propaganda how a conflict with outside powers might bring about an Israeli intervention.[8] Along with this, they learned from the Sinai operations what they may have perceived only dimly before: the crucial importance of mobility, armor, and air power. The deployment of the Egyptian troops in Sinai pointed to a war strategy that counted on the Israeli forces' wearing themselves out in attacks on static Egyptian positions, after which the Egyptian mobile and armored units would pass to the counterattack. The relative ease with which the Israeli forces by-passed the Egyptian strongholds and threw all the Egyptian defense plans into confusion by swift deep penetrations indicated that in the future, decisions would be reached essentially by slugging matches between mobile columns of armor and infantry working in close coordination with air support. That the Israelis had dared to execute their moves only because they counted in advance on Franco-British intervention at the other end of the peninsula and in the air over all of Egypt did not alter the fact that plans resting on linear static defense proved to be not so suitable to possible contingencies as alternative ones resting on mobility.

(2) Other aspects of the Suez-Sinai War confirmed the importance of air power while crystallizing the meaning of the task of confronting an attack by some Western power. Prior to the war, the Egyptian leadership may have envisaged an armed encounter with a power such as Britain or France, but if it did so it almost certainly conceived of the task of the armed forces as not more than salvaging Egypt's honor by going down fighting. The unfolding of the Franco-British operations demonstrated that, given certain international political contexts, the armed forces, particularly the air force, might achieve much more— they might, in fact, impose enough caution and delay on the enemy to deny him the time needed to accomplish his purpose before being stopped by international pressure. Hence, success in an encounter with major outside powers appeared as a serious enough possibility to be worth planning for, and planning for along the general lines that had proved effective. This was particularly necessary since developments in the sphere of inter-Arab relations demonstrated that armed conflicts

---

[8] Nasser confessed ten years after the nationalization of the Suez Canal that he had expected a French-British attack but not an Israeli one. (See *al Ahram*, July 27, 1966.)

with outside powers were not so unlikely, even after Suez, as many have supposed.

(3) The events set in motion by the conclusion of the arms deal with Russia and the nationalization of the Suez Canal not only pitted Egypt against Israel and Western powers but also thrust Nasser into a position of leadership in the Arab world and led to Egypt's committing itself to the cause of integral Arab unity. This involved, among other things, new military implications. To be sure, the Egyptian leadership knew that integral unity could not, in the circumstances prevailing in the Middle East, be achieved by force, but it also realized that the pursuit of that goal had a military dimension that called for some particular capabilities. Egypt had to be prepared to send troops by air and sea to countries that might wish to unite with it voluntarily—as was the case with Syria in 1958–1961. It also had to be able to deploy troops in such ways as to encourage friendly political groups to make bids for power or to protect such groups already in power—as it actually did in Syria in 1957, in the Lebanese crisis of 1958, in connection with Kassem's revolution first to protect it and then to overthrow Kassem himself, in Algeria in 1963, and in Yemen in 1962.

We may note parenthetically that the use of force on a large scale in Yemen in actual warfare to promote Arab unity has been the exception that proves the rule in two ways: First, such use of force could be practiced in Yemen because it was the one Arab country that was outside the sphere of influence of any big power; second, the Egyptians had intervened not expecting any serious fighting and thinking of their action principally as a political move similar to others we cited. Once things took the course they did, they of course necessitated a very great expansion of the capability to deploy troops abroad.

Summarizing, we may say that the years after 1956 witnessed the development of the Egyptian armed forces on the basis of the following principles, derived from the experience of the first arms deal, the Suez War, and subsequent events: (1) steady long range programming to allow for the acquisition of the latest weapons and the phasing out of obsolescent matériel, instead of improvisation; (2) heavy emphasis on armor and air power to meet the requirements of fighting on the Israeli front and of imposing caution on potential Western enemies; (3) the development of greater and greater capacity to mount expeditionary operations across air and sea routes; (4) general quantitative expansion. For help in these tasks, the Egyptians relied on several hundred Soviet and East European technicians stationed in Egypt and on access to training facilities in Russia and in other East European countries. To offset somewhat the resulting great dependence on the Soviet Union, the Egyptians also attempted during this period to develop their own military industries with the help of German and other technicians hired on an individual basis.

The results of these efforts are reflected in part in the over-all picture of the Egyptian armed forces by about the middle of 1965:

(1) Total mobilizable armed forces: 195,000
(2) Total regular armed forces: 180,000
(3) National Guard and organized reserves: 50,000–70,000[9]
(4) Army: 150,000, organized into two armored divisions (one still forming at the time) of 11,200 men each; three motorized rifle divisions of 11,800 men each, six area commands for static defense forces (not all up to strength); one parachute brigade; 12 artillery regiments; various support and HQ units.

The armored and rifle divisions were reorganized on the Soviet pattern. An armored division consists of a tank regiment with 99 T-54 medium tanks, a heavy support regiment with 25 JS-3 heavy tanks and 33 SU-100 assault guns, an armored infantry regiment (that is, borne by armored personnel carriers) that includes 10 SU-100's, an artillery regiment with 24 122-mm field guns, a battalion of 12 Katyusha rocket launchers, and an anti-aircraft battalion with 34 AA cannons. A motorized rifle division includes a tank regiment with 99 T-34 medium tanks, two armored infantry regiments with ten SU-100's each, an artillery regiment with 24 122-mm field guns, and an anti-aircraft battalion with 36 AA cannons.

Tank strength included 840 medium and heavy tanks, all but 30 of them (Centurions) Soviet-made, including 400 T-34, 350 T-54, and 60 JS-3 types. Other armored matériel comprised 150 SU-100 assault guns, 20 light French AMX's, over 1,100 Soviet-made armored personnel carriers BTR-152 and BTR 40, plus several hundred other personnel vehicles assembled locally.

The air force comprised some 10,000 to 15,000 men plus 3,000 to 4,000 reservists and over 650 planes, some two-thirds of which were operational, virtually all Soviet-made. The combat formations included:

2 squadrons of TU-16 medium bombers	25–30
4 squadrons IL-28 light bombers	72
2 squadrons MIG-21 interceptors	
(some with air-to-air missiles)	52

[9] It seems that part of the larger National Guard of 1956 was incorporated into the regular army and part was dismantled, leaving a smaller group remaining.

4 squadrons MIG-19 all-weather fighters	80
2 squadrons MIG-15/17, used in Yemen	50
1 squadron of converted Yak-9 trainers, in Yemen	25
AN-12, IL-14, and other transport planes	60
MI-2 helicopters	40
	404–409

In addition, there were several scores of trainers, reconnaissance and liaison aircraft, and a relatively large number of obsolete and apparently idle planes, notably MIG-15/17's.

The navy comprised some 11,000 men, including coast guards, plus reserves of 5,000. Naval units included:

6 destroyers (four ex-Soviet "Skoryi" class, two ex-British "Z" type)

3 frigates

3 corvettes

9 submarines (eight ex-Soviet "W" type, one ex-Soviet "MV" type)

6 ocean minesweepers

8 coastal minesweepers

2 inshore minesweepers

10 motor gunboats armed with sea-to-shore missiles of 10 to 15 nautical miles range (six ex-Soviet "Komar" class with two missiles; four ex-Soviet "Osa" class with four missiles)

33 motor torpedo boats and small patrol craft

19 landing craft

1 transport

2 miscellaneous

An entirely new development is the introduction of various kinds of missiles in the Egyptian arsenal. The Egyptian military industry with the help of German scientists and technicians acting as individuals was able to produce three models of ground-to-ground missiles: *al Zafir*, which carries a 1000-lb warhead 235 miles, *al Qahir*, which carries a comparable warhead 375 miles, and *al Ared*, which carries a one-ton warhead some 440 miles. The first two of these can be launched from mobile platforms, but the *al Ared* requires a static launching site. As of the end of 1965, 100 missiles were estimated to have been built, but expert opinion was agreed that the guidance system was inadequate for precision bombing while the conventional warheads, the only ones available then, made the missiles too expensive to use for saturation bombing of large populated areas. In addition to these missiles, which were operated under a separate command, the army and air force jointly operated an anti-aircraft command that had at its disposal ten batteries of Soviet SA-2 Guideline surface-to-air missiles plus 85-mm guns and a radar network. We have already mentioned that the navy's ten "Komar" and "Osa" gunboats were equipped with 28 sea-to-shore missiles of 15 to 20 miles range and that some MIG-21's were equipped with air-to-air missiles. Finally, the Egyptian air force was expected to acquire a number of Kennel air-to-surface missiles capable of being launched from TU-16 planes some 80 miles from the target. Such missiles are supposed to be good against targets in mid-sea but not very reliable when directed at land targets because of distortions caused to their guidance systems by concentrations of objects.

The preceding picture will have probably changed significantly by the time this work reaches the hands of the reader as a result of phasing out of obsolescent equipment, making more of the available equipment operational, and new acquisitions. Nevertheless, it can as it stands be very useful for the attempt to link real and financial magnitudes that will be undertaken later on. It can also, when juxtaposed with the pictures of earlier periods, give a good idea of the development of Egypt's armed forces over time. Table XVIII below attempts such a juxtaposition.

It will be understood, of course, that the table is meant to convey general trends rather than very precise relations. It would be wrong, for instance, to suppose that the Egyptian armed forces grew only threefold in 15 years, since their armament, mobility, and firepower obviously grew by much more than that as is evident from the number of armored brigades. Similarly, the quantitative changes in the number of weapons from one period to another reflect only partly the development in real strength since they do not convey the changes in the quality of the equipment that occurred through the phasing out of obsolescent and its replacement with advanced equipment. The 1955-1956 figure for tanks and assault guns, for example, includes about 50 percent Sherman tanks and Archer guns that were quite obsolete at the time whereas the figure for 1964-1965 includes none of these but relatively advanced and less obsolescent weapons. This is even more true of the figures for planes because of the much more rapid development in aircraft technology leading to a very rapid rate of obsolescence. All 30 fighters of the first period, for example, had been discarded long before the end of the second; and of the 205 fighters of

TABLE XVIII: *Evolution of Egypt's Armed Forces*

	1949–1950	1955–1956	1964–1965
Total Armed Forces	50–60,000	90–100,000	180–195,000
Regular	50,000	90,000	180,000
Mobilizable	60,000	100,000	195,000
Auxiliaries (National Guard and Reserves)	–	100,000	50–70,000
Army: Total men	45–54,000	88,000	150,000
Armored brigades (assembled or dispersed)	1	3–4	7–8
Medium and heavy tanks and assault guns	80[1]	730	1,000
Armored personnel carriers	?	200	1,100+
Air Force: Total men	2,500	6–8,000	12–15,000
Total planes	70	400	650
Combat planes	35[1]	275	300
Transport planes	10[1]	60	100
Others	25[1]	65	250
Navy: Total men	2,000[1]	3–4,000	11,000
Selected warships:			
Destroyers	–	4	6
Frigates-corvettes	2[1]	7	6
Submarines	–	–	9
MTB's, etc.	12[1]	30	43
Landing craft	–	–	19
Missiles			
Surface-to-surface	–	–	100
Surface-to-air	–	–	10 batteries
Sea-to-seashore	–	–	28
Air-to-surface	–	–	–
Air-to-air	–	–	Some MIG-21's equipped with them

[1] Estimate.

the second, only 50 were retained in the third period and even these were used only in Yemen, where there was no serious air opposition.

Israel

Israel, like Egypt, was hampered between 1950 and 1955-1956 from acquiring equipment in the quantities and of the qualities desired by the limitations imposed by the Tripartite Declaration. These limitations, however, had far less effect on the development of Israel's armed forces in those years than they had on Egypt's militiary effort because of the different structures of the defense establishments of the two countries. The Egyptian establishment rested entirely on a standing army and was therefore severely checked in its growth by the limitations on the supply of arms and equipment. The Israeli establishment, on the other hand, rested on a complex system that integrated civilian and military endeavors into a total defense scheme so that the limitations on the acquisition of arms still left ample scope for developing and perfecting the organizational machinery that underlay it.

Another advantage, not unrelated to the first, was the fact that Israel recognized from the outset the general strategy that ought to guide the development of its armed forces and geared all its efforts accordingly, thus avoiding much waste of resources. Moreover, unlike Egypt's general strategy, which had the multiple objectives of securing the home front against subversion, preparing against outside attacks, being ready to carry expeditionary operations in other Arab countries as well as confronting Israel, Israel's strategy had the advantage of having a single purpose, permitting maximum concentration of effort. This objective was, and still is, to defend the sovereignty and territorial integrity of the state against potential attack by neighboring Arab states.

Arab spokesmen are wont to raise periodically the spectre of Israeli expansionist ambitions at the expense of Arab territory in their effort to spur their peoples to making greater defense efforts. However, without questioning the sincerity of the leaders' apprehensions and without prejudice regarding future developments, the diplomatic record as well as the internal evidence derived from the development of Israel's armed forces do not support the view of an expansion-bent Israel. This does not mean that if Israel were to become involved in war with the Arab countries it would not then endeavor to capture and try to retain some enemy territory, as indeed it tried unsuccessfully in Sinai in 1956 and more successfully in 1948; it only means that there are no indications to suggest that Israel has adopted expansionism as a general strategic objective actively guiding the development of its armed forces. This conclusion is not altered by the possibility, indeed the likelihood, that Arab preparedness and international circumstances may have had much to do with Israel's confining its aspirations to maintaining its sovereignty in its present boundaries.

As a *status quo* country recognized by nearly all but the opponent Arab states, Israel has had no conflict with outside powers of a nature that might involve armed confrontation with any of them.[10] On a number of occasions, Israel's interpretation of the defense of the *status quo* affecting it to mean opposition to the entry of troops of neighboring Arab countries into Jordanian territory has involved it in political clashes with the United States and Britain; but only once, in October 1956, did such a clash threaten to lead to an armed encounter with Britain, who sought at the time to protect the movement of Iraqi troops into Jordan. On that occasion, developments in Jordan itself eventually rendered the Iraqi move irrelevant; but while the crisis lasted the Israeli authorities were particularly distressed precisely because they had not envisaged in their contingency planning any armed encounter with any Western power, indeed any non-Arab power.[11] The particular Jordanian situation apart, Israel has had no interest threatened by outside military power, nor has it entertained a conception of its interest and role in the area or elsewhere in the world that clashes with those of other powers so as to suggest the need to prepare expeditionary forces for intervention overseas.

In its pursuit of the single purpose of defense against potential Arab attack, Israel confronted two basic problems, the answers to which provided the main elements of Israel's strategy generally and the principles guiding the development of its armed forces in particular. The first of these problems was the tremendous disparity in resources between it and its enemies. On the morrow of the armistice agreements, Israel's Jewish population amounted to some 750,000 while that of the five surrounding Arab countries it had fought numbered over 30 million. Egypt alone had more than 25 times Israel's Jewish population and about five times its national income. True, Israel had just defeated the combined onslaught of its enemies and had been prevented from capturing all of Palestine only by fear of British military intervention.

[10] Clearly this has changed as a result of the Six-Day War. Since the prediction in the previous paragraph came true and Israel is trying to hold on to some captured territories, and since Russia is committed to the support of some Arab countries, the possibility of conflict between Israel and the Soviet Union is one that Israeli defense planners must now take into account.

[11] See Dayan, *op.cit.*, pp. 59–60.

But it had been able to do so only by mobilizing the absolute totality of its resources for the war when its opponents had only exploited but a minimal part of their potential capacity. Clearly Israel could not go on for long tying down 10 percent of its population, more than 20 percent of its labor force, and even a higher percentage of its national product to defense as it had done in the war; and the problem was, therefore, how to deter the Arab states from undertaking a "second round" while reducing its own mobilization to levels that could be endured indefinitely.

The Israelis met this problem by devising the reserve system, which has since become the hallmark of their armed forces. The essence of the system was the injection of a dual military-civilian purpose into almost every collective activity supported by public authorities or normally regulated by them; but the chief feature of it was the method of organizing manpower for defense and civilian pursuits. Starting with the 60,000 to 70,000 men and women who had been mobilized for the 1948 war and continuing with recruits conscripted since, people were not so much discharged after completing their military service as they were given leaves of absence from the armed forces. For the men were put in reserve units and had to return to active duty for at least one month a year until age 49 while the women were in principle liable to the same kind of duty after regular service until age 39 and in practice were called back until they married. A relatively small cadre of "permanent" (regular) officers and NCO's served to maintain the frames of the units, man the professional and technical services, and train the annual recruits. Frequent call up exercises and various devices developed the process of mobilization of the reserves into a fine art over the years, so that in 1956 it was possible to mobilize some 100,000 reserves in the course of 72 hours.

The success of this Israeli response was made possible by two sets of factors. After 1948, during the dangerous period of transition from total mobilization to an intricate permanent defense system that existed only as blueprint, Israel needed a period of respite free from the likelihood of attack. The timidity of the Arab states after their recent defeat, the political disarray within and among them largely caused by their failure in Palestine, the preoccupation of Egypt with its problem with Britain, the "guarantee" of the territorial status quo and the rationing of arms supply provided by the Tripartite Declaration—all these factors combined with the armistice agreements to give Israel five precious years in which it was able to build and perfect the machinery of its defense system before the danger of war became real. However, the entire effort would have probably been of not much

avail if the relationship of basic resources between Israel and its enemies had remained the same as in 1948-1949, because in that case a
marginal effort by Egypt alone would have sufficed to offset the total
effort of Israel. It was only the very rapid growth of Israel's population and economy during the respite period and after it that made it
possible for the ingenuity of the defense system to compensate for the
vast remaining gap.

The second basic problem that confronted the Israeli defense planners was due to the size and topography of the country and the shape
of its frontiers. Without entering into the details at this juncture we
should point out that the smallness of the country leaves little or no
room for strategic retreat and maneuver while the relatively very long
and mostly unobstructed frontline rules out any strategy based primarily on static defense. This is particularly true of the frontline with
Jordan's West Bank, which provides excellent mountainous terrain for
the concentration of enemy forces for attack and several points from
which they can sally to cut up Israel, especially where the Israeli territory forms a long narrow waist 10 to 17 miles in width. Even without
leaving their convenient defensive positions in the hills, enemy forces
could disrupt with massive use of long range artillery all movement
along the Israeli strip between the two main centers of Israeli life in
the north and the south and could hit most of Israel's airfields. This
difficult position is mitigated somewhat by the fact that Jordan's basic
military capacity is not sufficient to permit it to make full use of the
advantages offered by the territory under its control and that Egypt,
the strongest opponent of Israel, is separated from Jordan. Nevertheless, the danger of a forcible junction between the two across the
sparsely settled Negev had to be taken into account as well as the
possibility of Iraqi and Syrian troops moving across contiguous frontiers to reinforce Jordan and operate from its bulge.

To meet this whole problem the Israelis adopted a general strategy
involving a mixture of defense and offense that dovetailed with the essential character of the reserve system. The principal element of the
strategy was that, since retreat and maneuver on Israeli soil were almost impossible, the Israeli forces should be equipped and prepared to
take the offensive and carry the war into enemy territory even before
he moves, if intelligence and political circumstances permit, or as soon
as possible otherwise. To allow the concentration of the striking force
necessary for such strategy, local and regional static defense were entrusted mainly to a network of hedgehog settlements manned by their
year-round inhabitants, to be supported in wartime by army units
composed of elderly reserves and equipped with heavier and technical

weapons not available to the settlers. These settlements were meant to absorb the first shock of enemy attack, slow him down, wear him out, and compel him to disperse his forces. The hard core of the armed forces would thus be free of static defensive duties, have time to mobilize, and muster for counterattack at the proper time.[12] To provide against the eventuality of the country being cut up, three "Front Commands" were set up and provided with a degree of autonomy and means of self-support to permit them to carry on the war until the restoration of contact. The same principle was extended where appropriate to smaller areas going down sometimes to the level of a single village, where such is found in a position where it might be isolated. This general strategy, adopted immediately after the end of the 1948 war, has been retained ever since with modifications in particulars to meet developments in the enemy camp and at home. The escalation in the quality and quantity of motorized and armored equipment capable of off-the-road movement at the disposal of the enemy, for example, by increasing the danger of rapid breakthrough and junction between Egyptian and Jordanian and other forces, put even greater emphasis on the imperative of anticipatory attack or counteroffensive by means of mobile armored columns. The enhanced importance of speed and mobility in turn put a premium on air power and control of the skies while making an anticipatory strike against enemy airfields almost the only way to protect one's own essential air force.

Because of greater secretiveness and because of the integration of civilian with military endeavors especially in connection with local and regional defense, it is much more difficult to obtain data about Israel's defense forces and to assess their significance than in the case of Egypt. This was particularly true of the early years of Israel's existence, before Arab and other intelligence became sufficiently organized and interested to learn and let the world know the summary facts about Israel's forces. Consequently, the data presented here about the 1956 and 1965 periods should be read with caution, while the data about 1950, scant as it is, should be viewed as not more than a hopefully intelligent guess.

As of 1949-1950, the total strength of Israel's armed forces consisted of a standing army (regular cadres and conscripts) of some 30,000, plus recently discharged but as yet not-so-quickly-mobilizable reserves of some 50,000. Some 90 percent of the total—less in the standing army

---

[12] For an example of how this system worked in the Six Day War, see the description of the war on the Syrian front.

and more in the reserves—belonged to the army, the rest to the air force and navy. The army was organized into ten brigades, probably all but three or four of them only skeletal and designed to be brought to full strength in case of mobilization. One of the brigades was armored according to the standards of the antagonists at that time. The equipment of all the armed forces was very mixed, with a heavy dosage of Czech weapons. Armored equipment comprised some 40 to 50 medium tanks plus another 100 light tanks and armored cars of miscellaneous weights and makes and some 200 armored personnel carriers. The air force included some 2,000 to 3,000 men with 40 to 50 planes, mostly worn-out Spitfires, Mosquitoes, Harvards, and similar type and generation planes, plus a few B-17's, and some Commando and Dakota transports. The navy was still embryonic, and its equipment was of negligible proportions.

As we have already indicated before, the next five years or so were the period in which the Israeli defense establishment was formed and its character became fixed. During these years, Israel also managed to acquire substantial amounts of relatively modern equipment, including some 200 tanks and 200 planes, of which 50 were jets. These acquisitions allowed it to match or surpass Egypt until the latter's deal with Russia. The deal created an abrupt potential imbalance and precipitated a frantic effort on Israel's part to acquire matching equipment. Israel eventually succeeded in its endeavor, but much of the equipment it was able to obtain arrived only within weeks or days before the start of the Sinai-Suez War, too late to permit its full utilization. Thus, a supplementary order of 100 super-Sherman tanks, 200 personnel carriers, 20 tank transports, and 300 four-wheel drive trucks was *approved* by the French General Staff only as late as October 3, some three weeks before the start of mobilization in Israel.[13] During the six months before the campaign, Israel received from France five squadrons of Mystère jet fighters, probably some 60 planes.[14] Of these the Israelis could fly only 16 during the war and probably relied on French fliers to operate 20 more.[15] At any rate, it is clear that the picture of

[13] Dayan, *op.cit.*, pp. 5, 30.

[14] In his memoirs, Eisenhower gives a figure of 60 Mystères based on information obtained from high-altitude reconnaissance planes. See his *Waging Peace* (New York, 1965), p. 677.

[15] This is based on textual analysis of Dayan's diary. In Appendix 4, Dayan lists for the Israeli air force only 16 operational Mystères; but on p. 80 he says that the Israelis could "put into action in Sinai" five jet squadrons including 37 Mystères. The explanation of this discrepancy may well be that the rumors which circulated at the time that French fliers operated from Israel were true.

Israel's armed forces during the Sinài-Suez War presented below, which is based on information that has transpired in connection with that war, does not represent Israel's total capacity, though it is not very far from it.

The total size of the standing armed forces in 1956 was 50,000 to 55,000. A mobilization that included men in "essential" occupations but was selective with regard to men in "urgent" ones and that was only partial regarding women and the elderly brought in an additional 100,000 for a total of about 150,000. To these might be added some 20,000 settlers alerted to help man local and regional defenses. This would suggest that a *complete* mobilization of all usable men and women could have brought up the total defense forces to some 200,000, in any case considerably less than the often quoted figure of 250,000.

The standing army comprising about 45,000 seems to have provided the frames for 16 first line brigades. This at least was the number of first line brigades available after mobilization in addition to an equal number of battalions. It is very likely that most of the sixteen battalions represented each a "paper brigade" that was left under established strength by incomplete mobilization and by the annexation of battalions belonging to them to some of the 16 brigades in order to reinforce them. The total number of battalions mobilized was 73 in addition to some 24 batteries of artillery and heavy mortars, which would make a total of some 26 somewhat understrength brigades.

Of the 73 battalions, three constituted an elite paratroop-infantry brigade and eight were armored—six of them being constituted, together with motorized infantry battalions, into three armored brigades. Armored equipment available comprised some 300 medium tanks, mostly Shermans and super-Shermans, about 100 French AMX light tanks, some 60 self-propelled guns, and maybe 400 to 500 semiarmored half-track personnel carriers, half of them new and the rest in worn-out condition.

The mobilized Israeli air force comprised some 5,000 to 6,000 men and 200 planes. Half the planes were jet, including 60 Mystères, 25 Ouragans, and 25 Meteors, and the other half was composed of 20 Dakotas and Nord transports and a miscellany of Mustangs, Mosquitoes, Harvards, B-17's, and the like. About three-quarters of these planes were operational during the Sinai War.

The mobilized Israeli navy comprised 2,000 to 3,000 men and two destroyers, nine MTB's, two landing craft, and a number of coastal patrol vessels.

It can be seen from a comparison between Egypt and Israel that Egypt at this point had considerably more modern heavy equipment for a mobilizable force that was considerably smaller than Israel's. We shall dwell later on the reasons for this paradox—of Israel, which is numerically far inferior to Egypt, being able to mobilize more manpower, and Egypt, which is technologically inferior, being able to marshal more technical equipment.[16] Right now we will only point out that in the years after Sinai, Israel applied itself systematically to improving primarily the quantity and quality of the equipment of its armed forces since the possibilities of expanding the numbers of troops was limited by the relatively small absolute increase in the size of the population after all the available human resources had been tapped and organized. The air force and the armored corps in particular were the subject of constant attention intended to enhance mobility and striking power.

As of the middle of 1965, the standing armed forces were 70,000 and the promptly mobilizable reserves were estimated at about 200,000 —a relatively small increase over the 1956 numbers but probably comprising less women and elderly people. The organization and equipment, however, were changed considerably.

The standing army comprised 50,000 troops. These constituted several full-strength brigades, including one armored and one elite paratroop/infantry, and maintained the frames and stiffening elements for the reserve units. Total mobilization could produce some 23 first line brigades, nine of them armored and three elite paratroop/infantry, plus some 15 "second line" brigades or brigade-equivalents. All this was in addition to artillery, of which some ten brigades could be mustered.

The equipment of the army was greatly improved especially in armor. This included then some 700 tanks plus at least 200 on order (delivered after mid-1965), one-third of them M-48 Pattons, and the rest M-4 Shermans with 105-mm guns, Centurions, and AMX-13; and some 150 self-propelled guns and about 700 to 800 armored personnel carriers. Anti-tank equipment included large numbers of SS-10 and SS-11 missiles.

The air force numbered some 8,000 men plus a promptly mobilizable reserve of 5,000 to 6,000 with about 450 to 500 aircraft plus 50 to 100 on order. Combat formations included:

[16] See p. 261 ff.

3 squadrons of Mirage IIIC fighters (some with Matra air-to-air missiles)	72 planes
1 squadron Super-Mystère interceptor/ ground attack	24
3 squadrons Mystère IVA fighter-bombers	72
2 squadrons Ouragan fighter-bombers	55
1 squadron Vautour tactical bomber/ reconnaissance	24
2 squadrons Noratlas, Stratocruiser, and C-47 transports	40
1 squadron helicopters S.58 and Alouettes	20

In addition, there were some 60 Fouga Magister jet trainers that could be used in a strike role, and miscellaneous communication and transport planes. On order were 48 A-4 Skyhawk light bombers and an unknown number of Super Frelon helicopters capable of carrying 40 men fully equipped over 600 miles at 150 m.p.h.

The navy acquired some important equipment after the Sinai War but remained on the whole quantitatively "underdeveloped" by comparison with other branches of the armed forces and with the enemy's quantitative naval strength. This seems surprising on first sight since the sea is Israel's only avenue to the world, but the Israelis believe that a war with the Arabs would not last long enough to make blockade and counterblockade action very relevant. Furthermore, Israel's needs are different from those of Egypt, which fears outside power attack from the sea and can maintain contact with Arab countries to the east only by sea. Obviously this does not mean that Israel could not profitably use a strong naval capacity but only that Israel could afford to assign to the navy a lower order of priority in the allocation of defense resources.

As of 1965 the navy comprised 3,000 men plus 2,000 to 3,000 promptly mobilizable reserves with the following vessels:

2 destroyers, ex-British "Z" class
1 frigate, ex-Egyptian "Hunt" class (captured in 1956)
4 submarines—two ex-British "S" class and
    two ex-British "T" class
24 MTB's
24 armed motor boats
x landing craft

Israel is known to be working on missile development, but little has come to light about its achievement in this field. On July 5, 1961, Israel launched the *Shavit II* "meteorological" rocket, but nothing more has been heard since on the subject except that the Israelis were co-operating with some "private" French firms in developing short-range missiles. These crumbs of information, Israel's advanced technical know-how, and the fact that the country has a relatively advanced nuclear establishment should lead one to anticipate important developments in that sphere. Israel has acquired a battalion of Hawk ground-to-air missiles from the United States. Some of its Mirage aircraft are equipped with air-to-air missiles. Israel has no sea-to-sea/shore missiles and is not likely to acquire any in the near future.

The over-all development of Israel's armed forces from 1950 through 1965 is reflected in a summary way in Table XIX.

As we have observed in connection with Egypt, it should be kept in mind that the quantitative expansion expressed in the table reflects only part of the development of Israel's armed forces since later acquisitions were not simply added on to earlier equipment but replaced it altogether with more modern and powerful weapons.

Syria

Information about the armed forces of Syria and of other Arab countries is much more scanty than information about Egypt or Israel. This is not because of more effective secrecy measures on the part of these countries but because their armed forces, being of marginal relevance to most of the issues that have preoccupied students and observers of the area, were not given the sustained attention that the forces of Egypt and Israel received. Nevertheless, the little information we have been able to glean suffices for the purposes of this study.

Although Syria's defense effort as expressed in military expenditure has been as strenuous as that of most countries of the area, its general strategy has been the least coherent and consistent. The reason for this is most probably the notorious political instability that has plagued the country since 1949 and has engulfed the armed forces themselves, thus preventing the successive defense chiefs from developing a continuous systematic policy suited to the realities of Syria's position. Ultimately, the incoherence and inconsistency appear to be due to a wide disparity between the broad objectives of the Syrians and their actual or potential capacity and the consequent disconnection between policies and goals.

The broad objectives more or less vaguely entertained by Syrians generally since the early years of independence have been as radical as can be. They have included the urge to crush Israel, the desire to re-

TABLE XIX: *Evolution of Israel's Armed Forces*

	1949–1950	1956	1965
Total Armed Forces (standing/promptly mobilizable)	30,000/ 70,000	50,000/ 200,000	70,000/ 250,000
Army (standing/ promptly mobilizable)	25,000/ 63,000	45,000/ 190,000	60,000/ 230,000
Armored brigades (assembled or dispersed)	1.5	4	9
Medium and heavy tanks and assault guns	40	360	800–1,000
Armored personnel carriers	200	400–500	700–800
Air Force (standing/ mobilizable)	2,000/ 3,000	4,000/ 7,000	8,000/ 14,000
Total planes	67	200	500
Combat planes	40	160	250
Fouga trainers/ combat	--	--	60
Transport planes	12	20	60
Others	15	50	130
Navy (standing/ mobilizable)	1,000/ 1,500	2,000/ 4,000	3,000/ 6,000
Selected warships:			
Destroyers	–	2	2
Frigates	–	–	1
Submarines	–	–	4
MTB's	5 (?)	9	24
L.C.	–	2	?

gain the Alexandretta district that fell under Turkish sovereignty in
the thirties, the wish to annex Lebanon and Jordan in addition to Israel in order to restore "natural Syria," and the dream of forming part
of an Arab union extending ultimately from the Persian Gulf (the

"Arab Gulf" to the Syrians) to the Atlantic. To achieve these objectives, the Syrians have banked not on any commensurate resources but on their readiness, or at least what they think is their readiness, to surrender their country's sovereignty in order to promote Arab unity, which is thought as conducive to the realization of the remaining goals. In the meantime, however, the known disposition of Syria to "give itself away" has induced other Arab countries (Egypt, Iraq, Saudi Arabia) as well as big outside powers (Russia, the United States, Britain, France) to intervene in Syrian politics through the use of agents, money, intrigue, and occasional movement of troops and fleets to promote or fight competing Syrian political and military groups, and has thus made it impossible so far to achieve a minimum of national unity and political stability within Syria itself.

While government succeeded government and Syria was buffeted by conflicting currents and waves, the armed forces grew constantly, in size and equipment more than in capacity, more because there was no political force capable of checking the claims of the successive military chiefs on the country's resources than in order to meet clearly perceived tasks. For even the task of confronting Israel, which in principle commands general recognition, has been approached from the very limited perspective of seeking to score in border encounters rather than to insure the country's basic defense, much less to achieve the objective of destroying Israel. There is evidence, indeed, that the Syrian military have been aware that they cannot stand up to Israel in any open all-out encounter.[17] Yet the Syrian forces on Israel's borders have consistently provoked Israel by their extreme belligerence. All the possible explanations of this phenomenon—that the Syrians cannot resist taking advantage of the tactical superiority of their mountain positions to harass Israel, that the Damascus politicans seek to score with their own and with other Arab peoples, that the Syrian leaders count on Israel's not daring to retaliate with all-out war, or that they precisely wish to provoke Israel into an all-out war in order to force other Arab countries to join in a final showdown to liquidate Israel—betray either an extreme shortsightedness or a disposition to gamble with the security of the country, which are the opposite of what a coherent general defense strategy is meant to achieve.

[17] See, for example, the invaluable minutes of the unity talks between Egypt, Syria, and Iraq that took place in the spring of 1963 and were published by the *al Ahram* Foundation in August 1963 under the title *Mahadir Muhadathat alWihdah*. The Syrian military representatives spoke again and again—for example, p. 11, p. 68—of the "mortal danger" that loomed less than 60 miles from Damascus, and so on.

At the beginning of 1950, the Syrian armed forces amounted to some 15,000 men, but this was largely paper strength. The core of this force was the *Troupes spéciales* created by the French during their mandatory rule of the country largely from minority groups and inherited by independent Syria in 1946. Most of the officers above the rank of lieutenant had been French. The Syrian authorities had barely begun to reorganize, restaff, and expand these forces when the 1948 war broke out. Of the 8,000 troops in existence then, the only effective formation was a mechanized brigade that took a leading part in the Syrian invasion of Palestine and was stopped dead a few miles inside Israeli territory by lightly armed settlers and regulars. Subsequently the Syrians demonstrated a much more impressive defensive capacity against large-scale Israeli attacks.

After the war the effort to reform and develop the armed forces was resumed but was soon distorted by the first of the many military coups d'état that were to characterize Syrian politics ever since. These coups did not prevent the quantitative expansion of the Syrian armed forces, for this objective was shared by all the successive rulers. But they divided the army into cliques that engaged in a constant process of political intriguing and mutual purging, and submitted the acquisition of equipment and spare parts to the caprices of the changing policies of the various governments and their changing relations with the outside suppliers.

From 1950 through 1956 the Syrians were able to acquire enough equipment for an armed establishment of 45,000, including police and gendarmerie, but the equipment was very varied and much of it had come from dubious sources through dabblers in the international weapons market and lacked sufficient stocks of spares and ammunition. In any case, most of it became obsolescent the following year when the government of the time concluded a $110 million arms deal with Soviet Russia that converted the Syrian armed forces to reliance on Soviet equipment. By early 1958, when Syria joined with Egypt to form the United Arab Republic, the Syrians had already received 80 MIG-17 jets, 200 T-34 tanks and SU-100 assault guns, artillery equipment for three regiments, anti-aircraft and anti-tank guns plus infantry arms. At that time, the Syrian armed forces were broken down into an army of 35,000 organized in six brigades, all mobile, two of them armored. The gendarmerie and a desert force accounted for some 5,000 men. The air force comprised some 4,000 men with about 130 planes, including the newly received MIG's plus older Meteors and Vampires, Italian transport aircraft, training, and miscellaneous planes. Only a tiny proportion of the total number of planes was operational; a Soviet bloc advisory and training mission several hundred strong was engaged in forming the Syrian air force. The navy comprised several hundred men with a few patrol vessels and motor gunboats.

In the subsequent years of the United Arab Republic's existence, the Syrians received more Soviet equipment but much of it was diverted to Egypt, partly it seems because Egypt was having difficulties getting weapons from the Soviet Union as a consequence of a temporary political falling out over Iraq, partly because the Syrian armed forces could not absorb all of it. It is certain that two ex-Soviet "W" class submarines were thus diverted, and it is probable that 50 MIG-17's and 100 armored personnel carriers were too.

After seceding from the U.A.R. in the fall of 1961, the Syrian government concluded a new deal with the Soviet Union. Between the springs of 1962 and 1963, 40 MIG-17 fighters, several IL-14 transports and helicopters, 80 T-54 tanks, 40 SU-100 assault guns, and six minesweepers were delivered. Much more equipment was due to be delivered in 1963–1964, but the coming to power of the Ba'th party after a series of coups d'état and its persecution of Communists led to a stoppage of arms flow. After several coups d'état within the Ba'th coup d'état, deliveries were resumed in late 1964 and included MIG-21 planes, additional T-54 tanks, heavy artillery, and equipment for a combat paratroop school. In the interim period, when deliveries had been suspended, the Syrians had to cannibalize some equipment in order to get parts.

By the middle of 1965, the total Syrian armed forces had reached some 60,000 to 70,000 plus about 40,000 reserves. The gendarmerie accounted for 8,000 and the desert guard for 4,000 men.

The army comprised 50,000 men organized in two armored brigades, two motorized infantry brigades, five infantry brigades, six artillery regiments, and one paratroopers battalion. Armored equipment included about 400 tanks, of which 200 were T-34 and 150 T-54 models, plus 50 assault guns and some 200 armored personnel carriers.

The air force included 9,000 men and about 130 planes comprising:

1 squadron MIG-21F fighters with air-to-air missiles	26 planes
2 squadrons MIG-17 fighters of 24 planes each	48
Il-28 light bombers	4
IL-14 transports	6

in addition to Chipmunk, Yak-11, Yak-18, and L-29 Maya trainers and Soviet helicopters.

The navy included some 1,300 men with two ex-Soviet T-43 type minesweepers, six submarine chasers, twelve MTB's, and four landing craft.

Jordan

The development of Jordan's armed forces and the general strategy guiding it have been affected by peculiar political considerations. To begin with, Jordan, earlier Transjordan, could not afford to maintain its armed forces out of its own resources; these have always been supported by outsiders. First Britain, whose officers founded the Arab Legion and commanded it for more than two decades, provided the subsidy; then, in 1956, Egypt, Saudi Arabia, and Syria jointly undertook to replace the British subsidy after the British officers were dismissed; finally, in 1957, the United States took over the burden of providing most of the funds that maintain Jordan's forces. At the end of 1964, the Arab summit decided to contribute funds to strengthen Jordan's army, in addition to the American subsidy, but at the time of writing (summer of 1966) the whole policy of cooperative Arab military effort expressed in the summit meetings was already in serious difficulty.

The dependence of Jordan on outside financial support has meant that outsiders have largely set the pace for the development of its forces and limited its strategic choices. In recent years, for instance, the fact that the United States has been paying the bill has meant that Jordan's ruler could perhaps flirt with the offensive dreams of other Arab governments vis-à-vis Israel but in the final account could not commit himself to them seriously without forfeiting American support and putting himself in a position of total dependence on demonstrably unreliable collective Arab backing.

Another factor compelling Jordan's ruler to assume an essentially defensive orientation is the result of the strategic implications of the Jordanian West Bank. This bulge, we have already suggested, constitutes a potentially fatal threat to Israel; but precisely for this reason it is certain to be the first objective of an Israeli attack in case of a general Arab-Israeli war. Jordan by itself cannot prevent the Israelis from breaking through the flanks of the bulge and converting it into a trap for its forces while capturing it, and any attempt to strengthen it in advance by inviting other Arab forces is almost certain to precipitate an Israeli attack. Israel, it can be assumed, normally covets the bulge for strategic if for no other considerations but is inhibited from actively seeking to annex it by the presence in it of nearly one million Arabs with whom it would not know what to do, as well as by diplomatic considerations. But these inhibitions would almost certainly vanish and Israel would strive to keep that territory if it were to capture it in response to a threat developing from it. Knowledge of this entire situation, which involves a peril to Jordan's political existence, has forced its responsible leaders to resign themselves ultimately to the objective of maintaining the *status quo.* The lack of a sound offensive alternative has in turn made the dependence on United States financial support, with its implicit restrictions on Jordan's action, more palatable than it might have been otherwise, since the restrictions ultimately applied to what Jordan could not do anyway. Even the more intransigent Arab nationalists within and outside Jordan seem to have come to understand this, much as they find it galling.[18]

At the outset of the Palestine war of 1948, Jordan's (then Transjordan) Arab Legion was the most effective force involved in the fighting. Excellently drilled and ably commanded by British officers, it was then a model of the level of effectiveness that could be achieved with Arab soldiers through careful training and organization. Its most severe limitation was its size: It numbered then about 6,000 men with no reserves; and the whole population of Transjordan—300,000 at the time—was too small and poor to permit rapid expansion. The Legion was organized into a motorized brigade of three battalions and 17 independent infantry companies each about 200 strong. The equipment was all British and included a few score armored cars but no tanks. There was no air force and no navy.

The quality of the Legion enabled Transjordan to come out of the war undefeated and with an addition of one third of Palestine's territory and 800,000 Palestinians, half of them refugees. But by the time Jordan concluded an armistice agreement with Israel in 1949, it was already clear that it could not defend its gains or even its original territory with its own forces alone or with Arab support, and had to rely on its mutual defense treaty with Britain and on general diplomacy for that purpose. For though the Legion had been doubled in size, its responsibilities had overtaken its growth because of the much more rap-

---

[18] Need we point out that our reasoning was shown by the events to be correct in every respect, except the ultimate result? There is a lesson to be learned here regarding the limitations of our game-theory type of analysis: really unforeseeable factors such as a slight delay may alter the terms of the game. Jordan would have probably stayed out of the war altogether had Israel immediately responded to the closing of the Gulf of Aqaba with war. The delay in Israel's response allowed a buildup of such pressure in the Arab world and at home that King Hussein was placed in the position of being damned if he didn't and damned if he did; and since doing was at least more honorable, he did.

id increase in Israel's military strength, the prolongation of the frontiers, and the hostility of numerous elements of the Palestine population to the regime.

These factors determined the development of Jordan's armed forces in the course of the following seven years, until the dismissal of the British officers and the subsequent termination of the Anglo-Jordanian defense treaty in 1956-1957. Because of the political unreliability of the Palestinians, they were not admitted in any large numbers into the Arab Legion proper but were organized instead into a National Guard with static local and regional defense tasks. The idea was that, whatever their feelings toward the regime, the Guardsmen could be relied upon to fight for the protection of their immediate homes and lives. The Legion itself was not greatly expanded numerically but was reorganized and re-equipped to serve as a mobile strike force with great firepower. Its relatively small size betrayed the fundamentally defensive orientation of the whole system. The Legion was not intended to initiate offensive action against Israel but was meant to come to the support of the National Guard in case of Israeli raids, and, in case of an Israeli offensive, to launch counteroffensive actions designed to delay the Israeli advance sufficiently to permit British forces to come to the rescue under the terms of the treaty.

By the time of the Suez-Sinai War, the Jordanian armed forces consisted of the following:

The Arab Legion, now called the Arab Army even in translation (in Arabic it was always called the Arab Army), comprised some 14,000 men organized into four motorized infantry brigades and a small armored brigade equipped with Charioteer tanks and armored cars. Total armored equipment included probably some 40 of the former and 150 of the latter in addition to armored personnel carriers.

The National Guard included about 30,000 men equipped with small arms only. About one-third of the men were fully mobilized and the rest were used on a part-time basis.

An air force was begun and comprised less than 1,000 men with 20 Hunters and Vampires (one squadron) plus miscellaneous trainers and communication planes.

There was no navy to speak of.

The crisis of 1956-1957, when internal pressures drove the King to terminate Jordan's cooperation with Britain and when the army was shaken by the sudden removal of British officers and by political intrigues among its native staff, threatened to undermine Jordan's entire defense system and bring down the whole regime. Eventually, after a royal coup d'état supported by the United States, a short-lived union

with Iraq, and another crisis caused by the 1958 revolution in the latter country that was stemmed by the arrival in Jordan of British paratroopers, the situation was more or less stabilized along lines similar to
the pre-crisis period. This time, however, it was the United States that
provided the outside support in the form of an annual subsidy and an
informal guarantee of Jordan's security and sovereignty.

From 1958 through 1965, Jordan developed its armed forces mainly
in order to permit them to continue to follow the general strategy of
the pre-crisis period in the face of the constantly rising level of forces
of Israel and other Arab countries. After the Arab summit meeting in
1964, it appeared for a moment that Jordan was beginning to aspire to
a more ambitious military role. With King Hussein's assent and participation, the summit meeting decided to provide funds for doubling
Jordan's strength in the course of a number of years in order to permit
it at least to stem with its own forces alone an Israeli attack on its
front while other Arab forces attempted the destruction of Israel's
forces on other fronts. But at the time of writing (summer of 1966) it
had already become clear that Jordan did not intend to comply with
the spirit of the summit resolution to the extent of jeopardizing American support, though it was able to use the interlude of summitry politics in order to press the United States to provide it with more equipment than this country liked or thought necessary to do.

By the middle of 1965, Jordan's total mobilizable strength amounted
to about 65,000 men. The regular army had 38,000 men, and there
were plans for bringing it up to 53,000. The existing forces were organized into four infantry brigades, two armored brigades, and one Royal
Guards brigade composed of the presumed most loyal elements. Arms
and equipment were by then mostly American and included 200 Patton tanks present and to be delivered, plus about 80 Centurion and
Charioteer tanks and a considerable number of Saracen and Ferret armored personnel carriers.

Iraq

The development of Iraq's armed forces has been guided by a general
strategy that has altered gradually over the years to meet changing political conditions before falling into incoherence and chaos in the wake
of the revolution of July, 1958.

From the time of the creation of the modern Iraqi state after World
War I until about the end of World War II, the Iraqi armed forces
were designed exclusively to uphold the authority of the government
internally and to keep the country together in the face of strong cen-

trifugal tendencies. In theory, internal security became the exclusive responsibility of the Iraqi government after the country became formally independent in 1932, but in practice the British were called upon on several occasions after that date to help in suppressing Kurdish uprisings. External defense was in theory the joint responsibility of independent Iraq and its British ally, but in practice it was the exclusive concern of Britain.

After the end of World War II, when the eviction of France from Syria and Lebanon, the upsurge of nationalism in the Middle East, and Britain's need to revise its relations with Middle Eastern countries combined to put the political organization of the area on the agenda, Iraq's rulers, with discreet British support, began to pursue actively policies aimed at achieving a union of the Fertile Crescent countries that implied a new role for Iraq's armed forces: They were to be ready to intervene beyond the borders to support political moves designed to promote the unity scheme. In this context Iraqi troops intervened in the Palestine war of 1948 and were alerted several times thereafter to be ready to intervene in Syria, in Jordan, and in Lebanon.

In the course of the years after 1954, the role of the Iraqi armed forces was theoretically enlarged, as Iraq became a founding member of the Baghdad Pact alongside Britain, Turkey, Iran, and Pakistan and assumed with these countries and the United States a share in regional defense against the Soviet Union. In practice Iraq could and did contribute little militarily to the Pact, and this was in effect a new formula allowing Iraq to continue relying on others for its external defense while enhancing the capacity of its armed forces to play the roles of insuring internal security and promoting the intra-Arab schemes of the Iraqi leaders by obtaining military assistance and political support from other members of the Pact and from the United States.

The overthrow of the monarchy in 1958 by a military coup and the subsequent withdrawal from the Baghdad Pact significantly altered the general strategy and conditions of Iraq's armed forces. The task of internal security became aggravated as the new regime sought to purge beneficiaries of the old and to consolidate its hold on the country. More important, the perennial Kurdish problem became particularly severe since the new government could no longer count on the cooperation of Turkey and Iran, irked by Iraq's withdrawal from the Baghdad Pact, in controlling the Kurds, who inhabit the frontier territories of all three countries. Moreover the Soviet Union, who now replaced Britain as Iraq's friendly big power, was inhibited by its past sympathy with the Kurds from assisting the Iraqi government in suppressing them as Britain used to do. As a result, the uprising that began in 1961 developed into a full-fledged but inconclusive war that has occupied half of Iraq's army and all its air force on and off to the time of writing (summer of 1966).

The regional role of the armed forces also was aggravated by the fact that the new Iraqi regime soon became alienated from both the Egyptian-Syrian enemies and the Jordanian-Saudi friends of the old, and by Kassem's rash attempt to annex Kuwait. The role of defense against outside powers that the old regime had relegated to Britain became important for the first time as the new regime pursued policies considered hostile by the former British, Iranian, and Turkish allies.

While confronting these tasks, the Iraqi army was supposed to play the leading role in administering and developing the country, and at the same time to reorganize and assimilate vast quantities of new Soviet equipment when it had been brought up on British weapons and methods for more than a generation. It is surprising under these circumstances that Kassem's rule lasted for nearly five years. The Ba'th-led coup that overthrew him achieved some alleviation in the regional sphere by renouncing the claim on Kuwait, but caused enormous damage to the armed forces by alienating the Soviet Union, who stopped the supply of arms and parts because of the Ba'thist brutal suppression of Communists and Kurds. The present government, which came to power by overthrowing the Ba'thists, appears at last to be mending things with the Kurds, with other Arab countries, and with the Soviet Union, thus giving Iraq the promise of some coherent and manageable development for the first time since 1958. Whether it will be allowed to proceed in its policies remains an open question.

In 1949–1950, the Iraqi armed forces totaled about 38,000 men, more than 90 percent of whom were in the army. The army was organized into three understrength divisions, one mountain and two motorized. The equipment was all British and included some 40 tanks and 150 armored cars. The army was so tied down to internal security tasks that a year or two before, it could spare only 1,500 troops for the initial invasion of Palestine in May 1948. Subsequently, the number of Iraqi troops in Palestine was brought up to some 6,000 to 7,000, but the Iraqi command was careful to assign them to purely defensive garrison duties in what came to be the Jordanian bulge despite the great offensive opportunities offered by the occupied terrain.

The air force may have comprised some 1,500 men with 30 or 40 machines, mostly trainers and other noncombat planes. In any case, it had hardly stirred in combat in the course of the Palestine war. The navy included a few river and coastal patrol boats.

The next eight years, up to the overthrow of the monarchy, witnessed a considerable strengthening of the armed forces made possible by a dramatic increase in oil revenues due to a revision of the royalties agreement, and by improved opportunities for acquiring equipment due to Iraq's participation in the Baghdad Pact. Special attention seems to have been paid to the air force, apparently in view of past experience when the British R.A.F. proved decisive on several occasions in suppressing Kurdish uprisings that had long successfully defied the efforts of Iraq's land forces.

By 1958, the armed forces amounted to some 63,000 men. The army included some 55,000 organized into five understrength divisions, including one armored, two mountain, and two motorized infantry. The equipment was still essentially British with some American additions, and included about 200 tanks of various types. The air force comprised some 6,000 men with about 120 planes including three squadrons of Sea Furies (32 planes), one squadron of Venoms (11 planes), one squadron of Vampires, one squadron of Hunter VI's (12 planes), four Bristol freighters, plus communication and training planes. The navy was still negligible.

The July 1958 revolution led to an upheaval in the development of Iraq's armed forces. From 1958 to 1963, the Soviet Union essentially replaced Britain in providing arms and technical military assistance and the Iraqi forces converted to Soviet military patterns while receiving enormous amounts of Soviet equipment. Three agreements allegedly worth $370 million were signed in 1958, 1960, and 1962. Then, the overthrow of the Kassem government by a Ba'th-led coup brought about a freezing of Soviet aid and the abrupt withdrawal of all East European training and advisory personnel, leaving the Iraqi forces to fend for themselves with equipment that lacked adequate parts and ammunition. And since Iraqi forces were engaged in war with the Kurdish rebels, they had to resort to massive cannibalization of equipment for parts. Britain had continued to supply Iraq with some weapons after a brief interruption in 1958, but these were only of supplementary importance and could not, of course, prevent the incredible wastage of Soviet equipment in the period between the interruption and resumption of its flow.

By the middle of 1965, after Soviet military assistance had been resumed, the Iraqi armed forces numbered over 82,000 men. The army's strength was 70,000 organized in the same five divisions (two motorized infantry, two mountain and one armored) plus what was called "Ministry of Defense Troops"—presumably a kind of regime guard against coups composed of one mechanized brigade and two mechanized guard battalions. Equipment received after 1958 included 100

T-54 and 300 T-34 and JS-3 tanks, plus 120 SU-100 assault guns and several hundred armored personnel carriers; but because of cannibalization, faulty maintenance, and lack of competent training personnel in the 1963–1964 period, less than half of this equipment was operational by mid-1965.

The wastage in the air force appears to have been even more terrible. The Kassem government is supposed to have received 140 MIG-17's; yet by mid-1965 there was only one operational squadron of them. Altogether, the air force numbered at the latter date some 10,000 men with 200 planes organized as follows:

1 interceptor squadron MIG-21's
1 ground attack squadron MIG-17's
1 interceptor squadron Hunters
1 squadron TU-16 medium bombers
1 squadron IL-28 light bombers
2 squadron Westland Mk-22 and Mi-4 helicopters
2 squadrons Antonov, Ilushin, and Dakota transports

These squadrons accounted altogether for about 100 planes. The other 100 consisted of communications and training aircraft and grounded planes.

In the 1958–1963 period, Iraq received 38 Soviet SA-2 ground-to-air missiles. One report has it that when the East bloc technicians withdrew in the wake of the Ba'th coup they took away with them the missiles' electronic guidance gear and that in the hands of the untutored Iraqis all of them turned soon into a pile of rusty junk.[19]

In mid-1965, the navy comprised about 2,000 men with three ex-Soviet "S.O.1" type submarine chasers, a dozen ex-Soviet MTB's, and six ex-Soviet armored gunboats plus small patrol boats organized for operations in the Shatt al Arab and Persian Gulf sectors.

Saudi Arabia

The information available about the armed forces of Saudi Arabia is very fragmentary and refers only to recent years, making it impossible to give a picture of their development over time as we have done with other countries. However, the scarcity of information is itself a sign that little evolution was taking place and that therefore generalizations about the Saudi forces in recent years are applicable with some modifications to earlier periods.

The armed forces of Saudi Arabia have been rather small by comparison with the amounts spent on defense. Jordan, for example, has
had a considerably larger military establishment in the last ten years
though Saudi Arabia has spent two to three times more on defense.
This situation reflects undoubtedly a certain degree of inefficiency in
defense spending in Arabia; but it is probably due more to the particular nature of the country's defense strategy. This strategy has been
concerned first and foremost with the threat of subversion from within
rather than invasion from without, and has therefore called for covert
intelligence-type operations at home and abroad as much as for open
military preparedness in the form of a visible armed establishment.

The Saudi rulers have not actively entertained offensive plans
against Israel despite their unmitigated political hostility to the Jewish
state. This is due partly to their assessment of such an endeavor as
diplomatically and militarily impracticable, partly to their desire to
avoid an armed conflict that might result in the interruption of the
flow of oil revenue on which the country depends entirely. Defensively, the Saudis are not concerned with any immediate Israeli threat beyond the possibility of skirmishes in the Gulf of Aqaba. Although this
attitude does not rule out the possibility of Saudi participation in case
of an all-out Arab military confrontation with Israel, it remains true
nonetheless that the day-to-day concern of the Saudi rulers has been
with threats and possibilities originating in inter-Arab relations rather
than in Israel.

Although the House of Saud had had a long record of hostility to the
Hashimites of Iraq and Jordan prior to 1958, fought a war with the
Imam of Yemen, clashed with the British over the Buraimi oasis, and
has been engaged in a feud with Egypt since 1958, it has had little
fear of an outright invasion from the outside since it established itself
in Arabia in the 1920's because of the immense size of its territory and
its extreme intractability. On the other hand, its checkered history and
its alliance with the Wahhabi sect, once considered heretical, going
back to the eighteenth century, have rendered it extremely sensitive to
the threat of isolation from without and subversion of the delicate network of loyalties on which the regime rests from within. Defense
against such threat required diplomatic-political and financial exertions abroad and at home more than the building of armed forces. At
least until the recent involvement with Egypt in the Yemen conflict,
armed forces were needed for three types of action: (1) for noncombat
moves in support of diplomatic-political action designed to keep a balance among the Arab countries, such as when Saudi Arabia sent troops
into Jordan and Kuwait at the behest of their rulers to balance the

presence of other Arab troops; (2) to act as a deterrent against internal subversion; and (3) in order to operate at threatened or coveted border outposts.

The Yemeni conflict introduced a new element in the situation. The massive presence in that country of Egyptian troops, avowedly dedicated to the cause of Arab unity and social revolution, gravely intensified the threat of subversion in Saudi Arabia by creating a convenient base from which men and supplies could be easily channeled to support enemies of the regime, and from which troops could eventually be sent to back an initially successful coup. The Saudis countered this threat by turning it against the Egyptians in Yemen, and they were so successful at it that, without committing any troops of their own, they were able to contain 70,000 Egyptian troops and force them to go on the defensive after several years of exertion. For a moment, in the summer of 1965, it appeared as though the Egyptians were about to give up altogether and withdraw from Yemen under a formula acceptable to the Saudis; but the promise of opportunities in the South Arabian Federation opened up by Britain's declaration of its intention to withdraw from that country by 1968 contributed to inducing the Egyptians to change their plans, reform their front in Yemen, and threaten to launch an air war against Saudi centers. It thus appeared at the time of writing that the Saudi-Egyptian confrontation was to be extended to the South Arabian territory; and although the Saudi methods may be as successful in checking the Egyptians there as they have been in Yemen, they are of no avail against the threat of air strikes against Saudi territory. To face this new situation, the Saudi government launched a crash program to build an air defense system worth $500 million to be manned by foreign technicians and mercenaries.

As of mid-1965, the Saudi armed forces comprised some 55,000 men. The army numbered 50,000 troops organized into three separate bodies. The regular army comprised some 12,000 men organized into one armored brigade and one mechanized brigade. An internal security corps included a Royal Guards brigade and five infantry regiments, adding up to some 18,000. In addition, there were 20,000 tribal levies organized into 40 to 50 battalion-sized units, equipped with light arms only. Equipment of the regular army and the internal security forces included several hundred M-24 Chaffee light tanks and Staghound armored cars, and Vigilant anti-tank missiles.

The air force included some 4,000 men with 40 to 50 planes, organized into one squadron of 12 F-86 Sabre fighters, one squadron of nine B-26 Invader tactical bombers, one squadron of five C-123 Provider transports, plus communications and training planes. The crash

program to establish an air defense system already mentioned envisaged spending $140 million on a number of Lightning single seat
Mk.53 fighters, Mk.55 two-seat trainers, and Jet Provost trainers; $70
million on a radar system; $56 million on a technical and training staff
of several hundred; $100 million on Hawk surface-to-air missiles, and
$200 million on facilities, bases, installations, and the like.

The navy included about 1,000 men with three gunboats, six PT
boats, eight landing craft, two armed coastal transports, and several
patrol launches.

Yemen

Information about the Yemeni armed forces is even more fragmentary
than that on Saudi Arabia's and refers mainly to the years since the outbreak of the present civil-international war; but the little data that are
available are interesting from several points of view.

In the forties and early fifties, the Yemeni armed forces consisted, as
they had for decades before, of a more or less regularly organized royal
guard plus tribal forces bound to the ruler through the personal loyalty
ties of their chiefs. In the mid-fifties, the Imam, though ruling over one
of the most "backward" countries of the world, almost consistently
supported the policies of the revolutionary leader of Egypt in the inter-
Arab arena and in the positions he took in the struggle between East
and West. When Egypt united with Syria to form the United Arab Republic, Yemen was the only Arab country to join that union formally
in the form of a loose federal arrangement, and in that same year it
became the third Arab country after Egypt and Syria to conclude an
arms deal with the Soviet Union. The Imam's policy was motivated by
two considerations, which also guided the development of his armed
forces: One was his aspiration to take over Aden and neighboring territories occupied by the British, and the other was his desire to strength-
en his position at home in the face of opposition from "radical"
groups, many of whom found a haven and a base in Aden. Naturally, it
was the first of these two objectives of the Imam that induced the
Russians to provide him with weapons and assistance to modernize his
army, which included 30 T-34 tanks, 50 SU-100 assault guns, plus a
great deal of light infantry arms.

As things turned out, the modernization of the army made it possible for a group of officers to mount a coup d'état in 1962 that overthrew the Imam and proclaimed a progressive republican regime that
was immediately recognized and given support by the erstwhile
friends of the Imam, Egypt and the Soviet Union. But the Imam, who

miraculously survived personally, began immediately to rally tribal support in the country against the revolutionary regime and found strong backing not only from Saudi Arabia, but also from his former British enemies, who now saw the main threat to their positions in the Egyptian-supported republican regime.

This initial comedy of errors and misjudgments had its sequel in the unfolding of the resultant war. The Egyptians, who lightheartedly rushed in a small number of troops in the expectation that showing the flag would suffice to consolidate the republican regime, had not counted on the will and capacity of lightly armed tribesmen operating in a familiar cut up terrain to defy successfully a modern invading force.[20] They therefore found themselves compelled to escalate their commitment until it became a major military undertaking involving up to 70,000 troops and necessitating the mobilization of reserves and the creation of two new divisions, not to speak of the losses in men and money. At the time of writing, nearly four years had elapsed since the beginning of the Egyptian intervention, and things had settled down to a situation in which the Egyptians controlled a core area including the major towns while the royalists controlled the rest of the country with neither side in a position to bring about a decisive conclusion.

By the middle of 1965, the Yemeni forces involved in the civil war included the following:

On the republican side, some 25,000 regulars including an army of 23,000 men being trained and partly commanded by Egyptians. It constituted ten motorized rifle battalions with armored support comprising 30 T-34 tanks, 50 SU-100 assault guns, and 70 armored personnel carriers. Egyptian plans called for the formation of three motorized infantry divisions of about 35,000 men to take over the main burden of defense. An air force was being formed with some 2,000 men and some 40 aircraft, including 30 Yak trainers/fighter-bombers, plus a few IL-14 and C-47 transports, and MI-1 and MI-2 helicopters. Only a few of these planes were operational at the time. There was no navy.

---

[20] The innocent confidence of the Egyptians is reflected in a remark Abdel Nasser made to General Lu'iy al Atasi on March 9, 1963, in the course of the union negotiations between Egypt, Syria, and Iraq that were taking place then. General Atasi expressed his hope that, once an agreement on the union was reached, Syrian troops would take part in the fighting in Yemen. To this, Nasser replied: "No . . . the Yemen war is over." (*Mahadir Muhadathat al Wihdah, al Ahram* Foundation, August 1963, p. 69.) It should be pointed out, in fairness, that the Egyptians were not the only ones who miscalculated the situation. The United States recognized the republican regime shortly after its proclamation in the expectation that it would successfully establish itself if it had not done so already.

On the royalist side, "regular" troops were estimated at 30,000 divided into four "army groups," equipped mostly with rifles plus some anti-tank guns, heavy machine guns, and a few 75-mm recoilless rifles. In addition, the royalists could count on intermittent support from up to 300,000 friendly tribesmen dispersed in territory beyond enemy control. The royalists had no air force and no navy.

Kuwait

The importance of the armed forces of Kuwait is in diametrical contrast to that city state's potential importance in the economics of defense of the area. Although Kuwait's fabulous oil-derived wealth puts it in a position to make contributions that can decisively affect the economy and hence the defense capacity of even the largest and most powerful Arab state, its own real military capacity would not suffice to defend itself for one day against its potential enemies—its immediate neighbors. Kuwait's security has therefore rested ultimately on the support of Britain, who shares in its wealth, and the rivalry among Arab countries that covet its wealth, which leads them to neutralize one another. This is clearly demonstrated in the events that transpired immediately after Kuwait achieved its independence in 1962.

Prior to independence, Kuwait's defense was formally and practically Britain's responsibility. With the granting of independence, an informal agreement was concluded between Britain and the ruler of Kuwait committing Britain to come to the defense of Kuwait any time upon the ruler's request. This agreement was put to the test immediately thereafter when President Kassem of Iraq claimed Kuwait as Iraqi territory and concentrated troops on its border. The British rushed troops into Kuwait that immobilized the Iraqi forces until the Arab League formed a military contingent that took over from the British the task of confronting Iraq's threat. Eventually, after the overthrow of Kassem, the new Iraqi government recognized Kuwait's independence in return for a grant of 30 million sterling. But the Kuwaiti rulers have continued to look upon Iraq as the main source of danger to themselves and their country, especially if Iraq were to be effectively united with Egypt.

Kuwait's defense strategy, worked out in cooperation with the British, rests on two principles: (1) anticipation of trouble through extensive intelligence at home and in threatening neighboring countries in order to give sufficient warning to British intervention troops, and (2) the building of armed forces capable of imposing a sufficient delay on potential attackers to permit timely British intervention. In both instances, a time margin of less than a day is considered sufficient to bring in the first elements of British troops from nearby Bahrein. To permit maximum rapidity of movement a small contingent of British troops with a number of tanks is permanently loaded on ships operating from Bahrein, and heavy equipment for use by the intervention forces is kept in storage in Kuwait.[21]

By mid-1965, the Kuwaiti armed forces consisted of about 5,000 men. The army numbered 4,500 organized into an armored regiment with 24 Centurions, a battery of 25-pounder artillery, and several motorized battalions with Ferret and Saladin armored personnel carriers. In case of surprise attack from an Iraqi brigade permanently stationed in Basra with the help of a paratroop battalion, British sources estimate the Kuwaitis to be capable of holding on for 18 hours if they should have adequate air cover.

Kuwait had at that time an air force of some 500 to 1,000 men with 25 aircraft including four Hunter fighters, two Caribou twin-engined transport planes, six armed Jet Provost trainers, four Whirlwind helicopters, and one squadron of transport AOP planes.

Kuwait had no navy.

Lebanon

Although Lebanon is wedged in between Syria, which has irredentist claims on it, and Israel, with which it is still formally at war, its successive governments have endeavored since Lebanon's participation in the abortive Arab invasion of Palestine in 1948 to rely almost exclusively on diplomacy for external defense. Moreover, reliance on diplomacy did not, with one exception, include seeking any formal security guarantee or alliance; it has rather meant counting on the good will of outside powers and their interest in the preservation of the integrity and sovereignty of Lebanon on the one hand, and striving to avoid any policies or actions that might antagonize any of Lebanon's constantly squabbling neighbors on the other hand. This general strategy, if it can be so called, happened to be quite suitable to Lebanon's internal political need of maintaining harmony between the Muslim half of its population, which on the whole identifies itself with general Arab currents in the area, and its Christian half, which generally looks westward for its inspiration. It also paid handsome economic dividends by sparing the country the waste of military buildup and by permitting it

---

[21] This information rests in part on British staff papers that fell into the hands of the Egyptians and were published in *al Ahram*, July 11, 1965.

to pursue the role of middleman and banker to all the countries of the area regardless of fluctuations in their mutual relations and in the types of internal regimes.

Sane and sound as this policy proved to be, it has not been easy to adhere to strictly. The pressure of mutually contending Arab camps on Lebanon to take a firm position with one against the other drove President Chamoun in 1958 to seek protection in a close alignment with the West, and his policy in turn contributed to the disruption of the internal political balance, the outbreak of civil war, and the intervention of American troops. Lebanon returned then to its traditional posture, but this is now being threatened again by the pressure of the Arab summit meetings of 1964-1965 on it to allow the diversion of the Jordan River sources in its territory away from Israel and to double the size of its armed forces in the next few years in connection with collective Arab plans for a confrontation with Israel. Lebanon has thus been forced to face the unpleasant dilemma of either courting trouble with Israel, getting sucked into the arms race, and ultimately becoming dependent on other Arab countries for its defense, or appearing to be indifferent about problems of crucial common concern to the Arabs and thereby risking a disruption of the internal balance at home. At the time of writing (summer of 1966), the Lebanese government had succeeded in temporarily wiggling out of the obligation to start with the Jordan diversion work; but it apparently was able to do so only by taking the first step toward increasing its armed forces by availing itself of funds put at its disposal by the summit resolutions to order 12 of the latest type fighter planes. Given the Lebanese lack of enthusiasm for military involvement, this step will probably prove to be a temporizing device without much consequence. But the possibility that it may be the beginning of the end of Lebanon's avoidance of the arms accumulation game in the Middle East should not be excluded.

In view of this background, we need not concern ourselves with giving a quantitative account of Lebanon's armed forces over the years. The following facts, referring to the middle of 1965, suffice to demonstrate that these have been maintained at a level aimed at meeting little more than internal security needs.

The total size of Lebanon's armed forces in 1965 was 11,000, plus a gendarmerie and police force of 3,000. The army consisted of 10,000 men organized into eight infantry battalions and two armored battalions equipped with 42 light French AMX-13 tanks and a few odd Shermans. The air force consisted of 600 men with some 18 aircraft including five Hunter jet fighters, three Vampire fighter-bombers/trainers, one Chipmunk primary trainer, one Dove light transport, eight Alouette

II and III helicopters. As part of the Arab summit plans to double the armed forces of Lebanon, Syria, and Jordan, Lebanon was about to acquire with summit funds 12 French Mirage-III supersonic fighters— a serious addition to the arms stocks in the area if it should materialize. The Lebanese navy comprises some 300 men with four patrol boats and one landing craft.

Summary and Conclusions

PATTERN OF ARMS ACCUMULATION

1. The analysis in this chapter illustrates in concrete terms the point made at the beginning of the previous chapter about the nature and dynamics of the accumulation of military force in the Middle East. The analysis of defense concepts and the development of the armed forces of the individual countries shows the following intricate pattern:

(a) There is a primary competition between Egypt and Israel, which drives them constantly to raise their respective level of armament.

(b) The action of each side affects in its own way other Arab countries and induces a secondary wave of arms accumulation. Israel's action exerts pressure on Syria and Jordan, its immediate neighbors, to keep developing their armed forces. This resultant effect cannot be called an arms race since Syria and Jordan could not possibly aspire each by itself (or both together) to match Israeli strength. Their accumulation of force *as far as their relation to Israel* is concerned is undertaken with a view to enhancing their military capacity in the sporadic but continuous border clashes with Israel, and in order to slow down an Israeli all-out attack sufficiently to permit external forces—international and/or Arab—to come to the rescue. In the case of Syria, there is also the notion of being able to use its armed forces as a trigger for an all-out offensive war against Israel involving Egypt and other Arab countries.

Egypt's action has a wider effect than Israel's because of its pan-Arab ambitions. The accumulation of arms by Egypt exerts pressure, in degrees that vary with the constantly shifting constellations of inter-Arab politics, on Syria, Jordan, Iraq, and Saudi Arabia to strengthen their armed forces. But here, too, the result cannot be called an arms race proper. For, quite apart from the great disparity in military resources between each of them and Egypt, none of them envisages an all-out military encounter with Egypt partly because most of Egypt's armed forces are pinned down by Israel, partly because of the lack of geographic contiguity between Egypt and these countries, and partly because the current mythology of pan-Arabism runs counter to the idea of an invasion of one Arab state by another. What is possible is military operations by a segment of the Egyptian armed forces in support of a rebellious force in one of the other states (except for Jordan where the probability of an Israeli forceful reaction complicates matters), and this constitutes the chief contingency that has impelled now one country, now another, to develop its armed forces in response to the growth of Egypt's military power. The rise in Egypt's military power increases its ability to maneuver and the size of the forces it can spare for the inter-Arab arena, which in turn provides added encouragement to potential rebel forces; consequently the governments of the four countries that consider themselves potential victims of Egyptian action are impelled to strengthen their armed forces in order to achieve the opposite effect—deter potential rebels in various ways (for example, regime guards, air force, and the like) and deny Egypt the advantage of the added margin of force. And since air force and airborne troops can be brought into action quickly and be promptly shifted by Egypt back and forth between the Arab and the Israeli arenas, the growth of Egypt's capacity in this sector induces an especially marked secondary effect on the actions of Arab governments threatened. This is very clearly evident in the recent massive effort of the Saudi government to acquire an air force and an air defense system.

(c) The secondary effects of the arms race between Egypt and Israel on some other Arab countries induce, in turn, tertiary effects among all the Arab countries. Thus Kuwait is impelled to accumulate military strength in order to provide for defense against Iraq; and Iraq, Syria, and Jordan are impelled to take into account and provide against one another in the context of their respective pan-Arab maneuvers as the shifts in governments and policies combine and divide them. Because the political patterns shift constantly and because of various limitations on the possibilities of all-out military action, the result is even more certainly not an arms race but sporadic mutual stimulation to increase military capacity.

(d) The secondary and tertiary effects of the Egyptian-Israeli arms race have a feed-back effect on that race, which acts as an accelerator to it. The feed-back effect operates on Israel directly, and on Egypt by way of its impact on Israel. As we have pointed out earlier, Israel feels impelled to strive for superiority over Egypt in order to take account of possible Arab combinations, while Egypt endeavors to achieve at least parity with Israel without having to rely on the addition of other Arab military resources.

2. Taking into account that an all-out encounter will be a war of

speed and movement, considering the effect of distance, the internal needs of the various Arab countries, and the size and nature of their respective military establishments, and allowing for more concord and cooperation among them than has been demonstrated in the past, Israel has endeavored to provide against the following maximum possible additions to Egypt's forces: in land forces, the bulk of the operational forces of neighboring Syria and Jordan. Contributions from Iraq and Saudi Arabia are not apt to amount to more than the difference between the *bulk* and *all* the operational forces of Syria and Jordan. In the air, virtually all the operational forces of all these countries, assuming careful prior undetected planning that would rob Israel of the possibility of pre-emptive moves. A reflection of this differentiation in the Israelis' estimations is seen in the disproportionate attention they paid to their air force over the last ten years relative to other branches (see Table XX, p. 254).

ANTICIPATED WAR AND LIKELY PATTERNS

1. Our analysis of the accumulation of force shows that, at least so far, the potential parties to an Arab-Israeli war envisage symmetric concepts of war.[22] Both Israel and Egypt, as well as Syria and Jordan, anticipate a brief war of movement in which armored and motorized columns and air forces are expected to be the decisive factors. There has been repeated talk on the Arab side, especially recently, of the desirability for them to switch to a war conception that envisages the attrition of the enemy by protracted guerilla warfare in a preparatory stage to be followed by a slower type war in which the Arabs would rely on massive numbers of foot soldiers, where the Arabs have an enormous potential comparative advantage, instead of counting on quantities of expensive heavy equipment, where Israel can easily compete with them.[23] But the *actions* of the Arab countries, and especially of Egypt—the most populous of them all—demonstrate that they realize that a host of circumstances make such a war impracticable as a substitute for a panzer-against-panzer war.

Leaving aside the international political factors militating against such visions, military considerations make them unprofitable. In the first place, the size of Israel and the nature of its terrain—mostly easy and with no major forests or jungles—may permit infiltration of small groups of three to five men who could undertake *fida'iyyun*-type ac-

[22] Not to be confused with war objectives, which are *not* symmetric.

[23] See for example Nasser's speech on July 26, 1966, *al Ahram*, July 27, 1966.

tions but not significant guerilla operations: They may ambush a lone army truck but not an army convoy; they may blow up minor installations but cannot storm important guarded targets; in short they can be very annoying but cannot seriously disrupt Israel's life. In the second place, Israel would retaliate against such actions by raiding across the border on land and from the air, and the raids and counterraids would quickly escalate into major war, denying the possibility of attrition action.

As for the deployment of human masses against mechanically equipped smaller forces, this can be successful only in extremely cut up terrain unsuitable to the deployment of armored and motorized forces and providing concealment and cover from planes to foot soldiers, such as North Korea, Vietnam, or Yemen (Egypt's frustrations there were probably the source of inspiration for the *talk* about men against heavy equipment). Such terrain exists in Israel to some extent only in upper Galilee and in the vicinity of Jerusalem. In the second place, a condition for the success of such strategy is that the enemy should not be in a position to invade the home base of the "massive" forces or to effectively cut off their supply lines, which is not the case with Israel's forces, who can march up to Amman and Damascus and occupy or interdict the few supply lines of Egypt in Sinai. In the third place, the Arab leaders themselves acknowledge that the "human waves strategy" involves awful losses; these could shatter the morale and disintegrate all but armies that are very well cemented by idealism and reliable political cadres, and can be borne only by states with a firmly controlled and well integrated political system. With all the proper conditions present, the masses of Soviet forces nearly collapsed before the onslaught of German motorized forces in World War II; and the Arab states are more like Tsarist Russia in World War I than the Soviet Union in World War II, and have to fear the fate of the former.

2. The kind of forces that the two sides have been building up and the nature of the equipment they have been accumulating betrays not only symmetric concepts of war but also symmetric strategies. Egypt and Israel seem to have been driving each other inexorably toward a variant of the "Pearl Harbor strategy," where most of the stakes are placed on a successful surprise air strike aimed at destroying the bulk of the enemy's air force on the ground, to be followed by a swift movement of armored and motorized columns against an enemy whose own unprotected armored columns are constantly pounded from the air and prevented from mustering for effective counteraction.

Because of the small room for strategic retreat and maneuver, the Israelis have been inclined from the very beginning to favor a strategy of pre-emptive attack. The acquisition by Egypt of large numbers of jet fighters and bombers and of large quantities of armored equipment through the first arms deal with Russia further reduced the effective room for maneuver and drove the Israelis to actually launch a pre-emptive strike in Sinai in 1956. On that occasion, the Israelis counted on the French and the British to do the job of destroying or neutralizing Egypt's air force for them and used their own air force entirely to pound Egypt's columns and give close support to their own fast-moving forces; however, the success of this kind of strategy taught the Egyptians to put less stock on static defense and to switch the main emphasis to armor, mobility, and a strong air force in rebuilding and developing their armed forces after Suez-Sinai. This development converted the "Pearl Harbor strategy" from favored type to imperative necessity for the Israelis, which in turn made it crucial for the Egyptians to anticipate the likelihood of such strike with a pre-emptive strike of their own.

An indication of this development is the mounting emphasis that the two sides have come to place on the acquisition of more and better strikeplanes on the one hand, and more and better anti-aircraft defenses to protect air bases against surprise attack, on the other hand. In this respect, it is to be expected that, with evidence of the limited effectiveness of surface-to-air missiles revealed by the fighting in Vietnam, the two sides will put greater emphasis in the future on additional measures to protect air bases against surprise attack. For Israel this would mean underground hangars, and for Egypt, the same, plus dispersal of bases. In addition, both countries would probably maintain around-the-clock air patrols, acquire more and better fighters, and effect massive concentration of anti-aircraft guns.

3. A factor that enhances the crucial importance of control of the skies and puts an added premium on a Pearl Harbor strategy is the development by both sides of large units of paratroopers and airmobile helicopter-borne troops. Mastery of the skies by Egypt can mean, for example, rapid transfers of sizeable units to the Jordanian bulge where they can exploit any number of mortal possibilities against Israel. For Israel, mastery of the skies can mean havoc operations in the vast, unguarded, and largely unprotectable rear of Egypt and other Arab countries.

4. Looking at the *types* of weapons in possession of Egypt and Israel we notice that in terms of the *quality* of conventional weapons, the arms race between these two countries has reached the peak: In the most important categories of weapons both sides are now equipped with the

latest models in existence anywhere. This means that future competition is apt to push the two parties toward escalation into the sphere of "nonconventional" weapons. In theory, of course, it is just as possible that future competition should take the form of "equipment intensification"—increasing the quantities of weapons per unit of troops—and increasing the number of units; however, without excluding some development in these directions, several reasons suggest that the emphasis will probably be more on qualitative escalation.

In the first place it is a fact that the two sides have already begun to tread in the nonconventional fields even before exhausting the qualitative possibilities that were available to them in the conventional field. Thus Egypt and Israel have engaged on rocket development programs and have taken steps toward acquiring nuclear capacity, with Egypt making more apparent headway in the former and Israel in the latter. It is only natural to expect greater efforts in that direction after the peak in the quality of conventional weapons had been reached.

In the second place, Israel seems to be coming close to the peak not only in the quality of conventional weapons but also in the quantity of forces it can mobilize. As Table XX shows, while Egypt doubled the number of its troops and increased the number of tanks and planes in its possession by some 90 percent and 60 percent, respectively, between 1956 and 1965, Israel increased the number of its troops in the same period by only 25 percent and placed much heavier emphasis on "equipment intensification" by increasing the number of tanks and planes in its possession by 150 percent and 190 percent, respectively. This certainly still leaves room for further "equipment intensification," but unless new sources of immigration open up, the prospect of the exhaustion of the potential mobilizable manpower in the face of the vast human resources available to Egypt will certainly mean that, among the resources diverted for further intensification of equipment, larger and larger shares will go for the development of nonconventional weapons.

Finally, as is demonstrated by the fact that both sides have already begun to tread in the nonconventional field, the indecisive results of the conventional arms race so far induce each side to hope that it might achieve a breakthrough in the magic sphere of nonconventional weapons that would alter the power relations decisively. The side whose conventional possibilities are nearer the limit is apt to give way to this hope more readily, but its action will set the pace for the other side even though it might still have room for conventional quantitative expansion itself. A factor contributing to this tendency is the important psychological and diplomatic advantage that might be gained from the possession, the appearance to possess, or even the appearance of having the capacity to possess nonconventional weapons beyond the reach of the opponent.

BALANCE OF FORCES

1. One of the basic premises of this study is that, given a conflict in which the parties to it constantly drive one another toward maximum exertion, the relative capacity to spend on defense (which depends on GNP and its distribution) is one of the key determinants of the balance of relative military strength. Obvious as this proposition sounds, it has nevertheless been ignored (and sometimes even contested) by the principals to the Arab-Israeli and other Middle Eastern conflicts and by outside observers.[24] It is therefore useful to start this summary discussion with a table that illustrates the general relationship between defense expenditure and real armed forces for each of several key countries at two of the landmarks used in this chapter (see Table XX).

For obvious reasons, the table does not, and could not, indicate precise relationships between the defense outlays and the real armed forces of each country at different moments. One of these reasons, already cited more than once before, is that items of equipment in the later and earlier periods are not strictly comparable in quality or cost since those of the later period are more advanced and more expensive and are not simply added to those of an earlier period but replace them in varying extents. Another reason is that the inventory of the real armed forces of a country in any given year is not entirely accounted for by the defense bill of that particular year but is the cumulative product of the defense outlays over a much longer period of time. Nevertheless, these and other reasons that could be adduced cannot gainsay the obvious *gross* correlation reflected in the table between the magnitudes of defense outlays and real armed forces.

2. The relationship between defense expenditure and real armed forces is even better reflected by comparing the relative magnitudes of both among two countries over two different periods. We know already that because of the close competition between Egypt and Israel, the quali-

---

[24] In all the vast literature on the Arab-Israeli conflict there is not a single study of the balance of forces as a function of the relative capacity to spend on defense. All discussions of balance of forces focus exclusively on military inventory or gross size of population and natural resources. This is true of discussions by the parties concerned. For example, General Y. Allon makes no reference at all to the financial question in his otherwise excellent study of Israel's defense problems, *Masakh shel Hol.* Haykal's numerous studies of the question in his *al Ahram* columns also omit the subject entirely.

TABLE XX: *Defense Expenditures and Real Armed Forces*

	Defense expenditures (million $)		Armed forces 1. Total mobilizable 2. Medium and heavy tanks and assault guns 3. Planes	
EGYPT	**1956** 258	**1965** 507 [1]	**1956** 1. 100,000 2. 530 3. 400	**1965** 195,000 1,000 650
ISRAEL	**1956** 140	**1965** 409 [1]	**1956** 1. 200,000 2. 360 [2] 3. 200	**1965** 250,000 900 580 [3]
SYRIA	**1958** 77	**1965** 130 [2] (includes first summit con-tribution)	**1958** 1. 45,000 25,000 Reserves 2. 200 3. 130	**1965** 70,000 40,000 400 160
IRAQ	**1958** 87	**1965** 200 [2]	**1958** 1. 63,000 2. 200 3. 120	**1965** 82,000 650 200
JORDAN	**1956** 36	**1965** 75 [2] (includes first summit con-tribution of $15 million)	**1956** 1. 14,000 30,000 National Guard 2. 40 150 (armored cars) 3. 20	**1965** 38,000 30,000 180 50

[1] Figures adjusted from budget to calendar years.
[2] Approximate.
[3] Includes planes on order.

ty of the equipment possessed by each in 1956 and 1965 was roughly comparable. This permits us to isolate the factor of quantity and to examine it comparatively over the two periods in its relation to defense expenditure. Doing this, we find that in 1956, Israel had 50 percent as many planes and 67 percent as many tanks as Egypt for a defense outlay that amounted to 54 percent that of Egypt. In 1965, as Israel's defense outlay attained 80 percent that of Egypt, the number of planes in its possession reached 80 percent and the number of tanks 90 percent that of Egypt. The more or less constant relationship between quantity of hardware and defense outlay over the two periods is as striking as the magnitude of the change in Israel's favor over the span of time covered.

3. The point we are trying to make here regarding the relation between defense expenditure and real military establishment would have been much stronger if we could demonstrate it also in connection with number of troops. This, however, is precluded by the nature of the Israeli armed forces. Because these rest primarily on a reserve system, changes in them may take the form of changes in the internal structure and constitution of the reserve units as well as increases in the total reserve pool. On the other hand, we may draw some added confidence on this score by comparing changes in defense outlays and changes in number of troops between Egypt and some other country over two periods. Syria seems to be a good candidate for this since it increased the number of planes and tanks in its possession by roughly the same percentage as Egypt, thus permitting us to isolate the military manpower factor. In 1958, Syria spent on defense 30 percent as much as Egypt in 1956 and had 45 percent as many troops. In 1965, it spent 25 percent as much as Egypt and had 36 percent as many troops—the ratio between defense outlay and number of troops remains virtually identical!

4. The fact, underscored in the above comparison between Egypt and Israel, that the proportions of hardware in Israel's possession in 1956 and 1965 coincided with or exceeded the percentages of its defense expenditure in relation to Egypt should help dispose of a fallacious notion that the Israelis have themselves believed and have propounded among others to the effect that Egypt gets a "better bargain" out of its defense expenditures because it can buy weapons much more cheaply from the Soviet Union. It is certainly true that Egypt paid much less than Israel for comparable pieces of heavy equipment and got much easier payment terms, but evidently the "bargain" Egypt got in the hardware component of the defense bill was more than matched by the "bargain" Israel derived from the manpower component of the bill

through its reserve system. For where virtually all of Egypt's military establishment consisted of costly standing armed forces, only one-fourth to one-third of Israel's establishment was standing forces and the rest consisted of relatively cheaply maintained reserves. And while the reserve system has probably been getting more expensive because of the more frequent and more prolonged call-ups necessitated by the increasingly more complex equipment of the armed forces, it is equally probable that Egypt has been getting less and less of a "bargain" from the Soviet Union as its acquisitions have progressed from weapons that were obsolescent for Russia to weapons currently in operation there, and as the marginal political returns expected by the Soviets from each new deal naturally diminished. The first deal, for instance, represented for the Soviets a major political breakthrough in the Middle East at a time when the Cold War was at its apogee, and they could therefore afford to give big discounts on the price of equipment in return for such ample political gains. The most recent deal, by contrast, could only serve to maintain an acquired political position in an atmosphere of relative détente and in a situation in which Egypt could not easily turn elsewhere after having invested so much in Soviet equipment. Therefore, the incentive to make financial sacrifices in pricing the equipment is much less than before.

5. It seems clear from the preceding, therefore, that the comparative size of defense outlays has been related closely to comparative magnitudes representing real military establishments. This means that the conclusions we drew from the more complete data we have on defense outlays about the direction of past trends are essentially confirmed. It also means that projections of comparative capacities to spend on defense may be taken as significant indices of the comparative real military establishments that could be built by the countries in question *if they do not come up against limitations that could obstruct their capacity to translate outlays into real military force.*

Addendum on Population and Balance of Forces

Our analysis of the relation of forces between Israel and the Arab countries has focused entirely on defense expenditure and military inventory. The conclusions we have drawn from that analysis do not tell us everything about the relative real military capabilities—the actual war-making capacities—of the antagonists because these depend on a multitude of factors besides the sheer number of troops and weapons that can be maintained at any given moment. Such factors would include training, skill, and administrative ability; leadership, morale, and relative objectives in an actual conflict situation; geographical and topographical features; types of political systems; and population resources. However, our analysis is not intended to anticipate the outcomes of possible wars but to study the politics of threat and deterrence; it is not concerned with real war-making capacities but with these capacities as they might be perceived by the parties concerned. Such perceptions have tended for a variety of reasons to abstract in greater or lesser degrees all these additional factors except population and to focus mainly on military inventory with its underlying economic-financial underpinnings and on human resources.

The reasons why the parties concerned have tended to look at things in this way are easy to understand. Some of the additional factors mentioned above, such as basic political systems, topography, and geography are taken by them as given since they are not easily altered; certainly they are overshadowed by the constant changes in military inventory. Others, such as leadership, morale, and specific objectives in a conflict situation, on the contrary, are so susceptible to fluctuation or so difficult to estimate in advance in terms of their "power equivalent" that the antagonists cannot count on them in their calculations except in a very rough way and therefore seek refuge from them in the "certainties" of military inventory. The third type of additional factors—skill, training, and administrative capacity—are also neutralized by the difficulty of assigning a "power value" to them as well as by the presumption that they can be developed by all the antagonists at least to the extent of keeping the relation of capacities between them constant.

What then of the human resources factor? How does it affect our conclusions with regard to the shifting balance of power in favor of Israel?

Briefly, the answer is that it does not vitiate our conclusions, though many observers of Middle East affairs, and even some participants in them, have thought that the relation of populations pointed to a decisive actual or potential military advantage on the side of the Arabs.

One of the most frequent miscalculations of Israeli-Arab power relations is that which simply compares numbers of population on either side or even only between Egypt and Israel and suggests that the resultant ratio of 20:1 or 12:1 or whatever it may be tells the essence of the story. Those who make this argument may not be unaware that there is a qualitative component to the factor of population, but it is implicitly or explicitly assumed that so enormous is the quantitative disparity that no matter by how much it is reduced to compensate for the qualitative difference, the remaining gap would still be enormous.

The simplest refutation of this simple argument is to point to the *fact* that after eighteen years of exertion and after at least ten years of maximum effort, Egypt still cannot field as many troops as Israel as quickly.

A more sophisticated miscalculation takes its starting point instead from the fact that Israel has always disposed of more troops than Egypt and argues that the circumstances which have made that possible so far are now changing and turning against Israel. The relevant comparison to make, it is argued, is not between total populations but between "effective populations"—a term that is only partly and implicitly defined. Hitherto Israel has disposed of more troops because such have been the relevant conditions that all its adult population was "effective," whereas in Egypt conditions were such that only a tiny proportion of the total population was effective yielding an absolute total smaller than Israel's. In recent years, however, the argument goes, the Egyptian revolution has initiated such enormous improvements in the fields of health and education and has so altered other relevant conditions as to make the future pool of "effective population" many times larger than Israel's, which has very little room for expansion. The conclusion is consequently drawn that the balance of forces, which has been in Israel's favor in the past, will inexorably and increasingly swing decisively against it in the future.[25]

The central thesis of this argument—that effective manpower was the bottleneck that prevented the Egyptian forces from growing as fast as they might have in the past and that this bottleneck is in process of being removed—would appear on the surface to be substantiated by some of the facts brought out in our own analysis in the previous chapter. We have seen there that whereas the number of Israel's troops grew by only about one-fourth between 1956 and 1965, that of Egypt doubled in the same period; and we have ourselves volunteered the comment that Israel's more limited increase was probably due to its having approached the ceiling of its mobilizable manpower. But if it is true that Israel's relatively small numerical growth was due to its having reached close to the limit of its manpower resources, it does not follow that Egypt's much larger numerical growth is due to its having

---

[25] See, for example, William R. Polk, "The Nature of Modernization—The Middle East and North Africa," in *Foreign Affairs*, October 1965. Polk is perhaps alone in presenting such an analysis explicitly, and in boldly drawing the conclusions from it. But the notion that Egypt's inability to mobilize as many troops as Israel or more is due to an insufficient pool of "effective manpower" is very widespread. See, for example, David Wood, "The Military Balance in the Middle East," Adelphi Paper number 20, Institute for Strategic Studies, London, July 1965; O'Ballance, *op.cit.*, "Conclusion."

broken previously existing limits on *its* manpower resources. For, if we observe our data more closely, we will notice that the Egyptian defense expenditures, too, doubled in the same period, and we would have to allow for the possibility that *they*, rather than the size of the pool of "effective manpower," may have been the limiting factor that was expanded in the course of the ten years under consideration. If that is the case, the implications for the future would also be quite different, since they would mean that the future growth of Egypt's forces would be limited by the increments it would be able to make to its defense expenditure.

That it was in fact defense expenditure rather than the size of the "effective manpower" pool that set the limits on the expansion of the Egyptian forces should have been clear to anyone following Egyptian affairs closely. Well before the improvements brought about by the revolution there was a considerable amount of unemployment, open and hidden, among young graduates of secondary and higher schools who could have been taken into the armed forces. The number of unemployed among the educated young people has remained high after the dramatic expansion of education by the revolution even though the prevailing law guaranteeing jobs to school graduates gives redundant employ to very many who would have otherwise been listed as unemployed.[26] Unlike what one finds in the United States, Britain, Israel, and many other countries, one does not encounter in Egypt posters or other forms of publicity urging and luring qualified people to enroll in the armed forces, even though this kind of appeal is practiced with regard to some civilian occupations. The evidence is to the contrary effect—that there are many more applicants for entering the military academies than can be taken into them, and that admission to these academies is indeed a valuable privilege granted only to those with connections or as a reward for extraordinary service, such as political activity in the youth cadres of the Arab Socialist Union.

The question may be approached on an entirely different level by comparing Egypt with Turkey and seeing how many troops it is possible to "extract" out of similar populations. In terms of total population size, the two countries are very close, approximating 30 and 31 million

---

[26] See for example the study made by the Egyptian Institute of National Planning entitled *Employment and Unemployment Among the Educated*, Cairo, the Institute, 1963, especially Table 2, p. 45. The column headings and the decimals are misplaced in this table; but with a little effort and with the help of the text and other tables they can be straightened out. The table shows that 5.5 percent of people with secondary or higher education were unemployed in 1963, despite the law *entitling* graduates to employment.

respectively in 1965. The age distribution of the two populations is also very close.[27] As far as educational qualifications go, Harbison and Myers have shown in a series of indices that, if anything, Egypt's population is more advanced than Turkey's. A "composite index" of the population enrolled in schools that they have devised gives Egypt 40.1 points as against Turkey's 27.2 points.[28] The "orientation" of students at the higher levels of education is almost identical: 23.0 percent in science and technology and 34.8 percent in the humanities, law, and arts in Turkey against 24.0 percent and 35.2 percent in the respective categories for Egypt. The figures for the "stock" of higher level manpower, reflecting earlier educational capacities, show the following: teachers at first and second levels of education, Turkey 27.1, Egypt 40.8; engineers and scientists per 10,000, Turkey 5.8, Egypt 5; physicians and dentists per 10,000, Turkey 3.5, Egypt 4.6. In all these essential relevant respects, then, Turkey and Egypt seem then to have a comparable pool of "effective manpower." As far as the competition of the civilian sector with the military in the demand for such manpower, one would expect the Turkish civilian sector to demand a larger share since the level of the Turkish economy as measured by GNP per capita is about 70 percent higher than Egypt's. Yet, in the final account, and on the basis of the same requirement of two years of military service, Turkey is able to "extract" a military establishment of over 450,000 men out of its "effective manpower" pool, twice the Egyptian number, suggesting very strongly that Egypt could do at least the same but for some *other* limiting factor.

That the other limiting factor is financial may be easily seen by referring to the military finances of the two countries. Roughly speaking, Turkey's defense expenditures in absolute amounts *out of its own resources* over the last ten years have been comparable to those of Egypt (including Soviet credits), with a tendency for them to be less in recent years.[29] The big difference, however, is that Turkey has been re-

[27] See Harbison and Myers, below.

[28] M. F. Harbison and C. A. Myers, *Education, Manpower and Economic Growth*, New York, 1964, pp. 46–47. A composite index "is simply the arithmetic total of: (1) enrollment at second level education as a percentage of the age group 15 to 19, adjusted for length of schooling, and (2) enrollment at the third level of education as a percentage of the age group, multiplied by a weight of 5."

[29] See, for example, *The Military Balance, 1966-1967* published by The Institute for Strategic Studies, London, 1966. In 1963, 1964, and 1965 Turkey is reported to have spent $351, $382, and $402 million on defense out of its own resources. During the same years, according to our somewhat different computation, Egypt spent $400, $526, and $576 million on defense.

ceiving for much longer than this period American military aid in various forms, estimated at over $130 million per annum in the last six years. It is this difference that accounts for the fact that Turkey has had a military establishment so much larger than Egypt's. It is, to put matters the other way around, the smaller defense funds at the disposal of Egypt—*not* the lack of sufficient numbers of "effective manpower"—that has held back the quantitative growth of Egypt's armed forces. It follows that the future quantitative growth of Egypt's armed forces will be limited by the amounts its future economic growth will allow it to spend on defense, unless it alters significantly the character of its armed forces.

Altering the character of the armed forces so as to be able to get a larger military establishment out of the same amount of defense funds may be accomplished *in theory* in one of two ways: (1) by cutting down the costs of manpower through the adoption of a system like Israel's that maintains a relatively small standing army and relies for the bulk of its strength on quickly mobilizable reserves kept in a high state of preparedness; (2) by cutting down the costs of equipment through the "dilution" of the units' establishment in expensive heavy items and using the funds saved to increase the number of troops. In practice, neither alternative is feasible for Egypt to any really relevant extent, given its own internal conditions and the imperatives of its confrontation with Israel.

The supreme requisite of a system based on reserves is extreme speed of mobilization, counted by the hours rather than by the days. For Egypt, this imperative is imposed by the speed of the Israeli system and by the offensive orientation of Israel's armed forces, which are certain to make any delay in Egypt's deployment of its forces fatal. The Israeli mobilization system can achieve its extraordinary speed because of two essential conditions that do not obtain in Egypt. The first is the very small size of the country and its easy internal road and communication network that makes possible the very quick assembling of forces and their immediate deployment at the close-by frontlines. In Egypt, the relatively much larger size of the country and much poorer internal communications network practically rules out speedy assembling except in the main cities. The second condition has to do with manpower and has two facets. On the surface, the system depends on extraordinary administrative capacity, including prior organization and maintenance of level of readiness through regular call ups, intricate coordination of manpower and supply, and intelligent initiative down to the level of the messenger who delivers the call up notices. Beneath the surface, the administrative capacity itself rests on an extraordinary degree of motivation on the part of all concerned that reduces shirking and mere formal compliance to marginal importance and minimizes the inevitable snags that might otherwise run the whole system aground. *This* kind of motivation—which is quite different from the kind of "effectiveness" we discussed previously—is rather scarce in Egypt, *not*, we must hasten to add, because the Egyptian as an individual is not capable of soaring to any level of motivation, but because the entire Egyptian politico-socio-cultural system is still caught in a transitional situation in which the collective prompters and supports for such orientation and behavior are rudimentary. In its earnest moments, the supreme Egyptian leadership recognizes this and considers its most fundamental task as precisely endeavoring to remedy the situation. Such a task, however, is tantamount to a thorough social reconstruction and is not something that can be accomplished in a decade or two.

The second alternative—increasing the size of the armed forces by diluting their equipment—has already been dealt with and we only need to recall the argument here. If the alternative means carrying the dilution as far as possible and shifting to a strategy of eventually trying to swamp Israel with "human waves," we have seen that such strategy is neither suitable to the Egyptian-Israeli battlefield, nor to the insufficiently integrated Egyptian armed forces and regime. If the dilution is to be partial, it would have no point at all. We have seen that the trend is in the opposite direction—that in order to protect the heavy equipment already acquired against mounting Israeli capacity for surprise attack, more rather than less emphasis on more expensive equipment and basic investments are indicated.

Our analysis so far suggests, then, that because of the limitation imposed by the economic factor, the very restricted possibility for Egypt to economize on the costs of manpower, and the futility of substituting manpower for equipment, the argument that Egypt's much larger manpower resources imply an impending shift in the balance of forces in its favor and against Israel is erroneous. While this conclusion stands as far as the argument being refuted is concerned, there are yet two aspects to the manpower question that must be considered before any firmer conclusions on the subject can be drawn. The first has to do with the Israeli side of the manpower ledger. We have said that the relatively small growth in the size of the Israeli forces in the last decade was due to its having come close to the limit of its mobilizable manpower resources. This raises the question whether the increase in the size of Egypt's forces *that is possible within the frame of the econom-*

ic limits might not yet support the thesis of a significant future shift in the balance of power in Egypt's favor.

To answer this question, let us begin by looking at the kind of numerical growth that is possible for Egypt in the next decade within the economic limits. We have seen that Egyptian economic growth in the decade between 1956–1965 made possible the doubling of its armed forces—from 100,000 to nearly 200,000. Assuming Egypt should retain the same "mixture" of manpower and equipment as in the past, we would probably be erring on the side of exaggeration if we suggest that the next decade would make possible the redoubling of the 1965 number to 400,000, including quickly mobilizable reserves. This would be an exaggerated estimate because even though GNP may grow at a somewhat faster rate in the next decade than in the last, the *acceleration* of the *rate* of defense expenditure is not at all likely to be as fast as in the past, when it nearly doubled in the course of the decade, because it has already reached such a high level. An acceleration like that of the past would leave Egypt with hardly any capital resources for economic growth. Furthermore, in the past decade, Egypt has been buying equipment in deal after deal on credits the payment of which will mostly fall due in the next decade. Finally, we should recall that even the past increase in numbers of troops was accompanied by a certain amount of "dilution" of equipment relative to Israel.

On the Israeli side, the last decade saw an increase in the number of troops by 25 percent only—from 200,000 to 250,000. A conservative estimate, and one which does not take into account any immigration, suggests that in the next decade the number of mobilizable forces can be brought up to more than 350,000 without any dilution of their present combination of ages and sexes. This appears to be a suspicious estimate since it envisages the possibility of a more rapid growth in the next decade *without* immigration than in the past decade *with* immigration; but the explanation of the mystery is simple: The years ahead will see the coming to military service age of the offspring of the massive immigration that poured into Israel immediately after its creation —682,000 in 1948–1951 and 212,000 in 1952–1957[30] Indeed, if we look at the population statistics, we see that in 1965 the pool of men and women liable to military service under the existing system—that is, of men aged 18 to 49 and women 18 to 34—amounted to 728,247. The same pool in 1975, taking into account those who will enter and those who will leave these age groups in the course of the decade, will in-

---

[30] *Statistical Abstract of Israel,* 1966, p. 92.

clude 966,542 persons. By applying the ratio of "actually mobilizable" to "total pool" that prevailed in 1965 to 1975 we get a total of about 329,000. But actually, the percentage of men in the "prime military age" of 18 to 34 in 1975 will be considerably greater than in 1965, entailing a larger percentage of mobilizable people. Whereas such men amounted to 270,000 in 1965, in 1975 they will total over 385,000. By applying the same mobilization ratio for such groups in 1975 as in 1965, we get an over-all total of more than 355,000 mobilizable persons.[31] To these will be added whatever resources future immigration might bring, which, judging from past experience, will be at the rate of 10 to 12 mobilizable persons per 100 immigrants. Finally, if necessary, the present combination of ages and sexes in the armed forces can be altered back to include more women and more older men from among the very large pool of people liable to military service.

A final aspect of the manpower question that needs to be given consideration relates to the potential contribution of other Arab countries. What effect would the addition of the military manpower resources of these countries to Egypt's resources have on the Arab-Israeli balance? It would take infinitely more labor than is justified to try to make realistic assessments of the military manpower potential of all the Arab countries in the context of the two limitations of economic capacity and availability of "effective manpower" pools, considering that our entire discussion of the manpower question has been undertaken mainly to dispel some misconceptions on the subject resting on superficial assumptions. Suffice it for our present purpose to demonstrate the very small relevance of the question by showing how little the present *relation* is altered by adding to the potential size of Egypt's troops that of two other countries with the highest projected rates of expansion. It goes without saying that the change in the *relation* would be smaller if we were to add the potential of countries with a lower projected rate of expansion.

Jordan has increased the number of its regular forces by a factor of 2.7 in the last decade. And although Jordan has a limited "effective manpower" pool, already spends over 15 percent of its GNP on defense, and depends decisively on American subsidies for its defense budget, we shall nevertheless assume that it can duplicate this feat in the next ten years. This should give us about 100,000 troops by 1975. Syria has increased the number of its troops by some 60 percent be-

[31] These calculations are computed from the table on Jewish population by sex and age in the *Statistical Abstract of Israel*, number 17, 1966 p. 38.

tween 1956 and 1965. And although Syria was able to do that only by accelerating its rate of defense expenditure during that period from 6 percent of the GNP to 10.4 percent, we shall nevertheless assume that it can duplicate this feat in the next decade. This should produce about 110,000 troops by 1975. Adding the total for the two countries to Egypt's, we get 610,000 troops against Israel's easy potential of 400,000. The resultant 6:4 ratio is hardly a revolutionary alteration of the present 6:5 ratio (308,000 against 250,000), which is granted to be highly favorable to Israel.

To conclude this discussion then, we can see that at least in the coming decade, Israel can marshal enough soldiers to match Egypt and to preclude any drastic alteration of the present relation of number of troops between it and the Arab countries. This does not mean that we expect any of the countries concerned to increase the number of its soldiers in the next decade to its maximum potential; on the contrary, our conclusions to the previous chapter sought to stress that the emphasis in future years will most likely be on equipment, sophisticated weapons, and defense capital investments rather than on more manpower. We have engaged in this rather long analysis of manpower potentials less for its own sake than in order to dispose of certain superficial impressions on the subject that were apt to raise doubts about the conclusions we have drawn from the balance of economic capacities and military inventories.

VI

To the Brink and Over: The May–June 1967 Crisis

Introduction

In the first part of this study, we have seen that war between the Arab states and Israel was a possibility that was immanent in a multitude of causes. Mutual fears and suspicions; the unsettled problems of refugees and boundaries; the festering wounds of infiltration, boycott, navigation rights, and water disputes; the Arab urge to avenge the humiliation of past defeats, the entanglement of the issue of Israel with inter-Arab rivalries and conflicts and its escalation to the point of a clash of destinies between Egypt and Israel; the agitation of regional problems by big power policies in pursuit of their global contest—all these were so many powder kegs any of which could ignite a war.

Yet, except to those addicted to hindsight wisdom, the war that came in June 1967 was by no means inevitable; nor was it anticipated by the belligerents themselves a bare few weeks before it occurred. For, as we have seen in the second part of this study, almost all the tensions and potentials for hostility had fallen into place in a pattern of politics of threat and deterrence that effectively checked real war for eleven years, since 1956. Despite border incursions and various incidents, both Egypt, the chief Arab protagonist, and Israel seemed to be in agreement that full-scale war was not likely so long as the kind of politico-military balance that prevailed during that period continued to exist; and nothing in mid-May 1967 suggested that it had suddenly changed or was about to do so.

True, our analysis of the balance of forces revealed a long-range trend in favor of Israel in the capacity to sustain the arms race; however, this trend was more a portent of diminishing than of increasing chances of war because Israel was the party content with the *status quo.* A pre-emptive strike by Egypt on the grounds that time was against it was not to be altogether ruled out, but the attendant perils made it certainly much less likely than a number of other alternatives that had not been tried or exhausted, such as readjusting Egyptian diplomacy to try to secure more aid for economic development from East and West and from oil-rich Arab countries.

Fundamentally, Egypt could afford to wait because its pan-Arab aspirations, which underlay its urge to change the *status quo* in Palestine, were not a matter of now or never but had a long time dimension. Nasser himself had said so repeatedly, the last time not long before the war. Why then did the war occur when it did?

As we shall presently see, this war, like so many others, was the result of a whole series of miscalculations and misjudgments on the part of all the interested parties. Above all, however, it was the consequence of an elaborate self-deception that President Nasser perpetrated against his own better judgment. Ever since 1957 he had repeatedly warned zealous Arab interlocutors against the danger of taking any action against Israel that might set in motion an uncontrollable drift toward war before Egypt was prepared and circumstances were right. Yet, though he had acknowledged more than once not long before May 1967 that these conditions were not ripe, he did precisely what he had cautioned against, and again and again allowed the situation created by one of his moves to dictate to him the next until he found himself practically begging for a showdown. He did this by persuading himself that his swift tactical maneuvers created within the brief span of two weeks the ripe strategic and diplomatic conditions that he had previously thought would require decades of many-faceted effort to bring about. Not for the first time Nasser allowed his pride in his tactical virtuosity to blind him to strategic imperatives.

These general and somewhat cryptic remarks will hopefully become clear in the following detailed analysis of the course of events. That course was, naturally, determined to a large extent by the stands taken by the big powers, particularly the United States and the Soviet Union, and by other Arab countries. However, since our entire study has centered primarily on Egypt and Israel and since these two were the principals in the confrontation that led to war, we shall focus our analysis on them. We shall examine the evolution of the crisis critically from the perspective of Cairo and then Tel Aviv, bringing in the other actors and considering their effect on the behavior of the principals at the appropriate moments.

The Chronological Skeleton of the Crisis

Before proceeding with our analysis, it might be useful to review at a glance a chronology of the main events of the crisis:

May 14, 1967:   Egypt's armed forces are suddenly put in a state of "maximum alert" and Egyptian combat units are seen rumbling through Cairo on their way to the Sinai frontline. The Egyptian press explains that these measures are taken in view of reliable information that Israel planned to attack Syria and as a warning that Egypt would enter the battle if Israel did attack.

May 16, 1967:   As the Egyptian troop buildup in Sinai continues, the Egyptian Chief of Staff, General Fawzi, sends a letter to U.N.E.F. commander, General Rikhye, asking him to withdraw immediately the U.N. forces from "the observation points on our frontier." The authoritative "political correspondent" of *al Ahram* reports that the U.N.E.F. commander was asked to withdraw his forces to the Gaza Strip.

May 18, 1967:   Egyptian Foreign Minister Riad writes to Secretary General U Thant informing him of the decision of the government of the U.A.R. "to terminate the existence of U.N.E.F. on the soil of the U.A.R. and in the Gaza Strip." *Al Ahram* (May 19, 1967) reports that Riad's letter was sent in response to an inquiry from U Thant about the "scope, limits, and meaning" of the previous decision of the U.A.R. The Secretary General immediately signifies his compliance with the Egyptian request.

Israel, which had previously mobilized some reserve units in response to Egypt's troop movements, calls in more reserves for active duty.

May 21, 1967:   Egyptian forces complete the takeover of U.N.E.F. positions and Egyptian units reach Sharm el Sheikh, at the tip of the Sinai peninsula controlling entrance to the Gulf of Aqaba. According to *al Ahram* (May 21, 1967), Israel was proceeding with full mobilization and had already concentrated five divisions on its front with Egypt. In the same issue, *al Ahram*, in its first reference to the Gulf of Aqaba since the beginning of the crisis, reports Israeli contacts with the Western powers in anticipation of a possible Egyptian move to close the Gulf.

May 22, 1967:   In a speech at an Egyptian air base in Sinai, Nasser announces the closing of the Gulf of Aqaba to Israeli ships and to all ships carrying "strategic material" to Israel. "They, the Jews, threaten war; we tell them: welcome. We are ready for war," he said in the course of his speech.

In a speech made the same day but before Nasser's speech, Israeli premier Eshkol disclaims any aggressive intentions on the part of Israel and calls for the withdrawal of Egyptian and Israeli forces to their previous positions.

May 23, 1967:   Premier Eshkol says in a speech to the Knesset (parliament) that "any interference with freedom of shipping in the Gulf and in the Strait constitutes a gross violation of international law, a blow at the sovereign rights of other nations, and an act of aggression against Israel."

In Washington, President Johnson declares in a nationally televised statement that "the United States considers the Gulf to be an international waterway and feels that a blockade of Israeli shipping is illegal and potentially disastrous to the cause of peace. The right of free, innocent passage of the international waterway is a vital interest of the international community."

On the same day, the Soviet government issues a formal statement that reviews the origins of the crisis without making any specific reference to the blockade and warns that "should anyone try to unleash aggression in the Near East, he would be met not only with the united strength of Arab countries but also with strong opposition to aggression from the Soviet Union and all peace-loving countries."

In New York, the Security Council meets in an emergency session at the request of Denmark and Canada. The debate trails off in the following days without reaching any conclusion. Efforts of the United States to obtain a resolution essentially requiring Egypt to refrain from blockade action while the Council discusses the issue are blocked by Soviet opposition.

May 26, 1967:   Israeli Foreign Minister Eban arrives in Washington after meeting President de Gaulle in Paris and Prime Minister Wilson in London and confers with President Johnson and Secretary of State Rusk. Egyptian Defense Minister Badran arrives in Moscow and confers with leaders of the Soviet government.

May 28, 1967:   Following Eban's report on his trip to Washington, Prime Minister Eshkol declares in a speech to the nation that the Cabinet had decided on "the continuation of political action in the world arena" to find ways to reopen the Strait of Tiran to Israeli shipping and had drawn up policy lines designed "to obviate the necessity of Israel having to use armed forces for its defense."

May 29, 1967:   President Nasser declares before the Egyptian National Assembly that "the issue today is not the question of Aqaba, or the Strait of Tiran, or U.N.E.F. The issue is the rights of the people of Palestine, the aggression against Palestine that took place in 1948, with the help of Britain and the United States. . . . They [people] want to confine it to the Strait of Tiran, U.N.E.F., and the rights of passage. We say: We want the rights of the people of Palestine—complete." The President adds that Minister of Defense Badran brought him a message from Soviet premier Kosygin "in which he says that the Soviet Union stands with us in this battle and will never allow any state to intervene until things go back to what they were before 1956" (al Ahram, May 30).

May 30, 1967:   King Hussein of Jordan pays a sudden visit to Cairo and signs with Egypt a treaty of common defense that would put Jordan's armed forces under Egyptian command in case of war. On the same occasion, Jordan agrees to allow the entry of Iraqi troops into its territory in the present emergency. Ahmad Shukeiri, leader of the Palestine Liberation Organization and bitter enemy of King Hussein, is present at the signing ceremony and flies to Jordan in the king's plane.

May 31, 1967:   The United States is reported to be engaged in efforts to bring Western maritime powers into a scheme of action to contest the Egyptian blockade of the Gulf of Aqaba. The Soviet Union is reported to be sending additional naval units to the Mediterranean.

June 1, 1967:   A reshuffle of the government in Israel brings in a "wall to wall coalition" including all parties except the Communists. General Dayan, Chief of Staff during the 1956 war, takes over the defense portfolio from Premier Eshkol.

June 2, 1967:   Prime Minister Wilson of Britain confers with President Johnson in Washington. It is reported that the talks dealt with the project of issuing a *declaration* on freedom of navigation in the Gulf of Aqaba to which Western maritime powers would subscribe.

June 4, 1967:   It is announced that Egyptian Vice President Zakariya Muhieddin would visit Washington and American Vice President Hubert Humphrey would visit Cairo shortly to hold talks on the crisis.

A conference of eleven Arab oil producing countries opens in Damascus on Iraq's initiative to consider the prohibition of sale of oil to countries that would support Israel.

On the same day, Iraq adheres formally to the Jordanian-Egyptian common defense agreement. Thus, the armed forces of Syria, Jordan, and the Iraqi expeditionary force, elements of which had already entered Jordan, are placed under Egyptian command.

An airlift continuing throughout the day brings Egyptian equipment and officers into Jordan.

Algeria, Libya, and the Sudan are reported to be preparing to send contingents to Egypt. Kuwaiti forces had previously arrived.

June 5, 1967:   Hostilities begin at about 8 A.M. (Tel Aviv time) with an Israeli air strike against Egyptian airfields and several armored thrusts into Egyptian positions in the Gaza Strip and Sinai. Syria immediately begins bombarding Israeli settlements. Some two hours later, Jordan opens heavy artillery fire along its entire front with Israel.

For the course of the fighting, see next chapter.

June 8, 1967:   Cease fire on the Jordan-Israel front.

June 9, 1967:   Cease fire on the Egypt-Israel front.

June 11, 1967:   Cease fire on the Syria-Israel front.

The View from Cairo

In this section we shall attempt to examine the evolution of the crisis that led to war from the perspective of Cairo. Of course, the events with which we shall be concerned are too recent and the data on them are too scant to permit any thorough historical study; however, the freshness of the impressions of the moment and a sense of the climate of the situation may permit maximal use of the facts that are now available to produce an account that may be of help to future historians even if it does not qualify itself as strict history.

As a perusal of the chronology suggests, four questions constitute the key to an understanding of the crisis from the Egyptian side: (1) Why did Nasser mobilize his troops and concentrate them in Sinai? (2) Why did he demand the withdrawal of U.N.E.F.? (3) Why did he go on to proclaim the blockade of the Gulf of Aqaba? and (4) Why did he escalate the issue from the Strait question to the entire Palestine problem?

The answers to all of these questions would be greatly simplified were one to suppose that Nasser had deliberately sought a military showdown with Israel from the very outset. His moves would then constitute a logical succession of steps toward such a showdown, and the only question would be about the reasons behind his choice of time. However, all the evidence runs against such a supposition, and everyone, including Nasser, the Israelis, as well as interested and neutral observers, rightly rejects it. Rather, evidence and opinion concur that Nasser made his first move, at least, with a limited objective in mind, and that it was the repercussions of this move and the circumstances in which he had made it that suggested to him the next steps. Our analysis must therefore begin with the background for Nasser's decision to mobilize and proceed to explain how its repercussions suggested the next moves.

Nasser himself indicated on various occasions after the beginning of the crisis that he had ordered the mobilization and concentration of the Egyptian armed forces because he had received intelligence reports that the Israelis were planning an attack on Syria, and he wanted to deter them from carrying out their intent. In the speech he delivered on May 22 in an advanced base in Sinai, in which he proclaimed the blockade, he said: "I say that the sequence of events determined the plan. We had no plan before May 13 (the time he received the intelligence) because we believed that Israel would not dare attack any Arab country and that Israel would not dare make such an impertinent statement (threatening Syria)." [1] He repeated the same point in a letter to President Johnson about a week later. And he reiterated it in his resignation speech on June 9, 1967, and in the address he gave on the anniversary of his regime, on July 23, 1967.

There is no reason to doubt that Nasser was telling the truth in all these instances. On one occasion, on May 26, 1967, he did seem to convey the contrary impression that he had deliberately sought a military encounter with Israel. In a speech he made that day before a delegation of the Congress of Arab Workers he said:

> One day, two years ago, I stood up and said we had no plan for liberating Palestine and that revolutionary action is the only way to liberate Palestine. I spoke then about the summit conferences and I said that their purpose was to work toward enabling the Arab states to fulfill their goals. We have finally come to feel that our strength is sufficient, and that in any battle we enter with Israel we will win with God's help. Consequently, we decided in fact to take real steps. . . .

> The truth is that I had an authorization from the Supreme Executive Committee to execute this (blockade) at the appropriate moment; and the appropriate moment came with Israel's threats against Syria. [2]

It is obvious, however, that on this particular occasion Nasser was merely trying to impress his all-Arab audience. Since he was already in the thick of the crisis by that time and knew that war was highly probable, he sought to gain added credit by claiming that he had deliberately planned it all in advance. Even then, he still accorded to the Israeli threats to Syria a crucial role.

[1] See text in the *New York Times*, May 26, 1967.
[2] *al Ahram*, May 27, 1967.

Why did Nasser choose to respond to the Israeli threats in the manner he did?

This question would perhaps acquire more point if we recall that for eleven years Nasser had firmly held to the lesson he drew from the 1956 war not to allow himself to become entangled through a succession of incidents into a war with Israel before he was fully prepared and before the international circumstances were deemed right. Despite the taunts and ridicule of his Arab opponents and rivals, he persisted in a policy of caution and avoidance of any new provocation of Israel right down to a few weeks before the crisis, signifying thereby his conviction that he was not yet ready. A dramatic expression of this thinking was given in the course of the Arab summit meetings of 1964-1965, where Nasser argued vehemently against the Syrian proposal to launch large-scale guerilla warfare against Israel and saw to it that the United Arab Command established by the summit formally voted down the proposal. Also, the summit had decided to divert the sources of the Jordan River in Syria, Lebanon, and Jordan on condition that the Arab armies should simultaneously be strengthened in order to be able to confront the anticipated Israeli reaction. However, when that condition was not fulfilled to Nasser's satisfaction yet Syria proceeded with the diversion operations, he boldly dissociated himself from the Syrian initiative by stating openly on May 31, 1965, that the diversion operations should be postponed if the countries directly concerned could not assume by themselves the risks of Israeli retaliatory action.[3] More recently, when the Jordanian Prime Minister publicly admonished Nasser for failing to come to Jordan's assistance during the Israeli attack on the village of al-Samu', on November 13, 1966, Nasser's unofficial spokesman—Muhammad Hassanein Haykal—retorted that according to the plans of the United Arab Command the responsibility for repulsing Israeli raids rested with the individual countries concerned as long as the attacks did not involve occupation of Arab territory.[4] A week before, Haykal was careful to underline that the same principle applied to the recently concluded Joint Defense Agreement between Egypt and Syria: "I wish to say for the sake of precision and clarity that the Joint Defense Agreement does not mean the immediate intervention of the Egyptian army in any raid against Syrian positions. These raids must remain the responsibility of the various fronts even if there were one single army and not merely a joint command." [5] This principle was applied in practice as late as April 6,

[3] *al Ahram*, June 1, 1965.
[4] *al Ahram*, November 18, 1967.
[5] *al Ahram*, November 18, 1967.

1967, five weeks before the beginning of the crisis, when Egypt sat still while the Israeli air force pounded the Syrian positions in the Golan Heights and shot down six Syrian planes, some in the vicinity of Damascus itself.

The first step toward understanding Nasser's mobilization move is to clarify the question of his perception of the Israeli intentions toward Syria. Nasser has indicated on several occasions that the Russians had informed him on May 13, 1967, that the Israelis were planning to attack Syria on May 17 and that they had concentrated on the Syrian front 11 to 13 brigades for this purpose. He has also claimed that the Syrians had reported to him that they had identified 18 Israeli brigades in their sector and that his own intelligence confirmed the fact of very heavy Israeli troop concentrations.[6] All this, if true, would perhaps suffice to explain Nasser's mobilization move. One could then say that in view of the enormous size of the Israeli forces in question, the Israelis were bent on executing an invasion of Syria rather than a mere retaliatory raid and that he could not "sit out" such an operation without forfeiting any claim to Arab leadership. Consequently, instead of waiting for the Israelis to move, he chose to act first in the hope that he might thus deter Israel and obviate the entire dilemma.

It happens, however, that the alleged Israeli troop concentration did not take place. The United Nations Truce Supervision Organization, which had many times in the past checked on similar allegations and submitted reports that obtained the credence of Israelis, Arabs, and United Nations organs, explicitly reported this time that it had failed to detect any Israeli troop concentration.[7] American intelligence sources confirmed this negative finding. The Israeli government invited the Soviet ambassador to go out to the area and ascertain the facts for himself. Inquiries made on the spot by the author after the war failed to find the slightest indication to the contrary. The conclusion is inescapable that Nasser exceeded the truth when he said he had obtained independent confirmation, that the only source for his claim of Israeli troop concentrations was the Russians' report, and that this report was probably also the source of the Syrian information.[8]

[6] See his speech on May 22, 1967, reported in the *New York Times*, May 26, 1967, his resignation speech, reported in *al Ahram*, June 10, 1967, and the speech on the anniversary of the Revolution, reported in *al Ahram* July 24, 1967.
[7] See text of U.N.T.S.O. report in the *New York Times*, May 21, 1967.
[8] As these pages were being prepared for the press, this hypothesis received further confirmation from the testimony of Shams al Din Badran, the Egyptian Minister of War during the crisis, in the course of his trial in February 1968 for plotting with others the overthrow of Nasser's regime. Badran asserted that after receiving the information about troop concentrations from the Russians, General

The absence of Israeli military concentrations raises an important question about the Russians' intentions and, more important for our purpose, opens up a different and much more complex line of thought about Nasser's motives than he had himself publicly indicated. Taking up the first issue first, it is important to recall that May 13 was not the first time that the Russians had circulated word about Israeli troop concentrations aimed at Syria that proved unfounded. On October 14, 1966, for example, the Soviet Ambassador to the United Nations, Nikolai Federenko, had said in the Security Council:

> Since the time when the Syrian people started to consolidate its independence and ensure its social progress, military tension has begun to build up on the borders of Syria, and we know that, of late, Israel has been concentrating large military forces on the Syrian border. In areas adjacent to Syria, military maneuvers are being staged. A large number of land troops, equipped with artillery and minesweepers, have been thrown in. There has been a partial mobilization of reserves in Israel. In addition, there is information showing that an air attack is being prepared in Israel against neighboring Syrian territory in preparation for the intrusion of Israel forces deep in Syrian territory.[9]

Then, as on the occasion of the May crisis, the United Nations Truce Supervision Organization was asked by the Secretary General to investigate and reported no signs that could bear out the Soviet allegations. Why then this repeated cry of wolf on the part of the Russians? Why this almost obsessive solicitude for Syria's security?

We have already suggested the answers to these questions in our analysis of Soviet Middle East policy in the fading Cold War. We argued there that since the fall of Khrushchev there had been within Soviet councils muffled doubts about the wisdom of the policy of extending large scale assistance to several Middle Eastern countries on the grounds that the political returns were entirely disproportionate to the enormous investments made. Those responsible for the policy naturally wanted to show some tangible justification for it, and this was at last provided by the evolution of the regime in Syria after the left wing

---

Fawzi, then Egyptian Chief of Staff and currently Minister of War, reported from Syria, whither he had gone to check on the information and to coordinate action with the Syrian government, that there was no sign of Israeli troop concentrations and that the Russians must have been having hallucinations. This testimony, of course, strengthens considerably the probability of our analysis below being correct. See *al Ahram*, February 25, 1968.

[9] U.N. Security Council, Provisional Verbatim Record, October 14, 1966, p. 62.

faction of the Ba'th took over power in a coup d'état in February 1965
—in Federenko's diplomatic language in the previously quoted passage,
"since the time when the Syrian people started to consolidate its independence and ensure its social progress." This regime not only paid
loud and frequent homage to Marxist slogans and not only carried out
drastic socialist measures, but it also took into the government one or
two avowed Communist ministers, an unheard of event in the Middle
East. Defenders of the policy of large scale aid to Arab countries could
thus point to this achievement as presaging the communization of the
entire regime and therefore as a critical return in the kind of currency
no self-respecting Communist could deprecate. Hence, the protection
of Syria became in a sense a vested interest for those who had staked
their reputation on the policy of large-scale assistance.

Protecting the Syrian government might not have been as difficult a
problem if that government had been content with a passive policy toward Israel. But precisely because the measures that made the regime
desirable from the point of view of the Russians made it extremely un-
popular among most Syrians, it found it essential to compensate for its
weakness on other scores by currying public favor with a very militant
anti-Israeli policy. This, from the point of view of the Russians, involved the danger of creating a community of interest between Israel—
eager to check Syrian-supported terror—and the United States—presumed to be eager to get rid of a progressive-communizing regime—
that could translate itself into military action to overthrow the Syrian
government. For a while, the Russians apparently tried to ward off the
danger by counseling caution to the Syrians, but it seems that eventually they "understood" the political necessities that dictated militancy
and sought instead to support the regime by other means.

One of these means was the constant "unmasking" of the feared Israeli-American plot by means of advance "warnings" such as the one
given by Federenko in October 1966. Another means was to try to
make an attack on Syria much graver to contemplate for the potential
aggressors by linking Syria's security with that of other Arab countries,
notably Egypt. We have already referred to Kosygin's successful effort
to persuade Nasser to patch up his quarrel with Syria and constitute a
solid "revolutionary front," which led to the conclusion of a Syrian-
Egyptian joint defense agreement in November 1966. But since this
agreement did not apply to border clashes and was therefore of no use
as a deterrent to Israeli action such as they launched against Syria on
April 7, 1967 (when Israeli planes hit artillery emplacements, shot
down six Syrian planes, and nearly buzzed Damascus), and since even
a limited Israeli action could cause the Syrian government to fall, the

Russians sought to compromise Egypt into a closer, overt, and dramatic identification with Syria's security. The opportunity to try to do so came in May 1967, when they apparently got hold of an Israeli contingency plan for a large-scale attack on Syria. They conveyed the substance of the plan to the Egyptians without indicating to them that it was a contingency document with the object of inciting them to make a military demonstration that would express their association with Syria and hopefully deter, any type of Israeli action, large or limited.[10] As events were to demonstrate, however, the Russians succeeded in getting Nasser to move but could not prevent him from going beyond the token demonstration to which they had hoped he would confine himself.

Going back to Nasser's move, he must have had before him on or around May 13 two sets of intelligence: the "information" provided by the Russians, backed by the undeniable Israeli verbal threats against Syria, and the negative reports about actual Israeli troop concentrations backed by the precedents of false alarms raised by the Russians. Had he wished to act within the cautious frame of mind he had maintained for so many years, he might have easily put down the Russian "information" as another false alarm and interpreted the Israeli threats as foreshadowing perhaps a limited retaliatory raid of the "traditional" kind. That he chose to act on the opposite premise suggests that he actually had reasons of his own to proceed as if he believed the Russian information and the worst interpretation of the Israeli threats.

The first and foremost of these reasons is probably the very fact that the Russians had suggested to him to move by providing him with the

[10] The exact date of the alleged Israeli attack and the specific number of units intended to take part in it suggest that Russian intelligence must indeed have laid its hand on an Israeli General Staff document. However, the absence of troops and the circumstances of the political situation in Israel discussed below suggest that the document was a contingency plan rather than a command paper. The Russians probably did not show the Egyptians the actual document and did not indicate to them that it might be a contingency plan only for fear that the Egyptians might not act on it in that case and the pressure of the Israeli threats against Syria would continue unabated. Some evidence of this may be found in the fact that on May 20, 1967, after mobilization and the expulsion of U.N.E.F., the "political editor" of *al Ahram*—clearly Haykal—wrote: "the full content of the plot against Syria has *now* become fully clear" and went on to say that the plot involved the capture by Israel of a large piece of Syrian territory from which Damascus could be threatened. The Syrian government would fall as a result. Israel would then evacuate on condition of placing U.N. troops on the Syrian heights. That the plot became clear "now" and that its scope was less than what the Egyptian press had previously indicated suggests that the Russians had not previously shown the actual document to the Egyptians.

"information." Nasser must not only have known that the information was false but he must have also figured that the Russians knew that it was false, and knew he knew it was false. In that case, he could only interpret the Russian move as an invitation to him to join them in spreading the false charges against Israel and to use this as an excuse to stir up the question of Israeli-Arab military relations with their implicit support. This represented such a forward advance in Russia's position, which had always been rather cautious about actively encouraging the Arabs to contemplate an armed encounter with Israel, that Nasser must have felt it very difficult not to respond to it. And the fact that the Russian invitation was so indirect and subtle probably suited his purpose better than if it were specific and explicit, since it gave him a greater opportunity to stretch its purpose and scope.

A second, no less crucial reason why Nasser decided to act as if the Russian information were true is that in a certain particular sense he believed it to be *essentially* true. He knew that there were no Israeli concentrations at that particular time, but he was convinced that an Israeli large scale attack on Syria was very likely to take place sooner or later. The reason for this conviction is that for quite some time he had been expecting the United States to try to destroy him, and he looked on the tension between Syria and Israel as offering the United States a good opportunity to use Israel in order to hit him indirectly by hitting at Syria. In other words, Nasser had reached, through his own independent thinking, conclusions that were quite similar to those of the Russians. But although, as Nasser himself was to point out later, his suspicion of the United States went back at least two years before the crisis, he had not dared do anything to ward off the expected American blow for fear that he might find himself confronting the United States alone, without Russian backing. Now that the Russians themselves seemed to be urging him on and implicitly promising him their support, he gladly availed himself of the excuse of Israel's threats in order to take the initiative and attempt to throw his enemies' plans into confusion.

To substantiate this point it is necessary to digress from our main subject for a moment and put forth some background material that has received no notice at all from those who concern themselves with Middle Eastern affairs.

American public opinion, and a segment of the Administration itself, seemed to be quite shocked when Nasser perpetrated what appeared to them a barefaced lie about American participation in the war on the side of Israel. But to the Arab publics at large these charges were entirely credible because they were the logical sequel to what some of their governments and leaders had been telling them for a long time about the United States. In Egypt, for example, Haykal had been for years writing frequent columns on international affairs in which the world was essentially perceived in terms of the Soviet and leftist clichés about the struggle between the forces of light and the forces of darkness, with the United States naturally leading the latter and Egypt playing a prominent role in the former. In these imaginative and often imaginary analyses, Egypt repeatedly appeared as the legendary hero who was constantly exposed to the malevolent American giant but always emerged triumphant in the end thanks to faith in principle, courage, and wit.

For some time before the crisis, Haykal had been suggesting that the United States was leading a global counterrevolution which was somehow responsible for the overthrow of Sukarno, Nkrumah, and Ben Bellah as well as for the interventions in the Dominican Republic and the Congo, and for the Vietnam war. The most disconcerting aspect of this situation, in Haykal's mind, was the fact that the Soviet Union and the progressive camp seemed to be powerless to resist this counterrevolution effectively because of the nuclear balance of terror, the split in the Communist camp, and the disarray of the forces of the Third World. The timidity of the Soviet Union was a matter of particular concern to Haykal since he expected Egypt to be the next target of the counterrevolution. The reaction had already begun to prepare the ground for its blow from within the Middle East by promoting the project of an Islamic Alliance through King Faysal of Arabia. The military coup d'état in Greece signified the pounding at the door of Egypt and the Middle East from without.

The suspicion of the United States and its identification as Egypt's foremost enemy reached a climax in a series of eleven successive weekly articles by Haykal entitled "We and the United States," the last of which appeared on the very eve of the decision to mobilize. The series purported to be an analysis of American-Egyptian relations from the time of the 1952 Revolution to the present; and the reason Haykal gave for starting it then was that "American-Egyptian relations had rolled down in the past years to the point where they now stand on the brink or near it. . . ." The premise of the argument was that there was a violent clash between the United States and Egypt that would last for a long time and increase in violence because the United States entertained plans in the Arab countries that ran counter to the interests of the Arab nation, including of course the Egyptian people. This clash had to be accepted by Egypt, though it was important to prevent it, if possible, from becoming an absolute and complete confrontation so long as the entire Arab nation was not united in its will. Haykal's historical analysis depicted the United States as constantly bent on hurting Egypt, albeit in different ways and degrees. He divided the period since 1952 into four phases to which he gave titles expressing his perception of America's intentions: "the taming-cajoling phase" lasting from 1952 to 1955; "the punishment phase" lasting from 1956 to 1958; "the containment phase" lasting from 1959 to 1963; and "the violence phase" beginning in 1964 and lasting to the present. This particular analysis of American-Egyptian relations converged with the many preceding discussions of global politics at a point that showed the United States to be engaged in the fiercest attempt ever to subdue Egypt and the Egyptian Revolution.

To understand the workings of this state of mind, it is necessary to mention that Haykal, reflecting the views of the Egyptian leadership, attributed to the United States virtually unlimited powers and responsibilities. In the last piece in the series, for example, which appeared on May 12, 1967, under the revealing title "The Cobweb Broken," Haykal depicted the United States as having somehow a hand in the travails of the Egyptian army in Yemen, the economic difficulties in Egypt, the exploitation of the relaxed inter-Arab atmosphere of the summit meetings by Saudi Arabia and Jordan in order to launch the Islamic Alliance, the plotting by the Muslim Brethren to overthrow the regime in Egypt, as well as the intensified arming of Israel. Pulling these wires, taking advantage of the internal difficulties in Syria, Iraq, and Algeria, and capitalizing on the fall of Khrushchev, the Sino-Soviet conflict, and the counterrevolution it unleashed in Africa and Asia, the United States was prepared to deal Egypt the coup de grâce.

That the views expressed by Haykal reflected at least generally Nasser's own thinking can be easily established by scanning Nasser's speeches in recent years. Suffice it for our purpose here to refer to a speech the Egyptian chief made on July 23, 1967. After telling at some length how the United States practiced deception against him in the course of the crisis preceding the war, he added that he, nevertheless, was not "taken in" because "we knew that something was in the making and that it would not be long in coming. . . . In fact, I had felt for two years that something would be prepared against us since the cessation of United States aid and American warnings to us not to arm or enlarge our army." [11]

With this kind of view of the United States' disposition toward

[11] *al Ahram*, July 24, 1967.

Egypt, it did not really matter much whether or not Israel had actually massed its troops on the Syrian border on May 13, 1967. It was "logical" for the United States to use Israel as an instrument for invading
Syria and thus demonstrating Egypt's impotence and the hollowness of
its claim for Arab leadership; and if the plot were not ripe just then, it
would mature before long. It was fortunate for Egypt that the Soviet
Union, because of its interest in Syria's security, was prepared at last
to work with Egypt in order to foil the American plot; for this reduced
the risk to be faced and gave Egypt the benefit of surprise. As Nasser
revealed in his speech on July 23, 1967, he estimated the chances of
war at the point of asking for the removal of U.N.E.F. at not higher
than 20 percent.

In addition to his obsession with the threat of a forthcoming American blow and his confidence in Russian support, a number of other factors affected the climate in which Nasser made his mobilization decision and his subsequent moves. Most of these factors were mentioned
by Haykal in the "Cobweb" piece cited above, though, of course, he
treated them differently than we do. There was, first of all, the very
difficult economic conditions at home. The ten year plan to double
Egypt's national product, on which Nasser had pinned his hopes for
Egypt's future, had run into great trouble. The first five years plan, completed in 1965, had fallen far short of its targets and had set going severe shortages and inflationary pressures. The second five year plan,
begun immediately after, encountered in addition a great dearth of capital and had to be first prolonged, then altered to switch the emphasis
from heavy to consumer industries, and finally was scrapped altogether
as Egypt failed to meet its payments to foreign creditors. Compounding Egypt's difficulties, and incidentally lending all the more weight
to Nasser's suspicions, was the cessation of American wheat shipments,
which had saved for Egypt an average of over 150 million dollars a
year in foreign currency since 1960. Such was Nasser's predicament
that he was compelled to assent to a practical devaluation of the
Egyptian pound of about 40 percent as well as other stringent conditions on which an International Monetary Fund mission had insisted in
order to obtain a 65 million dollar loan, one-third of which was to go
immediately for the repayment of overdue debts. As the prospects for
the growth of what Nasser called "organic strength" thus appeared to
be dim, the temptation to look for shortcuts through political maneuver must have been great indeed. Moreover, Nasser, who was well
aware of the arguments Administration spokesmen often used in their
efforts to secure Congressional approval for aid to Egypt (which argu-

ments amounted to barely disguised submission to blackmail), might
well have hoped that by "making trouble" he would press the United
States into resuming wheat shipments.

Another factor, alluded to by Haykal, was the decline in Egypt's
standing in the Arab world and the apparent collapse of the drive for
Arab unity. As Nasser well knew from experience, and as he was to
demonstrate again brilliantly by both positive and negative proof in
the weeks ahead, the adage that nothing succeeds like success nowhere
holds more true than in the Arab world. The reasons for this phenomenon have not been explored, but the phenomenon itself is beyond
doubt. We have seen in the historical chapters of this work how constantly prestige has been the currency of the area's politics, capable of
buying anything from assistance from the big powers to local alliances
and political mergers. Now before May 1967, Nasser had been short of
success and prestige for several years because of the economic
difficulties at home, the failure to win the Yemen war or bring it to
honorable conclusion, and the loss of room for maneuver in the international political arena as a result of the decline in the role of the non-
aligned grouping of countries. A measure of Nasser's own sense of the decline in his position in the Arab world was the great seriousness with
which he took King Faysal's activities on behalf of an Islamic Alliance.
Barely taken notice of in the world at large, Faysal's project was the
subject of constant, frantic attacks in Egypt, which betrayed Nasser's
sense of vulnerability in the face of the appeal in the Arab world of
the religious aura, wealth, and diplomatic finesse of the Saudi king and
his success in checkmating the Egyptians in Yemen. This situation
made a dramatic move on the Israeli issue particularly attractive to
Nasser since it not only promised to put him back in the Arab limelight but was also likely to cast his chief opponent in the shadows. For
Faysal was in no position, materially or by dint of his close ties with
the United States and Britain, to offer any significant "contribution" to
the Palestine problem.

A third factor in the climate in which Nasser made his decisions was
the doubt that was beginning to shake his grand strategic concepts toward Israel on the basis of which he had adopted an extremely cautious position. We have indicated on several occasions that Nasser
sought to achieve military superiority for a showdown with Israel with
resources he could command himself, but that until such time he was
determined, since 1956, to avoid any action that might embroil him
in war. This position rested, of course, on the assumption that it would
in fact be possible for him to attain a position of superiority within

some measurable time, an assumption that seemed quite warranted in the late fifties. Egypt had vast resources of manpower and a superior economic potential, which it was about to mobilize systematically through development plans. In addition, there was the prospect of uniting the resources of several Arab countries under single leadership and command, which began to materialize with the merger of Syria and Egypt in 1958. By the mid-sixties, however, the assumption that superiority over Israel was within grasp as well as the grounds for it appeared very dubious indeed. On the one hand, the development of Egypt's economic potential ran into grave difficulties after what seemed to be a promising start, while Israel developed its own capacities so fast that the absolute gap between the two countries as expressed in Gross National Product narrowed rather than widened. On the other hand, as we have seen in previous chapters, the prospects of union between Egypt and other Arab countries, instead of improving, suffered grievous blows with the secession of Syria, the Yemen conflict, the abortive Egyptian-Syrian-Iraqi union, and so on. These developments reflected themselves in the relation of forces at the disposal of Israel and Egypt, as expressed both in capacity to spend on defense and in the actual level of armaments, which showed Egypt to be less well placed vis-à-vis its enemy in 1967 than in 1956.

Nasser himself gave expression to the failure of his expectations on this score in a speech he made on July 26, 1966. Speaking about the Palestine problem he said:

> Last year, in May, when I spoke at the meeting of the Palestine Liberation Organization, I said that we cannot liberate Palestine. Today it has become clear that whenever we bring a plane, the United States and the West give Israel a plane; whenever we bring a piece of equipment—whenever we bring a tank, they give them a tank; whenever we bring a rocket, they give them a rocket. They say they are determined to keep the balance of forces between the Arabs and Israel in this region. In other words, they ignore the rights of the people of Palestine.
>
> I said that the answer to this is our manpower capacity. We can use this manpower to build an army of two or three million; the United States will not be able to give Israel two or three million people. It can give her tanks, but it cannot give her men. We have 30 million people. In the Arab world there are 100 million. We can, if we wanted and if we were determined to liberate Palestine, mobilize three or four million men and enter the battle

without paying any attention to casualties. This, o brethren, is the path to liberating Palestine.[12]

The collapse of the hope of eventually achieving a sufficient margin of superiority in armament to win a decisive offensive war required a change of strategy if Egypt were to stick to its objective. Nasser clearly recognized this imperative in the passage just cited; but he must have realized that the specific alternative of "human waves" against modern equipment that he suggested was not feasible for reasons we have previously considered. In any case, neither he nor any of his associates spoke again of this approach, and Egypt's defense effort continued to stress the acquisition of more and more equipment rather than the building up of mass, minimally equipped armies.

As the search for alternatives continued, Nasser apparently began to reconsider the Syrian strategy of trying to undermine Israel by constant harassment and guerilla action instead of waiting for the conditions for an all-out encounter to ripen. In a press conference he gave jointly with Iraqi President Abdel Rahman Aref in February, 1967, he seemed to reverse his own previous views when he said: "The Palestinian people have the right to launch their own liberation war and no Arab state can put obstacles in their way." The guerilla strategy was suited to the present and prospective relation of forces as Nasser came to see them in that it required Egypt to have only a reasonable defensive capacity against Israeli retaliation, which he thought he certainly had; however, it was still open to two objections that had led him in the past to turn it down: One was the slowness and uncertainty of the method, and the other was the possibility of Israel's choosing a convenient moment for itself to launch a large scale surprise invasion of the guerilla bases, as it did in 1956.

The situation he faced on May 13 seemed to indicate that a surprise mobilization move on his part might meet these objections at least in part. By forcing, or appearing to force, Israel to desist from attacking Syria, he would immediately deal a severe blow to its morale and self-confidence and thus start the new approach with a telling success. In the longer view, by serving notice that future Israeli raids would risk large scale conflict with several Arab countries, he might deter Israel from undertaking such raids and thus give the guerilla fighters a safer sanctuary.

We have made several rather long detours in our attempt to explain why Nasser marched his troops into Sinai on May 14, 1967.

[12] *al Ahram*, July 27, 1966.

These detours should prove useful in explaining Nasser's subsequent moves as well as this particular question. To recapitulate briefly:

On or before May 13, 1967, Nasser was faced with intelligence about an impending Israeli attack on Syria. The information suggested that the attack was to be on a large scale, thus making it very difficult to remain passive; but the information itself was rather dubious and unconfirmed. Though he had been cautious vis-à-vis Israel for many years, Nasser decided to act as though the information were confirmed and to cite as justification for his action the fact that Israeli leaders had made repeated threats against Syria. Inquiring into the circumstances that may have affected his option, we pointed to a number of factors that were apt to suggest to him the necessity, desirability, and appropriateness of acting in the manner he did. First and foremost was his understanding of the false information conveyed to him by the Soviets as an invitation to him to make a dramatic move against Israel with their support. The invitation appealed to him because it seemed to augur a more active Soviet hostility toward Israel, and because a long standing suspicion of the United States disposed him to think that an Israeli attack of the kind envisaged in the information was a logical means for the United States to hit him indirectly, if not immediately, certainly later. Given Soviet support, he thought a pre-emptive mobilization would probably foil the plot at little risk. Such action also recommended itself as a shortcut to enhanced power as the process of building Egypt's strength "organically" seemed to have bogged down. It had the added merit of making him worth appeasing with renewed economic aid and held the promise of recovering for him the prestige and initiative he had lost in the Arab world owing to economic difficulties at home, failure in Yemen, and the rising prestige of his rival, King Faysal. Finally, as his hopes of building up a margin of military superiority over Israel to permit him to win a decisive war waned in the face of Israel's growing strength and the failure of Arab unity to materialize, an action aimed at intimidating Israel appeared to be a good opening for an alternative strategy of limited action which he had been considering.

The next question we must deal with is the removal of U.N.E.F. This subject has stirred much unnecessary controversy because its various elements have been confused by the disputants. To begin with, Egypt's intentions should be perfectly clear. There is absolutely no doubt that the Egyptian government initially wanted the U.N. troops to be removed only from the Egyptian border with Israel and concentrated in the Gaza Strip. This is clearly evident from the letter of the Egyptian Chief of Staff, General Fawzi, to the commander of U.N.E.F., General Rikhye, and from authoritative comments in the Egyptian press.[13] The reason for this Egyptian request was obviously to make the message of the mobilization move credible to all concerned.

General Rikhye conveyed General Fawzi's request to U.N. Secretary General U Thant, who ruled that the request was made by the wrong person to the wrong person and therefore considered it as not received officially.

The U.N. Secretariat was later to avail itself of this point in order to insist that U Thant had received only one Egyptian request, and this was for the complete removal of U.N.E.F. "Legally" the claim is, of course, correct; and it would have been equally correct substantively if the Secretary General had in practice treated Fawzi's request as if it had not been made at all. In fact, however, U Thant acted on the request to the extent of inquiring from Egyptian Foreign Minister Mahmud Riad about the precise intentions of his government and of taking the very important step of indicating to him that while he, U Thant, considered Egypt perfectly entitled to ask for the complete removal of U.N.E.F., he thought it was not entitled to order how the U.N. force should be deployed. Accordingly, on May 18, 1967, Foreign Minister Riad wrote to U Thant conveying officially his government's request "to *terminate the existence* of U.N.E.F. *on the soil of the U.A.R.* and in the Gaza Strip."

It has been argued that, in taking this stand, U Thant had sought to intimidate Nasser into canceling the unofficial request made through General Fawzi. If so, the Secretary General must have been incredibly ill advised about Nasser's motives for marching his troops into Sinai, and even worse advised as to Nasser's character. The one excuse that could be mentioned on behalf of U Thant's advisers is that they were not the only ones to misinterpret Nasser's intentions and earnestness; they shared this failure with most of the world press, commentators, and diplomats. Even the Israelis, who were the target of Nasser's move and who are not reputed for taking any threats lightly, did not, as we shall momentarily see, take Nasser's move seriously at first.

The Secretary General has also been criticized for, in effect, stretching his authority to assent completely on his own to the Egyptian official request when he might have stretched it in the direction of seeking delay by referring the matter to the General Assembly or the Security Council. The discussion of this issue is really beyond the scope of our interest and is better left to international lawyers. We might

[13] The text of General Fawzi's letter appears in *al Ahram*, May 17, 1967. The same issue contains an example of authoritative comment by this newspaper's "political editor."

merely venture the opinion that the retorts of the U.N. Secretariat, relying entirely on the letter of the law, are disingenuous since, after all, the Secretary General did go beyond the letter of the law and engage in diplomacy when he followed up General Fawzi's letter with inquiries and "intimidation" attempts.

The complete removal of U.N.E.F. created a new situation fraught with momentous consequences. The movement of Egyptian troops suggests that Nasser had not fully anticipated it. For while all of Egypt's forces had been put on maximum alert as of May 14, only two divisions had been marched into Sinai to reinforce the one already stationed there before May 18.[14] A new big wave of troop movements began only after the request for the complete removal of U.N.E.F., rushing additional troops into Sinai, reinforcing the frontline with Israel, parachuting forces to seize the Straits of Tiran, and dispatching a considerable fleet through the Suez Canal and the Red Sea.[15] With Egyptian forces in control of the Gulf of Aqaba and with the removal of the U.N. buffer along the Egyptian border and the Gaza Strip, two issues confronted Nasser: what to do with Israeli navigation through the Gulf of Aqaba, and what position to take regarding the possibility of infiltration of Palestinian fighters from the Gaza Strip.

Strange as it may seem in retrospect, it was the latter question that occupied the manifest attention of the world almost exclusively in the few days before the Egyptians announced their decision to close the Gulf. Even in Egypt, public attention remained focused on the issue between Syria and Israel, and the first mention of the problem of Israeli navigation was not made until May 21, 1967, and then only indirectly, when *al Ahram* reported about Israeli diplomatic contacts with Western powers in connection with the fear that the Gulf might be blocked. One reason for this was probably that people felt instinctively that the closure of the Gulf was too serious a step to be expected to be taken as a consequence of a far less serious move. As we shall presently see, this instinct was not without foundation, wrong though it turned out to be.

Nasser has argued in his blockade speech on May 22, in his correspondence with the American and other governments, and in his postmortem speeches of June 9 and July 23, 1967, that the closing of the Gulf followed inexorably from the occupation of Sharm el Sheikh by

[14] *Al Ahram* reported in its issue of May 16, 1967, that the state of alert entered into effect as of 6 A.M. that day; however, in its issue of May 17, 1967, it corrected itself by reporting that it entered into effect as of 2:30 P.M. May 14, 1967.

[15] See General Yitzhak Rabin, "Why We Won the War," *Jerusalem Post Weekly*, October 9, 1967.

Egyptian troops and that it was somehow impossible for Egypt to be in control there and allow the movement of ships to Israel. Strangely enough, the world has tended to accept this view, as is evident from the widespread attempts to shift the blame for the whole crisis back to U Thant. Yet, in Egypt itself the issue was by no means predetermined; the Egyptian government might well have acted otherwise had some relevant and by no means predetermined circumstances been different.

That the closing of the Gulf was not in fact an "inescapable" conclusion is evident from the fact that almost no mention of it was made in the Egyptian press, even after the removal of U.N.E.F., until it actually came about. The many explanations, almost apologies, Nasser found necessary to give his troops and people while proclaiming his decision in his resignation speech and in his post-mortem account on July 23, 1967, suggest that he felt his audience was by no means bound to see the action as self-evident. In his July 23 speech he also implicitly put some of the responsibility on other Arab countries: "This was one of the things our Arab brothers had always insisted upon." But the most telling evidence was a report by General Rabin that Egyptian prisoners of war testified that Field Marshal Amer had told a group of officers in Sinai, on May 20, that the Straits of Tiran would not be closed. It is possible, as Rabin cautiously added, that Amer may not have known the truth or may not have told it.[16] But the fact remains that Nasser's second-in-command either did not himself think, or was able to argue before Egyptian officers as if he did not think, that the closing of the Gulf was "inescapable."[17]

If things might have been otherwise, why did they go the way they did?

Probably the most fundamental reason for Nasser's decision to proclaim the blockade was the weakness manifested by Israel in its response to his previous moves. As we shall see more fully when we discuss the crisis from Israel's side, the Israelis did envisage *some kind* of

[16] See General Yitzhak Rabin, "Why We Won the War," *Jerusalem Post Weekly,* October 9, 1967.

[17] In the course of his trial, former Minister of War Badran provided further confirmation. He testified that in December 1966 or January 1967, Marshal Amer sent a cable from Pakistan, where he was visiting, in which he urged Nasser to dismiss the U.N.E.F. in order to stem criticism that Egypt was hiding behind it. Nasser was not convinced of the wisdom of this step. When Badran raised with Amer the question of the Gulf of Aqaba and war, Amer replied that dismissing U.N.E.F. need not require the closing of the gulf. See *al Ahram,* February 25, 1968.

action against Syria and had made a great effort to prepare world opinion by depicting the Syrian-supported incursions as intolerable. They had not counted at all on any serious Egyptian intervention and were, therefore, completely surprised when Nasser marched his troops into Sinai. For a few days they tried to "protect" their initial judgment by characterizing Nasser's move as an empty show; but when he demanded the withdrawal of U.N.E.F. all skepticism vanished. Caught off balance, the Israelis began to beat a rapid retreat. Clearly, they had not bargained for a showdown with Egypt; and much as the press and government officials had previously talked about the "impossibility" of remaining passive in the face of the Syrian provocations, they nearly all changed their tone now and began to speak of the need to defuse the crisis. The appeasement mood reached its climax in the speech Premier Eshkol made before the Knesset on May 22, in which he disclaimed any intention of launching any attack, referred this disclaimer specifically to Syria and Egypt, warned of the danger of the troop build-up, urged the mutual withdrawal of forces, and, instead of the previous warnings, expressed merely the "expectation" that the Arab countries would reciprocate Israel's good intentions.

Eshkol's speech occurred after Nasser had already decided on the blockade and so could not have influenced it (though it did influence Nasser's posture thereafter). But, as we have indicated, the mood expressed in the speech was already evident before, and it had a crucial influence. It encouraged Nasser to believe that Israel under its existing leadership might not fight, especially if it did not receive encouragement and support from the United States. As he revealed in his speech on July 23, 1967, he told the Higher Executive Committee, which he had convened in his house to decide on the question, that he estimated the chances of war as a result of the closure of the Gulf at 50 percent —not more.[18]

Given this low estimate of the chances that Israel would respond with war, the closing of the Gulf had great appeal to Nasser on all the grounds we mentioned in our discussion of his mobilization move, with some variation. His expulsion of U.N.E.F. after marching his troops into Sinai and his successful intimidation of Israel had, as if miraculously, restored him to the position he had occupied more than once in the past of the undisputed hero and leader of the Arab world. He knew, however, from his past ups and downs that to retain this position long enough for it to be of use for any purpose he had to retain

---

[18] Speech in *al Ahram*, July 24, 1967.

the momentum of his success. He also knew that as soon as his opponents in the Arab world recovered from the first gust of his regained popularity, they would seek to minimize his political victory over Israel by taunting him about Israeli shipping going through waters he controlled and that were closed before 1956. To retain the gains he had already achieved, he was impelled, *given his estimate of the kind of risk involved,* to seek more gains by closing the Gulf.

The closing of the Gulf was also centrally relevant to Nasser's long term confrontation with Israel. It will be recalled from our previous discussion that although Nasser was beginning to veer toward the Syrian guerilla strategy, he still had reservations about it because of its vagueness and slow pace and the possibility of Israeli massive retaliation. Given the timidity manifested by Israel, the closing of the Gulf appeared as an excellent corrective of these defects. Were Israel to go to war after all, he felt he had enough defensive power at least to prevent it from overrunning Sinai, as it did in 1956. After the fighting was over and troops had been forced to withdraw by world pressure, he would end up with the Gulf still in his control, and closed. The Suez Canal affair would have thus been repeated, with the addition that, in this case, he would not only have dealt Israel a tangible and severe economic blow but would have also so completely shaken its confidence in its armed power as to make possible further blows without great risk of massive retaliation. Basically the same result would be obtained if Israel decided *not* to go to war. For if its morale and self confidence could survive an Egyptian defiance on a matter such as the dispute with Syria, it could not survive a successful Egyptian challenge on the matter of the Gulf, because here the Israelis had ceaselessly repeated to themselves and to the world at large ever since 1957 that interference with navigation would be a *casus belli.*

If on May 22 Nasser proclaimed the blockade while wishing that it should not lead to war, in the course of the following week he seemed to be doing almost everything to goad Israel into war. After having escalated the crisis once by removing U.N.E.F. and a second time by proclaiming the blockade, he went on in the last week of May to escalate it still further by making sure that the issue at stake should be understood as being not simply navigation in the Gulf but the entire Palestine question, and by reasserting unequivocally the right of the Palestinians to fight for their homeland. He thus deliberately confronted Israel's government with the choice of fighting right away and risking Israel's very existence or facing blockade and generalized guerila warfare under conditions of certain internal demoralization and possibly political collapse. In the course of that week, he told his associates that the chances of war had risen to 80 percent.[19]

The evidence for this ultimate step to the very edge of the brink is unequivocal. We have already cited in the chronology Nasser's speech to the National Assembly on May 29 in which he said that "the issue today is not the question of Aqaba, or the Strait of Tiran, or U.N.E.F. The issue is the rights of the people of Palestine." To a delegation of the National Assembly that went to pay its respects to him, he added that, having restored the situation to what it was before 1956 (when the Gulf was closed), the next step was to restore it to what it was before 1948 (when Israel did not exist). The day before, he had given a world press conference in which he repeatedly stated that the real issue was Israel's existence, which was itself an act of aggression. On the question of guerilla action, the following exchange took place:

> *Q.:* "As long as it is impossible to stop the Palestinians from fighting to recover their homeland, how is it possible to prevent the war of liberation from developing into a general struggle in the Middle East?"
>
> *A.:* "I believe that the Palestinians who were expelled from their country in 1949 [sic]. . . . I believe that after 19 years in which not a directive of the U.N. was applied . . . they have the right to pursue themselves a war of liberation to restore their rights in their country. If things should develop into a general struggle in the Middle East, we are ready for this struggle."

Two days before, on May 26, Nasser had told a delegation of the Arab Workers Congress, which had come from Damascus to convey support for his position:

> One day, two years ago, I stood up and said we had no plan for liberating Palestine and that revolutionary action was the only way for liberating Palestine. I spoke then about the summit conferences and said that their purpose was to act so that the Arab states may gain the capacity to achieve their goals. We have at last come to feel that our strength is sufficient, and that we will

---

[19] See his July 23 speech in *al Ahram*, July 24, 1967. In the speech Nasser said he had told the Higher Executive Committee that on the eve of the blockade decision the chances of war were 50 percent; "later" he told them they were 80 percent; after the Israeli government reshuffle (June 1), he told them they were 100 percent. Clearly, then, the 80 percent estimate was made between May 22 and June 1.

> win, with God's help, any battle with Israel. Consequently, we
> have decided to take in fact real steps. . . .

After speaking of the closing of the Gulf and claiming that he had
been given authorization by the Higher Executive Committee to do
this sometime ago but that he had waited for the appropriate moment,
which came when Israel threatened Syria, he added:

> If Israel began with any aggressive action against Egypt or Syria
> the battle against Israel will be total and its basic objective will
> be the destruction of Israel.[20]

Two questions arise in view of all this: Why did Nasser decide to escalate the crisis and move closer to war? Why, if he was reopening the
whole Palestine issue and courting war, did he not take the initiative
of attacking?

Some two-and-a-half years before the crisis, Haykal had described in
one of his many revealing articles Nasser's views of the conditions that
needed to be met before Egypt could go to war with Israel. These
were: the concentration of superior military power; the isolation of Israel; Arab unity.[21] On the eve of the crisis, on May 13, none of these
conditions seemed to Nasser to obtain; but such was the course of
events unleashed by his moves, so rapidly did the situation develop,
and such was his almost incredible daring to draw far-reaching conclusions and swiftly act on them, that it appeared to him during that last
week in May that all three conditions were met. His tactics, he
thought, had changed the strategic picture.

Regarding the concentration of superior military power, three factors combined to cause Nasser to revise his views. The first was the
purely psychological one of becoming intoxicated by the deployment
of enormous quantities of men and equipment, which he witnessed in
the course of his tour in Sinai. Anyone who has seen a large military
concentration of troops, vehicles, and armor in a battlefield could easily understand this feeling. The second factor, also of a psychological
nature, was a downward revision of the impression he had of Israel's
might as a result of the sheepish reaction of Israel's government to his
expulsion of U.N.E.F. and its relatively mild response to his blockade
move.

Everyone involved in Arab-Israeli affairs, whether as observer or as
participant, had expected a blockade of the Gulf to bring a swift and

[20] *al Ahram*, May 27, 1967.
[21] *al Ahram*, September 25, 1964.

drastic Israeli counteraction, especially in a situation in which Israel's armed forces were already mobilized and deployed on the Egyptian frontier. This is why President Johnson, for instance, found it necessary to go on the air within hours of Nasser's blockade declaration to make clear the United States' position. This is why he characterized in his message Egypt's action as potentially disastrous to the cause of peace. And this is why the President immediately asked Israel to give him a delay of 48 hours before taking any action. Yet, though there were many in Israel who urged an immediate military response, the government's reaction was extremely mild under the circumstances. In a speech delivered by Eshkol to a packed Knesset on May 23, the Israeli Premier "admonished" Egypt by saying that "any interference with freedom of shipping in the Gulf and in the Strait constitutes a gross violation of international law, a blow to the sovereignty and rights of other nations, and an act of aggression against Israel." He reminded the world that this was a "fateful hour" not only for Israel but for the world too and called on the major powers and the United Nations to act without delay in maintaining the right of free navigation to Elath. "If a criminal attempt is made to impose a blockade on the shipping of a member state of the United Nations . . . ," he said in his punchline, "it will be a dangerous precedent that will have grave effects on international relations and the freedom of the seas." [22] The contrast between this kind of talk and the tough reaction generally expected, particularly the appeal to the world to act on behalf of international order as well as of Israel, could only convey the impression that Israel itself judged its strength to be inferior to the task of picking up the gauntlet thrown by Egypt.

The days that followed saw a toughening of the vocabulary used by Israeli spokesmen. Foreign Minister Eban, on his way to Washington on May 25, spoke for example of the "very grave" situation confronting Israel and of the threat to the "vital interests of Israel," while unidentified "senior officials" passed the word to reporters that Israel would be fully within its rights in breaking the blockade as an act of self-defense if the United Nations or allied maritime powers did not. However, when it came to the "crunch," the Israeli Cabinet decided on May 28 to heed President Johnson's request and allow time for "the continuation of political action in the world arena."

The third factor leading Nasser to believe that the condition of concentration of superior force had been met was much more real, though it too contained a psychological element. As soon as Egypt mobilized on May 14, Nasser's Chief of Staff flew to Damascus in order to put into operation the terms of the joint defense agreement, bringing the forces of Syria and Egypt under unified command headed by Egypt. Naturally, this brought a considerable addition to the forces at Nasser's disposal as well as a strategic advantage of being able to open a second front to the north of Israel. A much more important accretion of force, and a truly crucial potential strategic advantage, was gained after the blockade move, when King Hussein of Jordan signed a joint defense agreement with Egypt. This agreement placed under Egyptian command Jordan's relatively small but tough armed forces and, more important, put at the disposal of that command the Jordanian bulge with its invaluable strategic potentialities. True, for these potentialities to be exploited, it was necessary to concentrate in the bulge greater forces than Jordan disposed of, else it could become a liability in the same measure it was an asset; but Nasser and Hussein knew this and made arrangements for bringing in considerable Egyptian forces and an entire Iraqi division.

The Egyptian-Jordanian treaty was signed on May 30, but according to the testimony of *al Ahram* (May 31, 1967), Nasser knew from overtures of King Hussein that it was forthcoming at least four days before and had the agreement in the back of his mind when he made the belligerent speech before the delegation of Arab workers. Thus within two weeks of his mobilization move and less than a week after his blockade proclamation, Nasser not only saw the forces at his disposal increased or about to be increased by the addition of all the Syrian, all the Jordanian, and a sizeable portion of the Iraqi armed forces, but also saw his strategic posture immeasurably enhanced by the prospect of being able to press Israel on three fronts and from many critical directions out of the Jordanian bulge. Given a little time and some coordination, these changes in Egypt's military posture could indeed have been formidable, but the swirl of events apparently blurred the distinction in Nasser's mind between the potential and the actual, and led him to act as if he already effectively commanded advantages that were only partly secured.

Regarding the second condition that had to be met before initiating an encounter with Israel—the isolation of Israel from its Western friends—the decisive moment in Nasser's eyes seems to have been reached on May 28, when Premier Kosygin reassured him that the Soviet Union would neutralize the United States in the event of war. In his speech to the National Assembly on May 29, Nasser broke the news in these words: "When I met Shams Badran [the Minister of War just returned from Moscow] yesterday, he brought me a message from the

Prime Minister of the Soviet Union, Mr. Kosygin, in which he says that the Soviet Union stands with us in this battle and will never allow any state to intervene until things go back to what they were in 1956."[23]

The significance of this development in Nasser's eyes would be better appreciated if we recall the background against which it took place. We have argued that the Soviet Union had practically incited Nasser to move his troops into Sinai in order to deter the Israelis from hitting Syria in a big or limited action. The Russians had not counted on the complications that developed with U.N.E.F. any more than Nasser had, but, in view of the circumstances previously discussed under which Nasser asked for the removal of that force, they went along and supported his move after the fact. Nasser's further initiative in proclaiming the blockade, however, startled the Russians and caused them to pause. For one thing, they had already achieved their objective of forming a broad Arab deterrent to Israeli attacks on Syria and had no interest in this new move. For another thing, they, as everyone else, knew the gravity with which Israel had looked upon such an eventuality and feared that a war might ensue that could face them with difficult dilemmas. Above all, they were concerned about the reaction of the United States in view of its sympathy with Israel and the specific commitments it had assumed on this particular issue, especially after President Johnson responded immediately and forcefully with his May 23 statement. This is why the Soviet government, in *its* statement on the same day, went into a long diatribe against Israel and those backing it, specifically supported Nasser's mobilization move and his removal of U.N.E.F., but was conspicuously careful not to make any explicit mention of the closing of the Strait of Tiran.

As long as the Soviet Union maintained its reserve on the issue of the Strait, Nasser feared that the chances of a strong American intervention on behalf of Israel were very high. He well knew that the two superpowers wanted to avoid an open mutual confrontation and consequently saw the Russian reserve as doubly ominous: It reflected to him the Russian reading of the United States' intentions as firm and calling for great caution, at the same time that it bore the danger of encouraging the United States to suppress its hesitations and stick to a firmer position than it might otherwise. These fears of Nasser were reflected clearly in the press conference he gave before he had received Kosygin's message, in which he combined an absolutely unyielding position vis-à-vis Israel with a plaintive and flattering attitude toward the United States. By the same token, when the Soviet Union committed itself

[23] *al Ahram*, May 30, 1967.

to opposing American intervention, the act seemed to Nasser to be significant not only in itself but also as a reflection of a lowered Russian estimate of the probability of American intervention. These evaluations appeared all the more trustworthy because Nasser knew that the United States and the Soviet Union had been in touch over the crisis at the highest levels since May 22 in an effort to prevent a misunderstanding of each other's intentions and because the overt behavior of the United States appeared to confirm them.

The United States, we have seen, began by reacting quite strongly to Nasser's blockade proclamation. Besides the President's forceful statement of May 23, a strong verbal note was delivered the next day to the Egyptian government by the newly appointed American ambassador to Cairo, in which the United States government essentially insisted on a return to the *status quo ante* pending negotiations and made it clear that it did not rule out the use of force if Egypt insisted on applying the blockade. The Administration took this position and persisted in it until May 26 in order to give Israel reason to hope that a settlement might be achieved without its having to resort to arms. After that date it began to waver.

On May 26, in the course of discussions with Israeli Foreign Minister Eban, President Johnson and Secretary of State Rusk referred to specific American plans of organizing concerted action of Western maritime powers to break the blockade, by force if necessary; however, they asked Israel to abstain from any forceful initiative for about two weeks until the plan could be put into operation. In the circumstances of the time, the American request assumed the character of a test of Israel's mood; and when the Israeli Cabinet decided two days later to accede to it, most people in the Administration thought that the "worst of the crisis" was over. The fact that the Israeli government accepted the American thesis of a *collective* initiative of maritime powers, even more than its acceptance of the delay, persuaded these officials that the United States was "off the hook," that Israel must have deemed the cost of war prohibitive, and that, consequently, if a formula that would save everybody's face could be found, the crisis would be "licked." It did not take the Russians long to detect the weakening in America's position and to exploit it in order to undermine any possibility of collective action by firming up their stand in support of Egypt.

It should perhaps be mentioned in this connection that as far as President Johnson himself was concerned, he was strongly inclined at the outset of the blockade crisis to take forceful action in fulfillment of what he deemed to be existing firm commitments to Israel. The reasons for this inclination will remain a matter of speculation until he or his associates begin to explain his thinking and feeling at that time. However, no sooner did he reveal this inclination in his May 23 statement than a groundswell of opposition began to build up in Congress and outside of it against any unilateral American intervention. The President, promptly taking account of this mood, switched to the idea of collective initiative but remained quite earnest about forceful action, which is probably why he was able to persuade the Israelis to wait. Once he succeeded in this, however, the sense that the crisis had eased and pressures at home and abroad blunted the remaining edge of his position and led him to go along with efforts to "patch things up." On the one hand, there was continuing strong opposition to the use of force, even in a collective setting, in Congressional circles weary of another Vietnam, among officials who argued that America's position in the Arab world would be badly hurt, and among those who maintained that such action was not really needed since compromise was possible. On the other hand, all but two or three of the potential partners of a collective action first balked at making any threat to use force and then shied away from even a simple declaration asserting the right of freedom of passage for ships of all nations in the Gulf of Aqaba for fear of endangering their interests in the Arab world.

While the United States appeared to be engaged in a repeat of the Dulles performance of 1956—when the late Secretary of State started with tough talk in connection with Nasser's nationalization of the Suez Canal and then proceeded to paralyze Britain and France with ingenious schemes and verbal acrobatics—the Soviet Union went on to give Nasser and the world a token of its earnestness by moving additional naval units to the eastern Mediterranean. Western commentators had much to say at the time about the relative strength of the Soviet fleet and the American Sixth Fleet, the hollowness of the Russian naval threat, the significance or insignificance of the maneuver, and so on, but no one seemed to see the importance of the Russian navy's presence as a "trip wire" before the Sixth Fleet and therefore as evidence of a serious intent to oppose American intervention. Another function that the Soviet fleet fulfilled was to deter, by the same method, other maritime powers from joining the United States in any forceful collective action.

With the United States practically detached from Israel, Nasser did not need to worry about other friends of Israel. De Gaulle had already made it clear to Foreign Minister Eban on May 25 that he opposed the use of force and favored a Big Four effort to solve the crisis, which the Russians promptly opposed. Prime Minister Wilson had assured

Eban at the same time that Britain was willing to join the United States in any action to reopen the Strait of Tiran, but the position of France, the increasingly hesitating position of the United States, the reticence of maritime nations, the firming up of the Soviet stand, and concern with the fate of British oil interests led him to pull back shortly thereafter. Essentially, then, and despite continuing noises to the contrary, the incredible seemed to Nasser to have happened: In a week of tactical maneuvers, Israel was effectively isolated from the West.

The third and last of the conditions that Nasser had set for himself before seeking a showdown with Israel was Arab unity. The kind of unity Nasser had in mind in the years before the crisis was most probably integral unity—that is to say, a merger of at least several critical Arab countries—and, of course, such unity did not take place in the week or so following the proclamation of the blockade. However, the crisis he unleashed precipitated a manifestation of Arab solidarity of such scope and depth as to lead him to expect that solidarity to fulfill, at least for the moment, the same functions as Arab unity. At the same time, he saw this manifestation as preparing the ground for culminating a victory over Israel with the realization of the longed for integral Arab unity.

The extent to which the course of events itself led Nasser to readjust quickly his evaluations and his objectives is indicated by the fact that on May 21, the day before he announced the blockade, al Ahram reported authoritatively that Egypt had refused a proposal made by some conservative Arab countries to assemble the Arab Common Defense Council, on the grounds that "only those can confront Israel who can confront imperialism. All other talk is illusion and deception." Yet, only five days later, with the secret knowledge that Jordan was about to throw its lot with him and with other manifestations of Arab solidarity, Nasser could barely control his enthusiasm before the delegation of the Arab Workers' Congress:

> If Israel began with any aggression against Egypt or Syria, the battle against Israel will be total and its object will be the destruction of Israel. We can do this. I could not have spoken like this five years ago or three years ago; and since I could not, since I was not prepared, to have said it would have been to utter empty words. Today, eleven years after 1956, I say these words because I know what we have in Egypt. And what Syria has. I know that the other countries too—today Iraq has sent troops into Syria. Algeria will send us forces. Kuwait too will send us forces.

. . . This is Arab force; this is the true rebirth of the Arab nation, which had previously been feeling rather hopeless.[24]

Nasser's feeling that he had triggered a rebirth of the Arab nation must have been strengthened even more in the days that followed. Literally every single Arab country offered to contribute or actually began to contribute troops. To be sure, Nasser did not think much of the military value of such contingents as those that Kuwait actually sent and that Morocco, Tunisia, Libya, the Sudan and, belatedly, Saudi Arabia were preparing to send. However, the crucial thing for him was that even the contribution of a symbolic force committed the contributing countries tangibly to the confrontation with Israel and served notice upon the world that they would jointly react against the interests of any nation that supported Israel. Naturally, the fact that the oil producing countries—Libya, Kuwait, Iraq, and Saudi Arabia—joined in the act lent a particular weight to this collective Arab diplomatic deterrent. Indeed, that deterrent had much to do with frustrating the schemes of collective action by the maritime nations.

We have been arguing that in the last days of May, Nasser escalated the immediate issue at stake in the crisis from the problem of navigation in the Gulf of Aqaba, with its implications for a long-range confrontation with Israel, to the problem of Israel's political existence, and that he did so after the repercussions of his earlier moves had led him to believe that the conditions for a showdown with Israel had materialized. If this is true, two questions arise: (1) Why did Nasser agree on June 4 to send Vice President Zakariyya Muhieddin to Washington and receive Vice President Hubert Humphrey in Cairo to hold talks on the crisis? (2) Why did he not take the initiative to attack Israel first and thus gain for himself the military advantages that might be had from striking the first blow?

The answer to the first question is that Nasser thought there was much to gain from talks and little risk in them. Although he subsequently revealed, in his June 9 speech, that he had predicted to his Executive Council that Israel would strike on June 5, he also said in the same speech that he had thought the talks might delay the outbreak of war while they lasted. A delay, if it were achieved, would give him time to complete his preparations and would especially give the Iraqi troops the chance to reach Jordan and deploy on its West Bank, while it would only increase the psychological and economic pressure on Israel, whose life was completely disrupted by total mobilization. Moreover, the talks offered the chance of trying to split the United States

[24] *al Ahram,* May 27, 1967.

and Israel by a show of moderation on the Gulf issue and thus further isolate his enemy. The risk he ran was that of giving the American Administration the chance to trap him into a position of appearing to be intransigent and defiant and thus to press Congress to support a forceful response on its part. However, the preliminary talks that had led to the agreement on the exchange of visits and his reading of the Administration's mood at that point had rightly persuaded him that the risk was negligible.

As to the second question, the answer is simply that the isolation of Israel, which was one of the essential conditions for seeking a showdown with it, was operative only if he did not strike the first blow. Nasser well knew that the Russian commitment to neutralize the United States depended on a prior Russian assessment of America's inclination to intervene as weak, and that the weak American inclination to intervene depended on the issue's appearing to be free navigation in the Gulf of Aqaba. Were he, by attacking first, to convert the issue formally into a battle for the existence of Israel, the whole situation would be altered. The great leap in the odds for an American intervention that would occur then could very well scare the Russians into a passive position, which would in turn further increase the chances of American intervention to near certainty.[25]

This assessment of the Soviet and American positions was driven home to Nasser, if in no other way, through one of these bizarre incidents that are apt to occur in situations in which two mobilized armies stare tensely at each other. The Israeli intelligence captured or intercepted an Egyptian command order to one of the air force units to bring its preparations to the point of readiness to open offensive operations on May 27. The Israelis understood the message to mean that the Egyptians would attack on that day. On May 26, they wired the information to their Foreign Minister who was then visiting in Washington, and the latter, in turn, conveyed his information to Secretary Rusk at

[25] Former Minister of War Badran testified in the course of his trial that when he returned from Moscow on May 28, he went to G.H.Q., where Nasser was having a conference. Nasser pointed out that the chances of war had risen from 80 percent to 100 percent, but that political considerations dictated that Egypt should not strike the first blow because the Americans would interfere. General Sidki Mahmud, commander of the air force, objected that he could not risk being paralyzed by some Israeli "miracle operation." Marshal Amer asked the air force chief whether he preferred to strike the first blow and face the Americans, or to be hit first and face Israel only. Sidki Mahmud immediately agreed that the latter was preferable. Asked what losses he expected to suffer from an Israeli first blow, he said 20 percent! See al Ahram, February 25, 1968.

an urgently called meeting. The American government tended to doubt the conclusion drawn by the Israelis; nevertheless it thought it prudent to have Assistant to the President Walt Rostow immediately summon the Egyptian ambassador and warn him of the grave consequences of an Egyptian offensive action. At the same time, the American government alerted the Soviet government of its apprehension and —most important from Nasser's point of view—the latter had its ambassador in Cairo rush to Nasser's residence and wake him up at three in the morning in order to deliver to him a note from Premier Kosygin urging self-restraint. The Americans and the Russians made similar démarches with Israel for the sake of symmetry, but Nasser did not fail to get the significance of the entire episode. Two days later, in his speech to the National Assembly, when he broke the news of the assurance he had received of Soviet support, he was careful, unlike his press, to stress that the support was confined to bringing things back to what they had been in 1956.

It was clear to Nasser, under these circumstances, that if he were to have a showdown with Israel, he had no alternative but to press and provoke Israel so that *it* should attack first, to be ready to absorb the first blow, and then to pass on to the offensive. By June 2 he thought he had succeeded in the first part of the plan. On that day, he reported to the Higher Executive Council that the chances of war were 100 percent and that Israel would start it on June 5 with an air strike.

Shortly after the war, an Israeli author published the text of an allegedly captured battle order issued by Nasser's second-in-command, Field Marshal Amer, on June 2, 1967.[26] Internal evidence suggests that the document is authentic. But authentic or not, it echoes clearly the key points of our analysis and can therefore be used in lieu of summary. This is why we think it useful to reproduce it here integrally.

TOP SECRET

Office of the Deputy Supreme Commander
Cairo, June 2, 1967

IN THE NAME OF ALLAH THE MERCIFUL, THE COMPASSIONATE

BATTLE ORDER NUMBER 2

Officers and soldiers of the armed forces:

[26] Shmuel Segev, *Sadin Adom*, Tel Aviv 1967, pp. 88–99.

Israel has tried and is still trying to obtain from the United States direct support for its planned military operations against Egypt. It is now clear, however, that, in view of the strong position of the government of the Soviet Union and its readiness to intervene immediately if any big power should go to war against Egypt, it is no longer to be expected under any circumstances that the United States government should join in a military adventure on Israel's side.

Israel will not be able to bear the burden of mobilization for a long time. Mobilization has already brought total paralysis of the Israeli economy. In the meantime, two important developments have taken place in the Arab arena: Jordan has signed a defense agreement with Egypt; Iraq has decided to participate in the battle, and with great force, from Jordan's territory.

After the broadening of the national government in Israel, extremist elements have joined who call for war against Egypt. I estimate that Israel believes that the entry of the Iraqi forces into Jordan and their deployment along the Israeli border would take two weeks. Therefore, Israel plans to clash with Egypt before this deployment is completed.

Accordingly, I have completed my plans and issued my orders for the organization of the operations. I call on each one of you to fight with maximum aggressiveness, to fulfill with devotion the commands and orders in the frame of the general plan, until the completion of the task by the Egyptian command. Our objective is to defeat the main forces of the Israeli army. Our armed forces, in terms of their numbers and the means at their disposal, can fulfill this task.

I bless you all, and I am sure that each one of you will fulfill his duty to the end and will think of nothing except the completion of his part in the general plan. The battle before us is fateful for Egypt and fateful for the entire Arab nation.

On you depends the honor of the Arab armed forces. I have full confidence in our victory. May Allah protect you and bring success to your endeavors.

Signed: *Field Marshal Abdel Hakim Amer*
Deputy Supreme Commander of the
Armed Forces.

The View from Tel Aviv

If with regard to Egypt, a glance at the chronology led us to ask four key questions, corresponding to Nasser's rapid moves, with regard to Israel a similar glance suggests to us only one question: Why was there such a timid public reaction on the part of the government until June 1, and then a diametrical reversal in the following days? And if in attempting to answer the questions about Egypt we have had to range far and wide into various diplomatic and military spheres, in trying to answer the question about Israel we need not go too far away from its own internal politics and problems of decision making.

Underlying this last difference is the contrast between the real situation of the two countries. Unlike Egypt, Israel did not have much room for diplomatic maneuver to alter its over-all situation. Nasser, for example, was able through diplomatic action to improve radically his military posture by the addition of the forces and strategic potential of Syria, Jordan, and Iraq. Israel could not by any conceivable means bring about any addition to its own armed forces. Again, where Nasser was able through the appropriate moves to marshal the diplomatic weight of all the Arab world and its varied resources and use it to influence the big powers' positions, Israel could only throw her own weight in the scales. Nasser, having altered the *status quo*, needed only to persuade the United States to *remain inactive* and could count on the assistance of the Soviet Union, which had shown no compunction about being thoroughly one-sided. Israel, seeking to restore the *status quo ante,* needed to persuade the United States to *take forceful initiatives* on its behalf at a risk to its own interests in the Arab world, at a time when it was deeply involved in a very controversial war, and in the face of Soviet opposition.

In view of all this it becomes apparent why, in viewing the crisis from the perspective of Tel Aviv, the crucial issue should be the government's repeated decisions on the question of fighting or holding back. Even the limited room for maneuver that Israel had with respect to influencing the United States to intervene on its behalf depended, as it appears in retrospect, on the impression conveyed by its government about its disposition to act militarily. For the chief incentive for the United States to intervene was precisely to avoid the outbreak of war. Once the Israeli government conveyed the impression that it was fearful of action, the United States lost most of its incentive to take forceful action and, concomitantly, the Soviet Union lost most of its inhibitions about supporting Nasser.

As for the timidity of the Israeli government, this is undoubtedly explainable in some part by the character of the Israeli political system. Once taken by surprise, Israel's government could not by its very nature act as swiftly and as decisively as Egypt's. In the latter country, an authoritarian system, or at best a "guided democracy," permitted one man to make quick decisions or to arbitrate decisively between the views of advisers and assistants who did not question his supremacy. In Israel, on the other hand, an effective democracy, and one based on a coalition of minority parties at that, dictated the necessity to arrive at new decisions by a near-consensus of 18 Cabinet members, any dissenting minority of whom could bring down the government. Such a system naturally fostered compromises and encouraged equivocal stands.

This "structural" factor and the element of surprise do not, however, suffice to account for the indecisiveness displayed by Israel's government between May 15 and June 1. For after all, the same structure had not prevented that government from swiftly adopting fateful decisions in the past, nor was it to prevent it from acting with incredible boldness in the days and weeks that followed. For sufficient grounds to answer our question, we must look beyond the structure to the particular leadership of Israel and the specific circumstances under which it operated at the time.

On the basis of the scarce data available, supplemented by impressions gathered on the spot shortly after the war, it seems that the key to the evolution of the situation in Israel lay in the development of a "credibility crisis" regarding Eshkol's role, in his capacity of Minister of Defense, as a link between the military and the government. The crisis had been latent for several years before May 1967, but Nasser's surprising and swift moves brought it to the fore at a most critical moment and caused the inherent indecisive tendencies of the government to assert themselves.

It is important not to confuse this argument with others that may sound somewhat similar. Much nonsense has been written about the tendency of the Israeli military to interfere with policy making, which presumably has resulted again and again in foiling the moderate policies of men like Sharett and Eshkol and in forcing them to adopt aggressive, adventurous lines. This is not the view subscribed to here, certainly not in the crisis under discussion. The military leaders did have their own evaluations of Nasser's intentions and also had estimates of the capabilities of Israel's armed forces that differed, sometimes rather sharply, from those of some members of the government; but then it was their duty to make such evaluations and estimates and transmit them to the Minister of Defense. The question is whether they also attempted to force their views on the government by some devious ways, and on this there is no evidence whatsoever, with one possible exception we shall note below. Furthermore, neither in the past nor in this particular crisis was Eshkol himself the "moderate" man besieged by the intransigent military leaders. We may indeed say that half the problem of credibility we mentioned was precisely due to the fact that for several years Eshkol had worked so closely with the military that some in the government came to suspect that he had surrendered to them his independent judgment in defense matters. The other half of the problem was due to the fact that some of his political enemies accused him of having no judgment at all in any matter, including affairs of defense, about which the Israeli public was particularly sensitive.

The roots of Eshkol's problem went back to his quarrel with Ben Gurion, which had led to a secession in Mapai in 1965. After that time, Ben Gurion and his supporters, including people with a great deal of experience in various aspects of defense, such as Moshe Dayan, Shimon Peres, and Isser Harel, had periodically made more or less vague charges of negligence on Eshkol's part in matters relating to national security. Partly in reaction to such attacks, Eshkol had tended to lean over backward and respond favorably to requests made by the professional heads of the defense establishment concerning budgetary allocations, permission to undertake retaliatory actions, and so on. Thus it was that, in the course of Eshkol's three years of tenure as Defense Minister, the Israeli armed forces improved and increased their equipment faster than ever, acquiring among other items the Hawk missiles, the 48 Skyhawk bombers, hundreds of Patton tanks, two submarines, and a good deal of other sophisticated equipment. At the same time, they tried out new and more dangerous types of military action in the repeated border clashes with Syria, such as using air power to attack Syrian gun emplacements and penetrating deep into Syrian territory in pursuit of enemy planes. All this did not of course silence Eshkol's political opponents nor did it assuage the doubts they raised, but it had the effect of sowing seeds of suspicion among some of his partners in the government that he might in fact have gone too far the other way and fallen under excessive influence of the military chiefs. In "normal" times, Eshkol was able to tread confidently between the two opposite suspicions and use them to offset one another. As the crisis set in, however, his sharing with the military in an unfortunate but understandable misjudgment of Nasser's intentions caused him to doubt himself and allowed now one kind of suspicion and now

another to assail him and jostle his reactions. By the time he settled to
a firm position, he had already forfeited the confidence of his colleagues in his judgment not only regarding his evaluation of the situation but also regarding his estimate of the ability of Israel's armed
forces to execute what action seemed to be needed. Only a man of
trusted military capacity and total independence from Eshkol could
resolve the Cabinet's doubts; when such a man was found in Dayan
and was foisted upon Eshkol, Israel moved.

We have already intimated that the Israelis definitely contemplated
some kind of action against Syria in the course of the month of May.
Syrian-supported guerilla activity had become more serious in recent
weeks, as Secretary General U Thant had pointed out, and the Israelis
considered it a matter of cardinal importance to nip it in the bud by
denying to the terrorists any sanctuary in the territory of Arab states
across the border. The scope of the envisaged action had apparently
not been determined as yet by May 14, but it was clear from the intelligence gained by the Russians and from declarations of responsible Israelis that the alternatives under consideration included an air attack
or an unusually large scale raid by land forces against Syrian military
bases. Eshkol himself had threatened an air strike, but his Chief of
Staff, General Rabin, had hinted publicly that a different type of action
might be taken. Whether Rabin spoke with Eshkol's approval or
whether this was an instance—the only one on record—of the military
trying to force his hand is not known. It is generally known, however,
that the Prime Minister and Minister of Defense had excellent relations with his Chief of Staff, and this suggests the possibility that the
different types of threat might have been deliberately orchestrated. Be
that as it may, the military leaders had taken it as certain that Egypt
would not react to whatever action was contemplated and had impart-
ed that conviction to the Defense Minister, who must have conveyed
it to the Cabinet as his own considered judgment.

The assessment of the military rested on good grounds and was
shared by experts everywhere: the relative strength of Egypt and Israel, the presence of large numbers of Egyptian troops in Yemen, the
poor state of inter-Arab relations, the known position of the big powers, and last but not least, Nasser's own cautious behavior in relation
to Israel in the preceding eleven years. That it nonetheless proved
wrong might not have mattered under different circumstances. But in
the atmosphere of suspicion surrounding Eshkol's stewardship of defense it was to have crucial consequences.

The military were so sure of their initial prediction that Egypt
would not react that they stuck to it even after Nasser made his first

move. They explained away the Egyptian troop movements as most probably an empty show, and though they were careful to ask for authorization to take precautionary measures, which Eshkol immediately granted, they maintained that Israel was still free to act against Syria. Eshkol, who considered himself politically responsible for what appeared to be a wrong forecast of Egyptian passiveness, had a psychological interest in going along with this view of his military chiefs. Judging by his subsequent action, however, he must have already begun to wonder whether he was not following them too uncritically.

Nasser's demand first for the U.N.E.F. to be concentrated in the Gaza Strip and then to be removed altogether caused the first serious divergence between the views of the military and those of the government as a whole and the first manifestation of indecisiveness on Eshkol's part. There was no disagreement at this, or at any stage, of the crisis that precautionary measures should be taken on the basis of the worst assumptions, and consequently Israel's mobilization and deployment of troops proceeded automatically *pari passu* with the Arab military moves. The divergences in question referred to evaluations of the new situation and the policies indicated by these. The military now became convinced that Nasser meant to intervene in case of an Israeli attack against Syria and were inclined to explain this unexpected behavior on his part by referring to the Russian factor. Furthermore, they clearly saw that by removing U.N.E.F. Nasser served notice that henceforth his side of the frontier would no longer be inactive in guerilla operations. Precisely for these reasons, however, they thought it was crucial for the future of Israel's security not to be intimidated and to respond forcefully to the next act of guerilla warfare even if this meant a large scale encounter with Egyptian forces.

The government accepted the reinterpretation of Nasser's intent and agreed that the removal of U.N.E.F. created a new security problem but refused to follow the conclusion of the military chiefs, who appeared to be advocating action for one reason and its opposite. The government's concern with international repercussions, its suspicion of the role of the Soviet Union, and its disappointment with the forecast previously given to it led it to attempt to meet the new security problem not by asserting Israel's deterrent power in a certain clash with Egypt, but by diplomatic action designed to defuse the immediate crisis and then to restore as much as possible a semblance of the *status quo ante*. The government was not unaware that its line would concede an important diplomatic and moral victory to Nasser that would enhance his standing in the Arab world, but it comforted itself with the notion that "tomorrow is another day" and with the hope that once this particular crisis blew over, the Arabs would be "back at each other's throat again." Clearly, the difference between the military and the government was the difference in the perspective of those whose business it is to prepare for war and are therefore psychologically ready for it when it comes, and those whose concerns are with the labors of peace and need a long psychological preparation before they are ready to contemplate war. And the option of war and peace in this instance presented itself to the government and people of Israel with such stunning abruptness that their preference was almost predetermined.

The position taken at this juncture by Eshkol specifically is not known, but the character of the speech he delivered before the Knesset on May 22 suggests that he either sought himself or was persuaded by others to take as much distance as possible under the circumstances from the views of the military. In that statement, it will be recalled, Eshkol almost forgot the "unbearable" situation with Syria and renounced any intent to attack in any way Syria, Egypt, or any Arab country unconditionally except for indicating that Israel "expected" to be treated on the basis of reciprocity. Having identified himself publicly with this timid position, it was not easy for Eshkol on the very next day to speak tough before his colleagues in the Cabinet, his countrymen, and the world at large when word came of Nasser's closing of the Strait of Tiran.

What we have just said does not mean that the proclamation of the blockade was taken in any but the gravest seriousness by Eshkol, the government, and everyone in Israel. It suggests, however, that within the context of the heightened crisis there was already established a disposition to take a more limited pragmatic view of the situation that sought to dismantle the immediate crisis, instead of a broader theoretical-strategic view that would convert the specific blockade act into a basic confrontation and respond accordingly. The difference between these two approaches was clearly illustrated by the positions taken by the government and the military leaders.

At an emergency session of the Cabinet on May 23, everyone agreed in a general way that Israel confronted a grave crisis and that the Strait of Tiran must be reopened. There was some discussion of the possible broad implications of the issue, but for practical purposes the problem was put in terms of the specific question of how to restore free navigation. After a general discussion of the means that might be used to achieve this objective, it was agreed that since other nations had an interest in the question and since the United States in particular had given some assurances on the subject, an urgent and intense effort should be made to achieve the objective by diplomatic means. The outcome of this decision was Eshkol's speech of May 23—in which, as we have said, he "admonished" Egypt and called on the big powers and the United Nations to remove the blockade—as well as Eban's mission to Paris, London, and Washington.

As for the military leaders, their first preoccupation after the blockade proclamation was to keep track of new military developments on the enemy side and to order the expansion of the mobilization and the deployment of troops in accordance with the enemy's moves and the most likely requirements of the new situation. By May 24 they had already done this and were prepared with a new evaluation of the situation and a plan of action, which they submitted to the Minister of Defense. As they saw it, Nasser's latest move was not to be viewed merely as the specific act of blocking navigation to and from Israel, important as this might be, but was to be considered above all as a challenge to Israel's deterrent power. Consequently, unless Israel *itself* nullified Nasser's action, his challenge would prove successful, and it would be the signal for further encroachments and harassments that would sooner or later lead to war but under more unfavorable conditions. Israel was capable of acting alone, they argued, and they presented a plan for operations against the Egyptian concentrations in Sinai, which, they expected, would compel Nasser to desist from his blockade.

Eshkol, it seems from the later course of events, was persuaded by these arguments. But since the Cabinet had already decided on diplomatic action and since Foreign Minister Eban had accordingly made plans for his trip to Paris, London, and Washington, there was little Eshkol could do except to tell the military chiefs that he appreciated their position, to indicate to them that he would not allow the diplomatic effort to drag on too long, and to suggest to them the need, in any case, to explain Israel's position to its friends so as to avoid their turning against it afterward, as happened with the United States in 1956.

With regard to the last question, Eban's trip to Paris turned out to have an opposite effect. President de Gaulle not only refused to commit his government to action on behalf of Israel's navigation rights but took the opportunity to extend to it, through Eban, a "friendly" warning not to start shooting on penalty of forfeiting French sympathy and diplomatic support. Thus, instead of securing French understanding, Eban's initiative elicited advice from de Gaulle, the violation of which was certain to be penalized. In London, we have already said, Eban received a promise from Prime Minister Wilson to join the United States in action to secure free navigation.

By the time Eban arrived in Washington, on May 26, he found instructions awaiting him to switch the emphasis in his talks with the American government from the Strait problem to the possibility of an Egyptian attack. These instructions reflected the uncertain and contradictory currents of thought that were already sweeping the Israeli government. For certainly one reason for the instructions was the desire to avoid the trap in which Eban had fallen in Paris, where his emphasis on the question of the blockade elicited from de Gaulle "advice" that limited Israel's freedom ultimately to act on its own militarily. By switching the emphasis to the possibility of an Egyptian aggression, the instructions intended to preserve Israel's freedom of action and to get the Americans to speak about the Administration's position in case things did "somehow" come to blows. Yet, either simultaneously with these instructions or shortly thereafter, Tel Aviv also sent to Eban the information from which Israel's Intelligence had deduced that the Egyptians intended to attack on the 27th. Eban was asked to convey this urgently to the American government with a view to its taking preventive action. One intent bespoke a sense of willingness and capacity to act militarily while the other betrayed an alarm at the possibility of having to fight Egypt immediately.

Eban's discussion with President Johnson, to the extent that its content has become known, seems to have conformed, on the whole, with the intent of the instructions. But his talks with other officials gave vent to the impression of a frightened Israel. With the President, Eban raised in an academic fashion the question of America's attitude in case of an Egyptian invasion and received in reply a confirmation of the United States' commitment to the independence and integrity of Israel. The President however, added, echoing what had hitherto been the general view in the Administration, that he thought Israel was in any case capable of defeating Egypt all by itself. On the question of navigation in the Gulf of Aqaba, the President indicated that the United States considered itself to be an interested party in this issue and was determined to force Nasser to retreat. He told Eban that he planned to achieve this by organizing a group of maritime nations who would pass their ships through the Strait of Tiran, by force if necessary, and make possible the passage of Israeli ships too. The President was not worried about the possibility of Russian intervention against such action, judging probably by the caution that the Soviet Union had displayed up to that point on the blockade question. He pointed out that he had already begun on his project and received encouraging indications from England, Canada, and Holland; he suggested that he only needed some time to bring it to the operational stage.

The President's "request" for some indefinite but brief time and his tying of American action to the participation of other powers must have been slightly disappointing to Eban, but in other respects he had good reasons to feel gratified. The President was reassuring about Russia, sounded determined to take action, and was optimistic about getting enough participation to make his plan feasible. Above all, he demonstrated respect for Israel's military capacity and did not at any point seek to foreclose for Israel the alternative of acting alone. He merely suggested that if it was willing to wait it would not need to do so. But one thing that Eban apparently failed to realize was that whatever was satisfying in the President's position was predicated on the assumption that Israel had the will and the capacity to take things into its own hands, thus making it necessary for the United States to deliver on its commitment regarding Gulf navigation if it wanted to avert war. For Eban went on that same day, upon Tel Aviv's instructions, to dispel or cast doubt upon that assumption by raising an alarm about the prospect of an Egyptian attack, which betrayed Israeli fear and unpreparedness for war. As Eban departed, American officials juxtaposed the impression they had always held about Israeli determination with the new one and waited for confirmation of either from the decision of Israel's Cabinet. When that decision came out in favor of continuing diplomatic action rather than going to war, the conclusion was drawn that Israel thought the cost of war to be prohibitive and had no recourse on the navigation question other than what the United States was prepared to do for it.

What went on in the Israeli Cabinet meeting on that May 27 and on the following day was actually somewhat different. The decision in favor of diplomatic action was really taken under circumstances that contained the seeds of its own undoing a few days later. At that meeting, all the considerations that had affected Israel's decisions up to that point found a dramatic expression that prepared the ground for the denouement that was to follow. Two themes underlay the long and agonized discussion: the validity and desirability of President Johnson's plan, and the costs to Israel of the alternative of military action. Taking everything into account, Eban argued in favor of holding back until the outcome of the President's project became apparent. He found support for his view among some Cabinet members. A second group voiced something akin to the view of the military chiefs, doubting the effectiveness of the President's plan even if it could be realized and questioning its desirability in any case. Members of this group asked rhetorically how long the maritime powers would keep naval units in the Gulf of Aqaba just to insure Israeli free navigation and argued that even if such freedom were secured indefinitely, the fact that it would depend on others would imply a failure of Israel's own deterrent that would have other ominous consequences. This group therefore urged immediate military action and was confident in its outcome. It was less confident about the costs involved but was willing to pay the price anyway. Between these two groups there was a third one whose views were critical for the outcome of the discussion. This group strongly doubted that the President would be able to deliver on his promises because of the extreme difficulty of getting a group of maritime powers to agree on forceful action. Though their position suggested a military response by Israel, they were fearful of the outcome and even more fearful of the costs of such action.

Eshkol spoke for the second group, and his position as Prime Minister and Minister of Defense should have carried a decisive weight with the waverers of the third group. But it is indicative of the pass to which things had come that Eshkol's swing back to a "hawkish" position, far from reassuring the waverers, only confirmed them in their doubts by seemingly providing new evidence of his unsteady judgment. When the question of immediate military response was finally put to a vote, the result was a tie, with nine ministers for and nine against. Among those who voted against were three Ministers from the National Religious Front, who did so because they mistrusted Eshkol's competence as Minister of Defense and were intent on having him replaced.

Already before the Cabinet meeting of May 27 an effort had been made by the two main opposition parties, Gachal and Rafi, to persuade Eshkol to take Ben Gurion into the Cabinet as Minister of Defense. It was a measure of the prevailing sense of national emergency that the leaders of these two parties, Menachem Begin and Ben Gurion, who had been inveterate political enemies for more than 20 years and could never bring themselves to exchange a mere hello, were yet able to meet and work together on the idea of a governmental reshuffle. Eshkol flatly turned down the proposal conveyed to him with great feeling by Menachem Begin, on the ground that he could not possibly work with Ben Gurion—so deep can political passions run in Israel. But, just then, the leader of the National Religious Front, Moshe Shapira, who was Minister of the Interior in Eshkol's government, joined with the leaders of the two opposition parties in another effort aimed at placing General Dayan as Minister of Defense. Dayan, the victor of

the Sinai War of 1956, a man of supreme self-confidence and conta-
gious courage, was already preparing to make himself useful by reviewing the military dispositions of Israel and its enemies with Eshkol's specially granted permission.

During the Cabinet meeting of May 27 that we have just discussed,
Moshe Shapira found an occasion to raise formally the proposal of ap-
pointing Dayan as Minister of Defense. According to one report, this
move led to the following exchange between Eshkol and Shapira:

> Eshkol: Tell me at last just what you think. From my conver-
> sations with you I got the impression that you are inclined toward
> moderation. Yet now you come up and propose the candidacy of
> Moshe Dayan, who is known to favor a military response. Isn't
> there some contradiction here?
>
> Shapira: I trust Dayan and his judgment.[27]

The Minister of the Interior added, according to the report, that his
party would not vote for any military action as long as Eshkol continued in the post of Minister of Defense.

Eshkol's ordeal was to get much worse yet. After the Cabinet meeting broke up inconclusively, he attended a special session of the General Staff to report on what happened. It was now the turn of the military chiefs to question his leadership and determination and to argue
again before him that the issue was no longer, if it ever was, simply
the blockade but the very existence of Israel. The Egyptian army had
changed from a defensive to an offensive deployment. Every day that
passed without a riposte would increase the casualty rate by 200 in
case of war. Nasser had thrown the gauntlet in Israel's face; its failure
to respond would certainly invite new pressures.

Shortly after Eshkol reached his home late at night after these painful
meetings, he was awakened by the Soviet ambassador to be handed an
urgent message from Premier Kosygin that was a problem in itself. As
Eshkol might have expected, the message included a warning to Israel
to refrain from any aggressive action against the Arab countries, but,
contrary to his expectation, it was also couched in comparatively moderate tones and gave a hint of a suggestion that the Soviet Union
might be open to a less one-sided position in the future if Israel exercised self-restraint.

Eshkol, who had for years dreamed of a rapprochement with Russia,
was induced by this slight hint of possible Soviet understanding to pro-
pose to go to Moscow for further talks with the Soviet government.

[27] Shmuel Segev, *op. cit.*, p. 70.

Naturally, the ambassador could only promise to refer the proposal to Moscow. The episode indicated, however, that if Eshkol's discussion with the military leaders had stiffened his determination, the thin trace of hope from Moscow had countered that effect.

Hours after the nocturnal visit of the Russian, the American ambassador appeared in the dawn of a Sunday morning to deliver a message from President Johnson. The note apparently reiterated the promise made to Eban, spoke in hopeful terms about the progress of the project of collective action by maritime powers, and urged patience on Israel's part. Eshkol may not have known then the ironic origin of these two messages from the chiefs of the superpowers, which was nothing other than the alarm Israel itself had raised in Washington two days before about an impending Egyptian attack. The United States government had taken this occasion to caution the Egyptians and to ask the Russians to do likewise. The latter had agreed to do so on condition that a similar démarche should be directed at Israel for the sake of symmetry and in order to avoid any implication that Egypt had been singled out as the potential aggressor. In any case, the approaches of the two powers at that particular time helped sway Eshkol to go along with those who opposed immediate military action. The Cabinet was thus able to decide to continue with diplomatic efforts while stressing that time was running short.

Eshkol's apparent inability to stick to one clear conception as to just what the issue at stake was—whether it was desirable even if it were possible for Israel to rely on other powers for keeping the Strait open and what would be the likely outcome of war and its likely costs—ended up by causing the mistrust in his judgment to spread from his coalition partners to many of the leaders of his own party. Feeling in the country at large also flowed in the same direction in torrential strength after Eshkol went on the air on May 28 to report on the decision of the government. By that time, the failure of U Thant's mission in Cairo, the futile debates in the Security Council, the barrage of broadcasts from Cairo voicing Egypt's increasingly belligerent posture, reports of ever greater Egyptian troop concentrations, and the tensions naturally fostered by a state of total mobilization had built up an atmosphere of unbearable suspense that sought relief in the words of the Prime Minister. It so happened that Eshkol had to read his speech in bad lighting, from handwritten notes that had not been typed for lack of time, and while he was in a state of near physical and mental exhaustion. Consequently, besides his reporting what was taken as a "do nothing" decision, his delivery was painfully faltering. The nation that had been sitting on edge for so long and expected from its leader on this fateful moment a speech of Churchillian quality got instead what was dubbed "the mumbling speech," in which it was given nothing to hold on to. It is said that soldiers at the front smashed their transistors in a mixture of disgust and despair.

Acting under the impact of the enormous wave of popular disgruntlement, the Parliamentary Party of the Alignment, including Eshkol's own Mapai Party and Achdut Haavoda, urged at a meeting held on May 29 with Eshkol's participation that the defense portfolio be handed either to General Dayan or to Minister of Labor Yigal Allon, a hero of the war of 1948 and member of Achdut Haavoda. Overwhelmed, Eshkol resigned himself to handing the defense position to Allon; but when he proceeded to convey his decision to his coalition partners, he encountered determined opposition from Moshe Shapira, who suspected that Allon would be beholden to Eshkol and not sufficiently independent. The Minister of the Interior threatened to hand in the resignation of his party from the coalition immediately and bring down the government unless Dayan were appointed Minister of Defense without delay. The next day Eshkol called Dayan in and worked out with him an arrangement whereby the popular general would be appointed Commander of the Southern Front while Allon would become Minister of Defense, but after another day of wrangling, the Secretariat of the Prime Minister's own party rejected this and other proposed arrangements and voted for Dayan as Minister of Defense as well as for a "wall to wall" coalition excluding only the Communists. The die was cast.

While these internal political wranglings were going on, the events we have analyzed in the previous section were taking place: the apparent fizzling out of the project of collective action, the spreading notion in American governmental circles that the decision of the Israeli Cabinet of May 28 marked the passing of the worst of the crisis and opened the door to compromise, the mounting intransigence of Egypt, the rallying together of the Arab countries, and the conclusion of the Egyptian-Jordanian agreement. These developments, especially the beginning of an airlift of Egyptian troops and matériel to Jordan and the movement toward that country of large Iraqi troops, disposed even the most hesitant members of the Cabinet to think that military action could no longer be postponed. What Dayan's presence in the Cabinet at this point did was not so much to influence the nature of the decision as to allow the Cabinet to make it with an easier heart. On June 3, after Dayan presented to the Cabinet the outline of the military situation, the operational plans that the military chiefs had prepared, the dour alternative to immediate action, and his confident judgment that the Israeli armed forces could swiftly execute the task to be entrusted to them, it was with relief that it unanimously gave him the go ahead and left it to him to choose the exact timing. He chose June 5, 1967.

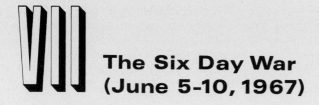

The Six Day War
(June 5-10, 1967)

Introduction

A truly reliable analysis of the course of the Six-Day War must await the publication of official documents or the records and recollections of people in a position to know the facts. After the Sinai War of 1956, it was ten years before the first such document became available in the form of General Dayan's *Diary*. Nevertheless, thanks to the modern media of communications and to the fact that their agents and workers were alerted well in advance to the likelihood of hostilities breaking out, the recent war was so well covered, at least on the Israeli side, as to permit the presentation already of a reasonably accurate and fairly complete preliminary picture of that amazing armed encounter.

The Armed Forces of the Opponents on the Eve of the War

The first step in the description and analysis of any war, from the standpoint of the actual military operations, should be a comparative account of the opponents' armed forces just prior to the outbreak of hostilities. However, such an account, if it is to be meaningful and reasonably complete, cannot be kept short, especially if one considers the great variety of military hardware available today. However, in the present case, such an account would be somewhat redundant since a complete tableau of all Middle Eastern states' military establishments as of mid-1965 was presented in Chapter V. Consequently, only a few general remarks will be made here about the quantitative and qualitative characteristics of the armed forces of Israel, Egypt, Syria, and Jordan as of the first half of 1967. The interested reader will find a detailed and complete picture of these countries' armed forces in Appendix B. In addition, Appendix C contains a technical description of the relevant military matériel (types, performances, and armaments of planes, tanks, and missiles), since it is clear that no meaningful inter-country comparisons are possible unless something is said about the capabilities of the weapons with which the opponents' armed forces were endowed on the eve of the war.

Looking first at sheer numbers, the military balance of power between Israel, on the one hand, and Egypt, Syria, and Jordan, on the other, as of the first half of 1967 is summarized in Table XXI.

One sees that, in terms of sheer numbers, the three Arab states that actually waged war against Israel had an appreciable numerical superiority in virtually all fields. Their smallest margin of superiority, paradoxically, was in manpower, and one of their largest margins over Israel was in the vital domain of supersonic interceptors/fighter-bombers. The Arab states had an infinite lead over Israel in the field of modern medium jet bombers, of which Israel had none. Thus, whereas the Egyptian Tu-16's were suitable for bombing strategic targets such as cities and big installations, the Israeli light Vautour bombers could really be used efficiently only against military targets, their bombloads being too small for anything approaching saturation bombing.

Insofar as air forces are concerned, it would seem that, except for Israel's Fouga trainers, which were not equal to the Arab subsonic fleet, neither side had a definite *qualitative* advantage over the other. However, General Hod said in an interview after the war that, after carefully testing the Iraqi MIG-21 that had earlier fallen into their hands, the Israeli air force had concluded that the Mirage was a somewhat better plane.[1]

It is clear that the Soviet armor supplied to Egypt and Syria was generally superior, qualitatively speaking, to the older and lighter Western armor in Israeli hands.[2] In the field of artillery too, the weight of evidence is that the Soviet-supplied Egyptian and Syrian hardware was qualitatively superior to the Israeli artillery.

Combining quantitative and qualitative information, it appears clearly that the three Arab nations had a decisive material advantage

[1] CBS-TV, July 18, 1967.
[2] See Appendix C.

TABLE XXI: *The Opposing Forces*

	Israel	Egypt	Egypt, Syria, and Jordan	(Egypt + Syria + Jordan): (Israel)
Armed forces upon mobilization	275,000	210,000	335,000	1.2 : 1
Tanks and assault guns	1,050[1]	1,300	2,100	2.0 : 1
Supersonic fighter-bombers and interceptors[2]	116	258	298	2.6 : 1
Subsonic fighter-bombers[3]	150	100	168	1.1 : 1
Light bombers[4]	24	43	47	2.0 : 1
Medium bombers[5]		30	45	(45.0 vs. 0)
Destroyers	2	6	6	3.0 : 1
Submarines	4	9	9	2.3 : 1

[1] Including 150 light tanks, not found in Arab countries.

[2] MIG-21; Sukhoi-7; MIG-19; Mirage-III; Super-Mystère.

[3] MIG-15/17; Hawker-Hunter; Mystère IVA; Ouragan; as well as 60 Israeli Fouga Magister trainers.

[4] IL-28; Vautour IIA.

[5] Tu-16.

Sources, criteria used, and comments: See Appendices B and C.

over Israel. Because of this, knowledgeable and qualified observers did not anticipate anything approaching the actual course of the war. Thus, for example, Hanson Baldwin estimated on May 24, 1967: "A comparison of tangibles and intangibles of military power in the Middle East would seem to indicate that neither side has enough superiority to court all-out war." [3] The *New York Times* Cairo correspondent, Eric Pace, wrote on May 22: "[The Egyptian forces now deployed] would presumably prevent any sudden humiliating defeat, like that of the offensive of 1956, when the Israelis overran the Sinai peninsula." The Administration's military experts took, in their majority, a similar view and expected that a series of swift initial moves, in which the opponents would destroy most of each other's air forces and

[3] See the *New York Times*, May 24, 1967.

armor, would be followed by a long war of attrition in which Israel would be bled white. This seems also to have been President de Gaulle's view, despite reports to the contrary that were published subsequently. Various indications suggest a similar Russian expectation.

The Air War

The War between Israel and its Arab neighbors started on Monday, June 5, with a series of Israeli air strikes, which, within 170 minutes, all but eliminated Arab air capacity.[4]

Observers and instant experts immediately went to work to discover the "gimmick" that made it possible for the Israeli air force to destroy several hundred enemy planes in a few hours—over four hundred in one day. There was thus talk of "Pearl Harbor," of devices to jam the Egyptian radar, of a new type of bomb, of special aiming instruments, of a wide flanking movement, and so on. Actually, a close analysis of the action would show that the Israeli success is attributable to nothing more than the superior quality of Israeli planning, training, and execution, and the extraordinary dedication of the Israeli flyers. The element of surprise might have been considered an extraordinary factor if, as in Pearl Harbor, the Egyptians did not expect an Israeli attack; but since, by Nasser's own admission, this was not the case, the *tactical* surprise achieved by the Israelis can only be considered a function of their qualitative superiority.[5] Even then, the element of surprise was operative only in the first wave of attack, not the subsequent ones, and only in the case of the Egyptian air force. The Jordanian and Syrian air forces were attacked, and knocked out, several hours after the Egyptian.

The first wave of Israeli war planes went out on Monday morning at 7:45 A.M. Tel Aviv time, 8:45 Cairo time. Its targets were the ten most important of Egypt's 18 military airfields. Three of these ten airfields were in the Cairo region (Cairo-West, Almaza, Inshass), three in the Canal area (Kabrit, Fayed, Abu Suweir), and four in Sinai (el Arish, Jebel Libni, Bir Thamada, Bir Gafgafa). The Israeli planes flew to their targets from many directions and reached them on the same instant.

[4] There is no doubt that Israel initiated the attack. Those who would draw from this the conclusion that Israel was the "aggressor" confuse attack and aggression —two different ideas. "The aggressor," as Taine put it, "is the one who makes war unavoidable." And Haykal wrote a whole column in *al Ahram* of May 26, 1967, to demonstrate that Nasser's moves had made war unavoidable.

[5] In his speech on July 23, 1967, Nasser said he had told the Higher Executive Council that Israel would attack on June 5 and that it would begin its attack with an air strike.

They observed complete radio silence and flew very low. This procedure meant increased fuel consumption (about one-third more than at height), but it had, of course, the great advantage that the attacking planes remained below the different radars scanning the area. These radars were quite numerous: The Israelis counted no less than 16 stations in Sinai and seven elsewhere in Egypt; there was the powerful Jordanian Marconi 247 radar station at Ajlun; and there were the British radars atop a mountain in Cyprus, the American airborne and naval radars of the Sixth Fleet, as well as the Russian naval stations nearby. If the latter had picked up the Israeli planes on their screens, they would most likely have passed that information on very quickly to the Egyptian air command.

But flying under all these radars was not sufficient; with the planes flying as low as 150 feet, air watches on the ground had to be taken into account. To avoid the possibility of detection, the Israeli planes of the first wave must have made their way to their targets over the sea and through the desert gaps between inhabited areas and military positions, such as west of Alexandria to reach Cairo and south of Port Said to reach the Suez Canal airfields. That targets in these areas were hit simultaneously with the airfields in Sinai—which were probably reached directly—is a measure of the accuracy of Israeli planning and execution. In subsequent waves as well as in attacks on other airfields (Cairo International, Dekheila, Ghurdaka, Luxor, Minia, Mansura, Bani Suwaif, Ras Banias), the Israelis must have flown by the most convenient ways, since surprise was no longer so possible or so important. The timing of the first wave of attack at such a late hour as 7:45/8:45 A.M. was probably due to several reasons: (1) the very fact that it was unusual; (2) a wait for the morning mist common over Cairo and the Canal area to dissipate; (3) the probability that this was a time when Egyptian air patrols were minimal or absent.[6]

---

[6] A possible fourth reason—and a very intriguing one—was mentioned by Haykal in *al Ahram*, September 13, 1967. Haykal reported that on June 5 at 8:00 A.M. (Cairo time) a military plane took off from a Cairo military airfield with Marshal Amer together with the commander of the air force and high general staff officers on board and headed for Thamada air base in Sinai. Seeing them off in Cairo were other high staff officers and waiting to receive them in Thamada were all the division commanders. Haykal speculated that the Israelis might have known about all this through breaking the Egyptian cipher and timed their attack so as to get as many of these officers as possible, or at least to take advantage of their absence from their command posts. In the event, the plane with its distinguished cargo arrived in Thamada but could not land, returned to its base of origin but could not land there either as both were under attack, and finally came down at Cairo International Airport, one hour and a half after the start of the Israeli air attacks.

The first wave caught all Egyptian planes on the ground, with the exception of four unarmed trainers.[7] Each of the ten Egyptian military airfields chosen as targets was attacked by successive groups of four planes, each of which made several running passes over the target to bomb, rocket, and strafe. Despite the sometimes heavy AA fire that met them, the Israeli pilots flew over their targets at low speeds to increase the accuracy of their fire (a few reports have it that some even lowered their plane's undercarriage to reduce speed to a minimum). The pilots of the first wave and possibly of those that immediately followed were instructed to disregard all targets except the Egyptian MIG-21 interceptors and the Tu-16 medium jet bombers. The planes of the first type were the only ones capable of posing a serious threat to the Israeli Mirages-IIICJ's, while the destruction of the Tu-16's robbed the Egyptians of the possibility to retaliate with large-scale bombing runs on Israeli cities.

The Israeli pilots found most of the Egyptian planes well dispersed over their fields, though none were in underground bombproof hangars (the Israelis have at least one airfield with such hangars). The ensuing destruction of matériel was so complete that only two flights of four MIG-21's each were able to take off, only to be destroyed after having downed two Israeli craft engaged in ground attack. Twenty Egyptian planes (12 MIG-21's and 8 MIG-19's) that shortly before the war had been shifted to the Ghurdaka air base on the Red Sea coast also managed to take off, presumably because that field was not attacked by the first wave; they headed toward their former bases in the Canal area only to find the runways there unusable. They were shot down. It seems that when some Israeli craft of the first wave arrived over their targets, they found a fairly large number of MIG-21's taxiing or getting ready to take off; the destruction of these planes was especially important because it meant the elimination of their highly trained pilots. The same thing of course holds for some of the pilots of the Egyptian craft shot down in the course of dog-fights, of which more in a moment.

According to all witnesses, including the author, who subsequently visited the Egyptian airfields in Sinai, Israeli gunmanship was remarkably accurate. Often only one or two 30-mm cannon shells were enough to shoot up one plane on the ground, even when it was surrounded by a protective concrete wall on all sides but one; the evidence of misses was rare.

[7] R. and W. Churchill in *Jerusalem Post Weekly*, July 24, 1967; and *Der Spiegel*, July 24, 1967.

Besides destroying grounded Egyptian planes, the Israeli aircraft bombed the runways in order to immobilize those planes that might have survived and to restrict the possibilities of redeployment or the bringing in of reinforcements. According to one story, the Israelis used a specially designed bomb to maximize damage.[8] General Hod confirmed the fact that his forces experimented with some home-designed bombing devices but asserted that this was not of any quantitative consequence since almost all the bombing was done with conventional means.[9]

While the first wave of Israeli craft was on its targets, another was already on its way, and a third was already airborne. From 7:45 A.M. until 10:35 A.M., one wave of incoming planes followed another at intervals of 12 to 19 minutes. Since planes were scheduled to stay over their targets eight to nine minutes, making at least three runs, some Egyptian airfields at least were kept under almost constant attack for two hours and 50 minutes, thus getting no chance whatsoever to recover.

As the first targets were destroyed, the list of targets was extended to all types of Egyptian planes, to radar installations, and to SAM-2 sites. Reportedly, all 23 Egyptian radar stations were destroyed but only a limited number of SAM-2 sites suffered a similar fate.[10] This, however, did not make much difference since, according to General Hod, all SAM-2's fired at Israeli planes missed, with one possible exception. Israeli flyers apparently learned how to dodge the missiles.

Simultaneously, the number of Egyptian airfields attacked was also increased until all 18 were covered. Thus, eight of the formidable TU-16 bombers that had been removed from Cairo West and Bani Suwaif to Luxor beyond the range of Israel's best planes met their doom there at the hands of lowly Vautours. A group of surviving Sukhoi-7's, MIG-19's and MIG-15/17's, which had been transferred to Cairo International Airport, were also visited and caught. In the afternoon of that first day, Israeli planes attacked some of the same air bases they had hit in the morning to mop up and prevent repair of the runways. More visits for the same purpose took place Monday night and Tuesday.

The devastating effectiveness of Israel's air blow can be gathered from Table XXII, which enumerates Egyptian losses:

In addition to these fighting planes, Egypt lost on that first day 32 transport planes, 56 during the entire war, including eight Antonov-12,

[8] R. and W. Churchill, *op. cit.*
[9] Hod on NBC-TV, Channel 4/Boston, July 23, 1967: "Israel's Victory."
[10] Two sites according to *The Sunday Telegraph,* June 11, 1967.

TABLE XXII: *Egyptian Aircraft Losses*

	Existing before the War	Destroyed on Monday[1]	Destroyed During Entire War[2]
MIG-21's	163	90	100
SU-7's	55	12	14
MIG-19's	40	20	30
MIG-15/17's	100	75	95
Tu-16's	30	30	30
IL-28's	43	27	30

1 Official communiqué by General Hod in D. Dayan, *Mé Hermon 'Ad Suetz*, Tel Aviv, 1967, p. 29.

2 R. and W. Churchill, *op. cit.*

31 Il-14, ten huge MI-6 helicopters, and seven MIL-4 helicopters.[11]

All told the Israeli air force destroyed somewhat over 450 Egyptian, Jordanian, Syrian, and Iraqi planes during the entire war: 410 were destroyed on the first day, 19 on the second, 14 on the third, and nine on the fourth.[12]

These figures speak for themselves and show clearly that, by Monday night, Egypt had only a vestigial air force. The Israelis had done in three hours what the British and the French air forces took three days to accomplish in 1956. With about one in three or four flyers killed, the command structure disrupted, the commanders demoralized, and many surviving planes damaged, it was surprising that Egypt was at all able to get a few planes into action in the closing days of the war, as for instance during the battle of Bir Gafgafa. How could such a carnage have been wrought by the smaller Israeli air force?

First, instead of dividing the air force into three parts, one each assigned to the tasks of attack, air defense, and ground support, the Israelis threw practically everything they had into the first strike. In General Hod's words, "we used all we had got." This can be seen from Israel's losses on Monday, June 5:

2 Mirage-IIICJ's
4 Super-Mystères

11 Shmuel Segev, *op. cit.*, p. 257.
12 General Hod, *Jerusalem Post*, July 2, 1967.

4 Mystère-IVA's
4 Ouragans
1 Vautour light bomber
4 Fouga Magister trainers

19 Total [13]

As one sees, even the very obsolete Ouragan fighters and the slow and lightly armed Fouga Magister trainers were put into action. All but two of these downed planes fell prey to AA fire. The fact that Israel's air force really "scratched the bottom of its drawers" in order to carry out as massive an attack as possible is the first element that explains its staggering success. How far this policy of total commitment was carried can be seen from the fact that only 12 Israeli fighter planes did not take part in the initial strikes and remained as a cover over Israel; of these, eight went up to provide a defensive screen, leaving four in reserve.[14]

This audacious piece of gambling was taken on the assumption that it would be an hour or so before the Egyptian High Command sorted out what was happening and another hour or so before it would notify its Syrian, Jordanian, and Iraqi allies and before these could go into operation. By then, most of the job in Egypt would have been completed, and attacks from other quarters could be adequately met. In the event, the assumption proved conservative.

The second factor underlying the success of Israel's strikes against Egypt is the very rapid rotation of the planes participating in the raids. According to Israeli plans, it had to take no more than one hour for a plane attacking an airfield in the Canal region to be back over its target after having returned to its base, refueled, rearmed and taken off again. This incredibly short time-lapse was made up as follows: approximately 22.5 minutes to reach the target, eight minutes for the attack, approximately 20 minutes to return to base (less than on the outbound leg of the trip because the planes were lighter), 7.5 minutes for refueling and rearming operations, leaving a safety margin of two minutes. That only 7.5 minutes were allowed for a plane to refuel, rearm, and take off on a new mission gives the measure of the proficiency of the Israeli ground crews. Another, even more important measure, is provided by the testimony—however one may discount it—of General Hod, who said: "At 7:45 on Monday morning the serviceability of our combat aircraft was better than 99 percent; and we maintained that

---

[13] *Le Monde*, June 7, 1967; report from Israel.
[14] S. L. A. Marshall, CBS-TV, Channel 5/Boston, July 18, 1967.

level of serviceability throughout the week of the war. Although it might have taken up to an hour to patch up holes in one or two of our aircraft, at no stage was any of our aircraft unserviceable, if you exclude our losses. Never did we have the situation of pilots waiting for aircraft." [15]

As a result, Israeli planes (and pilots) averaged about five sorties a day, and some made as many as eight. To appreciate this, one must remember that the normal number of sorties of American aircraft in Vietnam is on the order of two. Moreover, the Israeli air command had reckoned on the basis of prewar exercises that four to five Egyptian planes would be destroyed per raid on each airfield; in reality, the average during the first few hours turned out to be twice as high.

These two elements combined—total commitment and ultrarapid rotation—explain why the Israelis managed to keep most of 18 enemy airfields under almost constant attack for close to three hours, as can be shown by a rough calculation. Assuming that all ten airfields attacked by the first wave remained under attack for three hours, and assuming that each was attacked at an average interval of 15 minutes by four planes that could be back over their target inside one hour on the average (see above), one comes up with a total requirement of 160 planes (that is, 10 x 4 x 4 = 160). Since Israel had some 300 war planes, this would have still left 140 planes to deal with the other airfields, to allow for losses and mishaps, and to give us an ample margin of error.

It is interesting to compare these calculations with similar ones made by the military analyst of *al Ahram*. On June 5, at 9 o'clock (Cairo time), he argued, the enemy attacked simultaneously 11 bases. In addition, he hit on the first strike the Ferdan bridge over the Suez Canal, ferry number 6, the radar of Tal'at al Badan, the radar of al Hasanah, and an artillery scouting battalion at Kusseima. Taking these additional targets as the "equivalent" of two air bases, in terms of the planes they kept occupied, he arrived at 13 targets attacked simultaneously over a period of two hours.

The attack, he said, came in waves of 12 planes each. Consequently, in the first wave there must have been: 13 x 12 = 156 planes. During the first two hours, each base was subjected to at least three enemy sorties. Considering that a jet needs 30 to 40 minutes to refuel and rearm, and 25 to 30 minutes flying time to and from the target (for a total of 55 to 80 minutes), [sic] one plane could not have participated in more than one sortie in the course of the first two hours. Therefore, the number of planes participating in all three sorties was: 156 x 3 =

[15] London *Sunday Times*, June 8.

468. Since this number was almost double the number of planes of the
types that participated in the action possessed by Israel (250 to 280),
the "irrefutable" conclusion was that Israel was helped by the Western powers.[16]

It is obvious that the writer mistook three successive waves of four
planes each for a single wave of 12 planes—an excusable mistake, perhaps, since by the time one wave of four had completed its runs over
the target, there were only a few minutes (almost the time between
runs of a single plane) before the next wave of four arrived. Another
factor that distorted his calculations was the fact that he allowed 30
to 40 minutes for refueling and rearming when actually the Israelis
took close to 7.5 minutes to do so. Clearly, the analyst projected onto
Israel's air force the calculations accepted in the air force of his own
country. A captured operational plan revealed indeed that the Egyptian air command allowed 175 minutes between sorties for MIG-17's
and MIG-19's operating from Sinai against targets in the Elath region
of Israel.[17]

In the face of the extraordinary performance of Israel's air force, it
is not surprising that the Egyptians were thrown into some confusion.
The military analyst just cited, for instance, after having "proved" that
Western forces must have helped Israel in its first strike, went on to
explain that the reason why no American planes were shot down over
Egypt was because they cautiously avoided entering into action on the
Egyptian front and contented themselves with providing Israel with a
defensive umbrella that allowed it to throw all its own forces into the
battle! President Nasser, in his resignation speech, adopted at one and
the same time the themes that Israel must have relied on someone to
protect it against retaliation and that it used an air force "three times
its normal strength." Only four months after the war were the Egyptians finally able to persuade themselves that Israel alone, with its prewar air force, could inflict the blow it did, and thus put to rest the
myth about American participation.[18]

The preceding makes it partly understandable why on Monday, June
5, Egypt's guard was lowered. Given the comparative strength of the
Egyptian and the Israeli air forces and given the number of airfields
over which the Egyptian planes were dispersed, Egypt's planners did
not anticipate anything approaching Israel's devastating strikes; one
does not of course prepare for what is deemed to be entirely impossible. Nevertheless, the fact that practically all Egyptian planes were on

[16] *al Ahram,* June 21, 1967.
[17] Segev, *op. cit.,* p. 23.
[18] See the article by Haykal in *al Ahram,* October 13, 1967.

the ground shows that lack of serious preparedness and organization, overconfidence, and general irresponsibility were also a factor. Given the political situation after the Strait of Tiran had been closed, it was simply unforgivable that the Egyptian high air command should not have kept up intensive round-the-clock patroling over its territory.

In this context, it can be safely asserted that the same tactics would never have succeeded to nearly the same extent against Israel. In the first place, Israel, unable to rely on dispersal of airfields in its constricted territory, sought a measure of safety by putting some of its planes underground. Furthermore, the Israeli air command maintained a constant air watch; its state of preparedness was unequaled in the Middle East and lived up to the standards of any air force in the world. The record of Israeli-Arab air incidents in the years preceding the war shows this clearly: No sooner did an Arab aircraft cross the border by never more than a few miles than it was shot down by Israeli interceptors. Finally, the comparative quality of the Israeli flyers, as revealed in the war, was another assurance. In the dog-fights that took place during the war, the score was 60 to 1 in favor of Israel.[19]

The air war against Jordan, Syria, and Iraq can be disposed of briefly. The air forces of these countries did not intervene in the war until some three hours after Israel struck on Monday, June 5. Syrian planes made a number of ineffective forays against Megiddo and Haifa Bay. Two out of three MIG-15/17's were shot down over Megiddo and the third later crashed over Tawafik.[20] Tiberias also suffered a light bombing attack.[21] At 12:25 three Jordanian Hunters attacked Natanya with rockets, injuring seven persons in an insecticide plant and causing a fire, before being driven off by a single Israeli Mystère. The Israeli satellite air base of Kfar Sirkin, near the Jordanian border, also suffered a light air attack. But, by then, the bulk of the Israeli air force had become available again, and retaliation was almost instantaneous.

In a series of raids on the Jordanian airfields at Amman and Mafrak, the entire small air force of King Hussein was destroyed. Within the same hours, two-thirds of the Syrian air force was put out of action. The remaining Syrian planes fled to airfields outside the range of effective action in the area and left the skies over the Golan Heights to sole Israeli control. General Hod boasted: "It took us 25 minutes to deal with the air forces of Jordan and Syria," and added that the best Arab

[19] Segev, op. cit., p. 255. A different reckoning might make it 60 to 3.

[20] New York Times, June 6, 1967; Jerusalem Post, June 6, 1967.

[21] Général André Beaufre, Comment Israel a vaincu trois fois sur trois fronts, in Paris Match, June 24, 1967. General Beaufre was in command of the French forces against Egypt in 1956.

pilots the Israelis had to fight were the Jordanians. In these attacks the element of surprise was entirely missing; yet the results were swift and decisive.

On Tuesday, June 6, there occurred the only serious air penetration over Israel. An Iraqi Tu-16 bomber dropped three of its six bombs on the town of Natanya; the pilot, a colonel and one of the commanders of the Iraqi air force, apparently thought it was Tel Aviv. With his three remaining bombs, he then headed home, but was downed by AA fire in the Afula area. In retaliation for this raid, the Israelis staged an attack on the Iraqi air base at H-3, a pumping station on the Kirkuk pipeline near the Jordanian border, and destroyed most of the planes of the single Iraqi MIG-21 squadron that had been flown there earlier. In the process, they lost two planes, and their pilots were taken prisoners.

All told, the Israelis claim to have destroyed during the war nine MIG-21's and five Hunters belonging to the Iraqi air force, in addition to the Tu-16 brought down by AA fire. As to Syria, it is claimed to have lost no fewer than 32 MIG-21's, which must have been its entire fleet or close to it; in addition, some 23 Syrian MIG-15/17's were also destroyed.[22]

All told, the Israeli air force flew several thousand sorties during the entire war, of which more than one thousand occurred in the first day.[23] According to General Hod, about two-thirds of all sorties were in connection with ground operations. On Monday, few planes were available for close ground support except for the Fouga Magister trainers, which were called upon to silence enemy artillery and to crack up particularly tough positions. In the following days, however, the air force of Israel played a crucial role in connection with ground opera-

[22] An alleged incident about which not much is known concerns a flight of Algerian MIG's and transports which, on the second or third day of the war, presented themselves over the airfield of el Arish, by then in Israeli hands. After permission to land had been granted them, the Israeli troops on the ground supposedly captured both planes and occupants. In this version, the story is surely apocryphal. The Algerian MIG's were never exhibited nor seen by anyone, and the Israelis have not been inclined to hide whatever booty they took; neither has there been any subsequent word of Algerian prisoners. However, the curious thing is that Israeli authorities refused to either confirm or deny the report. So, we would speculate that what might have happened is that these planes indeed asked for permission to land, but then either the control tower of el Arish or some action on the ground (for example, AA fire) betrayed to the Algerians that the airfield had passed into Israeli hands, so that they turned back toward Egypt, while the Israelis belatedly realized that they had just missed a great opportunity.

[23] Segev, *op. cit.*, p. 25.

tions, although this has been so overplayed as to make the land operations appear subsidiaries. While the Israeli combat craft destroyed countless trucks and light vehicles and many tanks, they destroyed most of them late in the war, while they were fleeing. The Israeli armored forces made their decisive breakthrough without the benefit of air cover, as we shall presently see, and were responsible for most of the tanks knocked out or captured during the war.

The Land War

Simultaneously with the air strike against Egyptian air bases, Israeli columns crossed the armistice lines at several points to launch a general offensive against Egypt's land forces. A few hours later, Jordan opened an artillery barrage against Jerusalem and many other points on its border with Israel, and Jordanian troops seized the strategically located United Nations Headquarters in Jerusalem's no-man's land. The Israelis responded with a counterattack that expelled the Jordanians from the latter position and followed on with offensive operations in several sectors of their long front with Jordan. Sometime before, the Syrians had already entered into action with air attacks and massive artillery barrages against all Israeli settlements within range. The Israelis contented themselves then and later with defensive operations and air strikes until they finished off the Jordanian front and were in a position to transfer large numbers of troops for a massive offensive against the Syrians.

Except for the fact that Jordan and Syria entered the war when Israel attacked on the Egyptian front, the three Arab countries in effect fought their enemy on land in three separate wars. The lightning speed of Israel's attacks simply gave no chance to the Egyptian-led United Arab Command to even attempt any coordinated operations. On Israel's side, the land war against Egypt and Jordan was also fought as two separate wars; offensives were conducted on both fronts simultaneously and were terminated before there was time or need to shuffle troops between them. However, the land war against Syria was to some extent strategically linked with the war against Jordan in that operations on these two fronts were closely coordinated and required the maneuvering of a single pool of troops. But even here, serious operations against the Syrians did not begin until operations against Jordan were terminated.

Because of this essential disjunction of the theaters of war, we can follow the unfolding of military operations in each front separately without being concerned while dealing with one front about what was happening in another. We only need to precede our analysis with a sketch of the way in which the Israeli High Command assigned the forces at its disposal among the three fronts at the outset of the war and refer later on to the movement of troops from the Jordanian to the Syrian front, as these were the only inter-theater decisions in the entire land war.

It is impossible to obtain a truly reliable picture of specifics concerning the Israeli armed forces until the Israeli authorities themselves decide to divulge the facts. In the case of the Arab countries, defeat violated their military secrets. Documents were captured, prisoners talked, and the Israelis boasted. With Israel, however, victory has kept the veil of secrecy almost intact, and the accounts of hundreds of military reporters have only lifted corners of it for brief moments. It is from the glimpses of Israel's armed forces that could be caught at such moments that the following picture of the assignment of forces between fronts, as well as other specific information used later on, has been assembled.

Of the 11 armored brigades at its disposal,[24] the Israeli High Command assigned at the start of the war six brigades plus two armored "groups" to the Egyptian front, three brigades plus one or two armored groups to the Jordanian front, and one brigade to the Syrian front. Of four paratroop brigades, it assigned three to the Egyptian front and one to the Jordanian. Of about ten first line infantry brigades, it assigned three to four to the Egyptian front, five to the Jordanian, and one to the Syrian. Of a dozen artillery brigade-equivalents, six were assigned to the Egyptian front, four to five to the Jordanian, and two to the Syrian. "Second line" troops entrusted with static regional defense, garrison duties, protecting lines of communications, and the like, were assigned to fronts according to a reverse order of priority, with the Syrian front receiving about six brigade-equivalents, the Jordanian five, and the Egyptian three. In gross figures, the numbers of first and second line troops assigned on June 5 were 65,000 to the Egyptian front, 50,000 to the Jordanian, and 25,000 to the Syrian. Tanks were distributed approximately on the basis of 650 for the Egyptian front, 350 for the Jordanian, and 100 for the Syrian. Since our estimate of "first line" brigade assignment is derived mainly from identification of units that took part in military operations, we do not know whether there were any additional units held in strategic reserve. Some Israeli military writers have suggested that the High Command had held some of the troops we have accounted for in reserve

[24] See Appendix B for total Israeli and Arab forces.

until the swift air victory allowed it to commit everything and to rely on the air force as strategic reserve for the rest of the war.[25]

We are now in a position to consider the war in each front in turn.

THE EGYPTIAN FRONT

On the eve of the war, Egypt's buildup in Sinai had reached the level of some 120,000 men under the over-all command of General Mohsin Mortagui, formerly the commander of the Egyptian expeditionary force in Yemen. These troops were organized into two armored divisions (the 4th and the special task force under General Shazli), four infantry divisions (the 2nd, 3rd, 6th, and 7th), and the Palestinian "division" (composed of two brigades only), in addition to support, logistics, and service outfits and air force units in four air bases. These seven divisions comprised six armored brigades and five armored "groups." Together with miscellaneous armor attached to divisional headquarters, scout groups, and static defense positions, they included roughly some 900 tanks.

If one remembers that the Egyptian regular army was estimated at about 160,000, that some 30,000 of these were in Yemen (in addition to some 20,000 reserves), and that most of these were brought back only after the beginning of the fighting, then one sees that the 120,000 troops Egypt had concentrated in Sinai on the eve of the war constituted the great bulk of its army. In the course of the fighting in the vicinity of the Suez Canal, the Egyptian High Command threw into the battle additional troops that had been brought up from the west bank of the Canal. The crushing defeat of the Egyptian forces therefore entailed the destruction or dispersal of virtually the entire Egyptian regular army.

To understand the deployment of troops of the antagonists, their objectives, and the course of the operations, we must say a few words about the Sinai peninsula as a field of battle. The peninsula is a vast expanse of desert and mountain inhabited by not more than 50,000 people, mostly nomads. The part of Sinai south of an imaginary line running roughly west-east from the tip of the Gulf of Suez to the tip of the Gulf of Aqaba is roadless, wild, mountain country impassable to

[25] If we recall that the total size of the Israeli army is generally taken to be around 250,000 to 270,000 men (see Appendix B), the 140,000 men in first and second line fighting units appears to be plausible. This relationship of numbers is not quite what is referred to in military jargon as the "tooth-to-tail ratio." For, while the difference between 140,000 and the total number of the army may be considered almost all "tail," not all the 140,000 are strictly "tooth."

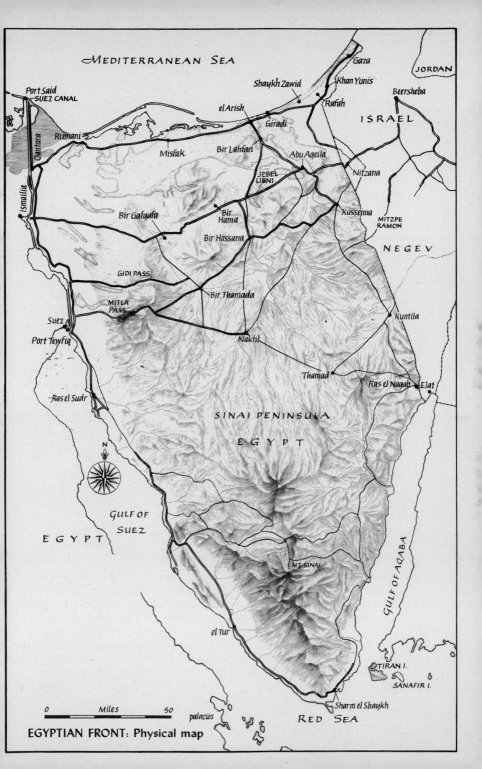

EGYPTIAN FRONT: Physical map

motorized vehicles except for a single paved road running along the western coast to Sharm el Sheikh at the tip of the peninsula and a difficult track along the eastern coast from the tip to a point north of the Israeli port of Elath. In 1956, Israeli troops that fought for Sharm el Sheikh descended upon it from both of these venues; but in this war, there was no land action at all south of our imaginary line. The Egyptian troops that had occupied Sharm el Sheikh evacuated it without fighting before the arrival of an Israeli naval unit, followed by airborne troops.

The northern part of our imaginary line is also in the main impassable to large motorized units except for short distances. However, it has a number of roads, tracks, and passes, which naturally served as the focal points for military action. Three main roads or axes running east-west in rough parallels were particularly important: (1) The northernmost connected Rafah, on the border of mandated Palestine, by way of el Arish, with Qantara on the eastern shore of the Suez Canal after running parallel to the Mediterranean shore for nearly all its length. (2) The central axis went from Nitzana, in Israel, to Ismailia, roughly halfway along the Canal on its western shore, after running through Abu Egeila, Jebel Libni, Bir Hama, and Bir Gafgafa. The southern axis had two starts near Israel's border, at Kuntila and Ras el Naqab, which joined before Thamad further west and went on through Nakhl and the Mitla pass to Suez, at the southern tip of the Suez Canal on its western shore.

In their eastern halves, the three east-west axes were linked by several north-south roads or tracks, which thus created important junctions. At their western end, the central and southern axes were bisected by prolongations of the southern Sinai ridges, giving rise to two or more bottlenecks: one south and west of Bir Gafgafa and the other at Mitla. The northern axis was hemmed in for almost its entire length west of el Arish by sand dunes and the sea.

The Egyptian troops were deployed both defensively and offensively in relation to these features. In the Gaza Strip, the Palestinian "division" of two brigades with tank and artillery support was dug in a network of fortified positions. To the southwest of the Strip, or at the northeast corner of Sinai, the 7th division, composed of four infantry brigades, one artillery brigade, plus tank support, occupied a series of fortified positions extending from Rafah to el Arish. These positions defended the northern axis and crucial road junctions and were thickly "settled." Equally thickly settled were the fortified positions of Um Katef, Abu Egeila, and Kusseima further south, which controlled the central axis and its road junctions. Here the 2nd division, composed of

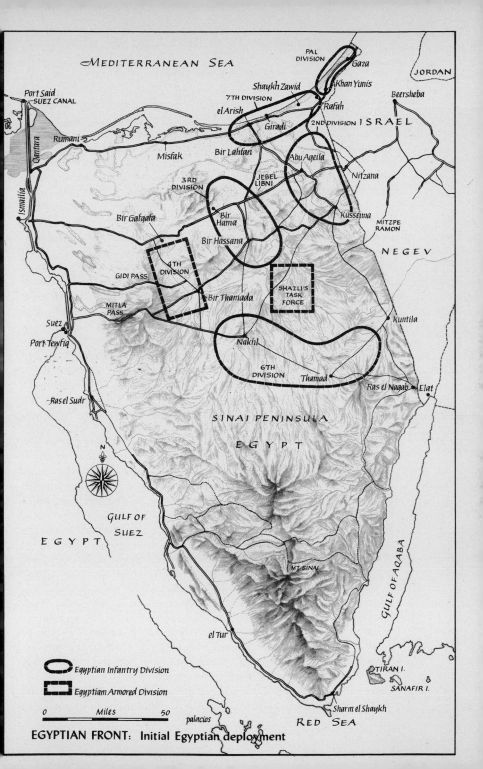

MEDITERRANEAN SEA

JORDAN

Port Said
SUEZ CANAL

Rumani

Qantara

Ismailia

Misfak

Shaykh Zawid

el Arish

7TH DIVISION

Giradi

PAL
DIVISION

Gaza

Khan Yunis

Rafah

2ND DIVISION ISRAEL

Beersheba

Bir Lahfari

Abu Ageila

3RD
DIVISION

JEBEL
LIBNI

Nitzana

Bir Gafgafa

Bir
Hama

Kusseima

MITZPE
RAMON

Bir Hassana

NEGEV

4TH
DIVISION

GIDI PASS

SHAZLI'S
TASK
FORCE

Bir Thamada

MITLA
PASS

Suez

Port Tewfiq

Nakhl

6TH
DIVISION

Kuntila

Thamad

Ras el Nagab Elat

Ras el Sudr

SINAI PENINSULA

E G Y P T

N

GULF OF
SUEZ

EGYPT

MT SINAI

GULF OF AQABA

el Tur

TIRAN I.

SANAFIR I.

⬭ Egyptian Infantry Division

▭ Egyptian Armored Division

0   Miles   50

palacios

Sharm el Shaykh

RED SEA

EGYPTIAN FRONT: Initial Egyptian deployment

two infantry brigades, two artillery brigades and two armored groups, was deployed.

The access to the southern axis was defended by the 6th division, composed of four motorized infantry brigades, one armored brigade, and one artillery brigade. One infantry brigade was positioned in Kuntila while the rest of the division was deployed along the sides of a triangle constituted by Kuntila–Nakhl–Kusseima, with the heaviest concentration at the base of that triangle.

Inside the triangle, General Shazli's mobile task force, composed of one armored brigade, one motorized commando brigade, and one artillery brigade, had been recently brought from the el Arish area. It occupied positions from which it could both reinforce the divisions defending the central and southern axes and spearhead a drive of all three divisions to cut off the Negev south of the Ramon canyon or through Nitzana-Dimona or Nitzana-Beersheba and link up with Jordanian forces.

To the west of all these positions, the 3rd division, composed of three motorized infantry brigades, one armored brigade, two artillery brigades, plus an armored brigade belonging either to the 2nd or the 7th division, was concentrated in the relatively small area between Bir Hassana and Jebel Libni. This very sizeable force was thus excellently placed to serve a triple purpose: (1) It could easily reinforce the units defending each of the three main axes; (2) it constituted the core of a second line of defense in case of serious Israeli breakthroughs; and (3) it could follow through any offensive action of Shazli's task force and the other divisions.

Finally, still further to the west, the crack 4th armored division plus one motorized infantry brigade and one artillery brigade was deployed in the vicinity of Bir Gafgafa-Bir Thamada, thus constituting a third line of defense near the crucial passes to the Suez Canal while being in a position from which it could move quickly in various directions to buttress the defenders of the two previous lines or to follow through any offensive action.

This over-all deployment revealed clearly the main lines of the Egyptian strategy. This was to provide a system of defense in depth which could absorb and smash the expected Israeli first blow, and also swing back promptly to a counteroffensive. The Egyptians, like the Israelis, were aware that they might be restricted to a limited time, perhaps a few days only, before international pressure forced a cease fire. Consequently, while they so deployed their troops as to be able to develop offensive operations in a number of directions, they betrayed a preference for at least an initial counterthrust with Shazli's force along the track crossing the Negev south of the Ramon canyon. This would allow them to secure the minimal objective of establishing a critically important land link with Jordan before a cease fire came into effect.

Like the Egyptians, and for the same reason of time limitation, the Israelis too had minimal and maximal political goals. The Israelis wanted, of course, to reopen the Strait of Tiran, but by the time the war started this objective had become secondary to and derivative from what had become the primary *political* goal of destroying either *a substantial part* or *all* of the Egyptian armed forces in Sinai. If the latter objective were accomplished, the capture of the entire Sinai peninsula and the reopening of the Strait would follow naturally. But even if only a considerable part of the Egyptian forces were destroyed before the onset of a cease fire, the Israelis thought this would put them in a favorable position to compel Nasser by a combination of diplomacy and military threat to desist from his blockade.

To accomplish these objectives, the Israeli High Command assigned the forces we mentioned before (six to seven infantry and paratrooper brigades, six armored brigades and two armored "groups" equipped with 650 tanks, plus six artillery brigades) under General Gavish, Commander of the Southern Front. These forces were organized into three task forces of divisional strength and two independent brigades. The Israeli planning called for the concentration of nearly all these forces against the northeastern corner of the Sinai peninsula with the object of destroying, at a minimum, most of the Egyptian forces deployed in the Gaza Strip and in the rectangle Rafah–El Arish–Jebel Libni–Kusseima. Once this was done and once that nodal sector had fallen under the control of the Israeli forces, they could, if time permitted, maneuver from the rectangle in a number of directions in pursuit of the maximum objective of destroying the remaining Egyptian forces and capturing all of Sinai.

General Gavish deployed the first of his three divisions, under the command of General Tal, opposite the Egyptian 7th division, at the southern end of the Gaza Strip. He deployed a second division, under the command of General Sharon, opposite the 2nd Egyptian division at Abu Egeila. The third division, under the command of General Yoffe, was poised between the other two divisions, facing supposedly impassable sand dunes between the Egyptian defense perimeters of Rafah and Abu Egeila. One "first line" brigade faced the rest of the Gaza Strip and only one reinforced armored brigade was deployed far from these concentrations in the south, facing Kuntila.

The Israeli military chiefs, like all strategists, sought to throw the enemy's plans into confusion and to dictate to him the conditions of the battle. In this instance, the Israelis wanted specifically to prevent the various *sectors* of the Egyptian defense lines as well as the various lines themselves from reinforcing and supporting one another; they wanted to flush the Egyptian units out of their prepared positions and force them into continual movement in open spaces where they would be much more vulnerable to Israeli maneuvers and air attack; they would then finally close a series of traps on them and destroy them piecemeal. Accordingly, the Israelis developed a three-phased master plan.

In the first phase, the divisions of Generals Tal and Sharon were to attack in coordination the two Egyptian perimeters of Rafah and Abu Egeila and thus restrict their capacity to reinforce one another. At the same time, even before the two perimeters were secured, one half of Yoffe's division was to move through the sand dunes between the Israeli forces attacking the Egyptian first line to threaten the second line in the vicinity of Bir Lahfan and prevent it from reinforcing the first. The second half of Yoffe's division was to pour through the Abu Egeila perimeter as soon as Sharon's forces had breached it and to fall with its fresh troops upon the Egyptian second line at the nodal point of Jebel Libni. Meantime, General Tal's forces, after breaking through at Rafah and smashing their way to el Arish, would turn south to close one pincer movement with Yoffe's first half-division at Bir Lahfan and another pincer movement with Yoffe's second half-division at Jebel Libni. Simultaneously, Sharon's forces, after mopping up the Abu Egeila perimeter, would attack the Kusseima defensive network and thus complete the occupation of the Rafah–el Arish–Jebel Libni–Kusseima rectangle and the destruction or rout of the Egyptian forces in it.

The second phase of the plan was left more flexible since it depended in part on the redeployments of the enemy as a result of the first, but its general idea was clear, and the Israeli forces were equipped and conditioned to launch into it and the next phase in one continuous breath. There was to be no special pause for regrouping and consolidating—only a quick conference among commanders for coordinating the assignments while the troops naturally paused for refueling and reprovisioning. The idea of the second phase was for the forces of Tal and Yoffe to complete the destruction of the second line of defense while rushing to block the passes to the Suez Canal and to meet the armored 4th Egyptian division defending them. As this movement would compel the Egyptian forces in the southern triangle (the 6th division and Shazli's force) to move rapidly in order to avoid being trapped east of the passes, Sharon's forces would move southwest to in-tercept them, while the independent reinforced armored brigade would advance from Kuntila and tail them so as to close a pincer with Sharon's troops.

The last phase of the plan was simply to force the remaining Egyptian armor to fight and to destroy it, to march on to the Suez Canal, and to complete the destruction of the fragments of the Egyptian army left behind. The capture of Sharm el Sheikh, the root of the whole war, was to be effected by naval units and an airborne contingent at some convenient time as a completely secondary and small side operation.

This description of the Israeli operational plans sounds more like a *post facto* summary of the actual movements of the Israeli forces. But the fact of the matter is that the execution of the operations was so perfect as to be hardly distinguishable from the planning itself. This, as we shall see, struck competent military observers like French General Beaufre as the unique achievement of the Israeli forces.

Israel's land offensive began on Monday, June 5, shortly after 8 A.M. with an attack on Khan Yunis, at the southern end of the Gaza Strip. Tal's main objective was the Rafah defense perimeter to the south and west, which consisted of a square of trenches, pillboxes, artillery emplacements, barbed wires, and minefields eight miles on each side, was defended by two infantry brigades plus abundant artillery and tank units, and controlled an important road junction leading to el Arish and the Suez Canal to the west, Gaza to the east, and Abu Egeila to the south. However, Tal decided to attack where he did in order to make his first breakthrough out of range of the Egyptian artillery in the Rafah perimeter. The Khan Yunis area was defended by Palestinian units.

After a brief bombardment that eliminated some of the mines, the Israeli armor surged forward and smashed its way through the town after suffering some casualties from mines and anti-tank guns. The motorized infantry that followed met with renewed stiff resistance, and tanks had to be called in again to complete the subjugation of the town.

Once Khan Yunis was overrun, Tal's forces wheeled southwestward for the assault on Rafah, while sending one brigade northward to clean up the Strip and capture the city of Gaza with the assistance of another brigade coming from without. Surprisingly, Gaza proved a tough nut to crack, and the city itself was not taken before dusk on Tuesday, after a midday air strike and some savage street fighting. Even after that, snipers continued to fire at Israeli troops as late as Saturday, June 10.

Tal attacked the Rafah perimeter using tactics that were to become the hallmark of Israeli operations throughout the war. The perimeter consisted of two fortified networks on either side of the el Arish road, and Tal attacked them both simultaneously. Against the northern network, he threw an armored brigade, which split into two forces, one coming from the front and drawing the enemy's fire while the other made a flanking movement through the sand dunes and fell on the Egyptian positions from the side and the rear. The Egyptians fought well from their entrenched positions and used their artillery effectively, but the accuracy and boldness of the Israeli tank crews, many of whom continued to advance and fire when their tanks were aflame, and the speed of their maneuver soon overcame the Egyptians. The commander of the Israeli armored brigade, with the unmartial name of Colonel Shmulik, having overrun the first of several Egyptian brigades he was to destroy, continued without interruption on a dash toward Shaykh Zawid, the next Egyptian position on the road to el Arish.

Against the southern network, Tal threw a brigade of paratroopers used as infantry and a tank force of battalion size. Once again, while the bulk of the paratroopers attacked the Egyptian positions from the side, the armored unit wheeled around and struck from the rear in an effort to knock out the Egyptian armor and artillery. Although the Israeli armored unit eventually succeeded in its mission, the paratroopers had a very difficult time getting through the minefields and barbed wires and combing miles of trenches and pillboxes step by step. Again the Egyptians fought well when dug in, and this time there were no Israeli tanks to finish off the job quickly. Before the day was over, however, the Israeli paratroopers, though bled, had completed their task, destroyed the second Egyptian brigade in the day, and were ready to take on a new assignment.

Meanwhile, Tal's armored forces, which had broken through earlier in the day, easily overran Shaykh Zawid and sped toward al Giradi, the last Egyptian fortified place before el Arish. At this place the Egyptians did some of their best fighting in the entire war. The Israeli armor had no difficulty breaking through the Egyptian lines, which lay astride the road to el Arish, but once the armor rode through, the Egyptians reconstituted their lines and fought off the next Israeli columns bringing in the supplies and ammunition of the armor that had just crossed. Once again, the Israelis brought up armor and smashed through with the supply convoy following, and once again the Egyptians reconstituted their lines and fought off the next Israeli columns. It was already night before the Israelis finally sent in their infantry to comb the trenches and emplacements one by one, finish off the embat-

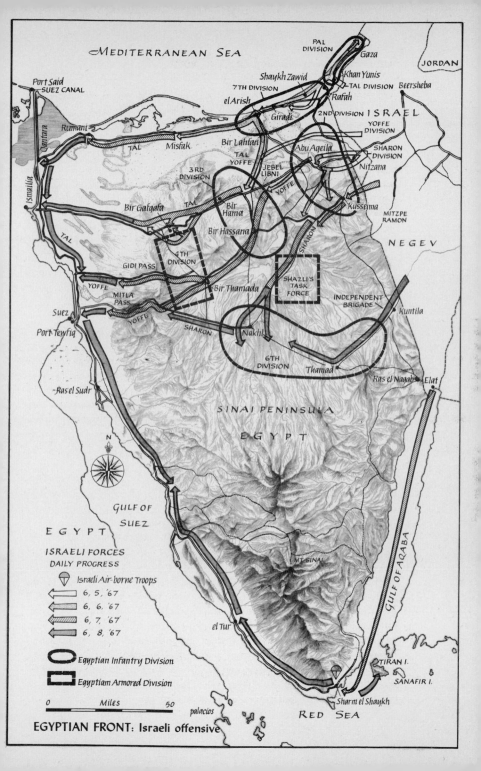

MEDITERRANEAN SEA

JORDAN

Port Said
SUEZ CANAL

Rumani

Qattara

PAL DIVISION

Gaza

Shaykh Zawid

Khan Yunis

7TH DIVISION

TAL DIVISION

Beersheba

el Arish

Rafah

Giradi

2ND DIVISION

ISRAEL

Misfak

TAL

Bir Lahfan

YOFFE DIVISION

Ismailia

TAL YOFFE

Abu Ageila

SHARON DIVISION

3RD DIVISION

JEBEL LIBNI

Nitzana

TAL

YOFFE

Bir Gafgafa

TAL

Bir Hama

Kusseima

MITZPE RAMON

Bir Hassana

NEGEV

TAL

4TH DIVISION

SHARON

GIDI PASS

SHAZLI'S TASK FORCE

YOFFE

Bir Thamada

INDEPENDENT BRIGADE

MITLA PASS

Kuntila

Suez

YOFFE

SHARON

Nakhl

Port Tewfiq

6TH DIVISION

Thamad

Ras el Nagab

Elat

Ras el Sudr

SINAI PENINSULA

EGYPT

N

GULF OF SUEZ

EGYPT

ISRAELI FORCES
DAILY PROGRESS

MT. SINAI

GULF OF AQABA

Israeli Air-borne Troops

6, 5, '67

6, 6, '67

6, 7, '67

6, 8, '67

Egyptian Infantry Division

Egyptian Armored Division

TIRAN I.

SANAFIR I.

0   Miles   50

el Tur

palacios

Sharm el Shaykh

RED SEA

EGYPTIAN FRONT: Israeli offensive

tled Egyptian brigade, and insure free movement for their forces. By then, the Israeli armored units that had passed earlier were already skirmishing at the outskirts of el Arish, which was to fall early the next morning. Thus at the end of one day of fighting, Tal's division had broken through the Egyptian defense line at one of its toughest points, fought its way through a 40-mile deep penetration, and destroyed in the process the bulk of the Egyptian 7th division. The Israeli losses in these operations are not known, except for the fact that they included 35 tank commanders, one of them a battalion commander—a measure of the dash of their leadership. But clearly the losses left Tal's division basically intact, as it was to prove in the following days.

About one hour after Tal's division had opened its attack on Khan Yunis, one half of General Yoffe's division—one motorized-armored brigade plus artillery under the command of Colonel Issachar—crossed the border some 20 miles south of Tal's forces in an area that sand dunes supposedly made impassable. Using the dry bed of a seasonal stream, the Israeli engineering corps managed to get Issachar's forces and their steaming engines across nearly 30 miles of difficult terrain in nine hours and allowed them to emerge in the vicinity of Bir Lahfan on the Egyptian second line of defense. Before reaching that position, Colonel Issachar had sent one of his armored battalions to help the Israeli division operating against Abu Egeila with an attack from the rear designed to confuse the enemy. He used the rest of his force to block the Bir Lahfan junction connecting Abu Egeila and el Arish with Jebel Libni, whence Egyptian reinforcements might be sent. And indeed, shortly after his reduced brigade had positioned itself, two Egyptian brigades, one armored and one motorized infantry, ran into it on their way to el Arish. In a night battle in which the Egyptians used infrared equipped tanks and the Israeli units kept firing and shifting positions and firing again, the Egyptian brigades failed to break their way through after losing some 14 tanks. With the approach of dawn, the Egyptian forces withdrew in fear of the Israeli air force, which actually appeared with the light of day and inflicted heavy blows on them.

While Issachar's reduced brigade was fighting off these two Egyptian brigades, a third Egyptian brigade entrenched in Bir Lahfan fired at its flank and rear without daring to come out of its positions to assist the Egyptian forces moving toward it. This lack of initiative appears even more incredible if we recall that by that time Tal's forces were already attacking el Arish and could be expected to descend upon Bir Lahfan from the north and catch it in a "sandwich." Were the Egyptian forces at Bir Lahfan not informed of what was happening? Did they expect el Arish to hold out? Or did they simply prefer to sit where they were and meet their fate without trying to break out of the nutcracker that was closing on them? No one knows the answer. The result, however, was that in the morning of the next day Tal's forces did come down and crush them against Issachar's forces.

While General Tal was breaking through at Rafah and half of General Yoffe's division was plodding through the dunes, General Sharon began with preliminary operations preparatory to assaulting the Abu Egeila defense network. This network, some 15 miles from the Israeli border at Nitzana, controlled a junction of roads connecting to the west with Jebel Libni, on the main road to Ismailia, with el Arish to the north, and with Kusseima to the south. Around the crossroads, the Egyptians had built over the years a formidable entrenched camp, which consisted of three successive, interconnected, lines of trenches two to three miles long, resting to the left on "impassable" sand dunes and to the right on hill positions extending to the comparable Kusseima perimeter. Around these lines, a series of interlocking outposts and minefields extended the camp's width and depth for several miles in each direction. The trench network was defended by an infantry brigade. Behind it, at least five battalions of artillery provided a powerful long arm. A force of some 90 tanks completed the system by giving it a strong mobile fist.

General Sharon's plan consisted of a series of coordinated indirect attacks on all three elements of the Egyptian defenses—infantry, artillery, armor—simultaneously. Before launching his main attacks, however, he spent the entire day of June 5 laying the ground for them. First, he captured or neutralized the relevant Egyptian outposts in the course of all-day fighting. Then he massed two brigades of artillery in front of the Egyptian lines in positions from which they could support the infantry advance. He also maneuvered a tank force in the same area in ways intended to deceive the enemy about the direction of the main attack. At night, he used helicopters to ferry some two battalions of paratroopers behind the enemy's lines with the mission of assaulting the Egyptian artillery from the rear. Finally, the engineers got to work under the cover of darkness to clear a way for the tanks and the infantry through the minefields in the areas chosen for attack.

These preparations completed, Sharon gave the signal at 10:45 P.M. for the opening of an artillery barrage that poured some 6,000 shells on the Egyptian positions within 20 minutes. Immediately after, an infantry brigade that had advanced through the "impassable" sand dunes at the left flank of the Egyptian positions split up into three battalions, each of which went into one of the lines of trenches from the sides. While the foot soldiers were rolling the enemy in the trenches in hand to hand combat, one-half of an armored brigade made a wide flanking movement and struck from the rear, where it appeared in time to help the paratroopers finish off the Egyptian artillery. After leaving small forces to block the routes against possible reinforcements, the armored force fanned out and went to meet the Egyptian tanks. By around midnight, when the advancing infantry had gone over the east-west road that cut across the three lines of trenches, the other half of the tank brigade advanced along that road from the front to meet the Israeli tank force that came from the rear and to squeeze the Egyptian armor between them. By 3:00 A.M. the Israelis had cleared the trenches and were everywhere in the perimeter, but tank fighting continued until about 6:30 A.M., when all resistance finally ceased. Hours before that, the second half of General Yoffe's division had galloped at full speed across the perimeter on the main east-west road heading toward Jebel Libni.

The Abu Egeila operation, with Israeli forces converging upon and cutting across one another at night in enemy terrain, was very complex and delicate and fraught with great risks of bad timing or of Israeli troops hitting one another. But the reward of successful execution was commensurate with the risks: The enemy forces were thrown into confusion and forced to fight as fragments without coordination. In a total of 20 hours of fighting, Sharon's division thus broke through the Egyptian defense line and opened the main way to the maneuver space of central Sinai while destroying over half of the Egyptian 2nd division and making untenable the position of the remainder of it. The price paid by Sharon's division in this particular operation is not known, but we do know that in the entire war that division suffered 58 killed and 192 wounded, and that most of these losses were incurred at Abu Egeila.

We have already intimated that on June 6, the second day of the war, Tal's forces completed the capture of el Arish in the early morning, finishing off the last brigade of the Egyptian 7th division. Subsequently, the division split into two: A small part consisting of one paratroop brigade with armor support continued to race west along the northern axis toward Qantara and covered almost half the distance by the end of the day. A larger part, composed of Colonel Shmulik's armored brigade, an additional armored brigade, an armored group, and artillery, wheeled south from el Arish and, after overrunning Bir Lahfan, linked up with Colonel Issachar's half of General Yoffe's division. The combined forces marched south toward Jebel Libni, and while Issachar began to attack the Egyptian positions in coordination with that half-division that had come through Abu Egeila, Tal prepared to swing westward toward Bir Hama and Bir Gafgafa.

In the meantime, Sharon's division began the second day of the war with preparations to destroy the Egyptian forces in the Kusseima fortified camp. General Sharon, aware of the hopelessness of the enemy's position, sought to save on casualties by avoiding a general attack. He planned instead to lay ambushes for the retreating enemy and to force him to leave his positions by means of strikes by the air force, which had by then become fully available for ground support, and limited prodding attacks with armor and motorized infantry. The deployments and air attacks took up the remaining part of the second day. The next morning, when the "prodding units" advanced on the Egyptian positions, they found them deserted. Failure of communications and coordination among the Israelis had allowed the Egyptians to escape the elaborately laid out trap.

On the morning of June 7, the third day of the war, Yoffe completed the capture of the Jebel Libni positions, linked up the two halves of his division, and marched south toward Bir Hassana. This last bastion of the Egyptian second line of defense had already been partly evacuated; it was quickly captured after an armor attack using the favorite Israeli tactic of assault from the front and the flank. With this, the first phase of the Israeli plan was completed: The first and second Egyptian lines in the crucial northeast rectangle were smashed, the 7th, 2nd, and 3rd divisions that manned them were destroyed or routed, while the 6th division and Shazli's task force further south were unhinged and forced to start retreating.

Even before this phase of the plan had been completed, the second phase had already entered into operation without any pause. Tal's paratroopers' column, which had raced some 40 miles west of el Arish the previous day, destroyed at the beginning of the third day the Egyptian fortified camp at Misfak, held by a battalion of Egyptian paratroopers plus artillery, and advanced another 40 miles to Rumani, about 15 miles from Qantara on the Suez Canal. The bulk of Tal's division and Yoffe's division, after the fall of Jebel Libni and Bir Hassana, rushed westward along two axes to the Bir Gafgafa and the Mitla passes. The positions protecting these passes, it will be recalled, constituted the third and last Egyptian line of defense; they were defended by the presumably still unshaken crack 4th armored division with additions. Since the capture of the passes by the Israelis would seal the fate of all the Egyptian forces in Sinai, the battle was expected to be both fiercely contested and crucial. In the event, it proved to be only crucial.

After a night and day gallop from Jebel Libni, Tal's forces reached the vicinity of Bir Gafgafa at about midday, having overrun on their way Bir Hama and a number of pockets of Egyptian resistance. What they confronted there was not a "regular" line of defense, such as the ones they had pierced before, but a cluster of military installations—including camps, depots, and an airfield—with relatively sparse fortifications, and large units of armor and motorized infantry deployed in and around these installations. General Tal personally took over command of the battle and advanced his armored troops in two concentric pincer movements. The wider pincers were intended to turn the enemy installations and block the "passes" behind him, while the narrower ones were intended to "squeeze" the installations themselves and to protect the wider pincers. These dispositions proved to be eminently successful.

As the columns of the wider pincers made their way to the passes, an Egyptian force of nearly brigade size set out after one of them but was intercepted by a tank force of the narrower pincers and cut to pieces. The narrow pincers then closed in on their targets, while the wider ones reached the passes and took blocking positions.

The blocking forces comprised a battalion of light AMX-13 tanks, which had been selected for the wide enveloping movement mainly because of the speed of its vehicles and their long range. Soon after the unit had deployed itself, it sighted an Egyptian armored brigade containing some 80 heavy tanks coming toward Bir Gafgafa from the west, presumably to secure or reopen that way of retreat for the Egyptian forces trapped to the east of it. The Israeli battalion lay in ambush for the superior Egyptian force and then opened fire on it from very short distances, but the shells of its light tanks simply slid over the thick armor of the Egyptian tanks. The Israeli tanks then dispersed and took advantage of their maneuverability and speed to buzz around the enemy tanks and try to hit them specifically in their vulnerable spots, often from distances of 15 to 20 yards. In this manner they held off the Egyptian brigade for several hours until a column of Israeli heavy tanks from the narrow pincers appeared on the enemy flank and the air force came into the action. The battle then took an entirely different turn, and after six additional hours of fighting the entire Egyptian force was annihilated.

Shortly after Tal had sealed the Bir Gafgafa exit, advance units of Yoffe's division blocked the Mitla pass and the "satelite" Gidi pass some 13 miles east and north. It will be recalled that on the same morning this division had fought at Jebel Libni more than 60 miles away; its incredibly rapid advance and the ease with which it achieved control of the crucial passes reflected the complete demoralization and collapse of the Egyptian army and the unbelievable nerve of a number of Israeli officers and men.

We have already reported how Bir Hassana, which was supposed to be the prop of the right wing of the Egyptian second line of defense, fell to Yoffe's forces in a brief engagement after most of the Egyptian forces had fled it. The same story was repeated at Bir Thamada, a large base with an airfield, the headquarters of the Egyptian Sinai command, and the supposed prop of the right wing of the third Egyptian line of defense. After Bir Thamada, one battalion of tanks and jeeps with recoilless rifles split off from the division and aimed for the Gidi Pass on a track road. The battalion reached the pass and entered it without problems; but once inside, it learned that 30 Egyptian T-54 tanks stood at the western exit ready to take its 14 Centurions one by one as they came out. The battalion commander asked for air support, but when two hours passed without anything happening, he got into the lead tank himself, drove at full speed out of the pass, received a salvo that missed, moved sideways, and provided covering fire while all his tanks filed out in a cloud of dust, fanned out, and charged. The air force appeared just then to help him and his men finish off all 30 enemy tanks without suffering a single casualty.

At the Mitla Pass, the story was different, though no less incredible and dramatic. In their effort to reach their target as fast as possible, Yoffe's armored columns outran their own supply units. But, the commander of the lead battalion, a certain Colonel Liska, decided not to bother waiting for fuel and rushed forward on the last leg of his advance with the tanks that could go. As one tank after another ran out of gas, it was left on the side of the road. After some time, Colonel Liska found himself approaching Mitla with only nine tanks, four of which soon dried out. Undaunted, he had the operative five tanks tow these four and continued his advance. When he came within sight of his objective, he observed small columns of Egyptian tanks and miscellaneous vehicles arriving every few moments and plunging in obvious panic into the 15-mile long pass. Too impatient to wait for reinforcements, he insinuated his limping column behind a row of Egyptian Centurions, got inside the pass, then veered off the road at one of the wide clearings in it, took up position, and opened fire at the next batch of Egyptian vehicles, causing their burning carcasses to block the way. This was how the most important and last avenue of escape for the Egyptian forces in Sinai was sealed off for many critical hours, until additional Israeli forces came to close it more securely. The reader may perhaps wonder why such an important strategic feature as the

Mitla was left undefended by the Egyptians. It transpired after the war that the Egyptian unit in charge of its defense had misunderstood a High Command order and withdrawn, and the mistake could not subsequently be corrected for, by that time, Egyptian communications had broken down.

While Tal and Yoffe were blocking the passes and all the Egyptian forces in Sinai were rushing toward them in greater or lesser disarray, General Sharon received orders to rush as fast as he could in a south-westerly direction from Kusseima in pursuit of the elements of the 2nd division that had retreated from there; concurrently, he was also to in-tercept elements of the 6th division and of Shazli's task force retreat-ing along the southern axis. Sharon spent the entire third day of the war in a mad gallop over bumpy terrain, catching up occasionally with the enemy's rearguard and destroying small forces left behind to slow his advance. By the morning of the fourth day of the war, he reached the vicinity of Nakhl, through which an entire Egyptian brigade of the 6th division, which was being tailed by the Israeli armored brigade from Kuntila, was expected to pass. There was a quick ambush, and a little while later the unfortunate brigade, caught from all sides and pounded from the air, was completely annihilated in the course of a battle that Sharon summarized as follows: "Between 10:00 A.M. and 2:30 in the afternoon we destroyed 50 enemy tanks—T-54s and Cen-turions—two regiments of artillery, anti-tank, and anti-aircraft bat-teries, and more than 300 vehicles. The enemy suffered over 1,000 casualties."

General Sharon, a veteran of two wars, went on to say: "This was a Valley of Death. I came out of it like an old man. Hundreds were killed. There were burning tanks everywhere. One had the feeling that man was nothing. A sandstorm had been churned up by our tanks. The noise was tremendous. Beside the din of tanks and guns, there was the roar of our heavy transport aircraft—Stratocruisers—dropping supplies of water and ammunition by parachute, and of helicopters evacuating the wounded. The shooting and fighting continued and vehicles loaded with fuel and ammunition were exploding all along the line."[26]

From Nakhl, Sharon's forces and the independent brigade continued westward, sweeping before them those Egyptian forces that had hith-erto managed to escape toward the Mitla Pass, where they met their doom at the hands of Yoffe's troops and the Israeli air force. What it meant for these Egyptian forces to be caught between Sharon's ham-mer and Yoffe's anvil, while being also pounded by the Israeli air

[26] R. and W. Churchill, op. cit.

force, can be gathered from the following account by an observer who visited the scene a few days later: "One 1.8-mile stretch of the Mitla Pass is so jammed with blackened Egyptian equipment that it is virtually impossible to get a vehicle through it. From a small rise, the scene resembles a huge junkyard. At one place in the pass there is a Soviet jeep-like vehicle. A truck is on top of it. On top of that there is another truck. On top of all three, there is a Soviet tank that was apparently driven there by a frenzied driver trying to find some way through the bottleneck."[27]

While the final destruction of the fragments of the Egyptian forces was proceeding, the other aspect of the last phase of the Israeli plan was concluded. Tal's force along the northern axis made its way to Qantara and the Suez Canal after destroying an improvised defense position manned by Egyptian commando units. The main part of Tal's division issued from Bir Gafgafa and made its way to the Canal at Ismailia over the carcasses of Egyptian tanks that fought a futile holding battle. Yoffe's forces remained at the Mitla the entire fourth day of the war to continue the reception and destruction of the fleeing Egyptians who kept coming.

By night time, when Yoffe sought to come out of the pass to go on to the Canal, he incredulously found the exit blocked by 30 Egyptian T-54 and T-55 tanks, which had belatedly come to defend it. Three hours later, the Egyptian tanks had been converted into so many torches illuminating the way to the Canal.

Thus came to an end the Israeli second Sinai campaign, which has been characterized with absolute superlatives by serious military analysts such as General Beaufre and General Stockwell, both leaders of the Anglo-French 1956 campaign against Egypt. In four days and three nights of relentless drive, the Israeli High Command achieved 100 percent of its objectives without a single serious hitch. The numerically inferior Israeli forces—at most two-thirds of the enemy—destroyed or shattered all Egyptian divisions found in Sinai at the beginning of the war plus all the reinforcements thrown into the battle in its last stages, captured the Sinai peninsula, and reopened navigation in the Strait of Tiran.

President Nasser specifically admitted in a speech before the Egyptian National Assembly on November 23, 1967, that the Egyptian army lost in Sinai 80 percent of all its equipment, 10,000 soldiers and 1,500 officers killed, and 5,000 soldiers and 500 officers captured.[28] Nasser did

[27] *New York Times*, June 18, 1967.
[28] *New York Times*, November 24, 1967.

not say, and perhaps he did not know, that about one-third of the equipment lost fell intact into the hands of the Israelis. Neither did he mention, though he must have known it, the number of officers and men wounded, and the number of soldiers whom the Israelis did not bother to take prisoner and allowed and helped to cross the Suez Canal at the end of the fighting. These two categories together must have accounted for at least three times the number of fatalities and prisoners that Nasser cited, thus bringing the percentage of losses in men close to the percentage of losses in equipment. The price that the Israelis paid for this astounding victory was 275 officers and men killed and 800 wounded. We do not know the Israeli losses in equipment except for tanks. Against the nearly 800 Egyptian tanks destroyed or captured, the Israelis lost 61.

It is still too soon to account completely and precisely for the thoroughness and speed of the Israeli victory in Sinai; however, some of the reasons that will certainly occupy an important place in any such account are already apparent. First and foremost we would mention the dash and fierce will to win of the Israeli soldiers, particularly the officers. We have seen a few examples of this in our account such as the blocking of the Gidi and Mitla passes, and we might have added many more illustrations. Suffice it to say that these instances were the rule rather than the exception, that the command phrase of Israeli officers is "follow me" rather than the usual "forward," and that tank commanders very often fought from open turrets in order to have a better vision of the field of battle than might be had through periscopes or tank slits. However, the best homage paid to the qualities of speed and dash of the Israeli army came from none other than President Nasser who said in a recent speech to the Egyptian National Assembly that on June 9, four days after the war broke out, there was not one Egyptian soldier on the west bank of the Suez Canal although the Israelis had advanced to the east bank, such was the speed of the Israeli advance and the paralysis of the Egyptian forces.[29]

The difference in the spirit of the Israeli and Egyptian leadership in battle is reflected in the fact that whereas Egyptian officers killed amounted to less than 15 percent of the total number of Egyptian soldiers killed, the corresponding percentage in the Israeli army was about two times higher.[30] Again, it is interesting to quote President Nasser: "It was this [Egyptian] army command that disintegrated into

[29] Speech delivered on November 23, 1967, al Ahram, November 24, 1967.

[30] 30 percent according to some sources, for example, Beaufre, Paris Match, June 24, 1967.

chaos within the first hours of the enemy attack, which, by Allah, was anticipated." He also alluded to the presence of corruption in the Egyptian officer corps, saying: "Inside the armed forces there were serious events, with commanders exploiting their position for private purposes." Since then, another example of deep-reaching corruption within the Egyptian high command has come to light in connection with the suicide of Marshal Amer, who was President Nasser's relative and closest friend.

In a war of movement, it is particularly important that the High Command should be able to revise its plans in accordance with a rapidly changing situation, which in turn requires that the lower echelons should be capable of making their own practical decisions on the basis of general directives. The Israelis knew the advantage that their officers and men had over their enemy on this score and planned their moves to make the most of it through strategies and tactics aimed at disrupting prepared plans and capitalizing on lack of initiative at the lower levels. The Egyptians did indeed fight with skill and courage from prepared positions in the first phase of the battle, but once their fixed lines of defense were smashed, they were never able to fight again in any coordinated fashion, and occasional displays of courage by various units notwithstanding, the bulk of the Egyptian troops that had not been affected by the first phase were reduced to a fleeing rabble by the swift Israeli maneuvers.

A large part of the credit for the speed and thoroughness of the Israeli victory must of course go to the Israeli air force, which had an uncontested mastery of the skies after the devastating blow it inflicted on the enemy's air force in the first day. Because of this mastery, much less attention had to be paid to Israeli units having to cover each other's flanks, to keeping a certain relation between vanguard and main force, and to matching the size of Israeli attacking units to the enemy to be attacked, and so on. There was always the possibility in case of serious trouble of calling in an air strike to help restore the situation. Moreover, the continual harassment of enemy columns by the preying Israeli planes had an incalculable effect in demoralizing the enemy and turning his retreats into routs. Some journalists and hasty military commentators have gone as far as to say that the entire second Sinai campaign was won by the Israeli air force. The reader who has come so far will know better. He will remember, for instance, that the first crucial breakthrough at Rafah was effected in the first half of the first day when the Israeli air force was busy elsewhere, and that the second and decisive breakthrough at Abu Egeila was achieved in night fighting when air support was unavailable. In these two battles alone, the Israeli armor put out of action about one-fourth of the Egyptian armor knocked out during the entire war.

A complete account of the war in Sinai would probably give considerable attention to the role of intelligence, communications, and logistics, all of which are crucial for effective rapid action. Little reliable data has transpired about these aspects except for a few suggestive facts and claims.

As far as Egyptian intelligence goes, we have the testimony of President Nasser himself who said in the previously cited speech to the Egyptian National Assembly: "Our intelligence services were rotten. They tried to set themselves up as a state within the state and exploit their position for gaining influence." In the same vein, it is also interesting to compare the total number of Israeli brigades that we estimated on the basis of numerous bits of information and identification of individual brigades on the three fronts with an estimate given shortly before the war by Haykal and evidently reflecting the findings of Egyptian intelligence:[31]

	Haykal's Estimate	Our Estimate
Infantry brigades	10	10
Armored brigades	7	10 plus 2 "groups"
Paratroop brigades	2	4
"Second line" brigades	7	36,000 men or about 12 brigades
Others	8 regional defense brigades 6 "Nachal" brigades	100,000 men, including some "tail"

Except for general claims and boasts, the Israelis have understandably remained rather discreet about their own intelligence services. However, what little evidence has emerged and the entire course of the war suggest that the Israelis were remarkably well informed about the enemy before and during the war. Thus, for example, a military airfield in Upper Egypt which had been completed only a few weeks before the war was included in those attacked by the Israeli air force on the first day of the operations.[32]

---

[31] Segev, op. cit., p. 263.

[32] Le Monde, June 11, 1967. Former Minister of War Badran said at his postwar trial that the Egyptian intelligence was responsible for the disaster. The Jews had been given 300 Mirages [sic] of which intelligence did not know. (Actually Israel received 30 Mirages shortly before the war; see Appendix B.) Badran added that the Jews had made reconnaissance, "through the Americans," of "every plane screw we had." See al Ahram, February 25, 1968.

As for communications, the story seems to be basically the same. The Egyptians have, for instance, argued that jamming of their communications was responsible for the failure of orders to hold on to the Mitla Pass to reach the unit concerned after this had been mistakenly ordered to withdraw earlier. The Egyptians attributed the jamming to the American ship *Liberty*, but it might very well have been the work of the Israeli intelligence. We know that the communications of the Egyptian army had so completely broken down by the third day of the war that orders to units had to be issued through radio Cairo. On the other hand, Israelis have boasted that their armed forces disposed of such a communications network that the High Command could listen in on orders being issued to field units down to the lowest levels.

As for logistics, we have on the one hand the incredible reports from Israeli sources that not a single Egyptian maintenance workshop was found in all of Sinai. On the other hand, we know that some of the Israeli tanks covered as much as 500 miles in the course of the campaign (though the direct route to the Canal is only 200 miles long), and that entire armored brigades advanced up to 60 miles in one day in war conditions and on mediocre roads and trails, which bespeaks of an extraordinary level of maintenance, engineering, and supply on a large scale. General Rabin even claimed in July that all the Israeli tanks that went into the war came out of it on their own power, except those destroyed in battle.[33]

A NOTE ON NAVAL WARFARE

As the reader may remember, the greatest disproportion of military might between Egypt and Israel was in the size of naval forces. Yet, and in spite of the short distances from Alexandria and Port Said to Tel Aviv, naval warfare was but incidental to the decisive operations in the air and on the ground. The first reason why this was so is that, prior to the war, Egypt shifted a part of its naval forces to the Red Sea, perhaps in the belief that Israel would strike toward Sharm el Sheikh. Later on, after the war, with the Canal blocked and the Israelis close to the town of Suez, these Egyptian naval forces were reported to have found shelter in the Yemeni port of Hodeida.[34]

The second reason is that the Israeli navy boldly took the offensive in spite of the numerical odds. On the night of Monday to Tuesday, an Israeli task force of one destroyer and a number of MTB's reached

[33] *Bammachané*, July 5, 1967.

[34] *Jerusalem Post Weekly*, July 24, 1967.

Port Said and engaged a group of Egyptian "Ossa" rocket boats moving westward along the Mediterranean coast. As soon as the Israeli gunners opened fire, the Egyptian boats retreated to the harbor after suffering some damage.[35] This action prompted the Egyptians to remove, on the next day, all their "Ossa" and "Komar" rocket boats to Alexandria, thus putting Tel Aviv out of their range.

In the same night from Monday to Tuesday, an Israeli naval force composed of one submarine reached the port of Alexandria. A group of frogmen then entered the harbor, succeeded in penetrating the main anchorage of the Ras al Tin naval base, and sank at least one craft of the "Ossa" type, as al Ahram acknowledged, and perhaps one or more Egyptian submarines. However, under circumstances still unknown, the Israeli frogmen were subsequently discovered and six of them were captured.

During the week, the Israeli navy detected three enemy submarines off Israel's coast. On Wednesday, a force of destroyers located one of them off Rosh Hanikra. After an attack with depth charges, an oil slick was sighted on the sea surface; this may either mean that the submarine was hit or that the slick was a feint. On Thursday, the Israeli destroyers fired depth charges at another submarine near Haifa Bay. Again, large patches of oil slick were sighted. A third submarine was sighted further to the south, attacked, and driven back. The three Egyptian submarines caused no damage. The fact that they were detected and destroyed or driven back must be weighed against the fact that there were only four Sonar devices in the entire small Israeli navy.[36]

In mid-afternoon, on Wednesday, June 7, there occurred the very unfortunate Israeli attack on the American vessel Liberty. At the time of the attack, the Liberty was moving slowly on a southeasterly course off el Arish, just outside the territorial waters. Its mission was to monitor communications in Sinai (one American seaman later put it more bluntly: "Let's face it," he said, "we were spying."). Arab sources accused it of having jammed Egyptian communications, a charge probably as true as the one that American planes helped Israel. As it subsequently turned out, the American naval command in Washington had earlier ordered the Liberty to move away from the Sinai coast, but the message was misrouted and did not reach it in time. Shortly after the outbreak of hostilities in Sinai, Israel had also asked via the American naval attaché in Tel Aviv whether there were any United States ships

[35] Jerusalem Post Weekly, June 12.

[36] Jerusalem Post Weekly, June 12, 1967; Le Monde, June 11, 1967.

in the area of the fighting, but for some reason no answer was received. As a final element explaining why this accident happened, it later turned out that, contrary to what earlier reports had asserted, there was one Egyptian vessel with a silhouette very similar to the *Liberty's*.

Thus it was that, at 2:05 P.M., two Israeli jets made several passes over the ship before strafing it with gunfire and rockets. The vessel sustained 81 hits. Twenty minutes later, three Israeli MTB's moved in at a fast speed; one of them challenged the *Liberty* to identify itself, but it signaled back "A-A," meaning "identify yourself first." The same signal had been given in 1956 by the Egyptian destroyer *Ibrahim el Awal* when it had tried to bombard Haifa. Thereupon, the Israeli boats attacked the *Liberty* with torpedoes, one of which hit it, tearing a 25 to 30 foot hole in its side, mostly below the water line. The Israelis were later to claim, both in official explanations and in the testimony of one MTB sailor, that at the time of the attack the *Liberty* was not flying the U.S. flag, but this was denied by American sources. Both versions may be correct in that no good view is possible from a low MTB sailing very fast through the waves, especially if the *Liberty* was still surrounded by some smoke following the air attack. After the vessel was hit, the Israeli boats recognized their mistake, apparently from an American life buoy floating in the sea, and one MTB stopped by the crippled vessel offering help, but it was understandably told to "go to hell."[37] In any case, it is now certain that the attack, in which 34 lives were needlessly lost, was a tragic mistake in spite of the fantastic tales that have been printed.[38]

THE JORDANIAN FRONT

The Jordanian front consisted of the West Bank of Jordan and the surrounding Israeli territory. Jordan territory on the West Bank formed two bulges in the shape of a turned-around capital "B," with the bigger bulge in the north. In contrast to Sinai, this battlefield was thickly settled on both sides with hundreds of villages and towns inhabited by hundreds of thousands of people in relatively close proximity. In divided Jerusalem, the Jordanian and Israeli positions were actually at most a few hundred yards apart, sometimes within a stone's throw of

[37] *New York Times*, June 9, 10, 11, 15, 20, 29, 30; July 7, 1967.
[38] Thus, *Newsweek* published an article saying that the attack had been deliberate, because the *Liberty* had gathered evidence that the Israelis had been the first to open fire in Sinai. But if that had really been so, would not the Israelis have sunk the vessel altogether?

one another. Also in contrast to Sinai, the terrain was completely mountainous, could be negotiated by motorized vehicles only along roads
and tracks and their sides, contained countless "bottlenecks," and was
therefore extremely ill-suited for swift, large scale, wide maneuvers by
armor.

The mountains of the West Bank are essentially a continuation of the
chain that includes the mountains of Galilee in Israel (and beyond
them those of Lebanon) and constitutes a kind of north-south spine,
from which the ribs slope down gently toward the west and more
abruptly toward the east. More or less along the spine runs a main
road on which are situated from north to south most of the important
towns of the West Bank: Jenin, Nablus, Ramallah, Jerusalem, Bethlehem, and Hebron. The two areas just north of Nablus and south of
Ramallah were the nodal sectors of the entire West Bank. From the Ramallah region, roads branched out in all directions. Eastward, just
north of Ramallah, went one of the two roads to Jericho, which then
continued to the Jordan River and constituted one of the two main
links between the western and the eastern banks. To the south, the
road led to Arab Jerusalem, cutting off completely the Israeli positions
in Mount Scopus, branched out to Jericho, and continued south to Bethlehem and Hebron. To the west, a road branched out to Latrun,
which lies on the old main road from Tel Aviv to Jerusalem at the
point where the Israeli coastal plain and the mountains of Judea meet.
Several tracks descended southward from that road to Jordanian positions that lay astride the Israeli corridor to Jerusalem. To the north,
the road went up to Nablus, where another network of roads, only
slightly less crucial, branched out. Just north of Nablus, the road
opened out into a pincer whose arms rejoined at Jenin, close to the
northern border of the bulge. From the eastern arm of the pincer,
the second main link between the West and East Banks descended to
the Jordan River. From the western arm, several roads and tracks descended to the narrow waist of Israel, including two main roads to
Kalkilya and Tulkarm.

We have already indicated on several occasions the crucial strategic
importance of the Jordanian bulges, and we need only recall that just
four miles separated the two Jordanian bulges at the corridor to Jerusalem; only ten miles separated Kalkilya from the Mediterranean at
Hertzlia, and 11 miles separated Tulkarm from the sea at Natanya.
From the mountains at the northwest corner of the bulge to Haifa,
the main port, it was only 25 miles, and from the mountains of Hebron
to the Gaza Strip and the Egyptian forces it was 24 miles. Quick

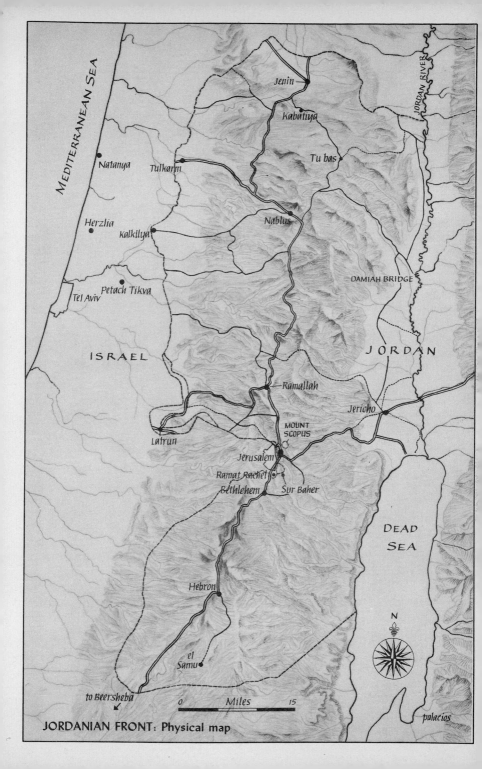

JORDANIAN FRONT: Physical map

breakthroughs along these axes could cut up Israel into fragments and isolate from each other the main centers of its population.

On the eve of the war, the Jordanians had concentrated ten of their 11 brigades on the West Bank, deployed as follows: In a broad arch roughly parallel to the border at the northern end of the bulge were three infantry brigades—one centered on Jenin, one spreading west and south to Tulkarm, and one spreading east and south to the Jordan River. In Jerusalem itself and in a north-to-south arch around it were two infantry brigades. East of these two concentrations, and in positions from which they could be reached quickly, were two armored brigades, one near the Jericho crossing of the Jordan and one near the crossing at the Damia bridge. The remaining three infantry brigades were deployed one in the triangle Nablus-Tulkarm-Kalkilya, one south of Kalkilya through Latrun to the northern edge of the Jerusalem corridor, and one south of Jerusalem to Hebron. In addition, two Egyptian commando battalions, which had been airlifted a few days before the fighting began, were deployed in the vicinity of Latrun. An Iraqi brigade, the spearhead of three more scheduled to come, was positioned on June 5 on the east side of the Damia crossing. The eleventh and last Jordanian brigade was deployed south and east of the Dead Sea, looking across the Negev to the Egyptian forces.

It is evident from this distribution of forces that as of June 5, the Arab forces on the West Bank were still basically deployed for defense but were beginning to develop the outlines of an offensive deployment. The eight infantry brigades thinly spread over a long front with the two armored brigades poised in the rear to come to the assistance of threatened sectors clearly pointed to a defensive orientation. At the same time, these two brigades, the Iraqi brigade near the crossing to the West Bank, the Egyptian commando battalions in Latrun, and the Jordanian brigade near the Dead Sea pointed no less clearly to the beginning of a process of assembling and deploying an offensive force meant to be completed in the following days. The Israeli attack on Egypt interrupted the process and forced the Arab forces on the West Bank to enter the battle in the subsidiary role of drawing Israeli fire in order to alleviate the pressure on the Egyptian front instead of mounting dangerous offensives.

We have said that the Israeli High Command threw against the Jordanian front some nine brigades, three of them armored, plus two armored groups. Actually, it had deployed against Jordan in the morning of June 5 a much less formidable force of only three infantry brigades and one armored brigade and did not decide to add the rest of the forces until the afternoon of that day and the following day, after

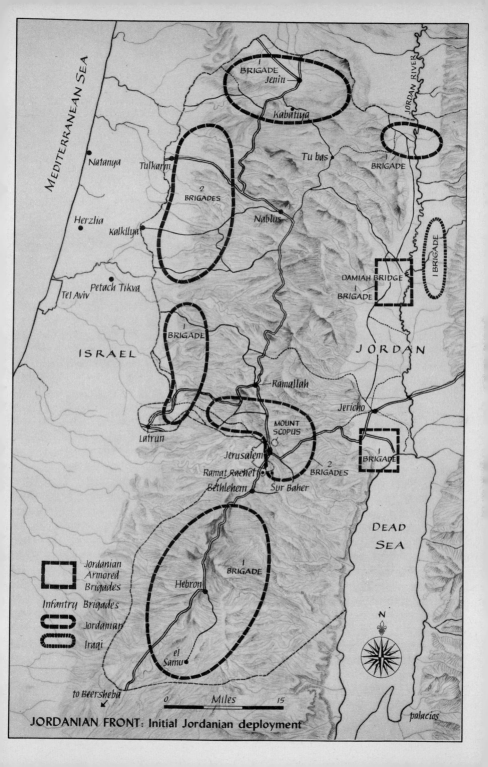

MEDITERRANEAN SEA

JORDAN RIVER

1 BRIGADE
Jenin
Kabatiya

Natanya
Tulkarm
Tu bas
1 BRIGADE

2 BRIGADES

Herzlia
Kalkilya
Nablus

Tel Aviv
Petach Tikva

DAMIAH BRIDGE
1 BRIGADE

1 BRIGADE

1 BRIGADE

ISRAEL

JORDAN

Ramallah

Jericho

Latrun

MOUNT SCOPUS

Jerusalem
Ramat Rachel
Bethlehem
Sur Baher

2 BRIGADES

1 BRIGADE

DEAD SEA

Jordanian
Armored
Brigades

Infantry Brigades
Jordanian

Hebron

1 BRIGADE

Iraqi

el Samu

N

to Beersheba

0   Miles   15

JORDANIAN FRONT: Initial Jordanian deployment

palacios

revising its initial strategy. For despite the Jordanian-Egyptian treaty, the Israelis stubbornly believed and hoped that King Hussein would content himself with a pretense of fighting; this is why the Israeli government asked General Odd Bull, Chief of the U.N. Truce Supervision Organization, to convey to the King a message to the effect that Israel would not attack if he held back his forces even while Jordanian fire was descending on Jerusalem. It was only after the King had given unequivocal indications that he was unable or unwilling to stay out—the capture of the U.N. Headquarters in Jerusalem, bombardment all along the front, attacks by Jordanian planes on Israeli military and civilian targets—that the Israeli High Command readjusted its thinking and put into operation contingency plans for such an eventuality. Whereas it had previously intended to give second priority to the Syrian front after the Egyptian, it now put the Jordanian front in second place and moved to it three or four brigades, two of them armored, initially intended for use against Syria. In addition, it rushed to Jerusalem one brigade of paratroopers that had been intended for use against the Egyptian front.

In number of brigades, the Israelis and the Jordanians were thus more or less matched. However, the Israelis, who relied heavily on their settlements, reinforced by "second line" units, for static defense, had the enormous advantage of being able to concentrate superior first line forces against selected Jordanian targets. Moreover, to Jordan's misfortune, by the time it decidedly joined the war, the Egyptian air force, which, according to the joint defense plans, was to provide the Jordanian troops with air cover, had already been knocked out, leaving these troops at the mercy of the Israeli air force. But not all the advantages were on the Israeli side. The Jordanian troops were entrenched in strong, prepared positions in terrain that was on the whole highly suited for defense and very difficult for the deployment of large motorized forces.

As with the Sinai offensive, the Israeli offensive against Jordan was planned in two continuous phases. The first was intended to secure a number of minimum objectives before any possible interruption of the fighting; this phase could at the same time serve as a prelude to the pursuit of the maximal objectives if time and circumstances permitted. The objectives of the first phase were: (1) to push the border back in the Jenin region, at the north of the bulge, in order to put the valley of Jezreel with its settlements and its important air base of Ramat David out of range of the Jordanian artillery; (2) to lop off the Latrun salient and sit on top of the Latrun-Ramallah road and thus remove a threat to one of Israel's main road junctions in the vicinity of Tel Aviv and secure and widen the corridor to Jerusalem; and (3) to establish a secure corridor to the Mount Scopus enclave, cut off from the rest of Jerusalem since 1948, and thus also improve the protection of Jerusalem itself. As may be readily seen, the achievement of these objectives would automatically cut off Arab Jerusalem from the north and east and place the Israelis in an excellent position to move on against the nodal sectors of the "spine" in pursuit of the maximal objective of capturing the entire West Bank and destroying or routing the Jordanian army in the second phase.

The Israelis began their offensive in the late afternoon and night of June 5 with a series of simultaneous attacks in the northern and southern ends of the upper bulge, including Jerusalem itself. In the north, they crossed the border in three prongs on a front some ten miles wide with Jenin as the target. The right and left prongs were secondary axes aimed at confusing the enemy's defenses; the main attack came from the center and was carried out by an armored brigade under the command of Colonel Moshe, which approached Jenin from the rear in the first hours of Tuesday, June 6. The Israelis planned to use their favorite tactic of sending the armor galloping in the streets of the city and spitting fire in all directions in an effort to shake its defenses. After this charge it would pull into key positions to block the ways before reinforcement and be prepared to lend assistance to the infantry coming in its wake to mop up. The Israeli tanks proceeded to execute their part of the plan, but as they issued from the city to block its approaches, they came upon an ambush of some 30 Jordanian tanks and anti-tank positions. For several hours the Jordanians fought bravely and skillfully and inflicted heavy losses on their enemy, but eventually Israeli reinforcements appeared on their flank and the two Israeli forces crushed them. The Israeli tanks then split up, with one force going back to the city to assist the infantry and the other rushing to hold blocking positions around it.

By about 8:00 A.M. Tuesday, June 6, white flags began to appear all over the city, but the Jenin battle was far from over. Before the Israelis had the city well in their hands, they received word of a column of some 60 Jordanian tanks, presumably from the armored brigade that was stationed near the Damiah bridge on the Jordan, approaching the city. The Israeli tanks raced out of the city in an effort to get to a road junction some three miles south of it before the Jordanians, but the latter had arrived there first and immediately engaged the worn-out Israelis. In the meantime, the Jordanian defenders of Jenin, encouraged by the news of the arrival of reinforcements and the withdrawal of the Israeli armor, resumed their resistance. The armor battle outside Jenin went badly for the Israelis for some time; it appeared for a while as though the Jordanian counterattack might recapture Jenin, or at least block any further Israeli advance to the south. However, the first of these possibilities was averted by the appearance of the Israeli air force—again and again the *deus ex machina* in the battles on the Jordanian front—which struck at the Jordanian armor and stunned it frequently and long enough to permit the Israelis to catch their breath, pull out their injured personnel and damaged equipment, reorganize, refuel, and reinforce their tank force.

Even before that battle was concluded in the afternoon of that day with the ruin of the Jordanian forces, the Israeli advance to the south was already proceeding relentlessly. Early on June 6, the Israeli authorities, having decided to move on beyond the first phase to the second, sent in a second armored brigade under Colonel Uri, which penetrated the bulge some 10 to 12 miles east of the point of entry of Colonel Moshe's armored brigade and moved rapidly along trails and tracks with the initial object of getting onto the eastern of the two roads connecting Jenin and Nablus. Sometime after 10:00 A.M., the vanguard of that force appeared in the rear of the Jordanian armor in the Jenin battle zone and cut off its way of retreat. The rest of the brigade got on the road to Nablus and began to tackle Jordanian positions and more of the armor of the valiant but overstrained Jordanian brigade.

The Israeli forces in the north of the bulge comprised by then two armored brigades, one infantry brigade, plus whatever forces were used for the diversionary attacks by the initial prongs. These formed two strong groups, which advanced toward Nablus along the two main roads leading to it from Jenin. Colonel Uri's force, moving along the eastern road, encountered fierce resistance from Jordanian armor, which tried desperately to prevent it from reaching the intersection of that road with the road going down to the Jordan River and the East Bank. A battle that lasted for seven hours, in the course of which the Israelis made generous use of their air force, exhausted both sides but stopped at nightfall on June 6 without decision. However, Colonel Uri decided to make his forces exert that extra effort that often determines the outcome of battles: Instead of using the night for resting and waiting for daylight and air support, he attacked shortly after midnight and smashed the enemy's resistance. As the sun of June 7, the third day of the war, approached its zenith, the forces of Colonel Uri had already split off into two, one of them rushing down the road to the Jordan valley and the other approaching Nablus.

The capture of Nablus, a city of 80,000 inhabitants and a crucial nodal point, was almost an anticlimax to the previous battles and fore-

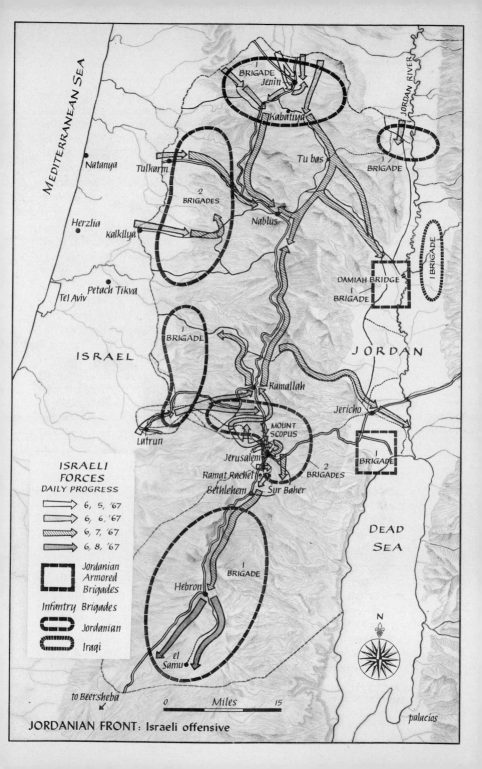

MEDITERRANEAN SEA

Natanya

Herzlia

Tel Aviv

Petach Tikva

ISRAEL

JORDAN RIVER

1 BRIGADE
Jenin

Kabatiya

Tu bas

Tulkarm

2
BRIGADES

Nablus

1 BRIGADE

kalkilya

1 BRIGADE

DAMIAH BRIDGE
1 BRIGADE

JORDAN

1 BRIGADE

Ramallah

Jericho

Latrun

MOUNT
SCOPUS

Jerusalem

Ramat Rachel
Bethlehem   Sur Baher

2
BRIGADES

1 BRIGADE

DEAD
SEA

ISRAELI
FORCES
DAILY PROGRESS

6, 5, '67
6, 6, '67
6, 7, '67
6, 8, '67

Jordanian
Armored
Brigades

Infantry Brigades

Jordanian

Iraqi

1 BRIGADE

Hebron

N

el
Samu

to Beersheba

0   Miles   15

JORDANIAN FRONT: Israeli offensive

palacios

cast the exhaustion of the Jordanian defense resources in this sector. The Israelis met with no resistance at its approaches though these included some narrow gorges excellently suited for defense. When their tanks warily entered the city, they were surprised to be met with cheering crowds rather than with fire. The people of Nablus mistook the enemy coming unexpectedly from the east for the Iraqi brigade, which was expected to arrive from an assembly point near the Jordan River. Little did they suspect that that brigade, which had come a long way from Iraq, would be entirely paralyzed by frequent visits of the Israeli air force alone. The Jordanian force defending the city apparently was no better informed than its population and concentrated its tank strength at the western approaches, thinking an Israeli attack more likely from that direction. When the Israeli armor appeared in their rear, the Jordanian tanks fought courageously as usual; but they were soon trapped into a bowl by the freely moving Israelis and leisurely destroyed by combined air force attacks and Israeli tank sniping. By 6:00 P.M. June 7, Nablus had settled to living under Israeli occupation after its mayor had signed an unconditional surrender and urged its population to observe order.

While these events were taking place, Israeli troops were converging on Nablus from all directions. Colonel Moshe's brigade, which had won the battle of Jenin the previous day and then moved to Nablus on the western road, reached it in the evening of the 7th without encountering serious resistance on its way. In the previous day, two Israeli forces consisting of "second line" troops had captured Tulkarm and Kalkilya without much fighting.[39] They then converged on the Tulkarm-Nablus road and climbed up to Nablus in their bus-studded columns spearheaded by a few tanks. The sight of scores of destroyed enemy tanks and vehicles on their way reminded them of the difficulties they might have encountered had not the Israeli air force passed there often before them. On the evening of June 7, these forces too reached Nablus after having mopped up pockets of resistance on their way. Finally, elements of an Israeli brigade that had fought in the south of the bulge in the previous two days and then marched northward through Ramallah also arrived and met the forces that had fought their way southward.

At the southern end of the upper bulge, the Israelis began their of-

[39] The lack of fighting did not, however, spare Kalkilya from extensive destruction. The Israeli forces that entered the half-deserted town blew up nearly half of its houses in retaliation for the alleged use of the town as a base for raiders, and for the shelling of Tel Aviv from it. General Dayan, during a visit in Kalkilya after the war promised help in the reconstruction of the demolished houses.

fensive late on June 5 and early on June 6 with two coordinated sets
of attacks, the one aiming at the critical nodal area of the "spine" between Jerusalem and Ramallah, the other aiming at the hills around all
of Jerusalem. The approaches chosen clearly reflected the desire of the
Israelis to secure the minimal objectives in that area to ensure themselves against a prompt cease fire or difficulties in achieving the maximal objectives.

At about 4:00 P.M. on June 5, an Israeli armored brigade under Colonel Ben Ari opened one set of attacks on a five-mile front in the
mountains at the narrowest end of the Jerusalem corridor just west of
the city. The brigade split up into three prongs and began its advance
along tortuous, steep, neglected roads and tracks toward the west-east
road to Ramallah known as "the height road." Between them and their
objectives stood a series of Jordanian positions that had been firing
their mortars all day on Israeli targets. The positions were relatively
thinly manned by pairs of platoons and companies rather than battalions and brigades, but they were well fortified with deep trenches,
pillboxes, mined barbed wires, and were endowed with good firepower
and excellent fields of fire. Moreover, the Israelis coming at them had
little room to maneuver their armor and had to attack in small narrow
formations. King Hussein, for one, thought that the Israelis should never have made it, for he fired the Jordanian commander of the sector after the war, but they did, and not for want of courageous fighting by
the Jordanians. By 3:00 A.M. the next day, the three Israeli battalions
were on the "height road" and wheeled eastward to the north of Jerusalem and the road from it to Ramallah, to help another Israeli attack
that was developing in an inner semi-arch.

While Ben Ari's armored brigade was advancing on the crestline,
the paratroopers' brigade began to attack at 2:00 A.M. from Israeli
Jerusalem in a northeasterly direction toward Mount Scopus. As its
name indicates, Mount Scopus commands a view of most of Jerusalem
and controls the Mount of Olives to the south of it and the road from
Jerusalem to Jericho and the East Bank. Between the paratroopers and
their objective were the large Arab quarter of Shaykh Jarrah and the
"American colony" defended by several lines of barbed wire, pillboxes,
lines of trenches, countless light and heavy machine gun nests and
firing positions, anti-tank guns, mortars, and artillery zeroed in on all
potential avenues of advance. The fighting that developed here was
among the fiercest and costliest in the entire war. The paratroopers suffered scores of casualties within the first minutes and their subsequent
progress was measured in yards paid for with much blood on both
sides. But the Israelis had the advantage of being able to throw in

reinforcements, including tanks, at the appropriate moments, and thus keep the pressure of the attack going until its successful conclusion. The Jordanians were denied such assistance by the simultaneous attack of Ben Ari's brigade on the crest and the far-reaching arm of the Israeli air force. The latter foiled the attempts of elements of the Jordanian armored brigade initially deployed in the vicinity of Jericho to come up to Jerusalem until Ben Ari's armored brigade arrived and sealed the road. In addition, Ben Ari's brigade attacked and captured Jordanian positions that could have helped the embattled forces in the city itself, and then converged on Mount Scopus to meet the paratroopers who fought their way up.

The left (northern) flank of Ben Ari's brigade was itself protected by yet a third Israeli attack, which started in Latrun and moved in a wide arch to the Jerusalem-Ramallah road in the vicinity of Ramallah. The attack began at about sunset on June 5 with a motorized infantry brigade reinforced with armor. The town and police fortress of Latrun, on which the Israelis had lost hundreds of lives in 1948 without ever succeeding in capturing them, were fairly easily crushed this time by Israeli armor, and their defenders, including the Egyptian commandos, fled in all directions. The Israeli armor climbed up the hills toward the supporting positions in Arab villages. Ghur al Fawqah, the strongest of these, was overrun after a sharp battle and its defenders too, also including Egyptian commandos, fled. By the time full daylight shone on June 6, however, Israeli infantry and supply columns moving in the wake of the armor in "soft-skinned" vehicles were surprised to discover that the Egyptian commandos, after having fled from their strong positions in Latrun and Ghur, had dispersed in the fields and groves in the vicinity and continued a sustained sniping fire that exacted a heavy toll and impeded "traffic." There was no alternative but to set aside a force of foot-soldiers to hunt the several hundred Egyptians by ones and twos for the next two days.

The bulk of the Latrun brigade continued its rapid advance along a good but narrow mountain road that offered many exceptional defensive opportunities. Due to a combination of thin Jordanian deployment and the speed and surprise of the Israeli movement, only one roadblock was encountered and overcome, and the brigade reached the vicinity of Ramallah on June 6. Earlier the same day Ben Ari's brigade, which had moved in the inner arch, had already raided the city.

On the morning of June 7, Ramallah was captured without difficulty and the two brigades, after meeting briefly, split again, one of them descending the eastern slope of the "spine" to go to Jericho the same day and block the second and last exit to the east bank, the other going up to Nablus to meet the Israeli forces that had descended upon it from the north.

We interrupted our discussion of the fighting in Jerusalem at the point where the paratroopers had fought their way through the built-up area north of Arab Jerusalem and reached Mount Scopus during the day of June 6. The paratroopers spent the rest of the day mopping up the snipers who still infested the areas they had captured and preparing for an attack on the Jordanian positions on the hills south of Mount Scopus—the Augusta Victoria hospital, the Mount of Olives, and Dir Abu Tor—prior to the assault on the old city of Jerusalem itself, at the feet of these positions. These moves were part of a coordinated set of attacks begun much earlier—that is to say, around noon the previous day—the over-all object of which was to completely encircle Jerusalem by capturing all the hill positions surrounding it.

We have said at the beginning of this narrative of the operations on the Jordanian front, that the war started in earnest when a Jordanian unit captured the U.N. Headquarters building, which lay on a strategic hill in the no-man's land south of Jerusalem. The Israelis responded quickly with a counterattack by elements of an infantry brigade—known as the Jerusalem Brigade—that expelled the Jordanians and inaugurated an offensive against the chain of positions south and east of the city. In a series of sharp battles that went on into the night of the 5th, the "sausage position" north of the U.N. Headquarters and the village of Sur Baher and the "bell position" to the south of it were captured. These two positions together with the Israeli outpost at Ramat Rachel cut off Jerusalem from the southern bulge and isolated the Jordanian forces assigned to the defense of the whole area from Bethlehem to Hebron.

In the course of the night of June 6–7, the Israeli air force and artillery intensified their action around Jerusalem. In the light of parachute flares and powerful projectors, flights of fighter-bombers streaked over the city delivering bombs and cannon fire while the artillery poured out shells on the Jordanian positions. By dawn, one part of the paratroopers went on to the assault of the Mount of Olives and Augusta Victoria while another part remained poised to break into the old city. At the same time, the Jerusalem Brigade advanced on Abu Tor and the neighboring village of Silwan, the remaining unclosed links in the chain around Jerusalem. The Israeli air force, artillery, and tanks were responsible for most of the noise and damage, with the infantry engaging in only sporadic fighting here and there, except at Abu Tor where some sharp clashes took place. The operation was soon over, and shortly after 9:30 A.M., June 7, the signal was given for the assault on the old city itself.

Militarily, the attack on the old city was an anti-climax to all the fighting that had taken place in preparation for this operation. The city capitulated minutes after the paratroopers smashed their way into it through Saint Stephen's Gate from the east. Emotionally, however, the operation was the climax of the entire war, and the appearance of the paratroopers at the Wailing Wall released a flood of feelings throughout Israel and among millions of Jews around the world that no one who witnessed it is apt to forget and that no one who was not moved by it himself is likely to comprehend truly.

While Israelis of all walks of life began pressing their way to the Wailing Wall in a mass pilgrimage that went on for months, the Jerusalem Brigade advanced south into the lower bulge, moving rapidly along the main highway without encountering any resistance. At about noontime Bethlehem capitulated without a shot being fired, and by sunset Hebron had followed suit. The Jordanian brigade in charge of this strategic and easily defensible area had abandoned most of its heavy equipment and simply melted away. When the cease-fire order of the Security Council, formally accepted by both Jordan and Israel, entered into effect that evening, the entire West Bank was in Israeli hands.

It thus took the Israeli forces slightly over 50 hours to rout the entire Jordanian army and capture the whole West Bank. Almost all the Israeli troops that fought on the Jordanian front were reserve units activated only a few days or weeks before the war; and they confronted an approximately equal number of regular enemy troops occupying formidable terrain features. The price paid by the Israelis for their success on this front was heavier than on the Egyptian front where they encountered and destroyed an enemy at least two and a half times larger. Against the 275 killed and 800 wounded they suffered on the Egyptian front, the Israelis had 299 killed and 1,457 wounded in the war against Jordan. About two-thirds of the Israeli soldiers killed and three-fourths of the wounded belonged to the forces of the Central Command, which fought primarily in Jerusalem and from the southern end of the upper bulge.

As for the Jordanian losses, King Hussein began by mentioning the total figure of 15,000, but later the Jordanian government officially listed 6,094 killed and missing, 762 wounded, and 463 prisoners. Among the killed and missing, the Israelis at first unofficially estimated about 1,500 killed, but then revised the figure downward to as low as 600, the remainder having thrown away their uniforms and just melted into the population. Regardless of computation, it is clear that most of the

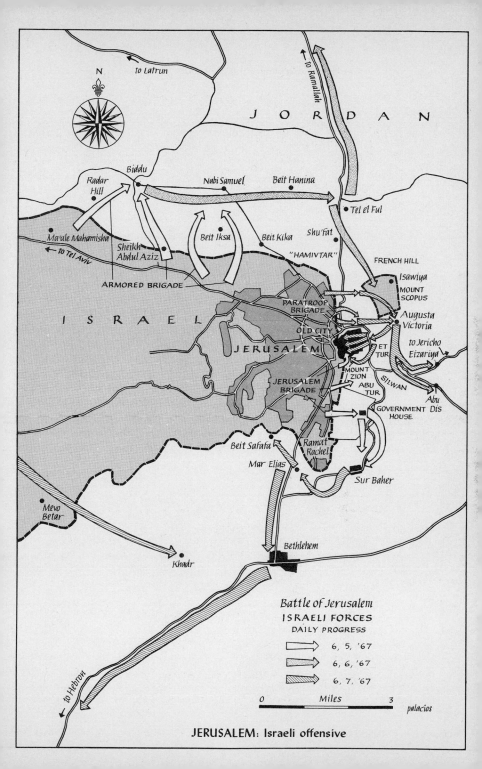

N

to Latrun

J O R D A N

to Ramallah

Biddu

Radar
Hill

Nabi Samuel   Beit Hanina

Tel el Ful

Ma'ale Mahamisha

Beit Iksa   Beit Kika   Shu'fat

to Tel Aviv

Sheikh
Abdul Aziz

"HAMIVTAR"

FRENCH HILL

ARMORED BRIGADE

Isawiya
MOUNT
SCOPUS

PARATROOP
BRIGADE

I S R A E L

Augusta
Victoria

OLD CITY

to Jericho
Eizariya

JERUSALEM

ET
TUR

MOUNT
ZION

JERUSALEM
BRIGADE

SILWAN

ABU
TUR

Abu
Dis

GOVERNMENT
HOUSE

Beit Safafa   Ramat
Rachel

Mar Elias

Sur Baher

Mevo
Betar

Khadr

Bethlehem

Battle of Jerusalem
ISRAELI FORCES
DAILY PROGRESS

6, 5, '67
6, 6, '67
6, 7, '67

to Hebron

0   Miles   3

palacios

JERUSALEM: Israeli offensive

ten Jordanian brigades found in the West Bank at the beginning of the war were badly mauled and two of them—the one in the Jenin area and the one in the southern bulge—were almost entirely destroyed or dispersed. Jordanian losses in equipment according to Israeli estimates included over one-third of the armor deployed in the West Bank. The Israelis say that they also captured 60 field artillery pieces out of a total of 90 initially deployed, 36 105-mm self-propelled guns, eight out of a total of 16 Long Tom long-range guns, and 20 tanks.

THE SYRIAN FRONT

The battlefield between Israel and Syria consisted of the region on both sides of the 40-mile long frontier or armistice line between the two countries. The Israeli side of the frontier is essentially constituted by the depression of the upper Jordan River and its tributaries. This is basically a flat, fertile, thickly settled valley. The Syrian side of the frontier is mainly constituted by the southwestern extension of the Anti-Lebanon range. Along the northern half of this side of the frontier, the mountains rise steeply at the frontier line itself or very near it, while along the southern half they tend to rise more gently for a few miles before accelerating the pace of their climb. Through most of the length of the frontier, the Syrians thus looked down from the hills on the Israeli plain below, which constituted an easy and tempting target for their artillery.

Although the Syrians made a few attempts to penetrate into Israeli territory and submitted the entire Israeli side of the frontier to heavy artillery bombardment, the real fighting took place entirely on the Syrian side, inside a rough rectangle as long as the border between the two countries and some 13 to 16 miles in width. This rectangle embraced the crestline of the Syrian heights, which stretched in a semi-arch close to its northern and eastern sides. On the crestline ran a crucial road which came into Banias, at the northwestern tip of the rectangle, from Beirut and Saida, continued inside the rectangle through Mas'ada, Kuneitra, and Rafid, and extended beyond it to Shaykh Maskin on the main Amman-Damascus road. At Kuneitra, a town of 60,000, this road was crossed by another main road that started from Acre, on the coast of Israel, and crossed into Syria near Mishmar Hayarden and then went on beyond Kuneitra to Damascus some 40 miles to the northeast. At Rafid, another road took off in a southwesterly direction and led through el 'Al and Fiq to Samakh in Israel at the southern tip of Lake Tiberias.

It can be seen from this schematic description that the heights were

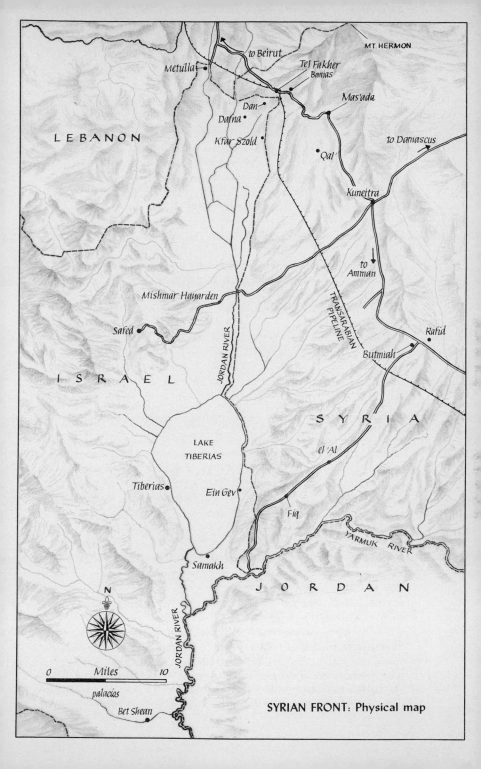

MT. HERMON

to Beirut

Metulla

Tel Fakher
Banias

Mas'ada

Dan

Dafna

Kfar Szold

Qal'

to Damascus

LEBANON

Kuneitra

to Amman

Mishmar Hayarden

TRANSARABIAN PIPELINE

Safed

Rafid

JORDAN RIVER

Butmiah

ISRAEL

SYRIA

LAKE
TIBERIAS

el 'Al

Tiberias

Ein Gev

Fiq

YARMUK RIVER

Samakh

JORDAN

N

JORDAN RIVER

0   Miles   10

palacios

Bet Shean

SYRIAN FRONT: Physical map

vital to the Syrians both offensively and defensively. They not only gave them positions from which they could harass at will the entire adjacent Israeli territory and entertain plans to break into Israel at convenient points, but they also protected the main avenues to Damascus from Israel. That the heights contained one of the sources of the Jordan River, whose waters have been the subject of dispute, and that the Transarabian Pipeline crossed them on its way to the terminals in Lebanon only added to their importance.

In view of this, it is not surprising that the Syrians deployed the bulk of their forces on the heights on the eve of the war. In "normal" times, the Syrians had three infantry brigades manning the defense positions in the area. In the days preceding the outbreak of the war, these were reinforced with two additional infantry brigades, which were deployed to the north and south of Kuneitra. Each of these five brigades either included or had added to it a battalion of T-34 tanks or SU-100 self-propelled guns. In addition, the Syrian High Command marshaled one armored brigade and one motorized brigade in the vicinity of Kuneitra in a position from which they could be used for defense or offense. Thus out of the total of nine brigades that comprised the Syrian army, seven were deployed on the heights. The remaining two brigades, one armored and one infantry, were held in the Damascus and Homs region by decision of the government and the Ba'th command, presumably to protect the regime itself against possible internal upheavals.

In the course of 19 years of tense and hostile relations with Israel, the Syrians had converted the heights into one huge fortified camp. These fortifications were described by some serious military experts, probably with some exaggeration, as stronger than the Maginot Line. General Rabin said they were the best and most formidable ever dug in the Middle East. There were three parallel lines of defense comprising dozens of fortified points with overlapping fields of fire. One such point, Tel Fakher, for example, was a promontory two miles south of Banias and two miles east of the kibbutz Dan, which looked out across the fertile Hulah valley to the hills of Galilee. The positions in this fortified point were almost entirely underground. They were connected by a series of interlocking trenches about eight feet deep and three feet wide. Most of the trenches were sided with the black volcanic stones that litter the fields in the area, but some were finished with smooth stone and mortar walls. Nearly all the trenches were roofed with curved steel plates that had been covered with a foot of soil on which wild grass and weeds had sprung up to perfect the camouflage. There was one large bunker that served as a command post and sever-

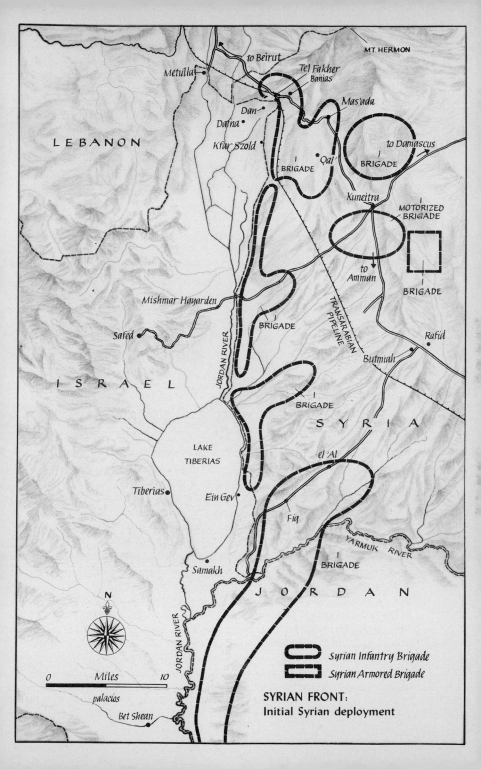

to Beirut

MT. HERMON

Metulla

Tel Fakher
Banias

Mas'ada

Dan

Dafna

to Damascus

Kfar Szold

I
BRIGADE

Qal'

I
BRIGADE

LEBANON

Kuneitra

I
MOTORIZED
BRIGADE

to
Amman

BRIGADE

Mishmar Hayarden

I
BRIGADE

TRANSARABIAN PIPELINE

Rafid

Safed

JORDAN RIVER

Butmiah

I S R A E L

S Y R I A

I
BRIGADE

LAKE
TIBERIAS

el 'Al

Tiberias

Ein Gev

Fiq

Samakh

YARMUK   RIVER

I
BRIGADE

J O R D A N

N

JORDAN RIVER

0   Miles   10

palacios

Bet Shean

Syrian Infantry Brigade
Syrian Armored Brigade

SYRIAN FRONT:
Initial Syrian deployment

al smaller ones used as sleeping quarters. The principal gun position in
the point was set in a concrete bunker with walls one yard thick. A
particularly deep trench led into the bunker from the east. The only
aperture to the west was a narrow slit with an overhanging roof. It
was slanted to make it safe from fire from the fields below. The perimeter of the point was surrounded by lines of barbed wire and mines
and afforded excellent fields of fire. In such fortified points the Syrians
had planted, besides infantry units, tanks, anti-tank guns, and a staggering array of artillery. It is estimated that 265 field pieces of various
calibers, capable of raining ten tons of shells in one minute, were entrenched in the heights, in addition to some 200 AA guns.

Against the heights, the Israelis had concentrated on June 5 a maximum of one infantry brigade and one armored brigade. The task of
these units was intended to be purely defensive so long as the Israeli
forces were engaged in the first and second priority fronts against the
Egyptians and the Jordanians. They were to come to the rescue in case
the Syrians menaced the Israeli defense line, which was manned by
the settlers in the area reinforced with second line units. As it was,
there was little occasion to use them for this purpose since the Syrians
never developed any serious offensive momentum.

On June 5, immediately after the Israeli attack on Egypt, Syria
joined the war by opening artillery fire against the Israeli settlements
and sending in, somewhat later, planes to raid targets in Megiddo and
around Haifa Bay. The Israelis responded with artillery fire and, in the
afternoon, with air attacks on Syrian gun emplacements.

On the second day of the war, June 6, the Syrians attempted their
only ground attacks against a number of Israeli settlements. In Dan,
Dafna, and Shear Yashuv, at the northeast corner of the Israeli border
with Syria, a force estimated at two infantry battalions and ten tanks
made a feeble attempt to advance on the villages but was repelled by
the settlers with the assistance of a force of tanks that came to the rescue. In Dafna, one Syrian tank succeeded in penetrating inside the
settlement before it was hit by bazooka fire. Further to the south, a
concentration against Kfar Szold was dispersed by volleys of mortar fire
before it attempted to move. Finally, at Ashmoreth, still further south,
the Syrians made a more determined attempt, which was repulsed by
the settlers and the soldiers of a second line unit; they left 200 dead
and seven tanks behind them. On June 7 and 8 the Syrians contented
themselves with heavy bombardments against all points within reach
of their artillery, which included some 130-mm guns with a 16-mile
range. But by June 8 the Israelis were already preparing a new and
much bloodier game for the Syrians.

Already on the 7th, as it became clear that the Egyptian and Jordanian fronts were collapsing, the Israeli High Command had ordered General David Elazar, Commander of the Northern Front, to prepare for an attack on the northern sector of the heights. Next day, while General Elazar was marshaling and deploying the two brigades he had on hand, other troops were being rushed full speed from the Jordanian front while the Israeli air force, now free of all other tasks, concentrated all its might on striking Syrian positions and troop concentrations. The Israeli offensive would have probably started on the same day but for political complications that put the whole operation into question.

After Egypt as well as Jordan had accepted the cease fire, some Israeli Cabinet members voiced the fear that an attack on Syria would be stopped immediately by the Security Council and would therefore cost Israel many casualties in vain, or that if the attack progressed satisfactorily the Russians might somehow intervene. We do not know how the Israeli government resolved these doubts, but we do know that when the decision came, it was made by Defense Minister Dayan, who had apparently been empowered by the Cabinet to determine the issue. We also know that Dayan himself hesitated and waited until 7:00 A.M. of June 9 before giving the go-ahead to General Elazar. The go-ahead thus came nearly four hours after the representatives of Syria and Israel in the Security Council had formally accepted a cease-fire injunction, which, however, could not be made to take effect in the field since each side charged that the other continued firing.

General Elazar's objective was to capture the Syrian heights up to their watershed along a line running east of the Banias–Kuneitra–Butmiah–Samakh road. Like all Israeli commanders, he favored a strategy of indirect approach, mobility, and envelopment, which meant in this case that he had to get onto the main Banias–Kuneitra road in the rear of the enemy where he could maneuver with his motorized columns. Two roads, we have seen, led from Israel to the Kuneitra road: one near Mishmar Hayarden at the center of the frontline, and one at the southern tip of Lake Tiberias near the Syrian-Jordanian border. However, these roads had two grave disadvantages: One was that they extended to relatively great lengths across the heights, and the other was that the Syrians, knowing them to be the only convenient approaches for motorized columns, had very heavily fortified them. To get around this problem, General Elazar decided to attempt a breakthrough to the Kuneitra road on an axis that was extremely difficult for motorized movement and was also heavily fortified, but at least had the advantage of being very short: the Banias area, where the Kuneitra road was only 2.4 miles from the Israeli border. Once that axis was secured, Israeli armor could pour in on the road, smash its way rapidly into the rear of the enemy, and facilitate the opening of new axes of movement by threatening the enemy's reinforcement and retreat lines.

The execution of the plan began with a five-pronged attack along the northern half of the front, three of which were designed to confuse the enemy about the direction of the main attack and to exert assisting pressure. Further pressure was exerted by the air force, which already the day before had begun to pound the enemy with all its might and continued to provide direct and indirect support to the ground forces. The excellently dug and camouflaged fortifications of the Syrians necessarily restricted the effectiveness of the air strikes against the entrenched enemy, but they gravely disrupted movements of troops in the open and gnawed at the morale of the defenders, who came to feel increasingly isolated, thus making possible the sudden total collapse that followed.

Before this collapse came to pass, however, the two prongs constituting the main attack had to engage in the most fierce and apparently hopeless fighting in the entire Arab-Israeli war. At 11:30 A.M., June 9, an armored brigade under Colonel Albert crossed the border in the vicinity of Kfar Szold and began fighting right away. Its immediate objective was the fortified village of Za'ura, some three miles uphill on the Kuneitra road, so as to cut off the Syrian positions to the north of its line of advance and protect the flank of a parallel advance by the second prong. Colonel Albert's brigade climbed up the roadless mountain behind mine removers and bulldozers who prepared the way for it foot by foot. The entire force moved on a single axis under intense artillery fire. Every now and then, the air force temporarily silenced the enemy fire, but it inevitably resumed after a moment. Less than half-way up, the lead battalion came upon the Na'mush position and literally ran over the Syrians, who continued to fire until the following tanks climbed on top of them. Then, one lead battalion wheeled to the southeast against Qal' in order to secure the flank of the brigade. As the battalion approached Qal', its commander was hit. The commander of the scout unit took over but was also hit minutes later. A lieutenant then assumed command and led the entire battalion in the continuing fight until the position was captured. Meanwhile, the remainder of the brigade continued its forward crawling and reached and captured Za'ura at 4:00 P.M., having covered three miles in five and a half hours.

While Albert's brigade was slowly making its way up, two battalions of the Golani infantry brigade supported by armor started fighting

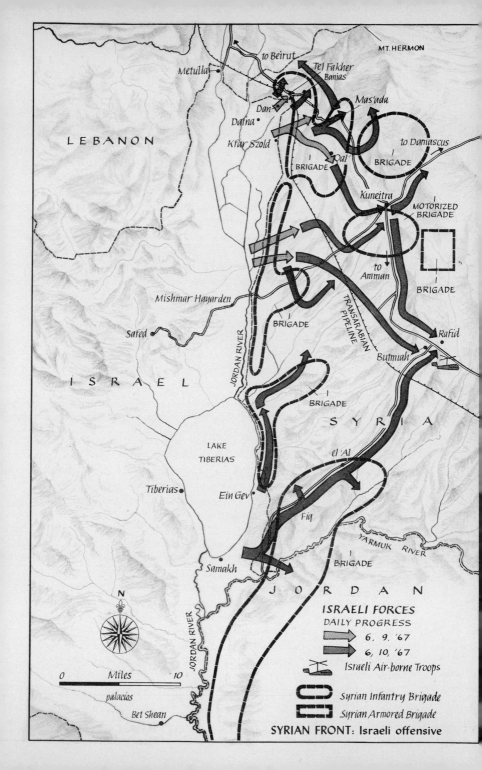

MT. HERMON

to Beirut

Metulla

Tel Fakher
Banias

Mas'ada

Dan

Dafna

Kfar Szold

to Damascus

I
BRIGADE

Dal

I
BRIGADE

LEBANON

Kuneitra

I
MOTORIZED
BRIGADE

I
BRIGADE

to
Amman

Mishmar Hayarden

TRANSARABIAN
PIPELINE

I
BRIGADE

Safed

Rafid

JORDAN RIVER

Butmiah

I
S R A E L

S Y R I A

I
BRIGADE

LAKE
TIBERIAS

el 'Al

Tiberias

Ein Gev

Fiq

YARMUK RIVER

Samakh

I
BRIGADE

J O R D A N

ISRAELI FORCES
DAILY PROGRESS

6, 9, '67

6, 10, '67

Israeli Air-borne Troops

N

Syrian Infantry Brigade

Syrian Armored Brigade

0   Miles   10

palacios

Bet Shean

JORDAN RIVER

SYRIAN FRONT: Israeli offensive

their way up a mile or so to the north with the immediate objective of
capturing the Syrian positions on the flank of Colonel Albert's armored
brigade and thus securing a corridor for more armor and troops to
erupt on the rear of the Syrians. There were 13 positions to overcome,
the most important of which were Tel Fakher, previously described,
and Tel Aziziyat, Burj Babil, Bahriyyat, and Banias. The battalions
moved in two prongs, one of them toward Tel Fakher, the other toward Burj Babil and Tel Aziziyat. The first of these advanced toward
its objective in half-tracks and tanks with the idea of swinging around
it and attacking from the rear. Immediately, the battalion came under
heavy artillery fire that hit several of its vehicles and stalled the whole
column. The commander, Colonel Klein, fearing to be caught in a
death trap, ordered his men to dismount and begin to advance on foot
for a frontal attack.

Tel Fakher consists of two promontories in the form of dromedary
humps. The battalion split into two; one force advanced on the northern promontory and the second on the southern. The first force tried to
charge across open terrain, suffered heavy casualties, and retreated.
The survivors got back into three halftracks that had been freed in the
meantime and renewed the charge. One half track was hit. Once again
the men dismounted and charged. The commander of the force as well
as his second in command were hit, but the attack continued and the
highest line of trenches was captured. From there the force made its
way slowly in hand-to-hand fighting to the rest of the positions.

The second half of the battalion advanced under very heavy fire in
seven halftracks on the southern promontory. Some 700 yards from the
objective, three of these were hit. Within another few yards, another
was hit. The force dismounted, and its commander discovered that he
had only 25 men left unhurt. The men split into two groups and
marched on the north and south of the promontory. The first group
broke into the perimeter after crossing the barbed wires over the
bodies of two of its members. After hours of fighting, all but one of the
men were hit. The battalion commander, who had appeared from nowhere to join the group, was among those killed. The second group too
penetrated the perimeter in the same way, fought its way among the
bunkers, suffered heavily, and ended up with only three men intact
but with the position in their hands. Finally, the battalion's scouting
unit, which had gone on a wide flanking movement, arrived from the
rear of the position to reinforce its assailants and complete its subjugation. The attack on Tel Fakher had lasted seven hours and cost the Israelis scores of casualties, including the battalion commander, his deputy, and most of its officers. But Tel Fakher was taken.

The other battalion of the Golani Brigade, which moved on Burj Babil and Tel Aziziyat, had a relatively easier time. It too saw its tanks and halftracks touch off mines and blow up, and it too had to dismount and advance on foot. Before it reached Burj Babil, most of its defenders had fled to Tel Aziziyat. But there was still a cruel hand-to-hand fight with the remainder. Moving on to Tel Aziziyat, the battalion was met by the Syrian commander and his second with a white flag. The Syrian ordered his men to cease fire, but they disobeyed him and continued to shoot. Another hand-to-hand combat developed in which 50 Syrians were killed before resistance ceased. By midnight the two Golani battalions had secured a sufficient breach in the Syrian lines to permit more armor to pour in on the next day.

While this was going on at the northern end of the front, a third battalion of the same Golani infantry brigade captured 'Urfiyya, some 20 miles south of the point at which Albert's armored brigade had penetrated the heights, thus making a breach through which another armored brigade under Colonel Uri was to penetrate the next day. Still further south, other units of infantry and paratroopers made additional breaches in the first line at Dubshiyyah and Tel Hilal. Thus by the end of the first day of fighting, General Elazar's forces had secured a pass to the Kuneitra road at the extreme north and had set up the stage for several new penetrations further south preparatory to the decisive fighting of the next day.

Early on June 10, with very heavy air support and artillery cover, Israeli forces began pressing in on all the axes opened up the previous day. The critical developments, however, took place in the northernmost sector. Through the breach made by the Golani brigade and Albert's force, a second and fresh armored brigade under Colonel Moshe moved in swiftly, helped in the capture of Banias, mopped up the sector up to the Lebanese border, then moved back south and east to help Albert's armored brigade in the assault on Mas'ada, on the main Banias-Kuneitra road. At this point, the Israeli plans called for a carefully concerted effort against Kuneitra, the hub of the Syrian heights and the gate to Damascus. They intended to use not only all the forces already engaged in the battle but also a fresh division of some two brigades under General Peled, including airborne troops, which was to open a new axis of advance along the Samakh-Butmiah road. However, the fall of Mas'ada unleashed a series of developments that made unnecessary any elaborate effort, as they led to the complete and abrupt collapse of the entire Syrian front.

At 8:45 A.M., June 10, Radio Damascus announced the fall of Kuneitra, six hours before any Israeli troops had reached it. The news was taken by the Syrian troops defending the positions throughout the heights as meaning that they could not expect any help from the rear and that the Israelis were in a position to move down rapidly from Kuneitra to close all avenues of escape and trap them in death pockets. Without losing a moment, they abandoned their positions and started a panic flight. At this point, the Israeli High Command ordered a general accelerated advance, and in an effort to realize the encirclement feared by the enemy, put in motion without much preparatory ado Peled's division, which was poised on the southern axis. However, despite the relatively rapid movement of the Israelis, and despite the fact that after a while they resorted to leapfrogging airborne units ahead of their troop columns, not many Syrians were trapped, and most of the damage suffered by them from this point on was inflicted by the Israeli air force, which kept hot on their trails all the way to Damascus. By the evening of June 10, the Israelis were sitting everywhere on the heights in positions that looked down on the approaches to Damascus, and a cease fire subsequently came into effect. The offensive against Syria had achieved its maximal objectives some 36 hours after it had started.

Why did the Syrian government announce the fall of Kuneitra prematurely? The unfolding of the operations up to that point allows no doubt that the general outcome of the battle for the heights would have been the same anyway. The Israelis would have probably suffered some more losses had they had to fight their way to Kuneitra and, by the same token, fewer Syrians would have been able to escape the Israeli traps; but Kuneitra and the heights were already doomed once the Israelis had captured Mas'ada, nine miles to the north, and had firmly established themselves on the crestline with two armored brigades and with a secure bridgehead behind them. Nevertheless, the question is intriguing if only because the premature announcement was so diametrically contrary to the habit of Syrians, and other Arabs too, to refuse to acknowledge even consummated reverses in the face of all evidence.

The most plausible answer appears to be the following: It is likely that the Syrian High Command itself realized that Kuneitra was doomed for the reasons we have just mentioned and decided to evacuate while there was still time, perhaps to salvage the troops for the defense of Damascus. Having reached this decision, it thought that announcing the fall of Kuneitra might have some advantages. It might precipitate a Soviet intervention by suggesting implicitly that the continuation of the fighting by the Israelis could only mean that they were aiming at Damascus. It might "satisfy" the United States and induce it to throw its weight in favor of an effective cease fire. It could shock the Syrians into exerting themselves to defend their capital by suggesting to them that it was in imminent danger and make more plausible a subsequent claim that the Israelis were forcibly stopped in their advance on Damascus. Finally, it gave several hours leeway to the Syrian forces spread all over the heights to scramble out before the Israelis actually took Kuneitra and began to cut them off. We might add that by that time Kuneitra was already in complete shambles as a result of Israeli bombing and that this might have satisfied the Syrians that they had already done much fighting for it. This at least is suggested by a subsequent article in the government's newspaper, *al Thawra*, which wrote after the war that the heroic defense of Kuneitra had been the most honorable fighting known to modern history, "even greater than the Russian defense of Stalingrad." [40]

An alternative explanation is that the Damascus regime, fearing an uprising, had withdrawn the brigades concentrated near Kuneitra to use them for self-protection. In order to cover up its intention and justify the moving of troops from the front to Damascus, it announced that Kuneitra had fallen after a heroic defense, thus implying that Damascus was the "logical" place for the troops to be.

According to an official Syrian communiqué, Syrian casualties in the war amounted to 145 killed and 1,650 wounded, a claim that is much more in the spirit of things Syrian than the premature announcement of the fall of Kuneitra. Later reliable reports from Damascus put the numbers at 2,500 killed and 5,000 wounded. [41] The Israelis held 591 prisoners of war whom they subsequently exchanged for a single Israeli pilot. The Israelis claim to have badly mauled and routed two out of the five infantry brigades and one-and-a-half out of the four motorized and armored brigades that constituted the Syrian army. They captured 40 tanks and claim to have destroyed 80 more, thus eliminating one-third of the tank force deployed by the Syrians. Out of 18 artillery battalions deployed on the heights, the Israelis destroyed or captured 15 in addition to most of the AA guns. The Israeli losses amounted to 115 killed and 306 wounded, the great majority of them suffered by the Golani brigade in its breakthrough in the Banias sector. Losses in equipment are not known. In addition, two civilians were killed and 16 wounded from the Syrian artillery bombardments, and a great deal of material damage was caused to 17 Israeli settlements.

We conclude this preliminary account of the three Israeli cam-

[40] *New York Times*, June 13, 1967.
[41] *Le Monde*, June 28 and July 1, 1967.

paigns, which no doubt constituted one of the most incredible feats of arms in modern times, with some words of General Beaufre who visited Israel, talked to its military chiefs, toured the battlefields, and wrote a tentative evaluation immediately after the war:

> In these three campaigns the Israeli armed forces demonstrated their high quality from the uppermost to the most modest levels. Such a series of successes rules out the idea of an accidental stroke of good luck. Sinai three days, Jordan two days, Syria two days—this decidedly is systematic lightning war.
>
> The recipes used are all well known: Surprise, resolve and speed, air superiority, a large degree of decentralization of command, ardent troops unencumbered by the complex of rigid and inhibited action which still prevails all too often in the European, and even the American armies, a simplified logistics system. The utmost of maneuver is thus made possible. . . .
>
> All this was known. But perhaps never before has an execution been seen which was so close to perfection; nor has a victory which was more rapid and more complete.[42]

[43] *Paris Match*, June 24, 1967.

The War and the Future
of the Arab-Israeli Conflict

Introduction

Immediately after the cease fire that ended the Six Day War, most competent observers expected a move toward peace to follow immediately. Israel's new defense minister, General Dayan, reflecting this mood, said that he expected a phone call from Cairo or Amman any moment. These expectations proved wrong, of course, and were very improbable in the first place. They were based entirely on the fact that Israel and its neighbors had fought a war without outside interference in which Israel achieved as decisive a victory as any in the annals of warfare. They did not, however, take into account the fact that the Arab-Israeli confrontation had never been an independent contest, and they allowed the absence of outside intervention in the war itself to obscure the near certainty that outside factors would reassert themselves after the war to try to inhibit the consequences of its outcome. Implicitly, these expectations were founded on a wrong analogy with other wars—World War II—for example, where the decision of arms left no room for further appeal.

A year after the war, when these lines were being written, General Dayan had long given up waiting for his phone calls and was speaking instead about convenient strategic borders to fight the next round. The Soviet Union had replaced the equipment Egypt and Syria had lost and was busy retraining their armed forces, while the United States had reaffirmed its commitment to help Israel match the Arab forces and had resumed shipping arms to it—as well as to Jordan. Guerilla fighting, reprisals, and border violence had become as rife as ever, and the sounds of fury and defiance echoed again. Opinion about the effect of the war on the prospects of peace had swung toward the opposite pole, summing itself in a heavy feeling of *plus ça change, plus c'est la même chose.*

The whole thrust of this study suggests that this last conclusion is no less rash than its previous opposite, although it may not appear to be so as obviously. It shares with its opposite the premise that a peace settlement ought to have taken place quickly after the war and takes the fact that it did not as evidence that it will not. It does not allow for the possibility, inherent in a conflict in which many variables were entangled, that not enough time had passed since the war for its implications to be assimilated and for things to be sorted out and rearranged in the light of them. It allows the surface sameness, which, as we have seen in this study, can mask momentous subsurface changes, to divert attention even from the obvious signs of change.

We have tried in this study to look at the Arab-Israeli confrontation as a conflict that has evolved from the interplay of three sets of factors: (1) the relationship of coercion between Israel and the Arab states, particularly Egypt; (2) inter-Arab relations as they centered on the meaning and mode of realization of the pan-Arab ideal, with special reference to Egypt's role; and (3) the competition among the big powers in the Middle East, with special attention to the Soviet-American rivalry. Our reading of the consequences of the Six Day War suggests that these have not only altered the latest prewar configuration of these factors, but have shaken their very foundations, creating a highly fluid situation. Whether this change will produce a viable settlement of the Arab-Israeli conflict or will merely give a new twist to a continuing confrontation, it is as yet too soon to predict. But it is quite apparent already that the change has made a settlement of the conflict a realistic option for the first time since 1949. This in itself is a far-reaching consequence of the war.

In this chapter, we will try to analyze the impact of the Six Day War on each of the three factors that shaped the Arab-Israeli confrontation. Because a new configuration of these factors has not yet definitely crystallized, we will devote the bulk of our analysis to a more or less independent treatment of each of them, trying to clarify whether the change in each factor and its components works for peace or for continuing confrontation. Only in the end shall we briefly venture into some speculation as to the configurations into which they might coalesce and whether these make for future peace or war.

The War, Pan-Arabism, and the Conflict

In the second chapter of this study, we argued that Egypt's commitment to the cause of integral Arab unity and its immediate attainment had the coincidental effect of escalating its conflict with Israel to a clash of destinies. Prior to that development, when Egypt understood pan-Arabism as signifying cooperation among sovereign Arab states, the conflict could in principle persist indefinitely in the state of neither war nor peace. After it, the issue between Egypt and Israel became an irreconcilable conflict which could be resolved only by war or the threat of war: Either Israel had to disappear as a political entity or at least change its character as a sovereign Jewish state, or Egypt had to renounce its commitment to integral Arab unity or at least pursue it in a long evolutionary manner that would skirt the Israeli obstruction to its achievement by military-political means. On June 5, 1967, war came, and within six days issued its verdict against Egypt, with its crucial implication of de-escalating the issue at stake in the Arab-Israeli conflict. The verdict was not immediately grasped in the confusion of defeat; but it gradually impressed itself upon the Egyptian leaders themselves.

"Objectively," the war was bound to affect Egypt's role as leader of the drive for integral Arab unity through the crushing blow it dealt to Nasser's charisma. We have seen in our discussion of the evolution of pan-Arabism that Egypt's commitment to the cause of integral Arab unity was not something it had thought out and sought in advance, but was rather an objective that was thrust upon it by the logic of Nasser's maneuvers and the spectacular successes he had achieved. Furthermore, since Egypt did commit itself to the cause of integral Arab unity, the striving for the realization of that ideal did not take the form of wide-ranging, systematic endeavors—such as those that characterized the evolution of the European Community, for example—nor did it assume any institutionalized form—as the striving for Arab cooperation had in the shape of the Arab League. Rather, it continued to depend primarily on Nasser's personal charisma and his capacity to maneuver in the fluid political conditions of the Arab world. Since Nasser's charisma itself had arisen out of real or imagined spectacular successes, and since it depended on continued successes for its maintenance, the spectacular defeat he suffered in the war was bound to explode it and thus deprive Egypt's drive for Arab unity of its major propellant.[1]

[1] The massive demonstrations following Nasser's resignation on June 9, 1967,

Once Egypt was launched on the pursuit of integral Arab unity and stumbled repeatedly on the Israeli obstacle, the realization of its goal came to depend in direct proportion to the failures in pursuing it on achieving sufficient military superiority over Israel to defeat it in an eventual showdown.

We have argued in Chapter VI that the fading of this hope after twelve years of trying was one of the factors that led Nasser to seize on the fortuitous opportunity that placed at his command in the last week of May 1967 what seemed to him to be superior Arab force in order to press the issue with Israel. When that apparently superior force fared so miserably in the actual war, any hope of eliminating by force the Israeli obstacle to Arab unity in the foreseeable future became completely unrealistic.

The results of the war placed Nasser's regime under tremendous immediate military, political, economic, and psychological pressures. To be able to withstand these pressures and avert immediate collapse, Nasser had to rely critically and in equal measure on Soviet support of various kinds and on massive financial assistance from the "reactionary" governments of Saudi Arabia, Libya and Kuwait, his opponents and potential victims of the day before. This dependence, in addition to the collapse of his charisma and his revealed military weakness, not only made it necessary for him to renounce any effort to achieve Arab unity by threat, force, and incitement to revolution, but also made it very uncautious for him to attempt to appeal to the Arab publics over the heads of their governments. Thus Nasser was forced to liquidate his military expedition in Yemen and to abandon his protégés in Aden and the South Arabian Federation. He was compelled to abide by a veto of King Faisal against the gathering of an Arab summit in Rabat in December, 1967, without daring to make this the occasion for a propaganda campaign against the Saudi monarch, as he certainly would have done in the past.

These "objective" realities gradually made their way into the consciousness of Nasser and his associates and led them to draw some basic conclusions about the future of inter-Arab relations as a conse-

---

which induced him to reconsider and stay in power, might seem to contradict the suggestion that his charisma was destroyed. Actually, these demonstrations took place under exceptional circumstances in which masses of people were gripped by a hysterical fear of disaster and an obsessive desire to hold on to the only certainty they knew in the form of Nasser's continued presence. Subsequent developments after things had somewhat subsided, which included plots, grumblings and demonstrations against Nasser and his regime, attest to an awakening to the sense that Nasser was just another leader, fallible and perhaps removable.

quence of the war. In July 1967, Nasser and his associates still clung desperately to the myth they had propounded during the war—that the United States had intervened on Israel's side—in order to explain to the public the "serious setback" suffered by Egypt. Concomitantly, they still addressed the Arab countries in the peremptory and threatening tones of yore. Thus Haykal on July 14, 1967:

> If this crisis should not lead to a start of a united Arab position to confront it until all its consequences had been eliminated, then it will certainly be the beginning of a great inter-Arab alienation. I would even say that inter-Arab affairs will not remain as they are but will deteriorate to the point of an Arab civil war—a far-reaching danger indeed.

In August 1967, Nasser attended the Arab summit at Khartum and obtained from Saudi Arabia, Libya, and Kuwait a commitment to pay him a subsidy to compensate for revenues he lost because of the war in exchange for his agreement to evacuate Yemen and not to oppose the resumption of oil shipments to the United States and Britain. This constituted a tacit agreement to refrain from pursuing Arab unity by subversion and force and a tacit acknowledgment that the United States might not, after all, have won the war for Israel. The agreement and acknowledgment were spelled out more and more in the course of the following months, and by the turn of the year were made quite explicit and were used as a basis for far-reaching political-strategic revisions. Thus, on December 29, 1967, Haykal culminated a series of *post-mortem* articles on the war with the startling admission that "the Israeli danger, with its local expansionist bent and its global links exceeds the possible capacity, present and future, of any part of the Arab nation." In other words, Egypt could no longer hope to be able to confront Israel alone. From this admission Haykal went on to draw the conclusion that "unity of action"—in the Egyptian ideological jargon, cooperation, as distinguished from "unity of rank," integral unity—on the part of the Arab countries had become the imperative necessity; not a necessity for a time, as it was sometimes in the past, but a basic strategy for all phases.

In the following weeks, Haykal took off into a discussion of Arab unity and inter-Arab relations which was no longer bound to the imperative of meeting the Israeli danger, but constituted an independent initial reappraisal of the subject. Thus, on February 2, 1967, he wrote that a distinction must be made between "the truth" [read the theory] of the unity of the Arab nation, and the objective fact of its being divided into separate entities:

No matter how great the [theoretical] unity of the Arab nation, the fact is that the Arab peoples live within independent boundaries and are subject to governments that exercise sovereignty in their homelands. It follows that Egypt cannot address itself to these countries over the heads of their governments. . . . Egypt had once abided by this style; but, to speak frankly, it has subsequently allowed itself to forget it and try a different one in view of various pressures, when it was fighting against imperialism in this region.

Contact with the *peoples* of the Arab nation must be made through the people of Egypt, not its government; and for this to be possible, the distinction between the people and the government must first be established in Egypt itself by evolving the Socialist Union. In the past, the mixing of the role of the state and the role of the revolution as embodied in the people caused each to come in the way of the other. "If . . . as happened in the past . . . secret apparatuses like the Intelligence should attempt to play the role of the revolutionary motor, the national action [read the striving for unity] would become degraded to the level of plotting." In the past, Egypt tried all too often to work with opportunistic elements "out of a desire to exploit them rapidly"; in the future it must distinguish between those it wants to choose and those who choose it.

On February 9, 1968, Haykal brought the discussion to a climax in which he explicitly urged a return to the pan-Arab concept of the Arab League. In a column revealingly entitled "Instead of Deepening Division or Depending on Night Adventurers," he began by arguing that in the existing conditions, political and social struggles (previously exalted as the only way to unity) only deepened the division of the Arab nation, which then tended to become consolidated by separate courses of economic development. This made for a situation in which the hope for Arab unity, "however much we may wish to deny it," rested on "the mood of an obscure military officer who would venture a coup at night, become the ruler in the morning, and be at the negotiations table in the evening signing a unity agreement." Such a notion thrust the hope for Arab unity into violent and dangerous currents to no avail. "A unity beginning in a coup . . . will most probably end in a coup." The only alternative was to work within the frame of the Arab League, "the only correct frame within which the common Arab action called for by circumstances can take place," provided the League should be conceived not as a substitute for Arab unity, but as the launching point for it. To make the League serve that function, a gradual, multistage program was necessary, starting with administrative reforms of that institution and moving on to establishing, by common agreement, various joint endeavors and enterprises, such as a center for the study of Israel, an Arab navigation company, unified efforts in atomic research, common basic curricula for schools, coordination of oil interests, an Arab strategic air force, and finally an Arab parliament like the European Assembly. Haykal recognized that this was a long-range program, and posed the question of its relevance to the immediate problem of "eliminating the consequences of aggression." His answer, obviously rhetorical, was: "If the Arab world could strike a new scientific spark in relation to its future, which is its unity, then the first step in that direction would be certain to produce sufficient capacity to remove the consequences of aggression."

Thus, after long and tortured meditation on the subject, the Egyptian leadership was compelled by the realities of the war's aftermath to reverse its commitment to pan-Arabism from a determination to achieve immediate Arab unity by all possible means, through a renunciation of the right to appeal to Arab publics over the heads of their governments, to the ideal of pan-Arabism embodied in the Arab League. The conditions it set for returning to work within the frame of the League are not as new as they were made to appear, and their realization is in any case beyond Egypt's control, so that the insistence on them seems obviously to be little more than an effort to palliate the return to institutions and procedures the Egyptians had vilified for many years.

The implications of this change are crucial for the Arab-Israeli conflict, and incidentally, also for inter-Arab relations and big-power politics. Regarding the latter, the change presages a period of relative freedom for the Arab countries from the kind of agitation and upheaval they have suffered since 1955, and this in turn suggests a diminished chance for big-power entanglement in Arab affairs. Regarding the Arab-Israeli conflict, the effect is to de-escalate it from a clash of destinies to a more conventional kind of international dispute susceptible to prolonged stalemate or even to solution. With integral unity a vision for the future rather than an immediate operational objective, it becomes possible for the Egyptian leadership to conceive of a settlement of the conflict with Israel without thereby forfeiting essential means and opportunities for the realization of unity. Working for Arab unity by gradual steps within the frame of the Arab League and accepting Israel's existence need not be incompatible in principle or in practice. This does not necessarily mean that Egypt has become prepared to settle with Israel; indeed, we have seen that the process of revision of Egypt's pan-Arab commitment was justified in the first instance by the need better to withstand Israel. But the change does mean that Egypt is no longer compelled actively to seek a showdown with Israel because it is Israel; it also means that if the leadership should find it necessary on pragmatic grounds to seek a settlement with Israel, it would not be held back by a sense that to do so would be to betray Egypt's destiny.

The War and the Relative Position of the Belligerents

The Six Day War not only indirectly de-escalated the issue at stake in the Arab-Israeli conflict, but also profoundly altered the relative position of the contestants in the conventional conflict that replaced the clash of destinies.

We have argued in our discussion of the evolution of the conflict (see Chapter I) that even before Egypt's commitment to the cause of immediate integral Arab unity had made war the only option, the relative position of the Arab states and Israel in 1949 and after ruled out peace as a realistic option. For Israel at that time, a move from armistice to peace promised emotional satisfaction and the prospect of serving its material interests, as well; but for the Arab governments, such a move held no prospect of significant material advantage, was psychologically painful to their people, and politically risky to themselves. Since there was no penalty attached to inertia, they preferred not to move and allow the situation to remain frozen at the armistice level. Jordan's ruler, who did stand to gain materially from peace and to suffer from the perpetuation of the armistice situation, tried to reach an agreement with Israel, but his attempt was foiled by emotional opposition among the public at home and the pressure of other Arab countries. The June war transformed this situation by giving the belligerent Arab countries something to gain from a peaceful settlement, be it only the recovery of losses suffered in it, and by attaching heavy penalties to the continuation of the cease-fire condition. To this extent, the war made peace at least a possible realistic option for the Arab countries for the first time in the history of their conflict with Israel.

The degree of validity of the option for peace has varied for each of the three belligerent Arab countries according to the interplay of a number of factors: the different degrees of emotional resistance to peace as a result of twenty years of confrontation, which in turn is related to different degrees of incentive and pressure at work on each of them, the different sense each has of the alternative ways open to it to recover its losses and get out from under the pressures, and the degree of independence each has in pursuing whatever course it chooses. The combination of factors in each case has itself been subject to change over a short period of time as a result of intervening events and experimentation with alternatives, including the responses of Israel and of the big powers.

The same situation that opened the option of peace for the Arab states afforded Israel the option of maintaining the cease-fire *status quo.* Israel did not cease to be interested in peace; but the gains it achieved during the war gave it at least the option of continuing with the cease-fire unless it could obtain a settlement on terms it considered satisfactory. As in the case of the Arabs' option for peace, the validity of this option for Israel is contingent upon a combination of factors, including its internal politics, the reactions of the Arab population in the conquered territories, the response of the Arab states, and above all, the attitude of the big powers. In Israel's case, too, the combination has varied over time.

In view of this great complexity of the postwar situation, it is not surprising that things have not yet jelled into a clear pattern that would permit a reliable prognostication as to the prospects for peace or continuing confrontation. This is why we are reduced in this section to trying to clarify the relative position of each of the belligerents without attempting to reach any firm definite conclusions.

SYRIA

The war put Syria under considerable disadvantages which should have given it an incentive to settle with Israel; but the entire ethos of the present regime opposes this logic. Since, at the same time, Syria is not in a position to contemplate war to recover its losses, the prospects are for a continuation of the *status quo* as long as the present regime remains in power.

The capture of the Golan Heights by the Israelis did some economic damage to Syria by causing the flight of 80,000 Syrians from the area. The capture of Syrian national territory by the enemy and the conversion of so many Syrians into refugees did greater political damage, although this is being suppressed, especially in view of the prewar attitude of the Syrian regime. Not only had that regime been a fervent advocate of war with Israel, but its action in supporting guerrilla operations was the immediate cause of the war.

Far more important than the economic and political effects have been the strategic consequences of the war. The occupation of the Golan Heights more than reversed the prewar strategic relationship between the two countries. When the Syrian forces held the Heights, their guns dominated a score or so of Israeli villages in the plain below, but they had no easy access to crucial centers within Israel. The roads from the plain to such places like Safed and Afula, Acre and Haifa are dotted with formidable natural obstacles that could be used by the Israelis to bar easy access to these cities by their enemy. Control of the Heights by the Israelis, on the other hand, not only removed the threat to their settlements and brought about the destruction and depopulation of Syrian villages and towns, but also put the Israeli forces within 40 miles of Damascus along roads that are almost free of natural obstructions. Moreover, with the Heights the Israelis gained control of the Banias source and tributary of the river Jordan, and of a portion of the Transarabian pipeline to boot.

All this should have put heavy pressure on the Syrian regime to try to recover its losses by devising some new strategy or by exploring the possibilities of a settlement. It has done neither. It has merely refrained from provoking Israel into taking advantage of its improved strategic position to widen its gains, relied on the Soviet Union to protect the country against unprovoked Israeli military pressure, and boycotted the United Nations' peace envoy. Toward its public at home, the regime has acted as if nothing happened.

The probable explanation of this behavior is that, since the Syrian leaders knew that their position at home did not rest on the quality of their performance in the first place, and since their credibility and standing in the Arab world were minimal anyway, it did not matter much if they did not confront the issue as long as they could count on the brigades they had actually pulled out of the battlefield to keep them in power at home and on the Soviet Union to protect them abroad.

An overthrow of the regime from within, a likely possibility in itself, would almost certainly bring about some change in Syria's position. The present regime owes its existence entirely to Soviet support; and this almost insures that any substitute for it would be at least temporarily alienated from the Russians and would look to Cairo if not to the West for support. This, and the pressures of the consequences of the war, which the new regime would have no interest in ignoring, would probably result in the aligning of Syria's position with Cairo's.

JORDAN

Jordan has been under much heavier pressures than Syria as a result of the war, and the emotional disposition of its ruler toward Israel has long been tempered by realistic considerations. King Hussein has been willing to envisage a final settlement with Israel, but he has been prevented so far from acting on his will by a delicate position at home and by the fear that Syria or Egypt might use it against him if he made a separate peace.

We have seen that King Hussein entered the war not out of choice but for lack of it. Unlike Nasser, who managed to deceive himself about its likely outcome, Hussein never had any illusions on this score. On May 28, 1967, for example, after he had decided to throw his lot with Egypt and Syria in case of war and had already been in contact with Nasser about the formal agreement he later signed to that effect, he gave vent before a group of foreign reporters to the feeling that he was heading for tragedy.[2] Consequently, he faced no problem after the war of admitting and comprehending the fact of defeat; nor did he need to agonize about its implications for the policies he had been pursuing throughout his career, and for the future balance of power between his country and Israel. He had known all along that Israel was and will be more powerful than his country, and even than any forces the Arab countries could jointly assemble. He had realized that the security of his country and his throne depended primarily on avoiding conflict with Israel and cultivating the support of the United States and other Western powers. His problem before the war had been how to avoid being driven by inter-Arab currents into the kind of trap in which he was eventually caught in May 1967; his problem after the war was how to get out of that trap and seek some settlement with Israel to recover his losses without courting perdition.

The pressures on Hussein to seek a settlement have been heavy. Contrary to the first impression, the economic pressure is not among the heaviest. Although the West Bank comprised most of Jordan's farmland and accounted for nearly half of its Gross National Product, it was no less of a net importer than the East Bank, and it had little scope for development except in the field of tourism. Financially, strangely enough, the war brought an improvement rather than a deterioration in Jordan's situation. It lost, probably only temporarily, the American subsidy, but it gained, probably also temporarily, a much higher subsidy from the Arab oil-producing countries.

Strategically, Jordan's loss of the West Bank was at most a mitigated evil. It deprived it of a critical base of operations against Israel which had not been exploited for lack of means, but which had served to focus on itself the unwelcome attention of everyone. The fall of the

[2] See report of interview by Dana Adams Schmidt in the *New York Times*, May 29, 1967.

bulge to Israel did bring Israeli troops to within 25 miles of Amman and did place them in a more convenient position to threaten Mafraq, some 45 miles from them, where they could cut off Jordan's main links with Syria and Iraq;[3] but this only made worse a military relationship to Israel that was already untenably bad.

The real damage and therefore the real pressure to settle has been of a political nature. The West Bank comprised half of Jordan's prewar population and was the source of most of its educated manpower. Moreover, the West Bank contains the most sacred places of Christianity and the third-holiest site of Islam after Mecca and Medina—the Dome of the Rock. These not only constituted a lucrative attraction for pilgrims and tourists, but endowed Jordan and its monarch with an international significance they would otherwise have lacked entirely. Although it seems clear even now that the Christian (and Jewish) holy places will not revert to Jordanian control under any foreseeable circumstances, resumption of control over the Muslim holy places is still possible and constitutes a crucial incentive for King Hussein to seek a settlement. Moreover, it is possible that even if the non-Muslim holy places were placed under a different regime, arrangements could be made in the final settlement to allow Jordan to benefit from the tourist movement they attract.

In view of Jordan's basic position vis-à-vis Israel before the war, and the consequences of the war itself, King Hussein has been eager to settle with Israel. However, his precarious political position at home has made it impossible for him to detach himself from Nasser's train and seek a separate peace. He has tried to persuade Nasser of the desirability of a joint settlement or to gain his assent to a separate Jordanian attempt; but so far Nasser has moved only slowly on the first and refused the second.

The weakness of Hussein's position at home has been due to the growth and activities of the *Fatah* (Organization for the Liberation of Palestine). This organization has used the East Bank as a base for guerilla attacks on targets in territories under Israeli control, and these have in turn provoked Israeli retaliation in the form of artillery and air action that have depopulated some of the best lands on the east side of the Jordan River, and massive raids by ground forces that could escalate into a hopeless, full-fledged war. Partly for these reasons and partly

---

[3] The Israelis were 45 miles from Mafraq at Samakh even before the war; but the capture of the West Bank secured their right flank and put them in a better position to threaten that crucial junction. The capture of the Golan Heights from the Syrians also helped, by securing the left flank of a potential Israeli drive.

because the organization has developed into a kind of unaccountable private army that could turn its weapons against him, King Hussein tried to suppress it. However, his attempt embroiled him with dissenting members of his government and with military personnel sympathic to the *Fatah*, and risked plunging the country into a major crisis.

Thus, whatever he does, King Hussein faces a threat to his regime. The question is whether he will continue to suffer this threat while remaining bound to Nasser's train and allowing the *Fatah* to operate and grow, or whether he will take his chances while detaching himself from Nasser, suppressing the *Fatah*, and attempting a settlement with Israel. Presumably, he would be able to count on American support in the latter case.

Should King Hussein be overthrown while pursuing either course, the immediate prospects of a settlement would suffer a setback while the longer-term prospects would get lost in a tangle of obscure contingencies. The new regime would almost certainly orient itself on the Cairo-Moscow axis and would replace whatever moderating pressure King Hussein is now able to exercise on Nasser with an opposite pressure. Its advent would probably lead to an intensification of the cycle of guerilla raids and Israeli reprisals, which might escalate into large-scale war that could drag Egypt and other Arab countries into a hopeless contest. Such an eventuality would in turn have serious implications for the big powers. Perhaps knowledge of the gravity of the consequences by the parties concerned would stop the chain reaction short. However, the evolution of the crisis of May 1967 should be a warning against taking too much comfort in this thought.

EGYPT

Heavy as the pressures on Jordan have been, the pressures on Egypt due to the outcome of the war have been even heavier. However, because of the previous expectations of the Egyptian regime and the position it thought it held in the region and the world at large, the idea of submitting to Israel's insistence on formal peace as the price of obtaining relief from these pressures has been too novel and too bitter for it to accept quickly. Consequently, it has tried to explore every alternative way of recovering its losses, has yielded to the pressures only gradually as it exhausted each alternative, and has endeavored to convert the concessions it was forced to make into a means of defeating Israel's objective. So far this rear-guard action has brought the regime to the point where it is willing to contemplate a mediated settlement that would legally terminate the confrontation with Israel, but not a formally negotiated peace that would legally terminate the political dispute with it.

Militarily, the Six Day War totally devastated Egypt's armed power. On June 9, 1967, when Egypt agreed to cease fire, the entire Egyptian army and air force had been completely destroyed as fighting bodies. Nasser was to say later that on that day there was not a single Egyptian soldier on the west bank of the canal to resist an Israeli crossing and march on Cairo. The statement certainly contained a good deal of hyperbole, since reports from Cairo for that day spoke of movements of troops in the capital and flights of air force units over its skies in connection with internal political maneuvers; nevertheless, it was essentially true that Egypt lay practically defenseless before the Israeli troops, who, however, had no intention of venturing beyond the canal. This particular consequence of the war proved to be the least enduring. On June 21, 1967, Soviet President Podgorny and Chief of Staff Marshal Zakharov arrived in Cairo and agreed with Nasser on a plan to rebuild Egypt's armed forces. Immediately after, the Soviets mounted a most impressive logistics operation by air and sea which brought the inventory of the Egyptian armed forces near to its prewar level within a few months. At the same time, a Soviet military mission several thousand strong set to work to help retrain and reorganize the Egyptian forces. These and other measures, such as posting Soviet naval units in Port Said, saved Egypt from the position of utter military impotence; but they did not rectify the strategic upheaval brought about by Israel's occupation of Sinai.

Strategically, the occupation of Sinai reversed the previous relationship between Egypt and Israel. It removed the threat of a rapid junction between Egyptian and Jordanian forces across the narrow part of the Negev triangle—a move that had been actually contemplated by the Egyptians before the outbreak of war. It gave Israel a more defensive frontier and an added depth of about 200 miles of desert, putting Tel Aviv, for example, 300 miles from the Egyptian forces on the west bank of the canal, while making Egypt much more vulnerable by placing Israeli troops on the east bank of the canal 80 miles from Cairo across mainly open terrain. Important Egyptian centers of population and large industrial complexes came now within Israeli gunshot, while the smallest Israeli settlement was safely tucked away. Air bases in the north of Israel fell out of range of Egypt's best combat aircraft, while the arm of the Israeli air force was correspondingly extended. Actual or potential air bases in Sinai added up to 15 precious minutes of loitering time to most Israeli combat planes over what they had before the war, while depriving Egyptian planes of comparable margins. How significant the difference can be may be gathered by reviewing the description of the Israeli air operations in the war (see pp. 324–327 above). The Egyptian navy, which could maneuver freely before the war between the Red Sea and the Mediterranean through the Suez Canal, was reduced to the same condition as the Israeli navy of having to operate in two independent forces. The Port Said and Suez naval bases became vulnerable to Israeli artillery; the Egyptian missile boats, removed to Alexandria, could no longer reach and threaten Tel Aviv and Haifa. Against all these advantages gained by Israel, the disadvantage of greatly extended lines of communications seems relatively small.

Economically, the initial impact of the war on Egypt was nearly catastrophic. The closing of the Suez Canal, the capture by Israel of the Sinai oilfields, and the loss of revenue from tourism, which dwindled in consequence of the persisting tension, deprived Egypt of more than $300 million annual revenue in hard currency. The significance of this loss may be appreciated if it is recalled that even before the war the Egyptian economy was in such trouble that the second five-year plan had to be scaled down, then completely scrapped; that the Egyptian government had defaulted on payments to foreign creditors, and that it was prepared to undertake a drastic effective devaluation of the Egyptian pound in order to qualify for a $65 million loan from the World Bank. The loss of $300 million in these circumstances spelled famine and disaster.

Egypt was saved from such a fate by an emergency supply of wheat from the Soviet Union and by the assumption on the part of Saudi Arabia, Libya, and Kuwait of the obligation to make up for most of the lost Egyptian revenue. However, leaving aside for the moment the political implications of having to depend for sheer economic survival on the munificence of governments who had been the object of Egyptian hostility and contempt until the day before, this arrangement still left Egypt under heavy economic pressure. The political uncertainty regarding the subsidy makes effective planning and execution more difficult than ever before, a problem not to be minimized in a completely administered economy; and the fact that it is fixed does not compensate for the growth potential of assets lost. More important than all this, the value of the Suez Canal—the biggest of these assets, accounting for $220 million in revenue—deteriorates rapidly the longer it remains closed. Silt accumulates at the canal's bottom which requires dredging at great cost. More significant, the blockage of the canal for the second time in ten years—this time for an apparently indefinite period—has greatly accelerated the process begun in 1956–1957 of shifting to supertankers which can carry oil economically around Africa. Should the canal remain closed much longer, most oil transport, which accounted for the bulk of its revenue, will by-pass it even after it is reopened. The construction of a large-diameter pipeline from the tip of the Gulf of Suez to Alexandria, said to be under consideration by the Egyptian government, may prove to be a profitable business venture in itself; but it would only enhance the trend toward supertankers by the suggestion that the Egyptian government itself has given up on the canal as a main oil-transit route. Moreover, the shippers might use the pipeline as long as it was there, but they would still want to retain the option of going around Africa in case the pipeline itself was disrupted by political and military crises.

Besides the strategic and economic aspects already mentioned, the two factors combine to produce an additional prospective pressure which must weigh very heavily on the thinking of the Egyptian government. We are referring to the prospects of a continuing arms race with Israel if the conflict is not settled peaceably. The Egyptian leadership must have learned from its experience since 1955 that the relevant relationships between Egypt and Israel are such that an arms race could accelerate to the limit of self-strangulation. Even before the war Egypt had felt the noose tightening, and the war bid fair to make things much worse in the future on at least two counts. Egypt's loss of nearly 80 percent of the equipment it had accumulated over a period of many years required it to make enormous acquisitions of new matériel over a period of a few months. Unless the Soviets provided the arms free of charge, which is rather unlikely, the economic resources of Egypt must have been more deeply mortgaged than ever before, no matter how easy the repayment terms. Moreover, the war has shown that even with its prewar strategic position, Egypt's military effort was far from sufficient to withstand an Israeli assault for more than two or three days, let alone give it any margin of superiority. With the much worse postwar strategic position, Egypt would have to exert itself infinitely more to continue the confrontation with Israel. While much of this exertion could be fruitfully addressed to improving the fighting qualities of Egypt's forces, there is no doubt that quantity and quality of equipment would also need to make big leaps to keep up with Israel, and this is very costly. These considerations probably underlay the statement of Haykal cited in the previous section (see p. 387) to the effect that Egypt alone was not in a position then or in the future to withstand the Israeli danger.

No less important than the economic and strategic effects have been the political pressures generated by the war and its consequences.

Internally, the outcome of the war initially caused Nasser to resign and nearly brought down the entire regime. Even after the initial shock wore off and Nasser resumed a measure of control over the situation, his charisma, the moral authority that had been the cement of the Egyptian political system, was deeply eroded. The consequences manifested themselves almost immediately in the disruption of the solidarity and cohesion of the armed forces, the material mainstay of the regime. Within days of the end of the fighting, various groups of officers, some dismissed in disgrace and some still in active service, engaged in conspiracies designed to overthrow the regime. The discovery of the plots and the public trials of the conspirators, by disclosing the abuses, cowardice and corruption of men of the highest ranks who had held key positions only a short time before, cast discredit upon the whole regime that had elevated them, and further undermined its foundations. For the first time since Nasser consolidated his hold on power in 1954, students and workers dared to defy the authorities and engage in large-scale demonstrations protesting various abuses and demanding far-reaching reforms. So far, Nasser has been able to stem the breaches with typical improvisation and resourcefulness; but his regime will most likely remain in a precarious condition until he can restore his authority, and he probably cannot do this without removing somehow the visible evidence of defeat in the form of Israeli occupation of Egyptian national territory.

Another kind of political pressure has been that stemming from Egypt's dependence on other Arab countries for economic survival. This has not only placed Egypt in a very humiliating position, but has also imposed more or less serious restrictions on its ability to pursue independent policies. We have seen a reflection of this in the regime's liquidation of its commitments in Yemen and South Arabia and its renunciation of the ambition to revolutionize and unite the Arab world for the more modest aim of seeking to promote Arab cooperation. Even in pursuing this more limited objective, the regime has had to suffer nullification of its initiatives by the objections of the Saudi king and other Arab chiefs. Nasser's erstwhile "feudalist, reactionary" opponents have apparently gone so far as to demand from him explanations for his moves vis-à-vis the Soviet Union, judging by the replies that he and Haykal have felt compelled to provide.[4] While it

---

[4] See, for example, Haykal's article in *al Ahram* of February 2, 1968, where he responded to anonymous Arab criticisms of Egypt for taking in so many Russian advisers and for allowing units of the Soviet navy to use Egyptian facilities. Haykal's argument about the advisers, also mentioned by Nasser in a public speech, was that they were not much more numerous than before the war, that

would be wrong to suggest that the Arab governments who provide the subsidy call the tune for Nasser, there is no doubt that Nasser has had to be careful in selecting his tunes, a galling limitation for a man whose chief talent has long been an extraordinary tactical dexterity.

The continuation of Israel's occupation of Egyptian territory constitutes yet another kind of pressure. The longer Israel continues in undisturbed possession of its gains, the greater the prospects of its wanting to hold on to them for good, or the more likely it would be to insist on harsher terms in an eventual settlement. On the other hand, to try to "disturb" Israel by trying to "keep the pot boiling," in Haykal's words, presents grave risks. Limited action by Egypt itself could bring Israeli retaliation in the form of bombardments that could turn the Suez Canal zone into deserted rubble, as was demonstrated after the Egyptian sinking of the Israeli destroyer *Elath*. Supporting *Fatah*-type action from Jordanian territory could produce an escalation into large-scale warfare that could involve the Egyptian forces prematurely and end in disaster. Nasser, indeed, must fear such a consummation as a result of the course events might take independently of any contribution on his part.

All these pressures have not so far produced among Nasser and his associates a willingness to settle the conflict with Israel permanently, as in the case of King Hussein. This is not because the pressures on Egypt have been lighter or because feelings of hostility toward Israel run deeper among Egyptians than among Jordanians—the contrary is true on both scores. The reason is rather that, whereas the Jordanians in power had long been conditioned by their weakness vis-à-vis Israel to suppress their feelings and, at bottom, to accept the existence of Israel as inevitable, the Egyptians have been conditioned by their view of themselves and of Israel to entertain a contrary attitude. The disparity in size and numbers between Egypt and Israel, the vast potential diplomatic, economic, and military resources of the Arab world that the Egyptian regime thought it could tap, the spectacular successes in the international arena the regime claimed to its credit, the real or alleged dramatic achievements it scored at home, and the boundless ambitions it entertained for Egypt had conditioned the regime

---

they had been invited, not imposed, and could be dismissed any time. As for the other point, Haykal argued that if the Arabs knew what was good for them, they should welcome the presence of the Soviet navy in the Mediterranean as a check against the American Sixth Fleet in that sea. This, however, he hastened to add, was not the true reason for what Egypt did. Egypt simply allowed Russian ships that were engaged in bringing arms to it to fill their tanks with fresh water in its ports, an elementary and logical courtesy under the circumstances.

and the people to indulge their feeling of hostility toward Israel, to think of its destruction as a real possibility, and indeed to publicly proclaim this as the war objective of Egypt before hundreds of international reporters ten days before the fighting broke out. (See above, pp. 291–292.) Because of this disposition, the outcome of the war literally proved almost more than Nasser and his associates could mentally withstand; and it is not surprising, therefore, that after the initial shock of defeat wore off, the regime tried its utmost to resist the drastic conclusions it seemed to dictate.

On the other hand, the Egyptian regime did not go so far in resisting these conclusions as to relapse into irresponsibility, as the Syrian regime did. For one thing, it had much more political credit to preserve at home, in the region and in the world; and for another thing the pressures on it and Egypt have been much more heavy and pervasive, making it impossible to ignore them without serious risk of collapse and chaos. At the same time, the Russians made it clear to the regime within two weeks of the end of the war that they would not go along with any desperate scheme to try to reverse its outcome by force, and made their absolutely vital assistance conditional upon Egypt's gradually moving toward a political settlement through the agency of the United Nations.[5] Consequently, the regime tried to grapple with the contradictory pressures it was under by adopting a line which objected to "the liquidation of the Palestine problem," refused reconciliation, direct negotiations with Israel, and formal recognition of it, but which sought to achieve "the liquidation of the consequences of the Israeli aggression," that is to say, some kind of limited diplomatic settlement short of peace. While it maneuvered in the diplomatic arena within these limits, it made a serious effort to take stock of what had in fact happened and to revise its thinking and strategy for the future in that light.

On this last score, the regime showed a remarkable capacity for self-criticism and realistic adaptation under very difficult circumstances. Thus, after desperate efforts, in the course of its *post-mortems* on the war, to salvage its own judgment and its view of Egyptian capabilities by blaming the defeat on American intervention, bad luck, or the misdeeds of individuals, the regime did finally acknowledge that Israel alone had done the impossible and crushed Egypt and its allies in a fair battle; and it drew from this the very painful conclusion that Egypt alone was not, and could not expect to be, in a position to withstand Israel. For a while the regime tried to take solace by pointing at the great

[5] More on this point below, pp. 411–412.

numerical superiority of the Arabs and their great potential resources; but before long, it turned round and itself questioned the avail of numbers against superior technology and the validity of the assumption that the Arabs constituted one force that Egypt could mobilize and lead. Concomitantly, the regime took the momentous step of renouncing the objective of immediate integral Arab unity as being beyond Egypt's capacity under the existing and foreseeable circumstances.

In the diplomatic arena, the regime's maneuvers took Egypt's formal position through four overlapping stages. First, the Egyptian government insisted on an unconditional withdrawal of the Israeli "aggressor" to the June 4, 1967, lines. Then, it informally agreed to some concessions in order to secure an Israeli withdrawal, including the right of free navigation for Israeli ships through the Strait of Tiran, renunciation of belligerence by unilateral proclamation, demilitarization of parts of Sinai and Israel, and perhaps allowing Israeli cargo to go through the Suez Canal on third-party ships. Later still, the Egyptians indicated their acceptance of the United Nations Security Council resolution of November 22, 1967, (which spoke in its preface of achieving peace and in its operative clauses linked the withdrawal of troops to termination of belligerence and safe and recognized boundaries), but insisted that withdrawal should precede any discussion of safe and recognized boundaries. Finally, in the fourth and current stage, the Egyptians have agreed to discuss both issues simultaneously, but only through United Nations envoy Jarring, not in face-to-face negotiations with Israel. The progression from stage to stage did not take place neatly and smoothly, but was accompanied by minor crises and reverses and by a constant drumming about the inevitability of war and various other psychological-war devices intended to enhance the effectiveness of each new step.

The transition from stage to stage has been related to the exploration or exhaustion of apparent opportunities. The first stage, for example, counted on the hope of a United Nations condemnation of Israel as an aggressor and a call for unconditional withdrawal; when the resolution to that effect introduced by the Russians failed to carry, the Egyptians moved to the second stage. The new position, in turn, counted on the pressures of the August 1967 Arab summit in Khartum, news of the Russians' rearming of Egypt, and other factors to impel the United States to reduce its support for Israel and thus leave it exposed to Soviet and world pressures; however, as this pressure failed to produce the anticipated effect because of the United States' eagerness to achieve a durable settlement, the Egyptian position moved to the next stage. The new position sought to yield something to the

American desire for a settlement by accepting the Security Council resolution in the hope of thus driving a wedge between the United States and Israel, who insisted on formal negotiations and peace treaties. Indications that the attempt might succeed in its aim if carried a little further led to the adoption of the next position.

As matters stand now, Egypt seems to have gone somewhat beyond the limits of the basic line it had set for itself. The acceptance of the Security Council resolution and the agreement to discuss its integral application imply a willingness to go beyond the notion of "liquidating the consequences of the Israeli aggression" toward a comprehensive settlement. On the other hand, the insistence on avoiding face-to-face negotiations, which is meant to avoid immediate tacit recognition of Israel and to preclude the idea of a formal peace treaty and explicit recognition, still safeguards the principle of opposing a basic settlement that would "liquidate the Palestine problem." The difference between the two ideas may appear academic, but is not. A settlement consecrated in a peace treaty would legally close the conflict and encourage outside powers to deal with Israel and treat with it on that basis without being inhibited by possible Arab reactions. A settlement by some other method, on the other hand, may legally outlaw belligerence and recognize frontiers, but it would permit the conflict to be carried on by political means and would thus leave the Palestine issue open and inhibit dealings by third parties with Israel. This is why Israel has opposed the Egyptian position.

ISRAEL

The cease-fire has put under Israeli control roughly 47,000 square miles of former Arab territory, nearly six times the 8,000 square miles that constituted prewar Israel. It has also brought in an Arab population of about one million which, when added to the Israeli Arab population of about 300,000, makes the ratio of Jews to Arabs in the entire area under Israeli control nearly 63:37, almost the exact ratio of Arabs to Jews in Palestine at the end of the Mandate period.

The new territories are devoid of any significant natural resources except for a relatively modest amount of oil in Sinai. Sinai itself, accounting for about 95 percent of the new territories, is mainly a forbidding desert, inhabited by some 20,000 people in the el Arish region and a comparable number of bedouins. The Gaza Strip can support less than half of its 350,000 population. The West Bank contains some potentially usable agricultural land if water could be found; in the absence of this, its presently cultivable land is overcrowded with the existing population of 600,000. The Golan Heights have some agricultural land, but the entire area is only a few hundred square miles.

The main significance of the conquered territories is politico-strategic and emotional. We have already dwelt on the crucial politico-strategic advantages bestowed on Israel by the conquests in the course of our analysis of the impact of the war on the Arab countries, and we need only add a remark about boundaries. Although the cease-fire lines multiplied Israeli-controlled territory by seven, they reduced the length of its prewar land boundaries by nearly one third, while making them much more defensible by resting them on the Suez Canal, the Jordan River and the crest of the Golan Heights. The coastal line has been prolonged severalfold, but only a small proportion of the additional length can be threatened by an enemy like Egypt. We have also mentioned that the cease-fire lines greatly lengthened Israel's supply lines across the Sinai desert.

The emotional significance of the conquered territories derives from their association with Jewish history and mythology since biblical times, and with Zionist aspirations since before the partition of Palestine. This is less true of Sinai than of the West Bank, and most true with regard to Jerusalem, the focal point of Jewish yearning since the days of the First and Second Temples. Quite apart from any final disposition of these territories, their being under Israeli control now is a fact of much more than practical interest to the Israelis.

Before discussing the views of the Israelis about the disposition of these territories, it is necessary to look into the question of their ability to maintain their occupation and the burdens, if any, that this entails.

The diplomatic dimension of this question is of critical importance, as was shown after the 1956 war, when Israel was forced by the combined pressure of the United States and the Soviet Union to relinquish Sinai and Gaza and go back to the 1949 armistice lines. We shall leave aside this dimension for the moment except for pointing out that Israel this time escaped United Nations censure and Soviet and other pressures to withdraw unconditionally thanks to the intercession of the United States, and for suggesting that as long as American support is forthcoming, diplomatic pressure on Israel to evacuate unconditionally will prove ineffective.

Economically, the occupation has not, on balance, been much of a burden on Israel. The disruption of the economy of the West Bank has required some expenditure to avoid disaster and concomitant political difficulties, but a policy of allowing free movement of funds, goods and people between the two sides of the Jordan River even in the midst of high border tension has reduced the need for such spending to the tolerable proportions of a few tens of millions of dollars. The need to maintain larger numbers of armed forces in a state of readiness to defend the conquered territories has probably added several tens of millions of dollars to the defense burden; but the total of these costs has been for the most part compensated by the proceeds from the Sinai oil field which fell to the Israelis intact.

Militarily, Israel is in a better position to defend the territories now under its control than the territory it controlled before the war, both because of the strategic advantages we have already discussed, and because the confidence and morale of the Arab armies have suffered a rude shock. Guerilla fighting, however, presents a more complicated problem.

Much nonsense has been written as to how the Israeli occupation of vast territories inhabited by about one million Arabs created conditions favorable for a popular war of liberation in the Algerian, Vietnamese, or Cuban style. Such views forget that Sinai, accounting for some 95 percent of the occupied area, is virtually empty and is climatically forbidding to the movement and survival of guerillas. They forget that the West Bank, the Gaza Strip, and the Golan Heights have added only about 3,000 square miles to Israel's original 8,000 square miles, and that no spot in that entire territory is so inaccessible to Israeli land and airborne forces as to permit the establishment of a large, open guerilla base as called for by that type of war. Above all, they forget that the entire Arab population in the West Bank and the Gaza Strip is relatively small by comparison to Israel's, that Israel's economy is totally independent of it, and that therefore Israel holds an ultimate sanction which none of the powers fought by guerillas elsewhere had: driving out the entire population. This need not be done in one fell swoop, but could be brought about over a period of a few years in the context of fighting back the guerillas. Interestingly enough, the Arab population in its mass has instinctively grasped this truth which has eluded the more sophisticated commentators, and has for this reason refrained on the whole from giving assistance to *Fatah* or other raiders, forcing them to confine themselves to hit-and-run tactics from bases in the East Bank.

From a strictly military point of view, then, the guerilla problem is ultimately no more difficult to handle after the war than it was or could have been before the war, and it may even be easier. For Israel can operate freely in the West Bank, which it could not do before, and it has that ultimate sanction on the population which it lacked before. From a psychological-political point of view, however, the problem may have become more difficult. Before the war, antiguerilla action was action to defend the Israeli homeland against incursions of foreign raiders; after the war, such action assumed the character of Israeli forces of occupation suppressing national resistance fighters. The transformation makes Israel's repressive and retaliatory measures less justifiable even in the eyes of friends abroad, and makes the casualties suffered in the process less bearable to its own population at home. Moreover, should the population in the occupied territory be swept by events into the resistance movement despite everything, the application of the ultimate sanction would, for at least some time, make things much more difficult in both respects. Finally, there is always the risk that the cycle of violence might explode into large-scale war which could create grave diplomatic complications even if the fighting should go in favor of Israel—in fact, precisely because it predictably would. The Russians may be much less prepared in such an eventuality to sit back and see the regimes under their protection crushed, especially since they would expect the United States to be much more inhibited in running interference for an Israel defending its conquests than for an Israel defending its existence.

With the occupation involving only slight real disadvantages by comparison with the very important politico-strategic and emotional advantages, the Israelis have felt no need to take the initiative to terminate the existing situation, and have responded to the initiative of others with an insistence on some general terms. These terms include peace and the final liquidation of the conflict plus modifications of the prewar boundaries. What kind of modifications, the Israelis themselves have been unable to decide, indeed, have not had to decide, since the Arab states have not yet accepted the idea of a final peace.

A small minority of Israelis has pressed for formal annexation of all the conquered territories in the full knowledge that this would nullify any prospects of peace in the foreseeable future. This position merits attention not because it might sway the majority, but because of the possibility that continued Arab opposition to peace may persuade many who now oppose the minority opinion that there is no other choice, and because it exercises a pull toward extremism even now.

The annexationists have organized as a pressure group under the name of "The Land of Israel Movement." Among their leaders are found many prominent personalities in all fields of endeavor, especially the literary world. The membership of the group cuts across the Israeli political spectrum—a new phenomenon in Israeli politics made possible by "liquification" of traditional structures and allegiances by the trauma of the crisis and the war. The movement includes extreme left-wing idealists harking back to the idea of a binational state, as well as right-wing chauvinists who dream of a "Greater Israel" stretching on both sides of the Jordan; pious Jews and romantic atheists; people who seek a Jewish-Arab symbiosis after the Christian-Moslem model of Lebanon, and people who seek *lebensraum* and incentive for massive immigration; "hard-nosed realists" who mistrust peace treaties with the Arabs, and deliberate "levantinizers" who wish to see Israel become a Middle Eastern state; and so on. The diversity and contradictory character of the group's motives would probably tear it asunder if it met with greater prospects of success; for the moment, however, it is able to exert a stiffening influence on many who do not accept its views integrally.

The great majority of Israelis, including all but one or two members of the Cabinet, differentiate between the Golan Heights and Sinai on the one hand, and the West Bank on the other. With regard to the former, they have not ruled out the idea of annexation in case Syria and Egypt should persist in refusing to negotiate peace. With regard to the West Bank, however, they have strongly opposed annexation on the grounds that Israel could not absorb one million Arabs in addition to its 300,000 Arab citizens without losing its identity as a democratic, egalitarian Jewish state. With a total Arab population of 1,300,000 growing naturally at about twice the natural rate of growth of the 2,300,000 Jewish population, it would not be long before the Arabs constituted a majority. Jewish immigration, having already dwindled to a trickle as a result of the exhaustion of all the previous sources of mass immigration, could not be counted upon to offset this development. Consequently, if the Arabs were given full citizenship rights, Israel would cease to be a Jewish state altogether after the Arabs became a majority, and its Jewish character would begin to change drastically even before that time due to the political play of a very large Arab minority. If the Arabs were denied full citizenship rights, Israel would lose its democratic character and enter upon a South African type of career. In either case, there would be the additional risk of ethnic conflict sooner or later, after the fashion of Cyprus, Belgium, or Canada.

Just as the minority has been united in pressing for total annexation but divided in the motives for wanting it, so the majority has been united in rejecting total annexation but divided in what it wanted instead. Some have argued in favor of setting up an autonomous Palestinian entity in the West Bank and making peace with it while ignoring the Arab states; others have argued for trading conquered territory for peace. The former have in turn been divided over the character and scope of the Palestine entity; the latter have differed greatly over the minimal terms for peace. The government itself has given little lead to its people and assumed no commitment abroad beyond insisting on full-fledged peace based on secure and recognized boundaries which would be better than those of June 4, but not necessarily identical with those of June 10, 1967.

Israeli diplomats have justified their government's reticence as unwillingness to reveal its hand before the Arab states have come to the negotiation table. Actually, the government has had little of a hand to reveal, because it has been unable to reach an agreement on just what it wanted. While this inability has been partly due to the lack of any sense of urgent need to agree as long as the Arabs continue to oppose peace, it has been also in great measure the result of a new, very fluid political situation at home.

The agonies of the days before the war which thrust Dayan upon Eshkol and brought about a national coalition government also undermined the traditional political views of the Israeli public and the alignments within and among Israel's parties. The outcome of the war and the issues it raised completed the disarray, and set in motion a comprehensive process of still uncompleted political readjustment in which the power positions in the country are at stake. In this situation, members of the government, having broken loose from party discipline and inter-party commitments, have tended to stick to individualistic positions and resist compromise out of genuine conviction or out of a desire to court popular opinion, thus making a consensus impossible.

The result of all this has been a drift toward more demanding positions and a tendency to let things happen which may restrict the possibilities of bargaining if and when the time for negotiations came. In June 1967, for example, when victory seemed assured but the fighting had not yet ceased, Prime Minister Eshkol, reflecting the mood of the country before the war, declared that Israel wanted only peace and sought no annexation. At about the same time, Defense Minister Dayan proclaimed in an emotional moment near the Wailing Wall that Israelis had returned to Jerusalem never to part from it again, and his words became a universal slogan overnight. Shortly after, the Cabinet considered a formal annexation of Old Jerusalem, but decided for the moment in favor of only its "administrative unification" with the new city; but Minister of the Interior Shapira, in charge of executing the Cabinet's decision, did everything possible to lend to the action the character of formal annexation. By now, absolute Israeli authority over Jerusalem has presumably become a "non-negotiable point."

A similar process has taken place in connection with several smaller issues, such as the resettlement of some Jewish quarters or villages and the creation of new ones in parts of the occupied territories, and also with very important issues relating to the future boundaries of Israel. On this last score, Minister of Labor Yigal Allon and Defense Minister Dayan, the leading competitors for the succession to the prime ministership, set the pace. Thus Allon for a long time publicly advocated a scheme for the establishment of a belt of semimilitary settlements alongside the western bank of the Jordan River and eventually forced the hand of Cabinet, which apparently decided in June 1968 that Israel's "military frontier" must be the Jordan River, wherever else its "political frontier" might be. Dayan has recently been urging that Israel's territory should extend from the Mediterranean to the Jordan, and that Israel should never give up physical control over the entry to the Gulf of Aqaba.

Thus the timing of the movement of the positions of Israel and the Arab states threatens to undermine the validity of the option for a final settlement opened by the war. While Egypt, whose position has determined that of Jordan and is apt to determine that of Syria in the future, advanced from an insistence on the restoration of the prewar *status quo* to a willingness to settle the military conflict with Israel but not the political dispute with it over Palestine, Israel has drifted into decisions and actions that could undermine the prospects of peace negotiations altogether. Unless this timing is corrected by an acceleration of the Egyptian movement and/or a slowing of the Israeli drift, the option for a final settlement may become purely academic.

The War, the Superpowers, and the Conflict

One of the most crucial consequences of the war was that it gave the Soviet Union as well as the United States an interest in a settlement of the Arab-Israeli conflict. However, despite the emergence of this common interest, tactical considerations and mutual suspicion have kept the two powers from coming to an agreement on the issue, and have pitted them, instead, in a contest paralleling that of Israel and Egypt.

Ever since 1954, the Soviets have allowed themselves to drift into playing a dangerous game with the Arab-Israeli conflict. Beginning with an effort to court the Arab countries through relatively innocuous political support in the Security Council in the course of its dealings with incidents arising from the conflict, they next acceded to an Egyptian request for arms that was consummated in 1955. Although they knew that the provision of arms was bound to inflame Arab-Israeli relations, they rationalized their action as being aimed not at Israel, but at the Baghdad Pact. When the 1956 war actually ensued, the Russians justified their next arms deal with Egypt and their first with Syria on the grounds of the defense needs of these countries in the face of proven Israeli aggressiveness. Once the arms race thus got going, there was no problem justifying further provisions of arms on the grounds of Israel's arming, though the Russians' refusal to consider proposals for concerted arms control betrayed their interest in maintaining a competition that made them indispensable to various Arab countries.

By that time Egypt's position evolved, and it and Syria spoke openly of their determination to destroy Israel in war; yet, although the Russians had no particular interest in this aim and a great fear of a war that might embroil them with the United States, they continued to provide their newly acquired friends with the unswerving political support, weapons, and military assistance that allowed them to consider it. By some reasoning that is not very clear, the Russians somehow trusted that they could handle things so as to have it both ways: to get all the benefits accruing from supporting the Arabs politically and militarily on an issue these people considered vital, without actually producing the armed clash they wished to avoid. Perhaps the Russians relied on the United States' commitment to Israel to deter the Arabs from attempting a war they themselves were making possible in the first place; perhaps they counted on the expectation that the Israelis would somehow manage to keep the level of their armament up to the levels they themselves kept raising with their arms provisions; perhaps they thought they could read signs of impending war and prevent it before it broke out; or perhaps they felt they could not refuse to provide arms without endangering their position, and simply acted accordingly and hoped for the best. Whatever their calculations, the game exploded in their face in May–June, 1967: Their own political manipulations triggered a chain reaction they could not control; Nasser tried to use them for a purpose they did not share; they, the United States, and Israel's deterrent failed to forestall war; Nasser tried to embroil them in a conflict with the United States with tales of American intervention; the regimes on which their position in the region rested suffered a defeat that threatened their existence and rendered them useless for a long time to come as instruments of pressure against America's position; and they then faced the choice of picking up the pieces, helping to restore the damage and paying the cost, or leaving the field free to the United States.

Their prestige in the world at large, the heavy investment they had made in the Arab countries, and perhaps some guilt at their share in triggering the crisis, not doing enough to stop its deterioration, and

then failing to save their friends, ruled out their remaining passive.
At the same time, however, if they were to bear a share of the consequences, they wanted to make sure this time that neither their action
nor the action of their friends should give rise to another debacle. The
specific measures translating this approach were agreed upon between
Soviet President Podgorny and President Nasser in the course of the
former's visit to Cairo on June 21–25, 1967, and were reflected in the
actions of the two countries in the course of the following year. These
suggest that the Soviets have come to see a continuing Arab-Israeli
confrontation as presenting greater dangers than opportunities to themselves and have therefore decided to try to liquidate it without jeopardizing too much their position in the Arab countries.

An interesting account of the highlights of the Podgorny-Nasser talks
that conforms closely to these general lines was written by the exceptionally well-informed Middle East correspondent of the Paris *Le Monde*,
Eric Rouleau, some six months after the event.[6] According to Rouleau,
Nasser began on a highly emotional and daring tone. He invoked the
example of the Soviet Union in World War II, when its troops suffered
defeats and retreated before the Nazi invaders but continued to fight,
recovered, pushed the enemy back and destroyed him. He boldly
offered to sign a mutual defense treaty with the Soviet Union and
proposed that the Russians should provide under its terms air support
to his troops in a campaign to push Israel back and liberate the conquered Arab territories. The Soviet President politely dampened Nasser's
spirit. He was not authorized, he said, to discuss a mutual defense
treaty with Egypt and thought that this was a rather delicate international matter. Against Nasser's use of the analogy of Russia in World
War II, Podgorny invoked, somewhat indelicately, the analogy of Brest
Litovsk, when revolutionary Russia realistically submitted to the German
diktat in order to salvage the essential that was the revolution.

Once these premises were established, the Russians reportedly specified
the terms under which they were prepared to assist Egypt. They would
meet much of Nasser's needs providing he took measures to purge the
government and the armed forces of incompetent, corrupt, and opportunistic elements; but they could not assume full responsibility for
Egypt's economy. They would help Egypt on an emergency basis to
rebuild its armed forces in order to withstand Israeli-American pressure; but they would not support any plans for initiated offensive military action. They would support Egypt in its effort to recover its lost
territories by diplomatic means; but Egypt was to renounce for good

[6] See *Le Monde*, Sélection hebdomadaire, February 1–7, 1968.

any aim of settling the Palestine conflict by force. Instead, in six months to a year, after it had put its house in order and placed itself in a more favorable bargaining position, it was to seek through the agency of the United Nations an "honorable settlement" that would not reward the Israeli aggressor with any territorial annexations.

Regarding the Soviet handling of Syria, nothing is known beyond what may be guessed from the few essential external facts. Syria has been rearmed by the Soviets, has rejected the November 22 Security Council resolution, and refused to deal with Ambassador Jarring, but has almost scrupulously kept its cease-fire line with Israel quiet. On the assumption that the Soviets were serious in their intent to avoid another Arab-Israeli explosion, we might deduce from these facts that the Soviets agreed to let the Syrians indulge in an irreconcilable posture on condition that they would not attempt to recover their lost territory by force, at least until the outcome of the issue between Egypt and Israel became clear.

While waiting for Egypt to recover internally, the Soviet Union began to skirmish and explore ahead of it. It tried to obtain a United Nations resolution in favor of unconditional Israeli withdrawal to weaken Israel's anticipated resistance to the Soviet plan; when its attempt was foiled by the United States, it began to explore the American disposition. The Russians found the Americans so amenable that they nearly worked out with them some formula of agreement at meetings between Foreign Minister Gromyko and Ambassador Goldberg on the margins of the United Nations session. However, an Arab protest spearheaded by Algeria impressed on them the notion that they might have moved too fast too soon. Subsequently, they continued their exploration at the Glassboro summit meeting, but apparently refrained from getting into specifics, preferring to wait for the Arab diplomatic position to catch up with them.

While waiting, the Soviets thought they detected a stiffening of America's position. Prime Minister Kosygin claimed in an interview with the editor of *Life* magazine in January 19, 1968,[7] that he had actually agreed with President Johnson at Glassboro on how to settle the conflict, but that the United States subsequently changed its views suddenly in favor of unreserved support for Israeli expansionist and aggressive designs. The American government denied the assertion of the Soviet Premier, who must have mistaken his own mental agreement with the position expressed by the American President with an express agreement, and must have read in the outward expres-

[7] See *Life*, February, 2, 1968.

sion of the American position since Glassboro a change of strategy rather than a tactical adaptation to the situation. Be that as it may, the assertion reflected a Soviet suspicion that the United States aimed at using Israel's victory to upset the balance of power in the region and the related balance of influence between the superpowers; consequently the Soviets decided to tread carefully and avoid exercising too heavy a pressure on the Egyptian side to signify its acceptance of a settlement in order not to risk alienating it in vain.

The United States, for its part, had always desired an Arab-Israeli settlement for the simple reason that it was deeply committed to Israel and also had important interests in Arab countries. In the fifties, the conflict had constantly hampered its efforts to recruit the Arab countries into a Western regional alliance. In the sixties, when it had settled down to a more conservative policy, the explosion of the conflict into war constituted the main threat to its interests. Throughout these years, it made countless efforts to promote a settlement of the conflict, or at least to insulate or contain it; but the lack of serious leverage with the Arabs and reckless Soviet policies defeated all its endeavors. In the absence of a better alternative, the United States had pinned its hopes to prevent a major explosion on diplomatic deterrence in the form of declarations of intent to resist aggression, coupled with an effort, first implicit and indirect and then increasingly explicit and direct, to maintain a balance of forces between Israel and the Arab states.

The war simultaneously demonstrated the failure of these preventive policies, dramatized the dangers they were designed to guard against, and opened a chance of achieving the long-sought basic solution of the problem. Balance of forces proved ineffective as a deterrent in a situation in which political combinations abruptly shifted within days. Diplomatic deterrence proved useless in the not unique circumstances in which it was tested. The inescapable minimal diplomatic support the United States gave to Israel in the prewar crisis embarrassed and endangered its Arab friends; while the outbreak of war put them in grave peril which could have been graver had the war taken a slower, let alone different course. Though the United States and the Soviet Union had agreed to stand aside in the war, the actual as well as alternative possible courses of events could have forced the hand of one or the other and possibly led to a confrontation. The worst American fears did not come to pass only because Israel's victory was unexpectedly swift and decisive; and that victory also afforded the first opportunity in twenty years for the United States to seek a basic settlement of the conflict by providing a leverage in the form of pressures on the Arab countries and the Soviet Union.

The United States had in effect decided to avail itself of that opportunity before the end of the war, when it opposed Soviet initiatives in
the Security Council to obtain an order for a cease-fire *and* withdrawal,
and helped the Israelis stall for time to complete their military operations. However, the kind of settlement it sought took specific shape
only in the following days. In hurried consultations within the Administration on June 9 and 10, 1967, there were those who, accustomed to
thinking of containment rather than solution of a conflict that seemed
to them intractable, urged that the United States should content itself
with seeking to end the military confrontation between Israel and its
neighbors. Others, buoyed by the news from Cairo about the disarray
of the regime, argued that the United States should strive to achieve
a complete settlement. The latter position essentially prevailed and
was given expression in the statement made by President Johnson on
June 19, 1967, the day Prime Minister Kosygin was scheduled to address
the Special Session of the General Assembly called at the request of
the Soviet Union. After serving notice that the United States would not
press Israel to pull back its armies until the Arabs joined Israel in a
peace effort, the President stated that the United States was committed
"to a peace that is based on five principles: First, the recognized right
of national life; second, justice for the refugees; third, innocent maritime
passage; fourth, limits on the . . . arms race; and fifth, political independence and territorial integrity for all." The President indicated that
"the parties to the conflict must be the parties to peace," but qualified
this by adding that "sooner or later it is they—it is they who must make
a settlement in the area"; in the meantime, the United States was
willing to see any method tried.[8]

The policy enunciated by President Johnson was very close to, but
not identical with, Israel's official position, which insisted on direct
negotiations leading to formal peace treaties. Certainly it did not condone
the stiffening of the terms for peace and the unilateral actions that
took place beneath the cover of the vague official Israeli position.
Nevertheless, in the course of the following months, several factors
combined to make it appear as though the United States identified
itself almost completely with what Israel did. The continued occupation by Israel of the conquered territories and the blockage of the
Suez Canal constituted the main leverage through which the United
States sought to achieve its own objective. The Administration did not
deem it tactically wise to weaken that leverage by stressing publicly

[8] For the text of the President's statement see the *New York Times*, June 20,
1967.

the difference between its official position and Israel's, or by openly taking strong exception to what was unofficially taking place in Israel as long as the Arab position remained distant from its own. At the same time, the Administration found it necessary to oppose Soviet-Arab maneuvers to eliminate or weaken the leverage held by Israel, which was also its own, by offering diplomatic resistance as well as by taking measures such as the resumption of arms shipments to Israel. The unsought appearance of complete identification that ensued has been the cause of considerable concern in the Administration, especially before the electoral campaign of 1968 got under way; but to the Soviets, accustomed to putting a sinister interpretation on whatever the United States did, the Administration's action appeared as a deliberate policy of support for Israeli expansionism and an effort to upset the balance of power in the region to the detriment of the Soviet Union and its friends. Naturally, this suggested to them the need to be particularly cautious not to get out of step with their own friends, thus unwittingly allowing them, in turn, to play the double game of official and unofficial positions.

Thus although the United States and the Soviet Union had come to share an interest in seeing the Arab-Israeli conflict settled, they have been unable in the course of the year that has elapsed since the war to find a way to a common agreement designed to realize their aim. In principle, they have been much closer to each other than the belligerents themselves. Both have been free from the passions with which their respective protégés have invested their positions, and both have reason to fear that their protégés might act on their passions in ways that could defeat the chances of a settlement and embroil the big powers more than ever before in a continuing Arab-Israeli confrontation. The Soviet Union, for itself, did not share the reservations of its Egyptian friend on the kind of settlement that was acceptable, and the United States, for itself, did not share the concern of its Israeli friend as to the specific way in which a settlement was to be sought or as to its particular territorial terms. Yet tactical considerations and mutual suspicion led them to line up with their respective protégés and to engage with each other in a contest by proxy which has set their positions much farther apart than they needed to be.

The contest has so far primarily taken the form of a test of endurance in which each has counted on the other to modify its position first. The Soviet Union has hoped that the United States would give way to its fear for the collapse of the Jordanian regime under the stress of the unsettled situation, the guerilla pressures on Israel and the embarrassments caused to the United States by Israeli reprisal raids across cease-fire lines in the territory of a friendly regime, the damage to American popularity and position in the Arab world generally as a result of its close identification with Israel's position, and the image of the Soviet Union entrenching itself deeply in the countries alienated from the United States. The United States has counted on the pressures on the Soviet Union stemming from the precariousness of the position of the Egyptian and Syrian regimes as a result of defeat and its consequences, the costs to the Soviet Union of propping and rearming these regimes, Russia's inability to help them recover their losses without assuming great responsibilities and risking a confrontation with the United States, the danger of an unpremeditated war being triggered by local incidents and exposing the Egyptian and Syrian regimes to another defeat, the blockage of the Suez Canal, shutting the newly developed soviet Mediterranean fleet out of convenient access to the Persian Gulf and the Indian Ocean at a time of opportunity when the British navy was pulling out, the enormous prolongation of the maritime supply line to Hanoi for the same reason, and finally the inconsistency of the position of resisting a final peace settlement after having accepted the need to terminate the confrontation and the futility of that position from a Soviet point of view.

Obviously, the waiting game has been heavily loaded in favor of the United States, a natural consequence of its being on the side of the victor. Although the United States has lost popularity among the Arab public, its influence with Arab governments has not been damaged as much as it might seem. Nasser's prewar pretensions in the Arab world have given several Arab governments reason to be thankful for his defeat, and this tempers their resentment of America for its support of Israel. Moreover, the United States was more than compensated for its loss of popularity with the withdrawal of Egypt from Yemen and South Arabia, and the lifting of Nasser's pressure on friendly Arab regimes such as Saudi Arabia, Kuwait, Libya and others as a result of his defeat and economic dependence on them. That the Soviet Union has held out this long and given Egypt the chance to evolve its formal diplomatic position as slowly as it has is a tribute to the patience and tenacity of its diplomacy—the much easier pressures on the United States have by contrast caused many experts to advise giving way. However, now that the Egyptian formal position has at last reached the point convened upon with Podgorny and has not made a decisive impression on the United States, much less on Israel, the Soviet Union is due to reconsider its stance. The position it will take will be crucial for the future of the Arab-Israeli conflict.

Conclusions: To War Again or to Peace at Last?

It is clear from our inquiry into the effects of the war that the situation is still unsettled. This means not only that the conflict itself has not been resolved, which is obvious, but that the *state* of the conflict has not yet settled into a pattern that would warrant any definite conclusion that it is headed for peace or for continuing confrontation and war. There are forces currently at work that favor both directions, and surprises are possible either way.

To take the surprises out of the way first, a coup d'état in Egypt is apt to have a decisive effect in favor of peace because it would leave intact the pressures on that country but would remove from leadership the man who has the strongest emotional interest in resisting a settlement. A coup in Syria is likely to help somewhat, and one in Jordan is most likely to have very damaging effects. The effect of an explosion of the cycle of guerilla raids and reprisals into large-scale war, another kind of surprise, depends on too many contingencies to warrant speculating about, and should probably be put down as a strike against peace.

Forces currently at work against peace include the intransigence of the present regime in Syria, King Hussein's delicate position at home in view of the great and increasing influence of the *Fatah,* Nasser's urge not to foreclose the future of the Palestine issue and to win at least a diplomatic victory over Israel in order to restore his battered prestige, the Soviet Union's public commitment to support the Arabs generally, its strong reluctance to risk alienating the regimes that constitute the mainstay of its position in the region, the mutual suspicion between it and the United States, and finally, Israel's drift into commitments by word and deed that may discourage the development of an Arab incentive for peace or frustrate the prospects of a successful conclusion of peace talks if these should take place.

Forces currently at work in favor of peace include Egypt's postponement of the objective of integral Arab unity to the remote future, King Hussein's willingness to make a final settlement with Israel, the pressure on Egypt to recover its losses and its inability to mount a military effort to recover them without the active participation of the Soviet Union—a situation that has already forced it to come a long way up to the point of agreeing formally to settle the confrontation in accordance with the Security Council November 22 resolution. This trend is enhanced by the emergence of active Soviet interest in a settlement, the strong American interest in peace and open commitment to seek it, and the underlying, longstanding, very strong Israeli urge to achieve peace and gain acceptance by its Arab neighbors, which is apt to prevail over the recent drift if given a realistic chance before too long and if buttressed by sound provisions to reassure Israelis about their security.

These forces for and against peace have not been in a static balance during the whole year that has elapsed since the end of the war—else they would have produced a settled stalemate situation. Rather, each component, although it may have been present from the outset, has changed in magnitude, expression, and relevance, causing the balance to swing up and down continually and, incidentally, deceiving and misleading observers who are disposed to think in simple, unidirectional terms only.

What of the future?

Leaving aside the surprises, which can swing the balance *either* way, there is nothing to suggest that any critical change is apt to originate from the side of Israel or the United States in the near future. On the other hand, our analysis suggests that the seesaw may soon be checked by new developments on the side of the Soviet Union and Egypt. The Egyptian formal diplomatic position having finally reached the point agreed to with the Russians immediately after the war, and having failed to produce the results sought, the two must soon reconsider their policy and make important decisions. Three logical alternatives will confront them: (1) moving on to accept negotiations with Israel aiming at peace; (2) deciding to attempt the recovery of the lost territories by force; and (3) sticking to the present intermediate course but introducing new measures to entice or press the United States to loosen its support for Israel's position and accept something less than a complete peace settlement.

If our analysis is correct, the second alternative may be favored by the Egyptians but will be firmly rejected by the Russians. Egypt alone or with Arab help cannot now or in the near future mount a successful "war of liberation" against Israel; so that a decision to go to war soon would require Russian participation in some form. With the United States' prestige so deeply committed on Israel's side now and in the near future, Russian participation in hostilities would be likely to invite an American response in kind and thus produce an extremely dangerous confrontation that would set back the entire process of détente that has taken place since the Cuban crisis. The difference between the position already accepted by Egypt and the final settlement on which the United States insists is not worth that kind of risk for the Russians.

Trying to build the armed forces of Egypt and its allies as quickly as possible to the point where *they* could contemplate a liberation war by themselves would not be a much more attractive alternative. The United States has already committed itself to keeping Israel's forces up to a deterring level, so that any massive shipments of arms to the Arabs would probably be countered by massive shipments to Israel, and the whole effort would merely accelerate the arms race and cost enormous sums to no avail.

The third alternative—sticking essentially to the present intermediate course—could be conceived either as a strategy or as a tactic. As a strategy it would mean accepting the indefinite prolongation of the present situation, decidedly turning down peace and taking precautions to avoid war under the present circumstances. Such a course would make sense only if the Russians and the Egyptians had reason to believe that they could win the "endurance game" against the United States in the long run, and it is hard to see such reason from our analysis. Otherwise the Egyptians would have no ground to adopt a course that would condemn them to continuing psychological and material strains, unless the Russians committed themselves to help them alter the balance of forces in the years ahead so as to put them in a position to press for the alteration of the *status quo*. This, however, would not be much different for the Russians from the delayed war alternative, and would leave them exposed to the risks of accidental wars and manipulated crises.

As a tactic, the third alternative would mean simply giving the present course another chance before abandoning it. Whatever course the Russians and the Egyptians ultimately choose, they will most probably adopt this tactic both in order to exhaust the possibilities of the present course and to prepare the ground for the alternative chosen. Moreover, if the two should fail to reach an understanding on any alternative course, resort to this tactic would be the logical way for them to temporize and avoid a crisis. In short, it is definitely to be expected that the Soviets and the Egyptians will attempt in the near future various measures designed to press and lure the United States away from Israel's formal position or to alleviate the pressures on themselves, before moving on to another course or facing each other again.

The first alternative—accepting direct negotiations and peace—would probably be the one most favored by the Russians and may not prove unacceptable to the Egyptians if they sense their partners to be unyielding on the other alternatives. But then it is certain that Egypt would insist on no territorial annexation whatsoever by Israel, and that the Russians would agree. This would be the Egyptians' way of scoring a diplomatic "victory" over Israel, a success they badly need to repair their battered prestige, and for both Russia and Egypt it would be a means to detach the United States, who is interested in peace much more than in its territorial terms, from Israel, who has informally come to expect far-reaching adjustments in its favor.

Should the Russians and the Egyptians opt for this course—and the odds seem to be distinctly in its favor—the prospects of peace will be bright, although not easy. Israel will certainly insist on sovereignty over the whole of Jerusalem and on other territorial modifications on the grounds of security, and the United States will probably let the bargaining take its own course until it reaches the predictable crisis point. Ultimately, however, the United States will throw its weight on the same side as the Soviet Union, and both will press hard for a settlement involving minimum territorial alterations. If the pressure should be accompanied by imaginative measures to assure Israel and the Arab states about their future security, it should in the final account work.[9] For the big powers will then find that they have strong allies among many in Israel itself who are weary of confrontation and are eager to be accepted by their neighbors under conditions of peace and reasonable security.

[9] The United States and the Soviet Union could, for example, sponsor a scheme of arms limitations involving all potential suppliers in addition to themselves. China would certainly stay out of such a scheme and may try to subvert it by offering to provide Arab countries with arms; but with the Soviet Union as well as the United States as sponsors, it is very unlikely that any Arab country should wish to defy both superpowers by accepting the Chinese offer. Both the United States and the Soviet Union have expressed interest in such a scheme as part of a comprehensive settlement. The two superpowers could also jointly and singly become formal guarantors of an Arab-Israeli peace treaty through some device like the 1925 Treaty of Locarno. That treaty resolved France's obsession with fear of German *revanchisme*, which had led it to insist on occupying the Rhineland, by providing a collective security guarantee to both France and Germany which persuaded the French to withdraw from the occupied territory and ushered in an era of reconciliation in Europe. The repudiation of the treaty by Hitler would seem to argue against the usefulness of such an arrangement; but in the Arab-Israeli case neither side would be strong enough to defy the other signatories by itself, especially since both depend on outside sources for their armament. The arrangement would, of course, fail if one of the superpowers should find it in its interest to subvert it and promote a resumption of the Arab-Israeli confrontation; but in such circumstances no alternative would be of much avail anyway.

APPENDIX A

SOURCES, METHODS, AND COMMENTS

TABLE I: Egypt

GNP, 1950/1-1962/3: Sources are: (1) Bent Hansen, "The National Outlay of the U.A.R. (Egypt), 1937–39 and 1945–1962/3," Memo No. 377
of the Institute of National Planning, Cairo, 12/8/1963, p. 12; (2) B.
Hansen and G. Marzouk, *Development and Economic Policy in the
U.A.R. (Egypt)*, Amsterdam, 1965.

For the years before 1952/3, Hansen and Marzouk reproduce (p. 10)
a GNP series for civil years:

1950	916
1951	1,016
1952	920
1953	888

By simple interpolation, we obtain the following figures for crop-
years:

1950/1	966
1951/2	973
1952/3	909

The figure thus obtained for the one over-lapping year, that is,
1952/3, is very close to that in the authors' own series: 909 vs. 905.

GNP, 1963/4-1964/5: Source is: U.N., "Monthly Bulletin of Statistics," May 1967, p. 173. Actually the figures are for Gross *Domestic* Product at current market prices rather than Gross National Product; however, the discrepancies between GNP and GDP are very small in the case of Egypt, as can be seen from the following figures:

	GNP	GDP
1959/60	1,372	1,376
1960/1	1,467	1,459
1961/2	1,550	1,513
1962/3	1,679	1,685
1963/4	...	1,888
1964/5	...	2,051

Defense Expenditures: Sources are: (1) "Draft of the State Budget for the Fiscal Year . . ." (in French and English), issues of 1950/1, 1954/5, 1956/7, 1957/8, 1959/60, 1962/3, 1963/4, 1965/6. Also more complete Arabic issues, "Mizaniyyat al Dawlah al Misriyyah" (up to 1957/8) and "Mizaniyyat al Iqlim al Janubi" (thereafter). (2) IBRD Report on U.A.R. Economy, 1965/6, mimeo (this source gives the usually undisclosed figures of actual expenditures in recent years). (3) Egypte/RAU: "Annuaires statistiques"; all issues up to 1960/61 (last available). (4) Numerous other sources such as: National Bank of Egypt, Quarterly Economic Bulletin, various issues; Central Bank of Egypt, "Economic Review," various issues; U.A.R. "Yearbooks," various issues; "The Middle East and North Africa," Europa Publications, London, published every second year, various issues; The Intelligence Unit of the Economist, "Egypt/U.A.R.," quarterly review and annual supplement, various issues; The Institute of National Planning, "Monthly Review of Economic and Social Events," various issues; ibid., Memo No. 209, "U.A.R. State Budget for Fiscal Year '62/3," August 1962; and the like.

The total figures reproduced in Table I under the heading of "Defense Outlays" are the sum of:

(1) Amounts spent by the "Ministry of War/Armed Forces."

(2) The net cost of military production in the Egyptian "Military Factories" (to obtain that net cost, account had to be taken of the civilian production of these factories; furthermore, double-counting had to be avoided, given that a fraction of the "revenues" of these factories is the counterpart of amounts spent by the War Ministry).

(3) A fraction of the expenditures of the Ministry of Interior. The outlays of this Ministry are divided between five departments: (1) General Office; (2) the Police College; (3) Police and "provincial administra-

tion"; (4) Gendarmerie; (5) Fire Department. Items (2), (3), and (4) usually account for about 75 percent of the total expenditures of the Ministry. In addition, the Prisons Department is a separate heading. Consequently, we have imputed to Defense: (1) 75 percent of the expenditures of the Ministry of Interior, and (2) the small allocation for the Prisons Department.

Thus for example:

	1956/7
Ministry of War	83.4
Military factories	3.3
Ministry of Interior	9.6[1]
	89.7

[1] 75 percent of 11.5 + 1.0 for Prisons Dept.

(4) Non recurrent items of a clear military nature; thus, for example, the War Ministry's "special allocation for emergency in Palestine" in the early years.

TABLE II: *Israel*

GNP: The source is: "Statistical Abstract of Israel," 1966, pp. 156–7. The figure for 1966 is an estimate derived from a slightly different GNP series published by the U.N., "Monthly Statistical Bulletin," Sept. 1967, p. 67.

Defense Expenditures: The sources are: (1) "Statistical Abstract of Israel," 1953/4 to 1966 issues; (2) for the years 1955–57, the above source is incomplete, certain expenditures incurred in connection with the Sinai campaign having remained undisclosed. So, in calendar years 1956 and 1957, we took the figures given by economist Don Patinkin in "The Israel Economy: The First Decade," and the Falk Project for Economic Research in Israel, 4th Report, 1957 and 1958. The figure for 1958 (calendar year) was obtained by combining data from the first source with the figure given by Patinkin.

The figure for defense outlays in each year is the sum of the following elements:

(1) Amounts spent by the "Ministry of Defense."

(2) The amounts reproduced under the heading of "Special budgets," both in the ordinary and in the development budget. Article 4

APPENDIX A

of the "Israel Draft-Budget Law, 1965-6" (in Hebrew) explicitly says that expenditures under headings 28 and 91—that is, special budgets on current and development account—will be allocated by the Knesset Finance Committee, on the basis of governmental recommendations, to: (a) the defense budget, and (b) the "special reserve" (p. 5). About this "special reserve," the same source says that the Ministry of Finance decides the objects to which these funds will be allocated. It is authorized, the source goes on to say, to use this special reserve for any purpose in the development section of the general budget. Thus, it is more than plausible that these secret development expenditures have some military relevancy (atomic research, rocketry, and the like). Consequently, there seems to be a clear case for reckoning the totality of both "special budgets" as a part of defense.

(3) Amounts spent on "police." It is granted that the case for reckoning such security outlays as part of defense is less clear for Israel than for the Arab nations. Nevertheless, we have decided to include them for the sake of symmetry. As an example, outlays in millions of Israeli pounds were as follows:

	1962/3	1963/4
Ministry of Defense	410.0	545.0
Special budget in ordinary budget	22.0	30.0
Special budget in development budget	104.0	123.7
Police	48.1	55.2
Total	584.1	753.9

The Israeli fiscal year goes from April 1 to March 31. Since GNP is given for calendar years, the defense expenditures had to be adjusted to a calendar-year basis.

TABLE III: Syria

GNP: The sources are (for GNP and the "deflator" used): "Statistical Abstract of the Arab Republic of Syria," 1962, 1963, and 1965 issues; "Economic Developments in the Middle East," U.N., N.Y., 1958; "Yearbook of National Accounts Statistics," U.N., N.Y., 1964 issue.

There seems to be no data available on the Syrian GNP at current prices, and only two series for GNP at *constant* 1956 prices are published. A first series, published in 1962, "Statistical Abstract," covers the years 1953 to 1962; then, starting with the 1963 "Statistical Abstract," a new series was published; it is said to be based on revised data for agriculture and communications. Consequently, we first had to link the two series in the following way: For 1956 to 1965, the revised series was used and, for the early years, the figures of the first series were adjusted to a comparable basis, since it was found that, for the overlapping years, the two series bore a very close relationship.

To derive GNP at current prices from the constant price series, a "deflator" had to be used. For 1953 to 1955, such a deflator was obtained from two National Income series (one at current prices and the other at constant prices). For 1957 to 1965, the deflator used was derived from two series for "Gross Domestic Capital Formation" (one at current and the other at constant prices). The deflator for these latter years is, of course, only an approximation to the true, but unknown, GNP deflator. Were it to be used for the purpose of economic analysis, this would be much too crude and uncertain a procedure, but, in the absence of better data, it may do for our limited purposes.

The procedure adopted to adjust the Syrian GNP for the years 1958 to 1961 so as to eliminate the effect of the slump due to the union with Egypt and, to a lesser extent, adverse climatic conditions was simply to take the linear trend of the Syrian GNP. This trend was estimated on the basis of a 1953–1963 sample by means of a simple regression, yielding the following equation: $Y_x = 1,826.86 + 146.78\ T_x$, where Y_x = GNP at constant prices in year X and $t_x = X$-1950.

Defense outlays: The sources used were primarily the "Statistic Abstract of the Arab Republic of Syria," 1959 to 1963 issues. Starting with the 1964 issue, the "Statistical Abstract" no longer disclosed any indication about the sums allocated to the "Ministry of War." So the sources used for the later years are: (1) "L'économie et les finances de la Syrie et des pays arabes," Beyrouth-Damas, December 1966 and March 1967; (2) the Intelligence Unit of the Economist, "1966 Annual Supplement on Syria, Lebanon, Jordan."

"Defense Outlays," as defined in Table III, comprise the amounts spent by the "Ministry of War," on "civil defense", on "gendarmerie" and by the "Directorate of Police." (Starting in 1958/9, the latter two items were consolidated under the heading of "Interior Security Forces"). Starting in 1961/62, the figures for the newly created "Allowances and Security Department" were included. The 1964 figure for that Department could not be found; consequently, the average for

1963 and 1965 was taken (1963 = 27.8; 1965 = 18.5; average = 23.2). All figures were put on a calendar-year basis by means of simple interpolation (over the years, the definition of the Syrian "fiscal year" underwent many changes).

TABLE IV: Iraq

GNP: The sources are: (1) "Yearbook of National Accounts Statistics," U.N., N.Y., 1965; (2) *idem*, 1966; (3) K. Haseeb, *The National Income of Iraq, 1953–61*, Oxford, 1964. The figure for 1965 is a projection on the basis of the average growth rate of GNP over the preceding six years.

Defense Outlays: Sources are: (1) "Statistical Abstract of Iraq," 1957 to 1964 edition; (2) "Middle East Economic Digest," April 1964 and October 1965; (3) The Intelligence Unit of the Economist, "1966 Annual Supplement for Iraq."

Defense expenditures are made up of the amounts spent by the Iraqi "Ministry of Defense" and the "Directorate of Police." No amounts were imputed for the "army factories" attached to the Ministry of Defense, for a continuous series could not be compiled. However, both expenditures and revenues of these factories were extremely small in those years for which data could be found (for example, in 1962/3: expenditures = .039 I.D. million; revenues = .020). All figures being given for the Iraqi fiscal year (March to April), they were adjusted to a calendar-year basis for the purpose of comparability with GNP.

TABLE V: Jordan

GNP: An official and continuous series for GNP exists for the years since 1959 only (source: Hashemite Kingdom of Jordan, Department of Statistics, *The National Accounts, 1959–1965*, Amman, 1966). Furthermore, two estimates are available for the years 1953 and 1954 (source: IBRD, *The Economic Development of Jordan*, Baltimore, 1957; estimates made by the Economic Research Institute of the American University of Beirut). As for the intervening years—1955 to 1958—a series had to be constructed. This we did by using the only price-index available on a continuous basis for Jordan, that is, the Amman wholesale price-index, to "inflate" another series for GNP at constant 1962 prices (source: A.I.D., "Estimated Annual Growth Rates," Statistical and Report Division, April 5, 1965, mimeo; *ibid.*, "Gross National Products, Growth Rates and Trend Data," June 15, 1966, mimeo). From a strictly economic point of view, this is of course a questionable procedure, but, given that discrepancies in overlapping years are small, it seems to be acceptable for our limited purpose.

Defense Outlays: The sources used are: (1) "Statistical Yearbook of Jordan," 1958, 1960, 1963, and 1964 issues; (2) "Middle East Economic Digest," London May, 1966, p. 28. Figures refer to "Defense and Police" and were adjusted to a calendar-year basis (the Jordanian fiscal year ends on March 31).

TABLE VI: Lebanon

GNP: Estimates of the Lebanese GNP are available for the years 1954 and 1957 (source: IRFED Report, "Besoins et possibilités de développement du Liban," Beirut, undated), as well as for 1962 and 1963 (source: A.I.D., Statistical and Reports Division, No. 5.5, '64 and No. 2.19, '64, mimeo). For the other years, the GNP figures were constructed on the basis of a series for National Income at current factor cost (sources: IRFED Report, *op.cit.;* "Economic Developments in the Middle East, 1961/3, U.N., N.Y., 1964; "Monthly Bulletin of Statistics," U.N., N.Y., May 1967, p. 172). Since the authors of the IRFED Report write that "it is likely that GNP exceeds National Income by approximately 15%," we have simply adjusted National Income data by that percentage to complete the GNP series. Finally, the figures for 1965 and 1966 are projections based on the average growth rate of the preceding six years.

Defense Outlays: This series is made up of the allocations for the "Ministry of Defense," for the "Gendarmerie," and for "General Security." Whereas the series for the "Ministry of Defense" is complete (source: U.N. "Yearbooks," 1961, 1964, and 1965 issues; "Middle East Economic Digest—Statistical and Documentary Service," May 1959 and November 1963), the figures for "gendarmerie" and "general security" could be found for the years 1954–1958 and 1962–1963 only (sources: Raja S. Himadeh, *The Fiscal System of Lebanon*, Beirut, 1961; "Etude mensuelle sur l'économie et le marché libanais," Beirut, No. 14, 1964). Consequently, the aggregate series was completed by extrapolation on the basis of the past observed relationship between the expenditures of the "Ministry of Defense," on the one hand, and "gendarmerie plus General Security", on the other.

TABLE VII: Kuwait

GNP: Official GNP figures exist only for the five years 1962/63 to 1966/67, where the year goes from April 1 to March 31 (sources: (1) State of Kuwait, Planning Board, "Statistical Abstract," 1965, pp. 91–3; (2) "Monthly Bulletin of Statistics," U.N., N.Y., Sept., 1967, p. 177). For the earlier years, the GNP series was constructed on the basis of Kuwait's oil revenues (sources: (1) The Intelligence Unit of the Economist, "Middle East Oil and the Arabian Peninsula," Annual Supplement, 1963; (2) *ibid.*, 1966). This admittedly roundabout and approximate method may be justified by pointing to the importance of oil in the Kuwaiti economy; a further check on its validity is provided by two National Income estimates for 1959 and 1962/3 (IBRD, *The Economic Development of Kuwait*, Baltimore, 1965). On the basis of 1959 = 100, we have a direct estimate of 125.0 in 1962/63 (April 1 to March 31) as against an indirect estimate based on oil revenues of 125.5 for 1962 (calendar year).

Defense Outlays: Figures refer to "Defense and Security" (that is, Defense and Interior Ministries). The sources used are: (1) IBRD Report, *op.cit.*, p. 73; (2) "Statistical Abstract", *op.cit.*; (3) "L'économie et les finances de la Syrie et des pays arabes", Beirut/Damas, Oct. '66, p. 123. The definition of the Kuwaiti fiscal year having undergone a change in 1959–60, the figures were adjusted to a comparable basis.

TABLE VIII: Kuwaiti Reserves

Source: IBRD Report, *op.cit.*, p. 81. The authors of that report comment: "The 1961 mission (of the IBRD) estimated that about 25 percent of the oil revenue earned since 1950 had been invested (by the Government in foreign State revenue-yielding securities). This percentage was actually a little higher in 1960/61 (25.8 percent), but it fell to a rate of about 11 percent in the following two fiscal years."

TABLE IX: Saudi Arabia

GNP: The only source giving a continuous GNP series is Herbert B. Woolley, "Past and Prospective Growth in Saudi Arabia," Riyadh, Sept. 30, '65, mimeo. For the years 1381–1383H (1962–64), GNP has been projected on the basis of oil consumption in Saudi Arabia, since the author of the above-mentioned study found a very close correlation between oil consumption and GNP in the 1370–1380H decade and used the same method for his projections to 1970 and 1975. The figures for 1384–1386H (1965–67) are our estimates based on an average growth rate of 11 percent in the preceding six years.

Defense Outlays: The sources consulted are: (1) "Middle East Economic Digest—Statistical and Documentary Supplement," Feb. '58, Jan. '60, Jan. '61, Jan. '62, Jan. '64, Nov. '64, and Nov. '65; (2) "L'économie et les finances de la Syrie et des pays arabes," Beirut/Damas, Nov. '66, p. 130, and Oct. '66, pp. 41–42. "Defense Outlays" are the sum of the following headings:
(a) Military Division of the Presidency of the Council of Ministers
(b) National Guard
(c) Intelligence
(d) Ministry of Interior (only "Civil Defense" and "General Security")
(e) Royal Body Guard
(f) Mujahideen Department (that is, Dept. of "Holy Warriors")
(g) Frontier forces (in early years: "Coast Guards")
(h) "National Defense, Special Allowance"
(i) Emergency expenditures (sometimes called "contingencies")
(j) Ministry of Defense and Aviation (excluding civil aviation and Saudi Arabian airlines).

Looking at the figures from year to year, it is apparent that budget appropriations are often shifted from one heading to the other. For 1386/7H (1967/8), the only figures available were for the most important headings (which, in previous years, made up 80 percent or more of the total defense expenditures); the appropriations for the missing minor headings were estimated on the basis of the preceding years. Since the Saudi Arabian fiscal year starts at mid-year (Hegira era), defense outlays have been converted to a full-year basis.

TABLE X: Comparative Defense Burdens

The estimates for the countries other than those of the Middle East were taken from the *Military Balance*, by the Institute for Strategic Studies, London; various issues. Comparing the Institute's estimates for Middle Eastern countries with those which we derived through a more detailed scrutinization of the sources, it appears that the Institute's estimates may sometimes be rather widely off-target. Thus, the figures of Table X should be taken *cum grano sali*.

TABLES XI, XII, and XIII: Defense Outlays, Investment, Education

See above, Tables I, II, III, IV, and V (sources for GNP also give investment figures; sources for defense outlays also give figures for education expenditures).

Figures 14 and 15; Tables XIV, XV, XVII: Tables A and B (below). Defense Expenditures in Content-Value Dollars

The series of defense outlays in 1962 dollars used in these figures and tables were derived in the following way: For each country, we had two GNP series, one at current prices and one at constant prices. This enabled us to derive the implicit deflators: (GNP at current prices)/(GNP at constant prices). The next step involved putting all implicit deflators on the base, 1962 = 1.00. In the case of Saudi Arabia and Kuwait, no constant-price GNP series was available; oil production measured in 1,000 tons was consequently used as a proxy. For Syria, the deflator used for the years 1955–1965 was the implicit deflator for capital formation, and the rather large fluctuations of this deflator lead us to think that it may not be a good proxy for the implicit GNP deflator; consequently, the data for Syria should not be trusted too much insofar as the year-to-year variations are concerned. The next step involved the use of the implicit GNP-deflators thus obtained to deflate the series of defense outlays in current national currencies. Finally, these constant-price defense expenditure series were converted into dollars by means of the respective 1962 exchange rates. The year 1962 was chosen as the base-year in the belief that the exchange-rates in that year did not distort too much the real purchasing-power parities, for the 1962 rates were post-devaluation rates in the case of Egypt and Israel, and there are some reasons to think that the new rates adopted just after a devaluation had not yet begun to undergo the process of erosion due to chronic inflation. It is clear that the procedure just described is at best an approximation: The implicit GNP-deflators are almost certainly not identical with the true defense-outlay deflators. Consequently, the deflated series in national currencies are probably but an approximation to the "real" content of defense spending. However, the procedure used is justified to the extent that one is interested in the "economic cost" of defense spending, for the resulting series are really in GNP-equivalent units. Finally, there is no assurance that even the 1962 exchange rates correctly reflect purchasing-power parities, so that the final series in 1962 dollars, when used for inter-country comparisons, give an indication of the order of magnitude involved but should not be trusted down to the last decimal point.

TABLE XVI; TABLE C (below): GNP Growth Rates

The sources used for the "real" GNP series are the same as those used for current GNP; see Tables I–XVII above. However, in the case of Saudi Arabia and Jordan, no series of GNP at constant market prices could be found. Consequently, we used oil production measured in 1,000 tons to derive the average compound growth rates for these two countries. This may be deemed an acceptable substitute, considering how large oil production looms in Saudi Arabia and even more so in Kuwait.

ECONOMIC COST OF THE ARMS RACE IN TERMS OF MAXIMUM FOREGONE GROWTH

For the years 1946 to 1962/3, Hansen and Marzouk (*op. cit.*, p. 8) have found the incremental capital/output ratio to be about 3:1 as can be seen from the parameters of the equation they estimated:

$$\Delta GNP = -0.027 + 0.326\ I$$

where ΔGNP = change in GNP and I = gross investment. In words, it would take an investment of about 3 £E. to increase total product by 1 £E. The above equation was used to compute the hypothetical increase in the Egyptian GNP had all defense outlays over and above 4 percent of GNP in each respective year between 1955 and 1964 been used for investment. Finally, the implicit average compound *per capita* GNP growth rate was derived for both the real and the hypothetical GNP figures.

The contribution of capital to the growth of Israel's total product has been estimated to lie between 13 and 24 percent for the period 1950–58, according to one source (Don Patinkin, "The Israel Economy: the First Decade" in The Falk Economic Research Project in Israel, 4th Report, 1957-58; p. 75, table 26), and between 24 and 36 percent for the period 1950–62, according to another source (Nadav Halevi and Ruth Klinov-Malul, "The Development of the Israel Economy," Vol. I, Jerusalem, 1965, p. 151). Using the average estimate of 24 percent (a lower value, it will be noted, than for Egypt), the hypothetical average compound GNP growth rate for Israel, under the assumption that all defense outlays over and above 4 percent were used for investment purposes, was computed in exactly the same fashion as for Egypt.

TABLE A: Comparative; "Real" Defense Expenditures; Israel and Each Arab Country

Year	Israel[1]	Egypt[2]	Syria	Iraq	Jordan	Kuwait	Lebanon	Saudi Arabia
			(million constant-value $)					
1950	40.9	...	...	...	...	...	...	...
1951	60.3 (100)[3]	114.2 (189)[3]	...	...	...	...	...	...
1952	58.6 (100)	121.8 (208)	...	...	...	...	...	...
1953	49.8 (100)	116.8 (235)	29.1 (58)	59.6 (120)	34.2 (69)	...	11.4 (23)	...
1954	64.8 (100)	129.0 (199)	31.5 (49)	65.8 (102)	34.2 (57)	...	12.5 (19)	...
1955	72.3 (100)	182.8 (253)	35.9 (50)	65.5 (91)	30.2 (42)	...	14.7 (20)	...
1956	161.9 (100)	217.6 (134)	49.4 (31)	80.1 (49)	38.6 (24)	...	18.6 (11)	...
1957	113.6 (100)	185.9 (164)	50.0 (44)	86.2 (76)	41.7 (37)	...	18.7 (16)	...
1958	116.8 (100)	170.9 (146)	91.3 (78)	89.0 (76)	45.6 (39)	33.9 (29)	19.8 (17)	...
1959	151.8 (100)	188.2 (124)	96.1 (63)	100.2 (66)	55.4 (36)	35.0 (23)	19.6 (13)	88.1 (58)
1960	161.1 (100)	214.3 (133)	77.5 (48)	121.0 (75)	51.5 (32)	43.1 (27)	20.9 (13)	77.9 (48)
1961	173.7 (100)	241.1 (139)	75.1 (43)	128.2 (74)	52.1 (30)	43.4 (25)	24.1 (14)	72.0 (41)
1962	218.1 (100)	285.1 (131)	91.6 (42)	135.2 (62)	53.2 (24)	52.4 (24)	28.0 (13)	80.3 (37)
1963	251.8 (100)	392.8 (160)	106.6 (42)	167.4 (66)	56.6 (22)	58.0 (23)	30.9 (12)	103.3 (41)
1964	295.4 (100)	501.4 (170)	99.3 (34)	199.1 (67)	56.6 (19)	59.4 (20)	34.0 (12)	129.5 (44)
1965	313.6 (100)	...	101.5 (32)	234.9 (75)	54.6 (17)	60.5 (19)	36.9 (12)	150.9 (48)

[1] Figures for Israel include amounts imputed for arms received free from West Germany between 1959 and 1964.

[2] For purposes of comparability, the figures for Egypt were converted to a calendar-year basis; it must be pointed out that such a procedure tends to "smoothen" increases and decreases; only in the case of a perfect trend will there be no such smoothening.

[3] Figures in parentheses are indices with the base: Israel = 100 in each year.

TABLE B: *Total Defense Expenditures Over Various Periods (million constant-value $)*

Country	1955-65 Israel = 100		1955-64 Israel = 100		1959-65 Israel = 100		1959-64 Israel = 100	
Israel	2,030	100	1,717	100	1,566	100	1,252	100
Egypt	...	...	2,580	150	...	...	1,823	146
Syria	874	43	773	45	648	41	546	44
Iraq	1,407	69	1,172	68	1,086	69	851	68
Jordan	536	26	482	28	380	24	325	26
Kuwait	...	...	...	...	352	22	291	23
Lebanon	266	13	229	13	194	12	158	13
Saudi Arabia	...	...	...	...	702	45	551	44
TOTAL	...		...		...		5,797	

TABLE C: *Average Annual Growth Rate of GNP* [1]

Country	1953-63	1954-58	1959-63
Israel	11.3	11.8	10.8
Egypt [2]	4.5	2.9	6.2
Iraq	6.6	7.2	6.1
Syria	5.8	3.1	8.5
Jordan	12.7	16.4	9.1
Lebanon	4.4	1.6	7.3
Kuwait	...	...	6.9
Saudi Arabia	7	4	10

[1] Gross National Product at constant market prices.

[2] 1953/4-1962/3; 1953/4-1957/8; 1958/9-1962/3

APPENDIX B

THE ARMED FORCES OF EGYPT, SYRIA, JORDAN, AND ISRAEL ON THE EVE OF THE WAR [1]

EGYPT

Whereas Egypt's total armed forces as of the middle of 1965 were estimated to number between 245,000 and 265,000 men, almost all evaluations published during the crisis that preceded the Six Day War quote a figure of 300,000 to 310,000—a not inconsiderable expansion, it would seem.[2] However, a closer examination shows that this expansion in Egypt's armed forces was largely illusory, for it concerned mostly the "national guards and reserves," which, from a level of 50,000 to 70,000 in 1965, reached a strength of 120,000 as of 1966-1967, whereas the regular forces showed but a slight increase from 180,000 to 190,000. The effective value of these "national guards and reserves" as fighting units is a matter of serious doubt on account of lack of training, encadrement, and equipment, and it is at least a plausible assump-

---

[1] Except where references are specifically mentioned, estimates are based on the collation of a large variety of open sources and the author's judgment.

[2] Thus: H. Baldwin in *The New York Times*, May 24, 1967; also *Boston Globe*, July 9, 1967; *Der Spiegel*, May 29, 1967. All these estimates are probably derived from: *The Military Balance 1966-67*, The Institute for Strategic Studies, London, September, 1966. The figures are given as of August, 1966.

tion that the only battle-worthy units among them were concentrated in Yemen where they accounted for almost half the Egyptian expeditionary force (20,000 men out of some 50,000).[3]

As to the remaining national guard and reserve units, it is probably realistic to consider them as nothing more than some sort of "Home Guard," whose main function was to ensure internal security, and which should not be reckoned as part of Egypt's "mobilizable and fieldable" armed forces except in the event of an Israeli drive into the Nile Valley or of protracted static warfare. Thus, Egypt's effective military establishment on the eve of the war numbered about 210,000 men—190,000 regulars plus 20,000 national guards and reserves—an increase of 15,000 over 1965.[4]

Of these, the regular army accounted for some 160,000, of which about 30,000 were in Yemen prior to the middle of May 1967. The army was organized into two armored divisions (the one still forming in 1965 had completed this process), six motorized infantry divisions (three more than in 1965), plus a Palestinian "division" of two brigades and an independent parachute brigade that was stationed in Yemen before the crisis.[5] Finally, one should also mention the testimony of an Egyptian general who, while in Israeli captivity, stated that on the eve of the war, 400 to 500 Soviet military experts were serving as advisers to the Egyptian forces.

Egypt's regular forces were remarkably well and abundantly equipped with the most modern conventional weapons produced by the Soviet Union and its East European allies. We have little data on the Egyptian artillery. Israel's Foreign Minister, speaking at the U.N., said that, "since 1955, Egypt alone has received from the U.S.S.R. 540 field guns, 130 medium guns, 200 120-mm mortars, and 695 anti-tank guns."[6] These figures seem to be not incompatible with the eight to nine artillery brigades that we were able to identify in Sinai. Some of that equipment had arrived very recently in Egypt; thus, for example, the new 122-mm howitzers, captured in Sinai and designated as D-30 by the Russians, were so new that the Egyptians had not had time to

[3] *The Military Balance 1966–67, op. cit.*

[4] This figure tallies with the estimates supplied just before the war by Israeli sources: *Le Monde*, Sélection hebdomadaire, June 22–28, 1967. However, no indication was found as to whether these figures include units of the Palestinian Liberation Army.

[5] An Egyptian division amounts to 12,000 men, not counting supporting units (*New York Times*, May 21, 1967); the national guards and reserves were said to be nominally organized into seven to eight divisions (*New York Times*, May 21, 1967).

[6] *New York Times*, June 20, 1967.

paint them in a desert color. Israeli experts said that this type of howitzer was a superb artillery weapon with a range of almost 19,000 yards. Further, it also turned out that the Egyptian army had recently received the newest Russian "Shmell" anti-tank wire-guided missile (known to N.A.T.O. experts as the "Snapper"). These missiles are mounted in groups of four at the back of a truck-like vehicle and their hollow-charge warheads are capable of penetrating the thickest tank armor at a range of up to 2,500 yards.[7]

Furthermore, the Egyptian field units had a wide range of equipment to protect them against gas and radioactivity. As the Israelis later found out in Sinai, Egyptian soldiers carried a Soviet-made gas mask and a special protective blouse to be used against certain kinds of gas and then discarded. A gas-identification kit was carried by each battalion. It could identify all the known kinds of nerve gas, including a brand-new type known to military experts as Soman. It also could identify mustard and other more conventional gases. The Russians also had provided the Egyptians (and the Syrians) with anti-gas and anti-radioactivity air filters for use in bunkers and emplacements. Moreover, each Egyptian battalion was equipped with a Geiger counter for measurement of radioactivity from nuclear weapons. At the brigade level, there was a truck-drawn mobile decontamination van, which had equipment to decontaminate against "all bacteriological and chemical warfare" as well as nuclear warfare, according to an Israeli account of what the Egyptians left behind in Sinai. It could be used to decontaminate weapons and equipment as well as men. At the division level, the Egyptians had a unit designed to decontaminate terrain.[8] The Israelis did not find in Sinai any equipment for generating or delivering poison gas. However, that the Egyptians have such a capability, and that they used it in Yemen against the Royalists, is a matter put beyond controversy by an official and public statement of the International Red Cross.

Turning now to Egyptian armor, it appears that in the two years after 1965 the Egyptian tank and assault-gun fleet had undergone a considerable qualitative as well as quantitative improvement. As of mid-1966, that fleet consisted of some 1,060 tanks composed as follows (figures in parentheses for mid-1965): [9]

---

[7] It is known that in the course of the fighting in Sinai one such missile knocked out an Israeli tank; the three other recorded launchings at Israeli armor all missed. (*New York Times*, June 27, 1967.)

[8] *New York Times*, June 27, 1967.

[9] *The Military Balance 1966–67, op. cit.*

350 medium T-34 tanks (400)
450 medium T-54 and T-54B tanks (350)
A few medium T-55 tanks (none)
60 heavy Josef Stalin III tanks (60)
150 SU-100 assault guns (150)
30 Mk-III medium Centurion tanks (30) [10]
20 AMX-13 light tanks (20) [10]

On the eve of the war, Israeli sources put the total number at 1,300 tanks, which suggests a not unreasonable increase after mid-1966.[11]

Turning to Egypt's air force, we notice here, too, a great increase, both quantitative and qualitative, over 1965. Because of the importance of air power, Egypt's capability has received more than ordinary scrutiny so that two series of figures are available for fighting planes, one for mid-1966 and one for May 1967. They are as follows when compared to mid-1965:[12]

	Mid-'65	Mid-'66	May '67
Sukhoi-7 supersonic fighter-bombers	–	a few	55
MIG-21 supersonic interceptors	52	130	163
MIG-19 supersonic all-weather fighters	80	80	40
MIG-15/17 subsonic fighter-bombers	150	150	100
Tu-16 medium bombers	25–30	30	30
IL-28 light bombers	72	40	43
TOTAL: Fighters	282	360+	358
Bombers	97–102	70	73

Especially striking is the large increase in the number of MIG-21's and Sukhoi-7's. Causally linked or not, this build-up followed Mr. Kosygin's visit to Egypt in May 1966. The decrease in the number of MIG-19's seems strange and may be due to the transfer of some of these planes to other countries, perhaps as a counterpart to increased shipments of MIG-21 and Sukhoi-7 planes (the Soviets have used Egypt as a base for re-export of military hardware to Algeria, for example). In any case, as a day fighter, the MIG-19 is not as effective as

[10] With the reserve units.

[11] Le Monde, Sélection hebdomadaire, June 22–28, 1967.

[12] Mid-1966: The Military Balance 1966–67; May 1967: New York Times, July 11, 1967, probably based on information from official U.S. sources.

the MIG-21, and its all-weather capability is of little import to the Egyptians, given the climate of the region.[13]

In the field of anti-aircraft defense, the Egyptian forces possessed vast quantities of Soviet 57-mm and 85-mm AA guns plus a number of Soviet SAM-2 "Guideline" surface-to-air missiles distributed in 27 sites over the Delta, the Nile Valley, and Sinai.[14]

As the events of the war proved, the Egyptian program for the local manufacturing of medium-range surface-to-surface missiles turned out to be a complete failure because of over-ambitious planning, lack of experience and know-how, ill-judged purchases of equipment abroad, and personal differences between many of the leading German scientists involved.

Finally, it seems, there was no accretion to the Egyptian naval forces after mid-1965 (see Chapter V), or at least no confirmed information on that score has come to light. Israel's Foreign Minister told the U.N. General Assembly that, starting in 1955, Egypt had received seven destroyers and fourteen submarines from the Soviet Union; but other estimates give six destroyers, four of which were ex-Soviet, and nine submarines, all ex-Soviet, as of mid-1965.

SYRIA

Much less attention has been paid to the development of the Syrian than the Egyptian armed forces. Estimates published just prior to the war show practically no change when compared with the figures for mid-1965.[15] Thus, the Syrian armed forces comprised about 60,000 to 70,000 regulars and 40,000 to 45,000 reserves. As in the case of Egypt, the battle-worthiness of these reserves is very dubious, and they probably added little or nothing to the fieldable forces. Just before the war, the Israelis put forward the figure of 65,000 for Syria's forces.[16]

The regular Syrian army of some 50,000 men comprised the same number of brigades and regiments as in 1965 (two armored, two motorized, five infantry brigades, and six artillery regiments) and had subsequently received the Soviet 130-mm medium gun, with its almost 29,000 yard range and its 70-lb projectiles. Neither does there seem to have been any drastic change in the Syrian tank fleet, which consisted of about 400 T-34's and T-54's, plus 50 SU-100 assault guns, as of Au-

[13] *Jane's All the World's Aircraft,* London, different editions.

[14] General Hod, interviewed on NBC-TV, July 23, 1967.

[15] H. Baldwin, *New York Times,* May 24, 1967; *Boston Globe,* July 9, 1967.

[16] *Le Monde,* Sélection hebdomadaire, June 22–28, 1967.

gust 1965. Israeli sources gave for 1967 an estimate of 500, including assault guns.[17]

As to the Syrian air force, it was estimated that, as of mid-1965, it comprised the following planes: 26 MIG-21's, 48 MIG-17's, and 4 Il-28's.

It is interesting to compare these figures with a statement by General Mordechai Hod, the O/C Israel Air Force, on the morrow of the war to the effect that "[Syria and Iraq] had about 40 MIG-21's, 40 MIG-17's, and a limited number of bombers."[18] Since Iraq is known to have had the equivalent of one squadron of MIG-21's, a total of 40 for both countries signifies that the above estimate for mid-1965 must have kept its validity as of May 1967. With the MIG-15/17's, however, there seems to be a considerable disparity in estimates since Iraq had one squadron of them in 1965 in addition to Syria's reported 48. The explanation is probably that Hod had in mind operational planes, whereas the 1965 estimate refers to number of planes in the possession of Syria. Such a low degree of usability of equipment is not uncommon in most Arab air forces.

JORDAN

An estimate of the total armed forces of Jordan is made difficult by the existence of the national guard, which, in 1965, comprised some 30,000 men as compared with a regular army of 38,000 men. Plans existed at the time to expand the army by incorporating into it part of the national guard. This seems to be what indeed took place in the meantime, since most reports on the eve of the war put the strength of the Jordanian army at some 50,000 to 55,000 men grouped into eleven brigades, two of them armored, plus support units. In addition there were reserves totaling 15,000 to 20,000 men, comprising the remnants of the national guard not amalgamated in the regular army. These half-trained Palestinians cannot be reckoned as part of Jordan's fieldable forces.

As far as armor is concerned, most reports said that Jordan had around 200 tanks on the eve of the war, of which some 70 to 80 were Centurions and the rest presumably M-48 Pattons received from the U.S., which had agreed to supply a total of 200. Our estimate for mid-

---

[17] *Le Monde*, Sélection hebdomadaire, June 22–28, 1967.
[18] *Jerusalem Post*, July 12, 1967.

1965 was 270 to 280 tanks. Israeli sources gave an estimate of 300 tanks on the eve of the war,[19] and King Hussein seemed to concur with this estimate when he stated shortly after the war that his armored forces amounted to "300 modern tanks, including 250 new Patton M-48's from the United States."[20] The fact that the King gave a figure for the Pattons that is higher by 50 than what the United States had reportedly promised him is puzzling.

By the eve of the war the Jordanian air force had undergone no change since mid-1965 and comprised 20 British-built Hawker Hunter jets, of which two were at the time in Britain for servicing.[21] None of the promised 36 refurbished American supersonic F-104 fighters had been received by Jordan when the fighting broke out, and prospective Jordanian pilots were still training in the United States—together with prospective Israeli pilots for the Skyhawk light bombers also ordered from the U.S. The first F-104's were to have been delivered in July, 1967.[22]

ISRAEL

The Israeli armed forces on the eve of the war added up to a total of some 275,000 to 300,000. Of that number, 71,000 were regular officers and soldiers and the rest reserves that had been called up in stages starting on May 14. Whereas most Arab reserves cannot be counted as part of the fieldable forces, the bulk of the Israeli reserves were as usable as the regular forces. It is said that the response of the reserves to the call to active duty exceeded 100 percent; people who were exempt from active service or from service in first line units showed up and begged to be incorporated.

The army accounted for some 250,000 to 265,000, of whom 60,000 were regulars. The latter constituted several entirely regular brigades and provided "scaffoldings" and stiffening elements to the reserve units. In all, the army was organized into some 24 to 26 "first line" brigades, of which 11 were armored and four were crack paratroopers, plus about 14 brigade-equivalents of "second line" troops and regional defense forces, plus support and auxiliary units.

[19] *Le Monde,* Sélection hebdomadaire, June 22–28, 1967.

[20] *New York Times,* June 26, 1967.

[21] Statement by King Hussein, *New York Times,* July 14, 1967. This was also the Israeli estimate.

[22] *Ibid.*

No estimate of any sort has ever been published about the Israeli artillery. From the fragmentary evidence of battle accounts and hopefully informed guesses, we estimate that Israel must have used about a dozen heavy mortar and field artillery brigades in addition to the integral support sections of infantry units. Virtually nothing is known about the quality of the equipment except that it had been greatly improved in recent years but still included many obsolescent field pieces, that generally speaking Israel's field artillery in Sinai was outnumbered and outranged by Egypt's, although the heavy mortars, largely made in Israel, were first rate.

Amazing as it may seem in the light of the reports that had been coming out of Yemen for a long time that the Egyptians were using gas against the Royalists, no adequate defensive provisions had been made in the Israeli army against gas warfare. Israel, it seems, counted exclusively on the deterrent capability it undoubtedly had until practically the last moment, when it made frantic efforts to secure a modicum of defensive equipment.[23] An airlift from France to Israel, which went into operation around May 15, ferried, among other items, loads of anti-gas equipment.[24] Israel also hastily "bought" (in fact, it was a gift) 20,000 gas masks for civilians from West Germany over the opposition of Defense Minister Schröder. The masks were delivered on June 3 and were allegedly shipped back one month later. Jordan also placed a similar "order" with the Federal Republic, but the war broke out before any decision was reached.

Israeli armor did not seem to have increased much since mid-1965. Its strength on the eve of the war is estimated as follows:[25]

[23] See in this connection the very interesting report of an Israeli reserve officer in *Life,* Special Edition on the War, June, 1967: "Two days before the war started, I was called with the commanders of other units and given some very quick anti-gas warfare training. I must say that we were not prepared for such a thing. We were told not to inform the soldiers of the possibility of a gas attack because there was no equipment and, therefore, it was useless to create a panic. My orders were that the moment I saw gas striking my unit, I was to inform headquarters so that perhaps other units could be saved. During the [subsequent] shelling I had to take risks in order to see if there was evidence of gas coming out of the shells."

[24] *Jerusalem Post Weekly,* July 31, 1967.

[25] It is interesting to compare this estimate with the following statement by General Dayan: "We have never revealed, and I hope we never shall, what the size and numbers of the Israel defense forces are. I had occasion before the events of the recent days to be asked whether it was true that we had 600 to 800 tanks, and I can only say that whoever relied on this estimation was mistaken." (*Jerusalem Post,* June 8, 1967.)

200 American M-48 Pattons
200 American M-4 Shermans
250 British Centurions
250 self-propelled guns, mostly British
            (150 in 1965)
150 light AMX-13

Total: 900 medium tanks and assault guns and 150 light tanks.

Regarding anti-tank weapons, the Israeli army is equipped with French Nord-Aviation SS-10 and SS-11 wire-guided missiles with a range of about 2 miles; they are similar to the Soviet-supplied "Shmell" missiles. Some of these missiles were supplied on the very eve of the war in the course of an airlift from France that started on May 15 and about which not too much has been said.[26]

Turning now to the Israeli air force, the most notable change since mid-1965 seems to have been the addition of some 20 Mirage-IIICJ interceptor/fighter-bombers to the 72 already there.[27] It is most probable that at least a similar number of older type Vautours and Mystère IV-A's were retired in the interim, so that the total number of fighting planes remained the same—around 300—though, of course, the over-all quality was greatly improved. The picture of Israel's fighting air force on the eve of the war appears thus as follows, with the 1965 figures in parentheses:

Mirage-IIICJ supersonic interceptor/fighter-bombers	92	(72)
Supersonic Super-Mystère fighter-bombers	24	(24)
Mystère fighter-bombers	50	(72)
Ouragan fighter-bombers	40	(55)
Vautour II-A light bombers	24	(24)
Fouga Magister trainer/ground-attack	60	(60)
Total:	290	(307)

[26] *Le Monde*, Sélection hebdomadaire, June 22–28, 1967, article by Ph. Decraene, who personally witnessed the execution of some shipments. Also: *Jerusalem Post Weekly*, July 31, 1967.

[27] *The Military Balance, op. cit.*, as well as most press sources continued to cite the figure of 72 Mirages for the eve of the war. However, *Le Monde* of June 10, 1967, cited the figure of "approximately 100," and two other sources indirectly explained the larger figures by reporting that 20 Mirages were flown to Israel on the eve of the war by French pilots, who immediately returned to France on commercial airlines. See *Le Monde*, Sélection hebdomadaire, June 22–28, 1967, article by Ph. Decraene; also *Der Spiegel*, June 26, 1967.

Israel had ordered 48 A-4 Skyhawk light bombers from the U.S. nearly two years before, but none had been delivered by the time the hostilities started. Finally, the Israeli air force also had one copy of the MIG-21, which had been flown to Israel in 1966 by a defecting Christian Iraqi pilot (Israel air force number for that unique MIG-21: 007 . . . !).

Something ought perhaps to be said about the reports that at the time the war started, Israel possessed some 50 delta-wing twin-jet Mirage-IV light bombers. This quite advanced, Mach 1.7 plane with a range of over 1,000 miles is the basic element in the vector of the French nuclear strategic force. The first source to report that story was the not-always-reliable French magazine *L'Express*.[28] Then the London *Sunday Times* also published it, saying that the purchase of some planes had been confirmed to a British air official by one of the directors of the French Dassault firm, which manufactures the Mirage-IV's.[29] The French Air Ministry, on the other hand, categorically denied these reports. The mystery was eventually cleared up after the war when it was learned that Israel had contracted for the purchase of 50 Mirage-V's, none of which, however, had been delivered by the time hostilities broke out. Evidently, the reports had confused the Mirage-V, an advanced version of the Mirage-III possessed by Israel, with the quite different Mirage-IV, and had failed to distinguish between purchase and delivery.

In the field of anti-aircraft defense, the Israeli airfields and cities were defended by two battalions of U.S. Hawk surface-to-air missiles, thought by the Israelis to be far better than the Russian SAM-2 in the Arab arsenals. In addition, Israel counted on a large number of radar-guided 40-mm AA guns, considered to be superior to the 57-mm and 85-mm guns in possession of the Egyptians and the Syrians.

[28] 12–18 June and 19–25 June, 1967.
[29] June 18, 1967.

APPENDIX C

THE OPPONENTS' MILITARY HARDWARE

A. AIR FORCES

1. Egypt and Syria

The *MIG-21*, which was and is the mainstay of Egypt's and Syria's air force, is a short-range single-seat delta-wing fighter whose single turbo-jet power-plant develops 9,500 lb dry (12,500 lb with after-burner). Its maximum level speed when clean is Mach 2 at 36,000 feet; the maximum level speed with missiles and under-fuselage fuel tank is Mach 1.5. Its combat radius when clean (that is, without extra fuel tanks) is 375 miles. Its armament consists of two 30-mm cannon and two "Atoll" air-to-air missiles similar in configuration and size to the U.S. Sidewinder.

The *Sukhoi-7* is a long-range multipurpose fighter-bomber that is larger and heavier than the MIG-21 and is equipped with a much more powerful turbo-jet engine. It is probably much less limited in range and all-weather capability than the MIG-21, and the two types are therefore complementary rather than comparable. Its speed is put at 1,060 m.p.h. at 36,000 feet by one source,[1] and at Mach 1.8 "at height" by another.[2] It is characteristic of the stage reached by the big powers' deliveries of arms to under-developed countries that, although the Sukhoi is not offered to the Russians' allies in Eastern Europe (no doubt because it is an offensive weapon), it has been made available to

[1] *New York Times*, June 1, 1967.
[2] *Jane's All the World's Aircraft, op. cit.*

Egypt and 200 of them have recently been offered by the Soviet Union to India.[3]

The *MIG-19* is a single-seat all-weather interceptor-fighter with two axial turbo-jets (6,500 lb each or 8,818 lb with after-burner). Its maximum speed at 20,000 feet is Mach 1.3, and it has a rate of climb of over 15,000 ft/min at sea level. Its armament consists of three 23-mm cannon (or two 23-mm and one 37-mm), and provision has been made for target-seeking air-to-air missiles on four underwing pods. The normal range of the MIG-19 is 600 miles, or 850 with external tanks.

The characteristic of the older *MIG-17* are as follows, the indications between parentheses referring to the earlier MIG-15. It is a single-seat interceptor-fighter with one turbo-jet engine developing a thrust of 7,590 lb (5,450–5,955 lb). Its armament varies but generally includes two 23-mm and one 37-mm cannon. There are provisions for two under-wing packs of eight 55-mm air-to-air rockets, or a total of 1,100 lb of bombs. Its maximum speed is put at Mach .975 and its rate of climb at 10,400 ft/min at sea level. The MIG-15/17's normal range is 510 miles and as much as 1,760 miles with external tanks.

Turning now to the Egyptian and Syrian bombers, the Tu-16 is a subsonic medium bomber equipped with two turbo-jet engines developing 20,950 lb each. It has been supplied to Egypt (and Iraq), but not to Syria. Its armament consists of no less than thirteen 23-mm cannon, and it can carry a bombload of up to 19,800 lb delivered from a bomb-bay 21 feet long. Its maximum level speed is estimated at 587 m.p.h. at 35,000 feet when fully loaded, and its range with the maximum bombload is of the order of 3,000 miles. The Tu-16 can also be made to carry the "Kennel" air-to-surface anti-shipping missile; this missile, which was supplied to Egypt by the Soviet Union sometime in 1965 or 1966 (see Chapter 5), can also be used against land targets. In this context, it should be mentioned that the Egyptian operational plans for an air offensive against Israel, which were seized at el Arish after this town was taken by the Israelis, mentioned an attack by "missile bombers."[4]

The older IL-28, which is found in both the Egyptian and the Syrian air force, is a light attack bomber with two turbo-jet engines (5,955 lb each). It carries four 23-mm guns, and its bombload is believed to total up to a maximum of 4,400 lb. Its maximum speed is 580 m.p.h. at 20,000 feet, and its range with a maximum bombload is about 1,500 miles.

[3] *New York Times*, June 1, 1967.

[4] *New York Times*, June 25, 1967.

2. Jordan

The *Hawker Hunter* is a single-seat fighter with one Rolls-Royce turbo-jet engine developing some 10,000 lb. Its armament consists of four 30-mm guns, and it can carry as external stores two 1,000-lb bombs, two 500-lb bombs, two clusters of six 3-in. rockets or two extra gas containers. Its maximum level speed is Mach .92, but the plane can become supersonic in shallow dives at height. Its range is put at 1,840 miles.

3. Israel

The *Mirage-IIICJ* is an all-weather interceptor and day ground attack fighter of the same general class as the MIG-21. It has a single SNECMA turbo-jet plant developing 14,110 lb and an optional and jettisonable rocket-motor (3,700 lb). Its maximum speed at 36,000 feet is 1,430 m.p.h. or Mach 2.15, and its maximum low level speed is a remarkable supersonic 925 m.p.h. The Mirage thus seems to be slightly superior to the MIG-21 on both essential counts of power and speed; the mission take-off weight seems to be about the same in both cases, that is, around 18,000 lb. The Mirage is equipped with a Cyrano Ibis radar and carries two 30-mm guns, three air-to-air Matra R-530 or two rocket-launchers with 72 rockets under the wings, and two 1,000-lb bombs or an air-to-surface AS-130 missile under the fuselage. Its maximum combat radius with attack at ground level is 560 miles or 745 miles when flying at a speed of Mach .9 at a height of 36,000 feet. One unconfirmed report has it that Israel's Mirage-IIICJ (and also the Super-Mystère) were equipped just before the war with the more advanced Matra-550/551 guided missiles that were picked up by three El Al jets at the Bordeaux airport just before the outbreak of the war.[5]

The *Super-Mystère* is a rather versatile fighter-bomber that is just supersonic when not using the after-burner with which it is fitted (that is, it has a speed of 748 m.p.h. at 36,000 feet). Its single turbo-jet power-plant develops 9,700 lb, and its armament comprises two 30-mm cannon and a pack of 35 air-to-air rockets in the fuselage, plus under-wing loads made up of 38 rockets in two honeycomb launchers, or two 1,100-lb bombs, or two napalm tanks, or 12 heavy air-to-surface rockets or two Matra air-to-air guided missiles. It is estimated to be able to stay aloft for about one hour when flying at 620 m.p.h.

The *Mystère IV-A* is an older subsonic fighter-bomber whose turbo-jet develops 7,700 lb. Its maximum speed at operational level is 615 m.p.h., and it carries two 30-mm cannon, 55 air-to-air rockets, one 1,000-lb or two 500-lb bombs under the wings, or two 480-liter Napalm containers, or two Matra rocket containers with 19 air-to-air rockets each, or two groups of six air-to-ground rocket projectiles. Its range is about 700 miles (350 miles, of course, if the plane is to come back to its starting point).

The old *Ouragan* is the first jet-propelled fighter built in France and has a power-plant developing 5,000 lb. Its armament comprises four 20-mm cannon, and there are provisions for 16 rockets under the wings. No information could be found on whether it can carry bombs, although that is quite probable. The Ouragan has a maximum speed of 575 m.p.h. at 40,000 feet, and its range is 600 to 700 miles.

The *Vautour IIA* is a two-seat subsonic light bomber with two turbojet engines (7,716 lb each). It can carry up to 240 rockets or 10 bombs in its bomb bay, and four 19-rocket packs or two 1,000-lb bombs under the wings. Its maximum speed is 680 m.p.h. No information on its range could be found, though it is known that it was the only plane that could reach the Luxor airfield in Upper Egypt.

Finally, the *Fouga Magister,* which is built in Israel under license from Potez/France, is a small two-seat twin-jet trainer that can be used for ground attack, and was very extensively so used by the Israelis. It carries two 7.5-mm machine guns and racks for two 55-lb air-to-ground rockets. One 110-lb bomb or one Nord-Aviation AS-11 guided missile may be fitted under each wing. Its maximum speed at 30,000 feet is about 450 m.p.h. with a maximum permissible diving speed of 535 m.p.h. Its range is somewhat under 600 miles with a fuel reserve.

B. MISSILES AND ROCKETS

Egypt

The Russian-built *SAM-2's* are two-stage anti-aircraft rockets; the solid fuel in the first stage burns for about four seconds and the liquid fuel of the second stage for about 22 seconds. The rockets can lift the warhead to an altitude of about 60,000 feet at a speed of approximately three and a half times that of sound, or about 2,600 m.p.h. Two radar systems and a computer are contained in one large mobile radar van. One "locks on" to enemy aircraft and the other guides the missile, which has a so-called "slant-range" of 21 to 30 miles. The missile has proved to be of some effectiveness in North Vietnam against U.S. planes by forcing them to lower altitudes and thus bringing them within range of conventional AA fire. However, according to a recent report, U.S. planes in mission over North Vietnam are now fitted with much improved "black boxes" containing highly classified electronic countermeasure equipment that temporarily blinds enemy radars and permits them to fly through areas guarded by SAM-2's while keeping above the range of the North Vietnamese AA guns.[6] A program to manufacture SAM-2's in Egypt under license got bogged down, it is reported, especially because of welding problems. At several trial launchings of the local product, the fins simply fell off the tails.[7] According to a statement by an Egyptian general in Israeli captivity, all SAM-2 sites were entirely in the hands of Egyptian personnel by the time the war broke out. Some 150 Soviet experts and instructors who accompanied these rockets to the UAR from 1962 onward had by then completed their tasks.[8]

The Egyptian program for local manufacturing of medium-range ground-to-ground missiles turned out to be a complete, and very costly, failure. Between 30 to 40 attempts had been made to test the liquid-fueled *Al Kahir* and *Al-Zafir* projects, but to little effect. Each time the rockets went out of control and landed in the desert or the sea because of the total failure of the guidance system. Difficulties were also experienced with the electronic equipment, the fuel containers (more than 100 of which burst), and with the graphite-lined combustion chambers. Consequently, the *Al Zafir* missiles shown during past military parades to a rapturously admiring Egyptian public must have been only mock-ups. The only exception to the chain of Egyptian rocket-testing failures is an air-to-air rocket designed by the German technician Moebus, the trials of which were successfully completed in early 1966. Although his rocket was scheduled to be put into production, Moebus himself has now left Egypt, perhaps yielding to pressures from the West German government.

C. ARMOR

1. Egypt and Syria
The *T-34* is a now obsolescent tank, its first appearance in battle going back to 1941 when it made for a rude awakening of the German armies invading Russia. It is armed with an 85-mm gun, which is a relatively small caliber as tanks go nowadays; its weight is 32 tons, and it has a maximum speed of 33 m.p.h.[9]

[6] *New York Times*, July 24, 1967.

[7] *Sunday Telegraph*, London, June 11, 1967.

[8] All these technical features are from Israeli sources and are based on the SAM-2 missiles captured in Sinai (*New York Times*, June 27, 1967).

[9] These and most other technical data on tanks are from: Dr. F. M. von Senger and Etterlin, *The World's Armored Fighting Vehicles*, Doubleday, 1962; translated from the German.

The *T-54* is a more modern tank of post-World War II design. Its armament consists of a 100-mm gun and three machine guns, including an anti-aircraft one, and it weighs 36 tons. This 240-centimeter high, exceptionally streamlined tank makes for a more difficult target in the open spaces of the desert than its Israeli equivalent, the American Patton M-48, which is higher by no less than 70 centimeters.[10]

The *T-55* is one of the latest Soviet tanks and quite a few captured in Sinai were manufactured in 1966 and had been driven only a few hundred miles, some evidently straight from Alexandria (the older T-54b is almost as good a tank, with its improvements, as the T-55). The T-55 is equipped with two infrared projectors, one for firing the 100-mm gun and one for observation by the tank commander. These projectors make it well-suited for night combat, and the Egyptians used them in that manner, though not very effectively. The T-55 has gyroscopic stabilizers in both horizontal and vertical planes that are designed to assist accurate shooting while in motion (the T-54 has a gyro-stabilizer in the vertical plane only). However, an Israeli source commented that this tank was deficient in "human engineering." It is a difficult vehicle to enter and to leave, and the gun loader must work in a cramped position relying largely on his left hand.

Both the T-54 and the T-55 have excellent gun-sighting equipment, with a wider field of view than the Western equipment used by Israel. They are low-silhouette models with very hard and well-contoured armor plating, which causes more shells to ricochet than do older Israeli tanks obtained from the West, which often present quite a few "shell traps." [11]

The *Josef Stalin III* heavy tank is a 46-ton monster armed with a formidable 122-mm gun. It is heavily armored (20-cm thick plates!) and, like all Russian tanks, has an exceptionally low silhouette and well-shaped hull and turret. However, this tank is more impressive in appearance than in reality because of its low power-to-weight ratio, its low speed (maximum of 23 m.p.h.), and its short autonomy.

The *SU-100* assault gun carries a 100-mm weapon. It is based on the T-34 chassis and, up to the introduction of the T-54, was the natural complement of T-34 tanks (which, as said above, are armed with an 85-mm gun). As is known, the difference between an assault gun (or tank destroyer or self-propelled gun) and a tank is that the former has no turret, so that the same chassis can carry a heavier gun.

The Egyptian armored fleet also comprised some 30 British-made

[10] *Der Spiegel*, June 12, 1967.

[11] *New York Times*, June 27, 1967.

Mk-III Centurions and some 20 French-built AMX-13 light tanks. Both are described below, in the section on Israeli and Jordanian armor.

2. *Israel and Jordan*

The *M-48 Patton* is a medium tank developed in 1953, armed with a 90-mm gun, one machine gun in the turret, and one extra AA machine gun. It is said to be a highly developed vehicle, well-shaped, but relatively heavy, with a small operating range (68 miles in the original version; 145 miles in the propped-up M-48A2 version) and a maximum road speed of 28 to 30 m.p.h. The complicated fire-control equipment is also reported to create some difficulties when the tank is used in the field.[12]

The *Centurion* is an even older British tank first used in battle in 1945. In its original version it was armed with a 83.4-mm, 20-pounder gun and a co-axial machine gun. It is rather slow (maximum road speed of 21.8 m.p.h.) and has a small range of action (68 miles). However, the Israeli Centurions were locally fitted with a very effective 105-mm gun, instead of the usual 83.4-mm cannon. This operation is more delicate than would seem, for mounting a heavier cannon on a tank that was designed for a lighter weapon carries a great danger of overloading the vehicle and putting too much stress on chassis and turret. However, the operation was fully successful in the case of the Israeli Centurions.

The M-48's in Israeli hands were said to be equipped with an excellent new optical range-finding device that allowed them to fire their heavy gun immediately without having first to determine the range of the target with tracer bullets, according to a report from Germany, the country that supplied them to Israel.[13] The same report said that the British Centurions had no comparable equipment and that the Soviet-supplied Egyptian tanks were equally devoid of any comparable device. Another technical source does indeed credit only the M-48 with a range-finder.[14]

The American *M-4 Shermans* are old medium tanks introduced in 1941 and used in large numbers by the Western armies during World War II (in N.A.T.O. countries, it was later replaced by M-48 Pattons). In the version supplied to the Israelis, it mounts a 90-mm gun, but the Israelis replaced it with a 100-mm gun. It is the approximate

[12] Dr. F. M. von Senger and Etterlin, *op. cit.*, p. 198.

[13] *Der Spiegel*, June 12, 1967.

[14] F. M. von Senger and Etterlin, *op. cit.*, p. 282.

equivalent of the Soviet T-34, though its hull and turret are not nearly so well-designed.

The French *AMX-13* is a light tank whose first prototype was built in 1948. It weighs only 15 tons but has a fairly high road speed (40 m.p.h.) and a range of action of 208 miles. It carries a small 75-mm gun and is used mainly as a reconnaissance vehicle or tank destroyer, or when a high-speed dash across open terrain is necessary.

INDEX

Abbas II (Khedive), 60, 63
Abdallah (King of Jordan), *see* King Abdallah
Abu Egeila, breakthrough at (1967), 338, 343–344, 351–352
Aden, Yemeni interest in, 242
Adenauer, Konrad, 167, 168
Albert, Colonel, 376, 378, 379
Algeria, relations with Morocco and Tunisia, 57–58; appearance of planes at el Arish (June, 1967), 329n
Allon, Yigal, 253n, 315, 409
Amer, Marshal Abdel Hakim, 288, 300n, 321n; text of battle order, 301–302; suicide of, 351
Anti-Communism, strategic role of in U.S. policy, 71, 113–115; *see also* Eisenhower Doctrine
Anti-Semitism in Soviet Union, 107
Arab Army, 234; *see also* Arab Legion
Arab boycott of Israel, 43–44, 87
Arab League, 29, 39, 63ff, 78, 80, 87, 97, 98, 138, 186, 385; concept of, 66–68; proposed return to concept of (1968), 388–389; intervention in Kuwait, 244
Arab Legion, organization of, 232; postpartition role, 29–31, 66, 99; role of in Palestine War, 233–234
Arab Union, 71, 72; vis-à-vis Iraqi crisis (1958), 116
Arab unity/disunity:
disunity, during 1948 war and aftermath, 29–36, 40, 66–67; interim (1954–1956), 58–59, 68–69, 77–78
Egypt's commitment to integral unity, 56, 72, 78ff, 101, 109, 207, 213, 247, 385–386
Egypt's renunciation of immediate "integral Arab unity" after 1967 war, 386–389, 402

Egypt's role in after 1967 war, 385–390
effect of existence of Israel on, 83–88; *see also* "Clash of destinies"
and patterns of arms accumulation, 145, 247–248
and Kuwait's oil-derived wealth, 185–187, 244
summit meetings: *re* cooperative military efforts (1964), 47, 232, 235, 246, 273; *re* Jordan River water diversion (1964), 47, 246, 273; at Khartum (August, 1967), 387, 402
"unity talks" (1963), 229n
meeting of Arab oil-producing countries (June, 1967), 270
see also Arab League; Arab Union; Ba'thist Party; "Class struggle"; Kassem; Nasser; Nationalism, Arab; Pan-Arabism; United Arab Republic
Aref, Abdel Salam, 78
Arms, flow of, to Middle East, 89–91, 128; from Western powers to Egypt, 48; from Western powers to Israel, 48, 50–52; from Soviet Union to Egypt, 49–50, 52, 55; big power motives for supplying, 90–91, 409–411
Arms, motives for acquiring:
Egypt, 145, 146, 152, 155–156, 169, 191, 208, 211–213, 218, 247–248
Iraq (pre-1958), 236, 237–238; (post-1958), 236–237, 238, 247–248
Israel, 145, 146, 165–166, 190, 191, 218–219, 249
Jordan, 232, 234, 235, 247–248
Kuwait, 244, 248
Saudi Arabia, 240–241, 247–248
Syria, 227–229, 247–248
Arms, rationing of, 48, 50, 146; effect

of, on Egypt's defense budget, 149; —on Israel's defense budget, 161–162; by U.S. and Soviet Union, future prospects for, 420n *see also* Tripartite Declaration

Arms control, future prospects of, 204

Arms expenditure, relative capacity for, 253

Arms exports by Western powers, economic motives for, 90, 166–167

Arms race, definition of, 144–145, 247–248

Egypt-Israel: 145–146, 155–158, 191, 247, 248, 251–252; trends in, 198–204, 253, 255; spill-over effect of, 191–198; secondary effects of, 247–248; feed-back effect of, 248; Egypt's "threefold task" vs. Israel's "single purpose," 218; prospects for Egypt after 1967 war, 398

Aswan Dam, U.S. role in, 50, 51, 69, 70, 110, 111; Soviet role in, 75, 124, 127

Atasi, Lu'iy al, 243n

Ataturk, Kemal, 94

Azarbaijan, 95

Azzam pasha, 39

Badran, Shams al Din, 269, 270, 274n, 288n, 300n, 352n

Baghdad Pact, 49, 51, 68–69, 73, 79–80, 87, 90, 109, 117 *see also* "Northern tier" alliance

Balance of power, Tripartite Declaration (May, 1950), 48, 50

Baldwin, Hanson, 319, 435n, 439n

Balfour Declaration, 23–26; reversal of by British White Paper (May, 1939), 26–27

Bandung Conference (April, 1955), 109, 141

Barker, A. J., 209n, 211n

Ba'thist Party, in Syria, 72, 76, 129, 130; in Syria and Iraq, 77–78, 82–83, 86–87; adoption of Marxism by, 130

Beaufre, André, 328n, 339, 349, 350n; evaluation of Israeli lightning war (1967), 382

Begin, Menachem, 312

Ben Ari, Colonel, 365, 366

Ben Gurion, David, 52, 167, 168, 305, 312

Ben Vered, Amos, 168n

Bernadotte, Count Folke, 32

Bevin, Ernest, 96, 98–100 passim

Big power rivalries, 49–50, 71–72, 80, 92–97 *see also* Superpower conflict; Soviet Union; United States

Border raids, after 1948 war, 44–46; after 1956 war, 55–56, 273

Boundaries problem, 36–37, 41–42

Bretholz, Wolfgang, 39n

Brinkmanship, 112

Bulganin, Nikolai, 109

Bull, General Odd, 360

Central Treaty Organization (CENTO), 125, 131

Chamoun, Camille, 246

China, conflict with Soviet Union, 121, 124–125, 141, revolutionary militancy of, 121, 122, 142; "third power" role in Middle East, 141–142; as potential arms supplier to Middle East, 420n

Chou En-Lai, 109, 141

Churchill, R. and W., 322n, 323n, 348n

"Clash of destinies" (Egypt-Israel), 22, 83, 85, 101, 385, 390

"Class struggle," and Arab nationalism, 75–77, 82, 85n, 145n *see also* Imperialism, Egypt's view of struggle against

Communism, Soviet promotion of, 94, 124–125, 126, 129, 132, 141–142; Arab fear of, 93, 131; Soviet failure to promote in Egypt (1955), 113

Communists, role of, in Arab countries, 125

"Containment Policy" (U.S.), 101–102; extension of, to Middle East, 103–104, 107–108; and "New Look" policy, 111

Cuban missile crisis, (1962), 121

Czechoslovakia, 69, 107, 111, 112

Dayan, Moshe, 44n, 209n, 211n, 219n, 223n, 305, 317, 364n, 383, 408, 409, 442n; role in 1967 crisis, 270, 312–313, 315–316, 375

Decraene, Philippe, 443*n*
De Gaulle, Charles, 97, 297, 309–310,
320; and French global policy,
1960's, 121
Detente, East-West, 109, 112, 135;
effect of, on client states and
third powers, 120–123, 140
Dulles, John Foster, 50, 51, 52, 101,
104–106 passim, 110, 297

Eban, Abba, 269, 293, 309–311
Economic assistance, as contribution
to arms escalation, 90
Eden, Anthony (Lord Avon), 50, 70*n*
"Effective populations" (Egypt-Israel),
258–265
see also Manpower; Israel, armed
forces, reserve system
Egypt
Internal: attempt at political and
economic consolidation (1961),
75–76; radicalization in 1960's,
129; unemployment among educated youth, 259; "effective manpower" compared with Turkey's,
259–261; internal politics after
1967 war, 399–400; projected
large-diameter pipeline, 398; *re*
possibility of coup in, 417
International: repudiation of 1936
treaty with Britain, 100, 102–103;
role in 1948 war, 32–33; rejection
of U.N. Security Council ruling
on blockade (1951), 43; rejection
of MEDO, 103, 107, 108; anti-
British Cairo riots (1952), 103;
overthrow of Faruq regime, 103,
106; attack on Baghdad Pact,
68–69, 79–80, 105–106, 110, 111,
207; arms deal with Russia (1955),
101, 109, 110–111, 112, 152, 210–
211,—political impact of, 49–50,
—list of matériel, 209; relations
with Britain (post-1956 war), 138;
and Eisenhower Doctrine, 113–
115; Egyptian-Soviet relations
(1958), 116–118; renewed rapprochement with U.S. (1959 and
after), 126, 132; deterioration of
U.S. relations (from 1964), 129,
133–135; Haykal's perception of

relations with U.S. (1952–1967),
278–281; arms deal with Russia
(1961–1962), 134; and Soviet economic aid (1965), 130*n*, 152*n*; Soviet aid after 1967 war, military,
89*n*, 396, 411, —economic, 397, 411
Inter-Arab: and pan-Arabism, pre-
World War I, 63; and inter-Arab
conflicts, 58, 73–74; commitment
to integral Arab unity, 56, 72,
78ff, 101, 109, 207, 213, 247,
385–386 (*see also* Nasser), —military implications of, 213; separa-
tion by Israel from other Arab
countries, 86–88, 146; "Summit
meeting" against water plan
(1963), 47; adjustment to post-
1967 realities, 401–402; renunciation of immediate integral Arab
unity (1967), 387–389, 402, 417,
—implications for relation to Israel, 389–390, —implications for
revolutionary role, 388–389, 399
(*see also* Yemen; Yemen war);
dependence on "reactionary" Arab
governments after 1967 war, 386–
387, 397, 399–400, 416; diplomatic
maneuvers following 1967 war,
402; vis-à-vis "liquidation of the
Palestine problem," 401, 403
vs. Israel military: post-partition
role, 29–33, 35, 40–41, 47–56;
and border raids on Israel, 45;
and refugee problem, 38; boycott
and partial blockade (post-1948),
43–44; motives for acquiring arms,
see Arms, motives for acquiring;
arms procurement from Russia,
256; missile development, 156;
lessons from 1956 war, 208, 211–
213; strategy for "four fronts"
(post-1956), 208, 218; "threefold
task" in post-1956 strategy, 211–
213; conditions for going to war
with Israel (pre-1967), 292, 298–
299; armed strength in 1949, 208,
—in 1956, 209–211, —in 1965, 214–
216; *re* armed forces reserve system, 261–262; naval power (1965),
215; minimal objective, 1967 war,
336–337; options for the future,
418–420

Egyptian High Command, failure of (1967), 350–351
Egyptian Institute of National Planning, 259n
Eisenhower, Dwight D., 223n
Eisenhower Administration, "New Look" approach, 104–106; anti-Soviet belligerence of, 108; vis-à-vis Iraqi crisis, 1958, 119; aid to Egypt (1959), 132
Eisenhower Doctrine, 71, 79, 90, 113–115, 118, 137
Elazar, General David, 375–376, 379
Emir Abdallah, see King Abdallah
Emir Faysal, see King Faysal I (of Iraq)
Eshkol, Levi, 269, 289, 293, 308–309, 408; and "credibility crisis," 304–306, 307, 312–315

Farid, Muhammad, 63
Faruq, see King Faruq
Fatah, 142, 394–395, 405, 417
Fawzi, General, 274n, 285–286
Federenko, Nikolai, 275, 276
France, Middle East interest, pre-World War I, 62, 63, —post-World War I, 24, 25, 64, —World War II era, 64, —post-World War II, 97, 138–139, —1950–1956, 48, 50–54 passim; arms sales to Middle East countries, 90; 1956 war, 70, 71, 110, 139; global policy (1960's), 121, 140; "third power" role in Middle East, 138–141
Fuad, see King Fuad

Game theory type analysis, unforeseeable factors, 233n
Gavish, General, 337
Gaza Strip, 45–46, 268, 285–287 passim, 307, 334, 337, 339, 403, 405
Geneva Summit Meeting (July 1955), 109
Germany (West), see West Germany
Gidi Pass, battle of (1967), 347
Glassboro Summit Meeting, 412–413
Golan Heights, see Syrian Heights
Great Britain, Middle East interest, pre-World War I, 61–63, —post-World War I, 64, —1917–1947, 22–28, 235–236, —World War II

era, 64–66, —post-World War II, 92–93, —1948–1956, 48–55; Palestine policy, 95–96; collapse of Middle East policy, 97–100; role in "northern tier" alliance, 104–106; arms sales to Middle East countries, 90; 1956 war, 70, 71, 110; intervention in Jordan (1958), 74, 115, 116, 137; intervention in Kuwait, 185, 186, 244–245; "third power role in Middle East, 137–138
Greece, Soviet interest in, 92, 94–95; U.S. intervention in, 95
Guerrilla war, 250, 284, 291, 394–395, 405–406, 417
Gulf of Aqaba, blockade of after 1948, 43–44; guarantee of right of innocent passage (post-1956 war), 55; May–June, 1967, 268–269, 287–291; Nasser's "authorization" to blockade, 272, 292; Soviet view of blockade, 295; U.S. view of blockade, 269, 293, 310; Israel's initial reaction to blockade, 233n, 292–293, 308–309; re Israel's physical control over entry to after 1967 war, 409

Halevi, Nadav, 432
Hansen, Bent, 421, 431
Harbison, M. F., 260
Harel, Isser, 305
Haseeb, K., 426
Hashim, House of (the Hashimites), vs. House of Saud, 63, 69
see also Hashimite family, as rulers
Hashimite family, as rulers, 62–67 passim, 72–73
see also Hussein, Sherif; Hashim, House of
Hawk missiles, from U.S. to Israel, 134
Haykal, Muhammad Hassanein, 54, 85n, 109n, 145n, 152n, 156, 167–169 passim, 185, 253n, 273, 277n, 292, 320n, 321n, 327n, 352; report on Iraqi crisis (1958), 116–119; re "class struggle" and threat of imperialism, 279–282; post mortems and prospects after 1967 war,

386–389, 398; defense of Soviet
influence in Egypt, 399–400
"Heartland countries," listing of, 91
Heiman, Leo, 239*n*
Herzl, Theodor, 23
Himadeh, Raja S., 427
Hitler, Adolf, *re* repudiation of Locarno
treaty, 420*n*
Hod, General Mordechai, 318, 323,
324, 325–326, 328, 329, 439, 440
Hussein, Sherif, 24, 61, 62
Hussein (King of Jordan), *see* King
Hussein

Ibrahim pasha, 60, 63
Imam of Yemen, 77, 133, 242–243
Imperialism, Egypt's view of struggle
against, 278–280, 298
see also "Class struggle"; Nationalism, Arab
India, 109
Institute for Strategic Studies, London, 260*n*
Internal security and external defense,
146–147; in Egypt, 207, 208, 218;
in Iraq, 179, 235–238 passim; in
Jordan, 182; in Kuwait, 185–186;
in Saudi Arabia, 240–241
International Monetary Fund, conditions for loan to Egypt (1967),
281
Iran, supply of arms to, 89; Soviet interest in (post-World War II), 92,
94–95, 125, 128, 131; British influence in, 93; U.S. intervention
in, 93, 95, 104, 125; defiance of
British interests (1951), 100, 102;
as part of U.S. global defense network, 112, 131; prohibition of
foreign missile bases (1962), 128;
relations with Soviet Union (1962),
128
Iraq, and the Hashimite family, 62,
72, 73; post-partition role, 31, 32,
33, 35; and inter-Arab conflicts,
58, 68, 73–74; and Baghdad Pact,
49, 51, 68–69, 73, 179, 236; arms
from U.S. (Baghdad Pact), 90;
support of U.S. intervention in
Middle East, 104, 105, 114, 236;
inaction during 1956 war, 54;

revolution in (1958), 73, 82, 115–
119, 235, 236; internal instability (1958–1963), 237; orientation
toward Russia, 74–75, 236; outlawing of Communist Party (1960),
126, 142; Ba'th effort to unite with
Syria, 77–78, 82–83; relations with
Soviet Union, 1960's, 126–127; arms
from Soviet Union, 90, 165, 179,
238–239; as threat to Kuwait, 244;
expeditionary force to Jordan
(June 1967), 270
Irgun, Dir Yasin, massacre by (1948),
35
Islamic Alliance (Jordan-Saudi Arabia),
279, 280, 282
Israel, establishment of state of, 22, 28
vis-à-vis Arabs: military effectiveness in 1948 war, 30–33; as potential economic competitor with
Arab states, 38; impact of on Arab
unity, 83–88; as wedge separating
Egypt from other Arab countries,
86–88, 146
vis-à-vis big powers: solicitation of
U.S. support (1949), 96; breakdown
of relations with Russia (1952),
96, 107, 108; opposition to Baghdad Pact, 105, 108; attempt to
join NATO, 105, 108; appeal for
arms from big powers (1955–
1956), 50–51; arms supply from
France (1955 and after), 139
military: pattern of arms accumulation, 145, 247–248; participation
with Britain and France in 1956
war, and reasons for it, 52; naval
equipment from Britain, 138;
arms gifts from West Germany,
90, —and relevance to arms race,
167–169, —effect of on defense
expenditures, 157, 158f, 159f,
160f, 163–164; arms from U.S.
(after 1960), 134; construction of
nuclear reactor, 47, 139, 166; motives for acquiring arms, *see* Arms,
motives for acquiring; armed
forces, "single purpose" strategy,
218–219, —reserve system, 220–
222, 255, 256, 261; armed strength
in 1949–1950, 222–223, —in 1956,

224, —in 1965, 225–226; naval power (1965), 226; topography and defense strategy, 221

1967 crisis and after: objectives in 1967 war, 337, 360–361, 365, 375, 380; attack on American vessel, *Liberty*, 354–355; significance of conquered territories, 404; defense and guerrilla problem, 405–406; internal politics and the May–June crisis, 304–306, 311–313, 315–316; internal politics after 1967 war, 408–409; division of opinion on post-war settlement, among the public, 406–407, —among government officials, 408, —consequences of, 409; growth of population and economy, 1949–1953, related to defense system, 221; growth of economy (1953–1963), 202

Issachar, Colonel, 342, 343, 344

Italy, 64, 97

Jenin, battle of (1967), 361–362

Jerusalem, partition of (1949), 34; capitulation of (1967), 367–368; *de facto* annexation of by Israel, 408, 420

Jewish immigration to Palestine, 95–96

Jewish National Home policy, *see* Balfour Declaration

Johnson, Lyndon B., statement on Gulf of Aqaba (May, 1967), 269, 293; inclination to forceful action, 296–297; talks with Eban, 310–311; diplomatic message to Israel, 314; statement on settlement, 414; Glassboro Summit Meeting, 412

Johnston, Eric, 46

Joint Defense Agreement, Egypt-Syria (1966), 273, 276, 294; Egypt-Jordan (May, 1967), 270, 294

Jordan (*see also* Transjordan), settlement of 1948 war, 33, 36, 40; settlement with Israel (1949–1950), 37, 233; and refugee problem, 37, 38, 233–234; attitude toward border raids, 45; and inter-Arab conflicts, 58; vis-à-vis Baghdad Pact, 69; vis-à-vis Eisenhower Doctrine, 71, 114; arms from U.S.

(Eisenhower Doctrine), 90; inaction in 1956 war, 54; arms from U.S. and Britain, 90; coup d'état (April, 1957), 114, 234; call for British military aid (1958), 115, 235; dependence on British and U.S. subsidies, 180–183, 232, 235; subsidy from Arab oil-producing countries, 393; U.S. influence in, 232, 233; internal politics after 1967 war, 394–395; *re* possibility of coup in, 417; vis-à-vis Egypt and Israel, 86, —after 1967 war, 394–395

Jordan River, dispute over waters of, 46–47, 87, 246, 273; Israeli access to Banias source (1967), 392; as Israel's "military frontier," 409

Jordanian West Bank, strategic importance of, 221, 232–233, 356, 393–394; topography and terrain, 355–356; significance of to Israel and to Jordan, 394, 403–404; Israeli views toward annexation of, 407

Kalkilya, devastation of (1967), 364

Kassem, Abdel Karim, conflict with Nasser, 73–74, 75, 82, 125–127 passim; outlawing of Communist Party in Iraq (1960), 126, 142; claim to Kuwait, 186, 237, 244

Kennedy Administration, and "preventive diplomacy" in Middle East, 132; rapprochement with Egypt, 132, 133; failure of rapprochement, 134–135

Keynesian argument, as inapplicable to poor economies, 196

Khrushchev, Nikita, reprimand of Nasser, 75; and *detente* policy, 109; vis-à-vis Iraqi crisis (1958), 116–118; meeting with Nasser (July, 1958), 116–118; call for big power meeting, 124; and Cuban missile policy, 121; on noninevitability of war, 121; and Egyptian aid policy, 128; on international versus Arab socialism, 129n

King Abdallah, 29, 37, 40, 62, 64–65, 66, 99, 100

King Faisal, *see* King Faysal (of Saudi Arabia)
King Faruq, 29, 47–48, 63, 65, 66, 103, 207
King Faysal I (of Iraq), 24, 25, 61, 62
King Faysal (of Saudi Arabia), 72, 279, 282, 386, 399
King Fuad, 63
King Hussein, *re* U.S.-aided coup d'état (April, 1957), 71, 114; and Iraqi crisis (1958), 115, 116; and U.S. support, 232, 235; defense treaty with Egypt (May, 1967), 270, 294; estimate of Jordan's armored forces, eve of 1967 war, 441; role in 1967 war, 233n, 360, 365; political options after 1967 war, 392–395, 417; political position in Jordan, after 1967 war, 417
King Saud, 72
Klein, Colonel, 378
Klinov-Malul, Ruth, 432
Korean War, 102, 103, 107
Kosygin, Alexei, as Egypt-Syria conciliator, 130, 276; crisis of May–June, 1967, 270, 294–295, 301, 313; Glassboro Summit Meeting, 412; statement on results of Glassboro meeting, 412–413

"Land of Israel Movement," 406–407
Lausanne Protocol, 36–37
League of Nations, Palestine Mandate, 24
Lebanon, post-partition role, 31, 33; and refugee problem, 38; attitude toward border raids, 46; vis-à-vis Baghdad Pact, 69; vis-à-vis Eisenhower Doctrine, 71, 114; arms from U.S. (Eisenhower Doctrine), 90; internal politics of, 73, 182, 245–246; civil war (1958), U.S. role in, 73, 115–116, 246; reliance on diplomacy as defense strategy, 245–246
Liberty, American vessel, Israeli attack on, 354–355
Liska, Colonel, 347

Manpower
vs. technological equipment (Egypt-Israel), 252, 255–256, 283–284, 401–402, –paradox of in 1956, 225; –Egypt/Syria/Jordan-Israel (1967), 318
"effective populations" in relation to, 30 (1948), 258–265
projected growth of in Israel, 263–264
projected growth of in Egypt, 263
potential contribution of Arab countries other than Egypt, 264–265
Marshall, S. L. A., 325n
Marshall Plan, 102
Marzouk, G., 421, 431
McMahon, Sir Henry, 24
Middle East Defense Organization (MEDO), 102–103, 108
see also "Containment Policy"
Missile development, in Egypt, 156, 215–216, 252, 449; –in Israel, 156, 226–227, 252
Mitla Pass, battle of (1967), 347–349 passim; and jamming of Egyptian communications, 353
Morocco, relations with Algeria, 57–58
Mortagui, General Mohsin, 332
Moshe, Colonel, 361, 362, 364, 379
Myers, C. A., 260

Nablus, capture of (1967), 362–363
Naguib, Mohammed, 51
Nakhl, ambush at (1967), 348
Nasser, Gamal Abdel
commitment to integral Arab unity, 22, 78ff (*see also* Arab unity/disunity: Egypt's commitment); 298–299 (1964); renunciation of as immediate goal after 1967 war, 386–387
as pan-Arab figure, 22, 51, 59, 69–73 passim, 78–83, 101, 109, 213; decline prior to 1967 war, 282; after 1967 war, 385–386, 416
as revolutionary, 68–69, 76–77, 82, 85n, 145n; *The Philosophy of the Revolution*, 79; support of Yemen revolutionaries, 77, 82, 87, 88, 241; overconfidence on Yemen war, 243n; *see also* "Class struggle"; Imperialism, Egypt's view of struggle against; Nationalism,

Arab pre-1956 war: attitude toward Western Alliance, 106; opposition to Baghdad Pact, 49, 68–69, 80, 110; arms deal with Soviet Union, 49, 110–111, 146; nationalization of Suez Canal, 51, 70, 110

1956 war and aftermath: explanation of Syrian inaction in, 54; comments on (1966), 211n, 212n; caution toward Israel prior to May, 1967, 55–56, 273, 282–283

1957–1967: vis-à-vis Iraqi crisis (1958), 116–119; meeting with Khrushchev (July, 1958), 116–118; conflict with Kassem, 73–74, 75, 82, 125–127 passim; establishment of control in Syria (1958–1961), 76, 81–82; vs. Ba'thists in Syria and Iraq, 76, 78, 82–83; warnings to Israel against manufacturing nuclear bomb, 47; view of necessary conditions for Egypt to go to war with Israel (1964), 292, 298–299; disdaining of U.S. aid, 134; manipulation of Soviet interest in Middle East, 110, 410; steps toward 1967 war, 267–270 passim, 272, —reasons for acting on Soviet "information," 277–278, —initial limited objective, 271, 274, 277, 284, 286, —suspicion and fear of U.S. counter-revolutionary intentions, 278–281, —economic and political troubles, 281–284, —factors in overconfidence, 292, 295, 297–299; invoking of Palestine liberation issue, 269–270, 272, 283, 290–292; prediction of June 5, Israeli air strike, 299, 301, 320; reflection on Israeli air strike, 327; statement on losses in Sinai, 349–350; statement on speed of Israeli advance, 350; denunciation of Egyptian High Command, 350–351; denunciation of intelligence services, 352; internal problems after 1967 war, 399–400; meeting with Podgorny, 411, 416; position of after 1967 war, compared to Egypt's position in 1949, 41n, 417

Nationalism, Arab, 39–40, 74–75, 83, 142, 394–395, 417; —Israeli, 23–26, 406–407

Nationalist upsurge, post-World War II, 92–93

Naval power, 1965: Egypt, 215; Israel, 226; —Egypt after 1967 war, 397

Nehru, Jawaharlal, 109

New Look Policy (Eisenhower Administration), 104–106; vis-à-vis "Containment Policy," 104, 107–108, 111

Nonalignment doctrine (Bandung Principles), 109

North Africa, and French interest in Middle East heartland, 139

North Atlantic Treaty Organization (NATO), 102

"Northern tier" alliance, 97, 104–106, 108
    see also Baghdad Pact; New Look Policy

"Northern tier" countries (Turkey, Iran, Iraq, Pakistan), 104

Nuclear capacity, China, 121; Egypt, 252; France, 121; Israel, 252; Soviet Union, 104, 109, 111, 120; United States, 104, 108–109, 111, 120

Nuclear reactor, Israeli construction of, 47, 139, 166

O'Ballance, E., 209n, 258n

Oil, importance of in Kuwait, 185, 187

Oil interests in Middle East: British, 98, 137–138, 244, 298; European, 102; United States, 95, 115, 133; vis-à-vis collective action in 1967 crisis, 297, 298, 299

Organization for the Liberation of Palestine, see Fatah

Ottoman empire, and Zionist efforts, 23; and rise of pan-Arabism, 24, 60–62

Pace, Eric, 319

Palestine, and the Hashimites, 62–63; Jewish National Home Policy (Zionist and British), 23–26; League of Nations Mandate, 24; British position in, 93; partition

of, 26–28, 96–100; British immigration policy, 95–96; consequences
of 1948 war, 33–36
Palestine, plans for liberating: statement by Nasser (July, 1966), 283–
284; statements by Nasser (May,
1967), 269–270, 272, 283, 290–292
Palestine Liberation Army, 166
Palestine Liberation Organization, *see*
Fatah
Palestine "problem," origins of, 22,
24–28; and failure of peace after
1948 war, 39–40; importance of
to Egypt, 204; Egyptian view of
after 1967 war, 401, 403, 417;
Israeli view of after 1967 war,
407–408; Soviet view of settlement
of, 411–412
Pan-Arabism, meaning of, 59–60
    see also Arab League; Arab Union;
    Arab unity/disunity; Ba'thist
    Party; "Class struggle"; Kassem;
    Nasser; Nationalism, Arab; United
    Arab Republic
Patinkin, Don, 423, 432
Peace options (post-1967), 390–391,
409, 417–420
Peace prospects, after the 1948 war,
22, —incentives, 37–38, 47–48,
—obstacles, 36, 38–42, 48–52; after
the 1956 war, 55–56; after the
1967 war, 219*n*, 415–416, 418–420
"Pearl Harbor Strategy," 250, 251
Peled, General Elad, 379, 380
Peres, Shimon, 168, 305
Pineau, Georges, 50
Podgorny, Nikolai, 411, 416
Polk, William R., 258*n*
Pre-emptive strikes, inducements to,
249, 251

Rabin, General Yitzhak, 287*n*, 288, 306,
353, 372
Rafah, breakthrough at (1967), 338,
340, 351–352
Reallocation of territory, after 1948
war, 33–34; —after 1967 war,
391–392, 394, 396–397, 403–409,
420
Refugee problem, after 1948, 34–38
passim, 41, 42

Riad, Mahmud, 286
Ribbentrop-Molotov Pact of 1939, 94
Rouleau, Eric, 411
Royal Commission of Inquiry (1937),
22, 25–26
Rusk, Dean, 296

al Said, Nuri, 64, 68, 70*n*, 74, 80
Saud (King of Saudi Arabia), *see* King
Saud
Saud, Emir Ibn, 62, 65
Saud, House of, vs. House of Hashim,
63, 69, 71
Saudi Arabia, and inter-Arab conflicts,
58; internal politics of, 72, 188–
189, 240; vis-à-vis Eisenhower
Doctrine, 114; support of Imam of
Yemen, 58, 77, 133, 241, 243
Schmidt, Dana Adams, 393*n*
Schroder, Gerhard, 442
Segev, Shmuel, 301*n*, 313*n*, 324*n*, 327*n*,
328*n*, 329*n*, 352*n*
Shah of Iran, 125
Shapira, Moshe, 312, 313, 315, 408
Sharon, General Arik, 337–345 pas-
sim; description of ambush at
Nakhl, 348
Shazli, General, 332, 336, 345, 348
Shelepin, Alexander, 128, 135
Shepilov, Dmitri, 123
Shmulik, Colonel, 340, 344
Shukeiri, Ahmad, 270
Sidki, General Mahmud, 300*n*
Sinai, Israeli views toward annexation
of, after 1967 war, 407
Sinai campaign, 1956 war, 44*n*, 45–
46, 54, 209*n*, 211*n*; 1967 war,
332–349
Sinai peninsula, topography and ter-
rain, 332–334
Soviet Union, Middle East interest,
post-World War I, Greece, Turkey,
Iran, 94, —post-World War II,
92–95 passim; interest in Israel
and heartland, 96–97; reaction to
U.S. Middle East policy, 106–111;
arms to Jews of Palestine (1948),
28, 96; support of Israel (1947–
1948), 96; breakdown of relations
with Israel, 96, 107, 108; development of nuclear capacity, 104,

109, 120, —second strike capacity, 111, 112; *detente* campaign, East-West (1953-1955), 109; policy in 1955-1956, 49-50, 53, 55, 71-72; interest in Egypt (1955-1958), 106, 109-110, 112-113; arms deal with Egypt (1955), 52, 55, 69, 101, —political impact of, 49-50, 109-111; reaction to 1956 war, 53, 111; relations with Egypt (mid-1958), 116-118, —in 1959, 75, 82; interest and policies in northern tier countries (before and after 1958), 123-124, —in Iran and Turkey (1960's), 128-129; new interest and policies in heartland (1958 and after), 124-128, —new approach (1960's), 128-131; position on Arab unity, 127; reaction to Syrian overthrow plot (1957), 114; vis-à-vis Iraqi crisis (1958), 116-119, 141-142; vis-à-vis Yemen war, 130; competition with U.S. in Middle East, 1960's, 122-123; vested interest in Syria (1965-1967), 275-276; role in 1967 crisis, 269, 270, 294-296, —intelligence on Israeli plan to attack Syria, 274, 274n, 275, 276-277, —diplomatic role, 301, 313-314, —deployment of naval forces, 297; problem of access for Mediterranean fleet to Persian Gulf, 416; arms provisions to Egypt (1955-1967), 409-410; rearming of Egypt (1967-1968), 196n, 396, 411; arms supply to Egypt and Syria (1967-1968), 89n, 383; economic aid to Egypt after 1967 war, 397, 411; terms for relations with Egypt, post-1967 war, 411-412; pressure on Egypt for U.N. solution, 401, 411-412; diplomatic support of Egypt, 412, 414, 416; prospects for armed intervention in Middle East, 406, 418-419; convergence of interest in Arab-Israeli settlement with that of U.S., 420; divergence of policy from that of U.S., 409, 415-416; options for 1968 and after, 418-420;

conflict with China, 121, 124-125, 141

see also Big power rivalries; Superpower conflict

Stalin, Josef, 75, 107

Statistical Abstract of Israel, 263n, 264n

Status quo in Middle East, Israeli vs. Egyptian interests in, 146, 157, 267; *re* Israel's "single purpose" strategy, 219; Jordanian interest in, 233

see also Israel, as wedge separating Egypt from other Arab countries

Stockwell, General, 349

Strait of Tiran, *see* Gulf of Aqaba

Strategic importance of Middle East, 91, 100ff, 108, 122ff

Strauss, Franz Joseph, 168

Suez Canal, blockade of after 1948, 43-44; nationalization of, 51, 70, 110, 111; economic losses on after 1967 war, 397-398

Suez-Sinai War (1956 war), lessons to Egypt from, 208, 211-213, 251

see also Sinai campaign, 1956 war

Superpower conflict, global level, 100-101, 111-112, 120-122; as it affects the Middle East, 122-123; costs of in Middle East, 127-128; vis-à-vis Soviet and U.S. proteges, post-1967 war, 415

Syria, and the Hashimites, 62-63, 65-67; post-partition role, 31-33, 40-41; and refugee problem, 38; and border raids, 46; and inter-Arab conflicts, 58; and inter-Arab unity, 71, 229; objections to Jordan River water plan, 46-47; vis-à-vis Baghdad Pact, 69; vis-à-vis Eisenhower Doctrine, 114; as object of big power rivalry (1957), 71-72; merger with Egypt, 70-72 passim; as part of UAR, 76; Ba'th effort to unite with Iraq, 77-78, 82-83; arms from Soviet Union, 89n, 90, 114, 165, 171, 230-232; plot to overthrow regime (1957), 71-72, 114-115; Soviet Union's vested interest in, 275-276; internal politics of, 227-229, 230; left-wing coup d'état

(February 1966), 129; militant anti-Israeli policy of, 276; guerrilla war against Israel, 130; alleged Israeli threats to (1967), 272, 273, 306; member United Arab Command (June 1967), 270; relations with Soviet Union after 1967 war, 412; internal politics after 1967 war, 392; *re* possibility of coup in, 417

Syrian Heights, topography and terrain, 370–371; fortifications, 372, 374; Israeli capture of, 375, 394n; Israeli occupation of, 391–392, 404; Israeli views toward annexation of, 407

Taine, Hippolyte Adolphe, 320n

Tal, General, 337–349 passim

Teheran Conference, 95

Thant, U, 268, 286–287, 306

Tito, Marshal Josip Broz, 101, 109, 117

Transarabian pipeline, 372, 392

Transjordan, and the Hashimite family, 62, 72; post-partition role, 29, 32, 33, 35

  see also Jordan

Tripartite Declaration, May 1950 (U.S., Britain, France), 48, 50–52, 102, 110, 146; effect of on arms buildup in Middle East, 149, 161–162, 218

Truman, Harry S., 96

Truman Doctrine, 95

Tunisia, relations with Algeria, 57

Turkey, Soviet interest in, 92, 94–95, 131; "effective manpower" compared with Egypt's, 259–261; and U.S. intervention in Middle East, 93, 95, 104, 114, 115; as part of U.S. global defense network, 112, 131; U.S. removal of missile bases (1962), 128; relations with Soviet Union (1962), 128; supply of arms to, 89; U.S. military aid to, 260–261

United Arab Command, *re* responsibility for repulsing Israeli raids, 273, 276; incapacity of in 1967 war, 330

United Arab Republic, formation of, 70–74 passim; effect of union on defense expenditures, 154, 156, 165, 171–175 passim

United Nations, Azarbaijan question, 95; Palestine issue, 96, 99, 100; Special Commission on Palestine (1947), 26–27; partition plan, 26, 27, 28, 33; role in 1948 war, 22, 27, 28, 30–34 passim; Conciliation Commission (1948–1949), 36–37; and 1949 armistice, 37–38, 42; Security Council enjoinder against Egyptian blockade (1951), 43; Emergency Force (UNEF) after 1956 war, 44, 46, 53, 55, —Egypt's acceptance of, 165, —as of May, 1967, 268, 285–287, 307 (*see also* U Thant); Truce Supervision Organization report (May, 1967), 274, —as of October, 1966, 275; Security Council, crisis of May–June, 1967, 269, 275, —cease fire injunction (June, 1967), 368, 375; capture of Headquarters in Jerusalem, 360, 367; role in settlement of 1967 war, 414; role in aftermath of 1967 war, 402–403, 404; Arab use of in Syria crisis (October, 1957), 72

United States, as viewed by Middle East countries, post-World War I, 92–93; first moves as Middle East power (1940's), 95; intervention in Iran, Turkey, Greece, 94, 95; American oil interests, 95, 115, 133; assumption of Britain's role in Middle East, 100–102, 137; and Palestine immigration question, 95–96; support of Palestine partition, 96; and Tripartite Declaration, 48, 50–51, 52; *re* Jordan River water plan, 46; development of nuclear capacity, 104, 108–109, 120, —second strike capacity, 104, 111; "Containment Policy" and its extension to Middle East, 101–104, 107, 108; "New Look" Policy and its application to Middle East, 104–106, 108, 111; interest

and policies in "northern tier"
countries, 104–106, 131; failure of
effort to contain Arab-Israeli
conflict (1950–1956), 48–55; position on 1956 war, 53, 110, 111;
policies toward Arab countries
(1950–1958), 69, 70, 71–72, 80;
relations with Egypt (1952), 105–
106, —reaction to Soviet-Egyptian
arms deal (1955), 110, —1957–
1958, 71, 113–115, —1959–1963,
126, 132, –1964–1966; 129, 133–
135, —Egyptian view of U.S. relations, 279–281; Congressional
criticism of aid to Egypt, 134,
281–282; role in Jordan coup d'état
(April, 1957), 114, 234; plot to
overturn Syrian government
(1957), 71–72, 114–115; intervention in Lebanon, 1958, 73, 74,
115–116; vis-à-vis Iraqi crisis
(1958), 115–119; vis-à-vis Yemen
war, 133–135 passim; provision
of arms to Turkey, Iran, Iraq,
Jordan, Lebanon, 89–90; policies
in heartland (1958–1966), 131–
137; supply of arms to Israel,
134; Defense Department promotion of arms sales, 90n; competition with Soviet Union in Middle
East (1960's), 122–123; role in
1967 crisis, 269, 270, 296–298,
300–301, 310–311, —diplomatic
role, 301, 314; arms to Israel
and Jordan after 1967 war, 383,
415; role in aftermath of 1967
war, 402, 404; diplomatic support
of Israel after 1967 war, 413–
415; vs. Soviet Union, post-1967
war, 409, 412–416; convergence
of interest in settlement with that
of Soviet Union, 420; divergence
of policy from that of Soviet Union,
414–416; prospects for armed intervention in Middle East, 406,
418–419
see also Baghdad Pact; Big power
rivalries; "Containment Policy";
Eisenhower Doctrine; "New Look"
Policy; Superpower conflict; Tripartite Declaration
Uri, Colonel, 362, 379

Vietnam, U.S. intervention in, 122;
lessons from warfare in, 251
Vital-interest areas, U.S.-USSR, 111–
112; and Eisenhower Doctrine,
113
see also Superpower conflict
von Senger, F. M. (and Etterlin),
449n, 451n

Wailing Wall, 368, 408
Wars of Liberation, comparison of
terrains: Middle East theater vs.
Vietnam, Yemen, etc., 250, 405
see also Guerrilla war
Weizmann, Chaim, 23
West Germany, arms gifts to Israel
(1958–1963), 90, —implications of,
167–169, —effect on of on arms expenditures in Israel, 157, 158f,
159f, 160f, 163–164
White Paper of May, 1939 (British),
reversing Balfour Declaration,
26–27, 98–99
Wilson, Harold, 270, 297–298
Wood, David, 258n
Woolley, Herbert B., 429
World Zionist Congress, first (1897),
23

Yemen, 58, 72, 250; vis-à-vis Baghdad
Pact, 69; revolution in (1962), 77;
"class struggle" and Egyptian
intervention in, 77, 82, 87, 88,
241; Egyptian agreement to evacuate, 387, 399
Yemen war, Soviet interest in, 130;
Egyptian role in, 213, 241, 242–
243; Egyptian expenditures in, 156,
175n; Saudi role in, 58, 77, 133,
241, 243; U.S. attitude toward,
133, 134–135
Yoffe, General Abraham, 337–349
passim
Yugoslavia, 109

Zaghlul, Sa'd, 63
Zhdanov Doctrine, 96
Zionism, Soviet attacks against, 107
Zionists, 23, 26; support of U.S. involvement in Palestine, 93;
aspirations of *re* Israeli control
of conquered territories (1967),
404